In the Beginning…

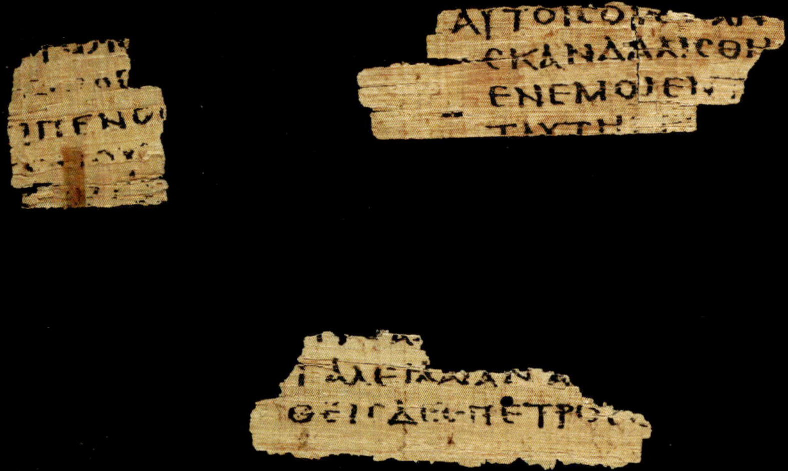

In the Beginning

BIBLES BEFORE THE YEAR 1000

Edited by Michelle P. Brown

Essays by
Michelle P. Brown
Harry Y. Gamble
Herbert L. Kessler
Monica J. Blanchard

With contributions from
Zaza Alexidze
Bruce C. Barker-Benfield
Malcolm Choat
Ann C. Gunter
Charles Horton
Martin Kauffmann
Richard A. Leson
Vrej Nersessian
Ben Outhwaite
Adolfo Roitman
Ilana Tahan
Olga Vasilyeva
William M. Voelkle

Published by the
Freer Gallery of Art &
Arthur M. Sackler Gallery

Distributed by
Smithsonian Books
New York and Washington

Published by the Freer Gallery of Art and the Arthur M. Sackler Gallery on the occasion of the exhibition *In the Beginning: Bibles Before the Year 1000*, October 21, 2006–January 7, 2007, organized by the Freer Gallery of Art and the Arthur M. Sackler Gallery in partnership with The Bodleian Library, University of Oxford.

Distributed by HarperCollins Publishers.

Publisher's note: Unless otherwise stated, all biblical quotations in the text are from *The Holy Bible. New Revised Standard Version* (1995). A list of bibliographical abbreviations used in the endnotes is given on page 319. Other abbreviations commonly used in the text are:

B.C.E. "before the common era"
C.E. "of the common era"
P Papyrus

In the catalogue entries, page dimensions are given in millimeters, height before width. Where variant spellings are possible, place names have been anglicized.

On the cover: *Washington Manuscript III—The Four Gospels (Codex Washingtonensis)*, back cover with the figures of Sts. Mark and Luke. Freer Gallery of Art, Gift of Charles Lang Freer, F1906.298; cat. no. 28.

Library of Congress Cataloging-in-Publication Data
In the beginning : bibles before the year 1000 /
Michelle Brown, editor.
p. cm.
Includes bibliographical references and index.
ISBN-13: 978-1-58834-240-9 (hardcover)
ISBN-10: 1-58834-240-9 (hardcover)
ISBN-13: 978-0-934686-03-7 (pbk.)
ISBN-10: 0-934686-03-3 (pbk.)
1. Bible–History. 2. Bible–Manuscripts–History.
3. Bible–Publication and distribution–History.
I. Brown, Michelle (Michelle P.) II. Freer Gallery of Art. III. Arthur M. Sackler Gallery (Smithsonian Institution)
BS445.I5 2006
220.4'074753--dc22
2006020112

Guest Curator: Michelle P. Brown
Coordinating Curator: Ann C. Gunter
Head of Design, Publications, and Digital Media: Dennis Kois
Art Director: Reid Hoffman
Editors: Alison Effeny and Jane Lusaka
Photo Researcher: Anna Leithauser
Image and Photo Services: John Tsantes
Rights and Reproduction: Cory Grace
Production Manager: Rachel Faulise
Exhibition Design: Kelly Webb
Catalogue Design: Studio A, Alexandria, Virginia

Typeset in Benton Sans and Verdigris.
Printed in Singapore by CS Graphics.

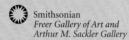

Smithsonian
Freer Gallery of Art and
Arthur M. Sackler Gallery

Contents

In the Beginning: Bibles Before the Year 1000 is generously supported by

Anonymous
The Friends of the Freer and Sackler Galleries
Mr. and Mrs. Ladislaus von Hoffmann
Constance Corcoran Miller
The Marriott Wardman Park Hotel
The Italian Cultural Institute, Washington, D.C.
The Ryna and Melvin Cohen Family Foundation
The Hassan Family Foundation.
The Federal Council on the Arts and the Humanities

Honorary Committee

Board of the Freer Gallery of Art and Arthur M. Sackler Gallery

Honorary Trustees

Foreword

Freer Gallery of Art & Arthur M. Sackler Gallery

In the Beginning: Bibles Before the Year 1000 is an exhibition that gathers many of the world's most important biblical manuscripts in order to examine the early history of the Bible—how it took shape, how different cultures participated in its development, and how different people experienced the Bible and its teachings during this formative period. En route, it opens up wide vistas, stretching from the Middle Eastern deserts to hermit's cells on Ireland's coast. These landscapes are populated with human stories that have become part of the history of the individual works on display—stories that unfold as we piece together, with the help of items that range from tiny fragments to beautifully preserved and lavishly decorated volumes, the process by which the Bible was born.

Thanks to the extraordinary generosity of lenders from four continents, the collaboration of the Bodleian Library at the University of Oxford, and the expertise and zeal of guest scholars, we have been able to approach this challenging task of surveying the first thousand years of the history of the Bible—both as text and as artifact.

In the Beginning also celebrates the centennial of Charles Lang Freer's purchase of four parchment manuscripts from a dealer in Egypt in 1906. The manuscripts formed the core of Freer's biblical collection, which he generously donated to the Smithsonian and the nation in that same year, though he made further additions that were included in his bequest in 1919. Although Freer's principal collecting interests lay elsewhere, in the arts of Japan and China and late-nineteenth-century America, his collection of biblical codices remains the most important of its kind outside Europe.

Immediately celebrated as major acquisitions, the codices received considerable press attention and played a key role in establishing the United States as an important repository of biblical manuscripts. They remained few, however, and culturally isolated from the substantial holdings of Asian and American art included in Freer's gift to the Smithsonian and his subsequent acquisitions. The works from other institutions on display in *In the Beginning* have allowed the Freer & Sackler galleries both to show the manuscripts to their advantage and to explain their significance to the history of the biblical text and the history of the codex.

We are deeply indebted to many institutions and individuals for scholarly advice and encouragement, generous loans of key works, and financial support. The exhibition is organized in association with the Bodleian Library, University of Oxford. For their enthusiastic support of, and contribution to, this project, I owe profound thanks to Bodley's Librarian Reg Carr, and to his ever-helpful staff, Ronald Milne, Richard Ovenden, Lesley Forbes, Martin Kauffmann, and Bruce Barker-Benfield. The British Library has also been a most generous lender, and I am indebted to Lynne Brindley, chief executive, and her staff, especially Scot McKendrick, Vrej Nersessian, and Ilana Tahan. All the lending institutions deserve our thanks for making available some of their most important treasures, and I hope none will mind if I single out the Holy Monastery of Saint Catherine's, Mount Sinai, which agreed to loan a number of items, including an inestimable fragment of Codex Sinaiticus. I owe special thanks to His Eminence Archbishop Damianos, Father Justin Sinaites, and Nicholaos Vadis, as well as to the Supreme Council of Antiquities of the Republic of Egypt, in particular to Zahi Hawass and Wafaa el-Saddik.

Michelle P. Brown has enthusiastically served as guest curator, ably assisted by Harry Y. Gamble and Herbert L. Kessler, and with contributions by Monica J. Blanchard. Many other scholars have supplied expertise and wise counsel along the way: Zaza Alexidze, James H. Billington, Sebastian Brock, Gudrun Buehl, Malcolm Choat, Guglielmo Cavallo,

Christopher De Hamel, Christian Förstel, Harald Froschauer, Triainos Gagos, Charles Horton, Ekaterina Krushelnitskaya, Richard A. Leson, John Lowden, Cyril Mango, Marlia Mango, Ben M. Outhwaite, Stefan C. Reif, Adolfo Roitman, Ihor Ševčenko, Olga Vasilyeva, William M. Voelkle, and Roger Wieck. Rita Venturelli and Michael L. Giacalone of the Italian Cultural Institute kindly facilitated visits to and correspondence with libraries and museums in Italy and provided support for scholarly exchange with Italian cultural institutions. Special thanks are due to our local advisory group—Gregory Nagy, William Noel, Andrew Oliver, and Alice-Mary Talbot—for all their help, particularly in the initial stages of the project, and to Georgi Parpulov for his assistance in gathering information on potential loans.

We owe considerable thanks to the Society of Biblical Literature and its executive director, Kent H. Richards, for sustained interest in our project; and to Larry Hurtado, who first proposed an exhibition of the Freer biblical manuscripts to celebrate the centennial of their acquisition, and who has edited a fine volume of essays devoted to them to coincide with this occasion.

This show focuses on material seldom studied or exhibited at the museum, and involved the forging of many new institutional partnerships. It has therefore proven especially challenging for the Freer & Sackler staff. I admire and appreciate the creative energy, resourcefulness, and attention to detail they have brought to every aspect of the exhibition and its publication and programs.

Above all, I must thank our generous sponsors. An exhibition with so many treasures is inevitably a costly affair, and I would like to thank Mr. and Mrs. Ladislaus von Hoffmann; Constance Corcoran Miller; The Marriott Wardman Park Hotel; The Italian Cultural Institute, Washington, D. C.; the Ryna and Melvin Cohen Family Foundation; and the Hassan Family Foundation. The exhibition also is supported by an indemnity from the Federal Council of the Arts and Humanities. We would not, however, have been able to mount this show without the support of a private donor whose stupendous generosity has been matched only by his desire to remain anonymous.

Julian Raby
Director
Freer Gallery of Art & Arthur M. Sackler Gallery
Smithsonian Institution

Foreword

The Bodleian Library

The Bodleian Library of the University of Oxford is proud to be associated with the exhibition *In the Beginning: Bibles Before the Year 1000*, which has been organized by the Smithsonian's Freer Gallery of Art & Arthur M. Sackler Gallery as a component of the Freer's anniversary celebrations.

It is fitting that the theme for this collaborative exhibition should be the Bible, for this book above all others has played a key role in the Bodleian's development over the past 400 years. Bibles were among the first books to be acquired by Sir Thomas Bodley for his new Library, even before its official opening in 1602, and the earliest printed catalogue of the Bodleian (published in 1605) listed bibles prominently among the *Libri Theologici* that took pride of place on the Library's shelves. The first of my predecessors as Bodley's Librarian, Dr. Thomas James, was a biblical scholar at heart, and his first subject catalogue was of the theological books acquired during the first decades of the Library's existence. In 1635, too, Dr. James's Sub-Librarian, John Verneuil, published his *Catalogus interpretum Scripturae*, which proved to be the first of many contributions to scholarship made by Bodleian Library staff.

The Bodleian has always taken the acquisition of bibles seriously. In 1793 a fifth of the Library's annual budget was spent on a single printed bible—a copy of the Forty-two-Line Bible produced in Mainz by Johannes Gutenberg. By complete contrast, however, the Bodleian bible manuscripts presented here all came into the Library's possession as gifts. Some of them—such as the Codex Oxoniensis (cat. no. 53), given by Sir Robert Cotton—were donated in response to the early efforts of Thomas Bodley himself as he "stirred up other men's benevolence"; others were added much later—like those from the outstanding bequest of Francis Douce in 1834 (cat. no. 55). And it is particularly pleasing to be able to contribute to the Freer Gallery's celebrations by exhibiting some of the finest of these great acquisitions, including both the Selden Acts (cat. no. 54) and the Caedmon (or Junius) manuscript (cat. no. 61), which are being seen outside Europe for the very first time.

The selection of works from the Bodleian for this exhibition has been made by the Bodleian's medieval specialists, Dr. Martin Kauffmann and Dr. Bruce Barker-Benfield. Working in close and fruitful collaboration with the staff of the Freer and Sackler galleries and with guest curator Prof. Michelle P. Brown, they have drawn with great skill on the riches of the Bodleian's extensive collections of late antique and early medieval manuscripts—the most extensive of any university collection in the world. The Bodleian's contribution to *In the Beginning* is the latest in a long tradition of international collaboration, and demonstrates our continuing commitment to the advancement of knowledge and the support of world scholarship. We are highly delighted to be part of such a unique and wonderful show.

Reg Carr
Bodley's Librarian
The Bodleian Library, University of Oxford

Introduction

Michelle P. Brown

The Christian Bible is the best-selling book of all time. It can sometimes seem as if it were literally written in stone, like the Ten Commandments. Yet it assumed the form we know today only gradually, over many centuries, as the result of cultural interaction and exchange between many different societies. Unlike the scriptures of certain other religions, the text of the Bible (from the Greek *ta biblia*, "the little books") is not generally considered to have been received as a single, ready-formed body of teaching, but rather to be the result of an ongoing process of transmission, study, interpretation, and revelation inspired by the Spirit of God.

The earliest Christians inherited from Judaism the Hebrew scriptures, which formed the Old Testament. During the first century C.E. they supplemented them with letters of instruction and exhortation from Christ's followers, and with oral accounts of his life and teachings that came to be written down as gospels (from Old English *godspell*, "good news"). Together, these came to provide the basis of the New Testament. Many other such accounts came into circulation, some composed by Christians and others by the Gnostics (a sect that conflated aspects of various religions with cabalistic magic and sought mystical enlightenment). During the fourth century the process to establish a biblical canon began, that is, determining which texts were acceptable for use in Christian worship. Some texts were accepted as part of the canon of belief, and others rejected as apocryphal, just as they had been in the Hebrew tradition, through scholarly debate among the Church Fathers and at the early ecumenical councils convened among the various local Churches to ensure a measure of uniformity of belief and practice.

Alongside the gradual crystallization of the biblical text a new form of publication emerged—the book (or codex)—which the Early Christian communities favored over the scroll or bookroll used in Antiquity. The advent of the codex was one of the greatest technological revolutions the world has known, but it achieved popularity only during the fourth century, along with edicts granting religious toleration within the Roman Empire and the rise in popularity of Christianity, which by the end of the same century had become the state religion.

Within decades the superpower of Rome was fragmenting, although the memory of its grandeur lingered on and continued to inspire the Semitic, Germanic, and Slavic peoples who formed or preserved successor states within its former territories. Likewise, the concept of empire, with a supreme ruler uniting and protecting both the state and the religious establishment, continued to beguile the papacy, the Christian empires of Byzantium and Carolingia, and the Muslim Caliphate. Many distinctive local Churches arose within their respective enclaves, with a significant measure of religious toleration being accorded to Christians and Jews living within those areas around the Mediterranean that came under Muslim rule from the mid-seventh century onwards. These Churches developed their own traditions of worship and patterns of belief, some orthodox and some deemed heretical for failing to observe the rulings of the early ecumenical councils. Their versions of the biblical texts varied, in accordance with the various routes by which they received them, and they gradually evolved their own distinctive scripts and decoration and translated scripture into their own languages.

A debate concerning idolatry and the appropriateness of imagery in religious contexts recurred in Judaic, Christian, and Islamic circles during the first millennium C.E. It is usually assumed that within Judaism and Islam sacred figural art was proscribed, although attitudes could vary according to period and conditions. Both faiths responded to the wider social context of art inherited from the late Greco-Roman world, adopting many classical motifs that can be found in the illumination of books as well as in public and sacred buildings. Christians, too, were heirs to this rich Antique tradition and faced a dilemma concerning the use of images. In the Christian Orient the Churches of Syria, Armenia, Georgia, Coptic Egypt, Ethiopia, and Nubia all formed their own influential traditions of illumination. Byzantium, which more than anywhere preserved the culture of late Antiquity, initially continued to employ images in worship, producing richly ornamented Christian scriptures and icons that functioned as living prayers during their making and contemplation. It was beset by iconoclasm for much of the eighth and early ninth centuries, during which time only the Cross and the Book were permitted as visible symbols of faith, but thereafter resumed its earlier enthusiasm for opulent ornament, figural narrative, and iconic symbolism. In Europe the tone was set by Pope Gregory the Great who, around 600, asserted that in images the illiterate might read. The issue continued to be debated, especially within Carolingian ecclesiastical circles in the late eighth and early ninth centuries, but the door had been opened to permit the burgeoning of a vibrant variety of book arts, in which sacred calligraphy and the adornment of Logos—the Word—were explored alongside a delight in ornament, a fascination with symbolism, an appreciation of narrative illustration that complemented a love of epic poetry, and a realization of the image's potential to bolster the authority of the state.

Out of this rich diversity and cultural complexity emerged the Bible as we know it: an approved grouping of texts arranged within an Old Testament and a New Testament. The Bible seldom took the form of a single volume, however, but usually circulated as manageable groupings of texts bound into book form (such as the Pentateuch, the psalter, the gospelbook, and the epistles). When the books of the Bible were enshrined together as one integral, harmonious whole in a single-volume pandect it was usually as the result of a major publication initiative associated with scholarly work to produce a new edition, such as the Hebrew Masoretic Bible of the Rabbanites or that of the Karaites; the Septuagint, in which the Hebrew text was translated into Greek for the Hellenic Jews of the diaspora; the Syriac Peshitta, which draws close to the Aramaic spoken by Jesus; or Saint Jerome's Latin translation, the Vulgate, and its successive reconstruction and revision under Cassiodorus, Ceolfrith, and Alcuin. In addition to the three "sacred languages" of Hebrew, Greek, and Latin, local vernacular languages were also used to share the scriptures, complemented by distinctive regional styles of script and illumination. Out of this array of diverse traditions emerges our modern babel of bibles, with each edition differing but all ultimately converging in harmony to form a single entity—the Bible, which speaks to so many people in so many ways.

In the Beginning: Bibles Before the Year 1000 presents the physical evidence of the development of both Bible and book, from fragile fragments of papyrus and humble early parchment codices to resplendent illuminated manuscripts and sumptuous jeweled bindings. Some have remained in ancient monastic libraries or cathedral treasuries since they were written; others have languished, concealed in desert caves, sealed up in long-forgotten rooms, or buried to await resurrection by archaeologists from the ground itself; many have passed from hand to hand down the centuries and are now preserved in great public libraries, museums, and private collections. Each has its own distinctive voice and a tale to tell.

A number of leading experts introduce themes covered in the exhibition in a series of essays. Ann C. Gunter discusses the acquisitions of Charles Lang Freer (1854–1919), whose collection of ancient biblical manuscripts is the most important of its kind outside the Middle East and Europe. Harry Y. Gamble examines the earliest biblical texts, the initial fluidity of the Bible's contents and its significance for the development of the book format familiar today. Monica J. Blanchard outlines the foundation of the early Churches of the Christian Orient and the evolution of their distinctive traditions of worship and scriptural transmission. My essay follows the journey of the Bible from its roots in the Middle East to its reception as far afield as Europe's wild Atlantic seabord, transforming societies as it went, and itself being shaped in its turn. On the way we learn what motivated those who lovingly made sacred books and how such volumes were used in public worship and private prayer. In conclusion, Herbert L. Kessler explores the processes by which the Word assumed splendid physical form and was explored and interpreted through its illumination.

By the end of our journey we come to appreciate how, during the course of the first millennium C.E., the Bible evolved out of the simple working manuals of early Christian communities to become a beautified and venerated symbol of faith. In the process, the Bible and the book achieved the status of cultural icons—roles that still endure to this day.

Charles Lang Freer's biblical manuscripts

Ann C. Gunter

Left to right: Dr. Frederick W. Mann, Charles L. Freer, Ibrahim Ali, and Ali Arabi, in Cairo, January 1907.

In December 1906, Charles Lang Freer embarked on his first trip to Egypt. He intended to pursue additions to his collection of early glazed ceramic wares but he also had a new mission for, early that year, the Smithsonian Institution's Board of Regents had finally agreed to accept his proposal to donate his remarkable collection of Asian art and the work of James McNeill Whistler to the national museum. Soon after Freer's arrival in Cairo, Giza antiquities dealer Ali Arabi showed him four parchment manuscripts written in Greek. Freer's diary for December 19, 1906, provides only a skeletal account of the transaction: "Bought manuscripts in forenoon & paid for them during afternoon." A letter to his friend and business partner, Frank J. Hecker, however, supplies a richer version. The normally circumspect Freer admitted that he was "carried completely off" his feet, spent two days examining the manuscripts with the aid of two local Greek scholars, and "fell by the wayside." [1]

Freer's 1906 purchases formed the nucleus of his collection of biblical manuscripts, although subsequent acquisitions made by him or on his behalf were to augment that core. The best-known and most important remains the Washington Codex of the Gospels (also known as the Freer Gospels or Codex Washingtonensis), a late fourth- or early fifth-century codex—the third oldest parchment manuscript of the gospels in the world—enclosed in painted wooden covers dating to the seventh century (cat. nos. 28, 29). He also bought a late fourth- or early fifth-century parchment codex of Deuteronomy and Joshua; a sixth-century codex of the Psalms; and a sixth-century codex of the Epistles of Paul (cat. nos. 27, 19, 20).

In autumn 1907, again home in Detroit, Freer began a serious quest for advice concerning the biblical manuscripts acquired the previous winter. He contacted Francis W. Kelsey, professor of Latin at the University of Michigan in nearby Ann Arbor, with whom he had long enjoyed a close friendship.

A past president of the American Philological Association and current president of the Archaeological Institute of America, Kelsey was well acquainted with experts in classics and biblical studies. He recommended that a young Michigan faculty member, Henry A. Sanders, examine the manuscripts and undertake their publication. In December 1907, Sanders presented to meetings of professional societies preliminary reports that generated considerable excitement in the popular press as well as in the scholarly world.[2] Several weeks later, Freer hosted a meeting devoted to the new discoveries for the Detroit Society of the Archaeological Institute of America. Kelsey's diary reports that at a small afternoon gathering before the evening event, he and others were allowed a closer examination: "Separated leaves of mss. of Deuteronomy and Joshua. Looked at other 3 mss., especially latter part of gospels, End of Mark.... With an ivory paper knife I loosened one cover, then the leaves of the mss; all opened up—wonderfully fresh and clear."[3]

In 1908, Freer undertook a second trip to Egypt with the primary aim of ferreting out the source of the manuscripts purchased in December 1906.[4] Since the beginning of the year, Freer and Kelsey had met and corresponded frequently about the publication of the manuscripts and the desirability of learning more about their provenance. Kelsey offered to enlist in advance the support of two British scholars, Sir Frederic G. Kenyon and David G. Hogarth, should Freer require expert advice while contemplating purchases in Egypt. Kenyon, of the British Museum, was a distinguished specialist in the Greek Bible and palaeography. Hogarth, a highly experienced field archaeologist, had excavated in Egypt with a British Museum expedition and also contributed to the Egypt Exploration Fund's *Fayum Towns and Their Papyri* (1900). Freer thanked Kelsey but declined: "I am a little in doubt as to the wisdom of letting it be known in Museum circles, that I anticipate visiting Egypt, as one can never measure the competition that may spring up if it is known a real search is being made for rareties."[5] He did seek advice from certain experts on this trip but they were, as in 1906, local scholars employed at the Greek College and the Khedival Library. Later, he was to correspond with other, internationally distinguished specialists in biblical manuscripts, including Kenyon.

While in Egypt, Freer wrote to Kelsey long and entertaining accounts of his adventures with Ali Arabi to track down the source of the manuscripts. The Giza dealer eventually produced the looters themselves as witnesses, who claimed that the manuscripts were taken from the ruins of a nearby monastery. Freer admitted in a letter to Hecker to "enjoying the quest greatly.... Poker and all other games are as nothing. It's real living, real experience—and beats winning a big contract for [railroad] cars quite out of sight."[6]

On this trip, Freer purchased from Arabi two important Coptic manuscripts: a large portion of a psalter of the fifth to seventh century (cat. no. 21) and part of a homily on the Virgin Mary written by Theophilus, archbishop of Alexandria. He also acquired over forty fragments of letters and other documents from the Cairo Genizah, the storeroom of the Ben Ezra Synagogue containing sacred and other medieval writings produced by the city's Jewish community.[7]

Beginning in 1908, Freer devoted considerable attention to the ambitious program of research and publication that he and Francis Kelsey had devised for the Greek and Coptic manuscripts and fragments acquired in 1906 and 1908. Kelsey recruited specialists to study and publish the material, initially in facsimile form and subsequently in scholarly monographs that appeared in the University of Michigan's Humanistic Series; Freer underwrote their research as well as the costs of publication and distribution. Under Kelsey's capable stewardship, Sanders completed facsimile editions of what became known as the Washington Manuscripts of Deuteronomy and Joshua, and of the Gospels, which were published in 1910 and 1912 together with scholarly commentaries on the texts. Sanders went on to complete his studies of the manuscripts of the Psalms and the Epistles of Paul, which appeared in 1917 and 1918. Freer's diary reveals that Sanders was a frequent guest at the collector's home in Detroit, where he conducted research on the manuscripts. William H. Worrell, a young specialist in Semitic languages appointed to the University of Michigan faculty, was charged with publishing the Coptic manuscripts and fragments.

Through a lively correspondence as well as occasional visits and telephone calls between Detroit and Ann Arbor, Kelsey consulted Freer on every aspect of the project: the selection of authors, plans for research and publication, and details of book design and photographic reproduction. Freer responded promptly and with equally meticulous attention to detail. When Kelsey sent Freer a sample of the Coptic font that would be used in Worrell's publication, Freer replied that it seemed to him "very artistic," having the quality of "'Notan,' a Japanese term expressing light and dark. I am sure the forthcoming publication will be admired by all who have a chance to study it,

Freer's purchases included this wooden bookstand, which likely was used to display early Christian manuscripts. Egypt, fifth–seventh century.

especially those who have the power to see beauty."[8] Freer's replies were invariably thoughtful and gracious, and he extended extraordinary courtesy and generosity to the young scholars who undertook the research and publication. When Sanders and Worrell traveled to Egypt and Syria, Freer provided advice on hotels and other practical matters and wrote letters of introduction to dealers and consular officials with whom he had established relationships on his own journeys. In response to a request from Kelsey, Freer supported Worrell's research travels in Egypt and the Levant and more than once expressed solicitude for the young scholar's well-being. In warmly avuncular fashion, he offered to obtain for Worrell a specially outfitted medicine case similar to one made for Freer himself.[9] In turn, Sanders and Worrell visited dealers to examine potential acquisitions of Greek and Coptic works and, with Freer's consent, occasionally made purchases on the collector's behalf. Freer acknowledged that his ignorance of ancient languages left him completely at the mercy of antiquities dealers. "You see I am at a great disadvantage! When Ali [Arabi] pulls from his cellar floor a ms in Coptic and calls it demotic or something else I am sitting in hot soup because I don't know the difference," Freer wrote to Kelsey.[10]

Freer made only a few acquisitions from Cairo dealers after 1909, usually with the assistance of intermediaries. In 1913, Sanders bought a fragment of a Coptic psalter from the Cairo dealer Maurice Nahman.[11] In 1916, a fifth Greek manuscript, the text of the Minor Prophets, was bought by Dr. David L. Askren from Nahman (cat. no. 10). Askren was a missionary and physician who worked in the Fayyum district south of Cairo during World War I, appointed by Francis Kelsey to purchase antiquities on behalf of the University of Michigan. At the time Askren purchased the Minor Prophets for Freer he also obtained Coptic manuscripts for the Pierpont Morgan Library. The entire group of manuscripts remained in Cairo until 1920, as a consequence of the perilous state of Mediterranean shipping brought about by the war.

James McNeill Whistler's Peacock Room, which Freer had purchased in 1904 and installed at his home in Detroit, was an early setting for the display of biblical manuscripts as well as other objects from Freer's collection. At a November 1912 exhibition in Freer's house, the room's shelves bore Persian, Chinese, Korean, Japanese, and Egyptian ceramics; a separate glass case contained the manuscripts of Deuteronomy and Joshua and the Gospels. Since the opening of the Freer Gallery of Art in 1923, the manuscripts have seldom been exhibited, and several have never been displayed. Were the current exhibition to consist solely of the Freer's own biblical manuscripts, it would still be a landmark event.

The Bible: The journey of the text

Hebrew

Greek

Latin

Vernacular languages

The Hebrew Bible *(Tanak)* composed of 39 documents—the Torah (5 books), the Nevi'im (or Prophets, 21 books), and the Ketuvim (or Writings, 13 books)—developed into Karaite and Masoretic editions from ca. 100 C.E. and later.

The Targum an interpretative reading of the Hebrew Bible into Aramaic

3rd century B.C.E.
The Septuagint, a Greek translation of Jewish scripture used by Hellenistic Jewish communities and early Christians, is begun. It is likely that different parts of the Hebrew scriptures were translated by different people at different times and places around the eastern Mediterranean in the centuries before Christianity. Includes 15 additional Jewish writings, mostly composed in Greek—the apocryphal books.

1st–4th century C.E.
Septuagint supplemented over several centuries by 27 Christian books in Greek, which assume canonical status ca. 350–400.

ca. 220 B.C.E.–250 C.E.
Revisions of the Septuagint by Aquila, Symmachus, and Theodotion. The **Hexapla,** a comparative edition of the Septuagint, compiled by Origen of Alexandria early in the 3rd century.

170–175 C.E.
The Diatessaron, a single, long narrative or harmony formed by conflating the gospels, is composed by the Syrian Tatian. It becomes the gospel of Christian communities in Syria until the 5th century.

4th century
Vernacular translations produced in languages of the Christian Orient and subsequently in Slavonic.

5th century
The Syriac Peshitta derived from the Hebrew Bible and Greek Septuagint.

The Old Latin *(editio vulgata)*
Many Latin versions of the Bible in circulation, all grouped under this name.

5th century
St. Augustine of Hippo's Latin revision is designed to bring the North African Old Latin version closer to the Greek.

ca. 382
St. Jerome begins his Latin translations, including his revision of the Old Latin (based on the Hexaplaric Septuagint) and his **Vulgate,** in which he purges Old Latin errors and variants with reference to earlier Greek and Hebrew versions.

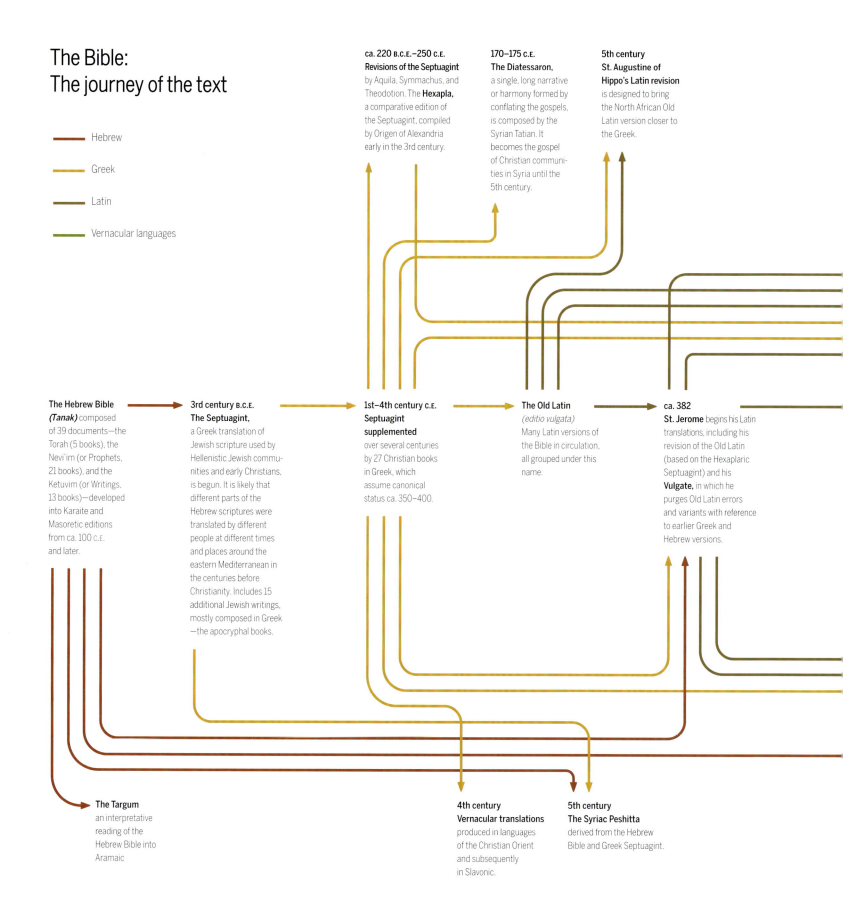

"Mixed" texts
Old Latin and Vulgate readings merge to produce many others with regional variations.

The Eastern Orthodox and Roman Catholic Bibles base their Old Testament upon the Septuagint, and include the apocryphal books. Many editions have been produced.

6th century
Cassiodorus produces several editions, drawing variously upon the Hexapla, the Vulgate, and the Old Latin.

ca. 700
The Italo-Northumbrian family of texts—Ceolfrith Bibles, Lindisfarne Gospels, etc.—reconstructs the Vulgate, with reference to Cassiodoran, Neapolitan, and other exemplars.

ca. 800
The Alcuin Bible, a single-volume edition of the Vulgate Bible completed by Alcuin of Tours, is copied throughout the Carolingian Empire and forms the basis of the **Paris Study Bible** in the 12th–13th century.

Many vernacular translations of both Greek and Latin editions are made during the Middle Ages and the Early Modern period.

1546
The Vulgate Bible is accorded authorized status by the Catholic Church at the Council of Trent. Several editions have been produced.

ca. 547
Victor of Capua produces a New Testament edition, conflating Vulgate readings to form a gospel harmony *(Diatessaron)*.

The Protestant Bible bases its Old Testament upon the Hebrew Bible, and excludes the apocryphal books. Many editions have been produced.

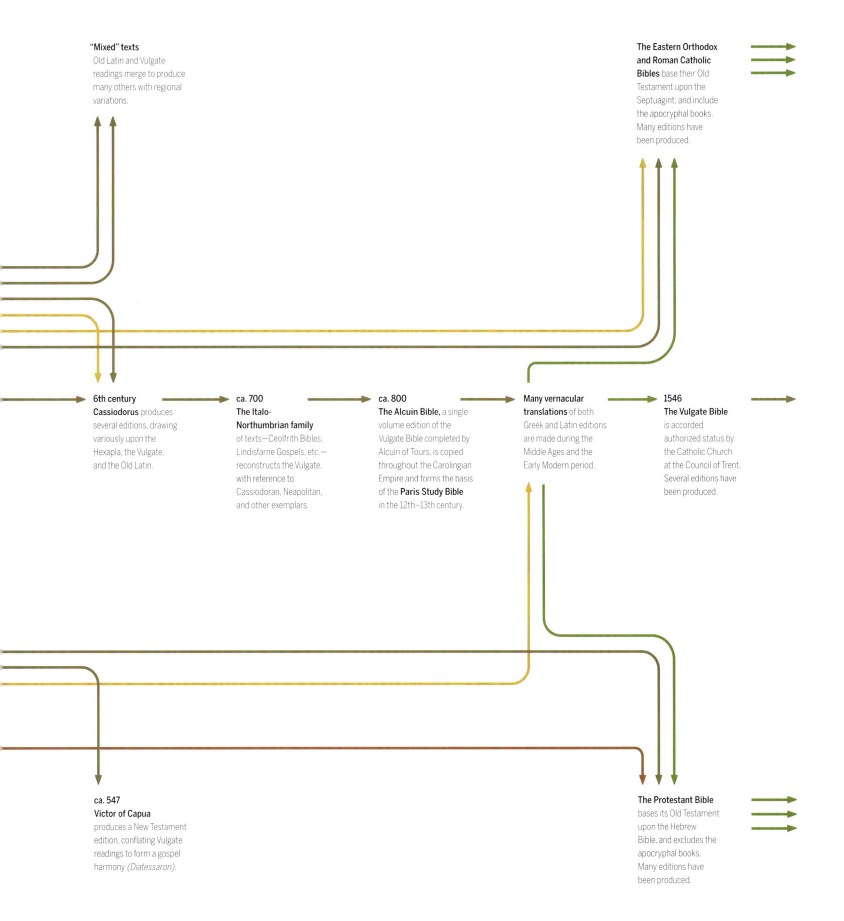

Europe and the Near East, circa 800 C.E. (and other sites mentioned in the text)

EUROPE
Slavs
Khazars
Avars
Danube
Black Sea
Caspian Sea
GEORGIA
Sinope
Ejmiacin
ARMENIA
Constantinople
Chalcedon
Nicaea
Mt. Athos
Caesarea of Cappadocia
BYZANTIUM
Smyrna (Izmir)
Laodicea
Ephesus
Edessa
Harran
Tigris
ASIA
Antioch
Euphrates
Tagrit
Beth Zagba
(St. John Monastery)
Baghdad
Damascus
Tyre
Mediterranean Sea
Caesarea
Jamnia
Jerusalem
ABBASID CALIPHATE
Alexandria
Persian Gulf
Fustat (Cairo)
Sinai
Fayyum
Mt. Sinai
Nile
Red Sea
Tiberias
Sea of Galilee
Caesarea
Jordan
Mediterranean Sea
Jerusalem
Qumran
Bethlehem
Dead Sea
Nahal Hever
Masada
Alexandria
Judaean
Desert
Deir el-Suriani
Wadi Natrun
Cairo
Giza
Sinai
Fayyum
Gulf of Aqaba
Fayyum
St. Anthony's
St. Catherine's
St. Paul's
Mt. Sinai
Oxyrhynchus
Gulf of Suez
Nile
Red Sea
0
100 mi
0
100 km
Nag Hammadi
Thebes (Luxor)

Harry Y. Gamble

Bible and book

Opposite:
Detail of fig. 2

In thinking simultaneously about the Bible and about the book, we are considering respectively content and form, or, as we might also say, a message and its medium. In the long history of the Bible and the equally long history of the book we have to do with an extraordinarily interesting interplay of content and form, such that neither Bible nor book can be well understood apart from their long-standing and dynamic synergism.

This close kinship between Bible and book is hidden in their very names, for "Bible" renders into English the Greek phrase, *ta biblia*, which means simply "the books" or, more accurately, "the little books." This plural designation may also usefully remind us that the Bible was not always conceived or known as a book—the single volume we customarily encounter and use—but at one time was known instead as a group of small books, physically distinct, not bound together.

This recognition may, in turn, evoke our curiosity about how and when and why these "little books" came to be gathered up and bound together to create a single volume, and indeed a sacred one—questions that inevitably force us back to the history of the book as the physical medium in which all ancient texts, including the Bible, have been inscribed, preserved, and transmitted. The development of the Bible and the evolution of the book are, as we shall see, intimately intertwined, and this holds true of the Bible far more than for any other text. That shared history is our subject.

THE MANY FORMS OF BOOKS AND BIBLES

The modern book—a series of leaves bound together at one edge and protected by covers—has a long history of its own. This, the leaf-book or codex, has been the principal form of the book in Western culture generally since the fourth century of the Common Era (C.E.). But in earlier centuries, reaching back to pre-classical times, the standard form of the book for all the peoples of the Mediterranean Basin was nothing at all like this. The ancient book was, rather, a roll (sometimes called a scroll) made of papyrus or animal skin upon which a text was inscribed by hand (FIG. 2), and this fact is subtly recalled whenever we refer to a book as a "volume," for in Latin *volumen*, from the verb *volvo*, "to roll," means "a bookroll." The gradual transition in Western Antiquity from the time-honored bookroll to the codex (FIG. 1) followed upon and imitated the popularity of the leaf-book in early Christianity, and specifically in connection with the formation of the Christian Bible.

This was a monumental change in the history of the book. In significance it is sometimes compared to the invention of movable type in the fifteenth century, and it is of some interest in our connection that the first book Johannes Gutenberg printed was the Mazarin Bible, produced in 1453–55. But the transition to the codex is perhaps more aptly compared to the advent of electronic texts in the late twentieth century, which even now is revolutionizing the way that texts are made, accessed, and stored. In both cases we have to do with a major change in the format of texts, and consequently in the means of producing and using them. It may well be that for readers of the not-too-distant future the word "book" will automatically conjure the meaning "e-book" rather than the leaf-book that it suggests to us, or the bookroll that it designated in pre-Christian Antiquity.

Just as the book has historically taken different forms, so has the Bible. The word "Bible" refers to no single thing, for there have been and there are today many forms of the Bible. Within Judaism the word Bible signifies thirty-nine documents that belong respectively to the Torah (five books), the Nevi'im (or Prophets, twenty-one books) and the Ketuvim (or Writings, thirteen books), all of which were composed and have been preserved in Hebrew. Such a tripartite arrangement of Jewish scriptures may have begun to develop in Judaism before the time of Christianity. It probably reflects the stages by which the Jewish Bible came into being, though its sequence also intimates the relative importance and authority of these writings within Judaism. It is with reference to these three components that the Bible is commonly known among Jews as the *Tanak*, a word formed from the initial consonant of the name of each part. This collection did not come into its final and definitive form before the late first century C.E., or even a bit later.[1]

This Bible, which we sometimes call the Hebrew Bible, was not, however, the only form even of the Jewish Bible in Antiquity. Many Jews lived outside Palestine in communities of the Mediterranean diaspora, and probably most of them knew little or no Hebrew, but spoke Greek. It was among and on behalf of these diaspora Jewish communities (especially the one in Egypt) that there arose another Jewish Bible, the Septuagint.[2] This was a Greek translation of the Jewish scriptures that probably began to be made in the third century B.C.E. It came to be called *Septuaginta* (Latin for "seventy") and is often designated by the Roman numerals LXX (70) because, according to the legendary account provided by the *Letter of Aristeas*, seventy-two Jewish translators were brought from Palestine to Alexandria in Egypt by the Egyptian king, Ptolemy II Philadelphus (285–246 B.C.E.), to render the Torah into Greek, which they reportedly did with inspired efficiency and accuracy.[3] This legend obscures, however, what was

Fig. 1
Codex. Coptic (Oxyrhynchite); Egypt (Oxyrhynchus), late fourth or early fifth century. William H. Scheide Library, Princeton University Library, M 144.

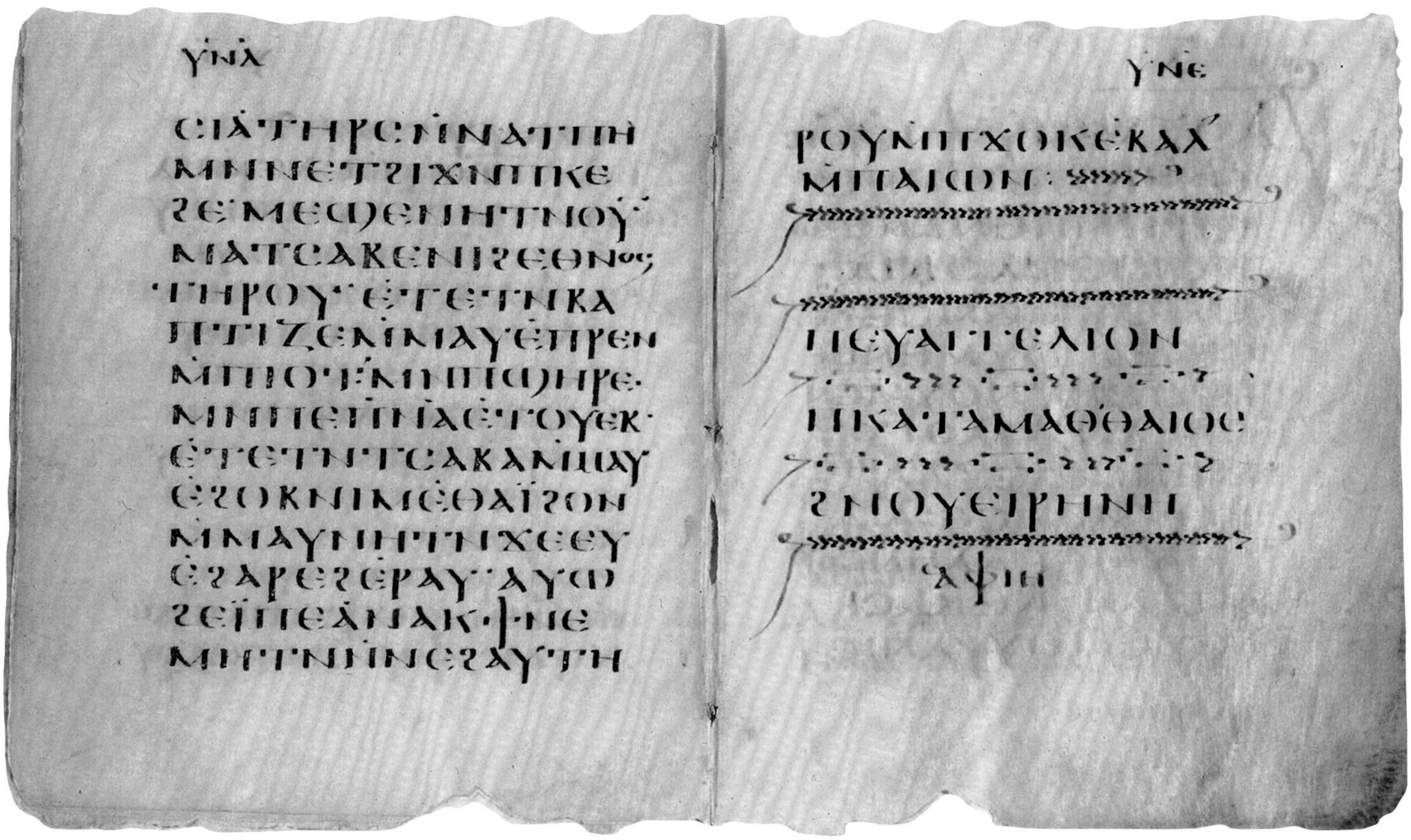

undoubtedly a far more lengthy and complex history, for the Septuagint shows considerable variations in style and accuracy, which suggests that there was no one, original translation into Greek, but rather that different parts of the Hebrew scriptures were translated by different people at different times and places around the eastern Mediterranean in the several centuries prior to Christianity.[4] The Septuagint differs from the Hebrew Bible not only in language but notably also in content: beyond the thirty-nine books of the Hebrew Bible, it offers fifteen additional Jewish writings, most of which were composed in Greek rather than Hebrew. These books are usually called the apocryphal or the deuterocanonical books. Furthermore, some of the documents of the Hebrew Bible have a longer or a shorter form in the Septuagint, and sometimes also a different order of materials within a given book. Hence for ancient Greek-speaking Jews who used the Septuagint, the Bible had a significantly different shape than for Jews who used the scriptures in Hebrew.

Fig. 2
Temple Scroll, Israel, first century B.C.E. Jerusalem, The Shrine of the Book.

Because Christianity emerged not as a new and independent religious movement but as a sectarian type of Judaism, the Bible of the earliest Christians was nothing more or less than the Bible of Judaism. Given the Palestinian roots of Christianity, this probably means that at the very beginning Christians had recourse to the Jewish scriptures in Hebrew. But from an early time Christianity began to find its larger constituency not within Palestinian Judaism but in the Greek-speaking Jewish diaspora where both Jews and non-Jews were recruited to the Church, with the result that the Bible of early Christianity quickly became and long remained the Septuagint.

Then gradually, over a period of several centuries, Christians began to supplement their use of the Septuagint with specifically Christian writings—gospels, letters, apocalypses, and the like, all composed in Greek. As such Christian writings acquired wider use and authority they were progressively gathered up, and finally shaped into a special collection consisting of twenty-seven documents. These were designated as writings of the "new covenant" or "New Testament," and Christians set this collection alongside the Septuagint, which, correspondingly, Christians began to call the "old covenant" or "Old Testament." Thus the Christian Bible, in its ultimate shape, was considerably more extensive than Jewish scriptures (whether in Hebrew or in Greek), and was characterized by two distinct bodies of literature, one Jewish and one Christian, but both in the Greek language.

Yet even after this development, the Christian Bible has taken different forms, and still has different forms today among the several streams of the Christian tradition. So, for example, in both Eastern Orthodox Christianity and Roman Catholic Christianity the Old Testament continues to represent the contents of the Septuagint, and so contains the apocryphal or deuterocanonical books.[5] In Protestant forms of Christianity, on the other hand, and contrary to ancient and medieval Christian usage, the scope of the Old Testament is conformed to the Hebrew Bible and excludes the apocryphal or deuterocanonical books.

Whatever forms it has taken, the contents and the arrangement of the Bible, as well as the uses made of it, have both influenced and been influenced by the media in which it has been transcribed and transmitted—that is, by the form of the book as it has evolved over the centuries. It is to that evolution that we now turn.

THE BOOKROLL

The only form of book known to the peoples of the ancient Mediterranean world was the bookroll, an object strange to the modern eye in substance and form.[6] Such a book could be made of various materials. By far the most prevalent was papyrus (whence comes our term "paper"), but leather or parchment was also used. The individual pieces of these materials were joined edge to edge to create a strip of the length needed to write out the text at hand.

The texts written in bookrolls were of the most various types: the great majority had a documentary character (administrative edicts, contracts, petitions, accounts, official and private correspondence, and the like); others were of a professional nature (medical, scientific, and philosophical writings, handbooks of astrology or magic), while still others were more literary (history, prose and poetry, drama). But if all sorts of texts were contained in bookrolls, not all bookrolls were precisely alike. Just as we are acquainted with many types of modern books, from deluxe leather-bound editions printed on fine paper to cheap paperbacks, or from large, handsomely produced and lavishly illustrated coffee-table books to smaller but serviceable manuals, so also in the ancient world the bookroll could be variously produced. But its production usually bore a relationship both to its content and to its intended use.

Depending partly upon the material from which they were made, and partly on the texts written on them, bookrolls varied in size—that is, in height and in length—but considerations of the convenience of the reader were clearly important and appear to have been determinative: bookrolls were commonly of small size so that they might be easily held and handled.

A bookroll made of papyrus was ordinarily between 25 and 33 centimeters tall, though many shorter and a few taller specimens are known. Its length was much more highly variable, and depended on the extent of the text inscribed on it. Some bookrolls were no longer than 3 meters, while others ran to more than 15 meters. There was no theoretical limit to the possible length since manufactured rolls of papyrus could easily be glued together, but there clearly were practical limits, and these were imposed by manageability, that is, relative convenience for reading, handling, carrying, and storing the book. The upper limit of length for such convenience was about 15 meters, but the vast majority of bookrolls were much shorter, usually not exceeding 9–10 meters. Hence very long texts were ordinarily divided and distributed into a series of rolls of more or less standard length. The extensive histories of Herodotus and Thucydides, for example, were divided respectively into nine and eight "books," that is, rolls. Bookrolls for official or ceremonial uses were often of larger dimensions than the common book: size suggested importance and such books did not have to be easy to manipulate.

Texts were inscribed upon papyrus rolls in tall, narrow columns (*selides* in Greek, *paginae* in Latin). The widths of these characteristically varied with the genre of the text: columns of prose texts typically range from 4.3 to 7.5 centimeters, while columns of verse tend to be wider, 8–14 centimeters. The height of columns likewise varied, in accordance with the height of the roll and with the sizes of top and bottom margins, but ordinarily they were in the range of 15 to 24 centimeters. The number of characters on a line (*stichos* in Greek, *versus* in Latin) varied with the width of the column and the size of the handwriting, and the number of lines in a column depended on the height of the columns and the size of the handwriting. Columns in bookrolls usually contain between twenty-four and forty-two lines. This manner of inscription, like the size of the bookrolls, was for convenience of reading: held in both hands at a comfortable distance apart, the book was progressively unrolled by the right hand and rolled up by the left, exposing only one or two columns at a time.

To the modern eye, it is a striking feature of ancient Greek and Roman books that they are customarily written in continuous script *(scriptura continua)*, that is, without divisions between words, and with little or no punctuation or paragraphing—aids that modern readers take for granted. Instead, in each column the characters appear as an undifferentiated block. It was the task not of the scribe but of the reader to determine what syllables constituted words, what words made up a sentence, and what sentences composed a paragraph. As daunting as this may seem to us, the skilled ancient reader was able to do it with relative ease. It has often been claimed that the presentation of ancient texts in continuous script required them to be read aloud so that the ear could assist the eye in the decoding effort. But this seems not to have been the case; ancient readers were able to read silently, just as we do. This does not, however, change another fact, namely that it was customary in Antiquity for texts to be read aloud, sometimes in private, but usually in company.[7]

The quality of a papyrus bookroll was determined mainly by three features: the quality of the papyrus itself, the layout of the text, and the type of handwriting. Manufactured rolls of papyrus were graded as to quality, taking into account the size of the sheets and the smoothness of the joins, but also the thinness, density, whiteness, and smoothness of the material itself.[8] As to layout, a well-produced book was provided with generous margins at top and bottom, and was written in uniform columns that were tall and narrow, with a good space between the columns. Stingy margins and irregularities of layout marked a book of lesser quality. Last but not least was the quality of the writing. Though there were many varieties of scribal hands, it suffices here to mention two general types: the documentary hand and the book-hand.[9] Both forms of writing were practiced by professional scribes. In their exaggerated forms they are easy to distinguish, but amid the gradations between them no sharp dividing line can be drawn. The book-hand was a careful script characterized by well-formed, separated, and upright letters evenly maintained along the line. Its clarity and regularity make it both aesthetically pleasing and easily legible. The book-hand required both more time and greater skill than the documentary hand, a more rapidly written cursive script, characterized by simplified and less careful letter formation, by the frequent use of ligatures (strokes connecting letters), and by the extension of some letters above or below the line. Legible, but neither careful nor artistic, the documentary hand was used, as the name indicates, mainly for recording purposes. Such features of bookrolls are signs of their relative quality.

Fig. 3
Lidded jars for storing scrolls, found at Qumran. Palestine, 1st century B.C.E.–1st century C.E. Jerusalem, The Israel Museum, inv. no. KhQ 1474.

Fig. 4a
Construction of a single-quire codex.

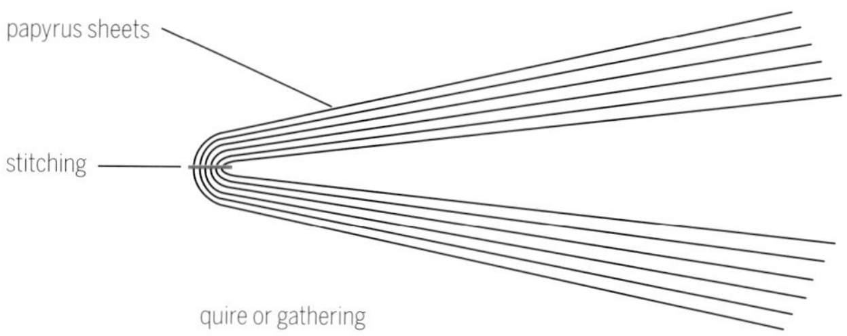

Fig. 4b
Construction of a multiple-quire codex.

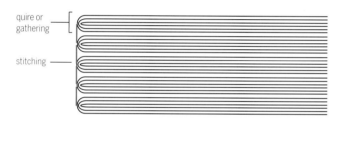

Matters were not altogether different if the bookroll were constructed of animal skins (leather or parchment) instead of papyrus. The many Jewish bookrolls, mostly fragmentary, that were discovered in the twentieth century in the Judaean Desert, including the so-called Dead Sea (Qumran) Scrolls (FIG. 3), are in the vast majority written in Hebrew on leather. Since prior to 1945 the only known early Jewish manuscript containing a portion of biblical text in Hebrew was the Nash Papyrus, four fragments containing the Decalogue and the Shema dating from the second century B.C.E., the manuscript finds in the Judaean Desert have enormously enriched knowledge about both book and Bible. Many of these books are scriptural: 202 copies of biblical books have been found at Qumran alone (almost a quarter of the total number of manuscripts found there), and nineteen copies at other sites. These are the oldest surviving manuscripts of those biblical documents.[10] But whether they contain scriptural or non-scriptural texts, these Jewish bookrolls are highly instructive.[11] They show that, apart from their preference for leather, in their bookmaking and scribal practices Jews generally followed conventions already noted in connection with papyrus bookrolls: though individual rolls vary in height and in length, they nevertheless fall well within the range of height and length typical of Greek papyrus rolls, and the texts are similarly inscribed in tall and relatively narrow columns.[12] It is also noteworthy that among these Jewish examples a single roll normally contains the text of only one document, whether biblical or non-biblical, which corresponds to broader practice.

Some significant differences, however, can be observed. In Jewish books the columns of text tend both to be wider (varying between 6 and 20 centimeters) and to have fewer lines per column (an average of twenty, though some manuscripts have many fewer or many more) than in Greek papyrus rolls. Moreover, these manuscripts were not written in continuous script; rather, there we find divisions between words and a common use of marks or spaces to distinguish paragraphs as well as smaller units of text.[13] Finally, since Hebrew is written and read right to left, Hebrew bookrolls run in the opposite direction to Greek ones.

FROM BOOKROLL TO CODEX

The centuries-long dominance of the bookroll and its ubiquity among the cultures of the Mediterranean region make it all the more surprising that in the first and second centuries of the Common Era a new kind of book appears, the codex or leaf-book. By the fourth century, the codex had virtually replaced the roll as the standard format of the book. How and why did this development occur?

This new form of book, the codex, is first mentioned in our sources by the Roman poet Martial, writing about 85 C.E., who recommends to readers who might wish to carry his poems when traveling "those that parchment confines in small pages," and mentions other literary works that are available "in pocket-size parchment" from certain booksellers (*Epigrams*, 14.184–92). We can surmise from this that in Rome small parchment codices had begun to be used for literary texts. The prototype for such a format was a set of two or more thin wooden panels, either whitened or slightly hollowed out and filled with wax, and fastened together with a thong through holes along one edge. This was called a *caudex* (literally "a block of wood"), and upon it one could write with pen and ink (if whitened) or a metal or bone stylus (if waxed). Such sets of tablets were the ancient equivalent of our scratchpad or spiral notebook, handy devices for jotting notes, keeping accounts, sketching first-drafts, or doing school exercises, because the writing could be washed or smoothed off and the tablets reused. These were utilitarian objects, not books in any proper sense, nor did their status change when parchment or papyrus was substituted for wood.[14] The innovation mentioned by Martial apparently did not catch on, for the format of the Greek and Latin book continued long after to be what it had always been, the bookroll.

The rich discoveries of ancient manuscripts that occurred, mainly in Egypt, in the last half of the nineteenth and the first half of the twentieth century greatly enlarged the body of evidence about ancient books, but it also provided a fresh and surprising recognition: while the vast majority of books were bookrolls, virtually all the early Christian books that turned up were not rolls, but codices.[15] Thus Christians appear to have written their books in codices at least as early as the early second century, and to have done so habitually, evincing an almost exclusive preference for this form of book.[16]

Consequently, if it cannot be said that Christians invented the codex, it was clearly Christianity that first adopted and exploited the codex and popularized its use. The subsequent slow and gradual displacement of the bookroll by the codex as the medium of non-Christian texts closely parallels the expansion of Christianity in the Roman Empire, and the triumph of the codex over the bookroll in the fourth century coincides with the establishment of Christianity as the official religion of the Empire later in the fourth century.

A codex was constructed on wholly different principles than a bookroll, regardless of the material from which it was made. The vast majority of early codices were made of papyrus. Single sheets of papyrus were cut, usually to the square, from a manufactured roll, stacked, folded vertically at the middle, and then stitched together along the fold. A single such gathering or quire could comprise a considerable number of sheets, but usually no more than about fifty. This would yield a codex of 100 leaves and 200 pages. In a single-quire arrangement, too many sheets proved unwieldy, making the central leaves protrude at the outer edge and causing the codex to spring open (FIG. 4a). To avoid such problems, a codex could be constructed by forming multiple quires, each consisting of only a few sheets (usually four, but as many as twelve), stacking these smaller quires and then stitching them together (FIG. 4b). Using the multiple-quire method a codex could contain many more leaves than the largest feasible single-quire codex. Still, the single-quire codex was simpler to make, and was probably the earliest form of the codex. It was a serviceable vehicle if the text to be written in it were not very lengthy.

Most of the earliest Christian codices were of the single-quire variety, which means also that they were not very capacious. The largest of these are the Chester Beatty codex of the Pauline Epistles (P 46), which originally ran to 208 pages; the Chester Beatty codex of Ezekiel, Daniel, Susanna, and Esther with 236 pages; and the Chester Beatty codex of Numbers and

Deuteronomy (P VI) with 216 pages.[17] But single-quire codices were usually much smaller than these. Our earliest copy of the Apocalypse of John is found in a codex (P 47) of only 46 pages, and two very early manuscripts of John's Gospel appear in single-quire codices of 130 pages (P 52, early second century) and 100 pages (P 5, third century).[18] Yet some quite early Christian codices are of the multiple-quire type. Examples are P 66 (ca. 200 C.E.), containing the Gospel of John and P 4+64+67 (all thought to come from the same manuscript, ca. 200 C.E.), containing the gospels of Matthew and Luke).[19] In the second and third centuries the extent of text to be inscribed appears not to have dictated the choice between single- and multiple-quire codices: so we find in P 75 (third century) the gospels of John and Luke in a single quire of 144 pages,[20] but in P 66 we find the Gospel of John alone in a multiple-quire codex of 156 pages. Only when a book of much more than 200 pages was wanted did it become really necessary to consider the advantages of multiple- over single-quire construction. P 45 (see below, page 29), which contained all four gospels and the Acts of the Apostles, was a multiple-quire codex with quires of only two leaves (four pages) each, providing a total of 220 leaves or 440 pages.

Beyond the number of pages, in their other dimensions, too, early Christian papyrus codices were small books, generally no taller than 20–25 centimeters and no wider than 10–15 centimeters, and so typically rectangular in shape. It was in consequence of such size and shape that in these early Christian codices texts were written out in a different way than in the traditional bookroll. Instead of deploying the text in a series of tall narrow columns, the page of a codex was customarily inscribed in a single broader column, yet the text was still offered in *scriptura continua*.[21] Furthermore, the type of scribal hand normally found in these early Christian codices is neither the elegant professional book-hand used in the finest non-Christian books, nor the merely functional cursive documentary hand, but something in the middle range between them, sometimes called "reformed documentary" or "informal round" script. A practical rather than an artistic hand, it is characterized by more carefully formed letters and a more restricted use of ligatures than the ordinary documentary hand, and is content to be legible without aspiring to beauty. Among these early Christian manuscripts there is a considerable variety in the quality of transcription, not only in the type of hand used but also in the degree of care and accuracy. The large number of textual corruptions that appear in these manuscripts—some accidental and some intentional—suggest that their scribes were not professional (or at least were not particularly well-trained and did not work to a high standard) and that early Christian books were not produced under highly controlled conditions.[22]

Two other inscriptional features of these early Christian manuscripts deserve mention. At least some of them show a tendency toward fewer lines to the page and fewer letters to the line than other manuscripts, and a somewhat more liberal use of accent, punctuation, and breathing marks. These traits may be intended to facilitate reading, perhaps especially public reading, from books of small size.[23] Far more arresting is the ubiquitous presence in early Christian manuscripts of the phenomenon of *nomina sacra* or "sacred names," that is, the practice of writing a select set of names in a peculiar way, above all the names *Iesous* (Jesus), *kyrios* (Lord), *Christos* (Christ), and *theos* (God). All of these words were regularly written in a distinctive contracted or abbreviated form, using only their first and last letters (and occasionally a medial letter), and placing a horizontal stroke above them.[24] No theory of the origin of this practice claims general consent, but it is broadly agreed that

Fig. 5
Codices with leather covers, found at Nag Hammadi in the 1940s. Egypt, fourth century. Cairo, Coptic Museum.

ultimately it derives in some way from Jewish reverence for the name of God, which in ancient Jewish scriptural manuscripts is frequently written in a special form. Since the use of *nomina sacra* regularly appears in the earliest extant manuscripts of Christian books, the convention must have originated quite early, and probably already in the first century C.E.

A codex, like a bookroll, could be provided with protective covers, though the two formats obviously required covers of different kinds. Bookrolls, especially valuable ones, were perhaps usually furnished with simple cylindrical sleeves of papyrus or parchment into which the bookroll could be slipped for storage. Covers for codices were more difficult to make: they required at least a front and a back, and attachment to the spine of the codex. Such covers could be made of wood, leather, or papyrus (in the case of thin leather or papyrus it was customary to stiffen the material by pasting used or discarded papyrus inside it—the origins of the limp vellum binding). No codex datable to the first three centuries has been found with covers, but this does not mean that they had none. This lack of evidence has been richly remedied by the discovery of the Nag Hammadi codices, which date to the fourth century. Their covers are made of leather cut in a single sheet slightly larger than the leaves of the codex itself, and with a leading edge that forms a flap that overlaps the outer edge of the codex when closed. An additional piece of leather is glued along the spine on the inside for strength, and thongs are provided to secure the codex inside the cover (FIG. 5). These covers, while very interesting, are not necessarily standard and representative,[25] and it is not to be assumed that codices were routinely furnished with covers beyond, perhaps, a blank page of papyrus.

Having briefly described how these earliest Christian manuscripts were constructed and inscribed, we may go on to ask: what do their features tell us about how these books were perceived, valued, and used in early Christian communities? Given their small size, their limited scope, their quasi-documentary scripts, their lack of adornment, and the notebook-like medium of the codex, it is clear that these were by no means fine books produced to a high standard. Their physical form gives no intimation that they were objects of reverence, let alone that they possessed sacral or iconic status. In the larger company of ancient books, these entirely unpretentious items would have been appraised as second-class books, or indeed as small pamphlets, poorly corresponding to conventional literary tastes or bibliographic practice. But at the same time these early Christian books are highly functional—economical, convenient, and legible—and clearly designed for practical use. Neither private texts nor products of the professional book trade, these books were produced within and for the small Christian communities that read them, and their principal interest was in the content, not the form, of their books.

But why was it that Christians initially adopted the codex and employed it as the standard medium for their texts? To us who are habituated to it, the codex or leaf-book is so obviously a more practical format than the bookroll that no other explanation is needed. The codex offers greater economy of material, greater capacity for text, greater convenience of reference, and, being more compact, greater ease of portability and storage. But its practical advantages, though many, seem an inadequate explanation for two reasons. On the one hand, a codex was significantly more difficult to construct than a bookroll, which came more or less ready-made. On the other hand, if the advantages of the codex were so self-evident, it is puzzling that, outside the early Christian context, the bookroll continued to be the dominant format for a long time. Consequently, it has been suggested that some early Christian document of recognized authority or high usefulness—perhaps a gospel, perhaps the collected letters of Paul, perhaps a collection of proof-texts extracted from Jewish scripture—was issued and became known in codex form, and that the authority or utility of its content carried over to the kind of book in which it was available, so that the codex was in this way promoted as the standard form of the Christian book.

None of these explanations has yet proved conclusive. For the present, it can be observed that Christianity adopted the codex at a time when it still had mainly utilitarian associations. Many of the very few early codices that are not Christian carry texts that give these books the character of manuals or handbooks, which is to say that in content as well as in form they retain practical associations with the notebooks that were the prototype of the codex.[26] By considering both content and form, perhaps we can say that Christians adapted a familiar, practical medium (the codex) to a new but still practical purpose. They inscribed their texts in codices not because they thought of these texts as "literature" in any aesthetic sense, nor because these texts were considered sacrosanct, let alone because such books were cult objects: the unpretentious status of the early codex belies such aims. Rather, we might suppose that the codex was the appropriate medium of these texts because what was wanted were practical books for everyday use—the essential handbooks or manuals of the Christian community.

THE FORMATION OF THE CHRISTIAN BIBLE

The scriptures of Judaism were the original written resources of Christianity, and from the outset they shaped Christian thinking and practice. Whenever Christian writings belonging to the first century refer to "the scriptures," it is the scriptures of Judaism that are meant.[27] Perhaps because of its heavy reliance upon Jewish scripture, early Christianity was slow to produce any writings of its own. The earliest extant Christian writings are the letters of Paul the Apostle, written between 50 and 60 C.E. It may be that about the same time oral traditions of Jesus's teachings or activities were collected and written down, but if so they have not survived as documents. In the last third of the first century other documents began to appear: the Gospel according to Mark was written sometime between 65 and 70, and perhaps a decade later (80–90) the longer and richer gospels according to Matthew and Luke were penned (the latter with a companion volume, the Acts of the Apostles), and probably later still (85–95) the notably different Gospel according to John. In addition to these, but still within the last few decades of the first century, there appeared other letters (of James, of Peter, of John, to the Hebrews), and an apocalypse, the Revelation of John (ca. 95 C.E.). Christian writings begin to multiply from this time on, with more letters (of Clement, bishop of Rome, of Ignatius, bishop of Antioch, of Barnabas), more apocalypses (the Shepherd of Hermas, the Apocalypse of Peter), a manual of church order (the Didache), and a variety of gospels (the Gospel of Thomas, the Gospel of Peter, the Egerton Gospel, the Gospel of the Hebrews, the Gospel of the Egyptians, etc.)—all belonging to the first half of the second century. No doubt still other Christian writings from this early period have been lost or, if they exist, cannot be firmly dated so early.

Several things may be said about these early Christian texts, all written in Greek, but very diverse of authorship, of place and time of composition, of genre and purpose. In form, style, and substance these writings make no pretense to be "literature" in the high sense of that term. Regardless of genre, they were intended not for a general, public readership but for the internal needs and uses of Christian communities themselves. And none of them was written with the idea of producing a document that might be incorporated into or placed alongside the scriptures of Judaism. Put bluntly, no early Christian writer was writing a "biblical" book.[28] Early Christianity had a Bible already, and it was the Hebrew Bible. Ultimately, of course, many of these writings did come to form what we know as the "New Testament" and to stand in Christian bibles alongside the Jewish scriptures, coming to share, for Christians, an authority at least equivalent to Jewish scriptures. But that result was long in the making, an outcome neither foreseen nor intended by any of these early Christian writers, who wrote what they did for the uses of their own communities. How, then, did that collection of Christian writings that we call the New Testament, and thus the Christian Bible as a whole, come into being? This occurred through a long and uneven process extending from the second through the fifth centuries, but we are able to discern important phases of it and some of its dynamics.

THE EMERGENCE OF SMALL COLLECTIONS

Early on, soon after they were written, various pieces of early Christian literature began to circulate among Christian communities. Because these communities were small, scattered over an increasingly broad geographical area, mostly illiterate and without much skill in producing or reproducing books, the circulation of these documents was both gradual and haphazard. There was no method of mass-producing books, each of which had to be handwritten, nor any method of mass-circulation. Documents came to be known and used, therefore, at first only locally around their points of origin, and then regionally—in Egypt, say, or Syria, or Asia Minor—as individual texts were reproduced and carried from one place to another by Christian missionaries or other travelers. In this unsystematic way Christian communities progressively gained acquaintance with various writings and made use of them for teaching, worship, evangelism, and self-defense.

Communities located in cities that were centers of trade or administration were the natural points for the confluence of Christian writings originating from diverse quarters. As these communities came to know more and more Christian documents, small collections began to be formed. Probably the earliest such collection consisted of letters of the Apostle Paul, for late in the first and early in the second century we encounter Christian writers who are familiar with groups of them. Clement of Rome, Ignatius of Antioch, Polycarp of Smyrna, and the author of 2 Peter all knew a number of Paul's letters, though it is unclear how many, and the notorious heterodox teacher Marcion of Sinope had a collection of ten Pauline letters by about 140 C.E.[29] The earliest surviving manuscript of the collected letters of Paul is the famous Chester Beatty Papyrus 46 (P 46), dated to 200 C.E. This codex of Egyptian provenance apparently lacked the Pastoral Epistles (1–2 Timothy and Titus), and not only ascribes to Paul the anonymous letter to the Hebrews but (uniquely) places that letter near the beginning of the collection, immediately after the letter to the Romans. The editions of the Pauline collection witnessed by Marcion and P 46 are variations on an earlier and perhaps original edition that contained only the community letters of Paul, not the private letters, that counted together letters to the same community (Corinthians, Thessalonians, Colossians-Philemon), and that arranged the letters in a sequence of decreasing length.[30] By the end of the second century more or less full collections of Paul's letters were known and valued in Christian communities throughout the Mediterranean Basin, from Antioch to Carthage, and from Alexandria to Gaul.

Very many gospels or gospel-type documents were current among Christian communities in the first half of the second century.[31] At that time many of those communities knew or preferred to use only one gospel, different ones in different places, and they persisted in this habit even when they became acquainted with other gospels, since they noted differences among them (even as we do) and were troubled by them.[32] Hence it is not surprising that many of the earliest papyrus manuscripts that carry gospel texts belonged to codices that contained only one gospel. Some early examples include P 1, P 70, and P 77 (all third century, but the last may be earlier),[33] each with Matthew only, and P 52 (ca. 120 C.E.) and P 66 (ca. 200 C.E.),[34] both from codices containing John alone. Yet a few early papyri show that sometimes two (perhaps more) gospels were transcribed in a single codex. For example, P 75 (third century) offers texts from both Luke and John.[35] If P 4, a third-century papyrus fragment of Luke, belongs with P 64 and P 67 (ca. 200 C.E.), which carry the text of Matthew, all having come from the same codex as most suppose, then that codex would have contained at least those two gospels.[36] Whether these codices may have contained more than two gospels, however, is uncertain.[37]

In such communities as possessed one or more of them, the gospels began to be used in the context of worship or instruction. Justin Martyr, writing near the middle of the second century, describes a Christian service of worship and says (*Apology* 1.67.3):

On the day called Sunday we have a common assembly of all those who live in the cities or outlying districts, and the memoirs of the apostles or the writings of the prophets are read for as long as time permits. Then when the reader has finished, the president of the assembly verbally admonishes and invites all to imitate such examples of virtue.

By "memoirs *(apomnemoneumata)* of the apostles" Justin doubtless means gospels (see *Apology* 1.66.3), though he does not say which ones, so that here we see gospels being read right alongside, or perhaps as alternatives to, prophetic books of Jewish scripture. This liturgical practice, which must have been traditional well before Justin's time, at once presumed and promoted among Christians a sense of the gospels as correlative to the scriptures of Judaism, and inevitably encouraged Christians to think of the gospels as themselves having a scriptural character.

Not long after Justin, perhaps between 160 and 170, there arose a collection of four gospels, those ascribed to Matthew, Mark, Luke, and John. Their collection was signified precisely by the act of transcribing them together in a single codex. The earliest known manuscript containing these four is the Chester Beatty papyrus P 45, dated to the early third century (cat. no. 14). This codex, though now largely fragmentary, originally contained not only these four gospels but also the Acts of the Apostles in 440 pages. The appearance of a collection of four gospels and the way in which it was understood were documented by Irenaeus, bishop of Lyon, around 180 C.E. He says in his *Against Heresies* (3.11.8–9):

It is not possible that the gospels can be either more or fewer in number than they are. For, since there are four zones of the world in which we live, and four principal winds, and since the church is scattered throughout the whole world, and since the pillar and support of the church is the Gospel and the Spirit of Life, it is fitting that she should have four pillars breathing out immortality all over and revivifying human beings. From this it is evident that the Word, the Artificer of all, he that sits upon the cherubim and controls all things, has given us the Gospel under four aspects, but bound together by one spirit.... For the cherubim were also four-faced, and their faces were images of the dispensation of the Son of God. For the scripture says, "the first living creature was like a lion," symbolizing his effective working, his leadership and royal power; the second was like a calf, signifying his sacrifice and sacerdotal order; "but the third had, as it were, the face of a man," an evident description of his advent as a human being; "the fourth was like a flying eagle," pointing out the gift of the Spirit hovering with his wings over the church. And thus the gospels correspond with these things among which Jesus Christ is seated.... For the living creatures are quadriform, and the Gospel is quadriform, as is also the course followed by the Lord.... These things being so, all who destroy the form of the Gospel are vain, unlearned and also audacious, those who represent the aspects of the Gospel as being either more in number than previously stated or, on the other hand, fewer.

It is apparent that Irenaeus strongly and cleverly rationalizes the relatively new collection of four gospels, appealing among other things to the visions of John in Revelation (4:6–10) and of Ezekiel (1:4–11). But at the same time Irenaeus construes this collection in a particular way: he does not speak of "four gospels" but of "the Gospel under four aspects" or "the quadriform Gospel." Here "the Gospel" is taken to be something singular that is distinctively deployed in (four) different perspectives, yet without becoming multiple. Just this sense is preserved in the traditional but secondary titles of the gospels ("the Gospel according to Mark" [or Matthew or Luke or John]), which allows for distributive authorship and literary diversity while yet maintaining the unity and coherence of the Gospel itself. We also see here the root of the symbols, richly exploited in later periods, of the different gospel writers: Matthew traditionally signified by the man, Mark by the lion,

Luke by the calf or ox, and John by the eagle.[38] The creation of a four-fold Gospel, understood on terms such as Irenaeus provides, was a solution to the problem of multiple gospel documents. But it was not the only possible solution, and it found a strong rival in another approach.

In the very period when Irenaeus was promoting a collection of four gospels, another Christian, a Syrian by the name of Tatian, created an entirely different form of "the Gospel." Prompted probably by the awkwardness of having numerous and divergent gospels, Tatian decided to combine their texts. Drawing mainly upon the same four gospels that Irenaeus acknowledged, but bringing in some additional material from other sources, Tatian broke the individual gospels down into their constituent parts, and restructured them into a single long narrative, which he called the *Diatessaron*.[39] Tatian's primary use of the same four gospels valued by Irenaeus shows that these had attained a wide recognition. But that Tatian could dismantle the individual gospels and recast their substance by transpositions, additions, and omissions, shows that they were valued chiefly for their contents and not as individual documents whose texts were inviolate. It is telling that Tatian was not criticized for his editorial project, and more telling still that the *Diatessaron* enjoyed broad and long-lasting popularity, especially in the Christian East: up to the fifth century, the *Diatessaron* was the gospel of Christian communities in Syria. Nevertheless, it was the four-fold Gospel commended by Irenaeus that became the standard form of the gospel collection of the early Church, and ultimately, even in Syria, displaced Tatian's *Diatessaron*.

A particularly interesting and important manuscript of the four gospels is the Washington Codex, a parchment codex of the late fourth or early fifth century, now in the Freer Gallery of Art, Washington, D.C. (see cat. no. 29). It offers the gospels in what is called the Western order—Matthew, John, Luke, and Mark—giving precedence to the authors who were apostles (the more familiar order, Matthew, Mark, Luke, and John is represented in P 45, discussed above). The text of the gospels in this manuscript is highly unusual, since different parts of it, even within the same document, have different textual complexions. Such a mixed text cannot be readily explained unless its scribe drew on various manuscripts (or parts of manuscripts) as he wrote out the codex, or unless the exemplar from which he copied had been made up in this way.[40] This manuscript also contains an apocryphal addition after Mark 16:14 (the "Freer logion"), a reading otherwise attested only by Jerome.[41] One can also observe in this codex a frequency of punctuation marks, spacing, and paragraphing, supplied to facilitate public reading. The covers associated with this codex, which depict full-length the four evangelists, two on the front and two on the back, are not original to it but come from a later period (cat. no. 28). It is likely, nevertheless, that parchment codices such as this were normally supplied with covers.

If by the early second century the letters of Paul were already available as a collection, and if around the middle of the second century four gospels had been brought together, early Christian communities were thereby furnished with two substantial bodies of Christian writings, each distinct in genre, but each capable of being written out in a single codex. It was this manner of transcription that gave tangible, visual form to these collections and served to represent them as "closed," that is, admitting of no further members. Thus the terms "the Gospel" or "the Lord" on the one hand, and "the Apostle" on the other, became shorthand ways of referring to these two collections, designations that, later on, would come to characterize a New Testament of rather larger scope.

THE CURRENCY OF OTHER WRITINGS

Beyond these two early collections, Christian communities of the late second and third centuries increasingly had at hand many other early Christian documents that were widely valued and used. Relatively well-known and popular in the second century were the letters we know as 1 Peter and 1 John, and, in addition, the Revelation of John and the Epistle to the Hebrews. But equally well-known and valued were the Shepherd of Hermas, 1 Clement, the Didache, and the Epistle of Barnabas.[42] On the other hand, we hear little or nothing during the second century about the smaller general epistles (2 Peter, James, Jude, 2–3 John), and not much about the Acts of the Apostles until near the end of the second century. Apart from the currency of these writings, the fund of texts available to Christianity continued to grow throughout the second century with the production of yet more gospels, acts of various individual apostles, and other documents.

This highly fluid situation persisted throughout the third century and well into the fourth.[43] If the authority of the fourfold Gospel and of the letters of Paul was almost everywhere acknowledged by Christians, the status of other writings continued to be largely indeterminate, and frequently also in dispute. Instructive examples are provided by the Revelation of John and the Epistle to the Hebrews. The Revelation of John enjoyed considerable early popularity as being both ostensibly written by an apostle and an inspired vision. Justin, Irenaeus, Clement of Alexandria, and Tertullian all accepted and used it. But in the first half of the third century it came under strong criticism with respect both to its authorship and to its materialistic millennialist outlook, and thereafter it was largely disused in the Greek-speaking East. The Epistle to the Hebrews, though it enjoyed an early popularity especially among Eastern Christians, was consistently neglected by Western Christians after the middle of the second century, partly because of doubts about its authorship, but even more on account of its rigorous teaching that sins committed after baptism were unforgivable, which conflicted with developing Western ideas about penance. Each case shows that issues of interpretation were at work in whether or not a given document was judged authoritative.

There are small indications that during the late third century there was a tendency to bring together a few of the non-Pauline epistles. Of these only 1 Peter and 1 John enjoyed much currency and use during the second and third centuries, the others (James, Jude, 2 Peter, 2–3 John) being mentioned only sparingly and sometimes with reservation. Yet early in the fourth century Eusebius (see below) could speak of "the seven letters called catholic" [i.e., general, without specific address].[44] This may mean that he knew of a discrete collection of these documents, but if so, it emerged far later than the collection of Paul's letters and the collection of the gospels.

THE FORMATION OF THE NEW TESTAMENT CANON

In application to the Bible, the word "canon" is taken by modern scholarship to mean a fixed and closed list of books that are understood to have unique status and exclusive authority. The word "scripture," on the other hand, is more general: it signifies writings that are accorded religious authority within a community, without regard to whether or not there is a fixed list of such writings, or whether any particular writing belongs (or should belong) to such a list.[45] Thus it is possible to have scriptures without having a canon of scriptures. We may say, then, that early Christianity had scriptures—both the scriptures of Judaism and some Christian writings—well before it had a canon of scripture, that is, before it had determined what writings to include in a fixed and final list. As it happens, the question of what writings constitute Christian scripture, and still more the question of which scriptures should be ruled in or ruled out of a canon of scriptures, were still open at the beginning of the fourth century.

Our most helpful witness to this circumstance is Eusebius, bishop of Caesarea (260–340 C.E.), a prominent churchman and author of the famous *Ecclesiastical History*, a treasure-trove of information about the early Church. In the midst of this work (3.25.1–7), Eusebius offers an assessment of the relative status of various documents in the Churches of his own day. He lists them in a three-fold classification. Among "acknowledged books" *(homologoumenoi)*, those received as authoritative scripture, he lists the four gospels; Acts; the letters of Paul, 1 John, and 1 Peter. Among "disputed books" *(antilegomenoi)*, those not received by all, he lists James, Jude, 2 Peter, 2–3 John, the Acts of Paul, the Shepherd of Hermas, the Apocalypse of Peter, the Epistle of Barnabas, the Didache, and the Gospel of the Hebrews. By saying that the Revelation of John might be put in either of these lists, Eusebius tacitly admits that it is a disputed book. Finally he refers to "spurious" *(nothoi)* and heretical books that are to be ruled out altogether, but mentions as examples only the gospels of Peter, Thomas, and Matthias, and the Acts of Andrew and of John. According to Eusebius, then, there were only twenty-one Christian writings generally agreed to be authoritative scripture, and so not yet the twenty-seven that eventually came to make up the New Testament.

With this discussion Eusebius was taking stock of the writings that had come down from the early generations of the Church to his own day. It was an opportune time for stock-taking in all matters concerning the Church, for the years 310–325 C.E. during which he wrote the *Ecclesiastical History* were momentous for Christianity. The "Great Persecution" of the Church, initiated in 303 by the emperor Diocletian and continued by his successors, had come to an end, and the Edict of Milan in 313 granted freedom of worship to all. Not less important was the accession of Constantine, who promoted Christianity, to sole imperial power in 324. The worldly circumstance of the Church was now radically different and infinitely more promising than ever before. With a new and actively Christian emperor who was fully prepared to favor the Church so recently and harshly repressed, it was time to assess the past and chart the future.

The question of what writings should count as Christian scripture was now more pressing than previously, for two reasons. The first was that Diocletian had recognized that books had a foundational importance for Christianity, and so in his edict of 303 he ordered the confiscation and destruction of Christian books.[46] The Church's repositories of texts, certainly including scriptural texts, were severely depleted through the systematic enforcement of this order and thus required some restoration. But second, in his intention to restore and promote the Church's fortunes, Constantine was enthusiastic to build new churches and to furnish them with copies of the scriptures. With this in view, in 332 he wrote the following letter to Eusebius, episcopal custodian of the famous Christian library in Caesarea (*Life of Constantine* 4.36):

Victor Constantius Maximus Augustus, to Eusebius. In that city which bears my name, by the assistance of God our Savior's providence, a vast multitude of people have joined themselves to the most holy Church. Whereas all things there receive a very great increase, it seems very necessary that there should be more churches erected in that city. Therefore do you most willingly accept what I have determined to do. For it seemed fit to signify to your prudence that you should order fifty copies of the divine scriptures, the provision and use of which you know to be chiefly necessary for the instruction of the Church, to be written on well-prepared parchment by copyists most skillful in the art of accurate and beautiful writing, which [copies] must be very legible and easily portable so that they may be used. Moreover, letters have been dispatched to the chief financial officer of the diocese giving instructions that he should take care to provide everything necessary in order that the said copies might be completed. This, then, shall be your responsibility, to see that the written copies be provided forthwith.

Eusebius must have found this letter gratifying, but also daunting, for the immediate production of fifty fine handwritten copies of "the scriptures" was a very tall order. No such effort had ever been undertaken, and even if the costs were to be covered from the imperial treasury, the logistics of such a project were enormous.

Constantine's request does not specify what was meant by "the divine scriptures" and, as we have noted, there was as yet no clear consensus about exactly what documents might come under such a rubric. In fact, we do not know either what Constantine intended or what Eusebius supplied. It has often been supposed that what was sought and provided were complete copies of the Bible, Old and New Testaments together, in a single volume. Indeed, some have wished to think that the famous fourth-century codices of the Bible, Sinaiticus (cat. no. 26), and Vaticanus, are surviving results of Constantine's requisition.[47] This is conceivable, but unlikely. Constantine wanted the books to be rapidly produced and easily portable, but neither could be expected if they were to be whole bibles. Probably, then, the books asked for and produced were codices of the gospels only.[48]

However that may be, the codices Sinaiticus and Vaticanus, both of the fourth century, exemplify a standard of book production far higher than any previously approximated by early Christian manuscripts. They are large format, written on high-grade parchment in careful book-hands of accomplished scribes, and laid out in three (Vaticanus) or four (Sinaiticus) tall, narrow columns to the page. In all respects these are magnificent specimens of bookmaking skill. It is interesting to notice, however, that the Codex Sinaiticus includes in its "New Testament" both the Epistle of Barnabas and the Shepherd of Hermas, books that, as we have seen, were in Eusebius's "disputed" category, and that Codex Vaticanus does not contain the "private" letters of Paul (1–2 Timothy, Titus, Philemon), and may possibly have included (like Sinaiticus) at least the Epistle of Barnabas and the Shepherd of Hermas.[49] Such variations show that the limits of the New Testament had not been determined when these manuscripts were produced.

Although these great codices and the comparable fifth-century Codex Alexandrinus make it clear that whole bibles (or pandects, from the Greek *pandektes*, literally an "all receiver") could be and were produced in the fourth and later centuries, such manuscripts were never produced in large numbers, owing to the magnitude of the scribal task and the unwieldy size of the product. There are no examples from the pre-Constantinian era of manuscripts containing even an extensive group of Christian writings, and in the post-Constantinian period it continued to be common practice for Christian scriptural books to be written in discrete smaller codices, whether of gospels only, or of the epistles only.

Nevertheless, in the production of pandects of Christian scriptures in the fourth and fifth centuries we have to do with another important point of convergence between Bible and book. Precisely in this period Christianity was in the late stages of deciding exactly which Christian writings should be reckoned as scripturally authoritative alongside the scriptures of Judaism. Nothing could more concretely define the scope of the scriptures, and nothing could more powerfully represent the unity of the scriptures, than transcribing everything in one large codex. Precisely in this period too had it become economically and technologically feasible, thanks to imperial patronage, to create such large-scale, multi-quire parchment codices as were required to include such an extensive body of texts as Christians esteemed. But once their extent was determined and their unity affirmed in the physical form of a whole-Bible codex, there were no compelling reasons to produce such large volumes, and thereafter the pandect played a mainly symbolic role but had little practical value.

It is only after the middle of the fourth century that we encounter a list of twenty-seven authoritative Christian writings corresponding exactly to the contents of the New Testament as we know it. This is found in the Thirty-ninth Festal (Easter) Letter written to his diocese by the famous Alexandrian bishop, Athanasius, in 367. It is probably not accidental that Athanasius was also the first to use the word "canon" for a limited body of authoritative documents. What Athanasius had in mind by this term was not the contents of a book, but rather simply a list of those writings that it was permissible to employ for public reading in the setting of Christian worship.

Athanasius drew up his list for his own diocese in Egypt, and it had no force elsewhere. But lists resembling his, though often different in content, begin to be frequent in the fourth and fifth centuries, and their appearance is symptomatic of a widespread interest in this period to make determinations that would finalize the form of the New Testament. The famous Codex Claromontanus (cat. no. 30), a sixth-century manuscript of the Pauline letters, is notable for several reasons: it is one of the earliest bilingual manuscripts, presenting the text in Greek and Latin on facing pages; it arranges the text in sense lines (*per cola et commata*, "by phrase and clause") as an aid to reading; and it preserves a list of Christian writings that is of much earlier origin than the manuscript itself and probably goes back to the fourth century. This list specifies, in order: the four gospels, ten letters of Paul, the seven catholic epistles, the Epistle of Barnabas, the Revelation of John, the Acts of the Apostles, the Shepherd of Hermas, the Acts of Paul, and the Apocalypse of Peter—a total of twenty-seven books, but a rather different twenty-seven than Athanasius listed. It must have been a mere oversight that three Pauline letters (Philippians and 1–2 Thessalonians) were not listed, and it is to be noticed that a scribal mark in the form of a horizontal line was placed before Barnabas, the Shepherd, the Acts of Paul, and the Apocalypse of Peter, which must indicate hesitation about these items, if not in the original list, then by a later copyist. If these things are taken into account, then the catalogue in Claromontanus closely resembles the list of Athanasius.

Another early list, the so-called Cheltenham Canon, comes from North Africa and may be dated to about 360 C.E. The list is introduced by the statement: "As it is said in the Apocalypse of John, 'I saw twenty-four elders presenting their crowns before the throne' [Revelation 4:10], so our fathers approved that these books are canonical [that is, "in the list"] and that the men of old have said this." The list includes four gospels, thirteen letters of Paul, Acts, Revelation, the three letters of John and the two of Peter—a total of twenty-four documents. The appeal to a vision of the Revelation of John, joined with an appeal to tradition ("our fathers," "the men of old") is reminiscent of Irenaeus's rationale for the collection of four gospels. Yet here tradition asserts itself in a further way, for after both the mention of the three letters of John and the two letters of Peter there is the notation *una sola*, "one only," in accordance with the early tendency to grant recognition only to 1 John and 1 Peter.

Finally, we may take note of pronouncements that were issued by several ecclesiastical councils during the fourth century. One comes from the Council of Laodicea in Asia Minor, held in 363. It stipulated for reading in the Church "only the canonical books," of which twenty-six were enumerated, Revelation being omitted in accordance with the old Eastern tendency. In the West, two North African synods promulgated lists of authoritative books. The Council of Hippo in 393 and the Council of Carthage in 397 both named the twenty-seven books of our New Testament.

All this evidence, taken together, indicates that a broad uniformity of usage, which closely approximates what we know as the New Testament, cannot be dated earlier than the period 350–400 C.E.[50] Yet the gradual emergence of an authoritative collection of Christian scriptures, and the final shaping of the New Testament canon in the late fourth century, were not consequences of official pronouncements of bishops or councils. Indeed, no ecumenical council of the Christian Church ever declared what precisely constituted the New Testament until the Council of Trent did so in 1546. Most, though not all, of the books that were finally included in the canon of the New Testament had been familiar to Christians for generations, and indeed had long been determinative of Christian conviction and identity. To that extent, the formation of the New Testament canon simply honored and enshrined usages that were long-standing in the majority of Churches. Even so, it was not merely a matter of collection, but also of selection, and therefore also of exclusion. Some books that had a long and broad history of usage, and had been valued as "scripture" by many, were finally disenfranchised by exclusion from the canon (for example, the Shepherd of Hermas), just as other books, perhaps less well-known, were included (for example, Jude or 2 Peter). Although various criteria—apostolicity, catholicity, orthodoxy (but not, however, inspiration)—were invoked to rationalize such decisions, the compelling basis for canonical recognition was, with few exceptions, traditional use.

Thus the New Testament, and with it the Christian Bible as a whole, was the cumulative result of the reading habits of Christian communities in their liturgical gatherings. Its contents represent those documents in which the Churches, through generations of public reading in worship, had discovered indispensable resources for the enrichment and enlargement of their religious life.

Monica J. Blanchard

The Christian Orient

In his monumental work, *Oriens Christianus*, published posthumously in 1740, the French theologian Michel Le Quien (1661–1733) described the ecclesiastical geography and listed the known bishops and heads of the Eastern patriarchates of Constantinople, Antioch, Alexandria, and Jerusalem.[1] Today the term "Christian Orient" remains a convenient descriptor for the ancient Churches of the Middle East. They shared in the heritage of the early Church but over time developed their own distinctive socio-confessional identities and their own languages of worship: Syriac, Coptic, Arabic, Armenian, Georgian, and Ethiopic. Their translations, exegetical texts, and manuscript decoration are important for the study of the earliest Bibles.

Opposite: Fig. 1 Cathedral of Ani, capital of the Bagratid kingdom of Armenia, tenth–eleventh century.

THE LANGUAGE THAT JESUS SPOKE

Syriac is the Aramaic dialect associated with Edessa in Mesopotamia (modern Urfa in eastern Turkey). In the second century it became the linguistic vehicle for an enormous body of Christian literature that extended from the Eastern Roman and Persian empires to southern India and China. Classical and later forms of the language continue to be spoken and written today by Christians of the Syriac tradition, who find in the Syriac gospels a special connection with the Aramaic language spoken by Jesus.

Geographical and political divisions and the controversies over the nature of Christ of the fifth through seventh centuries contributed to the formation of new ecclesial communities (see "Spreading the Word," page 53): the Church of the East (East Syriac or Syrian; so-called Nestorian), which rejected the Council of Ephesus in 431; the Syrian Orthodox Church (West Syriac or Syrian; so-called Monophysite or Jacobite), which rejected the Council of Chalcedon in 451; the Maronite Church of West Syriac liturgical heritage, which accepted Chalcedon; and the Melkite Church, which also professed Chalcedonian orthodoxy and kept Syriac among its liturgical languages until the seventeenth century.[2] Distinctive East and West Syriac language traditions and scripts also emerged in this period.[3]

The books of the Old Testament were individually translated from the Hebrew into Syriac beginning in the second century.[4] Later, the gospels and other books of the New Testament were translated from the Greek. Combined, these Syriac translations are called the Peshitta, i.e., "simple," which is the standard version for the Syriac-speaking Churches. In the sixth, seventh, and early eighth centuries, the prestige and influence of Greek-speaking Christianity was an incentive for revisions of the Syriac Bible towards the Greek, comparisons of the Syriac and Greek versions, and biblical translations from Greek into Syriac.[5] Translators attempted to "mirror" the Greek text in Syriac, and the "Syrohexapla" attests to their literal translation skills. Between 615 and 617, in a monastery outside Alexandria, Paul of Tella made this "mirror" translation of Origen's Hexaplaric revision of the Septuagint towards the Hebrew. In 616, Thomas of Harkel from the same monastery completed a revision of the entire Syriac New Testament, closely conforming it to the Greek by means of the same translation techniques.

The first Syriac gospel translation may have been the harmonized version composed by Tatian in the second half of the second century. Known as the Syriac *Diatessaron*, it has not survived, but an almost complete *Commentary on the Diatessaron* attributed to Saint Ephrem the Syrian (ca. 306–373) exists in Syriac (cat. no. 23). There is also an Armenian translation.[6] This *Commentary* brings us close to the early *Diatessaron*. In Syriac it was called the "Mixed Gospel" *(evangelion da-meḥalleṭē)*. By the middle of the fifth century Syriac translations of the "Separated Gospel" *(evangelion da-mepharreshē)* had replaced the *Diatessaron*. While the earliest Gospels of Matthew, Mark, Luke, and John in Syriac were influenced by the *Diatessaron*, they were gradually revised towards the Greek. By the fifth century a revised form had become the official Peshitta version of the gospels.

ARMENIA: A DOUBLE-ROOTED MESSAGE

Christianity was introduced into Armenia via Syriac and Greek influences.[7] The Armenian Church pays tribute to this double root by commemorating two founders of Christianity in Armenia. There is an Armenian tradition of apostolic foundation by Saint Thaddeus, known in Syriac as Addai, an apostle in the Eastern Christian Churches.[8] The *Teaching of Addai* tells the Syriac story of a correspondence between King Abgar V the Black of Edessa and Jesus, and how Jesus sent the apostle Addai to preach Christianity in Edessa.[9] Armenian versions of this story mention that after Thaddeus left Edessa, he brought the Christian faith to Armenia.[10] Gregory the Illuminator is honored as the founder and organizer of the Armenian Church. The son of a Parthian noble, he was raised as a Christian in Caesarea of Cappadocia. Gregory returned to Armenia around the year 298, when Trdat the Great claimed the Armenian throne. He eventually converted Trdat to Christianity and was ordained bishop of Armenia by Leontius, bishop of Caesarea of Cappadocia (ca. 314). Armenian Christian vocabulary,

Fig. 2
Tigris River at Diyarbakir (ancient Amida), Turkey.

literature, and liturgy reveal Syriac as well as Greek influences, as does the Armenian Bible.[11]

By the fourth century Syriac and Greek were the written languages of the Armenian Church; Armenian was one of its spoken languages. A passage from the *Epic Histories* attributed to P'awstos Buzandac'i describes the challenge for Armenian nobles (the *naxarars*) and peasants to grasp and accept Christianity:

... only those who were to some degree acquainted with Greek or Syriac learning [were able] to achieve some partial inkling of it. As for those who were without skill in learning and who were the great mass of the people—the naxarars *as well as the peasantry—even had spiritual-teachers sat night and day pouring the abundance of their teaching over [their heads] like a torrent of rain from the clouds, not one of them could keep in mind a single thing of what he had heard: not a word, not half a word, not a minimal record, not a trace!*[12]

Maštoc', later called Mesrob (died 440), created the Armenian alphabet at the beginning of the fifth century,[13] and he and the Armenian Catholicos Sahak (died 439) translated the Bible into Armenian. Literary sources from the fifth to eighth centuries preserve a montage of "snapshots" of this work. The two men—later named as saints—were aided by their pupils in collecting biblical and patristic literature and translating it from Syriac and Greek into Armenian. In Koriwn's *Life of Maštoc'*, which may have been composed in the mid-440s, Sahak and Maštoc' sent students named Hovsep and Eznik to Edessa to write down the traditions of the Church Fathers and translate them from Syriac into Armenian. The pupils did this and sent materials back to their Armenian fathers before heading to "the region of the Greeks" where they studied the Greek language and became competent translators:

Then they came to the land of Armenia, having brought authentic copies of the God-given book and many subsequent traditions of the worthy church fathers, along with the canons of Nicaea and Ephesus, and placed before the fathers the testaments of the Holy Church which they had brought with them.

Yet blessed Sahak, who had rendered from the Greek language into Armenian all the ecclesiastical books and the wisdom of the church fathers, once more undertook, with Eznik, the comparison of the former random, hurriedly done translations from then available copies with the authentic copies, and they translated many commentaries of the Bible.[14]

GEORGIA

Christianity was accepted as the state religion of Georgia circa 337 in the eastern kingdom of Kartli. The *Life of Saint Nino*, who brought Christianity to Georgia, tells of her birth and upbringing in Jerusalem, and her knowledge of Hebrew.[15] The Georgian alphabet was invented in the early fifth century and already by circa 430 the Georgian monk Peter the Iberian (ca. 413–491) had commissioned a large Georgian inscription near Bethlehem.[16] Around the year 600 Georgia accepted the Chalcedonian definition of Christ's nature that it had rejected at the Council of Chalcedon in 451. While Armenian and Syriac influences have been studied in the earliest Georgian translations of the Bible, subsequent revisions brought it into close conformance with the Greek. Georgian monks resident in Holy Land monasteries translated much Christian literature into Georgian (cat. no. 35). Texts no longer extant in their original languages of composition have survived in Georgian thanks to their efforts. At the same time many early Georgian manuscripts of the fifth through eighth centuries have also been preserved in these same monasteries.[17]

COPTIC EGYPT: TEXT AND CONTEXT

The Coptic Church in Egypt dates its foundation to the arrival of Saint Mark the Evangelist in Alexandria. The term Copt, from a later Arabic rendering of the word *aigyptos*, "Egyptian," came to identify the Christian Egyptian community and its Egyptian language. Greek was the earliest biblical language in Christian Egypt.[18] It was not until the end of the third century that a distinctive Coptic script of Greek letters, supplemented by letter forms from the Egyptian Demotic script, began to be used to translate the Bible into Coptic.[19]

When we speak of a Coptic language, we are actually referring to Coptic dialects. The configuration of the Nile river delta and valley fostered the development of multiple Coptic dialects, of which Sahidic and Bohairic are the most important for Coptic literature.[20] Sahidic Coptic became the classical literary form. Eventually it was replaced by Bohairic, which remains the liturgical language of the Coptic Church today.

The Coptic books of the Old Testament were translated primarily from the Septuagint, but no complete collection of the books of the Coptic Old Testament has survived from antiquity in any of the Coptic dialects.[21]

Egypt's climate and geography are nevertheless well suited for the preservation of papyri, parchment, leather, and other writing materials. Large groups of Coptic texts have been discovered in modern times, such as the 1910 find of the Coptic library of the ancient Monastery of Saint Michael near the modern site of al-Hamuli in the Fayyum district of Egypt. This collection of ninth- and tenth-century codices, now mostly in the Morgan Library and Museum, New York, made available for the first time a large and largely intact Coptic monastic library, with a variety of biblical resources with a secure *floruit* and provenance.[22]

Texts preserved in Egypt also tell a story of earlier scriptural diversity. In 1945 a fourth-century library of collections of Gnostic "scriptures" was discovered in Nag Hammadi in upper Egypt.[23] Arguably the most famous of these is a Coptic version of the Gospel of Thomas, one of a group of three Nag Hammadi texts with a Christian Mesopotamian (i.e., Syriac) provenance (FIG.3). The sayings of Jesus contained in this apocryphal gospel have attracted much attention (see cat. no. 15). Scholars have studied it alongside the canonical gospels and the *Diatessaron*, looking for parallels and cross-influences.[24] They have also drawn attention to its affinity with wisdom literature.[25] The scriptural value of the Gospel of Thomas within fourth-century Christian Egypt is unclear. It may have been read as edifying literature within Christian milieux.

ETHIOPIA: A NEW JERUSALEM

Christianity was introduced to Ethiopia from Egypt in the early fourth century. According to Rufinus's *Ecclesiastical History* (1.9–10) of circa 401, Frumentius and Aedesius, brothers from Tyre, were shipwrecked off the Ethiopian coast; they were rescued and became part of the royal court at Axum. Frumentius is said to have visited Athanasius in Alexandria to request a bishop for Ethiopia. Athanasius consecrated him, and he returned to Axum as the first of a long line of bishops, or *abunas*, who came to Ethiopia by way of Egypt.[26] The Ethiopian Church rejected the Chalcedonian definition of the nature of Christ; so did the Coptic Church of Egypt.

Most of the Ethiopic Bible was translated from the Septuagint into Geʿez or classical Ethiopic between the end of the fourth century and the end of the sixth century. It was subsequently revised on the basis of later Arabic versions that had been translated from Syriac or Coptic texts. The biblical canon

Fig. 3
Nag Hammadi Codex II, pp. 32–33. Left page: The end of the Apocryphon of John and beginning of the Gospel of Thomas. Right page: The origin of the world. Egypt, fourth century. Cairo, Coptic Museum.

Fig. 4
Detail, Church of the Holy Cross, 915–921, Ahtamar Island, Turkey.

includes more than eighty books—the largest of any of the Oriental Churches. Complete versions of the Book of Jubilees and the Book of Enoch are found only in Ethiopic.[27]

Ethiopian Christians cherish special connections to Jerusalem. The fourteenth-century *Kebra Nagast* (Book of the Glory of Kings) tells the story of Solomon and the Queen of Sheba, and their son Menelik, who took the Ark of the Covenant from Jerusalem to Axum in Ethiopia, making Axum the new Jerusalem and the Ethiopian nation the new chosen people of God.[28] The crucifixion scene in the Zir Ganela Gospels of 1400/1401 (cat. no. 40) is reminiscent of sixth-century imagery on small flasks and other pilgrimage materials linked to the veneration of the Cross and to the cult of the holy places in Jerusalem.[29]

MONASTERIES

It was only in 451 at the Council of Chalcedon that Jerusalem was recognized as a Patriarchal See. But it had been the earliest focus of Christian pilgrimage, and its Judaean desert environs became an important center of monasticism. Christians of different customs and languages worshipped here together.

The Judaean desert monasteries were at the center of Arabic-speaking Christianity, particularly among Melkite Christians, i.e., Christians of "Orthodox" or "Byzantine" faith. During the years between 750 and 1050 Melkites living under Islam were isolated from Constantinople and from their Greek-speaking co-religionists. In pre-Islamic times the Greek Bible had been translated into a local Aramaic language, Christian Palestinian Aramaic, which had been the Melkites' everyday language. After the rise of Islam Arabic eventually became the local vernacular, and Melkites became the first Christians to adopt it as an ecclesial language.[30]

The attraction of the Holy Land for all the Oriental Churches is exemplified by the Holy Monastery of Saint Catherine in Sinai, Egypt, where God appeared to Moses in the burning bush (see figure 2, page 48). The monastery's library holdings include manuscripts written or obtained by Greek, Arabic, Georgian, and Syriac-speaking monks professing Chalcedonian orthodoxy. Its relative isolation and arid climate helped to preserve many important biblical texts, including both the Greek and Syriac manuscripts known individually as Sinaiticus (cat. no. 26). The monastery's ecumenical spirit is demonstrated by Sinai Arabic MS 151, an Arabic translation and commentary on the Pauline Epistles, Acts of the Apostles, and the catholic epistles, written in 867 (cat. no. 32).[31] The translation was made from Syriac versions by Bishr ibn al-Sirri, who included a commentary drawing upon Eastern Syriac exegetical sources. Later, it was collated by a Syrian Orthodox writer, and at some point in time Melkite lectionary notes were added.

It is to Egypt rather than to the Syriac-speaking regions of Syria and Mesopotamia that we owe the preservation of one of the most important extant collections of Syriac Christian manuscripts. The library of the Monastery of the Syrians in the Wadi Natrun, Deir el-Suriani (see figure 3, page 48), sheltered these materials, many of which are now in the Vatican and British Library, London.[32] The general antiquity of the library selection is noteworthy, and it was well stocked with Syriac manuscripts of the fifth, sixth, and seventh centuries. It would be difficult to overstate the significance of this collection for the study of the Syriac Bible, and for Syriac literature more generally. Many of the earliest Syriac biblical manuscripts were found there, and manuscripts from Deir el-Suriani preserve early Syriac translations of lost or fragmentary Greek texts along with important early Syriac works.[33]

The Monastery of the Syrians originated in the sixth century as a Coptic monastic foundation, and owed its special cachet to the Wadi Natrun's association with the great monastic center of Scetis.[34] It was sold to a group of Syrian Orthodox from Tagrit (modern Tikrit in Iraq), perhaps in the early ninth century. Tagrit was the metropolitan see and center of the Syrian Orthodox Church in Iraq. It maintained a close relationship with Deir el-Suriani and with a community of Tagritan merchants resident in Fustat in Egypt. A special debt of gratitude is owed to the tenth-century abbot of the monastery, Moses of Nisibis (*fl.* 906–943), who spent five years in Baghdad negotiating a poll tax newly required of monks in Egypt by the Islamic Caliphate. His successful return to the monastery in 932 is commemorated by a series of notes written by him in books that he brought back. During the five years that he was away Moses collected 250 books from the churches, monasteries, and towns of Syria and Mesopotamia. His effort to build a great library for the Monastery of the Syrians ensured the survival of many early Syriac manuscripts.

The library of Deir el-Suriani also draws attention to an authentic meeting of the Syriac and Coptic traditions through the medium of translation activity (from Coptic through Arabic to Syriac) in the Monastery of the Syrians and other monasteries in the Wadi Natrun.[35] Like Saint Catherine's Monastery, Deir el-Suriani testifies to the interaction and communication between different Christian confessional groups brought together by a monastic calling and by the call of pilgrimage.[36] As in the Christian West, the monasteries of the Christian East were in large part responsible for the transmission and preservation of the Bible.

LEGIS HONORIFICA
THRONO FULTUS UBIQUE DO

Michelle P. Brown

Spreading the Word

The Bible, or rather the various biblical editions that we know today, took many centuries to evolve and assumed many forms. For Christianity is a religion of the Book, but one that has also relied on oral tradition—what people told one another, in Aramaic, Hebrew, Greek, Latin, and the vernacular languages. Written testimonies and individual books (or groups of books) of the Bible initially circulated as informally produced pamphlets of papyrus or parchment. It was not until attempts were made to gather them together, to assess their validity and "codify" them as complete bodies of work of a "canonical" (approved or standardized) nature, that complete Christian Bibles were produced, containing texts considered to embody authentic teaching inspired by God.

The first Christian emperor, Constantine, and his successors, who were intent on promoting clarity and unity within the new religion (and the Eastern and Western parts of their empire), played an important part in the gradual process of codification, as did the Church councils they convened to debate such matters. Complete bibles (pandects) were, however, rare and costly, until the rise of the European university book-trade around 1200 and, along with it, the "Paris Study Bible" (a densely written, more affordable, and portable one-volume bible, designed for use in the university syllabus). Prior to this, pandects were usually the result of well-planned programs of editing and publication associated with notable figures such as Emperor Charlemagne, Abbot Ceolfrith of Wearmouth–Jarrow, and Abbot Alcuin of Tours.[1]

Opposite:
Detail of fig. 10.

The codification of the Hebrew Bible underwent a similarly protracted process. For despite traditional claims that the Judaic scriptures were translated to form the Greek Septuagint in Alexandria in the late third century B.C.E. at the command of Ptolemy II Philadelphus,[2] it is now generally accepted that different parts of the Hebrew scriptures were translated at different times and places around the eastern Mediterranean during the centuries prior to Christianity and that the Hebrew Bible did not coalesce until the Council of Jamnia (ca. 100 C.E.) produced the canonical text. Subsequently, the Masorah, a body of notes on the traditions of the text, was compiled between 600 and 900 by Jewish scribes called the Masoretes.

Those unfamiliar with textual scholarship might assume that the earlier the copy of a text, the closer it will be to the original. But given the vagaries of transmission in the pre-print age, and the problems of ensuring copies free from scribal errors or editorial interventions, this need not be the case. Age alone does not guarantee authenticity or purity of text and the oldest surviving copy is not always the best. Sometimes all the available manuscript copies of a text need to be assessed to recapture an author's original intention.[3] What is more, it is necessary to consider the historical and social contexts in which individual copies were made. For, as we shall see, different cultures gave rise to different Churches, each with its own textual traditions, languages, and styles of book production and these in turn interacted with one another.

FROM LATE ANTIQUITY TO THE EARLY MIDDLE AGES

In order to appreciate the ways in which the dissemination of scripture occurred in the aftermath of the Roman Empire it may be useful briefly to consider aspects of its legacy in relation to book production and the ways in which the power vacuum it left behind was filled. With the fragmentation of the Empire in the early fifth century C.E. the urban nature of classical civilization was transformed into a new network of power-bases and intellectual centers. Some towns continued to trade, becoming bishoprics or royal centers, and were joined by rural manors, princely citadels, and monasteries, which proliferated throughout the Middle East and Europe. Literacy contracted among the general populace but book production—no longer undertaken by secular scribes and publishers—was perpetuated and carried beyond the old Empire's frontiers by the Church.

From the time that the codex achieved social acceptability along with Christianity during the fourth century, books were no longer just a cheap alternative favored by a persecuted underclass but the honored receptacles of sacred text for a powerful established religion (see "Bible and book," pages 32–33). Grand parchment books were made in response to the need for imposing volumes of scripture for prestigious churches, and whole bibles appeared—Codex Sinaiticus (cat. no. 26), Codex Vaticanus, and Codex Alexandrinus are the earliest known.[4]

Early Christian copies of scripture were undecorated, but during the fifth and sixth centuries images began to be applied to biblical books—with great picture cycles illustrating volumes such as the Byzantine Cotton and Vienna Genesis tomes (FIG. 1) and the Syriac Rabbula Gospels (cat. no. 62).[5] Pictures had not found favor with classical bibliophiles, but Italian publishers now even illustrated old literary favorites by Virgil, Terence, and Homer.[6] The use of opulent materials, with gold and silver scriptures on purple pages, also imparted imperial stature to the grandest Byzantine, Syriac, and Italian books, such as the sixth-century Italian Codex Brixianus (cat. no. 70) and the Golden Canon Tables made in Constantinople around 600 (see cat. no. 68).[7] The various peoples and kingdoms that emerged from the maelstrom of the Roman Empire's demise

Fig. 1
The Deluge, from the Vienna Genesis. Eastern Mediterranean, sixth century. Vienna, Österreichische Nationalbibliothek, Cod. Theol. Gr. 31, f. 3r.

also contributed their own distinctive forms of ornament to manuscript illumination.

In the Middle East and North Africa, book production increasingly became centered in remote monasteries founded by Christian communities that escaped persecution and tax hikes by following the lead of Saint Anthony, who had retreated to the Egyptian eastern desert in the late third century. In Caesarea, Armenia, Syria, Coptic Egypt, Nubia (an ancient region along the Nile in southern Egypt and northern Sudan), and Ethiopia monastic scriptoria developed distinctive styles of codicology (the ways in which books are put together), script, and illumination.[8] Some important monastic libraries survive, notably that at Saint Catherine's, Mount Sinai (FIG. 2) and Deir el-Suriani ("the Monastery of the Syrians") in the Egyptian Wadi Natrun (FIG. 3), where additional caches of long-lost manuscripts have recently been found in forgotten corners. Their contents graphically portray the varied cultural influences that had an impact upon these remote outposts (see "The Christian Orient," page 43, and below, page 54).

Christian bibliographic traditions in such areas, like those of Hebrew scribes, weathered the Islamic conquest of the eastern and southern Mediterranean from the seventh century onwards.[9] Although little survives from before the ninth century, Islamic book production was underway in the eighth. Muslim scribes, like their Jewish counterparts, did not use figural imagery in scripture for fear of idolatry, but evolved sacred calligraphy and decoration for the glorification of the Word. They also introduced paper—a technology learned from China during the eighth century, transmitted to Byzantium in the ninth and to the West from the eleventh—with cultural melting pots such as Iberia and Sicily serving as conduits for the exchange of ideas.

In Europe, book production became firmly established in the centuries between the retraction of the Roman Empire's frontiers in the early fifth century and the Viking raids, which commenced in 793 with the sack of Lindisfarne—a period often inappropriately termed "the Dark Ages," but one that was illuminated by its manuscript culture. One of the major achievements of the age was the construction of northern European successor states, underpinned by the Christian zeal of the newly converted and a re-emerging stability of administration and social structure based upon effective collaboration between Church and State. Crucial in this was the dissemination and reception of Christian scripture, with its emphasis upon law, social reform, and teaching by example. The great bibles, psalters, and gospelbooks of this age stand as its enduring monument.

The pagan Celts and the Germans of northern Europe had developed proto-writing systems of their own, ogam and runes, in response to Roman script but used them only for short commemorative or talismanic purposes, preferring to cultivate the memory and oral literacy.[10] They embraced written literacy along with Christianity and, faced with the challenges of learning Latin as a foreign language and how to write it,

Fig. 2
St. Catherine's Monastery,
Mount Sinai, Egypt.

Fig. 3
Deir el-Suriani Monastery,
the Wadi Natrun, Egypt.

made major contributions to book production. They evolved their own distinctive scripts and written languages, introduced word-separation and systematic punctuation,[11] promoted decoration to help navigate the text, and integrated their indigenous styles of art and poetry. Due largely to their enthusiastic espousal of its potential, the codex assumed much of its distinctive appearance and apparatus.

One of the most enduring successor states was that of the Franks in what had been Roman Gaul. The durability of the Merovingian dynasty (480–751), which paved the way for that of their Carolingian heirs (751–962), owed a lot to the continuity of much of the urban structure under the aegis of their bishops, whose dioceses perpetuated the Roman administrative divisions. The incoming Germanic settlers integrated, assisted by the rapid conversion of their leaders to Catholic orthodoxy, rather than to the Arian heresy concerning the nature of Christ (see below, page 53) favored by many other Germanic converts, thereby ensuring them the support of the post-Roman Church in Gaul.

The Merovingians' chancery script evolved from late Roman bureaucratic cursive—a rapidly written script with many loops and ligatures causing it to resemble the wanderings of a demented spider, while their books feature uncial script (a formal, rounded hand inherited from Rome) and a plethora of local scriptorium-specific minuscule scripts (less formal, lower-case hands, such as Luxeuil minuscule, Corbie "ab" minuscule, etc.). These were enlivened with initials and display lettering constructed from colorful birds, fish, beasts, and human forms that were derived from their own art and that of Byzantium and Italy.

Post-Roman Spain was occupied by Vandals and Visigoths. The latter converted and promoted Christian scholarship through the writings of figures such as Isidore of Seville. Visigothic scribes developed their own distinctive minuscule script, which they continued to use in many regions until the twelfth century as a sign of their independence from Carolingian dominance and their Christian identity under Islamic rule.[12] In the 780s Beatus of Liébana composed his influential commentary upon the Apocalypse of Saint John (Revelation) and the raw energy and Picasso-esque stylization of the images

Fig. 4
The Sealing of the Elect, from the Morgan Beatus. Spain, tenth century. New York, The Morgan Library & Museum, MS 644, ff. 117v–118r.

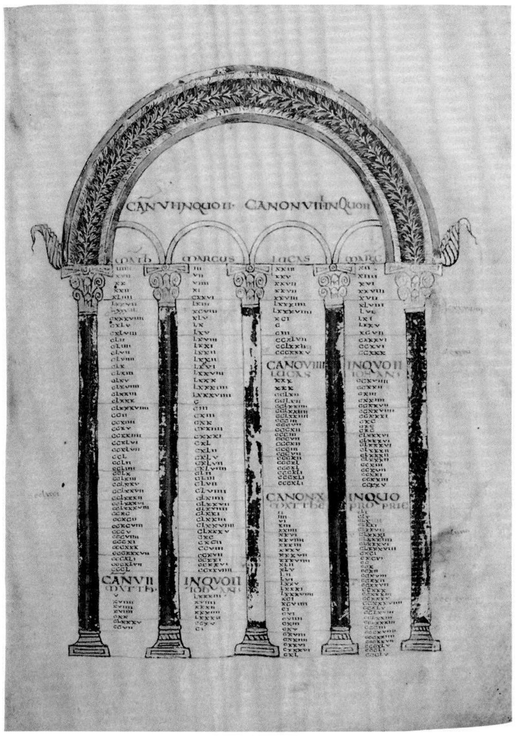

Fig. 5
Canon tables, from the Codex Beneventanus. Duchy of Benevento, Southern Italy, mid-eighth century (before 760). London, British Library, Add. MS. 5463, f. 3r.

Fig. 6
St. Luke, from the Corpus or St. Augustine Gospels. Italy (Rome?), late sixth century. Cambridge, Corpus Christi College, MS. 286, f. 129v.

in the resulting copies of the Apocalypse produced in Spanish scriptoria such as San Salvador de Tábara and Silos during the late tenth to early twelfth centuries (FIG. 4) speak both to the degree of cultural identity retained by the Mozarabic Christians under tolerant Muslim rule and their reception of certain stylistic influences.

In fifth- to sixth-century Italy power passed to the Byzantine Exarchate of Ravenna (a Byzantine province forming a bridgehead to the old Western Empire), the papacy in Rome, the Ostrogoths and the Lombards of northern Italy and Benevento and, from around 800, the Carolingian Empire. The romanophile Ostrogothic kingdom did not survive owing to its heretical Arianism, which alienated the indigenous population and its neighbors, but within it were written influential works, including those by the Italian biblical scholar and monastic founder Cassiodorus (see below, page 65), whose teachings exerted great influence upon early medieval scribes and authors.

The Lombards, resisting these other powers, fused influences from Mediterranean art with traditional Germanic animal ornament and favored their own Beneventan minuscule, which endured in the Duchy of Benevento in southern

Italy, notably in Saint Benedict's monastery of Montecassino, until 1300.[13] The eighth-century Codex Beneventanus (FIG. 5), a splendid gospelbook with skillfully painted classical arcades of illusionistic marble columns, is a tribute to their book culture.[14]

In Rome itself the Church, arts, and learning were given a tremendous boost under Pope Gregory the Great (died 604). This great missionary, intent upon reviving Rome's Western Empire in Christian guise, was a gifted theologian whose writings helped mold the Western Church. Books from Gregory's Rome feature elegant uncial script and initials decorated with crosses and fish. The Saint Augustine Gospels (on which the Anglican archbishops of Canterbury still take their oaths, FIG. 6), feature a classical author portrait and vignettes, resembling "cartoon-strip" scenes, from the life of Christ. The Gospels are traditionally said to have accompanied Augustine when he was sent by Gregory to convert the pagan Anglo-Saxon settlers of England in 597 and are certainly representative of the type of books his mission would have used— impressive in their way, but not of the highest quality (see cat. no. 53).[15]

Another force in the conversion of the English was Ireland, operating through monasteries such as Iona and Lindisfarne, founded by the Irish Saint Columba and his followers. Ireland had received Christianity during the fifth century, when Palladius was sent from Rome (431) as bishop to those who already believed and Saint Patrick launched his mission from the Romano-British Church.[16] Irish scribes developed decorated initials, formal half-uncial hands for scripture, and calligraphic minuscule scripts for less formal works. They, followed by their English neighbors, also introduced spaces between words and systematic punctuation to clarify legibility and meaning, stimulated by Gregory, Isidore of Seville, and Bede (the greatest English scholar of the age), all of whom promoted silent reading to facilitate meditation and comprehension, supplementing the classical emphasis upon reading out loud to foster oratory and rhetoric.[17]

The Anglo-Saxons further developed the range of scripts used, under renewed Roman influence via Canterbury and Wearmouth–Jarrow, adding Roman capitals and uncials, perfecting half-uncials, and evolving minuscules of varying levels of formality. Within this sophisticated system of scripts, termed "Insular" (i.e., of the islands of Britain and Ireland, ca. 550–850), form was suited to function, recognizing that it was inappropriate to use the same script for sacred texts as that used for informal correspondence or books intended for study in the library.[18] The power of writing was reinforced by the iconic nature of the book in a religious context. Secular rulers were quick to perceive the value of this new medium and enlisted the support of the Church in penning law-codes, charters, and genealogies to help establish secure states.[19] Augustine committed King Æthelberht of Kent's Germanic law-code to the "safe-keeping" of writing, and is credited thereby with inventing written Old English and beginning the process of integrating the Church into the social structure.[20] Unlike their continental counterparts, seventh-century English documents are written not in the excessively cursive scripts inherited from the late Roman bureaucracy but in the high-grade uncials used for scripture—perceptions of the importance of writing in the context of sacred text and liturgical ritual serving to imbue such instruments of government with enhanced authority.

Insular missionaries evangelized the courts and countryside of their islands and continental Europe through extensive monastic federations—monasticism having achieved tremendous popularity in western Britain and Ireland from around 500 through the influence of the Eastern desert fathers (founders of the monastic tradition in the Near East, such as

Saints Anthony, Pachomius, and Basil) transmitted via Italy and Gaul. Their inspirational preaching of the Christian message could lead seasoned warriors to embrace pacifism and kings to free slaves, radically transforming society—often at risk of assassination. The role models provided by such energized, charismatic, ascetic individuals—publicly acclaimed as saints during their lifetimes—set new levels of social and spiritual aspiration. Some of the most beautiful medieval gospelbooks (see FIG. 8 and cat. nos. 58, 59) were made as the focal points of their shrines and symbolized the processes of integration and transmission that characterized the transition from the Antique to the medieval period.

The Bible and the codex initially took shape in the world of late Greco-Roman Antiquity, within an empire that stretched from Syria to Scotland. Greek and Latin were the literary languages and Christianity had become the state religion. The world in which they would be developed was that of the early Middle Ages, when individual nations began to emerge, with their own languages, cultures, and religious traditions—orthodox Christian, heretical, and pagan—all influencing the ways in which Bible and book were perceived and produced. Many of these states were, in turn, subsumed within bigger territories as the concept of "empire" continued to beguile ambitious leaders who sought to bind together the diverse peoples under their rule, using faith as part of that process.

The discussion that follows charts the journey of the Bible during these "interesting times" through an examination of the following themes: the dissemination of scripture from the East to the West and the interlinked issues of the use of language and of local textual traditions; the gradual crystallization of the Bible through the work of successive editors; the emergence of the scribe's role as evangelist, situated within an ongoing process of transmission of scripture across the ages; and the changing status of the book and its role in society, as reflected in its physical form and appearance.

THE "SACRED" LANGUAGES AND THE RISE OF THE VERNACULAR

THE CHRISTIAN ORIENT

The Greek Church began to achieve ascendancy around the eastern Mediterranean from 381 C.E., when an ecumenical (universal) council declared that Constantinople exerted an equal authority in the East to that of Rome in the West. At the Council of Chalcedon in 451 five patriarchates were established: Constantinople, Rome, Alexandria, Antioch, and Jerusalem. Constantinople was accorded jurisdiction over Asia Minor and the eastern Balkans and evangelized there. In 588 Patriarch John IV of Constantinople declared himself Ecumenical Patriarch—a title retained by the leader of the Greek Orthodox Church to this day, while the leader of Catholic Orthodoxy in the West retains the title of "Pope." The authority of the other early patriarchates was severely curtailed by the spread of Islam, but the Coptic Orthodox (Monophysite) Church is still led by its own pope, the Patriarch of Alexandria.

During these and succeeding centuries the Greek language continued to play an over-arching, unifying role, but the hegemony of the Byzantine Church was disrupted by a number of factors. Jewish and Hellenistic influences may have been reconciled for Christians in the teaching of Saint Paul, but other Near Eastern cultural and religious traditions also had an impact upon the Eastern Empire. Early local Churches, such as those in Armenia, the first nation officially to adopt Christianity as its state religion in the early fourth century, and

Georgia, converted a little later, carefully guarded their established traditions.

More divisive, however, were the theological debates that dominated the fourth and fifth centuries and led to a hard-line condemnation of heretical sects by the "orthodox" Church, which in the process increasingly defined itself. Almost as soon as the Edict of Milan of 313 had sanctioned the existence of the Church, disputes concerning its beliefs and practices arose. Eager to prevent division, Constantine convened the first international ecumenical council at Nicaea in 325. This condemned Arianism—which taught that Christ was one of God's created creatures and that his nature was similar to but not the same as God's—and promoted the concept advanced by another Alexandrian prelate, Athanasius, that they were of one substance. The Council of Ephesus in 431 condemned the thoughts of Nestorius, Patriarch of Constantinople, concerning the relationship between Christ and the Virgin, whom he viewed as mother of the human part of Christ, fearing that the implications of this would split Christ's nature into two; this caused the East Syriac Church to splinter off. The crucial Council of Chalcedon, however, pronounced that Christ did indeed possess two natures, human and divine, which co-existed but were not merged. The Egyptians objected, championing the Monophysite belief that he possessed only one nature, causing a breach between the Orthodox and Monophysite (West Syriac or Jacobite, Coptic, Ethiopic, and some of the Nubian) Churches. The Armenians, busy fighting the Persians, did not attend Chalcedon and retained an ambiguous position regarding Monophysitism. Georgia broke with Byzantium following the Council, but resumed relations in 607, becoming an autocephalous Orthodox Church, as did the Slavic Churches that were subsequently established. A number of independent Churches therefore came into existence—each with its own languages and traditions.[21]

In the Christian Orient tension between "official" written languages and those spoken locally was not the issue it was to become in the West. Christ's teachings probably originally circulated orally in Aramaic,[22] a local language, even if the gospels were subsequently written in the literary Greek language of the eastern Mediterranean. There was no apparent concern about the appropriateness of communicating belief in regional languages. The Armenian Church employed Armenian; the Syriac Church employed Syriac; the Coptic Church employed Coptic (derived from the processes of writing the Egyptian language in Greek and translating the New Testament into Egyptian from Greek);[23] the Ethiopic Church employed Ethiopic (especially literary northern Ethiopic, Geʿez); the Nubian Church employed Old Nubian and Coptic; and so forth.

The adaptation of the Greek alphabet to produce those of Armenia and Georgia is ascribed to the missionary Saint Mesrob (or Mesrop) in the early fifth century. Likewise, Cyrillic script, which has been used for over sixty languages, is descended from the forty-character Greek-based Glagolitic alphabet, the invention of which is ascribed to Saint Cyril (ca. 827–69) and his companion Saint Methodius, sent as missionaries to the Slavs from Byzantium at the request of King Ratislaw of Moravia.[24] Other aspects of Greek influence can be seen in the way the books of these regions were constructed, written, and decorated.

The popularity of the early written vernaculars owed much to the desire among these groups for cultural definition and distinction (religious and ethnic). In short, centralized authorities tend to promote the use of a single unifying language, while those affirming local or group identity often use language as a means of signaling independent traditions and histories.

In the seventh century another important power emerged on the international scene. The Prophet Muhammad began preaching in Mecca around 610 and by 641 his followers had come to dominate much of the Middle East and were rapidly expanding around the eastern and southern Mediterranean. The toleration of religious and ethnic minorities by the Caliphate (the leading political power among Muslims) and its recognition of local religious leaders as simultaneously community representatives further promoted the development of self-contained regional Churches with inextricably interwoven ethnic cultures and traditions of faith, many of which survive still and periodically explode into conflict amidst the pressures and competition of our age. Positions became more entrenched during the Crusades of the late eleventh to late thirteenth centuries as Western forces sought to gain control of the holy places. Closer contact with the Churches of the East served only to deepen their estrangement, northern armies despoiling the heart of Byzantium in 1204. Finally, in 1453 Constantinople, the Christian city founded by Constantine in 330 as a bridgehead between Occident and Orient, fell to the Turks: the unfortunate, artificial rupture of the world into East and West was complete.

SAINT CATHERINE'S: A CULTURAL CROSSROADS

The Holy Monastery of Saint Catherine, Mount Sinai, one of the most important Byzantine monasteries, provides an extraordinary demonstration of the meeting of all these different traditions.[25] Its library has a remarkably polyglot, cross-cultural complexion. Founded by Emperor Justinian between 548 and 565 C.E., and originally dedicated to the Holy Virgin, it towers above the Sinai desert. This remote location has ensured its survival. Despite losses, it retains mosaics and icons from the time of its foundation and over 3000 manuscripts—part of the greatest library held by any Greek monastery.[26] The recent discovery of a further important cache of books from the medieval library, concealed in a long-forgotten sealed room, has added significantly to this number and, once conserved, will furnish a wealth of new research materials.

Mount Sinai (Horeb), where Moses encountered the Lord in the burning bush, has been a place of pilgrimage since Etheria, a Spanish noblewoman, visited in the fourth century and its international contacts continued after it came under Muslim rule in the seventh century. It has been home to Greek, Syrian, Arabic, Georgian, Slavic, and Latin monks—all espousing orthodoxy as expressed at the Council of Chalcedon. Their opposition to Monophysitism accounts for the comparative scarcity of Armenian, Ethiopic, and Coptic manuscripts.[27] Around two thirds of the extant works are Greek; some seventy percent of the rest are Christian Arabic texts; the remainder are written in Syriac,[28] Georgian, and Slavic, in descending order of frequency, and (in a couple of cases) Latin. The primary needs of the community were for scriptural and liturgical volumes, gradually supplemented by works written by the Church Fathers, exegesis and other study texts, and by materials in the native languages of incoming monks.

This remarkable library began to be known in the nineteenth century, especially after Count Constantin Tischendorf saw part of the famous Codex Sinaiticus there in 1844 (cat. no. 26).[29] This had been made in the fourth century, probably in Caesarea but, like other early volumes, had been acquired subsequently by the Sinai community. Many manuscripts, mostly servicebooks, were written at Sinai during the seventh to ninth centuries, some over the erased texts of earlier books (palimpsests). They are mostly in uncial script and do not contain figural imagery, probably as a consequence of Islamic influence and Byzantine iconoclasm (see below, and "Book as icon," page 80). However, decoration includes fish-shaped initials (an early Christian symbol of faith) resembling those of pre-Carolingian Italy and Gaul and perhaps inspired by gifts of books from these areas. Most are in Greek, but some are Greek–Arabic bilinguals for Arabic Christians and Greek monks raised in Muslim territories (such as Syria and Egypt) who spoke Arabic as their first language and Greek as their second (cat. no. 46).[30]

The end of iconoclasm in Byzantium, coupled with the wealth of Fatimid Egypt, meant that from the tenth century more opulent illuminated books were made at Sinai. One of the earliest was the Lectionary of Mount Horeb (cat. no. 52). It was written in Greek in 967 by Presbyter Eustathios, in uncial script adorned with decoration, including orientalizing initials and marginalia, among them Sasanian-style parti-colored griffins in the lower margins that recall Insular art such as the evangelist symbols of Saint Mark in the Book of Kells (in Trinity College Library, Dublin) and the Macregol Gospels (cat. no. 59).[31]

A significant number of tenth- to fourteenth-century Georgian manuscripts are also represented.[32] The Georgian kingdom was at its zenith, its monasteries flourishing in Syria and Palestine and producing recruits for the Sinai community, who required servicebooks in their own language or bilingually alongside Greek. A smattering of Slavonic books also survive, probably later imports to the library from Croatia and Macedonia, including two eleventh-century items in the Glagolitic language (a euchologion, Cod. Slav. 37, and a psalter, Cod. Slav. 38; see cat. no. 49)—among the earliest of extant Slavonic manuscripts. Their decoration recalls southern Italian and Byzantine foliate illumination.

A handful of pre-1000 Latin manuscripts survive, blending northern European, Visigothic, Greek, Syriac, and Arabic paleographical and ornamental influences, indicating that there were even Latin speakers present in the region, long before the Crusader kingdoms.[33] In 599 Pope Gregory the Great sent a legate bearing gifts to Sinai, so there were evidently early communications with the West.

By the end of the tenth century Constantinople had re-emerged as the central focus of Byzantine culture and its influence can be seen clearly in manuscripts imported into Sinai and produced there, including some of the finest illuminated manuscripts from the classicizing Macedonian renaissance.

Sinai has always been a meeting place of cultures and a destination of international pilgrimage. It is not surprising that its collections should reflect this, but perhaps miraculous that they should have survived the holocausts of history.

BIBLICAL TRANSMISSION IN THE MEDIEVAL WEST

What of the Western approach to the role of language in relation to unity and diversity? Social and ecclesiastical attitudes at this time were very different from those that prevailed at the end of the medieval period when Wycliffe, Tyndale, and Luther were condemned as heretics for publishing scripture in their native languages. Vernacular languages were deemed acceptable for biblical transmission in some areas at certain times, but nonetheless it was Latin that emerged as the main language in which biblical texts were copied in the medieval West. How did this come about?

The very concept of a linguistic "vernacular" is defined in relationship to universal languages. Around the Mediterranean these were Hebrew, Greek, and Latin—the "sacred languages" used for scripture. In medieval Europe it came to be Latin, the adopted vernacular of a diverse empire. The Italian monastic founder Cassiodorus wrote (*Institutiones*, Preface 4):

And so it appears that the Divine Scriptures of the Old and New Testament from the very beginning to the end have been expanded in the Greek language.... But with the Lord's aid we follow rather after Latin writers, that, since we are writing for Italians, we may most fitly seem to have pointed out Roman interpreters as well. For more gladly is that narration undertaken by every man which is told in the language of his fathers.[34]

This image of Latin as the early Italian vernacular reminds us that its primacy was by no means assured and that its rise was defined in relation to the Greek tradition, which itself interacted with Hebrew and other Semitic languages. When Saint Jerome produced his Vulgate it was so-named for its use of the common language of the day—Latin (the basis of the emerging "Romance" languages). The shift in perception of Latin's status owed a great deal to Jerome, Pope Damasus, and Pope Gregory the Great and their promotion in the West of Latin versions of scripture, raising "vulgar" Latin to literary heights.[35]

THE FORMATION OF THE LATIN BIBLE

One of the most important landmarks in biblical dissemination in the West was a Latin translation of the Christian Bible now known as the "Vulgate." This was one of several projects to produce reliable editions of the component books of the Bible, by studying Hebrew, Greek, and Latin texts, undertaken by Saint Jerome (ca. 347–419/20).[36]

Around 382 Jerome was commissioned to produce a new Latin Vulgate by Pope Damasus because there were "almost as many versions as codices,"[37] generally grouped under the heading "Old Latin" or *editio vulgata* (vulgar or vernacular), which themselves stemmed from Greek versions, notably the Septuagint. Their differences in wording, spelling, and punctuation could be significant, the variation being due to the numerous routes and sources of transmission, errors in translation and copying, and the inter-contamination of individual gospels. Jerome sought to purge them with reference to "ancient" Greek manuscripts, subsequently returning to the Hebrew to get even closer to the original meaning. In 385 he settled at Bethlehem and at Caesarea collated the Old Testament against the *Hexapla* compiled by Origen of Alexandria (185–254 C.E.), a critical edition of the Old Testament laid out in six columns of Hebrew and Greek comparative texts and transliterations. Jerome also partially revised the Latin Psalter with reference to the Greek Septuagint, and collated this, his "Romanum," against the Greek translation made from the Hebrew by the second-century Jewish scholar, Aquila, to produce the "Hebraicum."[38]

By the sixteenth century Jerome's new biblical translation from the Hebrew had acquired the title "The Vulgate" and the Council of Trent (1546) accorded it "orthodox" status. The Vulgate as we now know it (which is not quite the same as Jerome did) consists of Jerome's Latin translation of the Hebrew books of the Old Testament (except the Psalms); the Hebrew and Aramaic texts of Esdras and Daniel, and the Greek parts of the latter and Esther; Jerome's translation from Aramaic of Tobit and Judith; Psalms of the Gallicanum version, popularized in Gaul through the influence of Gregory of Tours and Charlemagne's circle, rather than Jerome's Romanum or Hebraicum; Wisdom, Ecclesiasticus, 1 and 2 Maccabees and Baruch from the Old Latin version; and Jerome's revised New Testament. The latter was conducted with reference to Greek sources and comprised Jerome's work on the gospels and, for the rest of the New Testament, the work of an anonymous editor probably based in late fourth-century Rome.

The oldest extant copy of the Vulgate, now in the Abbey of Saint Gall, an Irish monastery in Switzerland (MS. 1395), was

Fig. 7
Ezra, from the Codex Amiatinus. Wearmouth–Jarrow, northeast England, early eighth century (before 716). Florence, Biblioteca Medicea Laurenziana, MS. Amiatino 1, f. Vr.

probably made in early fifth-century Italy, but its early date does not mean that it is the most faithful representative of Jerome's work. Another important early witness to the Vulgate, the Harley Gospels (cat. no. 31), also contains a number of Old Latin textual passages, for Jerome's edition did not supplant earlier versions and his Vulgate merged with Old Latin readings, producing many "mixed" texts. By the time "The Vulgate" came to be printed, a complex process of distillation by Church councils and editors was needed to retrieve Jerome's original. Scholars had to compare a vast body of manuscripts copied throughout the Middle Ages, which they grouped into families with variant readings.[39] As a result, the Codex Amiatinus (FIG. 7) and the Lindisfarne Gospels (FIG. 8) emerge as particularly good representatives of Jerome's Vulgate.[40] These volumes were made in the Anglo-Saxon kingdom of Northumbria in northeast England during the early eighth century, the former at the twin monasteries of Wearmouth–Jarrow and the latter at Lindisfarne (Holy Island). They drew ultimately upon a gospelbook from Naples and various other exemplars (some by Cassiodorus), which were edited at Wearmouth–Jarrow to produce what is known as the "Italo-Northumbrian" family of texts. Christopher de Hamel has suggested that the popularity of the Vulgate in the "Italo-Northumbrian" family may stem from its use for readings in the reformed liturgy introduced to northern England from Rome around 700, which in some centers replaced or was used alongside earlier "Celtic" or other "mixed" liturgical traditions.[41] This demonstrates that another important factor determining textual variation was the liturgy—the public prayer-life of the Church. The version of the biblical texts used for readings in services would usually be those in general use by any given Church. If a new form of liturgy was introduced it sometimes brought with it a different version of the biblical readings.

The Vulgate, the Old Latin, and their "Mixed" hybrid offspring were not alone. Other early Christian authors also produced editions. Saint Augustine of Hippo revised parts of both Testaments to improve the fidelity of the Latin to the Greek, working from the Old Latin *editio vulgata* favored in North Africa. Victor of Capua produced a New Testament edition (ca. 547), conflating Vulgate readings to form a gospel harmony or *Diatessaron*, a genre originally pioneered by the Syrian Tatian (see "Bible and book," page 30) but which achieved influence only later via the studies of the medieval universities.

Texts might also be modified by scholars, in accordance with their own theological preferences: Gregory the Great states in his *Moralia in Job* that he used Jerome's text but varied it in accordance with the Old Latin where this agreed with his own moral interpretation, preferring, for example, "to us is born a savior" rather than Jerome's "to you" (Luke 2:11).[42]

Fig. 8 (detail below)
St. Matthew carpet-page and incipit page, from the Lindisfarne Gospels. Lindisfarne (Holy Island), northeast England, ca. 710–20. London, British Library, Cotton MS Nero D.iv, ff. 26v–27r.

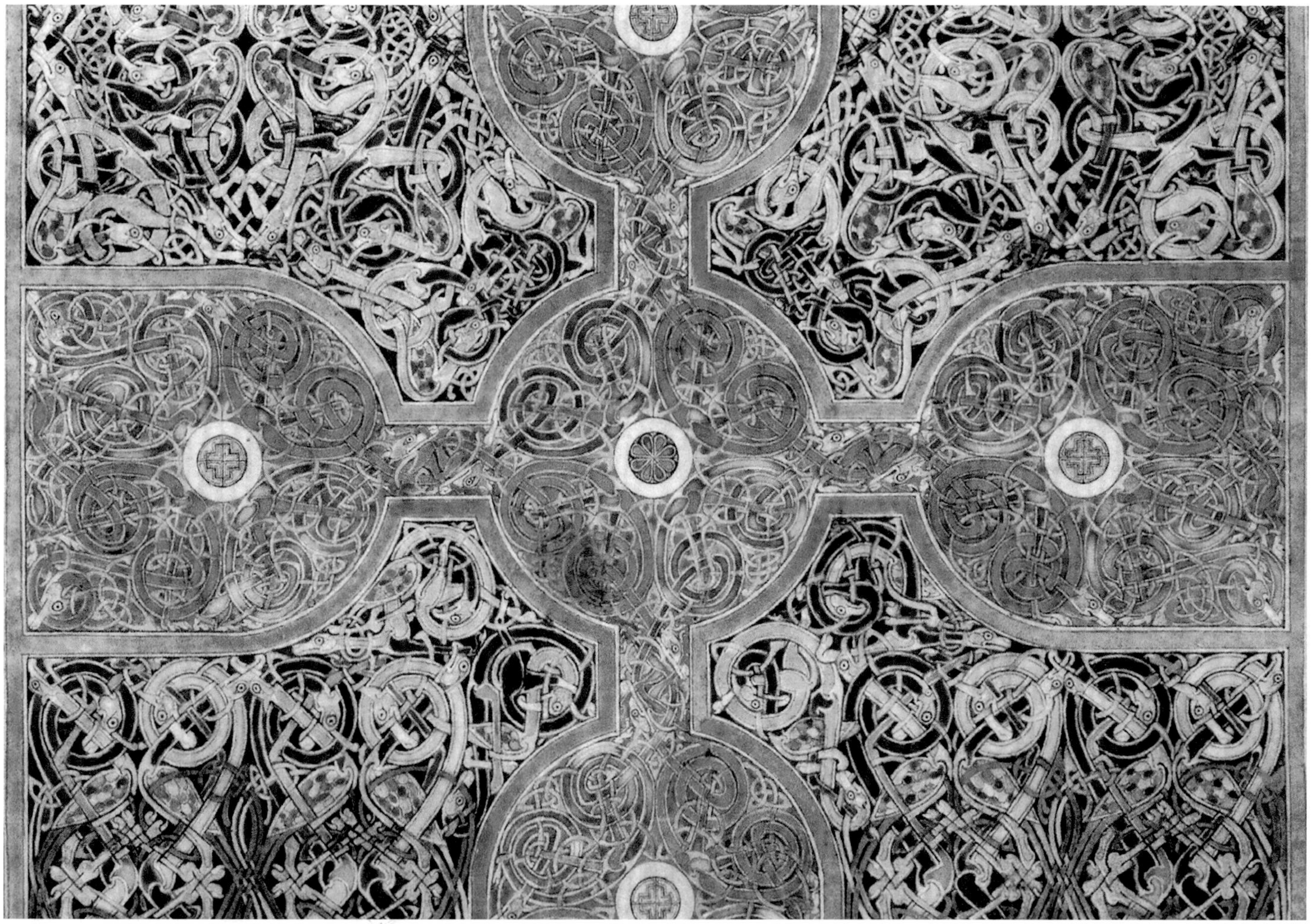

In the early Middle Ages, therefore, any consensus concerning the nature of "the Bible" was a long way off. Throughout the medieval world several different collections of canonically sanctioned biblical books circulated in a variety of languages—a veritable Babel of bibles, much like we still have today.

FROM BABEL TO PENTECOST

The initial rise to prominence of the Roman alphabet and the Latin language had been largely the result of the bureaucratic needs of the amorphous Roman Empire and its heir, the Christian Church. It remained to be seen whether the Church (or rather, Churches) would embrace the idea of a lingua franca or would accommodate its multilingual, diverse local parts within a latter-day Tower of Babel, with scripture circulating in many different languages. Its initial response is best charted in the way it reacted—through its missionary endeavors and the ways in which vernacular languages were employed—to Christ's sending out of the apostles (Matthew 28:19) to share his teachings with others. A biblical passage that helped to shape thinking in this respect was that relating to Pentecost:

All of them were filled with the Holy Spirit and began to speak in other languages, as the Spirit gave them ability. Now there were devout Jews from every nation under heaven living in Jerusalem. And at this sound the crowd gathered and was bewildered, because each one heard them speaking in the native language of each. (Acts 2:4–6)[43]

One of the foremost advocates of the use of vernacular languages in the service of the apostolic mission, Bede, was particularly interested in this episode. In his *Commentary on Acts* (Acts 2:6) he said that this passage could be read as meaning that the apostles went to many different peoples and preached in their various tongues or that they spoke only once and that, so to speak, the Holy Spirit simultaneously translated.[44] He was much criticized for this by his peers, who were not as well read as he and accused him of innovation rather than building upon earlier patristic thought. Bede subsequently justified his statement (in his *Retractio*, during the composition of which he invented the practice of footnoting to specify his sources) by emphasizing that he was quoting from an authoritative source, namely Gregory of Nazianzus.[45] Bede was not alone in his perception of the value of sharing scripture in the vernacular, in both oral and written forms. Indeed, as we have seen, some of the earliest examples of written vernaculars come from precisely this evangelizing context.

Disseminating a religion of the Word entails not only the translation problems of preaching in the field, for which interpreters are often initially required, but also the teaching of the necessary literacy skills for reading and copying texts. So it is hardly surprising that missionaries often resorted to the use of a written version of the spoken language of the area they were evangelizing, as a step on the path to achieving full (Latin) literacy. Different sounds in local languages often necessitated the creation of scripts to suit languages, as was the case with Saint Mesrob and Saint Cyril.[46]

The earliest written vernacular in the late Roman West was Gothic, invented by Ulfilas (ca. 311–383), "Apostle to the Goths," one of the migrating barbarian peoples that would shortly supplant the rule of Rome. Ulfilas drew upon the Greek and Roman alphabets to produce a written version of the Gothic language in order to translate the Bible. The great monument to the Gothic language is the Codex Argenteus (Uppsala, Universitetsbibliotek, DG 1), a splendid volume written in Ravenna for the Ostrogothic king, Theodoric, during the early sixth century.[47] Its stately script is indebted to Greek uncials and Roman capitals and the use of expensive materials is reminiscent of imperial dignity and Byzantine purple codices.[48] This is not surprising, given its origins in a major imperial center, but the promising cultural contribution of Ulfilas and his Gothic converts was curtailed by their Arianism, which restricted their influence among Catholic and Greek orthodox societies.

The English Church, along with those of the Celtic peoples, was open-minded in its approach to translating scripture. Saint Augustine's alleged role in inventing written Old English is perhaps best viewed in the context of his mission's instructions from Pope Gregory the Great to site Christianity within existing local tradition by adopting previously pagan festivals and places of worship and making them Christ's own.[49] The books that he took to England helped shape perceptions of the authority of writing in such a society, revolutionizing its oral literary traditions, its learning, and its administration (see cat. no. 53).

In a letter to Archbishop Ecgberht, Bede wrote that he had found it useful to translate the Pater Noster (Our Father) and the Creed into Old English for use by "illiterate" priests lacking sufficient Latinity to conduct services and to teach their flocks.[50] In his *Historia Ecclesiastica* (Ecclesiastical History of the English People) he also relates that the cowherd Caedmon, using the divine gift of song, turned scripture into English verse to make it more accessible.[51] Bede's interest in the vernacular relates to his recognition of the generosity of the Jews in sharing the Word with the gentiles through the Greek Septuagint, an impulse shared by the gentile races of Britain and Ireland who sought to share their faith with others (*Commentary on Tobit*, 12 and 2:6). On his deathbed, in 735, Bede was still sharing—translating Saint John: "the little Gospel that treats of the things that work by love."[52] This work has not survived, but may be recollected in the interlinear gloss added circa 950–60 to the Lindisfarne Gospels by the monk Aldred—the oldest surviving translation of the gospels into English —as well as the gloss added in the same period to a book originally from Ireland, the Macregol Gospels (cat. no. 59).

Aldred opened his colophon at the end of the Lindisfarne Gospels with a Latin synopsis of the "Monarchian prologues" attributed to Priscillian, which traditionally prefaced each gospel and reinforced the idea of committing oral tradition to writing, stating the authority from whom each evangelist was thought to have heard his gospel: Matthew from Christ, Mark from Peter, Luke from Paul, and John from the Holy Spirit. Aldred translated them into Old English and associated himself in the colophon with three figures to whom the original production of the volume is ascribed: the scribe, Bishop Eadfrith of Lindisfarne; the binder, his successor, Bishop Æthilwald; and the metalworker who adorned it, Billfrith the Anchorite. In so doing, Aldred presents himself by analogy as the fourth evangelist,[53] the inspired visionary Saint John. He thereby places himself, and the English language, in direct line of transmission from the divine to humankind.

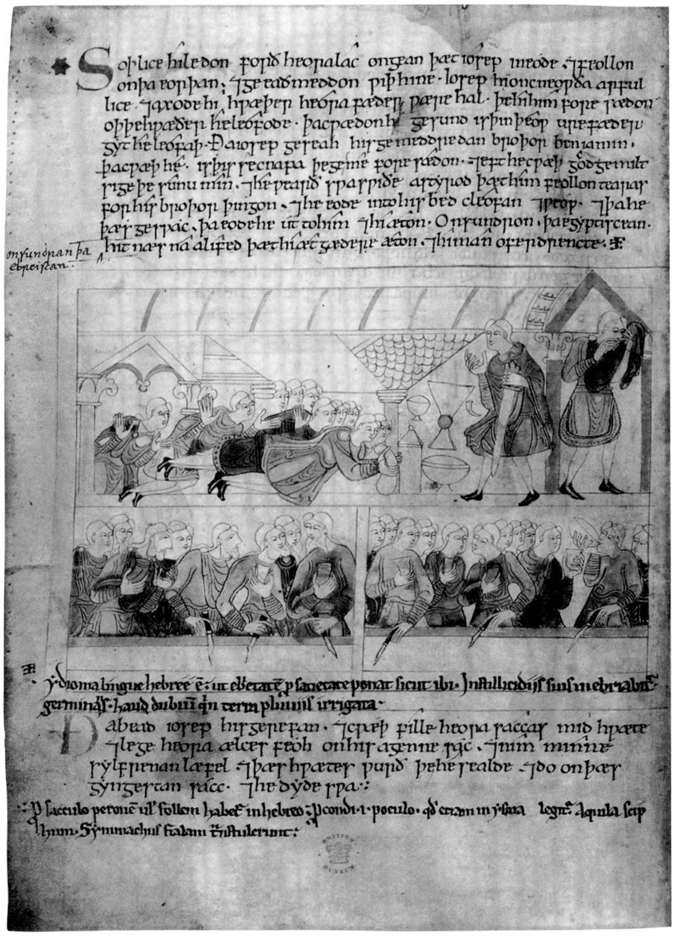

Fig. 9
Joseph and His Brothers, from the Old English Hexateuch. St. Augustine's, Canterbury, England, second quarter of the eleventh century. London, British Library, MS. Cotton Claudius B.iv, f. 63v.

The origins of the Anglo-Saxon tradition of glossing may be observed in copies of the Latin–Old English glossaries used in the schoolroom during the educational reforms implemented by Archbishop Theodore of Tarsus and his colleague, the North African Abbot Hadrian, at Canterbury during the seventh century—this was a truly cosmopolitan Church.[54] Incomers were not always so welcome, however. The escalation in the use of their written vernaculars by the English and Irish during the ninth century is perhaps best viewed as an ethnic response to Viking invasion and the establishment of a "state within a state." Ninth-century Wales and Cornwall witnessed a similar phenomenon in reaction to English expansionism. Such threats spurred a desire to preserve national cultural identity. They also stimulated the production of custom-written vernacular texts, including rousing sermons by Ælfric and Wulfstan designed to hearten and mobilize English resistance to renewed Viking invasion around 1000. At this time the Old English Hexateuch (FIG. 9), largely by Ælfric, and the Junius Manuscript, also known as the Caedmon Manuscript or Old English Genesis (cat. no. 61), were made. They conflated vernacular paraphrases of Old Testament texts with picture cycles of largely Early Christian origin, adapted to reflect the interests of contemporary "communities of reading," including women, and emphasizing the Anglo-Saxon people's own sense of exile and journey from their original Germanic and Scandinavian homelands to England as the new "children of Israel." They thereby asserted their cultural and linguistic identity and located themselves within the biblical landscape by using their own language and inserting details drawn from their own society and its artifacts into depictions of the biblical narratives—a proactive response to early Christian picture cycles seen by northern European pilgrims to Rome, Byzantium, and the Middle East.[55]

This raises the interesting issue of imperialism and regional identity in book production. Those areas that appear to have most consciously preserved their own script systems, decoration, and the vernacular were those that escaped absorption within the Carolingian Empire and its successors, namely Britain, Ireland, Visigothic Spain, and Benevento.[56] The corresponding reluctance of the East and West Franks and the rest of Italy to promote the vernacular has been ascribed to the gradual evolution of the Romance languages from the Latinity of the late Roman Empire and to a conscious Carolingian policy of promoting Latin, and caroline minuscule script, as a means of cultural cohesion and control throughout the amalgam of territories forged into the Carolingian Empire. Thus German identity, linguistic and otherwise, could and should not be unduly distinguished from that of Gaul, with its marked Roman legacy and mixed population. To quote Janet Nelson, "Not Frankish, therefore, but Latin could serve both to unite the Franks and to mark them out as a ruling *gens*, the chosen people of God—who of course had also chosen Latin as His medium."[57]

The written culture of the new Carolingian Empire did not, therefore, reflect that of its daily speech and oral transmission and explanation of texts remained an essential complement to written versions. Latin was the lingua franca throughout the Carolingian and Ottonian Empires, and the production of distinctively "vernacular" manuscripts would have to wait a while for the mainstream of European politics to shape-change. Meanwhile, in the peripheral regions of Britain and Ireland the Anglo-Saxon and Celtic peoples used everything at their disposal, including their own written and spoken languages, to share the "good news" (Old English, *godspell*), as did their counterparts at the eastern extremities of the former Roman Empire.

THE CONTINUING ORAL TRADITION

All this having been said, it should be remembered that most people's knowledge of scripture throughout the Middle Ages continued to be oral and visual, rather than written. They heard it through preaching, prayer, and images—adorning the personal belongings of the wealthy, carved on wayside crosses or in church buildings, which through their beauty afforded a glimpse of the world to come. Books were displayed prominently during public worship and used for contemplation by literate clergy and wealthy lay folk. The Psalms were the mainstay of public and private prayer and prayerbooks might feature psalm and gospel extracts. Gospelbooks might contain illuminated initials or scratched crosses in the margins, or both, marking lections (readings) for specific feast days.[58] They were gradually supplemented by evangelaries, lectionaries, and epistolaries containing readings in the order of the Church year. Other medieval servicebooks proliferated, including rituals, ordinals, pontificals, and benedictionals containing texts for particular services or prelates, and from the ninth century music was also written down, in neumatic notation, into books such as missals (texts for the Mass), breviaries (texts for the Divine Office of the monastic hours), choral antiphonals, and soloists' tropers. It was through such public recitation of snippets of scripture, sermons, poems, pictures, storytelling, and song that most people gained their knowledge of the Bible—just as many do today.

This oral dynamic is emphasized further in the First Bible of Charles the Bald (also known as the Vivian Bible), made at Tours in 846, which contains a miniature illustrating the inception and diffusion of Jerome's Vulgate, in which he is shown as an author, an oral teacher (of male and female pupils), and distributor of copies of his work to fill the churches (FIG. 10).[59]

Fig. 10
St. Jerome and the Dissemination of His Vulgate Version of the Bible, from The First Bible of Charles the Bald (or Vivian Bible). Tours, France, 846. Paris, Bibliothèque nationale de France, MS. lat. 1, f. 3v.

EARLY MEDIEVAL BIBLICAL CODICES

Throughout the early Middle Ages, biblical texts usually circulated in the form of individual books or collections, such as the gospelbook and the Pentateuch, the first five books of the Old Testament (the Judaic Torah). Single-volume bibles—or pandects ("all receivers," a term also used of Roman legal digests)—were unwieldy, imposing exceptions. They were powerful symbols of Christianity, physically embodying the integration of Old and New Testament books, just as the scroll epitomized Judaic scripture. This is visually affirmed in the Stockholm Codex Aureus (cat. no. 44), a resplendent mid-eighth-century gospelbook from southeast England, in which Saint Matthew is portrayed as an Antique author with his symbol, the man or angel, representing Christ's Incarnation. Matthew holds a scroll and the angel a book, emphasizing Christ's fulfillment of prophecy and transformation of the Law of the Old Testament (the scroll) through the Gospels of the New Testament (the codex).

GOSPELBOOKS

The type of biblical book that has survived most frequently from the early Middle Ages is the gospelbook, containing the four gospels and accompanying prefatory matter. This comparatively high rate of survival is probably due to its illumination and association with the shrines of saints, but also because the gospels were particularly revered. The four gospels that emerged as canonically sanctioned (those attributed to Saints Matthew, Mark, Luke, and John) were usually gathered together into one or two volumes, although John, used in the rites for the sick and the dying, also circulated separately (see "Bible and book" page 24).

Most early gospelbooks are classified as "mixed" texts, and grouped into families on the basis of variant readings, the origins of their exemplars, and their prefatory matter. These families include the "Mixed Italian" and "Mixed Irish/Celtic" groups and a distinctive Spanish family. Mixed texts incorporate Vulgate readings and it can be difficult to know which variants are significant and which incidental. Such classifications simply represent modern scholarly attempts to impose order on an organic process of textual transmission. In general, there are fewer differences between Jerome's Vulgate and the Old Latin versions in the New Testament than in the Old Testament. As we have seen, Jerome's Vulgate did not become an authorized version until the Council of Trent in the sixteenth century, and even then it did not become absolute. When such major changes in religious observance occur they are seldom uniformly adopted—for people generally prefer what they are used to hearing and reciting. Just consider the many printed orders of service and editions of the Christian Bible in use today.

In gospelbooks from the eastern Mediterranean (Greek, Armenian, Coptic, Syriac, and Georgian) each gospel occupied its own gatherings, perhaps emphasizing that they were by different authors and originally formed separate books.[60] In addition they were usually prefaced by one or more separate gatherings containing introductory matter consisting of canon tables and an explanatory letter from their compiler, Eusebius, to Bishop Carpianus.

Canon tables had been devised by Constantine's "court bishop" Eusebius of Caesarea (died 338/39) as a concordance system in which the gospels were divided into numbered sections with parallel readings, all displayed in tabular form (see cat. no. 68). Canon I lists passages appearing in all four gospels; subsequent canons show agreement between three gospels (canons II–IV), two gospels (canons V–IX), and passages unique to individual evangelists (canon X)—clearly indicating the non-synoptic character of John.[61] The numbers in the tables correspond to section numbers written in the margins beside the gospel passages. The numbering and agreements vary and canon tables are therefore also grouped into families.[62]

The prototypical early Western Vulgate gospelbook opened with prefaces by Jerome—the *Novum opus* and *Plures fuisse*—and a set of canon tables, and also included appropriate prologues and chapter lists preceding each gospel. Jerome had prefixed canon tables to his Vulgate and his *Novum opus* letter to Pope Damasus explained their use and the reasons for his textual revision. His *Plures fuisse* preface commented on the evangelists and potentially rendered superfluous the traditional Monarchian prologues summarizing the route by which each evangelist was thought to have received his gospel's teachings. The chapter lists preceding each gospel summarized their contents and refer to the Old Latin arrangement, although often accompanying the Vulgate. Additional texts, such as Eusebius–Carpiano, the Pseudo-Jerome preface *Sciendum etiam*, and Hebrew Names appear later and spasmodically.[63]

Prefatory lists of Hebrew Names mentioned in the text were a particularly "Irish/Celtic" feature.[64] The Old Latin featured Grecized versions of these names, but Jerome brought them into line with Hebrew originals. His *Liber de nominibus Hebraicis*, inspired by Philo and Origen, explained the meaning of the Hebrew Names in both Testaments and probably influenced Ireland (rabbinic tradition also expounded the meaning of such names).[65] It also addressed concerns among non-Hebrew speakers over correct pronunciation, given the absence of vowels in Hebrew.

Carl Nordenfalk has indicated that it was Eusebius's intention that the gospel harmony embodied in his canon tables should be "a full epitome of the Holy Writ" and that "in that capacity the Canon Tables partook in the sacredness of the Holy Word which they prefaced, and made them entitled to an unusually splendid adornment of their setting that pleases the eye and more than anything else accounts for the wide distribution of Eusebius' invention and the tenacity with which it survived."[66] Canon tables are often set within arcades, forming "an impressive atrium at the entrance of the sacred text itself"—an invitation and means of entering the Holy of Holies through a numeric encapsulation of Christ's ministry.[67]

Gospelbooks were often elaborately ornamented and in addition to canon tables (which were not always included) they might feature decorated incipits (enlarged initials and display lettering to mark the opening words of each gospel) or, in Byzantine-style books, headpieces at major text divisions; miniatures depicting the evangelists; and, occasionally, prefatory "carpet pages" (pages of ornament, perhaps with crosses embedded within it). Their visual impact was often further enhanced by the decoration of their bindings, rendering them symbolic statements of the unity of the gospels and shrines of Christ's teaching, whether they were displayed open or closed (see cat. no. 74).

THE PANDECT

The closest we come in this early period to an authoritative collection of biblical texts brought together in a single book known as the Christian "Bible" are a handful of early medieval pandects. Always a rarity, such massive single-volume bibles were costly, time-consuming, and intellectually difficult to produce and were usually linked to formal programs of codification and dissemination, such as those associated with the state sponsorship of Charlemagne or the monastic initiatives of Cassiodorus and Ceolfrith. They might be made as diplomatic gifts, like the Codex Amiatinus, which Ceolfrith took with him as a present for the pope in 716; for reference, like the two pandects Ceolfrith left for Wearmouth and Jarrow; or as exemplars circulated to foster the production of standardized copies, like Alcuin's Tours Bibles (discussed below).

Cassiodorus (ca. 485–580) was an Italian senator who withdrew from public life to found the monastery of Vivarium ("the fish ponds") on his country estate in Squillace, which was devoted to the study and copying of scripture. There he established an approach to biblical studies based on the classical liberal arts syllabus and the responsible copying and distribution of texts, being more concerned with orthography and Latinity than with textual revision. His nine-volume Old Latin Bible (Novem Codices) was made as his own reference copy and he also produced an illustrated single-volume bible, the Codex Grandior. Its Old Testament was based upon Jerome's earlier Hexaplaric revision of the Old Latin (based on Origen's version of the Septuagint, the *Hexapla*), the Vulgate was probably the basis for its gospels, and the rest of its New Testament was probably Old Latin. Cassiodorus also produced a smaller one-volume bible, Vulgate throughout, which he referred to as the *pandectam ... minutiore manu*, presumably meaning that it was written in minuscule script, prefiguring the use of caroline minuscule that we will encounter later in the Tours Bibles.

Abbot Ceolfrith (died 716) brought a copy of the Codex Grandior back from Rome to his twin monasteries of Wearmouth–Jarrow in the late seventh century.[68] The Codex Amiatinus that their scriptoria made in response preserved elements of its imagery but substituted a primarily Vulgate text compiled from a variety of sources.[69] For rather than simply copying one of Cassiodorus's editions, as is often suggested, the scriptoria of Wearmouth–Jarrow mounted a major editorial project, locating themselves within the prime lines of transmission of sacred text.[70] The Codex Amiatinus was no antiquarian facsimile or adaptation of one of Cassiodorus's editions into the codicological format of another (such as a reworking of the Novem Codices into the Codex Grandior's single-volume format). It was a dynamic work of scholarly editing and emendation.

The Ceolfrith Bibles achieved their version of the Vulgate by excavation, compilation, and interpretation, emulating Jerome's own distillation of different *vulgata* traditions.[71] They exhibit the influence of biblical commentaries by the leading scholar of the day, Bede (673–735)—undoubtedly a driving force behind the enterprise of his beloved abbot, Ceolfrith. Bede entered Wearmouth–Jarrow as a boy of seven and seldom ventured forth. The caliber of their libraries, his deployment of researchers, and his reader enquiries to the papal archives and other repositories nonetheless enabled him to undertake important work in biblical studies, history, and science—a joined-up approach to the meaning of life.

The famous "Ezra" miniature in the Codex Amiatinus (FIG. 7) has been read as an image of Cassiodorus adapted with reference to the great preserver of the Judaic scriptures, Ezra the Scribe (who memorized and "reconstructed" the Judaic sacred books after their destruction, with Solomon's Temple, by the Babylonians). But perhaps it should also be seen as a homage to the continued process of rediscovery and emendation of sacred text inspired by the Spirit.[72] The bookcase *(armarium)* behind the scribal figure contains nine volumes, alluding to Cassiodorus's Novem Codices but labeled as the editions of others, such as Augustine—indicating a living, ongoing tradition. This is an important adjustment to perception of the image, for it indicates that Cassiodorus and those responsible for the Ceolfrith Bibles were not attempting "authorized" editions, but authoritative ones, improving upon the best sources they could find in order to carry forward the process of revelation and understanding of the Word.

It would have been anathema to them to view their work as the "last word," for the process of transmission and exploration was a divinely inspired, perpetual one. The figure of the scribe represents Ezra, but also the Old and New Testament authors, Cassiodorus and other biblical editors, Bede, and the other Ceolfrith Bible scribes.[73] It also offers the viewer an open invitation to participate in the ongoing transmission of scripture.

THE CAROLINGIAN EDITIONS

The next major step in the transmission of the Bible in the West consisted of the editorial contributions made by the ecclesiastics attracted to the court of Charlemagne, who was crowned by the pope as the ruler of a new Christian empire in Rome on Christmas Day in the year 800. The most influential of these was Alcuin of York, the English Abbot of Tours (796–804), who completed a single-volume revision of the Vulgate Bible in 800. He drew upon the "Mixed Italian" and "Italo-Northumbrian" traditions familiar from England, and engaged in a process of scholastic correction: replacing Jerome's Hebraicum Psalter with the Gallicanum (based on the Hexaplaric Greek), and adding verse prologues and colophons. He is likely to have been influenced by the Ceolfrith Bibles, one of which he saw in Yorkshire, for one of his poems (*Carmina* 69) quotes the inscription surrounding the Ezra miniature in the Codex Amiatinus.[74]

Alcuin's was not the only early Carolingian version. The Court School established by Charlemagne at Aachen drew heavily upon English experience and Theodulf of Orléans relied upon the "Mixed Spanish" tradition of his homeland when preparing his revised text. Abbot Maurdramnus of Corbie also undertook a six-volume revision of the Bible, helping to devise a script for rapid copying and ease of legibility—caroline minuscule, the basis of modern typefaces.[75]

By 900 Alcuin's edition was becoming the norm throughout much of Europe, along with Carolingian influence and Church reform. Although not promoted as an "authorized" version, it approached the status of one. It formed the basis of the biblical studies conducted by the Victorines (the northern French scholastic followers of Hugh of St. Victor) and Paris University during the twelfth and thirteenth centuries.[76] There the Latin "Paris Study Bible" assumed the character with which we are familiar today: a small, portable, densely written single volume, its texts arranged (in both Old and New Testaments) in a threefold sequence of history and teaching (the Pentateuch and the historical books of the Old Testament, and the Gospels), praise and works (the Psalms and Proverbs, and Acts and the Epistles), and prophecy (the Prophets and Apocalypse/Revelation). The Christian bible had finally achieved a uniform character as a single book that formed the basis of study, liturgy, preaching, and prayer throughout Europe during the Middle Ages and Renaissance—and beyond.

THE MAKERS OF BIBLICAL MANUSCRIPTS

THE ROLE OF WOMEN

Monastic rules devised by Eastern fathers such as Saints Pachomius and Basil included time for study and scribal work, and in turn influenced European monastic founders such as Martin of Tours and Columbanus. Monasteries became the publishing houses of medieval Christendom. Patterns of work varied, from the solitary retreat of the anchorite to the communal endeavor of the monastic scriptoria that flourished especially with the rise of the Benedictine Order from the ninth century onwards. Male and female religious played their part and one of the earliest references to the monastic production of books relates to women. The *Life of Saint Caesarius*, the subject of which was Bishop of Arles during the first half of the sixth century, praises the bishop's sister:

The mother Caesaria, whose work with her community so flourished, that amidst psalmody and fastings, vigils, and readings, the virgins of Christ lettered most beautifully the divine books, having the mother herself as teacher.[77]

Caesarius composed the "Nuns' Rule" for their use, including provision for reading, conducting the daily Office, teaching the illiterate to read, and the custodianship of books (e.g., "Those who are put in charge of the wine cellar or of clothing or books, or of the gate or the wool work shall receive the keys upon a copy of the Gospels ...").[78] It makes no specific provision for the copying of books, but then neither do any of the influential early rules of common life, which perhaps subsume copying under the general heading of manual labor or study.

We know from Saint Boniface's correspondence with Eadburh, the abbess of Minster-in-Thanet in Kent, that the Anglo-Saxon monastery supplied his German mission with impressively penned, sumptuously gilded copies of scripture during the 730s. He requested that, following her earlier gift of books, she should have made for him a copy of the Epistles of Peter, elegantly penned in gold script to impress potential converts, using gold that he sent her for the purpose.[79] Minster-in-Thanet therefore probably produced some of the most beautiful early English illuminated scriptures (see cat. no. 54).

In Merovingian Gaul the supply of liturgical books to cathedrals and monasteries was likewise undertaken by women—the nuns of Rebais, Faremoutiers-en-Brie, Jouarre, and Chelles.[80] Rosamond McKitterick suggested that the role of women in the production of writing on the European continent may have been molded by the example of English women who participated in missionary work there, such as Leoba and Walburg in the circle of Boniface, and Harlindis and Relindis of Aldeneik in Flanders, who were associated with Willibrord and are said to have copied a gospelbook themselves.[81]

The distinctive structure of Germanic and Celtic society and law meant that women enjoyed a comparatively enhanced status that enabled them to participate actively in biblical dissemination. In the West there is slight, but significant, evidence that women made biblical manuscripts and acted as patrons, readers, and teachers in convent school and the home.[82] King Alfred the Great of England is said by his biographer, Asser, to have first conceived a love of learning and religion when attracted as a boy by a book that was being read by his mother, who promised to give it to him if he learned to read. By the end of the ninth century he had implemented a program of spiritual and educational reform that included copying books and translating them into English and founding schools—for boys.[83]

BEING THE BOOK: THE SCRIBE AS EVANGELIST

For those who dedicated their lives to God's service, to be entrusted with the transmission of his Word, as preachers and as scribes, was a high calling indeed. In a letter to Bishop Acca of Hexham concerning his commentary on Luke, Bede wrote, "I have subjected myself to that burden of work in which, as in innumerable bonds of monastic servitude which I shall pass over, I was myself at once dictator, notary, and scribe."[84] This revealing passage shows that he regarded such work as an act of *opus dei*, and that he differentiated between the functions of author, secretary, and scriptural transmitter.

Cassiodorus in his *Institutiones* said that each word written was "a wound on Satan's body," thereby assigning the scribe the role of *miles Christi* (soldier of Christ). In the same work he says that in those who translate, expand, or humbly copy the scriptures the Spirit continues to work, as it did in the biblical authors who were first inspired to write them.[85] Cassiodorus also advocated (in the *Institutiones* and his *Commentary* on Psalm 44/45:1–2; FIG. 11) that the scribe could preach with the hand and "unleash tongues with the fingers," imitating the action of the Lord who wrote the Law with his all-powerful finger.[86] Bede pursued this theme in relation to Ezra the Scribe, who fulfilled the Law by restoring its destroyed books, dictating them from memory and thereby opening his mouth to interpret scripture and teach others. The act of writing is therefore presented as an essential act for the preacher-teacher-scribe.[87]

Such exhortations may have influenced the production of the Lindisfarne Gospels, for this remarkable book is the work of a single artist-scribe.[88] Some modern scribes estimate that at least two years of full-time work in optimum conditions would be required to make it.[89] Contemporary scribes in the South Gondar region of Ethiopia, employing much the same methods and materials as when Christianity became their state religion during the fourth century, can write an undecorated religious codex of some 400 leaves in around eight to twelve months. They write for two or three hours per day amid farming and other church duties, in primitive conditions and simply resting the leaves on their knees as they squat to write.[90] Undertaking such an heroic feat of patience alongside the monastic duties of the Divine Office (celebrated eight times each day and night), prayer, study, and manual labor, suggests that making the Lindisfarne Gospels may have taken closer to five years, depending on how much exemption was granted from other duties, such as that accorded to anchorites. If, as seems likely, Bishop Eadfrith of Lindisfarne (698–721) both conceived the vision for its gospelbook and physically made it himself around 710–720, his role overseeing one of the largest dioceses in Britain would have made such work additionally challenging. Some of it was probably undertaken on "Cuddy's Isle", a tiny windswept tidal islet in the bay beside the monastery on Holy Island, where for the seasons of Lent and Advent the bishop retired on retreat—a watery northern wilderness in which the hermit-bishop was emptied out in order to be filled with the Spirit and the energy to recommit to the world.

Such eremitic scribal activity may have been a distinctive "Celtic" response to viewing such work as a living act of prayer.[91] Whereas the copying of other texts was the communal work of the scriptorium, transmitting scripture was entrusted only to the most senior members of the community. The Irish saints Canice and Columba were acclaimed as hero-scribes,[92] the former winning fame for writing out a complete gospelbook single-handed, for copying the gospels was seen as the highest scribal calling. In accordance with the teachings of Cassiodorus and others, the scribe became an evangelist and, by study, contemplation, and meditation upon the text *(ruminatio, contemplatio,* and *meditatio)*, might actually glimpse the divine

Fig. 11
King David Composing the Psalms, from the Durham Cassiodorus, *Commentary on the Psalms*. Northern England, mid-eighth century. Durham Cathedral Library, MS. B.ii.30, f. 81v.

(revelatio). This accorded with the patristic concept of the "inner library" in which each believer became a repository of the divine Word, a sacred responsibility that the Irish sage Cummian referred to as "entering the Sanctuary of God" through studying and transmitting scripture.[93] Books became the vessels from which the believer's inner ark was filled—enablers of direct Christian action, channels of the Spirit, and gateways to revelation: for "In the beginning was the Word, and the Word was with God, and the Word was God" (John 1:1).

Other forms of revelation might also be taken into account alongside the Bible: an Irish saint, Columbanus (ca. 543–615), who evangelized in Ireland, Gaul, Switzerland, and Italy, wrote that Nature was a second revelation, to be "read" alongside scripture to deepen our knowledge of God.[94] An affinity with Nature and the opportunities that it offered for solitary contemplation and communion with the divine are a distinctive feature of the "Celtic" response to Christianity. Along with many other aspects of Celtic eremitic monasticism inherited from the East, some of the communities producing the great Insular sacred manuscripts may have adopted something of the Syro-Palestinian monastic tradition, with its semi-eremitic *lavras*. This was especially apparent in remote outposts such as Skellig Michael off the southwest coast of Ireland (FIG. 12), whose members came together for communal worship but lived separately as quasi-anchorites in their stone beehive-shaped cells. The gospelbook became the scribal desert (Old Irish *disert*) and, via the "desert" islands of Britain and Ireland, influences from the Middle East, where the Bible was born, were transmitted to the West, alongside the latinized, imperial influences of Rome.[95]

Such books are portals of prayer. Just as Saint Cuthbert struggled with his demons on the rock of Inner Farne on behalf of all Creation, so the bishop-monk who produced the Lindisfarne Gospels as Cuthbert's cult-book undertook a heroic feat of patience and of spiritual and physical endurance. In this he participated in the apostolic mission of bringing the Word of God to the furthest outposts of the known world, enshrining it there within the new Temple of the Word and embodiment of Christ—the Book. He devised new technologies (the pencil, the lightbox, and a chemical mastery of pigments achieved through an understanding of the natural resources within his environment) to achieve a complex vision. Within this, lections from several sources were synthesized, in ecumenical fashion, into a new decorative program designed to celebrate Jerome's Vulgate and lections from the liturgy, incorporating some up-to-the-minute papal thinking. Unity and the avoidance of schism were major considerations, apparent in the careful balancing of iconic and aniconic features at a time when iconoclasm was rife. The Lindisfarne Gospels' evangelist miniatures sit like framed icons on the

Fig. 12
Early Christian monastery, Skellig Michael, County Kerry, off the southwest coast of Ireland, with detail of monks' cells (below).

page, portraying aspects of Christ's nature obliquely through their symbolism. Texts are introduced by exquisite cross-carpet pages, indebted to Coptic art and recalling the *Crux Gemmata* (the jeweled cross, symbol of the Second Coming) and the prayer mats sometimes used in northern Europe at this time as well as in the Middle East (see FIG. 8).[96] They prepare the entry onto the holy ground of sacred text, while the facing incipits explode in a riot of ornament, the letters themselves becoming a celebration of the divine—the Word made flesh or, rather, the Word made word.

The presence of the Lindisfarne Gospels on the altar, like that of other Insular gospelbooks such as the Book of Durrow, the Book of Kells, the Rawlinson Gospels, and the Macregol Gospels (see cat. nos. 59, 60), evoked the presence of God and celebrated the transmission of the gospels and their use in preaching and prayer. Pilgrims to Saint Cuthbert's shrine would have been greeted by the Lindisfarne Gospels' subtle blending of Celtic, Germanic, Pictish, Roman, Greek, and Middle Eastern ingredients. They would have been welcomed by motifs from their own cultures, woven into a harmonious and exotic synthesis embracing an ecumenical union that stretched from the deserts of Syria and Egypt to the Atlantic seaboard. This was a gospelbook that enshrined ideals and inspired devotion and wonder.

A SYMBOL OF FAITH AND AUTHORITY

IMAGES, MONARCHY, AND THE LAW

The problem of idolatry was actively discussed in Judaic, Islamic, and Christian circles during the early Middle Ages. It was also hotly debated in the West, despite the teaching of Gregory the Great, who wrote around 600 to Bishop Serenus of Marseilles that "in images the illiterate read." Nonetheless, early medieval copies of Christian scripture are among the most beautiful examples of the illuminator's art, their precious contents often enshrined within similarly precious covers—an acknowledgment of their symbolic power.

Byzantine book production flourished during the Early Christian period, readily embracing imagery (although little now survives), but hit an all-time low during the Iconoclast Controversy (726–87). Imagery was largely outlawed, with only the Book and the Cross being considered acceptable public manifestations of belief and art. With the Council of Nicaea in 787 and the accession of Empress Irene (797–802) images were reinstated and, despite an iconoclastic resurgence in 814–843, book production increased. Gospelbooks were graced with illuminated headpieces and initials and portraits of the evangelists as bearded scribes, and psalters were enlivened with marginal illustrations, as in the Theodore Psalter, written in Constantinople in 1066 (FIG. 13), stimulating the inclusion of imagery in their Western counterparts.[97]

The Carolingians' stance on imagery was conflicted. They used it to emphasize the interdependence of Church and State, the emperor combining the symbolic roles of king and priest, but remained troubled by idolatry. The Carolingian response to the Council of Nicaea took the form of the *Libri carolini* by Theodulf of Orléans, in which the primacy of the word was asserted over images, which were permitted but deemed to possess no inherent holiness or iconic value.[98] Copies of scripture produced from this time until circa 810 (when the Lorsch Gospels once more dared depict Christ in Majesty) are noticeably devoid of pictures of the divine, featuring instead illustrations of biblical narratives or evangelist portraits. This made way for the development of royal iconography.[99] Among the most opulent of ninth-century books were the First Bible of Charles the Bald, made at Tours in 846 as a gift for Charles from Abbot Vivian, and the Lothar Gospels, also made at Tours circa 850 as a gift to its monastic community from Charles's rival sibling, Lothar.[100] Such books, designed for

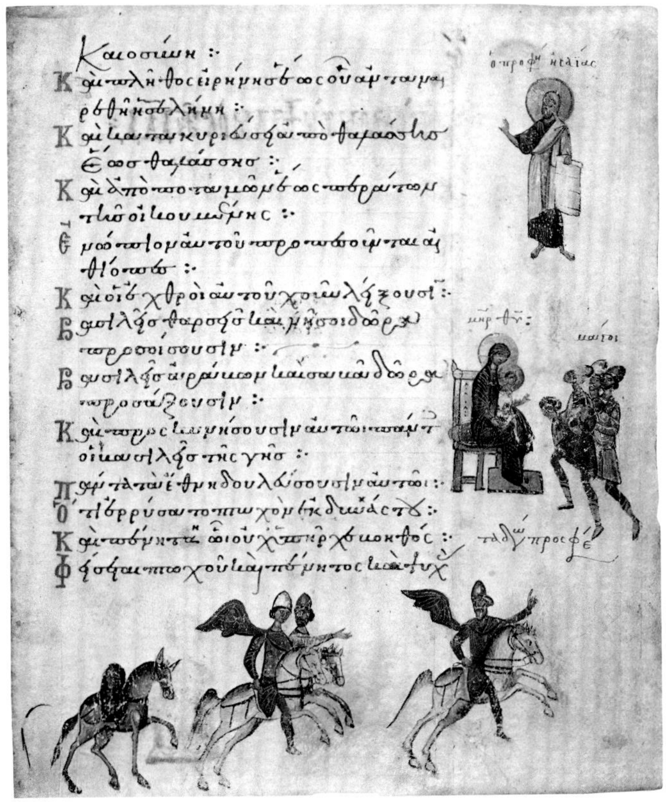

Fig. 13
Marginal images depicting *Isaiah* and the *Adoration of the Magi*, from the Theodore Psalter. Constantinople (Studios Monastery), 1066. London, British Library, Add. MS. 19352, f. 92r.

Fig. 14
St. Luke, from the St. Chad Gospels, with a document freeing slaves added in the margins during the mid-ninth century at Llandeilo Fawr, Wales. England (perhaps Lindisfarne or Lichfield), mid-eighth century. Lichfield Cathedral, MS. 1, p. 218.

Fig. 15
Christ at the Last Judgment, from a Carolingian treasure binding with relics set into the binding boards. Tours, France, first half of the ninth century (with some later decorative additions). London, British Library, Add. MS. 11848, upper cover.

public display, promoted royal iconography as an adjunct of power, depicting the ruler enthroned, like Christ in Majesty, and acknowledged by supporting figures representing Church and State or personifications of subject lands.

Royal oaths were sometimes sworn upon the Bible during coronation ceremonies: for example, a little ninth-century gospelbook from Carolingian Lobbes (the Coronation Gospels) was used at the coronation of Anglo-Saxon kings from the 920s.[101] "Books of the high altar" served as the sacred ground upon which legal transactions were enacted (we still swear oaths in court upon sacred texts) and in which they were sometimes recorded. Around 850 a Welshman named Gelhi swapped his best horse for the Saint Chad Gospels (FIG. 14), made circa 750 probably in Northumbria, and presented them to the altar of Saint Teilo at Llandeilo Fawr in Carmarthenshire.[102] They contain the earliest written Welsh in the form of legal documents added in the margins, including a manumission freeing slaves that is perhaps the earliest such document in the post-Roman world. Such books themselves became relics, through their association with saints. A particularly evocative example is an early ninth-century gospelbook from Tours in a splendid treasure binding (FIG. 15), depicting Christ enthroned at the Last Judgment, with the bones of saints recessed within its boards—allowing it to serve as both shrine and altar.

The Ottonians, successors to the Carolingians in the northern and eastern (essentially German) part of their empire from circa 962 to 1056, perpetuated the imperial concept. Ottonian scriptoria, such as those at Trier, Cologne, Echter-nach, Regensburg, and Reichenau, produced imposing illuminated volumes for use in public liturgy and the private devotions of royalty, aristocracy, and leading church people.[103] Among the most important to survive are the Gospels of Otto III, made at Reichenau (ca. 996), the Sacramentary of Henry II made in Regensburg (1002–14), and the Gospels of Abbess Hitda of Cologne (ca. 1000).[104] As in their Carolingian and late Anglo-Saxon counterparts, these volumes reveal a taste for classically inspired but stylized figures and lavish use of imperial purple and some books are written entirely in gold ink (chrysography). Such trends received a stimulus from renewed Byzantine influence following the marriage of Emperor Otto II and the Byzantine princess Theophano in 972.

THE PASSAGE INTO ETERNITY IN EAST AND WEST

An eastern Mediterranean appreciation of the iconic status of the book as an object of veneration was also transmitted to the West through the practice of enshrining sacred texts within treasure bindings. Ivories or bejeweled metalwork plates attached to wooden binding boards are found on Byzantine, Coptic, Armenian, Irish, Anglo-Saxon, Carolingian, and Ottonian books.[105] In Coptic Egypt and Ireland metalwork shrines (Old Irish *cumdach*) were also made (see FIG. 18.)[106]

In general, however, books were simply constructed from gatherings sewn together, either onto supporting leather bands—the preferred Western technique—or unsupported with only the sewing thread linking them together. The latter technique is known as "Coptic sewing," although it was widely practiced in eastern Mediterranean lands and is still employed in Ethiopia. The gatherings were then contained within wooden boards, often tied with thongs to keep the pages flat. The boards were covered with leather, perhaps tooled or molded to form a pattern, as on the earliest extant Western binding, that of the Saint Cuthbert Gospel (FIG. 16), a little copy of John's Gospel found alongside the body of Saint Cuthbert within his coffin.[107] This was made in Wearmouth–Jarrow in the

Fig. 16
The St. Cuthbert Gospel of St. John. Wearmouth–Jarrow, northeast England, ca. 698. British Library, Loan MS. 74, upper cover.

690s and employed not the Western but the "Coptic" binding technique, providing tangible evidence of communication between these far-flung regions.

The Saint Cuthbert Gospel was found inside the saint's coffin in 1104 and had probably been placed there in 698 when his relics were translated to the new shrine beside the High Altar at Lindisfarne. On one end of the wooden coffin (known as a *theca*, or box, like the *bibliotheca* for storing books) is one of the earliest Western depictions of the Virgin and Child, resembling Egyptian effigies of Isis and Horus. When the Copts moved into the ancient Pharaonic temples they did not redecorate, but applied new meanings to much of the imagery they encountered. The invisible presence of the book inside the coffin—like those in metalwork shrines—was evidently of powerful significance. An earlier case of scripture included in a burial is the oldest surviving complete Coptic psalter (see FIG. 17).[108] Around 400 it was placed open as a pillow beneath the head of an adolescent girl in a humble cemetery at Al-Mudil, forty kilometers northeast of Oxyrhynchus. An ancient analogy, for both, might be the Egyptian practice of interring the Book of the Dead with the deceased to aid their passage into the afterlife. The small bone peg, shaped like the ancient Egyptian key of life, that was used to unlock the Coptic psalter in question reinforces this connection.[109]

CHANGING PERCEPTIONS

The books of the bible had first begun to circulate as informal scrolls and pamphlets. That was a far cry from the way approaches to the sacred nature of scripture developed between 500 and 1000 C.E., producing phenomena such as the Jewish *genizahs*—sealed rooms within which even flawed copies of Judaic scripture were carefully stored prior to ritual destruction, so sacred were their contents (see cat. no. 1), and the

Fig. 17
"Pillow Psalter," found in a girl's grave. Egypt, fourth or fifth century. Cairo, Coptic Museum, MSS. Library 6614.

Fig. 18
The Lough Kinale Book-shrine. Ireland, late eighth century. Dublin, National Museum of Ireland, 1986:141, upper cover.

Christian use of splendid biblical codices upon which the most solemn and binding of legal rituals were enacted and validated.

The designs on some early Coptic bindings resemble the decoration of their cross-carpet pages, the sacrality of their texts reinforced by the sacred symbols that introduced them and adorned their protective covers. A late eighth-century Irish metalwork book-shrine, the Lough Kinale Book-shrine (FIG. 18), also carries a design resembling the Lindisfarne Gospels' carpet pages. It was tossed into an Irish lake during the ninth century when a disappointed Viking raider found that it only contained an old book.[110] This marked the beginning of a challenge to the iconic status of sacred texts. It may have come initially from "outsiders" who did not belong to any of the Abrahamic religions and did not respect their scriptures; but it would escalate in the late Middle Ages with the rising demands of believers to have access to the Bible in their own languages so that they could read and interpret it themselves, and with the advent of printing and the mass-production of affordable bibles.

At the dawn of the modern era, the bible was once more the unpretentious working manual of ordinary Christian communities, just as it had begun. In the interim it had revolutionized perceptions of the role and appearance of the book, which endures today as one of our greatest cultural icons.

Herbert L. Kessler

The book as icon

THE WORD MADE FLESH

Opposite:
Detail of fig. 4.

In a poem at the end of the gospel lectionary he had transcribed and decorated for Charlemagne in 781–83, the scribe Godescalc characterized his book:

Golden words are painted [here] on purple pages,
The Thunderer's shining kingdoms of the starry heavens,
Revealed in rose-red blood, disclose the joys of heaven,
And the eloquence of God glittering with fitting brilliance
Promises the splendid rewards of martyrdom to be gained.[1]

For Godescalc, the gold and silver letters on stained vellum, not just the sacred message that they communicated, were an image of the incarnate God. Godescalc's conception was rooted in Saint John's description of Christ as the Word, the pre-existing Logos who entered the world through the Virgin Mary, lived on Earth, and rendered visible the ineffable Divinity (John 1:13).

The idea was introduced directly through two miniatures that face each other at the start of the volume (FIG. 1). On the right is a picture of the enthroned Christ, holding a book in his left arm

Fig. 1
Christ Enthroned and
St. John the Evangelist, from
the Godescalc Lectionary.
781–83. Paris, Bibliothèque
nationale de France, MS. nouv.
acq. lat. 1203, ff. 2v–3r.

Fig. 2
Painting of Christ known as
the *Acheropita*. Rome, late
eleventh century. Tivoli,
Cattedrale di San Lorenzo.

and blessing with his right. This was fashioned after a famous sixth- or seventh-century painting of the Savior known as the *Acheropita* (see below, page 88) that was housed in the Lateran in Rome, where Pope Hadrian I had just baptized Charlemagne's son Pepin. Because of its ruinous condition, it is best known today through several replicas, including the late-eleventh-century version in Tivoli cathedral, which, like the original and Godescalc's version, shows the youthful Lord seated on a jeweled throne (FIG. 2).[2] On the facing page, the Evangelist is portrayed inscribing the beginning of his inspired text in gold letters on the purple leaves of an open codex, in this instance purposely repeating *verbum* (word) three times:

When all things began, the Word already was and the Word and the Word [sic] *dwelt with God.*

The figure of John pointing toward the enthroned Lord on the right shutter of the Tivoli triptych proffers the same sermon, which had become a proof-text of icon theory.[3] As articulated by Pope Hadrian I this theory stated that because of Christ's dual nature, the faithful who looked at physical images of him with bodily eyes were raised to a contemplation of the invisible Divinity.[4] For Godescalc, the book of sacred scripture functioned the same way; the glimmer of light off words "painted" on blood-red animal skins created an image of the incarnate God.

An exceptional image in a two-page opening in the Book of Kells (FIG. 3),[5] which is roughly contemporary with Godescalc's Lectionary, elaborates the same idea. On the right-hand page, Christ is pictured holding a book and actually enthroned atop the words that introduce John's Gospel: IN PRINCIPIO ERAT VERBUM ET VERBUM.[6] Christ's body frames the facing page, his face (badly trimmed) at the top, hands at either side, and feet below; the Lord literally incorporates the Evangelist and his inspired words into his very person.

How different this concept of scripture was, toward the end of the first millennium, from that of the earliest Christians who had written their sacred texts on fragile papyrus or wax tablets free of ornament and who treasured the writings not for their material value and physical elaboration but because they transmitted God's covenant to his chosen people. The product of a long evolution away from the initial concept of the sacred text as God's direct communication to his followers, the notion of the book as both an image of the Lord and as a repository of images was driven by diverse cultural considerations and fed by many sources.[7] Reaching maturity at just the moment around 800 when the Godescalc Lectionary and Book of Kells were illuminated, and developed even more completely in the next centuries, the conception of the Bible as icon as well as text was, in essence, an expression of the foundation of Christian belief that in Christ:

And the Word became flesh and lived among us, and we have seen his glory (John 1:14).

THE BOOK'S PHYSICAL PRESENCE

This evolution was enabled by the Christian preference for the codex form. In contrast to the scrolls favored by Jews and pagans, the firm pages of the manuscript book provided flat surfaces suitable for permanent adornment; and, bound together between sturdy covers, they could be fashioned into an impressive physical object suitable for processions and display. The potential of ornamented volumes of scripture had already been exploited under Constantine the Great; the first Christian emperor ordered the distribution of biblical books written in gold and silver on purple vellum, encased in expensively worked containers (see "Bible and book," page 32). Reported in Eusebius's *Ecclesiastical History*, moreover, Constantine's action made a lasting impression on his successors, who continued to commission luxurious biblical manuscripts to reflect the status of the official religion and, at the same time, symbolize Christ, the celestial ruler. Derived ultimately from an exemplar produced for Emperor Theodoric, the sixth-century Codex Brixianus (cat. no. 70),[8] for instance, perpetuates the tradition of regal books of scripture; and a bible produced in ninth-century Asturias, Spain, containing five blue- and purple-stained folios, has been associated with Alfonso II of Oviedo.[9]

The covers of Constantine's manuscripts were undoubtedly made of precious metals, gems, or ivory; the latter, a preferred material for the ceremonial "notebooks" known as consular diptychs, would have added to the regal aura of scriptural codices. Fifth- and sixth-century ivory gospel covers in Paris, Yerevan, and Milan (FIG. 4)[10] mimic the five-part format used for the most lavish imperial ivories but replace the image of the ruler with a representation of Christ. The practice was revived during the reign of Charlemagne when a five-part diptych was used on the Lorsch Gospels; the ninth-century cover imitates the great ivory icon of Justinian, now in Paris, but replaces the mounted ruler vanquishing a barbarian at the center with an image of Christ Trampling the Beasts (Psalm 91).[11] In an act of

Fig. 3
The beginning of the Gospel of John, from the Book of Kells. Iona (?), Scotland, ca. 800. Dublin, Trinity College Library, MS. 58, ff. 291v–292r.

appropriation rife with significance—many later book covers were actually fashioned from reused diptychs—the covers of a gospelbook adorned circa 900 by the monk Tuotilo, of the monastery of Saint Gall, were carved on an enormous piece of Late Antique ivory and, appropriately, substitute the ruler found on ancient carvings with a depiction of the majestic Lord of heaven (FIG. 5).[12]

Taking full advantage of the flat page offered by the codex, Constantine's court poet Publius Optatianus Porphyrius (also know as Porphyry) had composed in 324 a volume of verses in which sacred words were formed into diagrams to express visually the reciprocal relationship between word and sign, in a way that was to become fundamental to Christian art.[13] A copy of Porphyry's *Carmina figurata* was known in England by the mid-eighth century when it influenced (at least indirectly) the adornment of the gospels in the Stockholm Codex Aureus (cat. no. 44),[14] which are written on colored parchment and decorated with texts that are actually shaped as crosses of various forms.

While the material embellishment of books had been anticipated at the very start of the imperial Church, the status of manuscripts as icons was boosted by the more general discussion of the role of props in Christian worship that took place during the period of Iconoclasm (726–843). One side in this debate largely dismissed the role of physical devices in spiritual life while the other promoted the usefulness of precious substances and sacred icons. An Armenian defense of images written during the final third of the seventh century, for instance, likened icons to "Gospel books painted with gold and silver, and more, bound with ivory and of purple parchment"; and, as Godescalc and Pope Hadrian were to do a century later, it elaborated on the relationship between their material splendor and spiritual content:

When we bow down before the holy Gospel, or when we even kiss it, we do not venerate the ivory and the shellac, brought by the winds from barbarian lands, but we bow down before the word of the Savior written on parchment.... In the same way, it is not because of the colors that one bows down before icons, but because of Christ in whose name they were painted.[15]

Not everyone accepted such ornamented scriptures, of course; indeed, many considered decoration to be of no religious value or, worse, a distraction from the text's inherent sacred meaning. Porphyry himself believed that rich decoration would detract from poetic inventions, which he thought should be written in black and red ink on ordinary vellum.[16] Later in the fourth century, no less an authority than Saint Jerome, the translator of the Bible into Latin (Vulgate), criticized such books because they transgressed Christian austerity and risked polluting the divine message. Jerome deplored the fact that in his day "pages are stained the color of purple, gold is

Fig. 4
Ivory manuscript covers.
Northern Italy,
fifth century. Milan, Duomo
treasury.

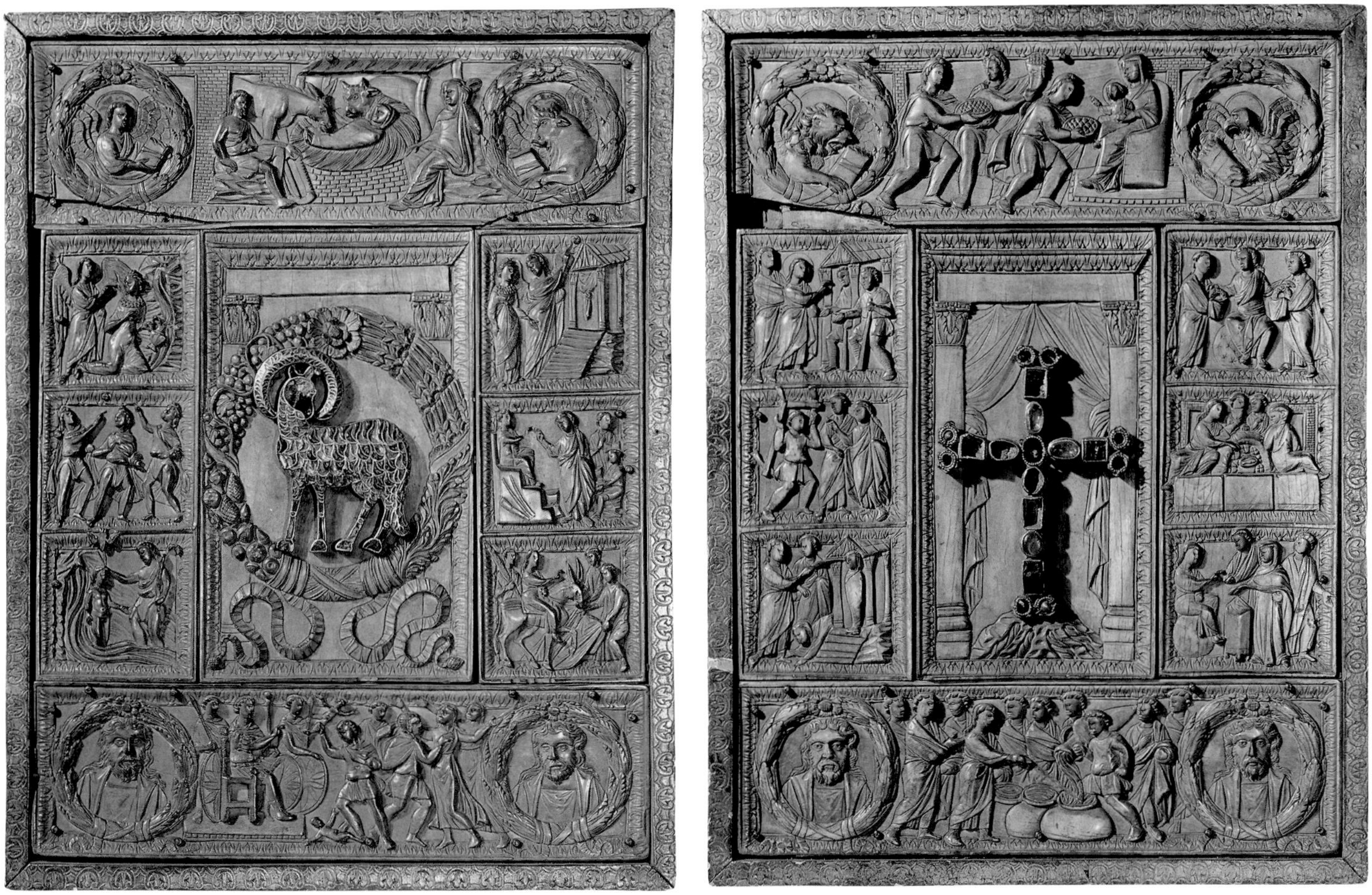

Fig. 5
Ivory manuscript cover from Tuotilo's Gospels. St. Gall (Switzerland), ca. 900. St. Gall, Stiftsbibliothek, MS. 53.

melted for lettering, manuscripts are decked with jewels; and Christ lies at the door naked and poor."[17] He advised Christians to "prefer correctness and accurate punctuation to gilding and Babylonian parchment with elaborate decorations."[18] Half a millennium later, Godescalc's contemporary Theodulf, bishop of Orléans, made a similar distinction between the ornament and text in books. In the tract on sacred images known as the *Libri carolini* that he coordinated on Charlemagne's behalf, he acknowledged the widespread practice of adorning books with figured covers and painted pages, but argued that, while such ornament added material worth, it had no other function.[19]

In the end, the production of luxury volumes continued even in the face of the scornful rejection by a Father of the Church of "books laid out on purple skins in gold and silver." Ironically, Jerome's criticism is actually transcribed in one of the most elaborate of all early manuscripts, the Codex Amiatinus prepared in the first decades of the eighth century at Wearmouth–Jarrow, which includes purple pages written in precious metals.[20] Despite his disparagement of the spiritual value of ornamented books, Theodulf also commissioned lavishly adorned manuscripts, even boasting that the bible made for him around 800 "shines with jewels, gold and purple."[21] Indeed, in Theodulf's bible in Paris, the Book of Psalms and the four gospels are written on purple-dyed vellum, the rich, imperial material signaling that these are the most important sections of the Old and New Testaments because they bear directly on the celestial ruler's life.[22]

ANIMATING LETTERS

Jerome seems also to have objected to another form of ornament that was just becoming popular in the late fourth century: decorated initials. Taking over a tradition from monumental inscriptions, these—like ornamented pages and decorated covers—were a means of providing books with a visually imposing aspect.[23] According to the earliest surviving witness, the late-fourth-century Virgil manuscript in the Vatican,[24] the enlarged letters were first inserted mechanically at the beginning of each page and therefore served no practical function; but in the slightly later Codex Alexandrinus,[25] they were deployed to set off major divisions of the biblical text and to mark key passages and, hence, to facilitate the uniquely Christian need to cross-check textual passages quickly—to compare the prophecies recorded in the Old Testament with their fulfillments in the New, for instance, or to coordinate the diverse accounts of Christ's life in the four gospels.

From the sixth century, enlarged letters were developed in diverse ways to ornament, animate, and even narrate the words of scripture. Working circa 700, for example, a scribe of the Lectionary of Luxeuil constructed the *T* that begins the text "Tempore illo" from a fish and two birds set atop a long stem filled with vegetal spirals (FIG. 6); the initial is made to frame the whole text and simultaneously to evoke Christ's cross and its life-giving power. The scribe also created a smaller initial *E* for the next phrase beginning "exsurgens," decorating it with more abstract elements that, nonetheless, still suggest that the words are actually alive.[26] In fact, the scribe used four sizes of letters to organize a single page, creating a hierarchy of scripts that forms a stark contrast to the unbroken lines of uniform letters found in pagan, Jewish, and even early Christian books. Whereas this *scriptura continua* was intended to be read fluidly and with the meaning alone in mind, the ornament in the Luxeuil lectionary stops the reader and forces her or him to ruminate on the forms and their symbolism—here, the cross as an emblem of life, a symbol of Christ, and a sign of paradise; and, in so doing, it transforms the text page into an image of its own underlying message, namely that God himself had entered the world through the Logos imprinted in flesh.[27]

The treatment of letters as images was generated, at least in part, by a practice by Hellenistic Jews of retaining the original Hebrew and Aramaic characters for epithets of God in the Greek translations of their Bible known as the Septuagint; Christians treated sacred names the same way (see "Bible and book," page 24).[28] Porphyry constructed many of his diagrams around such *nomina sacra* as the *Chi-rho*, a contraction for *Christos*; and in a page of the late-sixth/early-seventh-century gospels now in Munich, known as the Valerian Gospels (FIG. 7),[29] the eponymous scribe abbreviated the words for Lord and Jesus Christ in the fourth and fifth lines as *DNI* (for *Domini*, Lord) and *IHI XPI* (a transliteration of the Greek for Jesus Christ). In the Stockholm Codex Aureus, as in many other manuscripts, the same names and epithets are written in silver and gold; and the letters *IHS XPS* (for *Ihesus Christos*)—literally "golden words painted on purple pages"—are prominently inscribed behind Christ in the Godescalc Lectionary (see FIG. 1), providing a strong visual link between the icon and the text about the Savior's life that follows, which is also punctuated with the same hieroglyphs.

Nomina sacra were also elaborated as separate elements of decoration, particularly in Anglo-Saxon England. In the eighth-century Echternach Gospels, for instance, the word *Christi* at the start of Matthew's Gospel is written in intertwining Greek characters set out from the rest of the sentence, *autem generatio sic erat*; and even the abbreviation symbol above it participates in the sense of mysterious animation (FIG. 8).[30] The succeeding letters, diminishing in size and degree of ornamentation, appear to be generated by the iconic initials and only gradually to be transformed into legible text. The *Chi-rho* occupies an entire page in the slightly later Book of Kells (f. 34r); and, in the opening of John's Gospel, the reader is led step-by-step from an image of Christ as the book itself, to an icon of the Savior enthroned in the opening words in which he is called the Word, and then to the words that describe his earthly history (see FIG. 3). Alive with swirling whorls and filled with interlace ornament, moreover, the sinuous, interlocking letter forms themselves brilliantly express the idea that Christ is the living Word, realizing the concept advanced at the time by the Venerable Bede who, in the wake of Byzantine iconoclasm, had defended art by noting that *zoographia*, the Greek word for a painting, literally means "living writing."[31]

Fig. 6
Page from the Lectionary of Luxeuil. France, ca. 700. Paris, Bibliothèque nationale de France, MS. lat. 9427, f. 144r.

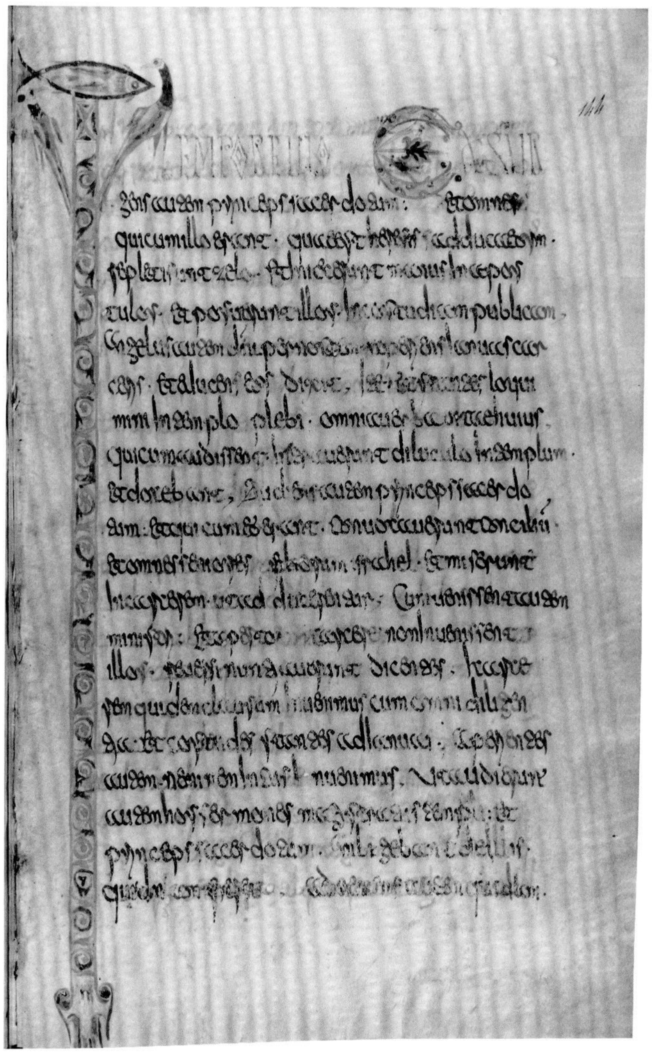

SIGN OF SALVATION

In these manuscripts, the *X* of the *Chi-rho* is presented as a cross, the powerful symbol of the Savior that seems to hold in check the serpentine figures (imported from pagan art) that reinforce its magical power over the chaotic mundane realm full of dangerous forces, both real and imagined.[32] The frame of the evangelist portrait in the Book of Kells features four crosses filled with interlace ornament; and another cross on the bridge of the letter *N* provides the support for the enthroned celestial Lord on the facing page. Calling to mind Christ's earthly travail reported in the words that follow, crosses and icon represent Christ's dual nature, which is the very essence of the *In principio* ("In the beginning"), the allusion to the Book of Genesis that opens John's Gospel.[33] A somewhat different conception is conveyed in the Luxeuil lectionary, where the cross serves as the initial *T* and is actually formed of images, amalgamating letter, picture, and apotropaic sign.

In turn, the jeweled cross in the Valerian Gospels in Munich (see FIG. 7), adorned with the *alpha* and *omega*, evokes the passage in the Book of Revelation (1:8) in which Christ identified himself with the first and last letters of the Greek alphabet and hence, once again, with words. Words, cross, and icon are brought together in a similar way at the end of a Syriac gospel-book, completed in 633/34 in Damascus: they provide a visual colophon—a pictorial closing—for all the gospels and also offer an image of the focus and ultimate destination of the prayer transcribed on the page, Christ himself.[34]

Hovering between image, sign, and letter, the cross had been used from the beginning to mark the outside of books of scripture. The gemmed cross set into the ivory cover in Milan, like Godescalc's glimmering letters on purple-dyed skin, evokes Christ's dual nature; shown set into a doorway, it also signals the entranceway to heaven that Christ's salutary death

Fig. 7
Explicit page from the Valerian Gospels. Northern Italy, late sixth/early seventh century. Munich, Bayerische Staatsbibliothek, MS. lat. 6224, f. 202v.

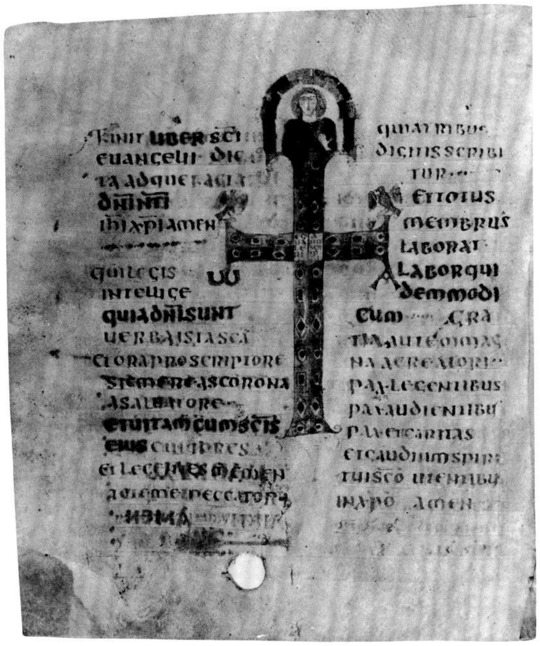

Fig. 8
The beginning of the Gospel of Matthew *(Chi-rho)*, from the Echternach Gospels. Lindisfarne (?), northeast England, eighth century. Paris, Bibliothèque nationale de France, MS. lat. 9389, f. 19r.

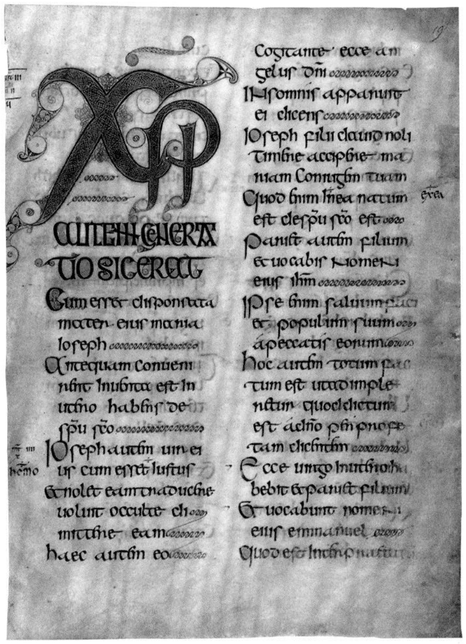

provided (see FIG. 4). Gilt-silver covers from the Sion Treasure offer the same message, depicting the life-giving cross and living plants within arched gateways (cat. no. 66).[35]

A simple, memorable geometrical shape, the cross had the additional advantage of dividing a surface into four equal fields and in that way conveying with elegant economy the harmony in Christ of the four gospels within.[36] A modest leather binding from fifth-century Egypt, now in New York, takes advantage of that potential,[37] as does the book Christ is shown holding in the magnificent sixth-century icon on Mount Sinai.[38] By the eleventh century, when the eighth- to ninth-century pocket-sized Gospels of Saint Molaise were refurbished as a relic contained in the book shrine known as the Soiscél Molaise, the cross had become a virtually universal element on book covers.[39] In fact, any ornament comprising four elements organized around a center point conjured up the sign of Christ, as on the book Christ is shown holding in the Godescalc Lectionary (see FIG. 1).

Influenced by their presence outside, crosses of various shapes became basic features of full-page decorations inside books. Coptic manuscripts incorporate decorative crosses as frontispieces and as explicit pages, as at the close of the Glazier Codex.[40] The painted, gemmed cross sprouting vegetation beneath a painted arch at the start of the Bible of Leo the Sacellarios imitates the form found on the Sion Treasure covers.[41] Crosses were used to mark the beginnings and ends of constitutive texts in seventh- and eighth-century Hiberno-Saxon manuscripts such as the Lindisfarne Gospels;[42] orchestrated in a series of elaborate variations in so-called carpet pages, they knit together individual gospels even while subtly asserting differences.

Ultimately, the cross came to be elaborated as the Crucifixion; both inside books and on covers, the simple geometric sign now actually incorporated figures, transferred from icons. In the Book of Kells, for instance, the dismembered face, hands, and feet emerging from the frame conjure up Christ's sacrificial death; and, developing the system found in a nutshell in the Luxeuil lectionary, the eighth-century Gellone Sacramentary represents Christ hanging from the letter *T*, the blood flowing from his side rendered with the same red pigment as the adjacent words and thus furthering the connection between icon and scripture.[43] A Crucifixion proper serves as a kind of carpet page in the Durham Gospels, there taken over directly from a painted panel;[44] and full-page depictions of Christ on the Cross are included in the eighth-century epistles in Würzburg[45] and in the ninth-century Gospels of Francis II.[46] The intricate symbolic Crucifixion in the early eleventh-century Gospels of Abbess Uta of Niedermünster is a culmination of this development (FIG. 9).[47] Set against a vine, it structures the entire page in a series of oppositions: life and death, Church and Synagogue (actually shown being bitten by a branch of the Cross), king and priest—realized in an intricate interweaving of word, symbol, image, geometrical schemata, and the sheer dazzle of gold on vellum.

Covers also came to feature the Crucifixion, further reinforcing the long-standing association between the volume of sacred scripture and the processional cross. The binding of the Lindau Gospels, for example, brings together an abstract back cover based upon the cross, constructed circa 800, and a magnificent gold repoussé depiction of the Crucified Lord, from circa 870, on the front.[48] From the Carolingian period on, elaborate Crucifixions were among the most common subjects on book covers, condensing into a single image the essential message of salvation.

Crosses also cued the reading of the text itself. One of the ornamented pages in the Codex Amiatinus, for instance, arranges the titles of the books of the Old Testament, as well as those of the New, within cruciform frames sprouting flowers, to signify that the Hebrew Bible is to be understood as a prophecy of Christ (FIG. 10). The point is underscored by portraying the ultimate source of all the biblical books in an icon of Christ, pictured as on the Tivoli panel as a youthful bearded man with his flowing hair parted in the middle, but here rendered entirely in gold to convey a sense of his divinity.[49] Likewise, in Theodulf's Paris bible, the harmony and differences of the two revelations are given visual form at the beginning in a perfect iconoclast's icon (f. 3r), words themselves forming a picture devoid of images, the preface *Vetus testamentum* by Theodulf's compatriot, Isidore of Seville, written out in the form of a cross:

The Old Testament cannot be understood without the renewals of the New through the grace that belongs to them through the New Testament, which is the kingdom of heaven.[50]

JEWISH WORD, CHRISTIAN GRACE

Art's capacity to embody the basic harmony of all scripture made the decorating of manscripts virtually irresistible. In Theodulf's Paris bible, for example, the simple forming of Isidore's preface in the shape of a cross conveys directly the message that the whole Old Testament that follows in the book is to be understood as a Christian prophecy. Diagrams, concordances, and typological illustrations did the same. In the Codex Amiatinus, the intricate table of contents not only asserts that Jewish scripture—from Genesis to Maccabees—

Fig. 9
Crucifixion and *St. Erhard Celebrating the Mass*, from the Gospels of Abbess Uta of Niedermünster. Regensburg, early eleventh century. Munich, Bayerische Staatsbibliothek, MS. Clm. 13601, ff. 3v–4r.

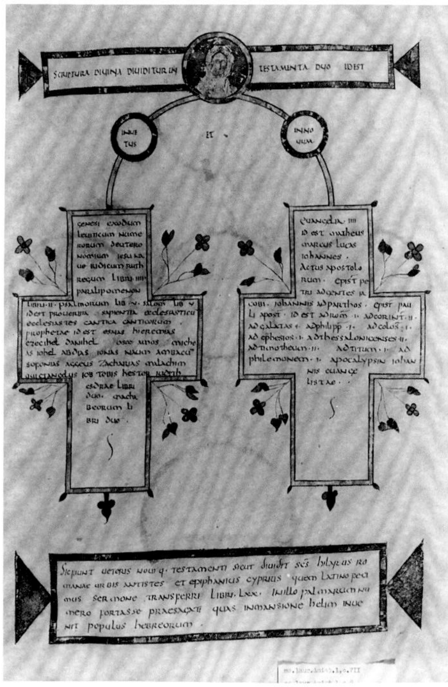

Fig. 10
Ornamented table of contents, from the Codex Amiatinus. Wearmouth–Jarrow, northeast England, early eighth century (before 716). Florence, Biblioteca Medicea Laurenziana, MS. Amiatino 1, f. 6/VIIr.

is to be read as the revelation of profound mysteries, but it also makes clear that both Testaments are more or less equal gifts to humankind from the Almighty.[51] Unity underlies the imagery of the Milan ivory covers, too, where the four streams flowing beneath the Cross allude to the fountain at the center of the Garden of Eden (Genesis 2:10) and, in turn, to the tree of the knowledge of good and evil from which, it was believed, the Cross had been made. The Fountain of Life is given an entire page in the Godescalc Lectionary, significantly on the verso of the page depicting Christ enthroned in a walled garden; there the representation also includes birds and a deer around a shrine topped by a cross, extending the reference to the words of "Psalm 42:1-2"

As a deer longs for flowing streams, so my soul longs for you, O God. My soul thirsts for God, for the living God.

Four rivers from which harts drink are also pictured beneath Christ's feet on the Tivoli *Acheropita*, symbolizing the new paradise established by Christ and its accessibility to the faithful.

A shrine with curtains drawn aside frames the cross-fountain on the Milan covers, another emblem of scriptural harmony and difference. This motif had impressive longevity; it was repeated quite precisely half a millennium later, for example, as the frontispiece to a Greek gospelbook in Messina.[52] It evokes the Temple in Jerusalem and the veil that closed off the *Sancta Sanctorum* (Holy of Holies) where, to expiate the chosen people's sins each Yom Kippur, the Jewish high priest had anointed the Mercy Seat with the blood of sacrificed animals.[53] According to the Epistle to Hebrews (9–10), Christ's sacrifice on the Cross had abrogated the old Jewish cult, opening up the Holy of Holies to all the faithful, a fundamental theological concept pictured literally in the lower right medallion of the Crucifixion page in the Gospels of Abbess Uta, where the Temple is represented with its curtain ripped open. The idea that the Incarnate God had replaced the rites previously closed off in the Holy of Holies also governed icons such as the Tivoli panel, which shows Christ enthroned on the Mercy Seat and—in an allusion to Mark's report that Christ himself had declared that he would replace the Jewish sanctuary with his own person—was called an *acheropita*, that is, an "image-not-made-by-hand":

I will destroy this temple that is made with hands, and in three days I will build another, not made with hands (Mark 14:58).

Evoked on the cover of Tuotilo's Gospels by the flanking cherubim that adorned the Ark of the Covenant, Christ (and icons of him) takes the place of the sacred vessels formerly hidden from sight inside the Temple (and its predecessor, the desert Tabernacle).

In many books of Christian scripture the reference to the Jewish cult marks the transition from the Old Covenant to the New. A full-page miniature of the Old Testament Tabernacle in the sixth-century Ethiopian gospelbook in Abu Garima, for instance, is paired with a depiction of the Fountain of Life (remarkably like that in the Godescalc Lectionary) to make the point;[54] and the ninth-century Valenciennes Apocalypse begins with an elaborate diagram of the Jewish Tabernacle that doubles as a decorative frame for the entire volume and as a precursor to the depiction at the end of the codex of John's vision of "the holy city, new Jerusalem, coming down out of heaven from God" (Revelation 21:2; cat. no. 72).[55] In the Codex Amiatinus the theme of supersession governs the opposition of a two-page diagram of the desert Tabernacle placed before the Old Testament (ff. 2v–3r)—entirely devoid of figural elements but with the curtain in front of the inner sanctum marked by a cross—and an icon of the enthroned Christ in heaven before the New Testament (f. 796v). The trope also underlies the dedication miniature in the Gospels of Abbess Uta, where the seventh-century saint Erhard is shown vested in the elaborate breastplate of an Old Testament priest (see Exodus 28:30) and celebrates Mass at the church's altar beneath an enormous canopy labeled "Holy of Holies" (see FIG. 9).[56] Thus Erhard, the founder of Uta's convent, is depicted as the precursor of all priests and simultaneously as the successor of Christ, "the high priest of good things to come," whose own death on the Cross (pictured on the facing page) had abrogated the Jewish cult and is symbolized by the Lamb in the medallion, the paschal offering in the Temple that Christ himself had superseded in a perpetually renewed sacrifice.

ONE VOICE

Tables and charts, like those in the Codex Amiatinus, also served the purpose of rendering textual concordance visual. The most important of these—because they allowed the user to find corresponding passages in the several gospels, as well as those unique to individual accounts—are the ubiquitous canon tables devised by Constantine's bishop Eusebius in the fourth century (see "Spreading the Word," page 64). Many canon tables deployed architectural forms to suggest the structural integrity of the four accounts, as in the woefully fragmentary but magnificent gilded canon tables in London (cat. no. 68);[57] and others included symbols and pictures as well to convey spiritual harmony. The Rabbula Gospels, painted in 586, offer a particularly elaborate example.[58] This set of ten tables consists of arches resting on columns filled with crosses and other signs and, in the margins, paradisiacal animals, figures, and scenes from the Old and New Testaments (cat. no. 62).

Following a tradition that may go back to classical scrolls, the Rabbula Gospels also included portraits of the authors of the texts; and these, too, helped to assert the fundamental point that, for all their apparent diversity, the books that constitute the Bible were products of men appointed by the One Almighty to bring his message to humankind. The adornment of the fragmentary Syriac bible in Paris,[59] for example, focuses largely on the inspired authors of each book: Moses, Joshua, Job, Solomon, Jeremiah, Ezekiel, and other prophets in their proper places in the translated Hebrew texts, and James in the largely lost New Testament section. Moses is portrayed at the start of the Book of Exodus in the ninth-century Moutier-Grandval Bible, first receiving the Law from the hand of God and then delivering it to the Levites.[60] In an imaginative move, he is portrayed with a balding head, widow's peak, and rounded beard, the easily recognized features of Saint Paul, to link his message to that of his Christian successor.[61] The prophets are pictured at the start of their writings in the now dispersed tenth-century Niketas Bible: before the Wisdom Books (Job, Psalms, Proverbs, Ecclesiastes, Song of Songs, Wisdom of Solomon, and Sirach/Ecclesiasticus), for instance, Jesus Sirach is shown in conversation with King Solomon, who is inspired by a personification of wisdom in the guise of the Virgin Mary;[62] and Jeremiah is portrayed before his prophetic text, engaged in a dialogue with Christ who appears to him from heaven (cat. no. 69).[63]

In like fashion, David is represented in psalters composing his sacred songs accompanied by four co-psalmists to establish a visual parallel with Christ and his evangelists.[64] In the ninth-century Chludov Psalter, Christ appears above David's head;[65] like the similar figure in the Codex Amiatinus, the round icon leaves no doubt that the Old Testament poems should be read as prophecy of Christian grace. Paul is portrayed in an epistolary now in Munich, not writing his letters but—in a message of continuity that would not have been missed by ninth-century missionaries to the Saxons—preaching them to barbarians unable to read.[66]

Most important, portraits of the four evangelists were included in gospelbooks to realize the claim—largely settled around the year 200 after a century of debate—that their accounts alone tell the same, doctrinally correct, story (see "Bible and book," page 29). Introducing the "symphony" of the canon in the sixth-century Rossano Gospels, for example, bust portraits of Matthew, Mark, Luke, and John holding books are tethered together in a circle filled with abstract ornament signifying the divine source.[67] In the same manuscript, a personification of wisdom is shown standing over the Evangelist Mark, guiding his hand as he writes the opening of his Gospel in red letters—starting with the word "beginning" in reference to the Book of Genesis.[68] The evangelists painted on the wooden panels covering the Codex Washingtonensis are in style and concept hardly different from icons; shown standing side-by-side, they not only recall the blessed authors of the gospels but also conjure up Christ, whose presence once lay in holy texts between them (cat. no. 28).[69]

In the Latin West, the evangelists were generally shown accompanied by winged symbols derived from Ezekiel's vision of "something like four living creatures ... of human form ... the four had the face of a human being, the face of a lion ... the face of an ox and the face of an eagle" (Ezekiel 1:4–11) and its rephrasing in the Book of Revelation (4:6–8). These mystical sightings of the celestial Deity from the Old and New Testaments were consistently cited in scriptural prefaces to justify the canonicity of the four accounts. The winged man (Matthew), lion (Mark), ox (Luke), and eagle (John)[70] are included together with the portraits of the authors in the corners of the Milan ivory covers, for example (see FIG. 4); and the Godescalc Lectionary pictures the four inspired authors in succession, each with his symbol. Hiberno-Saxon gospelbooks include pages of the four symbols alone; but generally, the evangelists' shared subject is actually pictured, the symbols positioned around the Almighty in the well-known iconography known as the *Maiestas Domini*.[71] The front cover of Tuotilo's Gospels exemplifies the image of unity; holding a book and flanked by the *alpha* and *omega*, the cosmic Sovereign is envisioned as he is described in the text within the volume, written by the four evangelists and inspired by their symbols (see FIG. 5). Christ is both the source and the fulfillment of scripture.

Distinctions are also given visual form within these general assertions of unity. On the cover of Tuotilo's Gospels, for example, Mark and Luke are shown along the bottom edge, the former sharpening his pen and the latter holding his upward, while at the top Matthew is already engaged in writing his text, as is John who inscribes a long roll. The first two were considered to be the more terrestrial authors, the second two celestial ones. These distinctions are not always consistent. In the Lindisfarne Gospels, beards designate Matthew and Luke as the terrestrial evangelists, and Mark's youthful appearance indicates his higher status.[72] John is consistently shown as the most elevated because, unlike the authors of the

Detail of fig. 11.

Fig. 11
Symbolic illustration from the Moutier-Grandval Bible. Tours, mid-ninth century. London, British Library, MS. Add. 10546, f. 449v.

three "synoptic gospels," he alone "in speaking of Christ's temporal acts also recognizes the eternal power of his divinity."[73] Thus, on Tuotilo's cover, John's symbol is given special treatment; the eagle bears, not a jeweled codex as the others do, but a *rotulus* (bookscroll). By recalling the vision of the sky that "vanished like a scroll rolling itself up" (Revelation 6:14), the *rotulus* refers to the belief that John alone had risen to the very limits of time and space, where he saw the entirety of sacred history—from the Creation (alluded to by the words "In the beginning" at the start of his Gospel) to the Second Coming (Apocalypse) and understood its truth in a way that even the most acute reader of scripture never could. In the Book of Armagh, this point is made by picturing the eagle grasping a fish in its talons, an allusion to the bird's perceptive faculties which were thought to be so keen that it could see prey even while it soared to the heavens.[74] John's special status is established in the Godescalc Lectionary by the placing of his portrait on the same opening as the icon of Christ and, in the Book of Kells, by the Evangelist's unmistakably Christ-like appearance.

The idea that, for all their diversity, the various texts of scripture speak of a single God is pictured explicitly in an extraordinary miniature at the close of the Moutier-Grandval Bible (FIG. 11). The "book sealed with seven seals" (understood here to be the whole Bible, both Old Testament and New) is shown atop an altar, surrounded by the four evangelist symbols holding their books being opened by the Lamb and the Lion of Judah, as was prophesied to happen at the end of time (Revelation 6). Below, the symbols are pictured unveiling the hidden truth (literally, "apocalypse"), namely that the God revealed in scripture is a single person. As the ox and lion tug at a cloth symbolizing the curtain of the Holy of Holies, the eagle lifts the cloth to reveal the face and the angel raises a horn to the man's mouth. Divine scripture, the miniature proclaims, is a single *persona*, one "sounding-through" despite its many authors and diverse tongues.[75] A few years before the miniature was painted, Beatus of Liébana explained its message this way:

The face of the Bible was veiled from Moses until Christ, and in the end of this Bible it is revealed. John reveals that the entire Bible is one book, veiled at the beginning and manifest at the end. Which book is called two testaments, Old and New, the law and the gospels, that is, the whole Bible.[76]

In the icon at the close of the Moutier-Grandval Bible, the reader sees the single "face of the Bible" in an image whose words he had only "heard" from the beginning of the book.

To lend authenticity to versions of the sacred text written in new languages (which had a linguistic consistency not found in the originals), their translators were also pictured. Eleventh-century Byzantine manuscripts of the first eight books of the Old Testament (Octateuch) include sequences of pictures representing Ptolemy II Philadelphus commissioning the Greek text of Hebrew scripture from Jewish elders.[77] Jerome is shown on the back cover of the Dagulf Psalter being commissioned by Pope Damasus to prepare his Latin translation and then dictating it to his scribe, the privileged counterpart to David and the co-psalmists depicted on the front cover composing their original Hebrew poems.[78] In this way the Dagulf Psalter, which was intended as a gift from Charlemagne to Pope Hadrian and contained Jerome's Vulgate text recently edited at the Frankish king's behest, also pictured current scriptural activity and honored the living pope. In the First Bible of Charles the Bald and the San Paolo Bible from Reims, Jerome's activities as translator are elaborated in prefatory frontispieces that picture his studies of Hebrew and distribution of the Vulgate pandects (see figure 10, page 63).[79] A remarkable portrait in the Codex Amiatinus depicts Ezra, who memorized scripture and then restored it after the Israelites returned from captivity in Babylonia (see figure 7, page 57). He is shown seated in front of a bookcase containing nine large codices, a barely disguised reference to the sixth-century exegete Cassiodorus, whose Codex Grandior had served as one of the models for the monks who made this enormous bible at Wearmouth–Jarrow under the watchful eye of the Venerable Bede (see "Spreading the Word," pages 65–66).[80]

Commissioning copies of and transcribing the Bible were sacred acts that assured the accurate transmission of God's word and, therefore, merited recognition and sometimes also recompense. Valerian (see above, page 84) inscribed his own name at the center of the gemmed cross under the sign of Christ himself in heaven;[81] and a monk and layman who transcribed the gospelbook in Bremen are portrayed at work in the scriptorium.[82] The monks at Saint Martin in Tours had themselves pictured at the end of the enormous First Bible of Charles the Bald, like the Magi, delivering the gift they had prepared to

Fig. 12
Monks of St. Martin at Tours Presenting Their Work to Charles the Bald, from the First Bible of Charles the Bald. Tours, 845. Paris, Bibliothèque nationale de France, MS. lat. 1, f. 423r.

Detail of fig. 13.

Fig. 13
Aaron Conducting the Ark of the Covenant, from the Bible of Leo the Sacellarios. Constantinople?, tenth century. Vatican, MS. Reg. gr. 1, f. 85v.

their ruler (FIG. 12). As the accompanying poem makes clear, the brothers hoped that their offering would induce the king to renew the privileges his grandfather Charlemagne had bestowed on their monastery, not because of its lavishness, but because it comprehended God's law, which they hoped the king would incorporate into his very person by reading "the two testaments again and again."

PICTURING SACRED HISTORY

Narrative illustrations were another means to render the fundamental unity of the Bible, to reveal the reciprocal relationship of the Old and New Testaments, in particular, and to harmonize the four gospels. In the fifth-century Ashburnham Pentateuch (Genesis, Exodus, Leviticus, Numbers, and Deuteronomy),[83] the pictures negotiate between different translations of the Hebrew scripture; inscriptions written in ink are transcribed from the Old Latin version of the Bible, while the painted captions are copied from Jerome's Vulgate. The miniatures themselves go further, still; the Creation of the World (FIG. 14), for example, provides a complicated reading of Genesis 1–3, portraying the Creator as a Binity (the Father and Son), a theological interpolation that the ninth-century owners of the manuscript later found unacceptable and emended by painting over one of the twinned figures in each pair.[84] In the Cotton Genesis, painters working in late fifth-century Egypt represented Christ as the agent of Creation, revealed the three angels who visited Abraham to be the disguised Trinity by providing one of them with a cross-nimbus, and gave particular prominence to Tamar with her children, Perez and Zarah, not because of their importance for the Book of Genesis but because, in Matthew's genealogy (1:3), these obscure persons are identified as ancestors of Christ.[85] The frontispiece to the Book of Leviticus in the Bible of Leo the Sacellarios represents Aaron conducting the Ark of the Covenant borne on the shoulders of six Levites and followed by Moses (FIG. 13); in so doing, it not only integrated Joshua's later account of the Levites entering the Holy Land (Joshua 3) into the Pentateuch, but also incorporated an allusion to the Christian liturgy that superseded the old order. The tall building with an attached apse in the background is clearly a church into which the ark containing scripture is being brought; and, swinging a censer in front of the procession, Aaron is figured as the precursor of Christian priests.

To disclose Christ in David's inspired poetry was particularly important for illustrators of psalter manuscripts. The Chludov Psalter, for example, conceives the phrase in Psalm 47, "God has gone up with a shout ... God sits on his holy throne," as a prophecy of Christ's Ascension by introducing into the margins a pictorial formula used also on early icons (FIG. 15). As the apostles and Mary look on, Christ rises from Mount Olivet, borne heavenward by angels—already transformed into an icon through his frontal pose and blessing gesture.[86] The effect is not only to provide a gloss for the words of the Psalm, but also to convey a fundamental belief that, while God communicated to the Jews through words, he manifested himself to Christians through the Incarnate Lord. In fact, the ninth-century Chludov Psalter was a reaction to the attack on Christian art that had recently preoccupied Byzantium in the period of Iconoclasm, during which such defenders of images as John of Damascus made the point precisely:

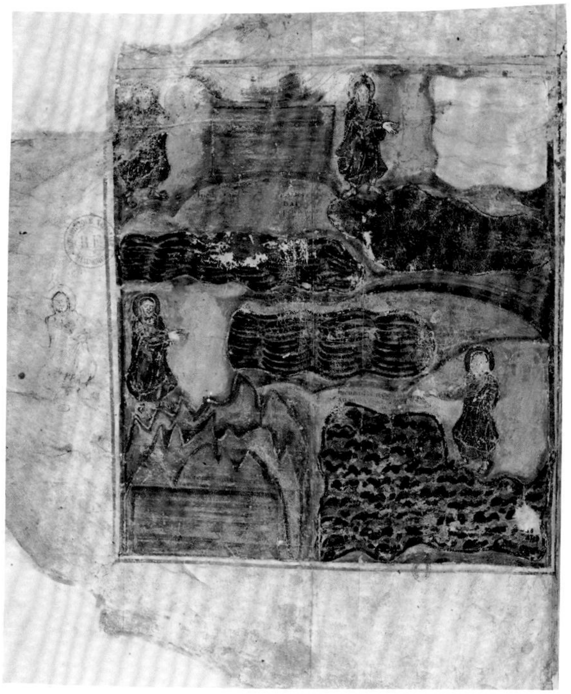

Fig. 14
Creation of the World, from the Ashburnham Pentateuch. Italy(?), fifth century. Paris, Bibliothèque nationale de France, MS. lat. nouv. acq. 2334, f. 1r.

Fig. 15
Ascension of Christ, from the Chludov Psalter. Constantinople(?), ninth century. Moscow, State Historical Museum, Cod. 129, f. 46v.

They truly are in error, brothers, for they do not know the Scriptures, that the letter kills, but the Spirit gives life. They do not find in the written word its hidden, spiritual meaning.[87]

The idea that images provided a spiritual understanding of the words they accompany was repeated at the Second Council of Nicaea convened in 787 to restore the cult of icons:

If it is pious to venerate [the prophecies about the Savior], how much more is it necessary to venerate what is the fulfillment of the prophetic reflection which we see in an icon?[88]

And the claim was made explicit in a miniature in a contemporary psalter on Mount Athos: this portrays David, the author of the words, "Their idols are silver and gold, the work of human hands" (Psalms 115), pointing to a representation of the Jewish Tabernacle fully furnished with the *vasa sacra* manufactured by Besalel (Exodus 31), who is pictured beside him. Such a depiction was intended to prove that God had ordained sacred objects as instruments of veneration, against the claims of the iconoclast John the Grammarian, who is also shown, pointing to an idol.[89] Christian understanding of scripture not only allows material representations including icons, the miniature asserts, it also requires them.

Illuminated Latin psalters also presented the words of Hebrew poetry as a prophecy of Christ whose incarnation fulfilled and abrogated them. The early ninth-century Parisian manuscript in Stuttgart, for instance, illustrates Psalm 104:2, "You stretch out the heavens like a tent," by showing Christ standing on the earth and lifting up the firmament, his own body making the transition between heaven and earth.[90] The coherent set of pictures of the Old Testament text in the slightly later Utrecht Psalter, in turn, engaged specific mid-ninth-century doctrinal disputes. Picturing David raising a chalice to Christ's side in the illustration of Psalm 115, for instance, engaged contemporary disputes over the nature of the Eucharist.[91]

New Testament narratives were most important as demonstrations of the Lord's earthly sojourn and the consistency of the four gospels; hence, they were generally treated in a straightforward manner. At the start of the fifth century the Milan ivory covers already framed the symbolic depiction of the Crucifixion with scenes of Christ's infancy and ministry; and the lavish ninth-century gold binding of the Codex Aureus of Saint Emmeram not only presents the *Maiestas Domini*, but also recounts in a series of reliefs Christ's terrestrial teachings: the Woman Taken in Adultery, the Cleansing of the Temple, the Raising of Lazarus, and the Healing of the Blind Man. In

Fig. 16
Moses Receiving the Law and *Doubting Thomas*, from an ivory manuscript cover. Germany(?), early eleventh century. Berlin, Staatliche Museen-Preussischer Kulturbesitz, inv. nos. 8506, 8505.

the Rabbula Gospels, events from the four texts are presented as a continuous history accompanying the canon tables and leading up to full-page depictions of the culminating moments, the Crucifixion and also the Ascension, Selection of Matthias, and the Pentecost described in the Book of Acts. A similar pictorial agenda governs the placement of narrative pictures in the Gospels of Saint Médard of Soissons produced in Charlemagne's court around 800; the Gospel of Luke (ff. 123v–124r) provides a running history, beginning with scenes of the Annunciation to Zacharias, the Annunciation to the Virgin Mary and, in the letter *O* of the opening word, the Visitation.[92] A depiction of Doubting Thomas on an ivory cover in Berlin (FIG. 16)[93] vividly demonstrates the belief in the reality of the Resurrection by showing the Apostle pulling Christ's cloak down and pushing his finger into his exposed wound (John 20:24–29). Looking at the depiction was intended to reassure the viewer of the cover in much the same way that Christ convinced the skeptical Thomas, "Have you believed because you have seen me?" (John 20:29); and touching the high relief would further have reinforced the sense of his or her belief in the Lord's presence.

The illuminators of the Rossano Gospels drew on all four gospels to provide a coherent account of Christ's life, and also included Old Testament prophets holding scrolls bearing texts related to the events toward which they point.[94] An illustration of the Last Supper (FIG. 17), reported in the three synoptic gospels, is preceded by depictions of the Five Wise and Five Foolish Virgins, recounted by Matthew alone (25:1–12), and followed by the Washing of the Feet, found only in John (13:2–11): David is shown below three times with verses from Psalms (22:2, 40:10, and 40:7–8) to make the same point that, in psalters, is realized through narratives placed beside the texts themselves. A miniature picturing the Annunciation to Zacharias (Luke 1:9–11), painted around the year 600 and stitched into the tenth-century Armenian Ēǰmiacin Gospels (FIG. 18) turns the idea around by starting the series of miniatures devoted to Christ's incarnation with a glance back to the Old Testament through the picture's emphasis on the temple and its curtain and Zacharias's elaborate vestments—including the belled fringe mentioned in Exodus 28–29.[95] The father of John the Baptist, considered by Christians to be the last Old Testament prophet, is in this way figured as the hinge between the Jewish cult and Christian priesthood.

Fig. 17
Last Supper, from the Rossano Gospels. Constantinople(?), sixth century. Rossano, Museo dell'Arcivescovado, f. 3v.

Fig. 18
Annunciation to Zacharias, from the Ējmiacin Gospels. Armenia, tenth century. Yerevan, Matenadaran, MS. 2734, f. 228r

Fig. 19
Detail, Canticle of Habakkuk, from the Utrecht Psalter. Reims, mid-ninth century. Utrecht, Rijksuniversiteit, MS. 32, f. 85v.

AMPLIFYING THE MESSAGE

Just as it engaged the diverse accounts of the Bible itself, so too art incorporated elements from extra-canonical sources to augment, interpret, and normalize the reading. To establish a pictorial link between the Old Testament and Christ's ministry, the Ējmiacin Gospels, for example, drew on the *Armenian Infancy Gospel*,[96] an apocryphal account of the sort illustrators frequently used to augment the canonical narratives, harmonize the various versions, and make them more readily accessible to readers. A stylized depiction of the Garden of Eden behind Jacob's tomb in the Ashburnham Pentateuch alludes to Jewish legends that identified the patriarch's grave as the portal to Paradise.[97] And the poetic paraphrase of the Book of Genesis in the tenth-century Junius Manuscript comprehends a pictorial preface that elaborates the creation of the angels, which is not recounted in scripture at all, the Fall of the Rebel Angels, and Satan's role in the Temptation of Adam and Eve (see cat. no. 61).[98]

An effective way to demonstrate the unity of scripture, of course, was simply to bind all of it in a single volume, as in the Codex Amiatinus and Moutier-Grandval Bible (see "Bible and book," pages 33–34). Referred to as *bibliothecae* (literally, "boxes for storing books," i.e., libraries) and also as "pandects" (juridical digests) because they comprehended all of divine law, such bibles were generally too cumbersome for practical purposes, however; and, by-and-large, they served only special functions such as gift-giving.[99] The Codex Amiatinus, for example, was made at the behest of Abbot Ceolfrith for presentation to Pope Gregory II; and the monks at Tours produced the Moutier-Grandval Bible for Hugo of Tours, just as later they would prepare a manuscript for Charles the Bald. The elaborateness of the Theodulf Bible in Paris suggests a similar special purpose. And, as the dedication miniature showing Leo the Sacellarios presenting his lavish book to the Virgin Mary attests, it was an *ex voto*; the epigram reads, "God with the Mother who gave birth, the God-bearer, in exchange for his mercy."[100]

Another harmonizing procedure was to arrange the diverse texts themselves in a coherent fashion, as in the Luxeuil and Godescalc lectionaries, where the gospel texts were ordered according to the liturgical calendar, or in the Utrecht Psalter, where canticles culled from other biblical texts—Exodus, Kings, Deuteronomy, Daniel, Matthew, Luke, etc.—were appended at the end and harmonized with the Psalms through a consistent style of textual presentation and illustration.[101] The rendering of the Canticle of Habakkuk (Habakkuk 3:2–19), for instance, glosses the Old Testament words in the same manner as in the preceding Psalm illustrations (FIG. 19); the phrase "You came forth to save your people" is understood as a prophecy of Christ by being pictured as the history of Christ's life from the Annunciation, through the Nativity, Passion, and return to heaven at the Ascension, and then, the casting down of demons. Such books served the liturgy more directly than the full Bible; psalms (including the canticles), the gospels, and the epistles were read in the Divine Office more, say, than Joshua or Revelation; and the new arrangement accommodated the Church rites.

More common was the introduction of prologues by Church fathers, contemporary poems and *tituli* (composed picture captions), and in certain instances even secular texts, that guided the reading of the scriptures and accompanying pictures. For example, a letter Jerome sent to Paulinus in which he set forth a comprehensive reading of scripture is included in the Moutier-Grandval Bible and many other manuscripts; Isidore's *Vetus testamentum* arranged as a cross in Theodulf's Paris bible details the relationship of Hebrew scripture to the New Testament; the anonymous *Origo psalmorum* compares David and Christ; and Jerome's *Novum opus* and

Plures fuisse prefaces, found in numerous gospelbooks, cite the fountain of four rivers in paradise and the Ark of the Covenant to argue for the harmony of four gospel texts (both themes alluded to on the ivory covers in Milan). Bound in the tenth-century manuscript of the Book of Maccabees from St. Gall, a late-fourth-century tract on military practice, Vegetius's *Epitoma rei militaris*, indicates the contemporary understanding of the Old Testament battle against the enemies of Israel as a universal example of spiritual struggle and as a paradigm of just war.[102]

Scripture, exegesis, and picture are often brought together in verses written *ad hoc* for inclusion in the lavish manuscripts. Epigrams composed by Leo the Sacellarios, for example, declare at the very beginning of his bible that:

Moses in drafting the law already presents in figure the manifest fulfillment … and David, who plays his harp, foretelling his own son, the Christ.[103]

Other verses in the same book direct the reading of specific miniatures, those framing the Leviticus frontispiece (see FIG. 13), reinforcing the meaning indicated by the pictured church and liturgical elements:

The priests and the Levites of the Old [Covenant] thus prefigure the treasure of the New; they prescribed carrying the Ark to Christ. For as within [the Ark] were the tables of that [Old] Law, so Christ, the human nature doubled with the divinity, proceeds from the Virgin.[104]

Other texts include verses from Sedulius's *Carmen paschale* describing the character of each author and his symbol and inscribed on many evangelist portraits;[105] and captions on depictions of the *Maiestas Domini* in the Lothar Gospels, Nancy Gospels,[106] and other Carolingian gospelbooks that make the spiritual meaning clear:[107]

Here are the four rivers flowing from one source, the books of Matthew, Mark, Luke, and John.

Likewise, Godescalc's dedication poem provides a cue for understanding, not the text, but its decoration; and, later, the 316 lines of poetry distributed throughout Charles the Bald's great bible provide a complex guide to the whole book and its illustrations.[108] *Tituli* in the Codex Aureus of Saint Emmeram were apparently composed by the great Carolingian theologian John Scottus Eriugena, offering especially sophisticated interpretations of the complicated miniatures.[109] The verses around the *Maiestas Domini*, for example, proclaim:

The ranks of the saints arranged in four-fold order,
as shown in the various drawings, behold great joys.
Now the present page shows with ornate splendor
Those things which the eight leading saints shout from pious lips.

Geometrical schemata and portraits rendered in gold and brilliant color, the poem proclaims, are equivalent to the inscribed words as a writing-down of the prophetic voices. Provocative verses in an early eleventh-century sacramentary in Paris almost taunt the viewer to find the spiritual message underlying a seemingly ordinary depiction of the Nativity:

This material picture demands diligent scrutiny from the eye of the human mind, exemplifying in itself, through the humble birth of his incarnation, how he who lives immortal and timeless in heaven, sought out the mortals of the world as a mortal himself.[110]

Fig. 20
Temple Instruments, from a Hebrew Pentateuch. Palestine or Egypt, dated 929. St. Petersburg, National Library of Russia, MS. Firk. Hebr. II B 17, f. 5r.

In these and many other manuscripts, sacred writings and splendid icons come together in Christ.

BOOK AND BODY

In the miniature showing Charles the Bald receiving his gift bible, the pandect is bound in red and studded with gems; the *ex voto* miniature in the Bible of Leo the Sacellarios pictures an even more lavishly adorned volume, covered in gold set with pearls and gems, being offered to the Virgin Mary (represented explicitly in the manner of an icon). These very materials were used on altars during this period, as the miniature in the Gospels of Abbess Uta actually shows, depicting the Codex Aureus of Saint Emmeram alongside the chalice and paten. The ivory used for many covers functioned in the same way; not only did it reinforce associations with the ruler, but it also suggested purity because of its color and because, according to medieval animal lore, elephants (from which it came) were considered chaste.[111]

As the embodiment of Christ, gospelbooks adorned with these materials were ceremonially carried into the church. A sixth-century mosaic in San Vitale, Ravenna, pictures the liturgy, where the scripture bound in gold and adorned with pearls and gems is shown together with the cross and paten being censed as part of the imperial procession to the altar, the ritual later mapped onto the depiction of the Jewish Levites bearing the Ark of the Covenant in the Bible of Leo the Sacellarios. In Rome, deacons and acolytes carried the books of the Bible in procession before the pope and set them up on the altar alongside the chalice, paten, and cross;[112] and in 855, Pope Leo IV stipulated that the gospelbook, reliquaries, and pyxides for the sacraments were all that were allowed on altars.[113] The enormous codex being opened by the sacrificial Lamb atop an altar in the Moutier-Grandval Bible reflects this tradition of the book as liturgical presence (see FIG. 11).

Many books directly engaged themes that connected them to altars. When the gospelbook covered by the Milan ivories was set up on the altar, for example, the cross and lamb depicted would have connected it directly to the Eucharist, reinforced by the image of the living waters, the reference to the site of Jewish sacrifice, and the narratives of incarnation, including the one (directly beneath the cross) of the Miracle at Cana, where Christ transformed water into wine.

Ivory covers in Tournai, carved circa 900,[114] picture the Crucified Christ actually bleeding into a chalice held up by Church beside the defeated Jerusalem and the Lamb of God borne heavenward by angels; and its back cover represents the church's patron Nicasius, whose relics were protected in the altar, as a type of Christ, clutching a book and venerated by two priests. The cover of Tuotilo's Gospels engender a similar chain of associations; Mary is pictured on the back ascending to heaven and beneath her, narratives of the local saint, Saint Gall, again anchor the book to the monastery and to the altar containing his remains.

In their form and function, as in their specific pictorial repertory, then, the elaborately decorated volumes both presented and made real the argument that Christ had replaced Jewish scripture in his very person. The achievement is made clear by a comparison of the Bible of Leo the Sacellarios or Tuotilo's Gospels with two miniatures in a Hebrew Pentateuch painted in Palestine or Egypt in 929 (FIG. 20). Rare, indeed unique, examples of Jewish book art from the early Middle Ages, the illustrations are entirely aniconic; deploying the visual language of Abbasid art, they picture the pedimented Temple with its menorah, incense shovel, manna jar, and other implements and even allow a glimpse into the Holy of Holies, where the tablets of the Law are pictured with their protective cherubim.[115] The miniatures perpetuate a tradition going back to Late Antique synagogue decoration in the Holy Land; and, recalling the ancient past, they engender a longing for the re-instatement of the Temple cult in the Holy Land that must still await the coming of the Messiah.[116]

The contemporary Christian books, by contrast, assert that the Messiah has already come, fulfilling Jewish scripture, abrogating the Temple cult and carrying the Lord's message to the entire world. Accordingly, the seventh-century Armenian tract in defense of images (see above, page 80) pointed out that books and icons are essentially alike, the one appealing to the ears and the other to the eyes, and when understood spiritually engender faith;[117] and Byzantine theologians labeled those who would destroy images "Judaizers." In the Gospels of Abbess Uta, Synagogue is shown turning away from the crucified Christ while Church looks up at God incarnate (see FIG. 9); and the same point is made in the opposition of subjects on the Berlin ivories carved two centuries later (see FIG. 16); Moses is portrayed within an aedicule representing the Holy of Holies receiving the tablets of the Law—inscribed by the finger of God—from the invisible Almighty while Thomas affirms that God had indeed become a man.

DARK MIRRORS

Christians understood that icons and even books of sacred scripture were only interim devices, useful for engendering faith, but destined to yield to a direct vision of God at the end of time. Paul declared in 1 Corinthians 13:

For we know only in part, and we prophesy only in part....
For now we see in a mirror, dimly, but then we will see face to face.

And John reported a similar vision at the close of the Book of Revelation (21:22 and 22:3-4), at the end of the entire Bible:

I saw no temple in the city; for its temple is the Lord God Almighty and the Lamb ... the throne of God and of the Lamb will be in it, and his servants will worship him; they will see his face.

Picturing God in mirror-image reversal at the gateway to heaven, the Valerian Gospels (see FIG.7) illustrate the idea; so does the final image in the Moutier-Grandval Bible, depicting the book of scripture sealed between covers and yielding to an icon of the enthroned God. Jerome put the principle this way in his influential letter to Paulinus, which is inserted at the start of the volume:

The Law is spiritual, one must lift a veil in order to understand it and, in order to, with its face uncovered, we contemplate God's glory.

As defenders of art maintained during the Iconoclastic period, if they were to lead to a contemplation of "God's glory," books had to be elevated through an allegorical reading of the literal account and the base matter of icons had to be spiritualized through meditation. Thus, when the eleventh-century author of the *Liber translationis Dionysii Areopagitae* looked at the cover of the Codex Aureus of Saint Emmeram, he saw in it a realization of John's final vision as "the image of the omnipotent Christ, the cornerstone and the true sun that illuminates the Heavenly Jerusalem."[118] A century earlier, when he depicted Christ with his head flanked by the *alpha* and *omega* enthroned between sun and moon and earth and sea, Tuotilo engaged the same conceit. So did Godescalc's "golden words on purple pages ... that open up the starry heavens," which not only broadcast the material value of his beautiful book of scripture but also made vivid the spiritual worth of their contents. They could carry the faithful only so far, however. Godescalc went on:

In this way the teaching of God, written with precious metals,
Leads through to the entrance rooms of the light-beaming kingdom
Following with a receptive heart the light of the Gospel,
And climbing above the steep constellations of the heavenly heights
It gathers [us] *in the inner sanctum of the king of heavens forever.*[119]

Like other things of this world, ornamented books and icons transport the faithful into the atrium of the inner sanctum; but, like the God of the Jews, Christ made visible in these things remains beyond the curtain, above the firmament, fully apprehensible only by an active mind that transforms them into a still higher contemplation.

Discovering the Bible

THE CHRISTIAN CONCEPT OF THE BIBLE was established before many of its earliest materials were discovered in the Middle East during the nineteenth century. It was only then that European and American explorers, archaeologists and laypeople, stimulated by scientific advances such as the publication of Charles Darwin's *Origin of Species*, embarked on a quest to prove that the biblical narrative was literally "true."

Teams of archaeologists from London, Oxford, Paris, and Berlin were dispatched to excavate in late-nineteenth-century Egypt. Exciting discoveries included an incredibly rich deposit of papyrus and parchment documents and book fragments from the outlying garbage mounds of a city known as Oxyrhynchus (modern al-Bahnasa) in Middle Egypt. These were excavated by scholars of Oxford University between 1896 and 1897 and today are housed in institutions such as the Bodleian Library in Oxford and the British Museum and its Library (now part of the British Library). As many as thirty-six basketfuls of manuscript fragments could be excavated in one day. The first Oxyrhynchus papyrus to be published (in 1897) was the single leaf containing "Sayings of Jesus," from a codex dating from the third century C.E. (cat. no. 15)

Another amazing find was the Cairo Genizah. Within Judaism copies of scripture containing scribal errors were not simply thrown away; until they could be ritually destroyed they were carefully stored in a sealed room known as a *genizah*. The synagogue of Old Cairo (to the south of the modern city) was founded in 882 C.E. and its associated *genizah* was not discovered until the late nineteenth century. The bulk of its contents were purchased in 1896–98 by Cambridge University academics Solomon Schechter and Charles Taylor, who shipped them home to Cambridge for further research. Photographs taken at the time poignantly convey the excitement of the scholars who were the first to study these long-lost works.

The fragmentary nature of these early documents provoked a crisis of confidence among some believers, who feared that this might leave the canon of scripture open to challenge or revision. In fact, more recently discovered materials, such as the Dead Sea Scrolls, support many of the textual relationships established by biblical scholars in earlier centuries.

The role of American collectors

The thrill of the chase was also felt by a number of Western collectors, who relished the often clandestine dealings surrounding their acquisitions. The American mining engineer Alfred Chester Beatty (1875–1968) was a prominent collector of early biblical materials, which he purchased from Egyptian dealers and peasants. Consequently the find sites of these items are unknown, though most are thought to have come from the Fayyum (an area southwest of Cairo). His collection, now housed in Dublin Castle, includes twelve important early Christian codices dating from the third to the fourth century: their discovery was announced in *The Times* of London on November 17, 1931.

Detroit industrialist Charles Lang Freer (1854–1919) made an outstanding purchase of early biblical codices and related items from a dealer in Giza, Egypt, in 1906. It remains the most important collection of its kind outside the Middle East and Europe and includes two substantially complete Greek codices from the fifth century. One contains the books of Deuteronomy and Joshua and the other the gospels. Known as Codex Washingtonensis, the Freer Gospels are among the principal early witnesses to the Greek Bible. Freer also acquired fifth- or sixth-century codices of the Psalms and of the Epistles of Paul; two important Coptic manuscripts; and, in 1916, a fifth Greek codex of the Minor Prophets. He even bought an early Coptic bookstand on which such early volumes would have been displayed.

Solomon Schechter at work in Cambridge University Library, 1898; see cat. no. 1.

Scroll and Codex

The earliest Hebrew scriptures

THE HEBREW BIBLE IS COMMONLY KNOWN TO JEWS AS THE TANAK, a word formed by the initial consonants of the three groups into which the Hebrew scriptures are divided—the Torah (five books), the Nevi'im (Prophets, twenty-one books), and the Ketuvim (Writings, thirteen books). This tripartite arrangement may have developed before the time of Christianity but the collection of texts did not assume its definitive form until the Council of Jamnia (ca. 100 C.E.) produced the canonical Hebrew biblical text. On this the Masorah, a body of notes on the traditions of the text, was compiled by Jewish scribes called the Masoretes between 500 and 900 C.E. The Aleppo Codex and the St. Petersburg Pentateuch (cat. nos. 6, 7) are among the significant early witnesses to the Masoretic text.

The Hebrew Bible was not the only version known to the Jews in Antiquity. Many Greek-speaking Jews lived outside Palestine in communities around the eastern Mediterranean. Among these groups, especially in Egypt, there arose a Greek translation of the Hebrew scriptures, probably begun during the third century B.C.E. It was called *Septuaginta* (Latin for "seventy", also denoted as "LXX") because, according to legend, seventy-two Jewish scholars were brought from Palestine to Alexandria in Egypt to translate the Hebrew scriptures into Greek, their individual versions all miraculously agreeing. The actual translation process was undoubtedly much lengthier and more complex: variations in style and accuracy suggest that different parts of the Septuagint were translated by different people at various times and places during the centuries before Christianity.

The Septuagint differs from the Hebrew Bible in its content. It includes fifteen additional Jewish texts, mostly composed in Greek, known as the apocryphal or deuterocanonical books. Furthermore, parts of the Hebrew Bible are longer or shorter in the Septuagint, which sometimes also orders materials differently within a given book. So, for Greek-speaking Jews and early Christians who used the Septuagint, the Bible had a significantly different shape than for Jews who used the Hebrew Bible.

Until 1945 the only known early Jewish manuscript containing Hebrew scripture was the Nash Papyrus, dating from the second century B.C.E., now in Cambridge University Library. But thereafter many fragmentary Jewish scrolls, mostly written in Hebrew on leather, were discovered in the Judaean Desert. Many are scriptural and are the oldest surviving copies of biblical documents to have been found, providing important evidence for the pre-Masoretic Hebrew Bible. These, the so-called Dead Sea Scrolls or Qumran Scrolls, were discovered by Bedouins in a cave in 1947 and are thought to represent the library of a community of Essenes, a Jewish sect, at Qumran, or that of a nearby Early Christian monastery established by Saint Pachomius. They include 202 manuscripts of biblical texts, such as the Second Isaiah Scroll (cat. no. 3), and may have been hidden at the time of the overthrow of the Jewish stronghold of Masada by the Romans in 73 C.E. In 1954, an advertisement appeared in the *Wall Street Journal* offering them for sale; they were purchased by the government of Israel for $250,000.

Detail: Fragment of a Genesis Scroll. Cambridge University Library, T-S NS 4.3. Hebrew; vellum. Palestine or Egypt; sixth–seventh century, cat. no. 2.

3

The Dead Sea Scrolls: Second Isaiah Scroll.
Jerusalem, The Shrine of the Book, 95.57/26B, The Hebrew University of Jerusalem (owner), MS.B (1QIsab [1Q8]). Hebrew; leather. Judaean Desert, Israel, before 73 C.E.

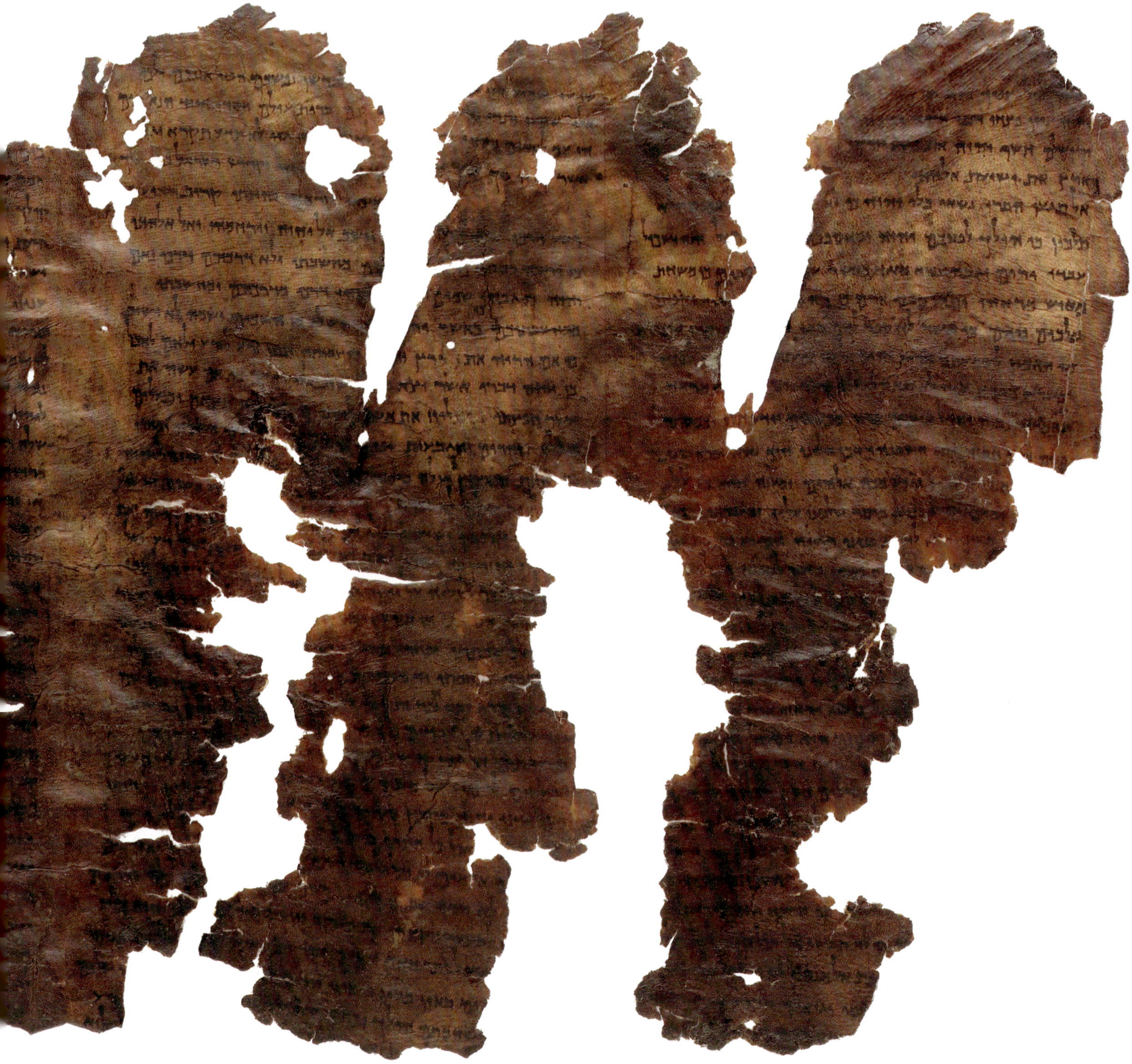

4

Fragment of a Genesis scroll.

Cambridge University Library, T-S NS 3.21; Hebrew; parchment. Palestine or Egypt, sixth–seventh century.

T-S NS 3.21
T-S NS 3.21

5

Palimpsest of Aquila's translation of the Bible.
Cambridge University Library, T-S 20.50. Overwritten with poetry by Yannai. Greek beneath Hebrew; parchment. Palestine or Egypt, sixth century (lower script), ninth–tenth century (upper script).

6

The Aleppo Codex: Second Book of Chronicles.
Jerusalem, The Shrine of the Book, 96.85/211, Ben-Zvi Institute (owner), f. 241r. Hebrew; parchment. Tiberias, Israel, tenth century.

7

St. Petersburg Pentateuch.
St. Petersburg, National Library of Russia, Firkovitch MS. Hebrew II B 17, f. 185v. Numbers 35:10–Deuteronomy 1:7. Hebrew; parchment. Palestine or Egypt, 929.

8

Bifolium from a biblical codex.
Cambridge University Library, T-S NS 246.26.2. Hebrew; parchment.
Du Gunbadan, Iran, 903–904.

9

Quire from the "Firkovitch Compilation."
St. Petersburg, National Library of Russia, Firkovitch MS. Hebrew II B 49.
Illuminated carpet page depicting the Ark of the Covenant. Hebrew; parchment.
Egypt, late tenth century.

Scroll and Codex

The earliest Christian scriptures

EARLY CHRISTIANS RELIED ON THE SCRIPTURES OF JUDAISM, and perhaps because of this were slow to produce writings of their own. The earliest to survive are the letters of Saint Paul, written between 50 and 60 C.E. (cat. no. 13). Other texts soon began to appear: the Gospel according to Mark was written some time between 65 and 70 C.E. Around 80–90 C.E. Mark's formed the basis for the longer gospels of Saints Matthew (cat. no. 11) and Luke (the latter accompanied by the Acts of the Apostles) along with a lost, shared source that has been termed "Q," which contained sayings and parables of Jesus and some episodes from his life, such as the Temptation. Around 85–95 C.E. the Gospel according to Saint John appeared, as did the letters of James, Peter, and John, Paul's letter to the Hebrews, and the Revelation of Saint John (also known as the Apocalypse, cat. no. 16). Christian writings then proliferated, with more letters—from the bishops Clement and Ignatius, and the disciple Barnabas—and more revelations or apocalypses. Also in circulation during the first half of the second century were a variety of gospels—including those of Thomas (cat. no. 15), Peter, the Hebrews, the Egyptians, and the Egerton Gospel (cat. no. 12)—and the Didache, a treatise containing summaries of the teachings of the Apostles along with instructions relating to rituals and the liturgy. Other known writings by Christians and Gnostics (a sect that fused aspects of several religions and sought mystical enlightenment as a means to salvation) cannot be firmly dated this early, while others have been lost. Sects such as the Gnostics often attributed their writings to known Christian figures including Mary Magdalene, Peter, and Judas.

The early Christian texts were composed in Greek, by various people for various purposes. They were written not for a general readership but in response to the needs of local Christian communities, and were not intended as "biblical" books as such, for Christianity had a Bible already—the scriptures of Judaism. Ultimately, of course, many of these writings came to form the New Testament in Christian Bibles. But that was the result of a long process not envisaged by their authors.

Christians were among the earliest to adopt a new vehicle for their writings—the book or codex. The Roman poet Martial was advising readers to buy literary works in this form as early as the first century C.E., but at first only the Christians favored it. Perhaps inspired by the sets of wooden writing tablets used in ancient times for rough notes, letters, or school exercises—and occasionally for Christian texts such as the Epistle Tablet from Vienna (cat. no. 18)—the papyrus codex was a practical and humble object and its use demonstrates the early Christians' utilitarian attitude to their texts. It also made cross-referencing, between the Old and New Testaments or between gospels, much easier, and it was more readily portable than the many scrolls required to carry the same amount of text. This appealed to Christian audiences, particularly during times of persecution.

Detail: The Washington Codex of the Minor Prophets, Freer Gallery of Art, F1916.768, p. 37. Habakkuk 2:4. Greek; papyrus. Egypt (Fayyum?), third century C.E., cat. no. 10.

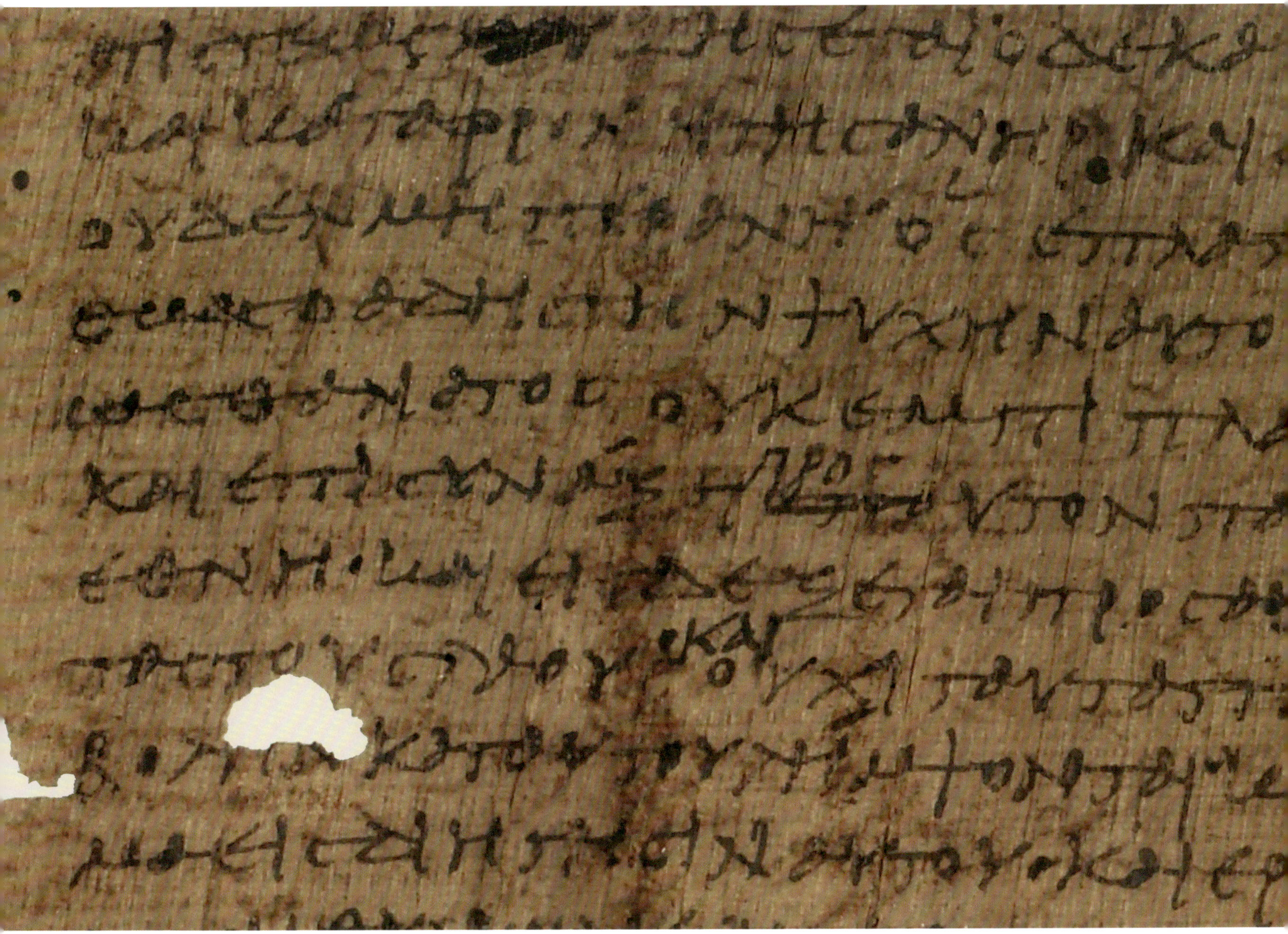

11

Early fragments of the Gospel of Saint Matthew.
Oxford, Magdalen College Library, P. Magd. Gr. 17 (P 64). Greek; papyrus. Egypt (?), ca. 200 C.E.; possibly somewhat earlier.

12

The Unknown Gospel (*alias* The Egerton Gospel).
London, British Library, Egerton Papyrus 2, 608. Greek; papyrus. Egypt, second century C.E.

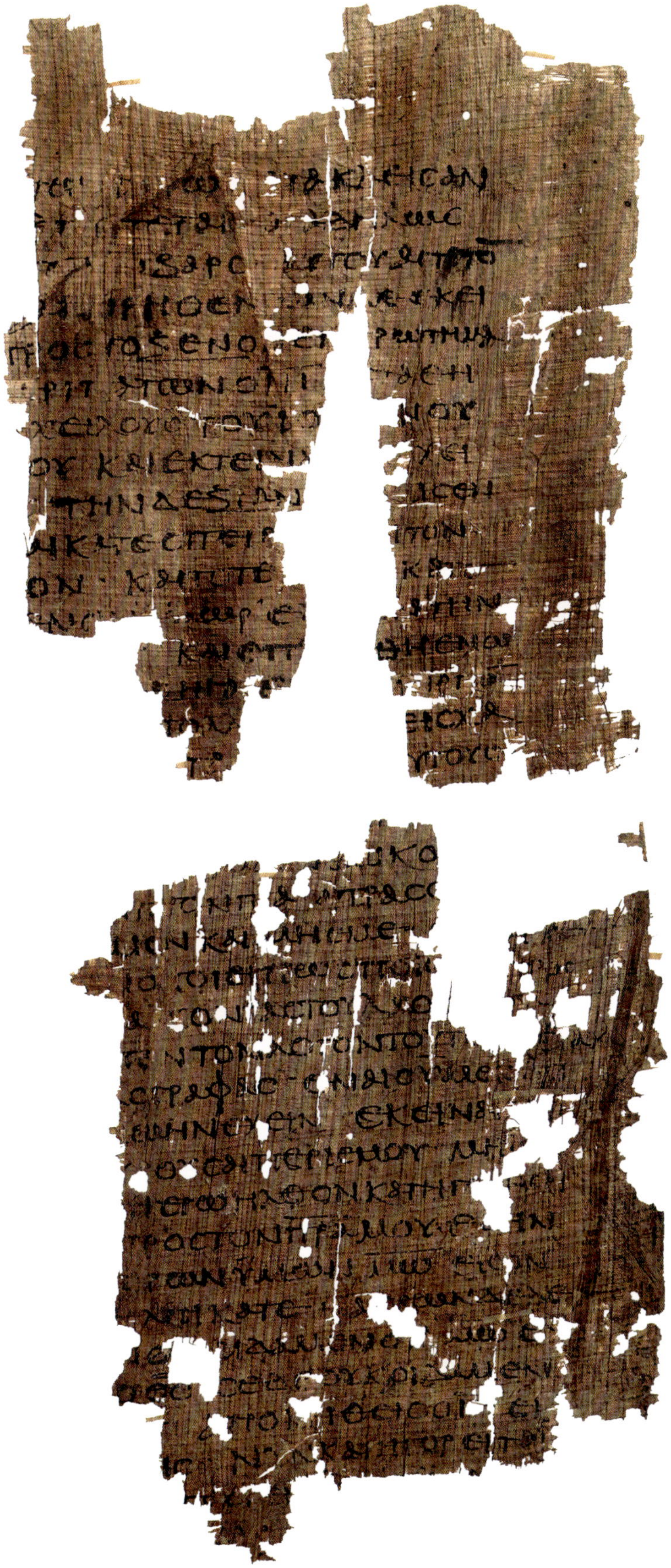

13

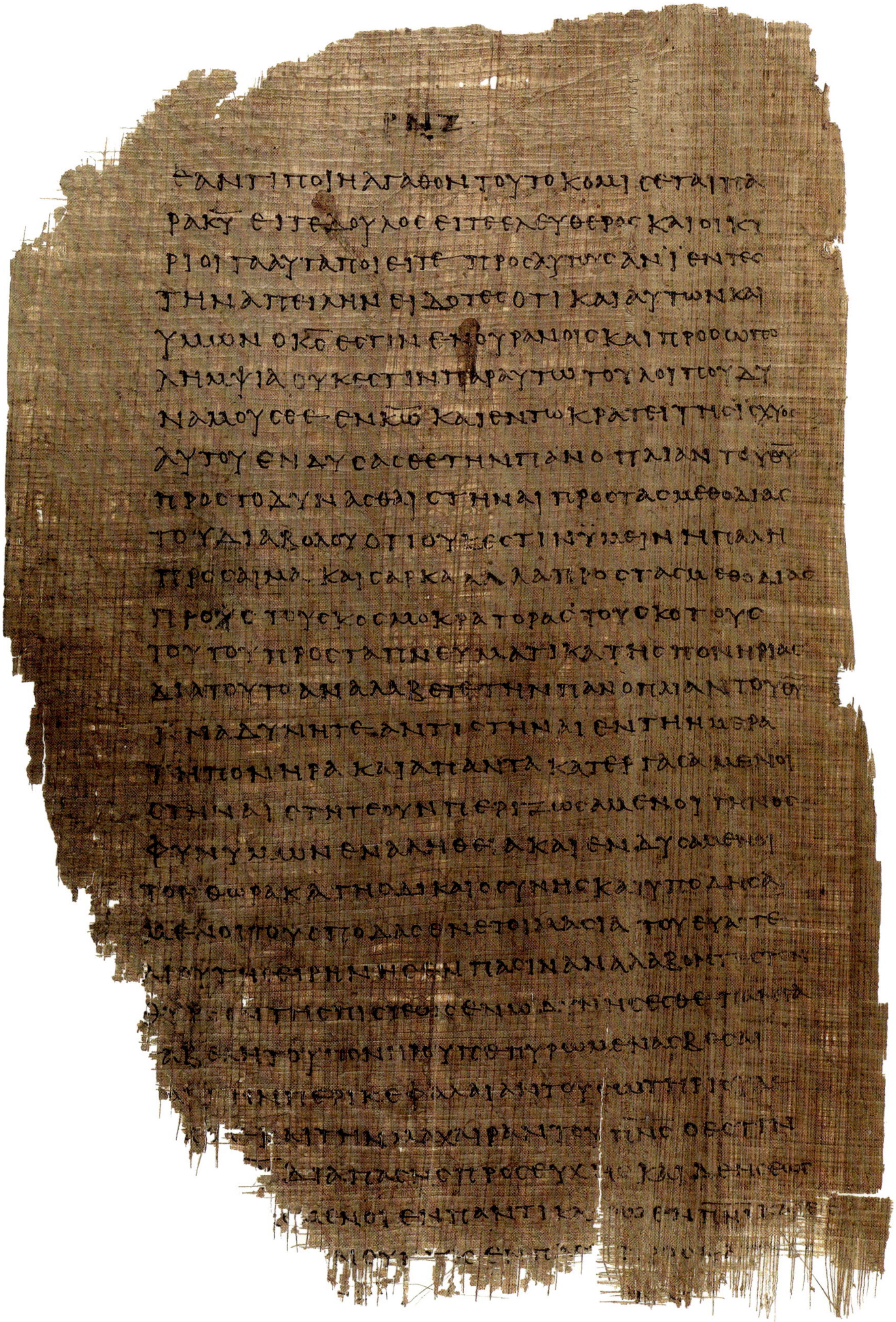

An early codex of the Epistles of Paul.
Ann Arbor, University of Michigan, 6238 (P 46), ff. 157v–158r. Ephesians 6:8–Galatians 1:8. Greek; papyrus. Egypt (the Fayyum), ca. 250 C.E.

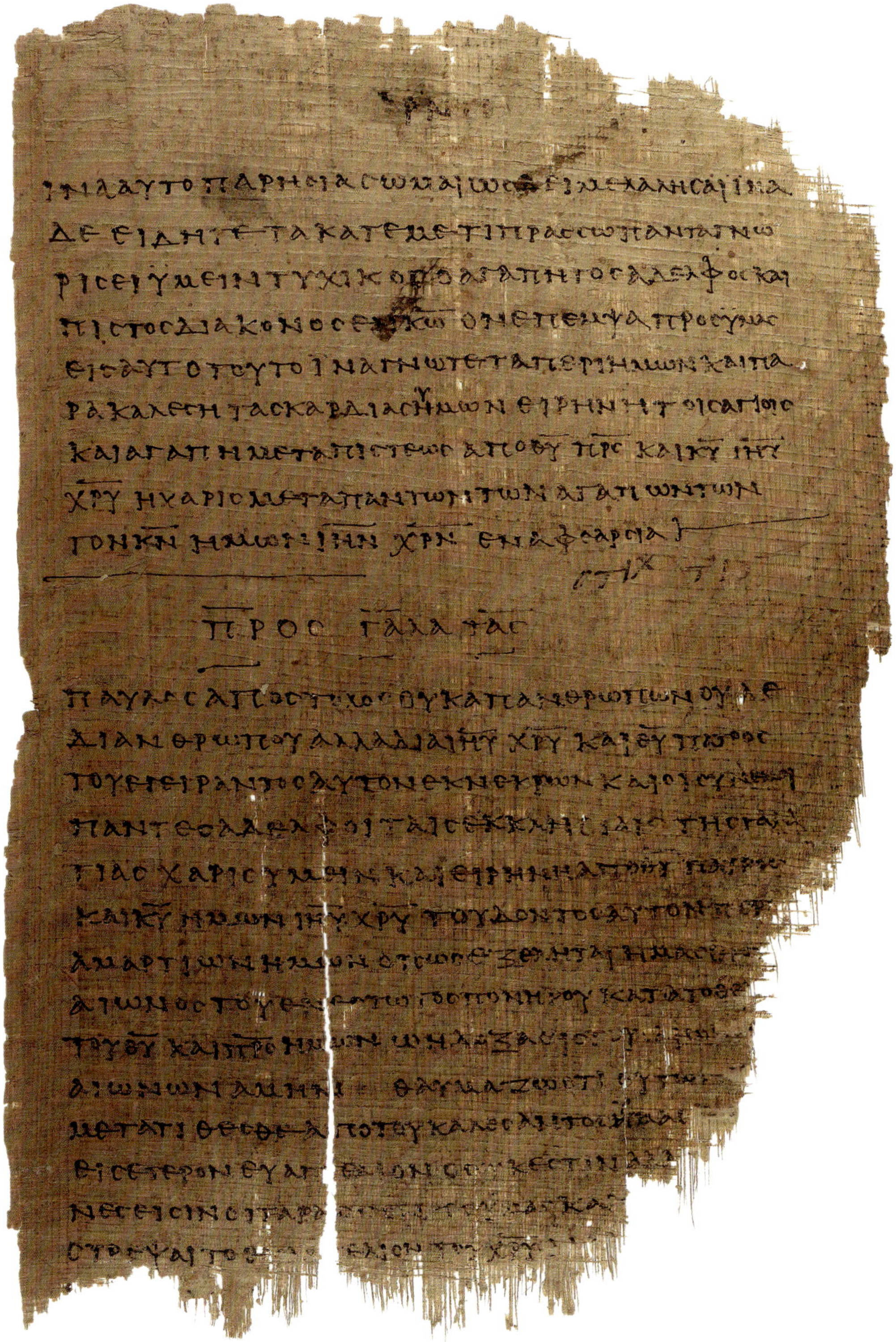
ΠΡΟC ΓΑΛΑΤΑC

14

The Chester Beatty Codex of the Gospels and Acts.
Dublin, Chester Beatty Library, MS. Biblical Papyri I (P 45), f. 7r. Mark 8:34. Greek; papyrus. Fayyum or Aphroditopolis (modern Atfih), Egypt, ca. 250 C.E.

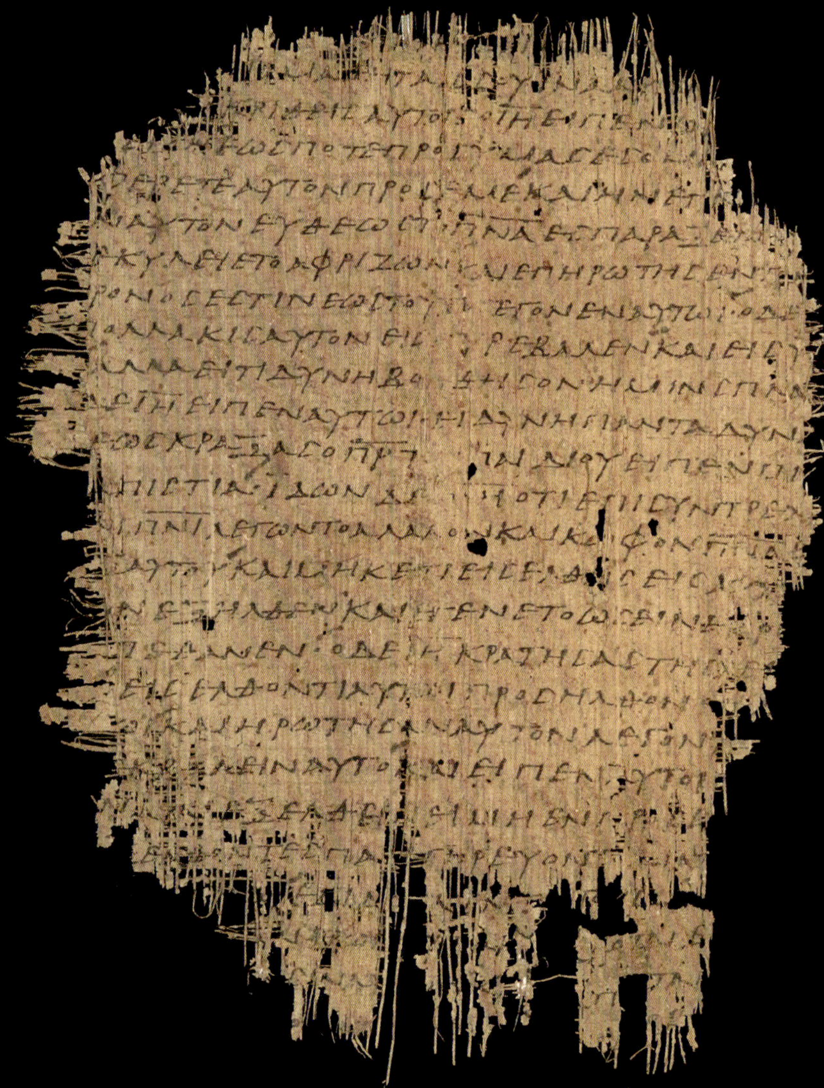

15

The Sayings of Jesus
(Logia Jesou).
Oxford, Bodleian Library,
MS. Gr. th. e. 7 (P). Greek;
papyrus. Oxyrhynchus, Egypt,
third century C.E.

16

An Early Christian bookroll.
London, British Library, P2053r (Exodus 11:26–32) and 2053v (Revelation 1:4–7) (P 18). Greek; papyrus. Oxyrhynchus, Egypt, third–fourth century C.E.

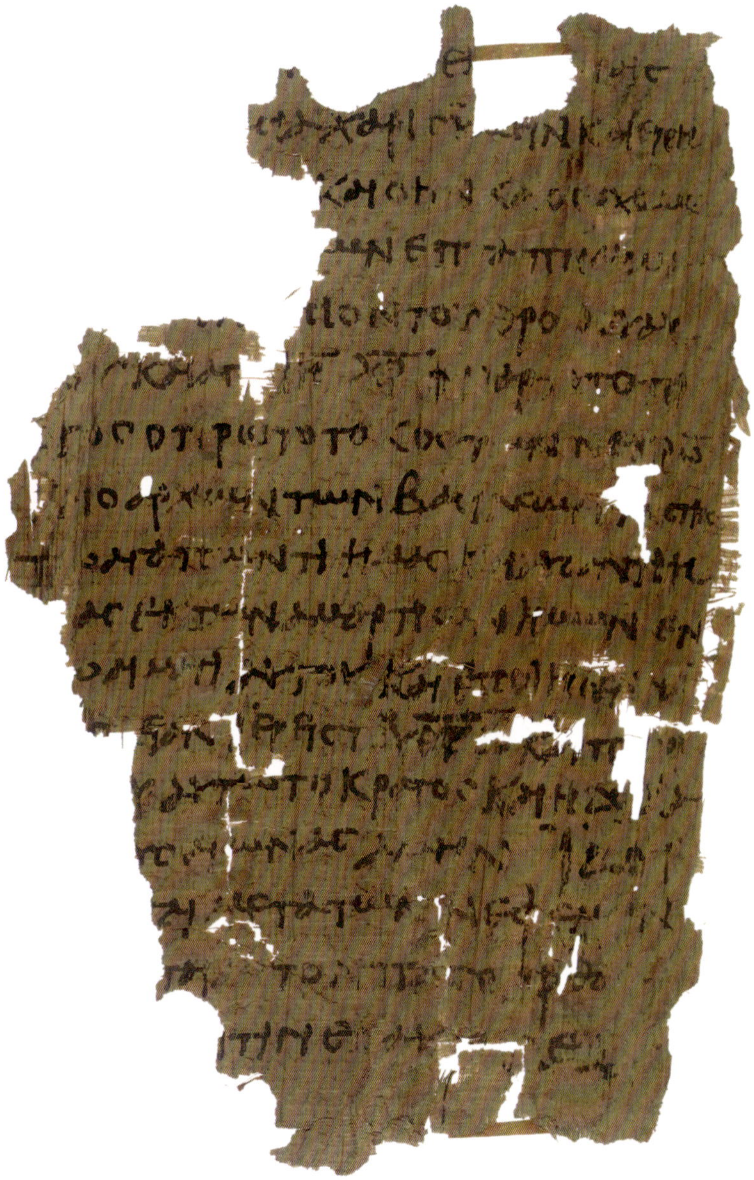

17

The Chester Beatty Codex of Numbers and Deuteronomy.
Dublin, Chester Beatty Library, MS. Biblical Papyri VI (Rahlfs 963), ff. 63v, 64v. Fayyum or Aphroditopolis (modern Atfih), Egypt, ca. 150 C.E.

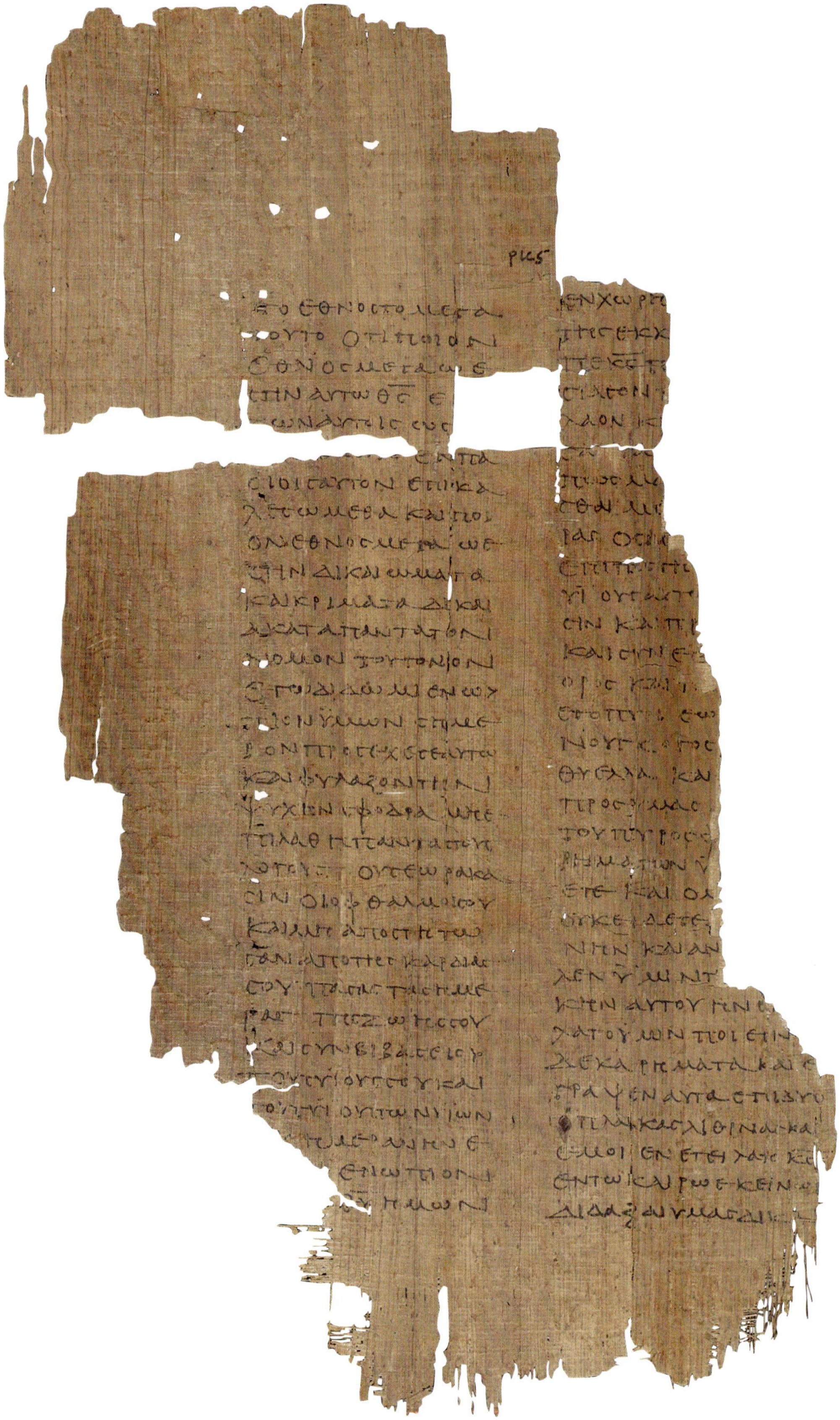

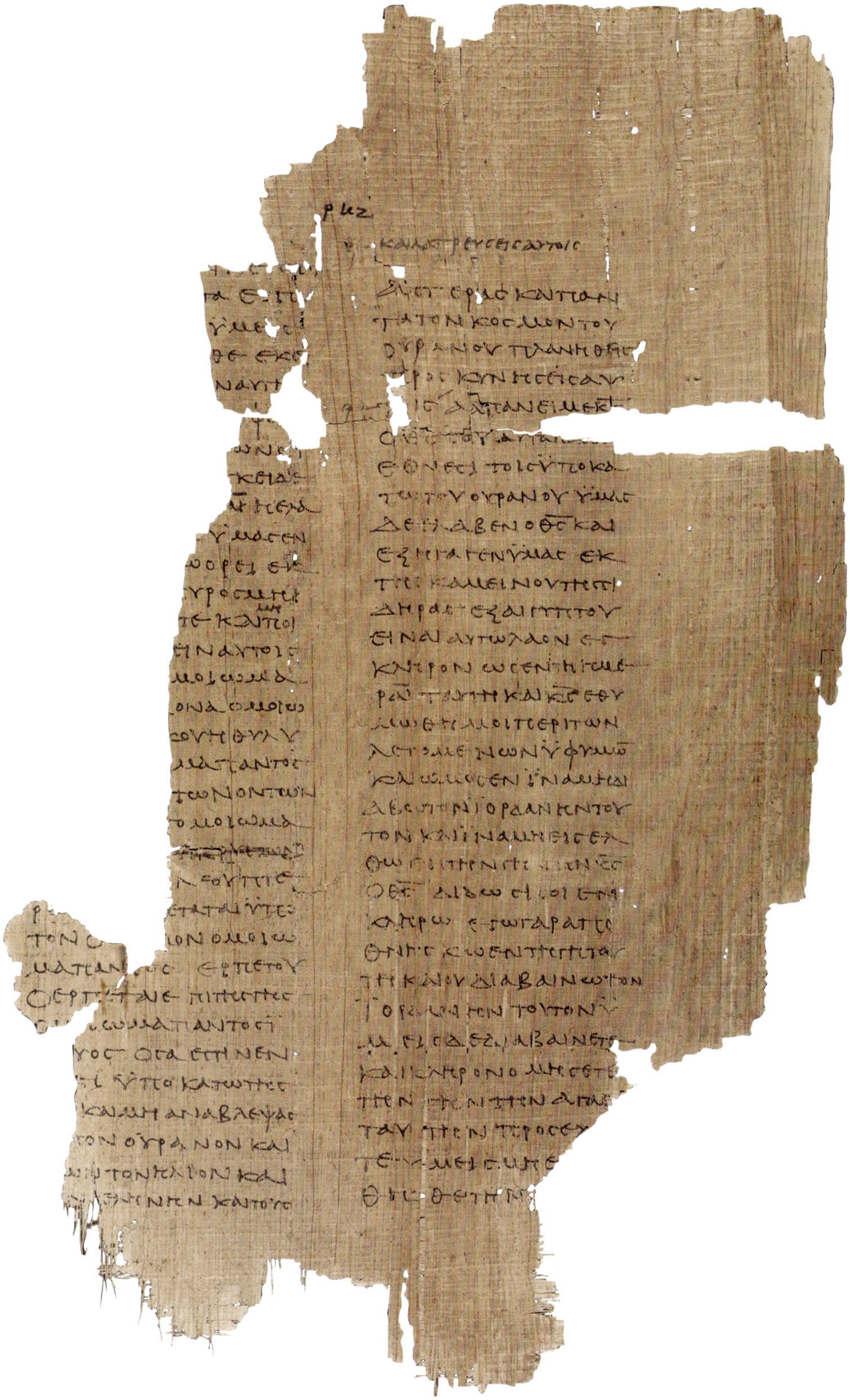

18

A tablet of texts.
Vienna, Österreichischen Nationalbibliothek, P. Vindob. KHT 1. Greek; wood. Egypt, seventh century.

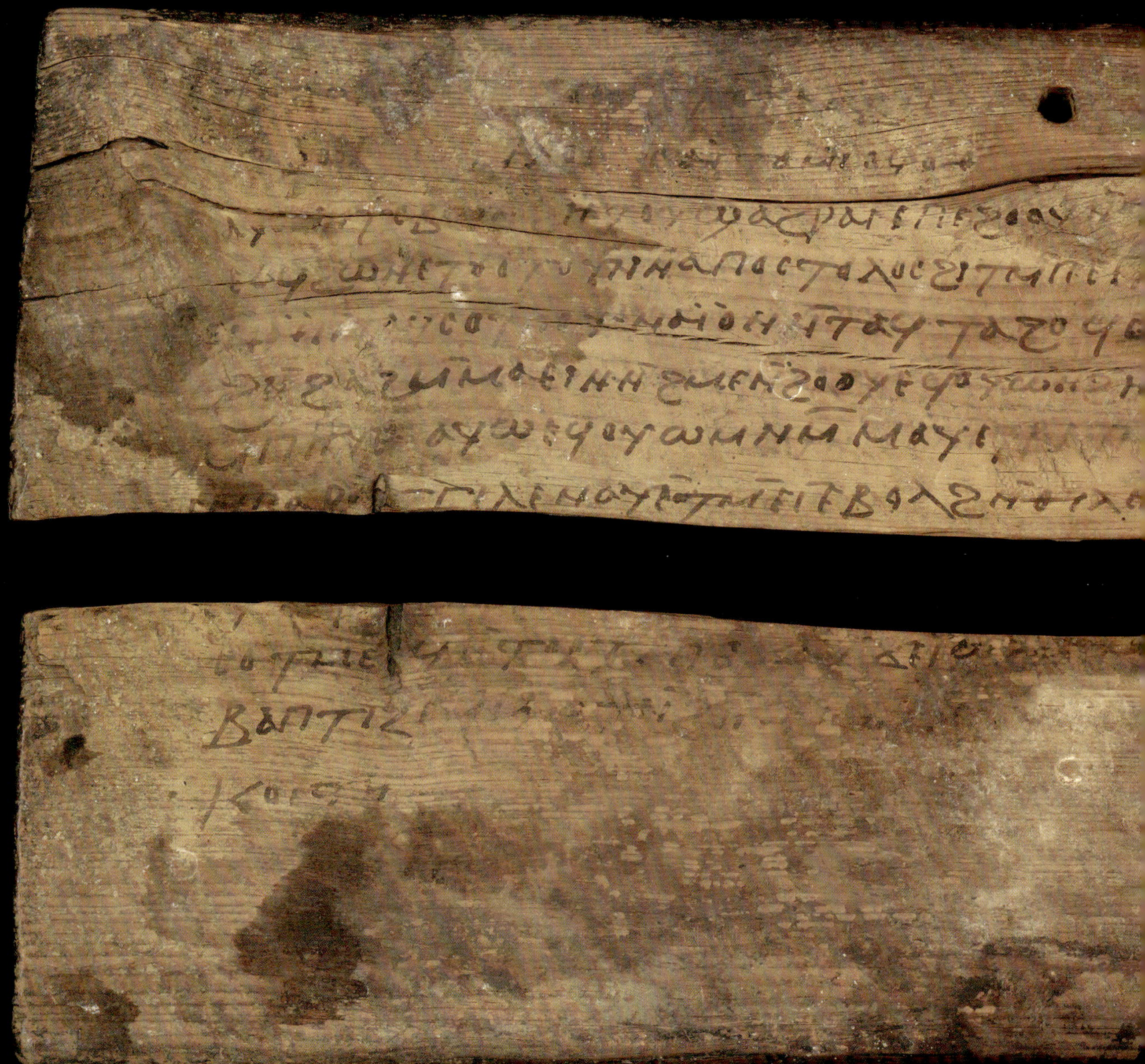

The Washington Codex of the Psalms.
Washington, D.C., Freer Gallery of Art, F1906.273, p. 171. Psalm 110. Greek; parchment. Egypt, fifth century.

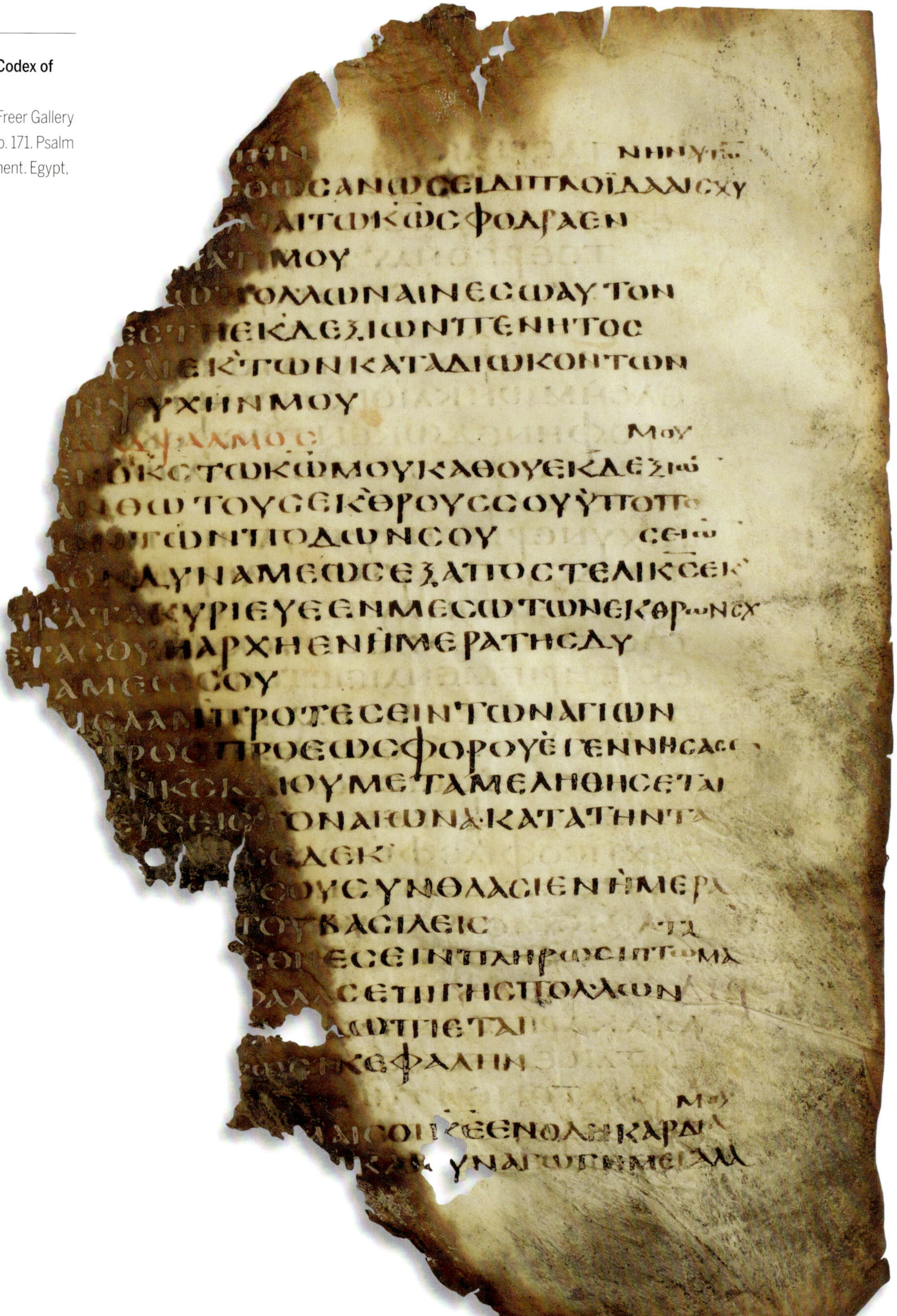

20

The Washington Manuscript of the Pauline Epistles.
Washington, D.C., Freer Gallery of Art, F1906.275, ff. 104v–105r. End of 2 Thessalonians and beginning of the Epistle to the Hebrews. Greek; parchment. Egypt, fifth or sixth century.

Formation and codification:
The evolution of the Bible

IN 303 C.E., DURING THE "GREAT PERSECUTION" OF CHRISTIANS, the Roman emperor Diocletian ordered the destruction of Christian books. But only ten years later—following his vision of the Cross and his subsequent victory at the Battle of the Milvian Bridge—Emperor Constantine (assisted by his counterpart in the Eastern Empire, Licinius) granted religious toleration throughout the Western Empire through the Edict of Milan. This toleration was extended in 324, when Constantine defeated Licinius and united the empire's two halves, establishing a new "Rome" at Constantinople. Constantine and his successors convened the early Church Councils to determine the nature of Christian belief and ritual and to counter heresy and schism; many churches were founded, all requiring acceptable collections of Christian texts. In 332 C.E. Constantine commissioned from Eusebius, bishop of Caesarea, fifty copies of Christian scriptures for his foundations in Constantinople. Christian writings began to be gathered in larger, more expensively produced books, fit for use in such prestigious surroundings.

The adoption of Christianity as the state religion of the Roman Empire later in the fourth century gave further impetus to the production of the biblical "canon," that is, a fixed list of books understood to have unique status and authority by virtue of divine inspiration. Before this time, a great number of texts had been in circulation, bearing out the words of Saint Luke that "many" had undertaken to write about Jesus. Some texts came to be rejected on grounds of dubious authenticity or association with sects such as the Gnostics. More of these have come to light in modern times, including, most recently, the Gospel of Judas.

In his *Ecclesiastical History* Eusebius recorded the status of the known biblical texts of his day. He divided them into the categories of "acknowledged books" and "disputed books," tacitly admitting that the Revelation of John was disputed by saying that it might be placed in either list. He also ruled out five, as he referred to them, "spurious" and "heretical" books (see "Bible and book," page 32).

According to Eusebius only twenty-one Christian writings were generally agreed to be authoritative scripture—that is, fewer than the twenty-seven books that eventually came to form the New Testament.

This longer list first appeared in the thirty-ninth Festal (Easter) Letter from Bishop Athanasius to his Alexandrian diocese in 367 C.E. It was Athanasius who first used the word "canon" to refer to texts that were specified for public readings during worship. Lists resembling his, though often different in content, were also compiled during the fourth to fifth centuries. One of these, probably of fourth-century composition, is preserved in Codex Claromontanus, a sixth-century copy of the Pauline Epistles (cat. no. 30). It specifies the four gospels, ten letters of Paul, the seven catholic epistles, the epistle of Barnabas, the Revelation of John, the Acts of the Apostles, the Shepherd of Hermas, the Acts of Paul, and the Apocalypse of Peter—twenty-seven books, but some different from those in Athanasius's list.

Clearly the question of which writings constituted Christian scripture—and which ones should be ruled out—was still open around 400 C.E. Accordingly, Gnostic texts, such as those contained in the Nag Hammadi Codices, and other apocryphal works continued to circulate.

Detail: The Washington Codex of Deuteronomy and Joshua, see cat. no. 27.

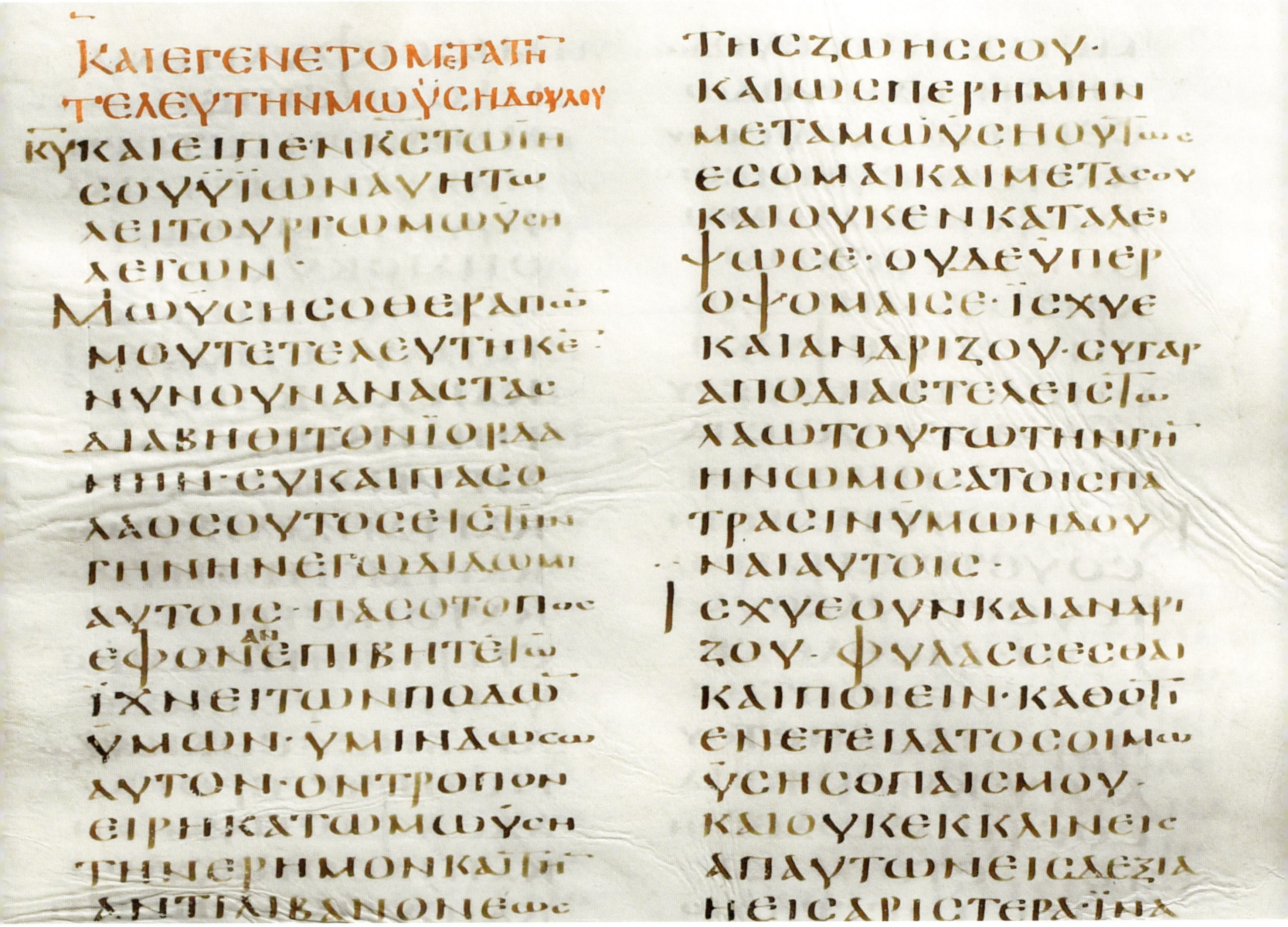
ΚΑΙΕΓΕΝΕΤΟΜΕΤΑΤΗΝ
ΤΕΛΕΥΤΗΝΜΩΥΣΗΔΟΥΛΟΥ
ΚΥ ΚΑΙΕΙΠΕΝΚΣΤΩΙΗ
ΣΟΥΥΙΩΝΑΥΗΤΩ
ΛΕΙΤΟΥΡΓΩΜΩΥΣΗ
ΛΕΓΩΝ·
ΜΩΥΣΗΣΟΘΕΡΑΠΩΝ
ΜΟΥΤΕΤΕΛΕΥΤΗΚΕ·
ΝΥΝΟΥΝΑΝΑΣΤΑΣ
ΔΙΑΒΗΘΙΤΟΝΙΟΡΔΑ
ΝΗΝ·ΣΥΚΑΙΠΑΣΟ
ΛΑΟΣΟΥΤΟΣΕΙΣΤΗΝ
ΓΗΝΗΝΕΓΩΔΙΔΩΜΙ
ΑΥΤΟΙΣ·ΠΑΣΟΤΟΠΟΣ
ΕΦΟΝΑΝΕΠΙΒΗΤΕΤΩ
ΙΧΝΕΙΤΩΝΠΟΔΩΝ
ΥΜΩΝ·ΥΜΙΝΔΩΣΩ
ΑΥΤΟΝ·ΟΝΤΡΟΠΟΝ
ΕΙΡΗΚΑΤΩΜΩΥΣΗ
ΤΗΝΕΡΗΜΟΝΚΑΙΤΟΝ
ΑΝΤΙΛΙΒΑΝΟΝΕΩΣ

ΤΗΣΖΩΗΣΣΟΥ·
ΚΑΙΩΣΠΕΡΗΜΗΝ
ΜΕΤΑΜΩΥΣΗΟΥΤΩΣ
ΕΣΟΜΑΙΚΑΙΜΕΤΑΣΟΥ
ΚΑΙΟΥΚΕΓΚΑΤΑΛΕΙ
ΨΩΣΕ·ΟΥΔΕΥΠΕΡ
ΟΨΟΜΑΙΣΕ·ΙΣΧΥΕ
ΚΑΙΑΝΔΡΙΖΟΥ·ΣΥΓΑΡ
ΑΠΟΔΙΑΣΤΕΛΕΙΣΤΩ
ΛΑΩΤΟΥΤΩΤΗΝΓΗΝ
ΗΝΩΜΟΣΑΤΟΙΣΠΑ
ΤΡΑΣΙΝΥΜΩΝΔΟΥ
ΝΑΙΑΥΤΟΙΣ·
ΙΣΧΥΕΟΥΝΚΑΙΑΝΔΡΙ
ΖΟΥ·ΦΥΛΑΣΣΕΣΘΑΙ
ΚΑΙΠΟΙΕΙΝ·ΚΑΘΟΤΙ
ΕΝΕΤΕΙΛΑΤΟΣΟΙΜΩ
ΥΣΗΣΟΠΑΙΣΜΟΥ·
ΚΑΙΟΥΚΕΚΚΛΙΝΕΙΣ
ΑΠΑΥΤΩΝΕΙΣΔΕΞΙΑ
ΗΕΙΣΑΡΙΣΤΕΡΑ·ΙΝΑ

21

Coptic Psalter.
Washington, D.C., Freer Gallery of Art, F1908.32, ff. 50v–51r. Coptic; parchment. Egypt, fifth–seventh century.

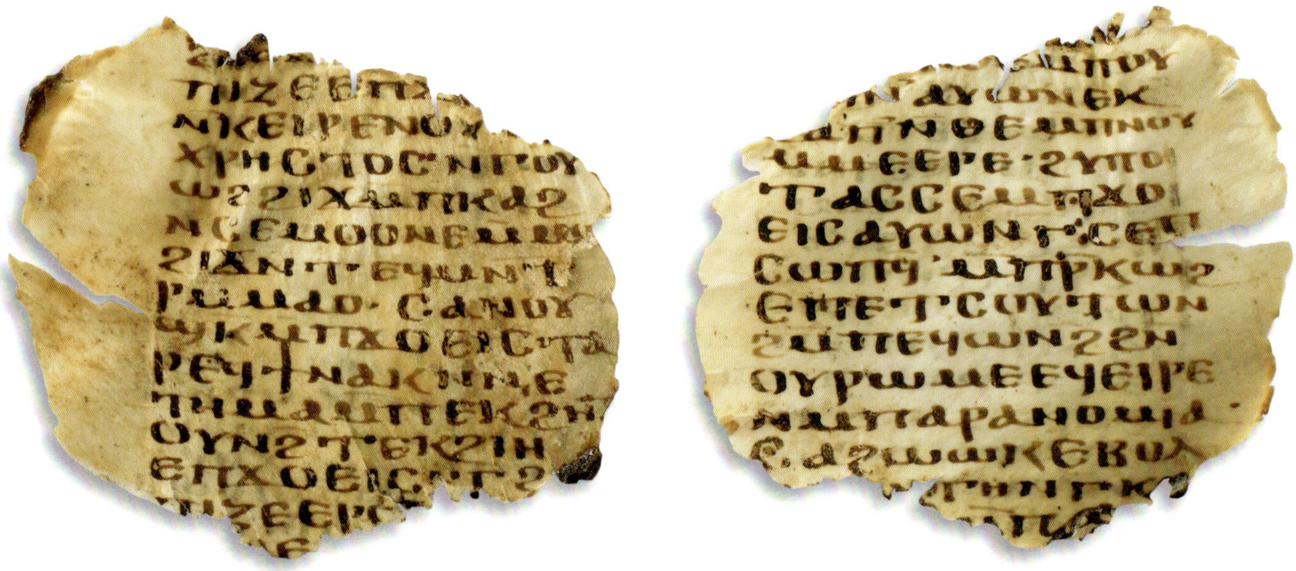

22

Codex Bruce (Codex Brucianus).
Oxford, Bodleian Library, MS. Bruce 96, f. 6r. Gnostic text; Coptic (Sahidic); papyrus. Egypt, fifth or sixth century.

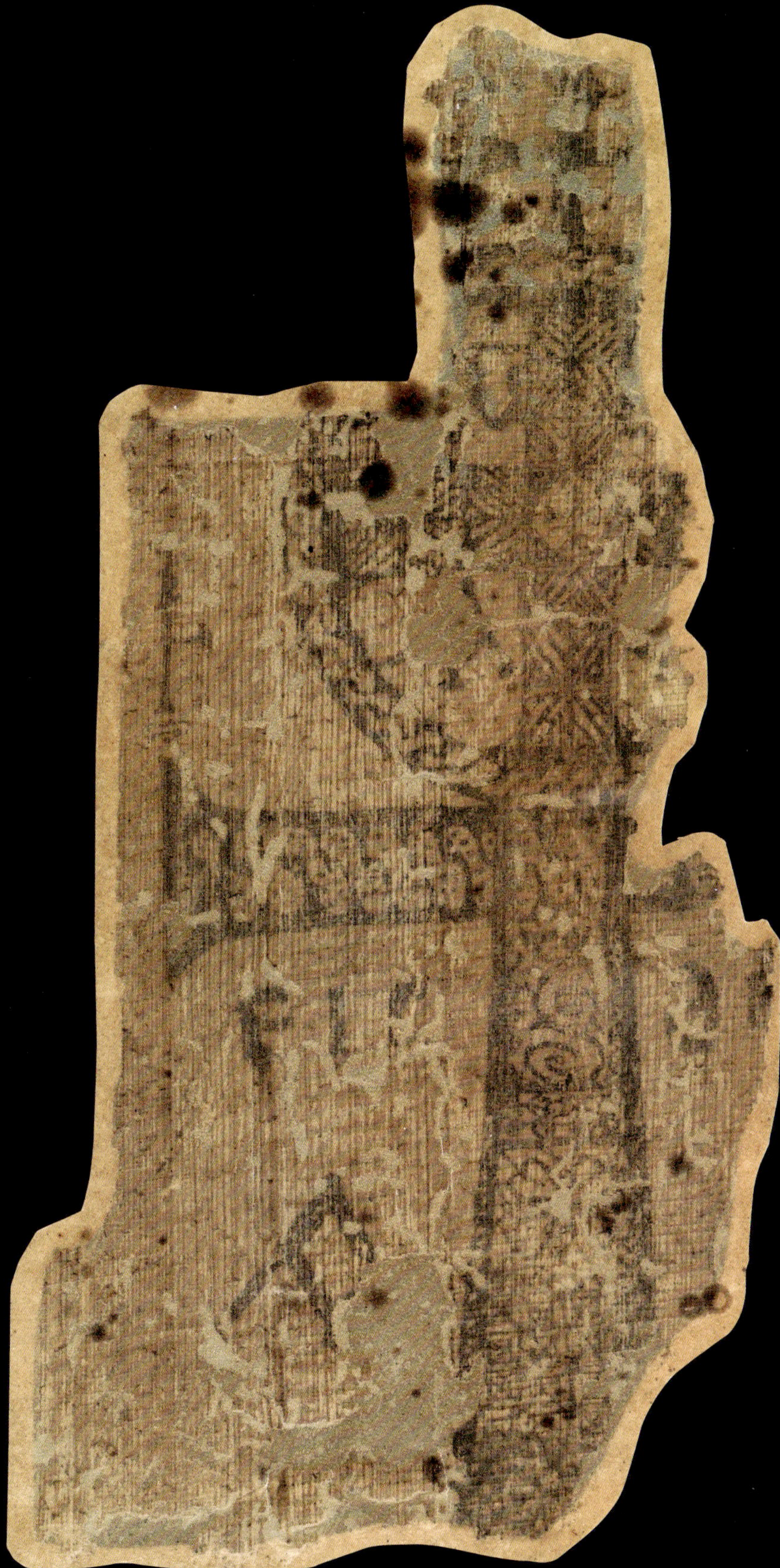

23

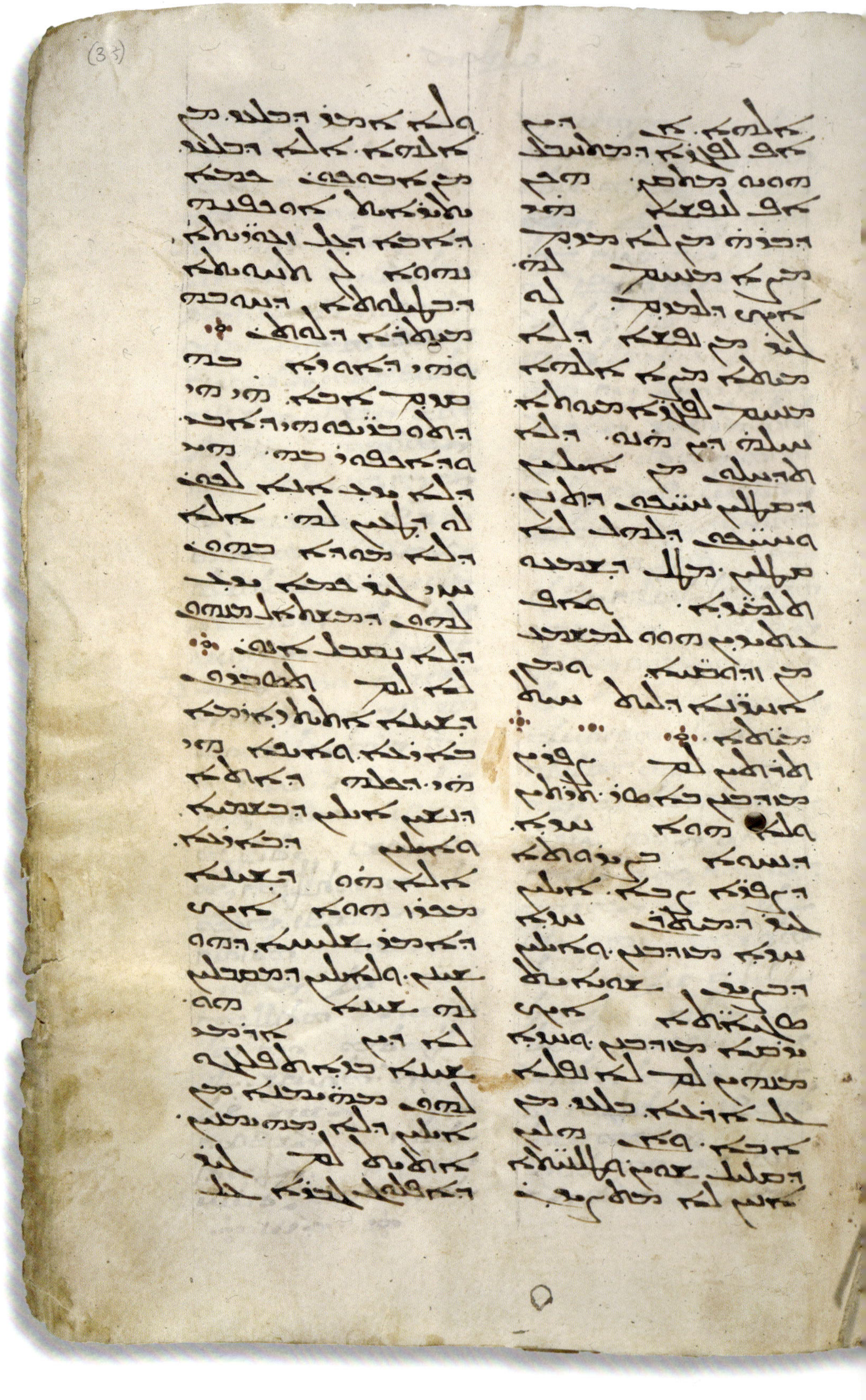

Saint Ephrem's commentary on Tatian's *Diatessaron*.
Dublin, Chester Beatty Library, MS. W 709, Syriac, 480–500.

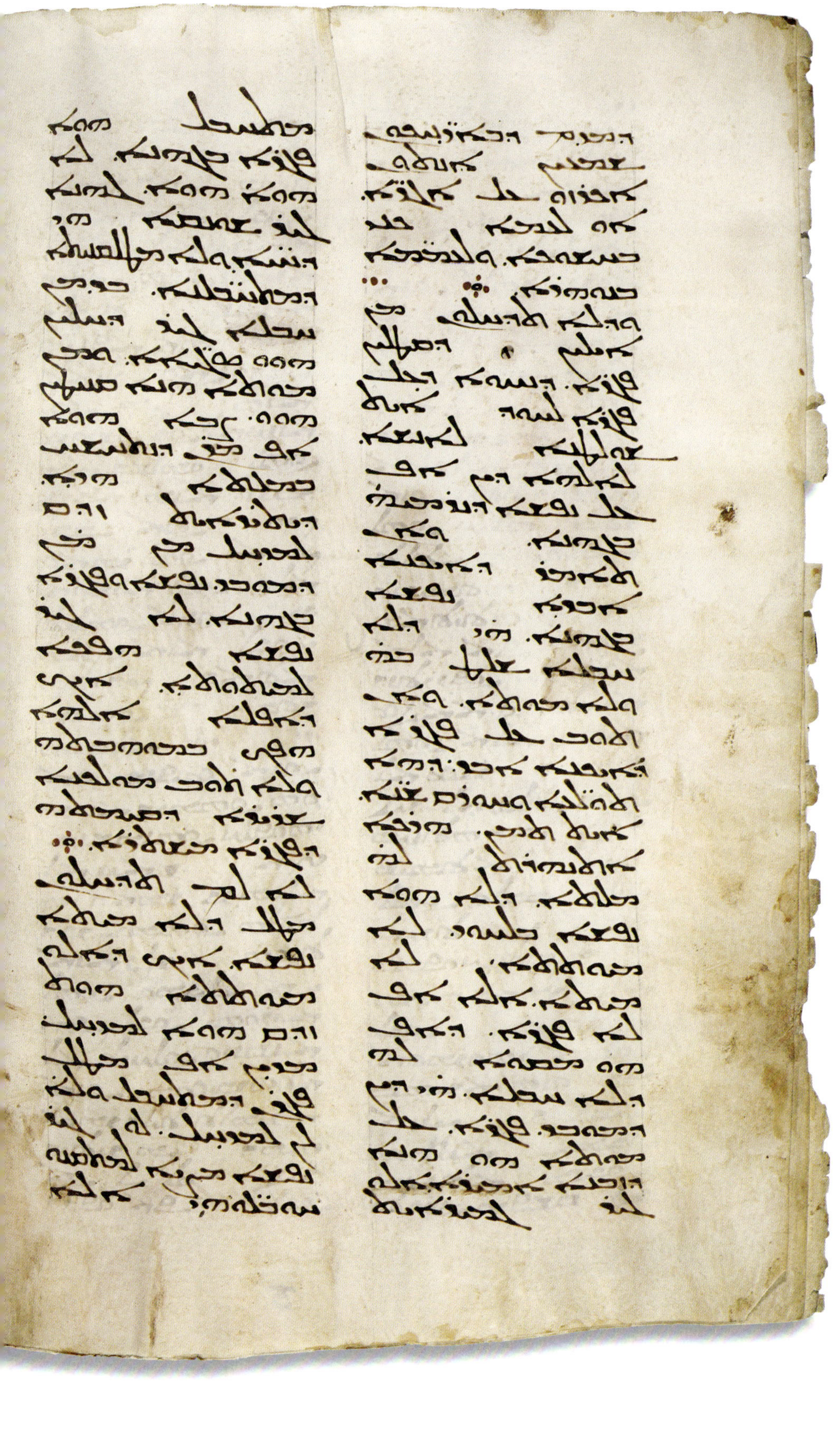

24

Syriac Pentateuch.
London, British Library, APA, Syriac MSS. Add. 14425, ff. 105r–106v. Syriac; parchment. Amida, 463.

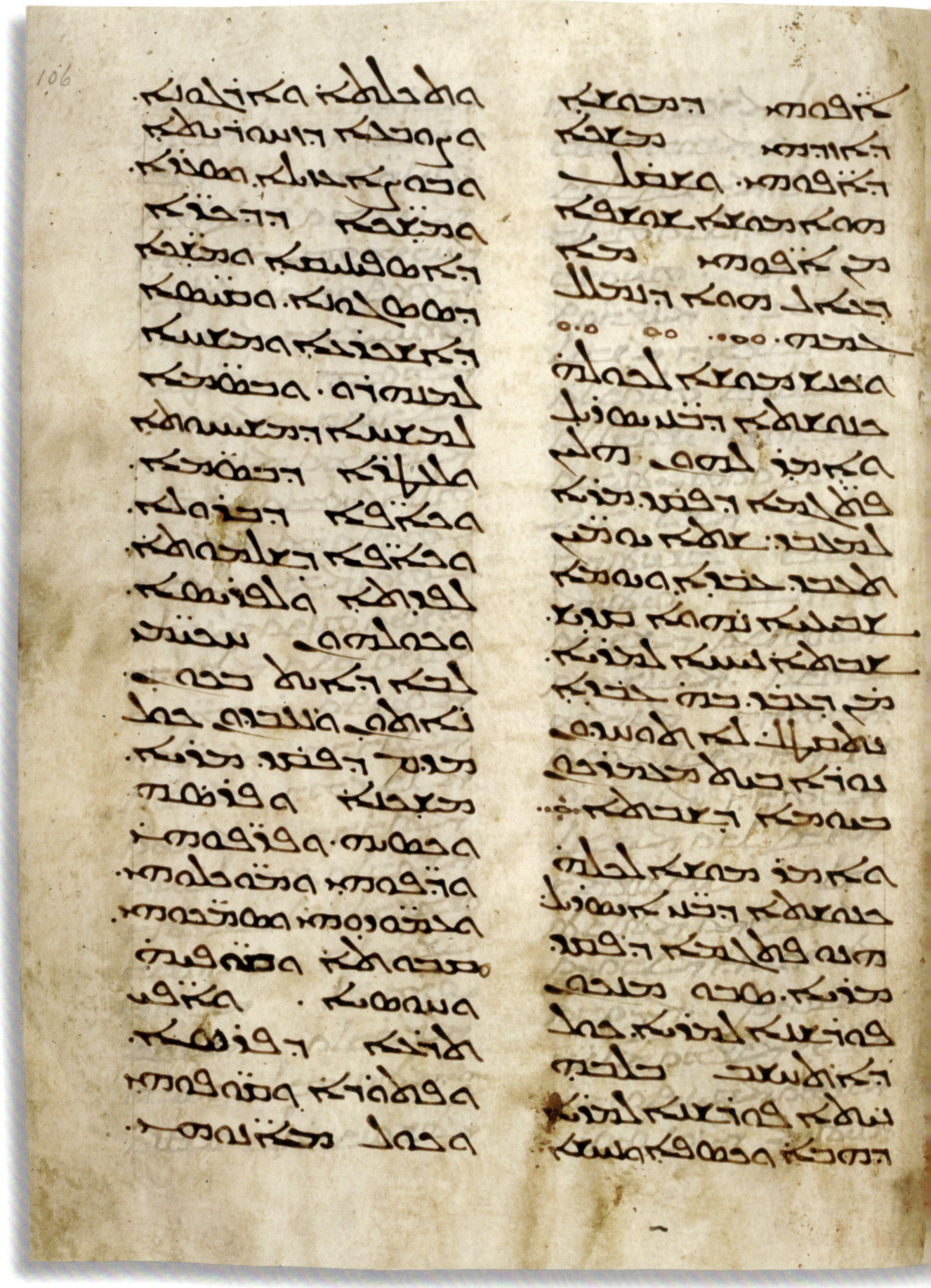

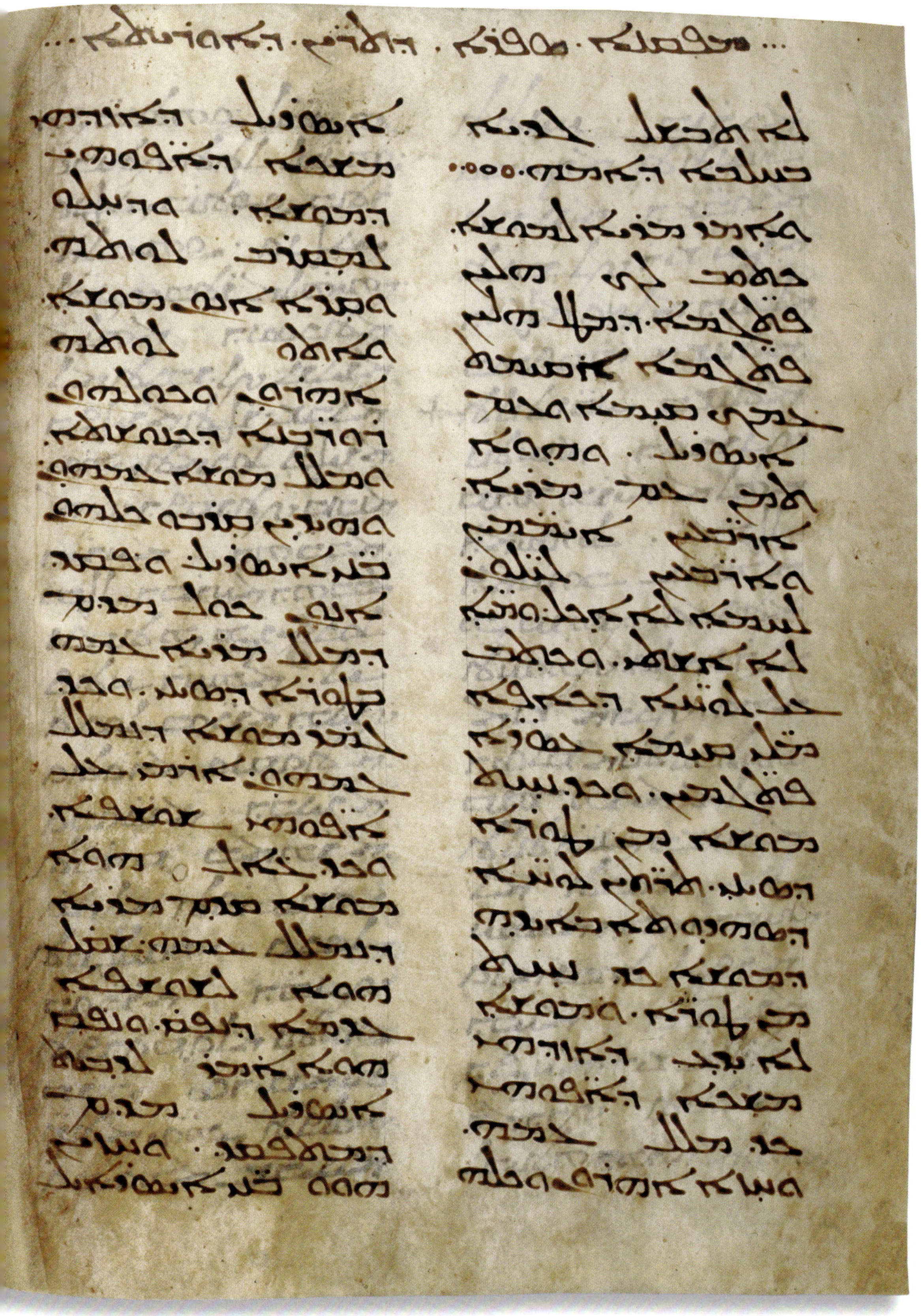

25

Syrohexapla Exodus.
London, British Library,
APA, Syriac MSS. Add. 12134,
ff. 132v–133r. Syriac;
parchment. Syria, 697.

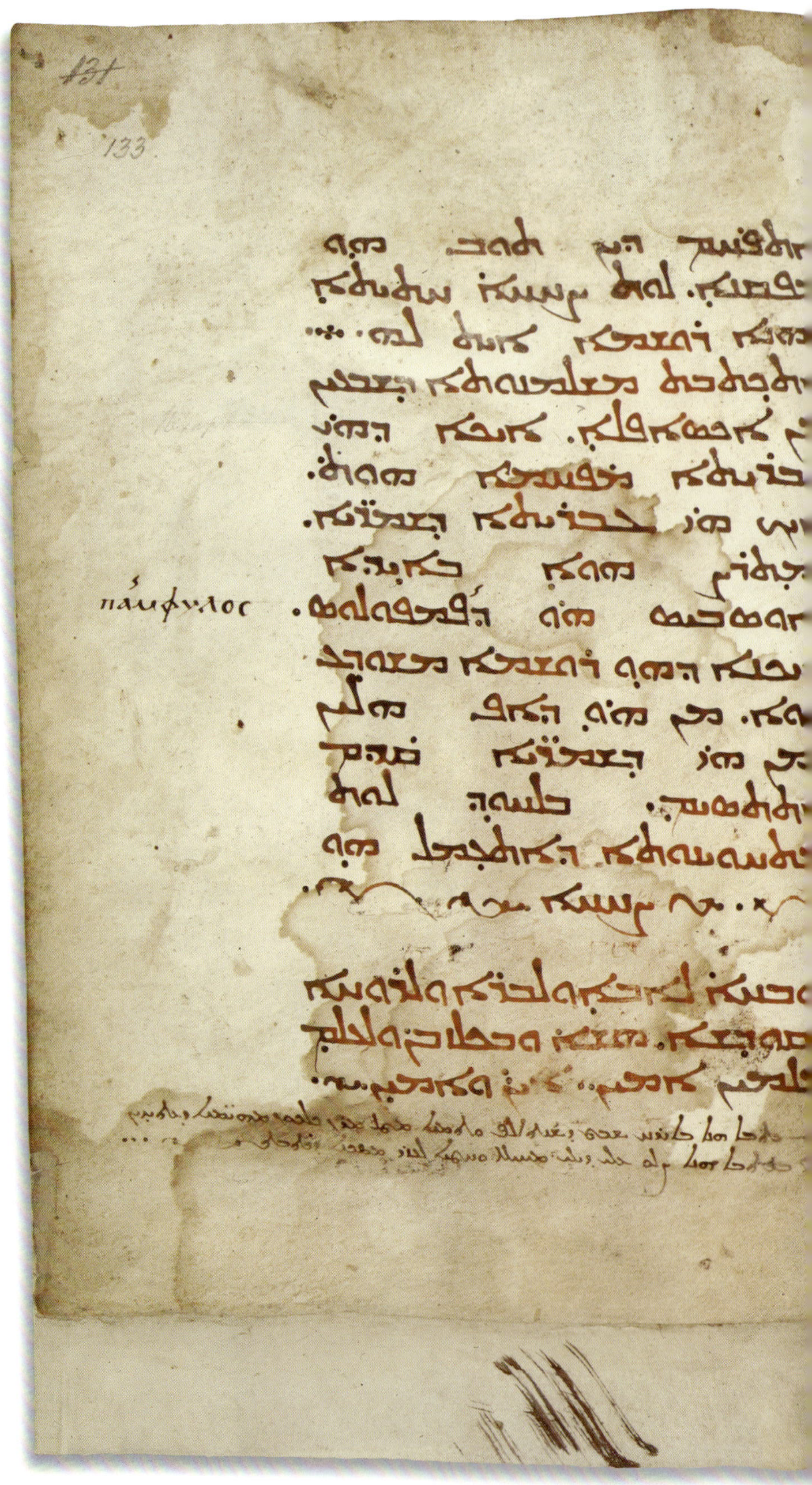

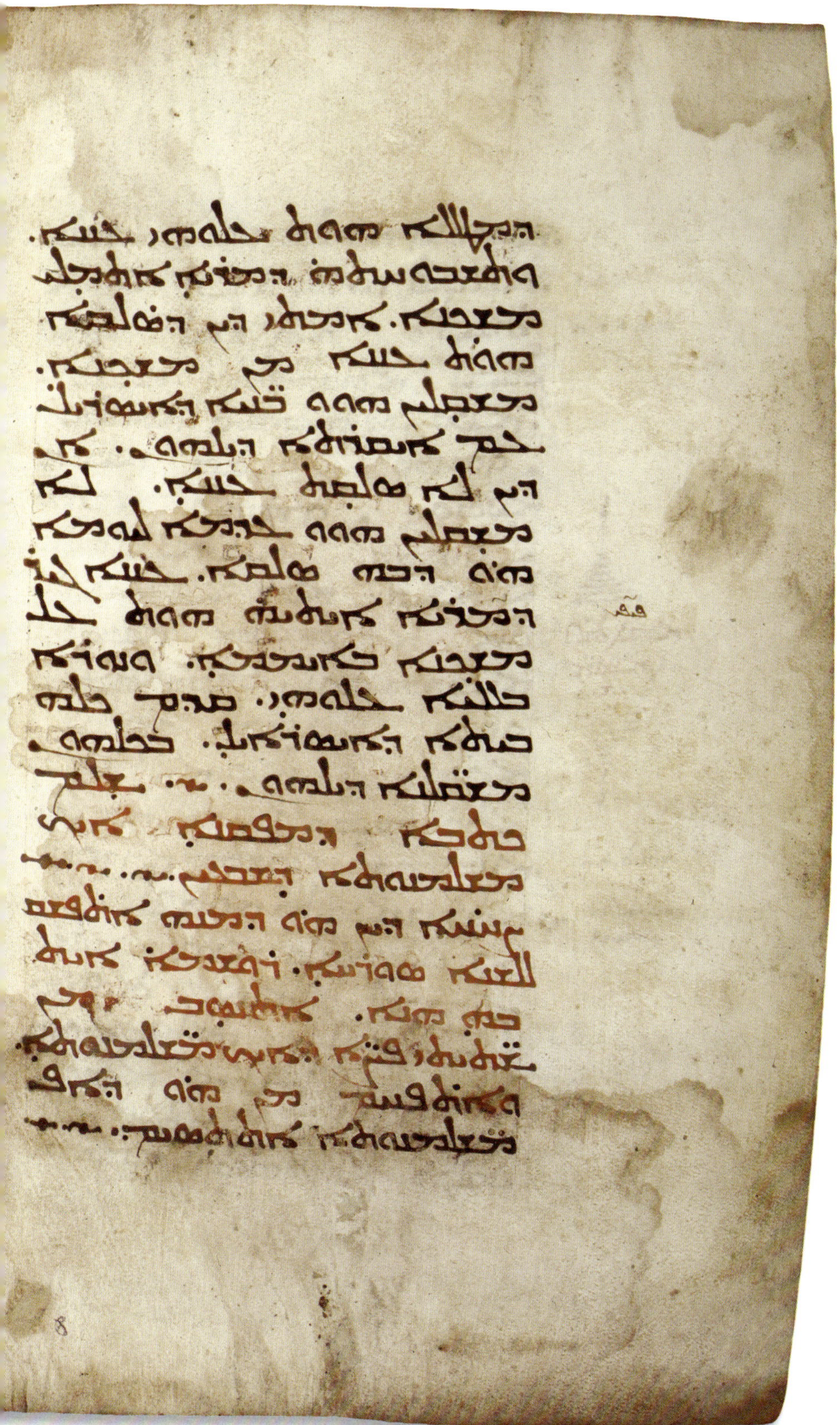

Formation and codification:
The earliest Christian bibles

THE EARLIEST COMPLETE CHRISTIAN BIBLES or "pandects"—Codex Sinaiticus, Codex Vaticanus, and Codex Alexandrinus—were written in Greek and date from the fourth to fifth centuries. They were powerful symbols for Christians, physically expressing the unity of the Old and New Testaments, but they were rare even in their own time, being impractical to use and expensive to produce.

Codex Sinaiticus is the earliest known and is thought by some scholars to have been made in Caesarea during the fourth century (cat. no. 26). This area hosted much of the research and writing conducted by two influential Early Christian scholars of the day, Bishop Eusebius and Saint Jerome. Although the production of Codex Sinaiticus cannot be proven to be directly connected to either of them, they all probably flourished in the same fertile intellectual soil.

It was more usual for Christian scriptures to circulate in the form of smaller collections of gospels or epistles, along with Old Testament collections such as the Pentateuch (cat. no. 24) and the psalter. Important early gospelbooks include the fourth- to fifth-century Codex Washingtonensis (cat. nos. 28, 29), written in Greek and contained within a remarkable later binding, its wooden boards adorned with luminous images of the evangelists painted in colored wax in seventh-century Egypt. Another is the Harley Gospels, which were written in sixth-century Italy and are an early witness to Jerome's Latin "Vulgate" edition (cat. no. 31).

Detail: The Four Gospels, right cover painted with the figures of Sts. Mark and Luke, see cat. no. 28.

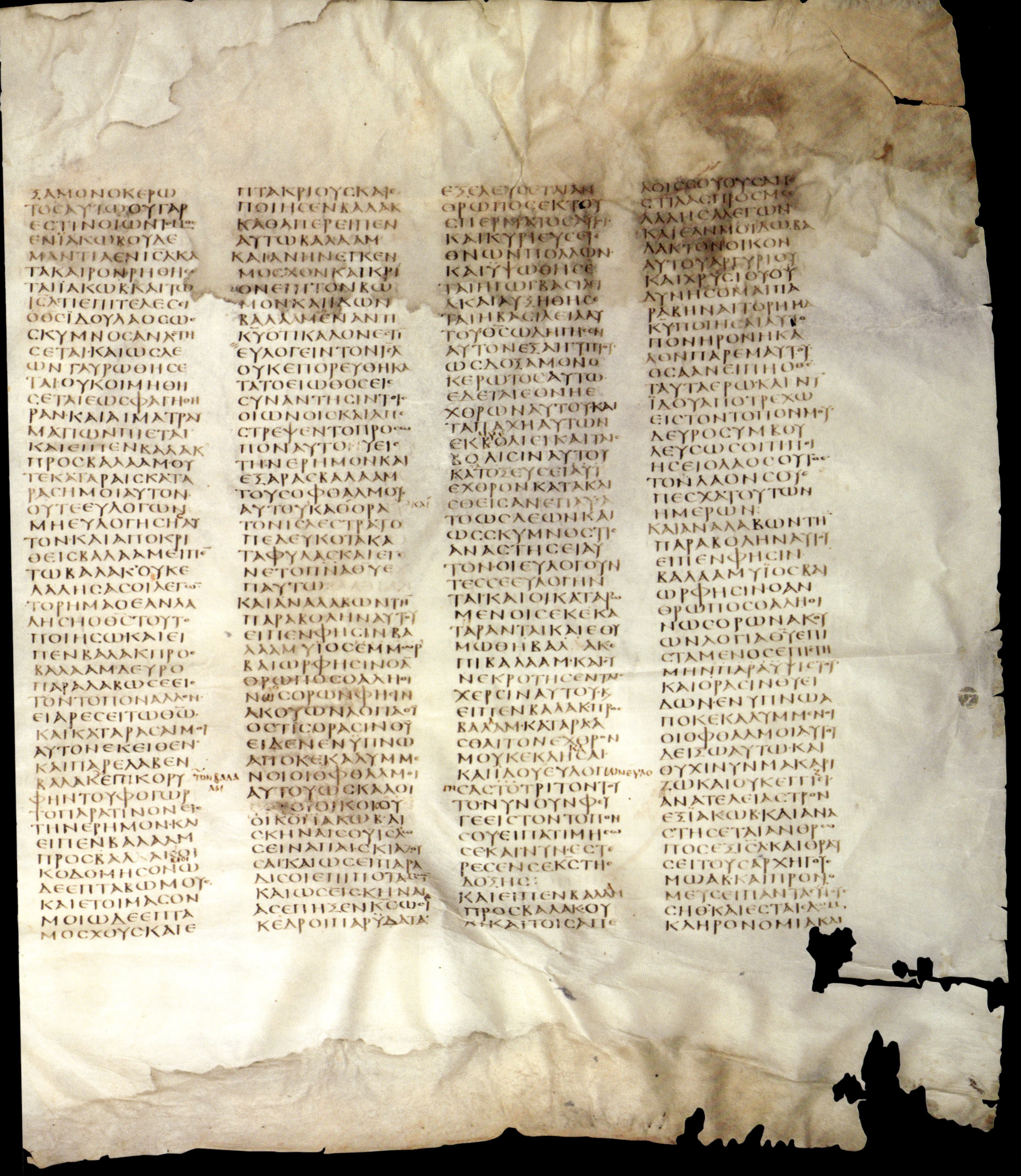

26

Previous pages.
Part of Codex Sinaiticus.
Mt. Sinai, Holy Monastery of St. Catherine, Codex Sinaiticus. Numbers 20:2–13. Greek; parchment. Caesarea (?), fourth century.

27

The Washington Codex of Deuteronomy and Joshua.
Washington, D.C., Freer Gallery of Art, F1906.272, ff. 117v and 119r. End of Deuteronomy and beginning of Joshua. Greek; parchment. Egypt, late fourth-fifth century.

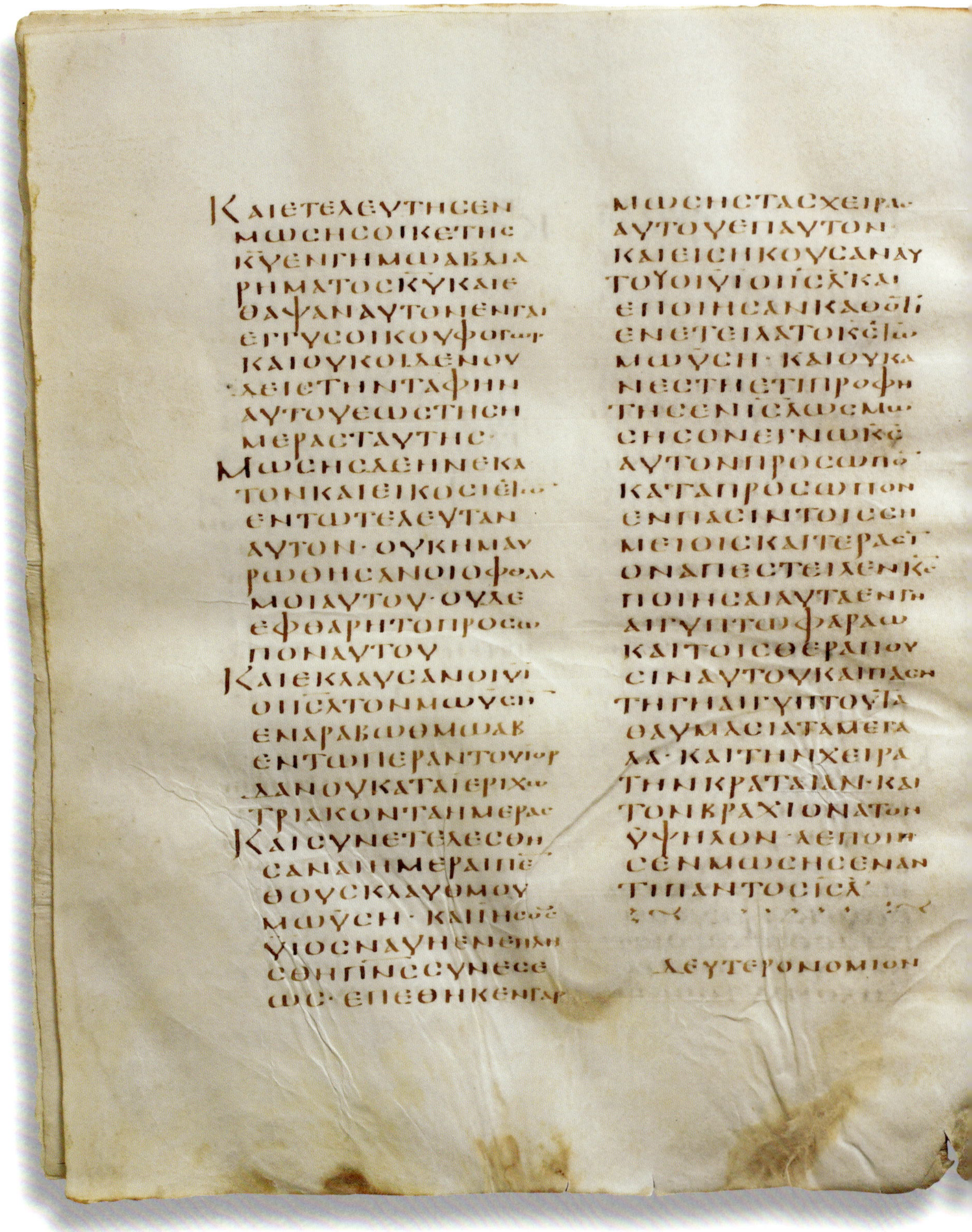

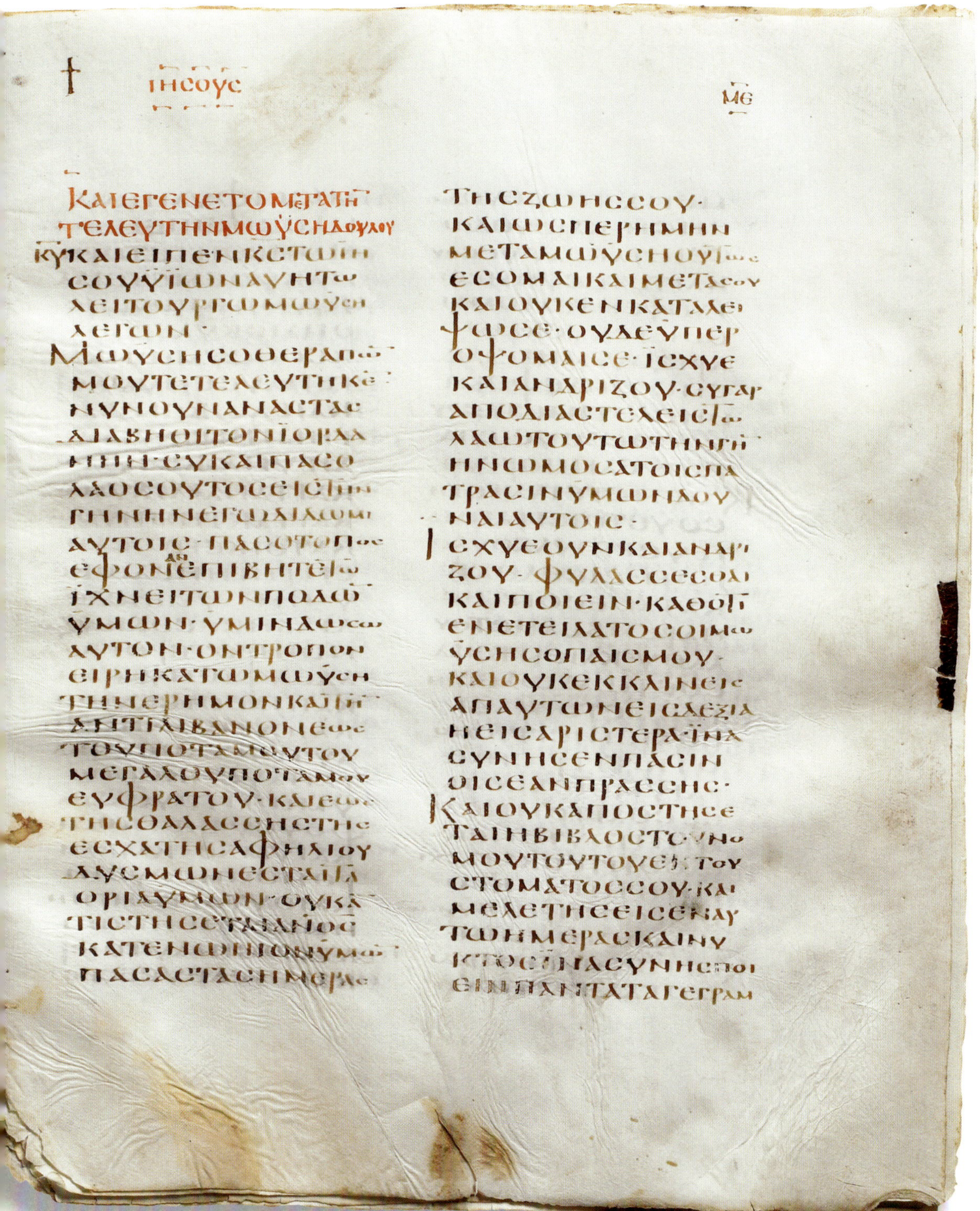

ΙΗΣΟΥΣ

ΜΕ

ΚΑΙ ΕΓΕΝΕΤΟ ΜΕΤΑ ΤΗΝ
ΤΕΛΕΥΤΗΝ ΜΩΥΣΗ ΔΟΥΛΟΥ
ΚΥ ΚΑΙ ΕΙΠΕΝ ΚΣ ΤΩ ΙΗ
ΣΟΥ ΥΙΩ ΝΑΥΗ ΤΩ
ΛΕΙΤΟΥΡΓΩ ΜΩΥΣΗ
ΛΕΓΩΝ·
ΜΩΥΣΗΣ Ο ΘΕΡΑΠΩΝ
ΜΟΥ ΤΕΤΕΛΕΥΤΗΚΕΝ
ΝΥΝ ΟΥΝ ΑΝΑΣΤΑΣ
ΔΙΑΒΗΘΙ ΤΟΝ ΙΟΡΔΑ
ΝΗΝ ΣΥ ΚΑΙ ΠΑΣ Ο
ΛΑΟΣ ΟΥΤΟΣ ΕΙΣ ΤΗΝ
ΓΗΝ ΗΝ ΕΓΩ ΔΙΔΩΜΙ
ΑΥΤΟΙΣ· ΠΑΣ Ο ΤΟΠΟΣ
ΕΦ ΟΝ ΑΝ ΕΠΙΒΗΤΕ ΤΩ
ΙΧΝΕΙ ΤΩΝ ΠΟΔΩΝ
ΥΜΩΝ· ΥΜΙΝ ΔΩΣΩ
ΑΥΤΟΝ· ΟΝ ΤΡΟΠΟΝ
ΕΙΡΗΚΑ ΤΩ ΜΩΥΣΗ
ΤΗΝ ΕΡΗΜΟΝ ΚΑΙ ΤΟΝ
ΑΝΤΙΛΙΒΑΝΟΝ ΕΩΣ
ΤΟΥ ΠΟΤΑΜΟΥ ΤΟΥ
ΜΕΓΑΛΟΥ ΠΟΤΑΜΟΥ
ΕΥΦΡΑΤΟΥ· ΚΑΙ ΕΩΣ
ΤΗΣ ΘΑΛΑΣΣΗΣ ΤΗΣ
ΕΣΧΑΤΗΣ ΑΦ ΗΛΙΟΥ
ΔΥΣΜΩΝ ΕΣΤΑΙ ΤΑ
ΟΡΙΑ ΥΜΩΝ· ΟΥΚ ΑΝ
ΤΙΣΤΗΣΕΤΑΙ ΑΝΘΡΩΠΟΣ
ΚΑΤΕΝΩΠΙΟΝ ΥΜΩΝ
ΠΑΣΑΣ ΤΑΣ ΗΜΕΡΑΣ

ΤΗΣ ΖΩΗΣ ΣΟΥ·
ΚΑΙ ΩΣΠΕΡ ΗΜΗΝ
ΜΕΤΑ ΜΩΥΣΗ ΟΥΤΩΣ
ΕΣΟΜΑΙ ΚΑΙ ΜΕΤΑ ΣΟΥ
ΚΑΙ ΟΥΚ ΕΓΚΑΤΑΛΕΙ
ΨΩ ΣΕ· ΟΥΔΕ ΥΠΕΡ
ΟΨΟΜΑΙ ΣΕ· ΙΣΧΥΕ
ΚΑΙ ΑΝΔΡΙΖΟΥ· ΣΥ ΓΑΡ
ΑΠΟΔΙΑΣΤΕΛΕΙΣ ΤΩ
ΛΑΩ ΤΟΥΤΩ ΤΗΝ ΓΗΝ
ΗΝ ΩΜΟΣΑ ΤΟΙΣ ΠΑ
ΤΡΑΣΙΝ ΥΜΩΝ ΔΟΥ
ΝΑΙ ΑΥΤΟΙΣ·
ΙΣΧΥΕ ΟΥΝ ΚΑΙ ΑΝΔΡΙ
ΖΟΥ· ΦΥΛΑΣΣΕΣΘΑΙ
ΚΑΙ ΠΟΙΕΙΝ· ΚΑΘΟΤΙ
ΕΝΕΤΕΙΛΑΤΟ ΣΟΙ ΜΩ
ΥΣΗΣ Ο ΠΑΙΣ ΜΟΥ·
ΚΑΙ ΟΥΚ ΕΚΚΛΙΝΕΙΣ
ΑΠ ΑΥΤΩΝ ΕΙΣ ΔΕΞΙΑ
Η ΕΙΣ ΑΡΙΣΤΕΡΑ· ΙΝΑ
ΣΥΝΗΣ ΕΝ ΠΑΣΙΝ
ΟΙΣ ΕΑΝ ΠΡΑΣΣΗΣ·
ΚΑΙ ΟΥΚ ΑΠΟΣΤΗΣΕ
ΤΑΙ Η ΒΙΒΛΟΣ ΤΟΥ ΝΟ
ΜΟΥ ΤΟΥΤΟΥ ΕΚ ΤΟΥ
ΣΤΟΜΑΤΟΣ ΣΟΥ· ΚΑΙ
ΜΕΛΕΤΗΣΕΙΣ ΕΝ ΑΥ
ΤΩ ΗΜΕΡΑΣ ΚΑΙ ΝΥ
ΚΤΟΣ ΙΝΑ ΣΥΝΗΣ ΠΟΙ
ΕΙΝ ΠΑΝΤΑ ΤΑ ΓΕΓΡΑΜ

28

The Four Gospels, left cover painted with the figures of Sts. Matthew and John. Washington, D.C., Freer Gallery of Art, F1906.297. Coptic; encaustic (wax) painting on wood. Egypt, seventh century.

28

The Four Gospels, right cover painted with the figures of Sts. Mark and Luke.
Washington, D.C., Freer Gallery of Art, F1906.298. Coptic; encaustic (wax) painting on wood. Egypt, seventh century.

29

The Four Gospels (Codex Washingtonensis or Freer Gospels).

Washington, D.C., Freer Gallery of Art, F1906.274, ff. 108v–109r. Mark 16:14. Greek; parchment. Egypt, fourth or fifth century.

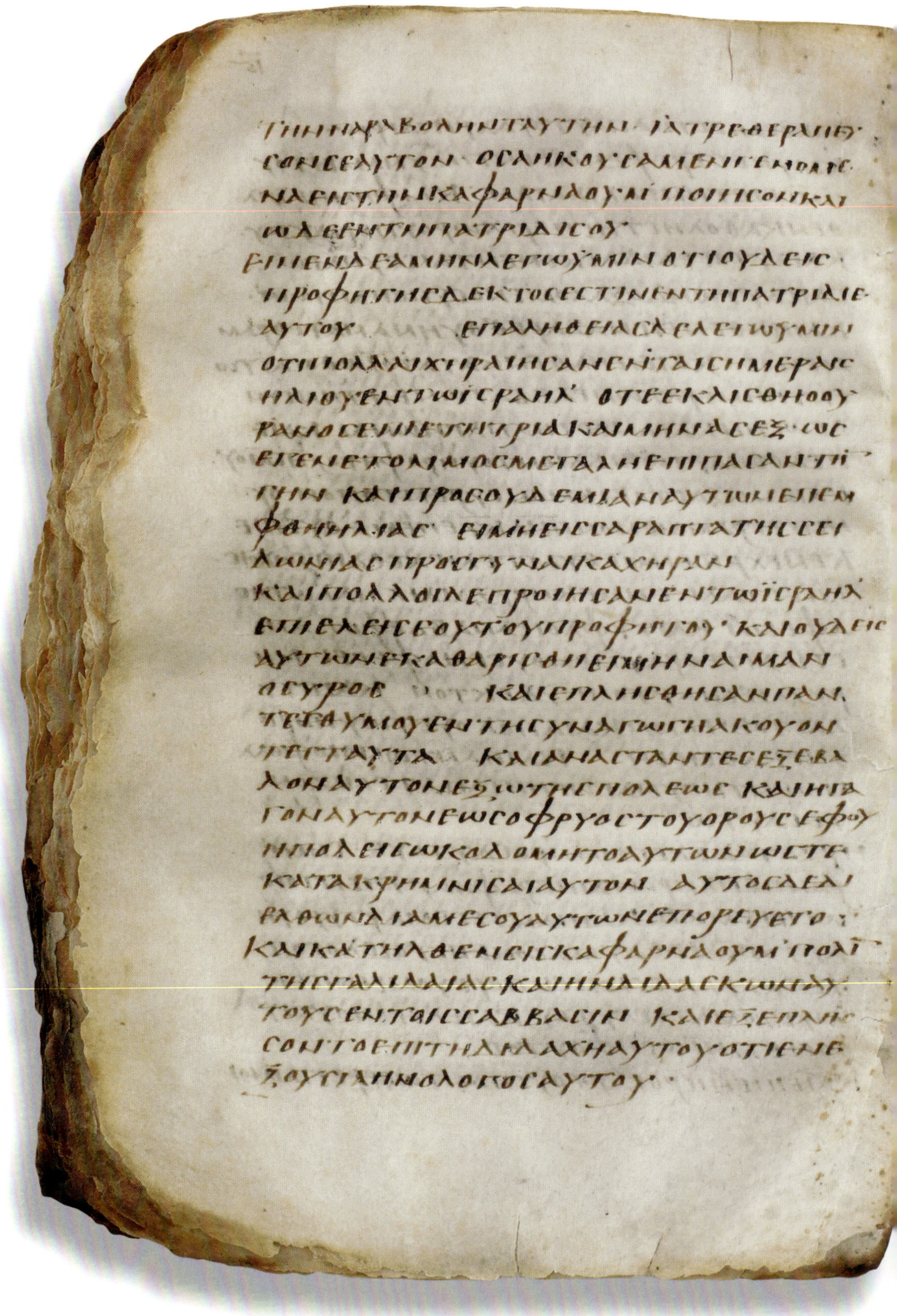

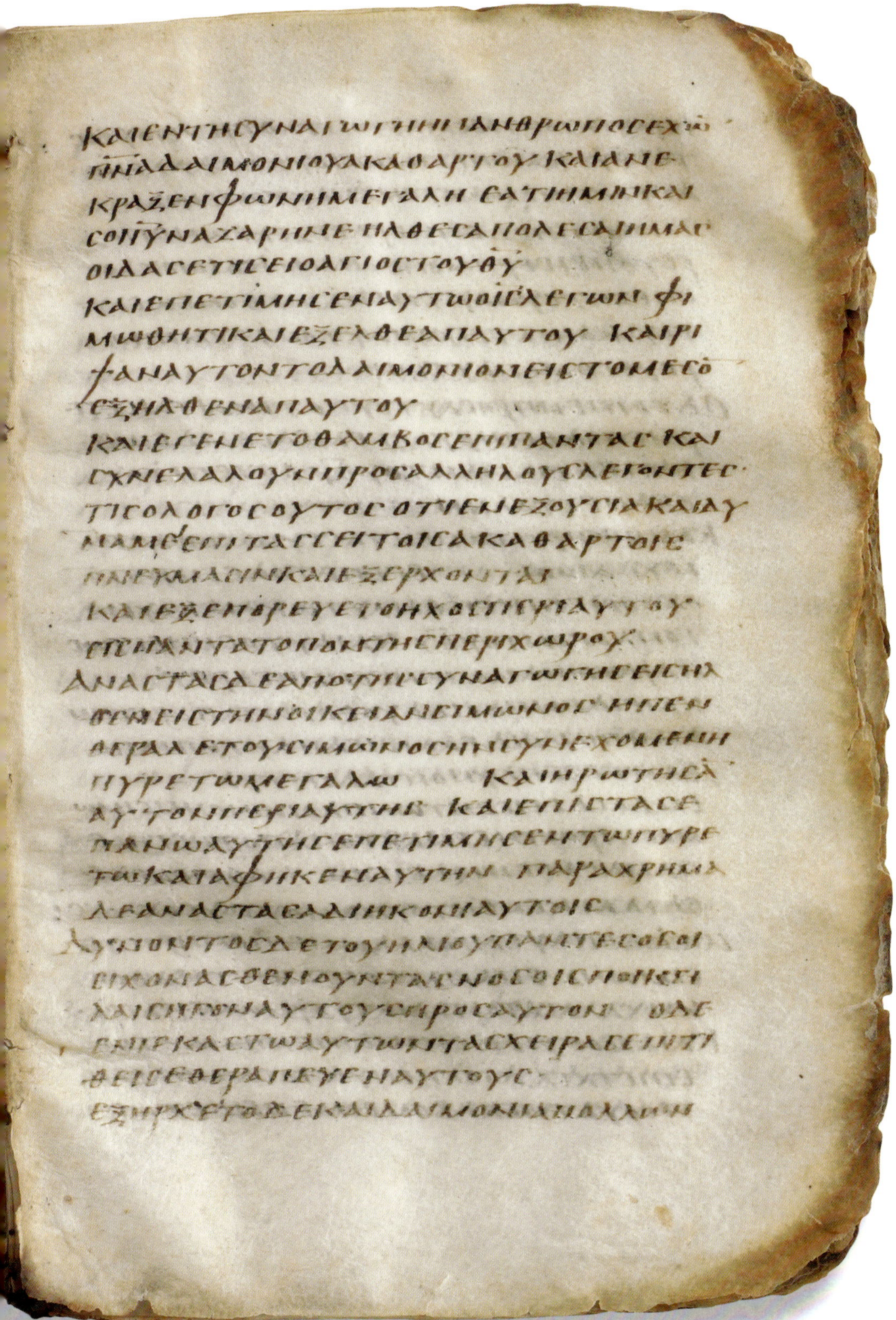
ΚΑΙΕΝΤΗCΥΝΑΓΩΓΗΗΝΑΝΘΡΩΠΟCΕΧΩΝ
ΠΝΑΔΑΙΜΟΝΙΟΥΑΚΑΘΑΡΤΟΥΚΑΙΑΝΕ
ΚΡΑΞΕΝΦΩΝΗΜΕΓΑΛΗΕΑΤΙΗΜΙΝΚΑΙ
CΟΙΙΥΝΑΖΑΡΗΝΕΗΛΘΕCΑΠΟΛΕCΑΙΗΜΑC
ΟΙΔΑCΕΤΙCΕΙΟΑΓΙΟCΤΟΥΘΥ
ΚΑΙΕΠΕΤΙΜΗCΕΝΑΥΤΩΟΙCΛΕΓΩΝΦΙ
ΜΩΘΗΤΙΚΑΙΕΞΕΛΘΕΑΠΑΥΤΟΥΚΑΙΡΙ
ΨΑΝΑΥΤΟΝΤΟΔΑΙΜΟΝΙΟΝΕΙCΤΟΜΕCΟΝ
ΕΞΗΛΘΕΝΑΠΑΥΤΟΥ
ΚΑΙΕΓΕΝΕΤΟΘΑΜΒΟCΕΠΙΠΑΝΤΑCΚΑΙ
CΥΝΕΛΑΛΟΥΝΠΡΟCΑΛΛΗΛΟΥCΛΕΓΟΝΤΕC
ΤΙCΟΛΟΓΟCΟΥΤΟCΟΤΙΕΝΕΞΟΥCΙΑΚΑΙΔΥ
ΝΑΜΕΙΕΠΙΤΑCCΕΙΤΟΙCΑΚΑΘΑΡΤΟΙC
ΠΝΕΥΜΑCΙΝΚΑΙΕΞΕΡΧΟΝΤΑΙ
ΚΑΙΕΞΕΠΟΡΕΥΕΤΟΗΧΟCΠΕΡΙΑΥΤΟΥ
ΕΙCΠΑΝΤΑΤΟΠΟΝΤΗCΠΕΡΙΧΩΡΟΥ
ΑΝΑCΤΑCΔΕΑΠΟΤΗCCΥΝΑΓΩΓΗCΕΙCΗΛ
ΘΕΝΕΙCΤΗΝΟΙΚΕΙΑΝCΙΜΩΝΟCΗΠΕΝ
ΘΕΡΑΔΕΤΟΥCΙΜΩΝΟCΗΝCΥΝΕΧΟΜΕΝΗ
ΠΥΡΕΤΩΜΕΓΑΛΩ ΚΑΙΗΡΩΤΗCΑΝ
ΑΥΤΟΝΠΕΡΙΑΥΤΗC ΚΑΙΕΠΙCΤΑCΕ
ΠΑΝΩΑΥΤΗCΕΠΕΤΙΜΗCΕΝΤΩΠΥΡΕ
ΤΩΚΑΙΑΦΗΚΕΝΑΥΤΗΝ ΠΑΡΑΧΡΗΜΑ
ΔΕΑΝΑCΤΑCΑΔΙΗΚΟΝΙΑΥΤΟΙC
ΔΥΝΟΝΤΟCΔΕΤΟΥΗΛΙΟΥΠΑΝΤΕCΟCΟΙ
ΕΙΧΟΝΑCΘΕΝΟΥΝΤΑCΝΟCΟΙCΠΟΙΚΙ
ΛΑΙCΗΓΑΓΟΝΑΥΤΟΥCΠΡΟCΑΥΤΟΝ ΟΔΕ
ΕΝΙΕΚΑCΤΩΑΥΤΩΝΤΑCΧΕΙΡΑCΕΠΙΤΙ
ΘΕΙCΕΘΕΡΑΠΕΥΕΝΑΥΤΟΥC
ΕΞΗΡΧΕΤΟΔΕΚΑΙΔΑΙΜΟΝΙΑΑΠΟΠΟΛΛΩΝ

30

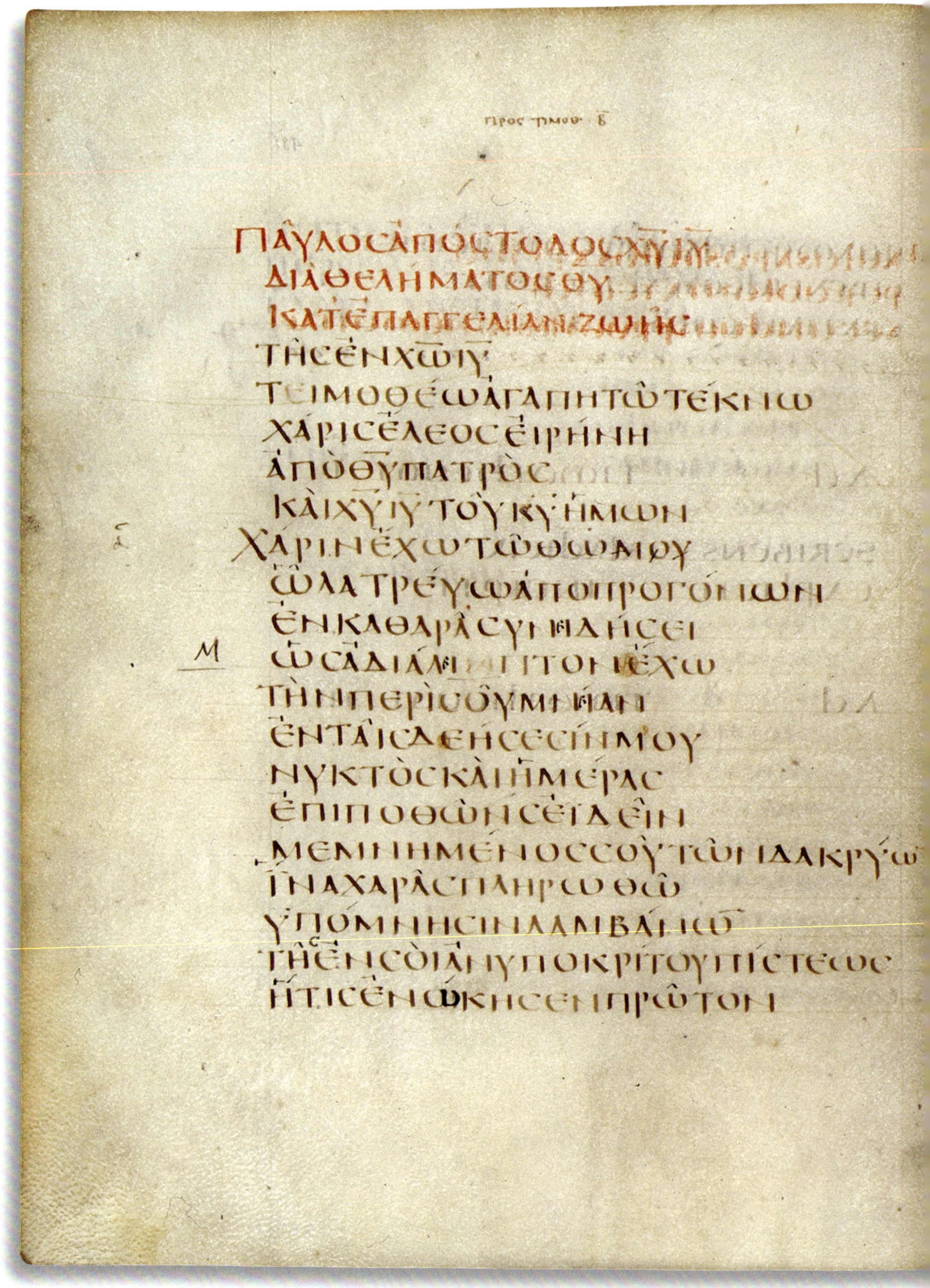

Codex Claromontanus.
Paris, Bibliothèque nationale de France, MS. Gr. 107 A. Bilingual manuscript of the Epistles of St. Paul. Greek and Latin; parchment; sixth century.

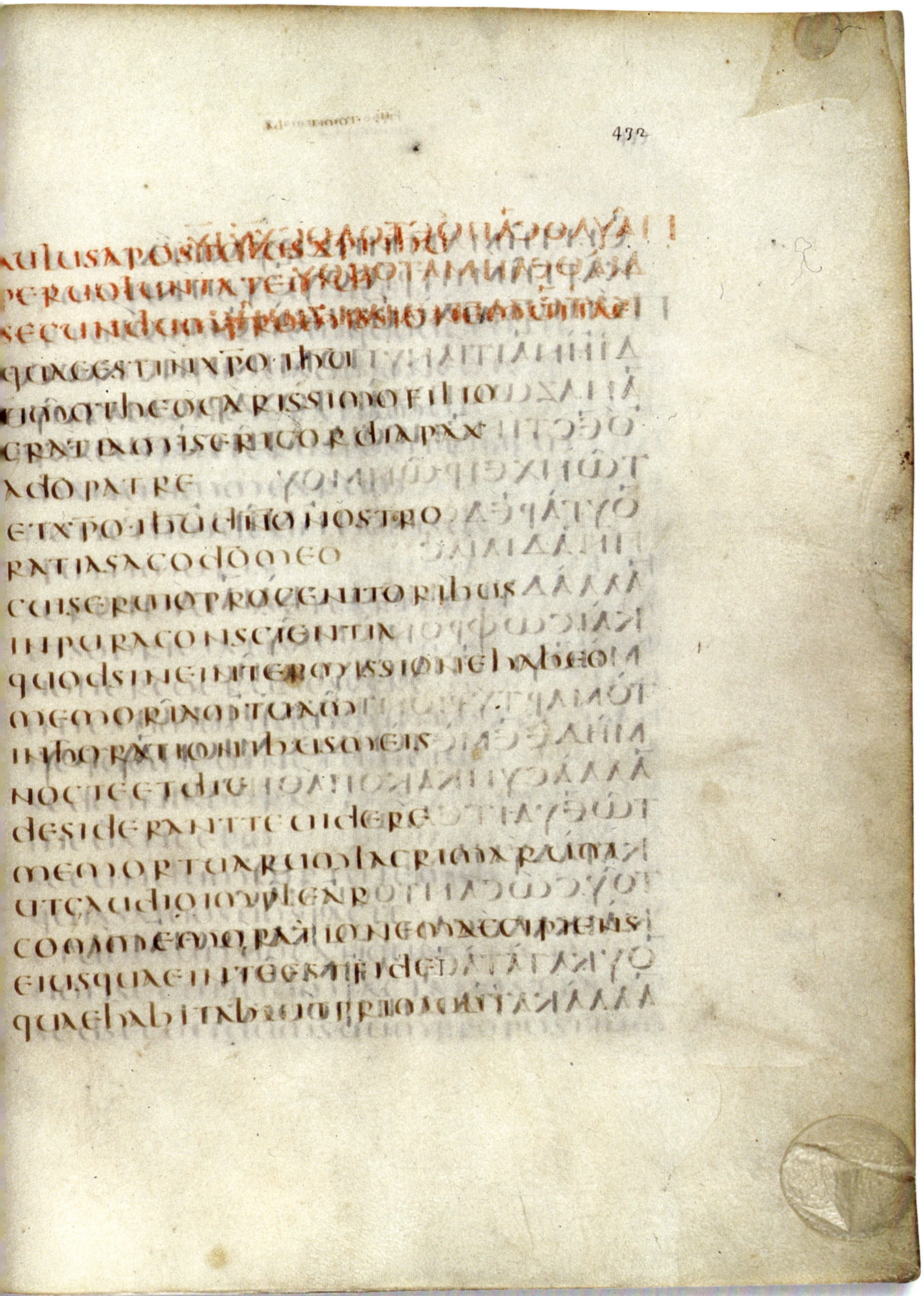

31

Codex Harleianus
(*alias* The Harley Gospels).
London, British Library, Western MSS., Harley MS. 1775, ff. 223v–224r. Gospelbook. Latin; parchment. Italy, late sixth, possibly early seventh century.

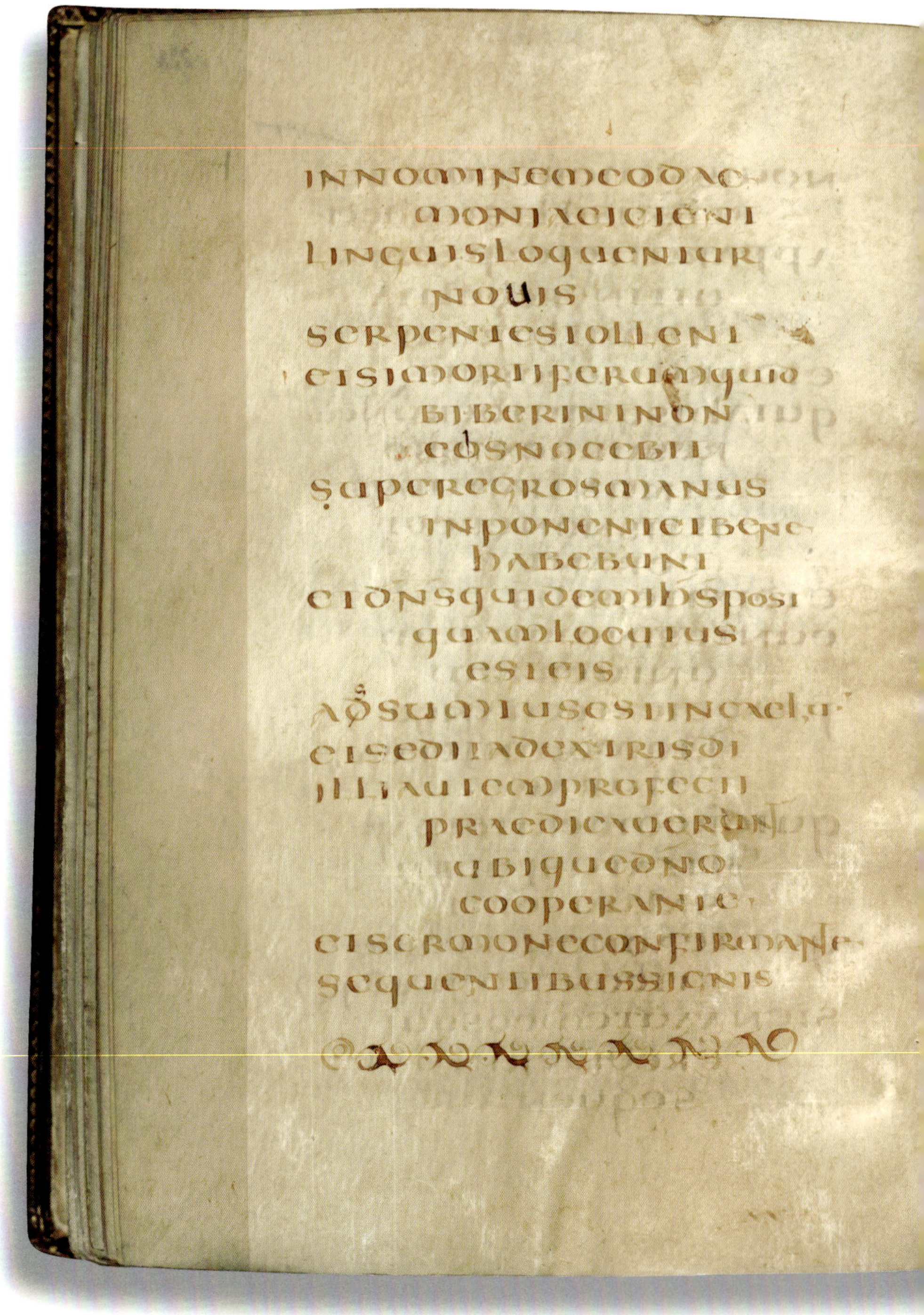

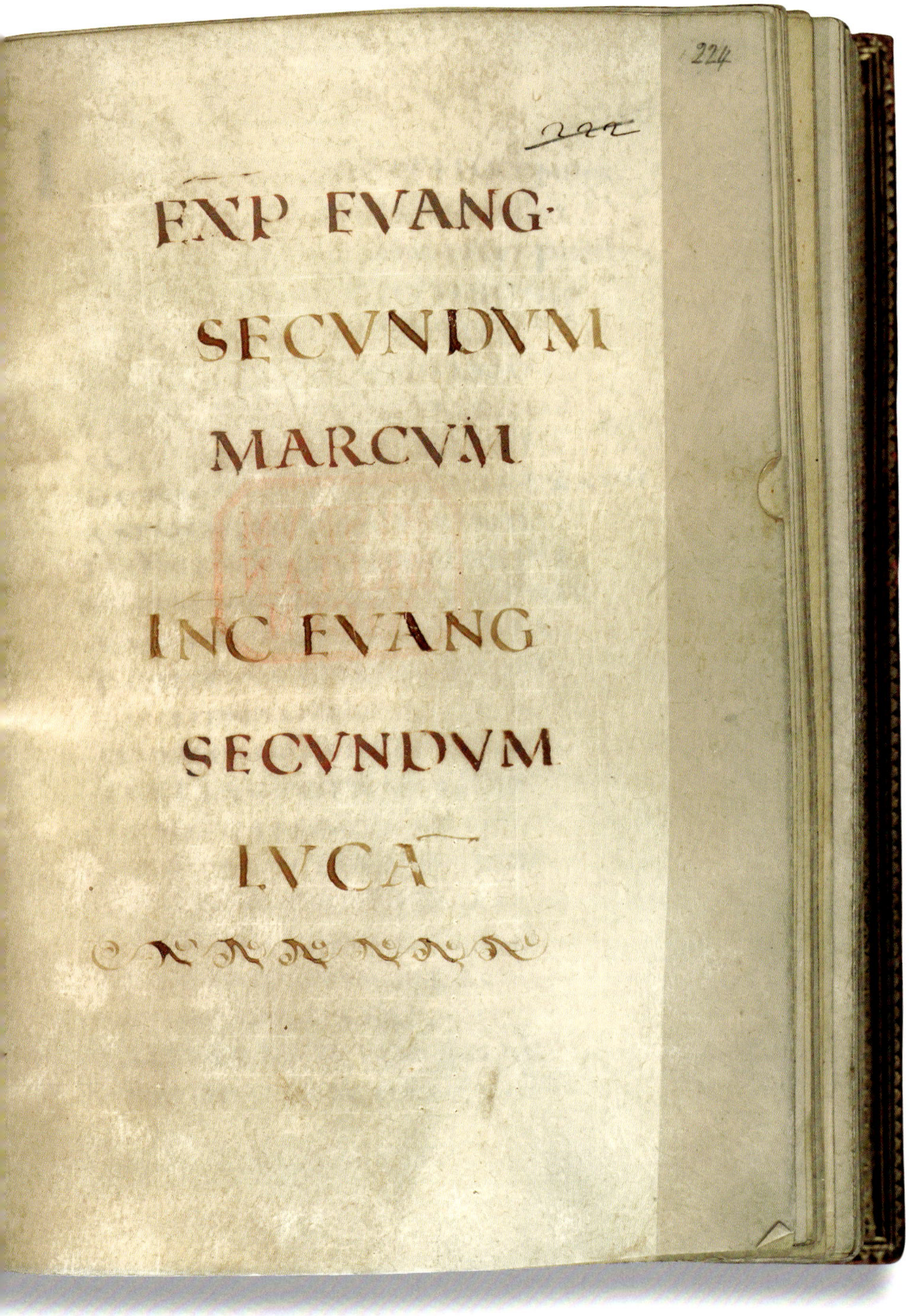
224
EXP EVANG·
SECVNDVM
MARCVM
INC EVANG
SECVNDVM
LVCA

From Babel to Pentecost:
"Sacred languages" and the vernaculars

THROUGHOUT THE MIDDLE AGES, most people's knowledge of scripture continued to be oral and visual rather than written. They heard it through the public recitation of snippets of scripture and in sermons, poems, storytelling, and song; or saw it in the images beautifying church buildings, carved on wayside crosses or adorning the possessions of the wealthy. Most books involved in public and private worship took the form of psalters and customized prayerbooks, while gospelbooks graced the shrines of saints and were read from during services or displayed on the altar, where they also served to solemnify legal transactions and oaths.

In the same period, however, the use of written vernacular (local) languages was promoted by the transmission of scripture. This development took on a different character in the West and East, shaped by varying cultural attitudes.

Around the Mediterranean, Hebrew, Greek and Latin were traditionally the "sacred languages" used for scripture. In the medieval West, Latin—the common language of the Roman Empire—came to assume this role. Its rise to literary heights owed a great deal to the efforts of Saint Jerome, Pope Damasus I, and Pope Gregory the Great, who promoted Latin versions of scripture in western Europe. Around 382 C.E. Damasus commissioned Jerome to produce a new Latin translation of the Bible because there were "almost as many versions as codices" in circulation. These were generally grouped under the heading "Old Latin" or *editio vulgata* (the vulgar or vernacular edition). Jerome sought to purge errors and variants with reference to earlier Greek and Hebrew versions, but his "Vulgate," so-named for its use of the "vulgar" Latin language of the day, merged with Old Latin readings to produce many "mixed" texts of regional complexion. By the time the Vulgate became an authorized version at the Council of Trent in 1546, a complex process of scholarly reconstruction was needed to retrieve Jerome's original translation.

While tension between "official" written languages and those spoken locally was to become an issue in the later medieval West, leading to the persecution as heretics of translators such as Tyndale, in the Christian Churches of the Near East (the Christian Orient) there was no apparent concern about the appropriateness of communicating beliefs in regional tongues. Indeed, the popularity of early written vernaculars owed much to the desire of such regional Churches to preserve their own identities.

Christ's teachings probably originally circulated orally in a local language, Aramaic, although the gospels subsequently were written in literary Greek. The Greek language continued to play a unifying role in the East, but as a result of the theological debates that dominated the fourth and fifth centuries a number of independent Churches had come into existence, and each carefully guarded its early traditions. These local Churches, in Armenia (which had been the first nation to adopt Christianity as its state religion in the early fourth century), Georgia, Syria, Coptic Egypt, Nubia, Ethiopia, and the Slavonic areas, all produced books in their own languages and with their own distinctive styles of script, decoration, and binding. They also had their own textual traditions, such as the Peshitta ("the simple one"), a translation of the scriptures into Syriac based upon the Hebrew Bible and the Septuagint (cat. no. 32).

Jews and Christians living under Muslim rule in the ninth and tenth century also used texts written in Arabic, the language of local currency, as in the Arabic Gospelbook from Mt. Sinai (cat. no. 35) and the Karaite Bible (cat. no. 33). The Karaites were a Jewish sect for whom the Hebrew Bible was the sole source of religious law. Their transcription of its text into Arabic may have been an attempt to produce a superior reading tradition for the Bible than that of established rabbinical Judaism.

Detail: Arabic Epistles and Acts, see cat. no. 32.

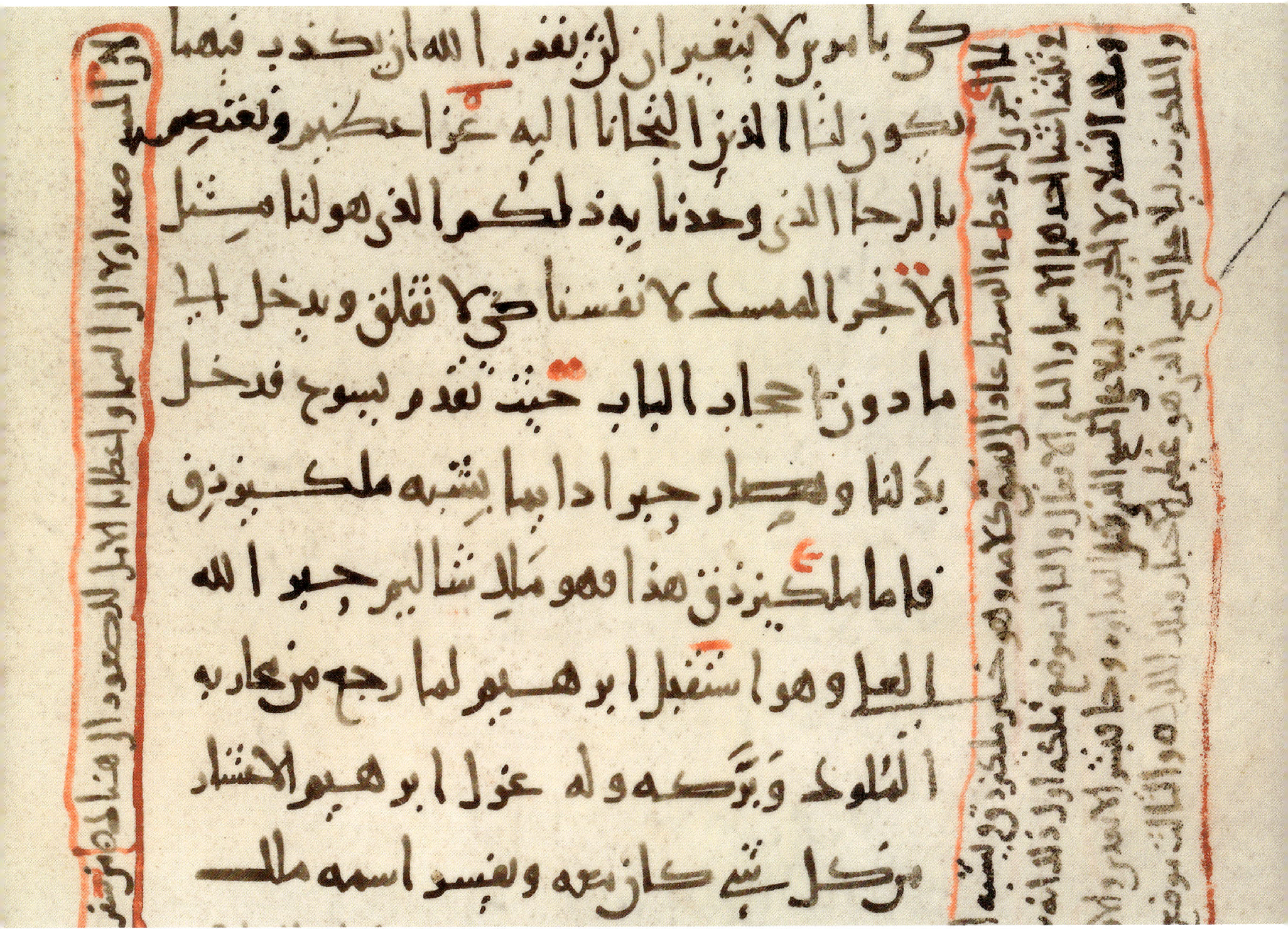
كي بامور لا يتغيران لن يقدر الله ان يكذب فيهما
يكون لنا الذين التجانا اليه عزا عظيما وليعتصم
بالرجا الذي وعدنا به ذلكم الذي هو لنا مثل
الانجر المسدد لانفسنا حتى لا تقلق ويدخل الى
ما دون حجاب الباب حيث تقدم يسوع فدخل
بدلنا وصار حبرا ابدا بما يشبه ملكيزدق
فاما ملكيزدق هذا فهو ملك شاليم حبر الله
العلي وهو استقبل ابرهيم لما رجع من محاربه
الملوك وبركه وله عزل ابرهيم الاعشار
من كل شي كان معه ويفسر اسمه ملك

32

Arabic Epistles and Acts.
Mt. Sinai, Holy Monastery of St. Catherine, Arabic MS. 151, ff. 171v–172r. Epistles and Acts. Arabic; parchment. Damascus, Syria, 867.

33

Karaite Book of Exodus.
London, British Library,
APA, MS. Or. 2540, ff. 18v–19r.
Hebrew in Arabic script;
paper. Palestine or Egypt,
ca. tenth century.

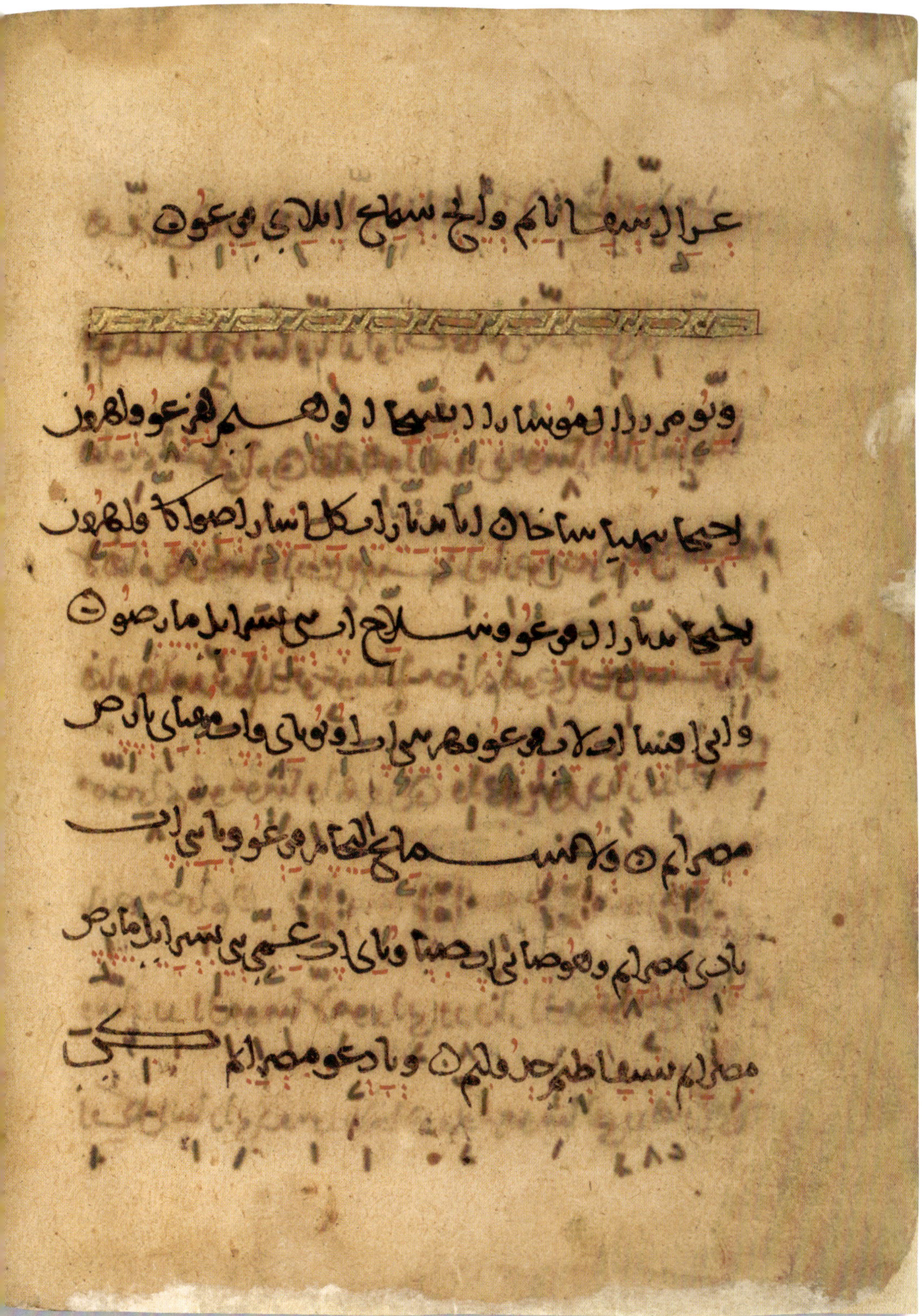

34

Pauline Epistles from the Syriac Peshitta.

London, British Library, APA, Syriac MSS. Add. 14478, ff. 85v–86r. Syriac; parchment. Haluga in the district of Serug, Syria, 622

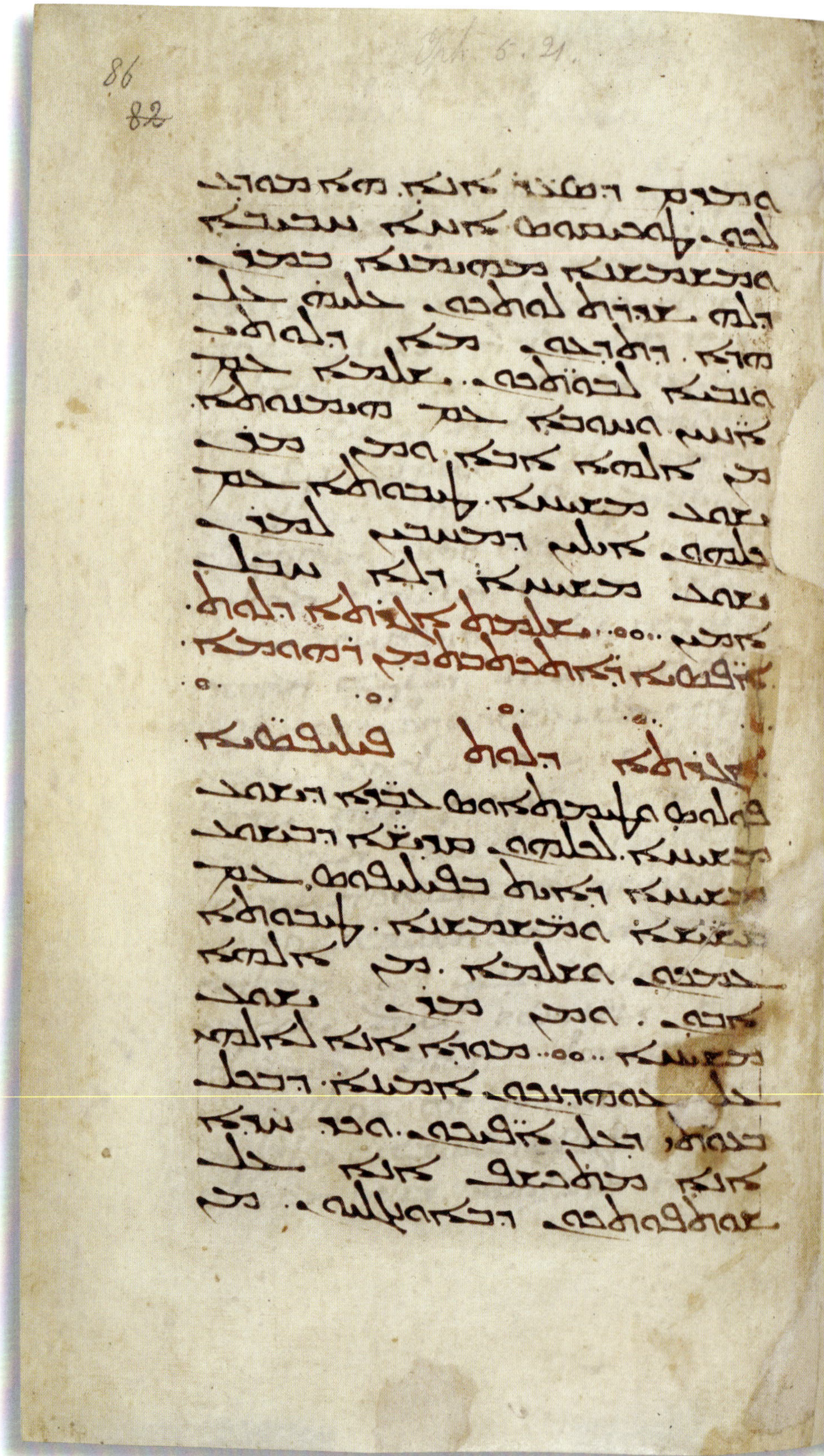

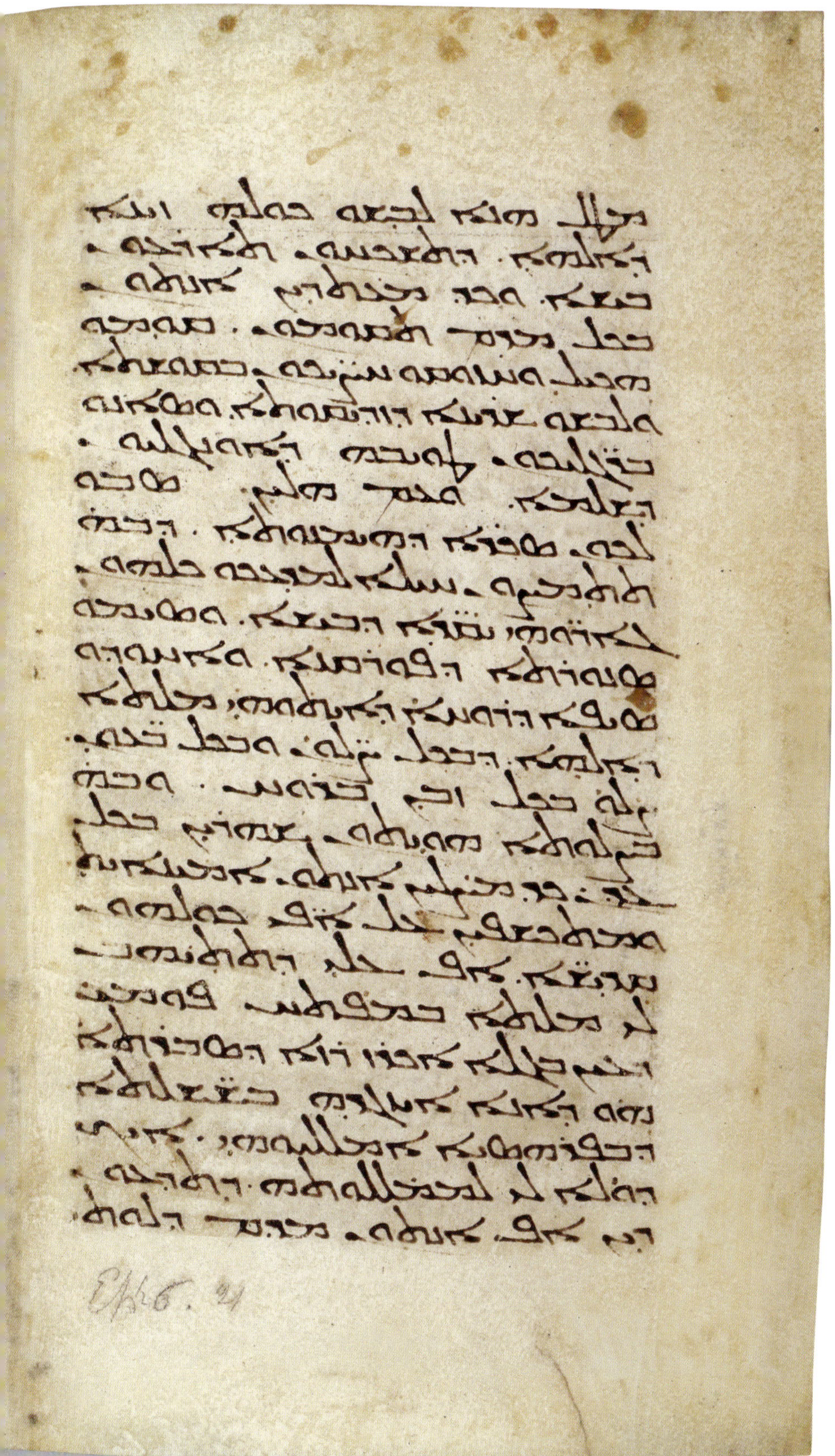

35

Arabic Gospelbook.
Mt. Sinai, Holy Monastery of St. Catherine, Arabic New Finds M. 14, ff. 23v–24r. Gospels. Arabic; parchment. Sinai, 859 (?).

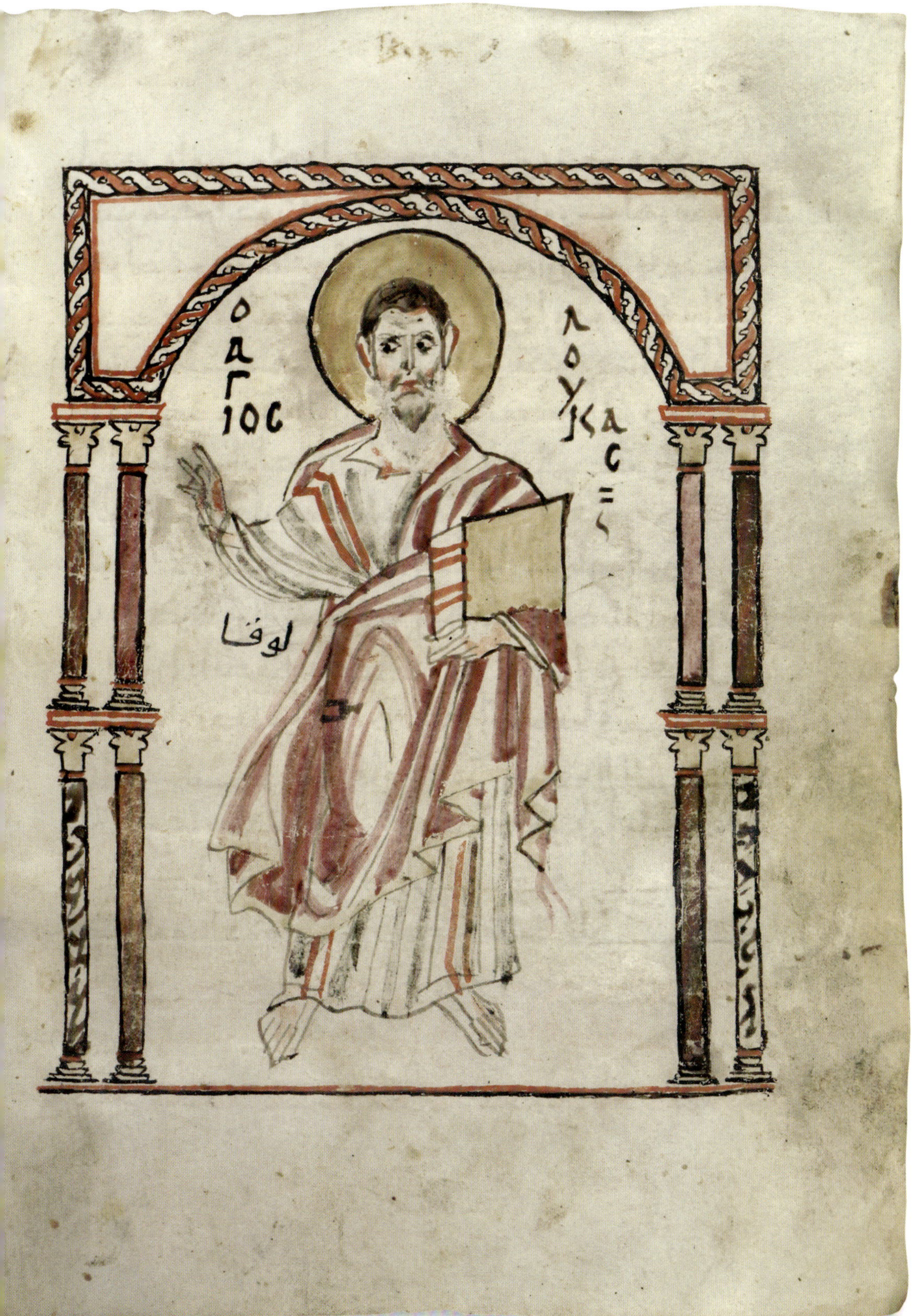
Ο ΑΓΙΟϹ
ΛΟΥΚΑϹ
لوقا

36

Georgian Psalter.
St. Petersburg, National Library of Russia, MS. Gruz new series 10. Georgian; papyrus. Probably Palestine or Sinai, Egypt; eighth century.

37

Opposite:
Armenian Gospelbook.
Baltimore, Walters Art Museum, MS. W. 537, f. 2. Virgin and Child. Armenian; parchment. Armenia, 966.

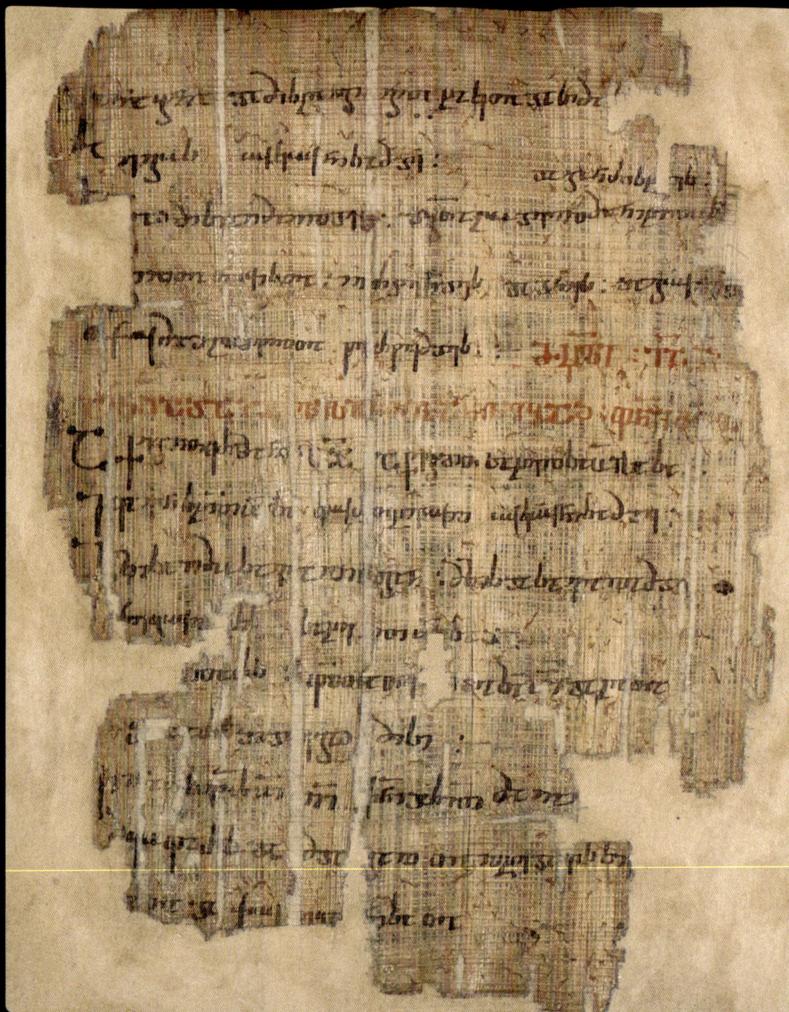

38

Armenian Gospelbook.
London, British Library, APA, Armenian MSS. Add. 21932, ff. 118v–119r. Armenian; parchment. Armenia, ninth–tenth century.

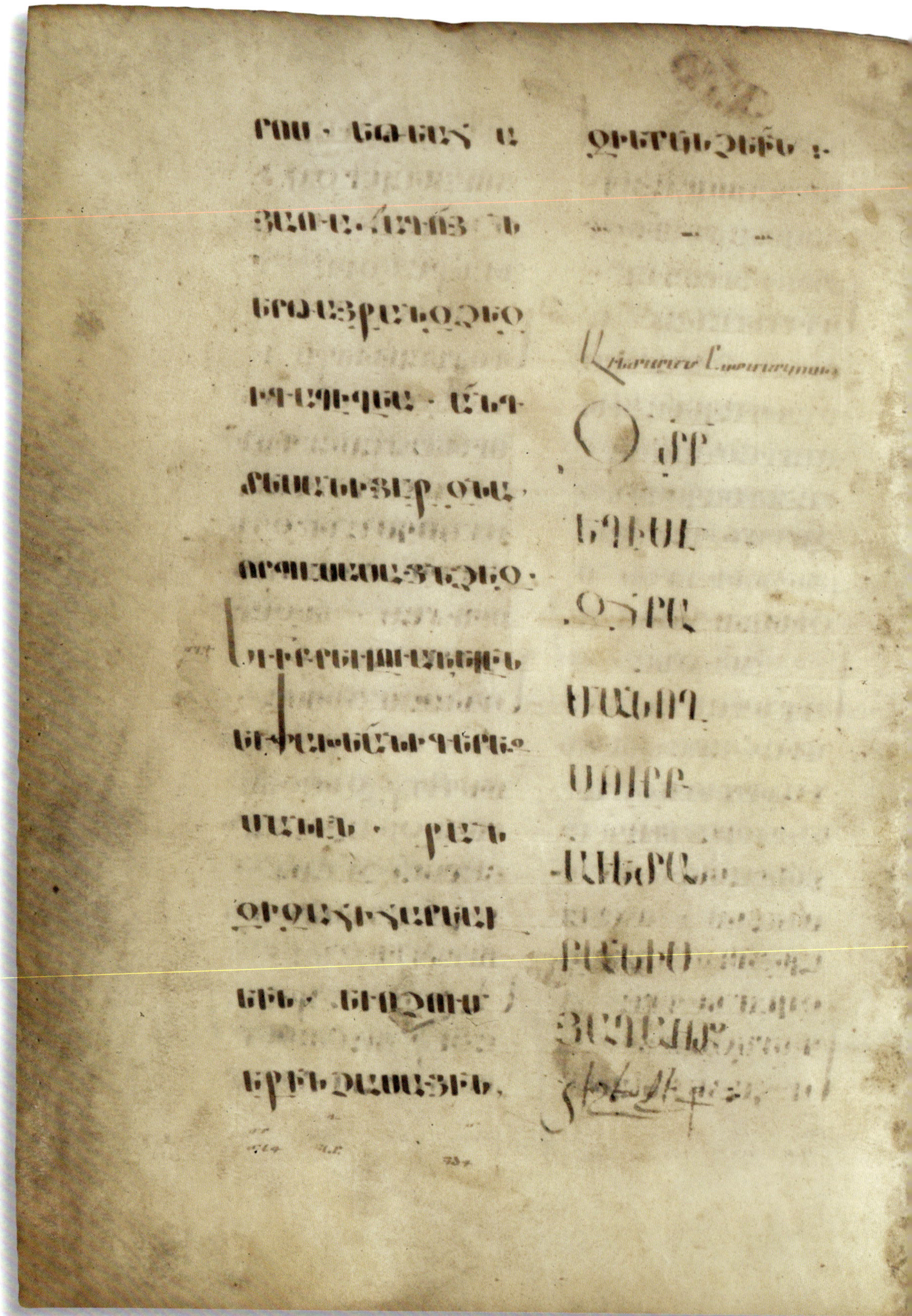

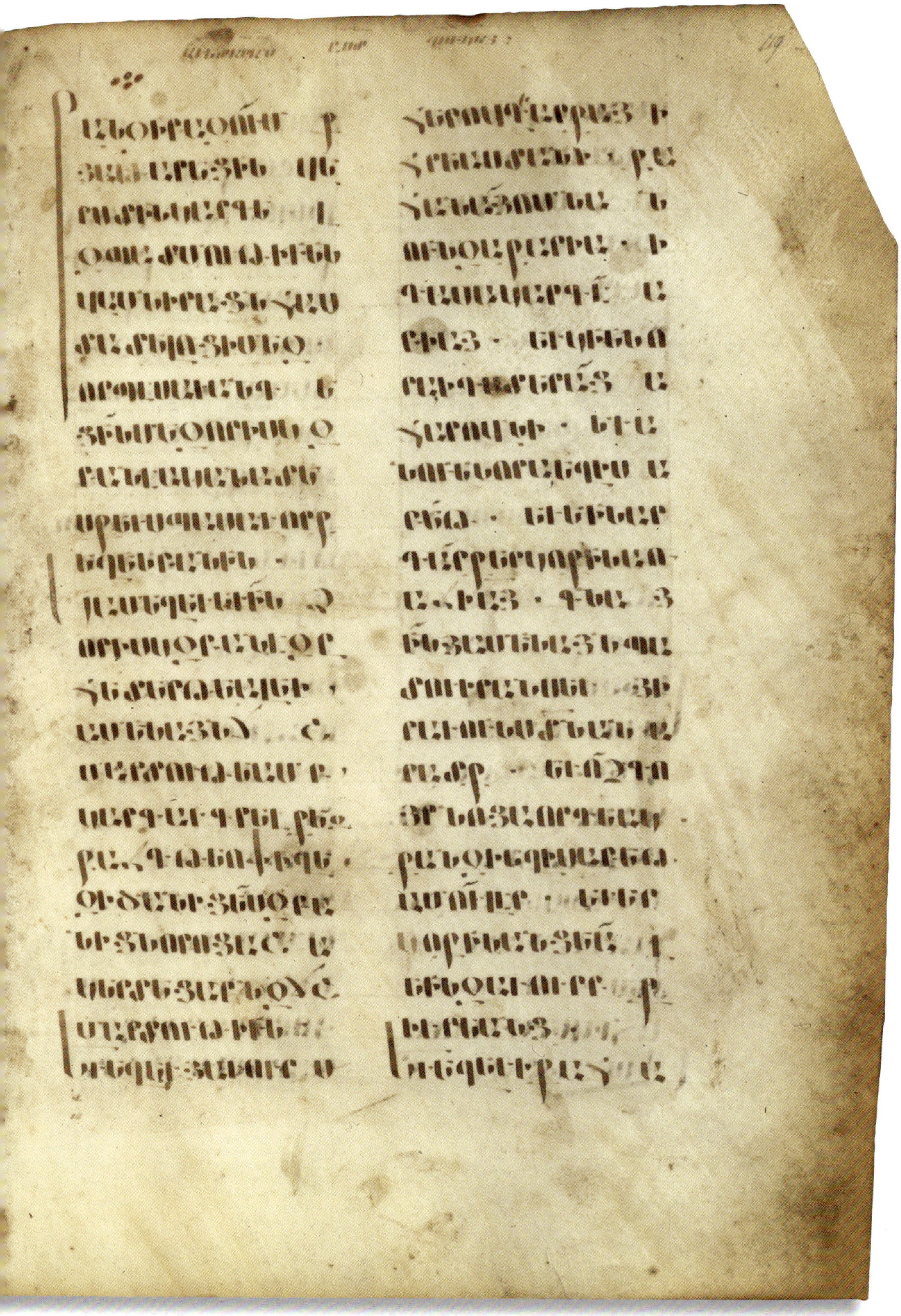

39

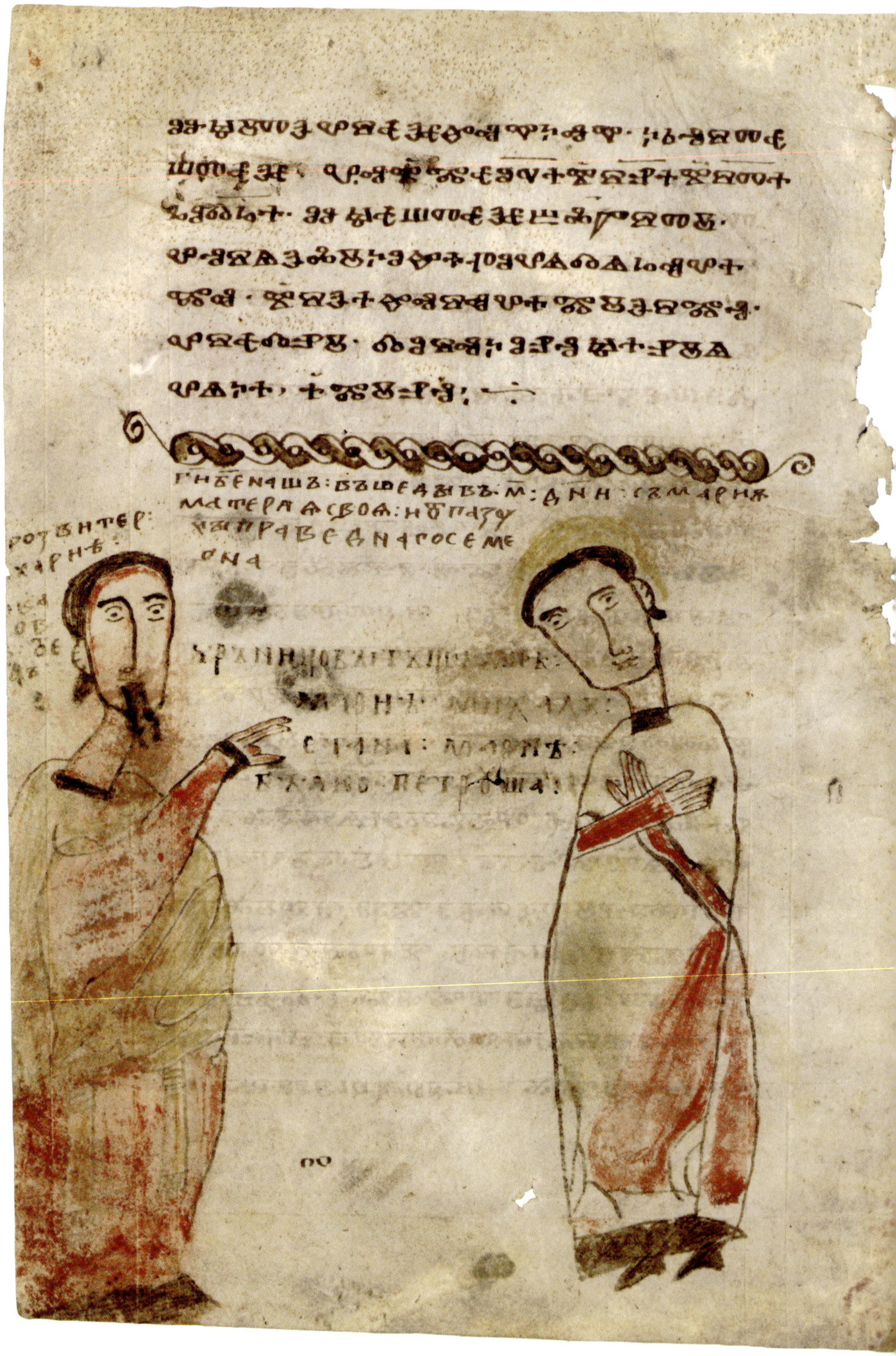

Codex Zographensis.
St. Petersburg, National Library of Russia, MS. Glag. 1, ff. 76v–77r. Gospels, inspiration of St. Mark. Glagolitic; parchment. Macedonia, late tenth–eleventh century.

Ethiopic Gospelbook (Zir Ganela Gospels).
New York, Morgan Library and Museum, MS. M.828, ff. 13v–14r, Ethiopic; parchment. Ethiopia, August 29, 1400–August 28, 1401 (canon tables, perhaps eleventh century).

Spreading the Word:
The single-volume bible

THE CONCEPT OF GATHERING THE CANONICAL TEXTS of the Old and New Testaments into a massive single volume, or pandect, only crystallized during the early Middle Ages. Too large for practical use, such books were for reference and display and symbolically enshrined Christian reception of the Word. Their production was usually linked to specific programs of codification and dissemination, undertaken under state sponsorship or as monastic initiatives begun by influential individuals.

Three important biblical editions were produced by Cassiodorus (ca. 485–580), an Italian senator who retired to found a monastery called the Vivarium ("Fishponds") on his estate in Calabria. There he established an approach to biblical studies based on the responsible emendation, copying, and distribution of texts. His Novem Codices was a nine-volume bible; the Codex Grandior was an illustrated single volume; and a smaller single-volume Vulgate bible, now lost, is presumed to have been written in minuscule script, anticipating the use of caroline minuscule script in the later Tours Bibles of the Carolingian Empire (cat. no. 43).

Abbot Ceolfrith (died 716) brought a copy of Cassiodorus's Codex Grandior back to Anglo-Saxon England from Rome circa 700, stimulating the production of three massive pandects at his twin monasteries of Wearmouth and Jarrow—the Ceolfrith Bibles (cat. no. 41). His foundations kept a copy each, of which mere fragments remain; the third was given to the pope as a gift in 716 and still survives intact. Known as the Codex Amiatinus, it was thought to be Italo-Byzantine work until identified in the 1880s as of English manufacture. Yet despite its mastery of Mediterranean features, the Codex Amiatinus was no mere antiquarian facsimile but a dynamic scholarly edition in its own right and exhibits the influence of the leading theologian of the day, Bede, who was probably one of the scribes. In the light of this, the famous image of a priestly scribe in the Codex Amiatinus can be interpreted as representing not only Ezra (who "reconstructed" Judaic scriptures from memory after their destruction by the Babylonians), but also the various authors of the Old and New Testaments, Cassiodorus, Bede, and other editors of the Bible across the ages, symbolizing the ongoing transmission of scripture.

This process was perpetuated in the Carolingian Empire. Around 800 Alcuin of York, Abbot of Tours, completed a single-volume revision of the Vulgate, and initiated the production of the Alcuin or Tours Bibles throughout the first half of the ninth century. Alcuin's was not the only early Carolingian version. Theodulf of Orléans relied upon the "Mixed Spanish" tradition of his homeland, which conflated Old Latin and Vulgate readings, when preparing his edition (cat. no. 42). Abbot Maurdramnus of Corbie also undertook a six-volume revision, in the course of which he helped to devise a multi-purpose script for ease of copying and legibility, caroline minuscule, which replaced the multitude of local hands in use around the Empire and later became the basis of modern typefaces.

The scriptorium at Tours had the resources to produce three massive Alcuin Bibles per year, as part of a publishing program that was designed to bring unity to the disparate territories of the Carolingian Empire. By 900 Alcuin's edition was becoming the norm throughout much of Europe. It subsequently formed the basis of studies conducted by the Victorines and Paris University during the twelfth and thirteenth centuries, and led to the production of the "Paris Study Bible," which finally assumed the character with which we are familiar today—a small, affordable, portable, densely written, single-volume bible.

Detail: Alcuin (Touronian) Bible, see cat. no. 43.

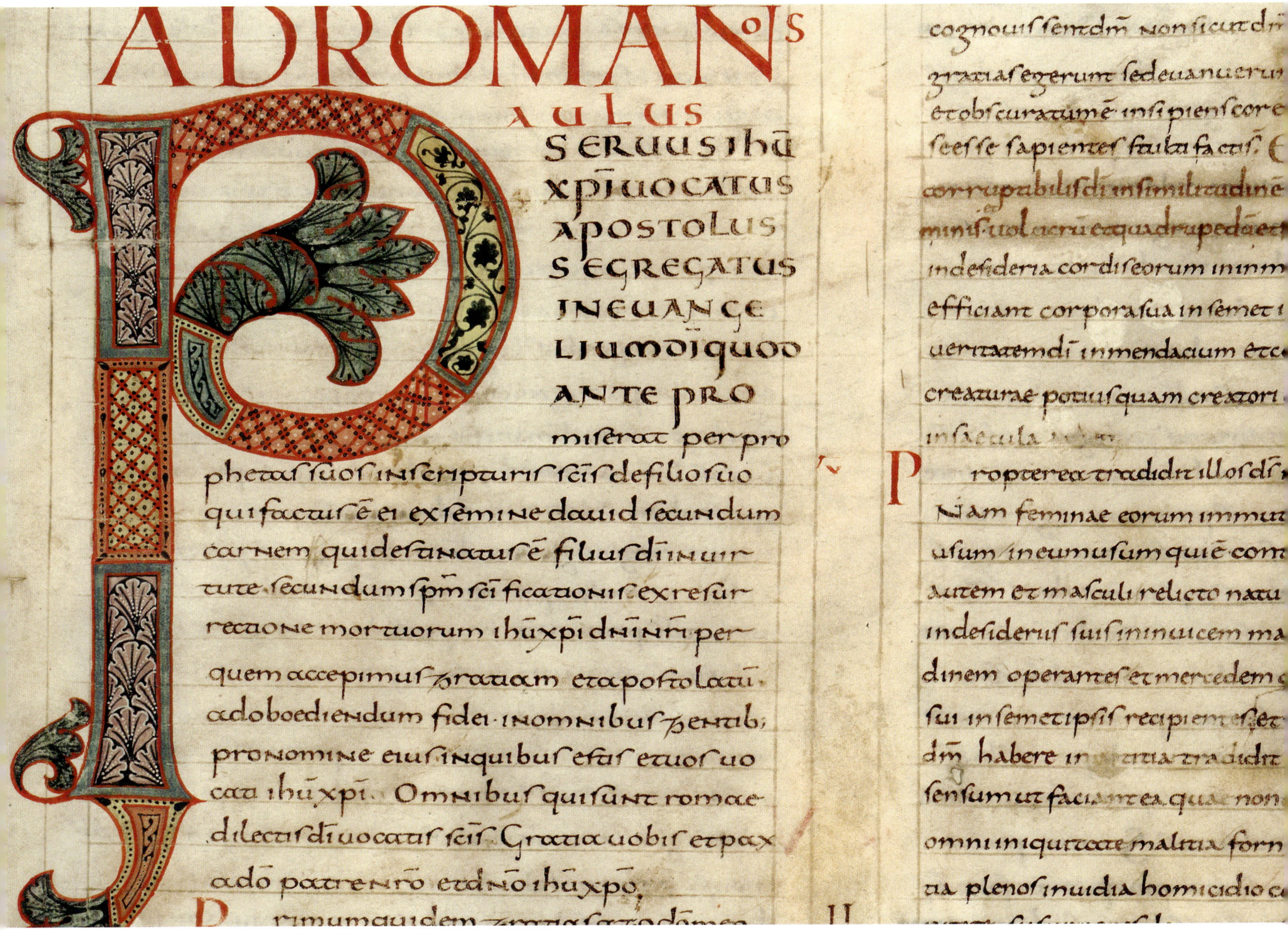
AD ROMANOS
PAULUS

Paulus seruus ihū xp̄i uocatus apostolus segregatus ineuange liumdiquod ante pro miserat per pro phetas suos inscripturis sc̄is defilio suo qui factus ē exsemine dauid secundum carnem quidest natus ē filius dī inuir tute secundum sp̄m sc̄i ficationis exresur rectione mortuorum ihū xp̄i dn̄i n̄ri per quem accepimus gratiam et apostolatū adoboediendum fidei inomnibus gentib; pronomine eius inquibus estis etuos uo cati ihū xp̄i. Omnibus quisunt romae dilectis dī uocatis sc̄is. Gratia uobis et pax adō patre n̄ro et dn̄o ihū xp̄o.
Primum quidem gratias ago deo...

cognouis sem dm̄ nonsicut dm̄ gratias egerunt sedeuanuerū et obscuratum ē insipiens core eesse sapientes stulti fac. sunt Ē corruptabilis dī insimilitudinē et minis uoluc̄ru et quadrupedā et indesideria cordis eorum inim efficiant corporasua insemet ī ueritatem dī inmendacium et c creaturae potius quam creatori insaecula

Propterea tradidit illos dr̄s ñi am feminae eorum immu usum ineum usum qui com autem et masculi relicto natu indesideriis suis ininuicem ma dinem operantes et mercedem sui insemetipsis recipientes et dm̄ habere in gratia tradidit sensum ut faciant ea quae non omni iniquitate malitia forn ta plenos inuidia homicidio c

41

The Ceolfrith Bibles: Middleton Leaves

London, British Library, Add. MS. 45025, ff. 2v-3r. Middleton leaves, third and fourth Book of Kings. Latin; parchment. Wearmouth–Jarrow, northeast England, early eighth century, (before 716).

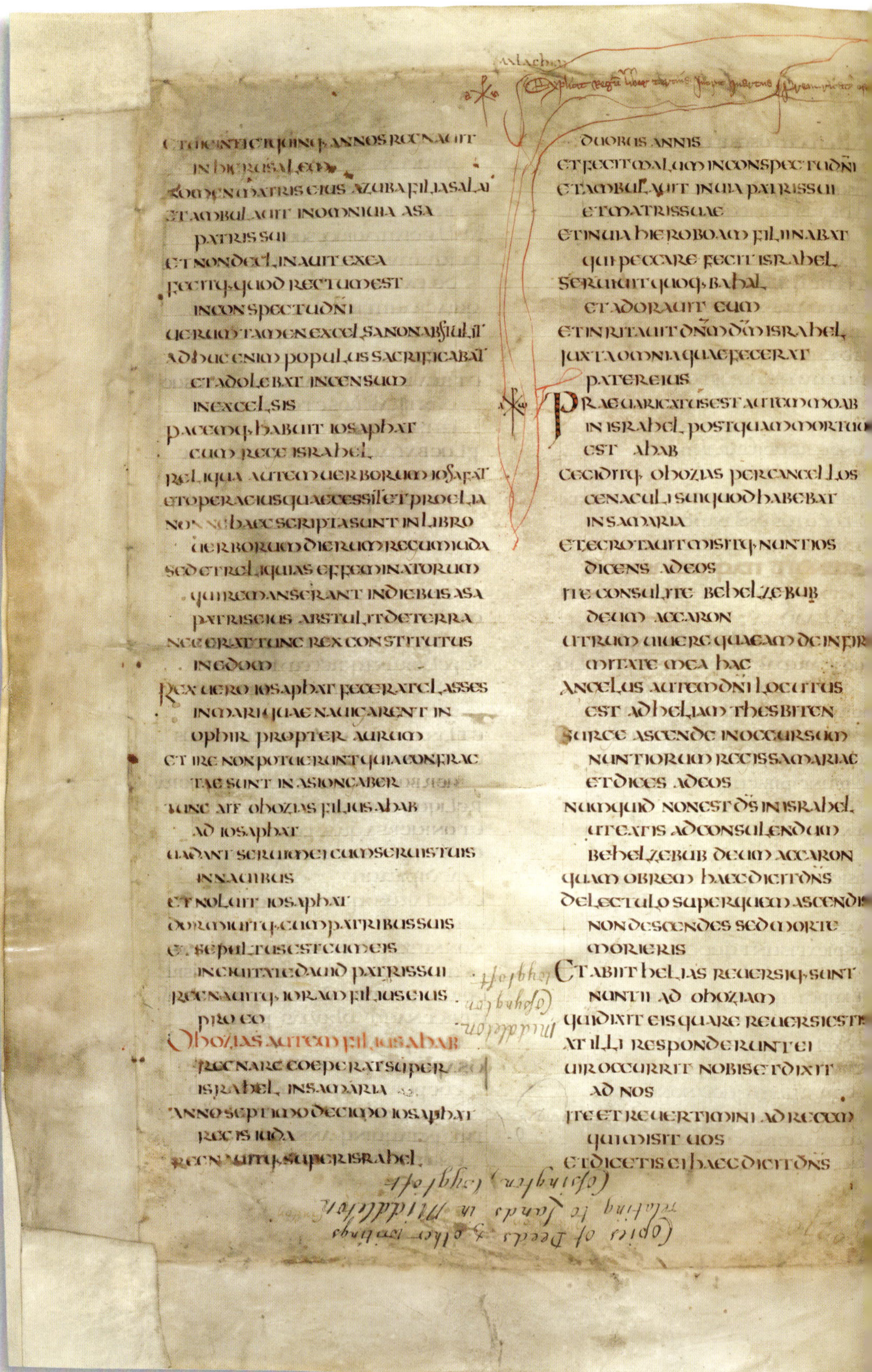
ET TRIGINTA ET QUINQ. ANNOS REGNAUIT
IN HIERUSALEM
NOMEN MATRIS EIUS AZUBA FILIA SALAI
ET AMBULAUIT IN OMNI UIA ASA
PATRIS SUI
ET NON DECLINAUIT EX EA
FECITQ. QUOD RECTUM EST
IN CONSPECTU DNI
UERUM TAMEN EXCELSA NON ABSTULIT
ADHUC ENIM POPULUS SACRIFICABAT
ET ADOLEBAT INCENSUM
IN EXCELSIS
PACEMQ. HABUIT IOSAPHAT
CUM REGE ISRAHEL
RELIQUA AUTEM UERBORUM IOSAFAT
ET OPERA EIUS QUAE GESSIT ET PROELIA
NONNE HAEC SCRIPTA SUNT IN LIBRO
UERBORUM DIERUM REGUM IUDA
SED ET RELIQUIAS EFFEMINATORUM
QUI REMANSERANT IN DIEBUS ASA
PATRIS EIUS ABSTULIT DE TERRA
NEC ERAT TUNC REX CONSTITUTUS
IN EDOM
REX UERO IOSAPHAT FECERAT CLASSES
IN MARI QUAE NAUIGARENT IN
OPHIR PROPTER AURUM
ET IRE NON POTUERUNT QUIA CONFRAC
TAE SUNT IN ASIONGABER
TUNC AIT OHOZIAS FILIUS AHAB
AD IOSAPHAT
UADANT SERUI MEI CUM SERUIS TUIS
IN NAUIBUS
ET NOLUIT IOSAPHAT
DORMIUITQ. CUM PATRIBUS SUIS
ET SEPULTUS EST CUM EIS
IN CIUITATE DAUID PATRIS SUI
REGNAUITQ. IORAM FILIUS EIUS
PRO EO
OHOZIAS AUTEM FILIUS AHAB
REGNARE COEPERAT SUPER
ISRAHEL IN SAMARIA
ANNO SEPTIMO DECIMO IOSAPHAT
REGIS IUDA
REGNAUITQ. SUPER ISRAHEL
DUOBUS ANNIS
ET FECIT MALUM IN CONSPECTU DNI
ET AMBULAUIT IN UIA PATRIS SUI
ET MATRIS SUAE
ET IN UIA HIEROBOAM FILII NABAT
QUI PECCARE FECIT ISRAHEL
SERUIUIT QUOQ. BAAL
ET ADORAUIT EUM
ET INRITAUIT DNM DM ISRAHEL
IUXTA OMNIA QUAE FECERAT
PATER EIUS
PRAEUARICATUS EST AUTEM MOAB
IN ISRAHEL POSTQUAM MORTUUS
EST AHAB
CECIDITQ. OHOZIAS PER CANCELLOS
CENACULI SUI QUOD HABEBAT
IN SAMARIA
ET AEGROTAUIT MISITQ. NUNTIOS
DICENS AD EOS
ITE CONSULITE BEELZEBUB
DEUM ACCARON
UTRUM UIUERE QUEAM DE INFIR
MITATE MEA HAC
ANGELUS AUTEM DNI LOCUTUS
EST AD HELIAM THESBITEN
SURGE ASCENDE IN OCCURSUM
NUNTIORUM REGIS SAMARIAE
ET DICES AD EOS
NUMQUID NON EST DS IN ISRAHEL
UT EATIS AD CONSULENDUM
BEELZEBUB DEUM ACCARON
QUAM OB REM HAEC DICIT DNS
DE LECTULO SUPER QUEM ASCENDISTI
NON DESCENDES SED MORTE
MORIERIS
ET ABIIT HELIAS REUERSIQ. SUNT
NUNTII AD OHOZIAM
QUI DIXIT EIS QUARE REUERSI ESTIS
AT ILLI RESPONDERUNT EI
UIR OCCURRIT NOBIS ET DIXIT
AD NOS
ITE ET REUERTIMINI AD REGEM
QUI MISIT UOS
ET DICETIS EI HAEC DICIT DNS

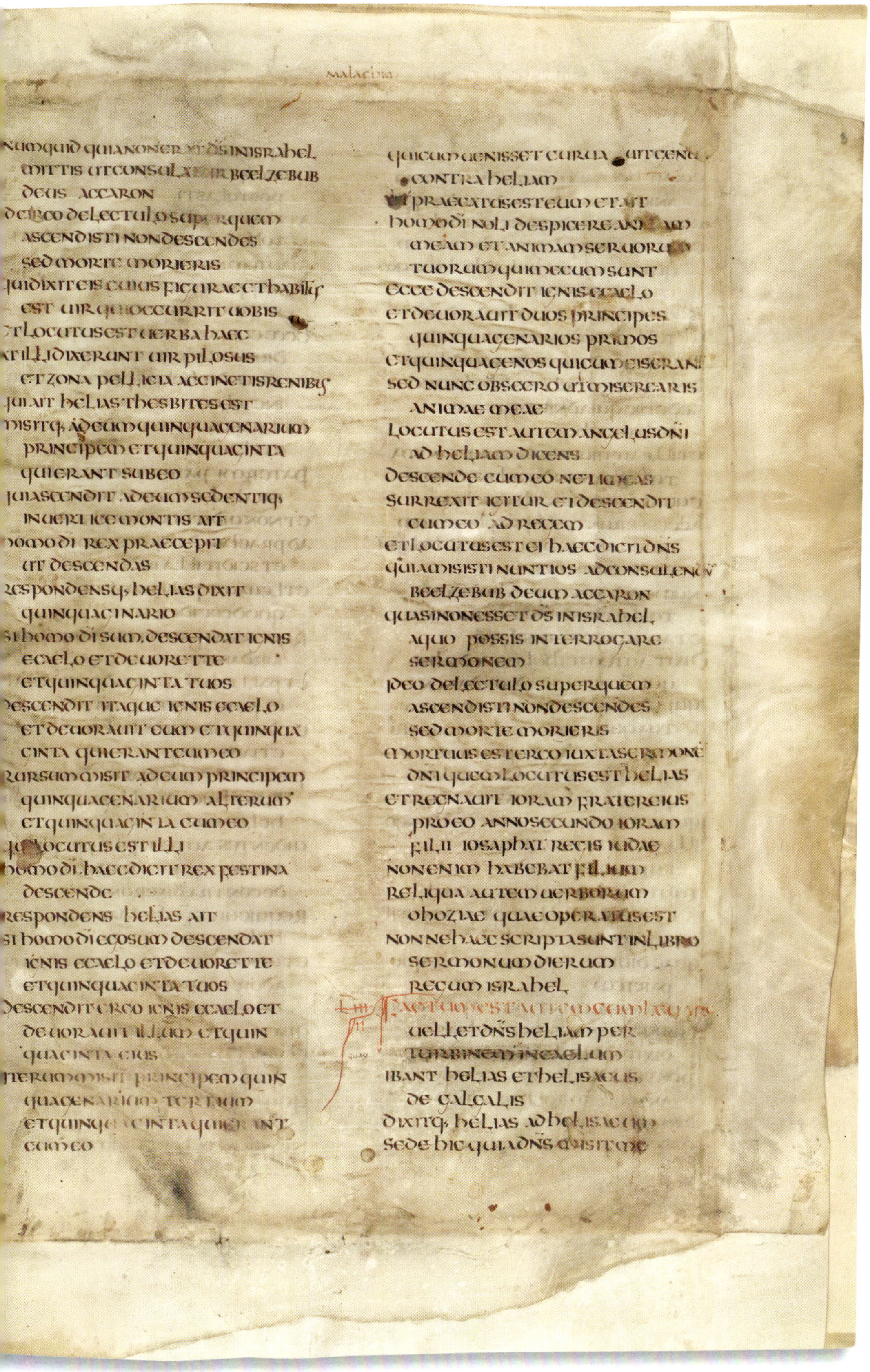
numquid quia non erat ds in israhel
mittis ut consulatur beelzebub
deus accaron
ideirco de lectulo super quem
ascendisti non descendes
sed morte morieris
qui dixit eis cuius figurae et habitus
est uir qui occurrit uobis
et locutus est uerba haec
at illi dixerunt uir pilosus
et zona pellicia accinctis renibus
qui ait helias thesbites est
misitq; ad eum quinquagenarium
principem et quinquaginta
qui erant sub eo
qui ascendit ad eum sedentiq;
in uertice montis ait
homo di rex praecepit
ut descendas
respondensq; helias dixit
quinquagenario
si homo di sum descendat ignis
e caelo et deuoret te
et quinquaginta tuos
descendit itaque ignis e caelo
et deuorauit eum et quinqua
ginta qui erant cum eo
rursum misit ad eum principem
quinquagenarium alterum
et quinquaginta cum eo
qui locutus est illi
homo di haec dicit rex festina
descende
respondens helias ait
si homo di ego sum descendat
ignis e caelo et deuoret te
et quinquaginta tuos
descendit ergo ignis e caelo et
deuorauit illum et quin
quaginta eius
iterum misit principem quin
quagenarium tertium
et quinquaginta qui erant
cum eo
qui cum uenisset curuauit genua
contra heliam
et praecatus est eum et ait
homo di noli despicere animam
meam et animam seruorum
tuorum qui mecum sunt
ecce descendit ignis e caelo
et deuorauit duos principes
quinquagenarios primos
et quinquagenos qui cum eis erant
sed nunc obsecro ut miserearis
animae meae
locutus est autem angelus dni
ad heliam dicens
descende cum eo ne timeas
surrexit igitur et descendit
cum eo ad regem
et locutus est ei haec dicit dns
quia misisti nuntios ad consulendum
beelzebub deum accaron
quasi non esset ds in israhel
a quo possis interrogare
sermonem
ideo de lectulo super quem
ascendisti non descendes
sed morte morieris
mortuus est ergo iuxta sermonem
dni quem locutus est helias
et regnauit ioram frater eius
pro eo anno secundo ioram
filii iosaphat regis iudae
non enim habebat filium
reliqua autem uerborum
ochoziae quae operatus est
nonne haec scripta sunt in libro
sermonum dierum
regum israhel
Factum est autem cum leuare
uellet dns heliam per
turbinem in caelum
ibant helias et heliseus
de galgalis
dixitq; helias ad heliseum
sede hic quia dns misit me

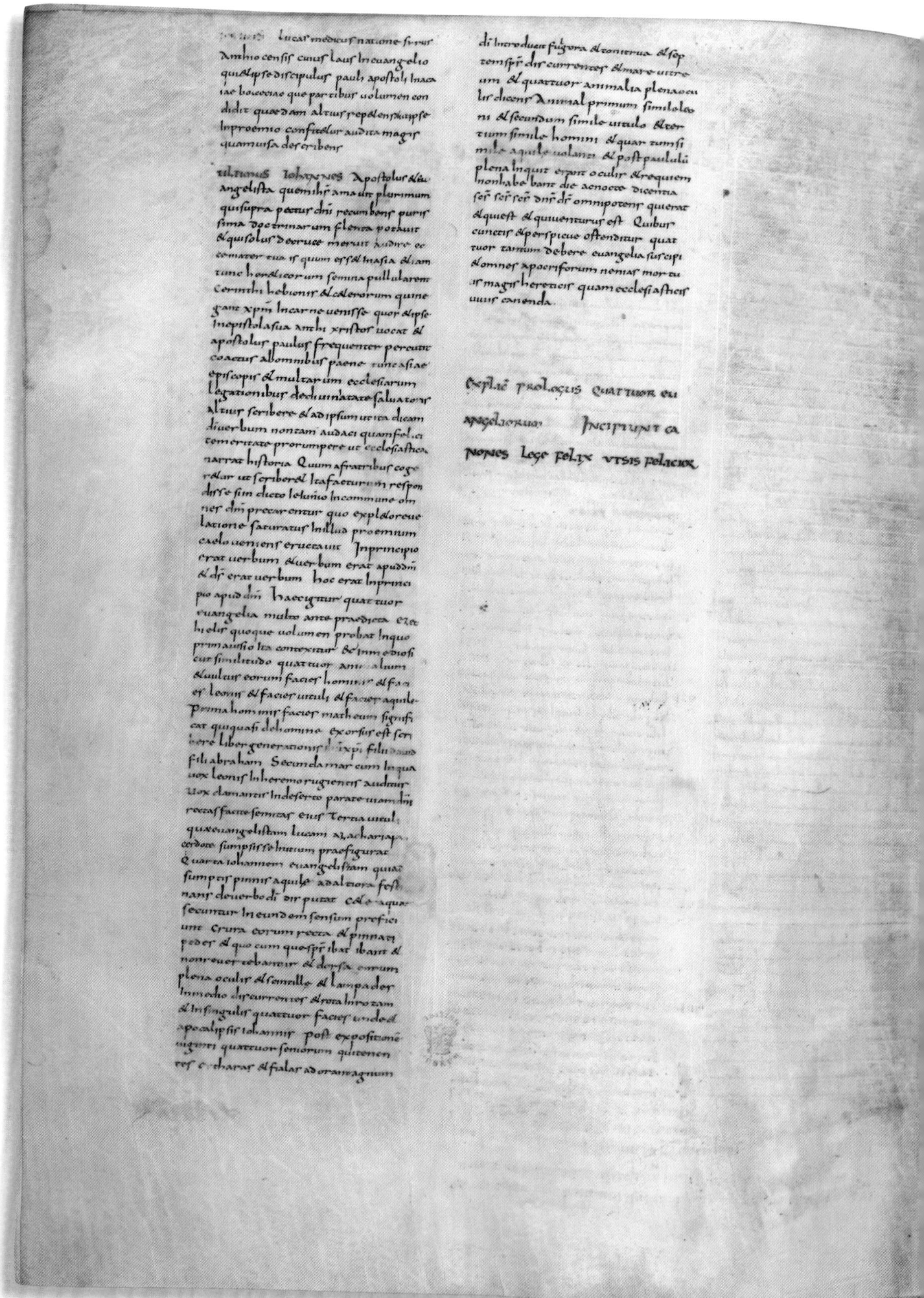

The Theodulf Bible (Codex Hubertianus).
London, British Library, Western MSS. Add. MS. 24142, ff. 197v–198r. Latin; parchment. Orléans or Fleury, France, ninth century.

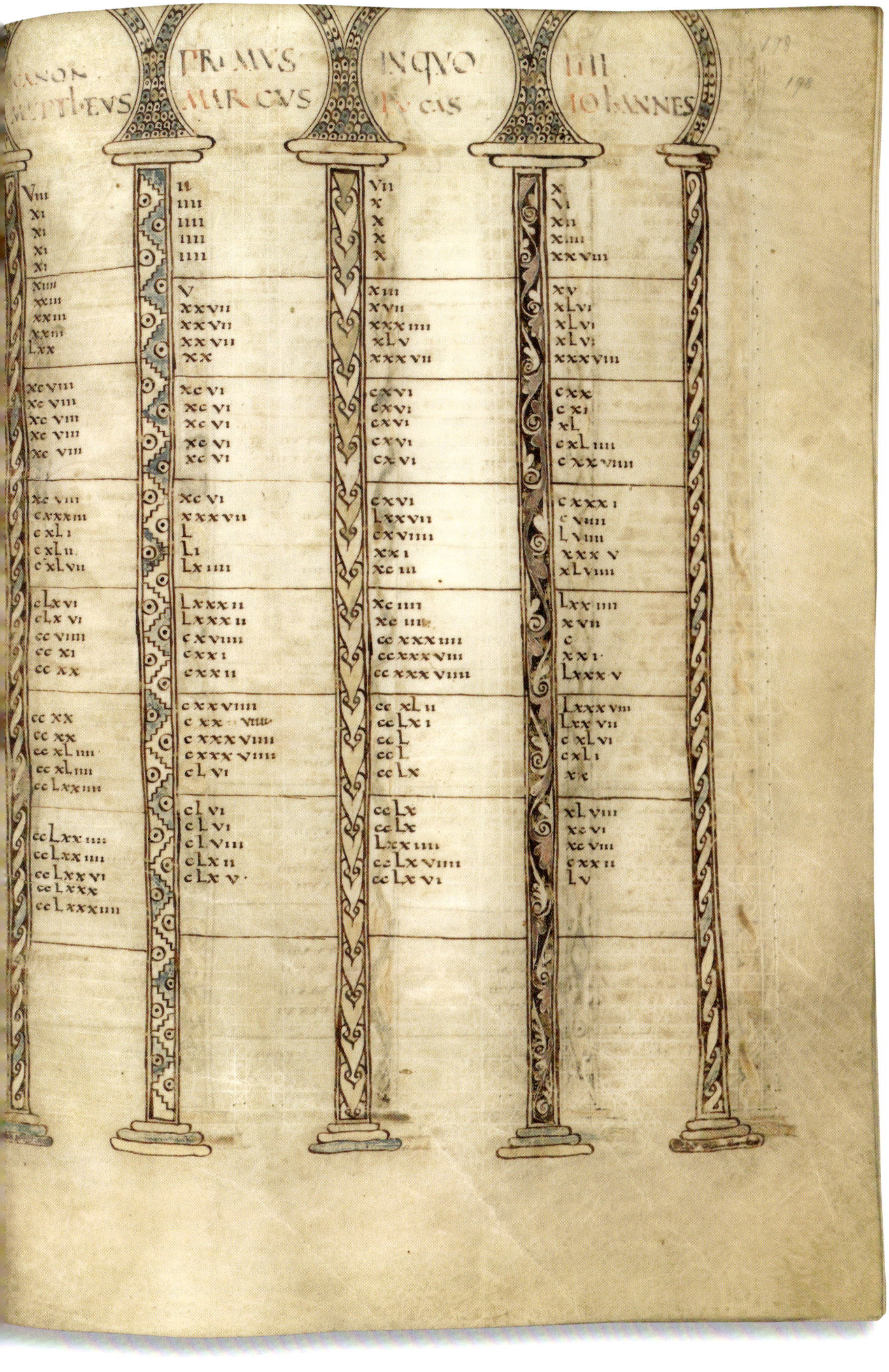
PRIMUS
INQUO
IIII
MARCUS
LUCAS
IOHANNES

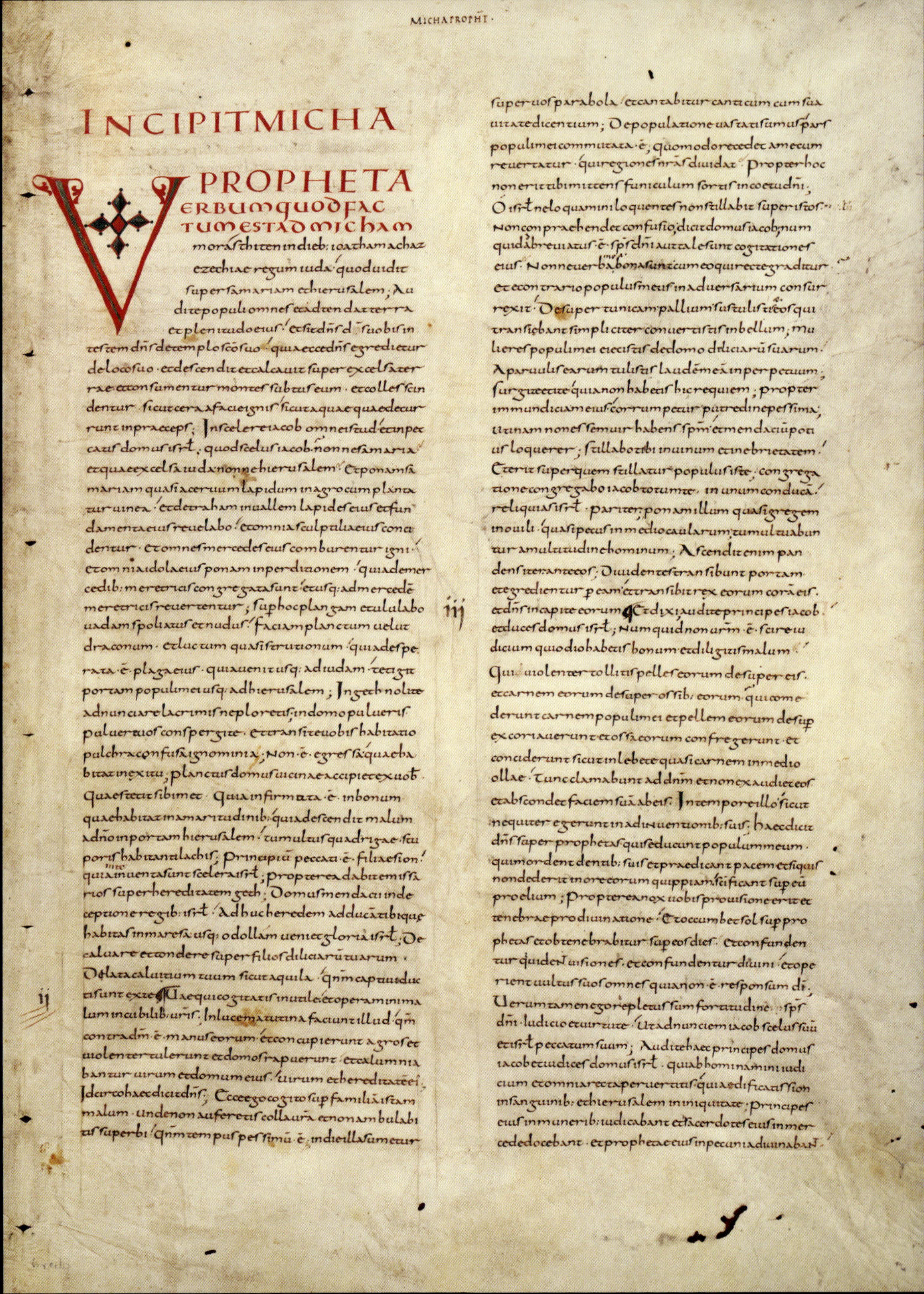

MICHA PROPHT

INCIPIT MICHA

V PROPHETA
VERBUM QUOD FAC
TUM EST AD MICHAM
morasthiten in diebus ioatham achaz
ezechiae regum iuda; quod uidit
super samariam et hierusalem; Au
dite populi omnes et adtendat terra
et plenitudo eius; et sit dñs uobis in
testem dñs de templo sco suo; quae ecce enim egredietur
de loco suo; et descendit et calcabit super excelsa ter
rae et consumentur montes subtus eum; et colles scin
dentur; sicut cera a facie ignis; sicut aquae quae decur
runt in praeceps; In scelere iacob omne istud et in pec
catis domus isr̃l; quod scelus iacob nonne samaria;
et quae excelsa iudae nonne hierusalem; Et ponam sa
mariam quasi aceruum lapidum in agro cum planta
tur uinea; et detraham in uallem lapides eius et fun
damenta eius reuelabo; et omnia sculptilia eius con
tundentur; et omnes mercedes eius comburentur igni;
et omnia idola eius ponam in perditionem; quia de mer
cedibus meretricis congregata sunt et usque ad merce
dem meretricis reuertentur; Super hoc plangam et ululabo
uadam spoliatus et nudus; Faciam planctum uelut
draconum; et luctum quasi struthionum; quia despe
rata est plaga eius; quia uenit usque ad iudam; tetigit
portam populi mei usque ad hierusalem; In geth nolite
adnuntiare lacrimis ne ploretis; in domo pulueris
puluere uos conspergite; et transite uobis habitatio
pulchra confusa ignominia; Non est egressa quae habita
bat in exitu; planctum domus uicinae accipiet ex uobis
quae stetit sibi met; Quia infirmata est in bonum
quae habitat in amaritudinibus; quia descendit malum
a dño in portam hierusalem; tumultus quadrigae stu
poris habitantibus lachis; principium peccati est filia sion
quia in te inuenta sunt scelera isr̃l; Propterea dabit emissa
rios super hereditatem geth; Domus mendacii inde
ceptione regibus isr̃l; Adhuc heredem adducam tibi que
habitas in maresa usque odollam ueniet gloria isr̃l; De
caluare et tondere super filios deliciarum tuarum;
Dilata caluitium tuum sicut aquila; qñ capti uiducti
sunt ex te;

super uos parabola; et cantabitur canticum cum sua
uitate dicentium; Depopulatione uastati sumus pars
populi mei commutata est; quomodo recedet a me cum
reuertatur; qui regiones nr̃as diuidat; Propter hoc
non erit tibi mittens funiculum sortis in coetu dñi;
O isr̃l nelo quam uim loquentes non fallabit super istos;
Non comprehendet confusio; dicit domus iacob num
quid adbreuiatus est sp̃s dñi aut tales sunt cogitationes
eius; Nonne uerba bona sunt cum eo qui recte graditur;
et e contrario populus meus in aduersarium consur
rexit; Desuper tunicam pallium sustulistis eos qui
transiebant simpliciter conuertistis in bellum; Mu
lieres populi mei eiecistis de domo deliciarum suarum;
A paruulis earum tulistis laudem mea in perpetuum;
Surgite et ite quia non habetis hic requiem; propter
immunditiam eius corrumpetur putredine pessima;
Utinam non essem uir habens sp̃m et mendacium po
tius loquerer; stillabo tibi in uinum et in ebrietatem;
Et erit super quem stillabitur populus iste; congrega
tione congregabo iacob totum te; in unum conducam
reliquias isr̃l; pariter ponam illum quasi gregem
in ouili; quasi pecus in medio caularum; tumultuabun
tur a multitudine hominum; Ascendet enim pan
dens iter ante eos; Diuident et transibunt portam
et egredientur per eam; et transibit rex eorum coram eis;
et dñs in capite eorum; Et dixi audite principes iacob
et duces domus isr̃l; Numquid non uestrum est scire iu
dicium; quod odio habeatis bonum et diligatis malum;
Qui uiolenter tollitis pelles eorum desuper eis;
et carnem eorum desuper ossibus eorum; qui como
derunt carnem populi mei et pellem eorum desup
excoriauerunt et ossa eorum confregerunt; et
conciderunt sicut in lebete quasi carnem in medio
ollae; Tunc clamabunt ad dñm et non exaudiet eos
et abscondet faciem suam ab eis; In tempore illo sicut
nequiter egerunt in aduentionibus suis; haec dicit
dñs super prophetas qui seducunt populum meum
qui mordent dentibus suis et praedicant pacem et si qui
non dederit in ore eorum quippiam sanctificant supeu
proelium; Propterea nox uobis pro uisione erit et
tenebrae pro diuinatione; Et occumbet sol sup pro
phetas et obtenebrabitur super eos dies; et confunden
tur qui uident uisiones; et confundentur diuini et ope
rient uultus suos omnes quia non est responsum dñi;
Uerumtamen ego repletus sum fortitudine; spū
dñi iudicio et uirtute; Ut adnuntiem iacob scelus suū
et isr̃l peccatum suum; Audite haec principes domus
iacob et iudices domus isr̃l; qui abhominamini iudi
cium et omnia recta peruertitis qui aedificatis sion
in sanguinibus; et hierusalem in iniquitate; principes
eius in muneribus iudicabant et sacerdotes eius in mer
cede docebant; et prophetae eius in pecunia diuinabant;

Alcuin (Touronian) Bible.
Los Angeles, J. Paul Getty Museum, 83.MA.50, f. 8. Micah 1.1–3.11, Latin; parchment. Tours, France, ca. 845–850.

Alcuin (Touronian) Bible.
Los Angeles, J. Paul Getty Museum, 83.MA.50, f. 10. Romans 1.1–2.8. Latin; parchment. Tours, France, ca. 845–850.

INCIPIT
EPISTOLA
AD ROMANOS
PAULUS
SERUUS IHU
XPI UOCATUS
APOSTOLUS
SEGREGATUS
IN EUANGE
LIUM DI QUOD
ANTE PRO

Spreading the Word:
The book as desert, the scribe as evangelist

THERE WERE NO RULES governing how scriptural books were made in the Middle Ages. For some scribes it was a communal exercise, part of the daily round of monastic life, conducted in the scriptorium in collaboration with colleagues. For others, the more solitary model of the eastern desert fathers held sway. Where those early saints, such as Paul and Anthony of Egypt, had gone into the wild desert places of the Middle East to find spiritual challenge, scribes living in the watery wildernesses of northern Europe would sometimes work alone, as both artist and scribe, performing heroic solitary feats of patience and toil within the scribal desert of the book—a place of meditation, prayer, and encounter with the Divine.

Such scribal endeavor, accuracy, and creativity might be inspired by commentators from East and West, notably the Italian monastic founder, Cassiodorus. He wrote that "the scribe preaches with the pen" and "unleashes tongues with the fingers," and asserted that "each word written is a wound on Satan's body"—the pen being mightier than the sword. Such injunctions even reached the Atlantic seaboard where, in monasteries such as Iona and Lindisfarne, people such as Saint Columba were acclaimed as hero-scribes.

Byzantine depictions of the evangelists helped to promote this image of the importance of the scribe, his labors set against a timeless spiritual background of gold, as in a lavish early example from the Bodleian Library in Oxford (cat. no. 45). The Stockholm Codex Aureus (cat. no. 44), made in southern England in the mid-eighth century, also displays splendid evangelist portraits, which affirm that the image of the book had come to epitomize the scriptures of Christianity, just as the scroll did those of Judaism. Saint Matthew is shown as an Antique author with, above him, his symbol of a man or angel. Matthew holds a scroll and the angel a book, emphasizing Christ's fulfillment of prophecy and transformation of the Old Testament Law (the scroll) through the New Testament Gospels (the codex).

The Stockholm Codex Aureus may have been made by the nuns of Minster-in-Thanet, in Kent, close to where Saint Augustine first landed in 597 to begin his conversion of the Anglo-Saxons. Female scribes are known to have supplied books for leading churches in Merovingian Gaul and England and for the Germanic mission fields. Women, too, could be called to be scribal evangelists.

Detail: Byzantine Gospels, St. Matthew, see cat. no. 45.

44

The Stockholm Codex Aureus.
Stockholm, Royal Library, MS. A.135, ff. 9v–11r. Gospelbook; St. Matthew miniature. Latin; parchment. Canterbury or Minster-in-Thanet, Kent, southeast England, mid-eighth century.

XPI AUTEM
GENERATIO
SIC ERAT CUM ESSET DS
PONSATA MATER EIUS
MARIA IOSEPH ANTEQUAM
CONVENIRENT INVENTA
EST IN UTERO HABENS

45

Byzantine Gospels: Excerpt from St. Matthew's Gospel.
Oxford, Bodleian Library, MS. Cromwell 16, ff. 30v–31r. Greek; parchment. Byzantium, Constantinople, mid-tenth century.

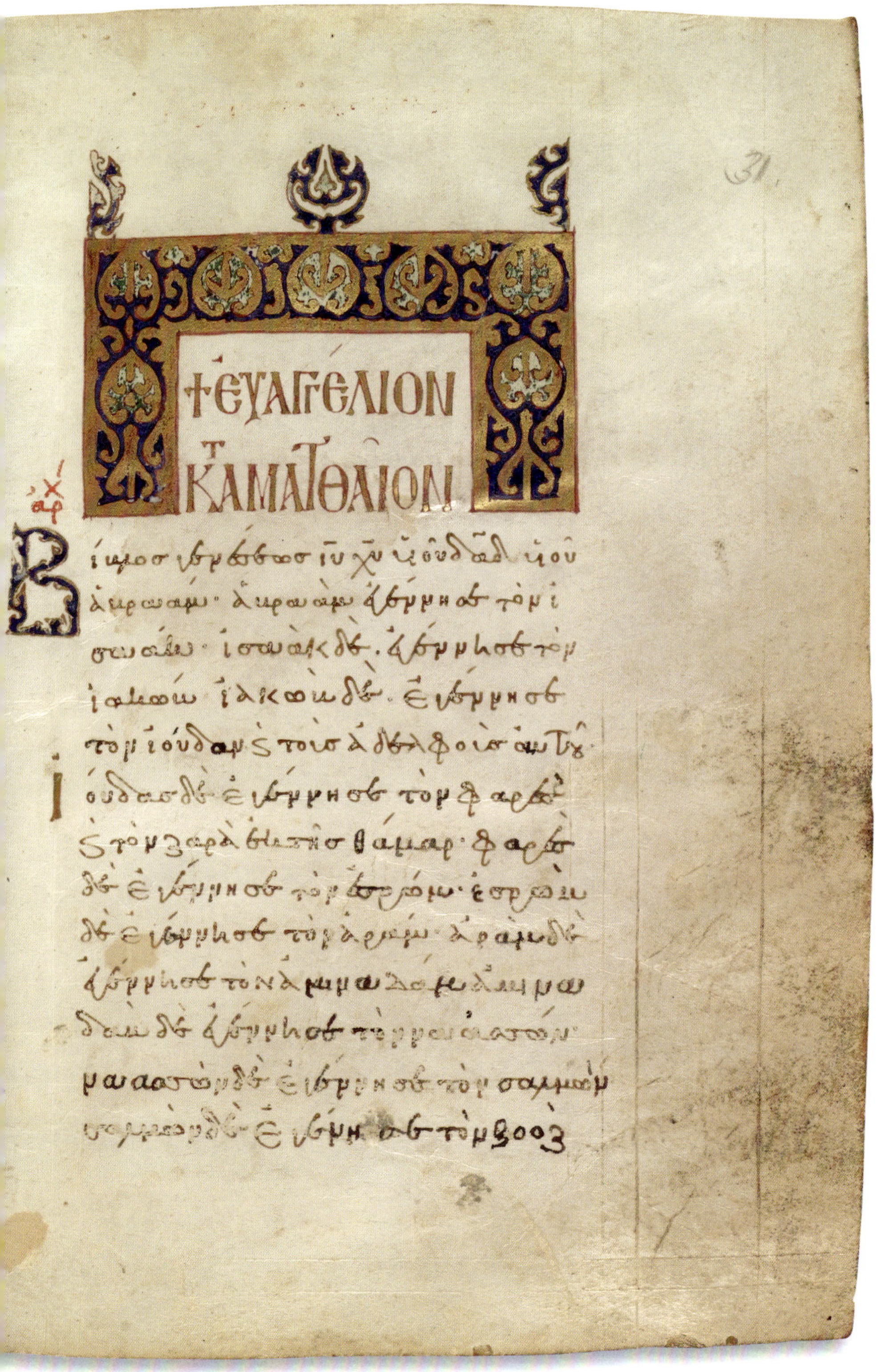
ΕΥΑΓΓΕΛΙΟΝ
ΚΑΤΑ ΜΑΤΘΑΙΟΝ

Spreading the Word:
From Eastern deserts to Western isles

DURING THE EARLY MIDDLE AGES, the Christian monastic cultures of two far-flung regions, Egypt and the islands of Britain and Ireland, were both shaped by the blending of the asceticism of the desert fathers, the legacy of the late Roman world, and their own local traditions and styles. They seem often to have shared perceptions of the role of the book. The desert sands of the East were translated into the watery seascapes of the North Sea and the Atlantic, where the beehive huts of the Skellig Michael monastery clung like gulls to a rock in the storm-tossed ocean around Ireland's southwest coast, in emulation of eastern high places such as Saint Catherine's monastery on the lower slopes of Mount Sinai. The allure of the Holy Land and their remoteness from the Mediterranean world may have contributed to the fertile reception of eastern influence in Britain and Ireland.

The Coptic Church of Egypt pioneered desert monasticism from the late third century and perpetuated many ancient Egyptian customs that were transmitted to western Europe. Around 400 C.E. a Coptic psalter was lovingly placed beneath the head of an adolescent girl, as a pillow in her grave, reflecting the ancient Egyptian practice of interring the Book of the Dead with the deceased. When the relics of the hermit-bishop-monk Saint Cuthbert were translated to the high altar at Lindisfarne in northeast England in 698, a little copy of Saint John's Gospel, made at Wearmouth–Jarrow but bound with a complex Coptic sewing technique and a tooled leather cover, was buried with him. Book-shrines were also made in both regions, the books they contained being revered as relics themselves.

Alongside liturgical and devotional influences, connections between the artistic styles of East and West can be traced. For example, the colorful Sasanian-style griffins in the margins of the Lectionary of Mount Horeb (cat. no. 52), from Sinai, find parallels in early gospelbooks from Irish and other Insular scriptoria, such as the Macregol Gospels (cat. no. 59) and the famous Book of Kells.

Saint Catherine's Monastery, Mount Sinai

The Holy Monastery of Saint Catherine is an extraordinary crossroads at which the traditions of East and West have met over centuries. Founded by Emperor Justinian between 548 and 565, the Byzantine monastery towers 1,500 meters above the Sinai desert. Its remoteness has ensured its survival, and it retains mosaics and icons from the time of its foundation and over three thousand manuscripts.

Mount Sinai (Horeb) has been home to Greek, Syrian, Arab, Georgian, Slavic, and Latin-speaking monks. The monastery's scriptural and liturgical volumes were supplemented with works by the Church Fathers, exegetical and study texts, and books in the languages of incoming monks. Around two thirds are in Greek; most of the rest are Christian Arabic texts.

Many manuscripts were copied at Sinai from the seventh to the ninth century, mostly in a rounded uncial script, inherited from Greece and Rome (cat. no. 47). Although they do not contain figural imagery, probably influenced by Islam, they include fish-shaped initials, inspired perhaps by pre-Carolingian Italy and Gaul. Beginning in the tenth century more opulent illuminated books were made at Sinai, including the Lectionary of Mount Horeb. Sinai also possesses Syriac and Georgian works (cat. nos. 50, 51) dating from the tenth to fourteenth centuries, when Georgian monasteries flourished in the region. Sinai's Slavonic books include two early items in the Glagolitic language, from which Cyrillic script is derived (cat. no. 49). A few Latin manuscripts made before 1000 provide valuable evidence for the presence of Latin speakers in the region, long before the Crusades (cat. no. 48). In 599 Pope Gregory the Great sent a legate bearing gifts to the monastery, so there were evidently early communications between Sinai and the West.

Detail: The Lectionary of Mount Horeb, see cat. no. 52.

46

Greek–Arabic Diglot of the Psalms and Odes.
Mt. Sinai, Holy Monastery of St. Catherine, Greek 36, ff. 38v–39r. Arabic and Greek; parchment. Sinai (?), eighth–ninth century.

47

Greek Psalter.
Mt. Sinai, Holy Monastery of St. Catherine, Greek 30, ff. 252v–253r. Greek; parchment. Sinai (?), ninth century.

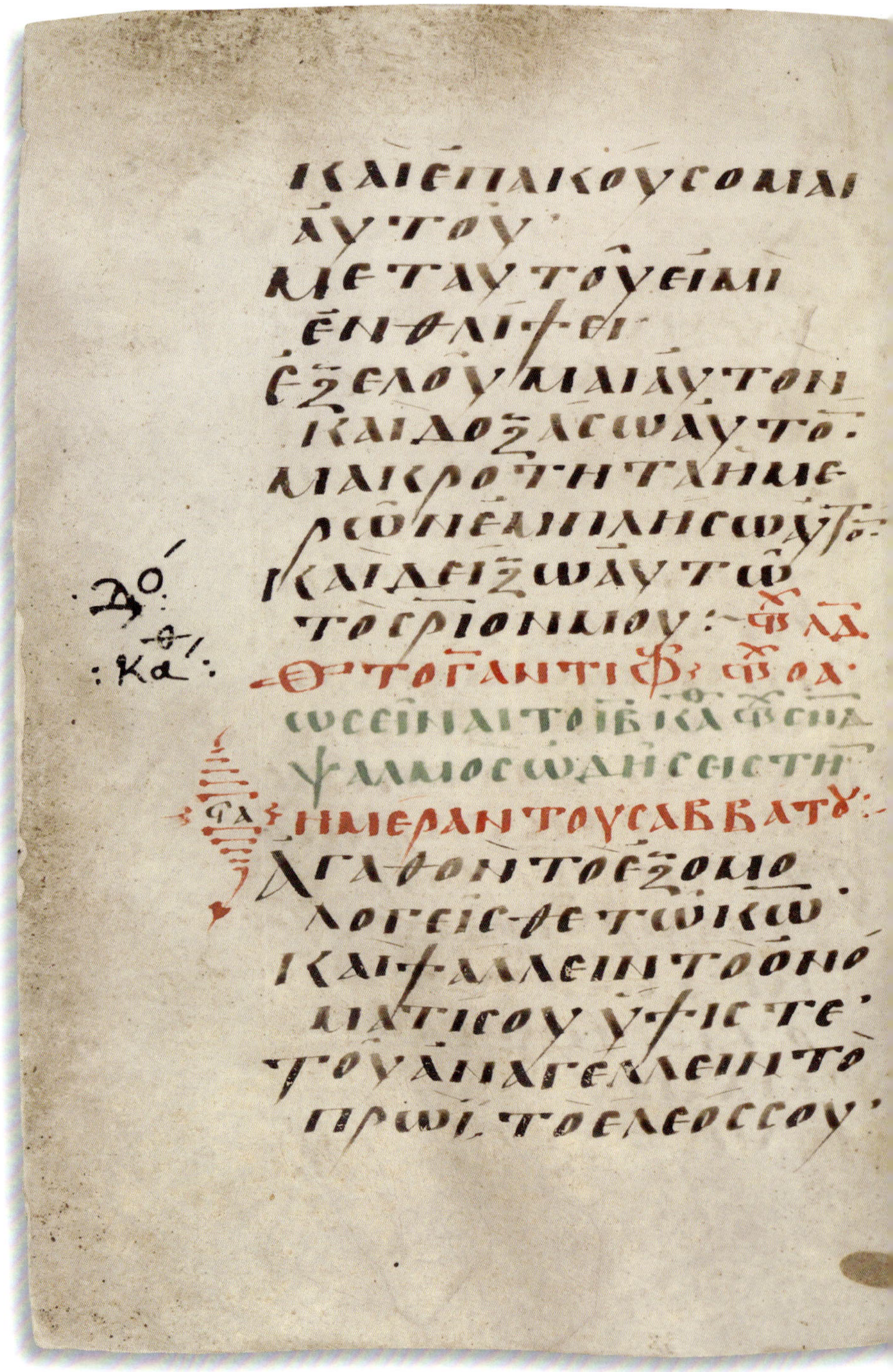

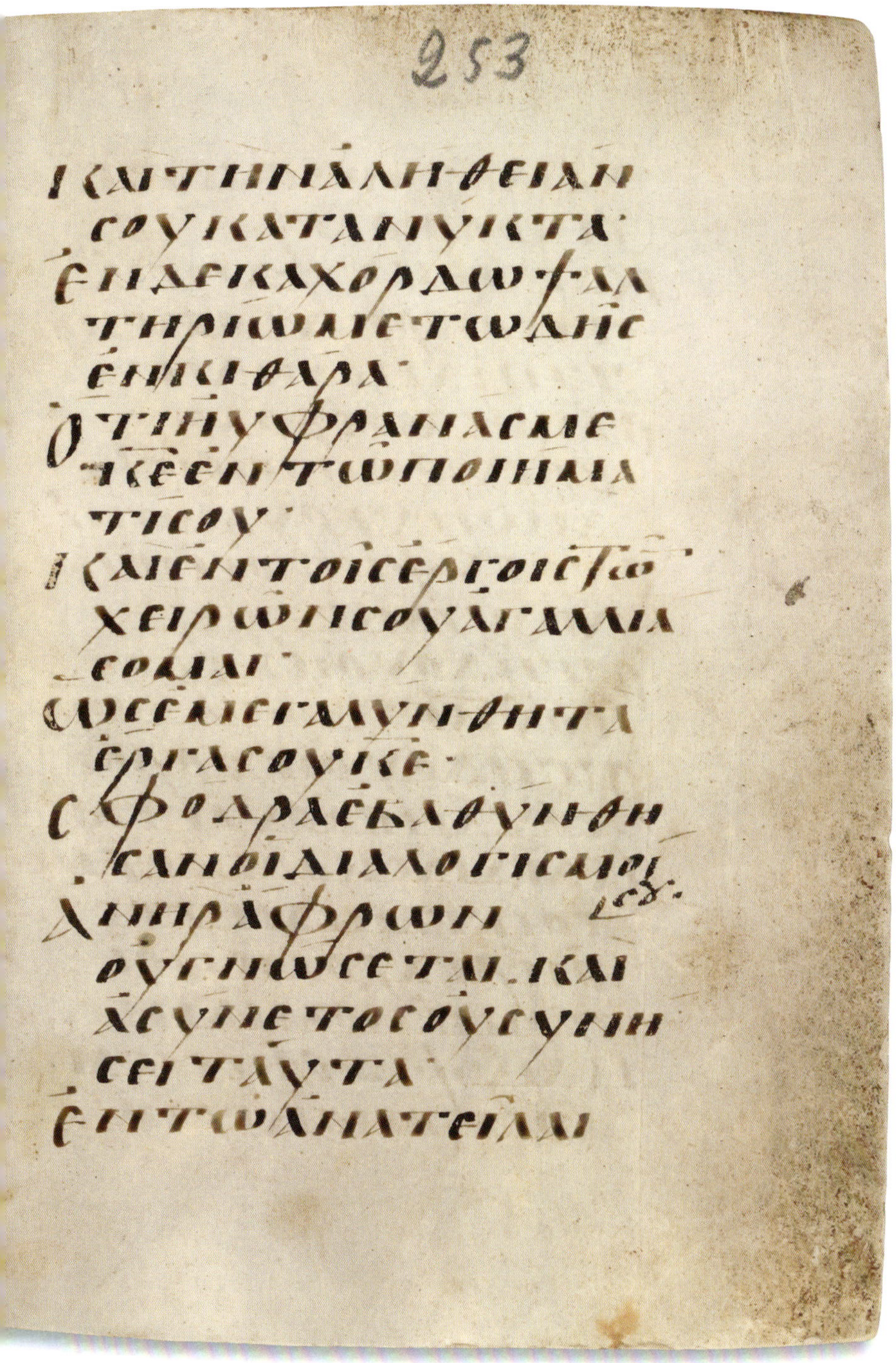
253
ΚΑΙ ΤΗΝ ΑΛΗΘΕΙΑΝ
ΣΟΥ ΚΑΤΑ ΝΥΚΤΑ
ΕΝ ΔΕΚΑΧΟΡΔΩ ΨΑΛ
ΤΗΡΙΩ ΜΕΤ ΩΔΗΣ
ΕΝ ΚΙΘΑΡΑ
ΟΤΙ ΗΥΦΡΑΝΑΣ ΜΕ
ΚΕ ΕΝ ΤΩ ΠΟΙΗΜΑ
ΤΙ ΣΟΥ
ΚΑΙ ΕΝ ΤΟΙΣ ΕΡΓΟΙΣ ΤΩΝ
ΧΕΙΡΩΝ ΣΟΥ ΑΓΑΛΛΙΑ
ΣΟΜΑΙ
ΩΣ ΕΜΕΓΑΛΥΝΘΗ ΤΑ
ΕΡΓΑ ΣΟΥ ΚΕ
ΣΦΟΔΡΑ ΕΒΑΘΥΝΘΗ
ΣΑΝ ΟΙ ΔΙΑΛΟΓΙΣΜΟΙ
ΑΝΗΡ ΑΦΡΩΝ
ΟΥ ΓΝΩΣΕΤΑΙ ΚΑΙ
ΑΣΥΝΕΤΟΣ ΟΥ ΣΥΝΗ
ΣΕΙ ΤΑΥΤΑ
ΕΝ ΤΩ ΑΝΑΤΕΙΛΑΙ

Latin Psalter.

Mt. Sinai, Holy Monastery of St. Catherine, Latin New Finds 1, ff. 19v–20r.
Latin; parchment. Sinai or Christian Orient (displays Visigothic, Frankish, Insular, and Italian influences), tenth century.

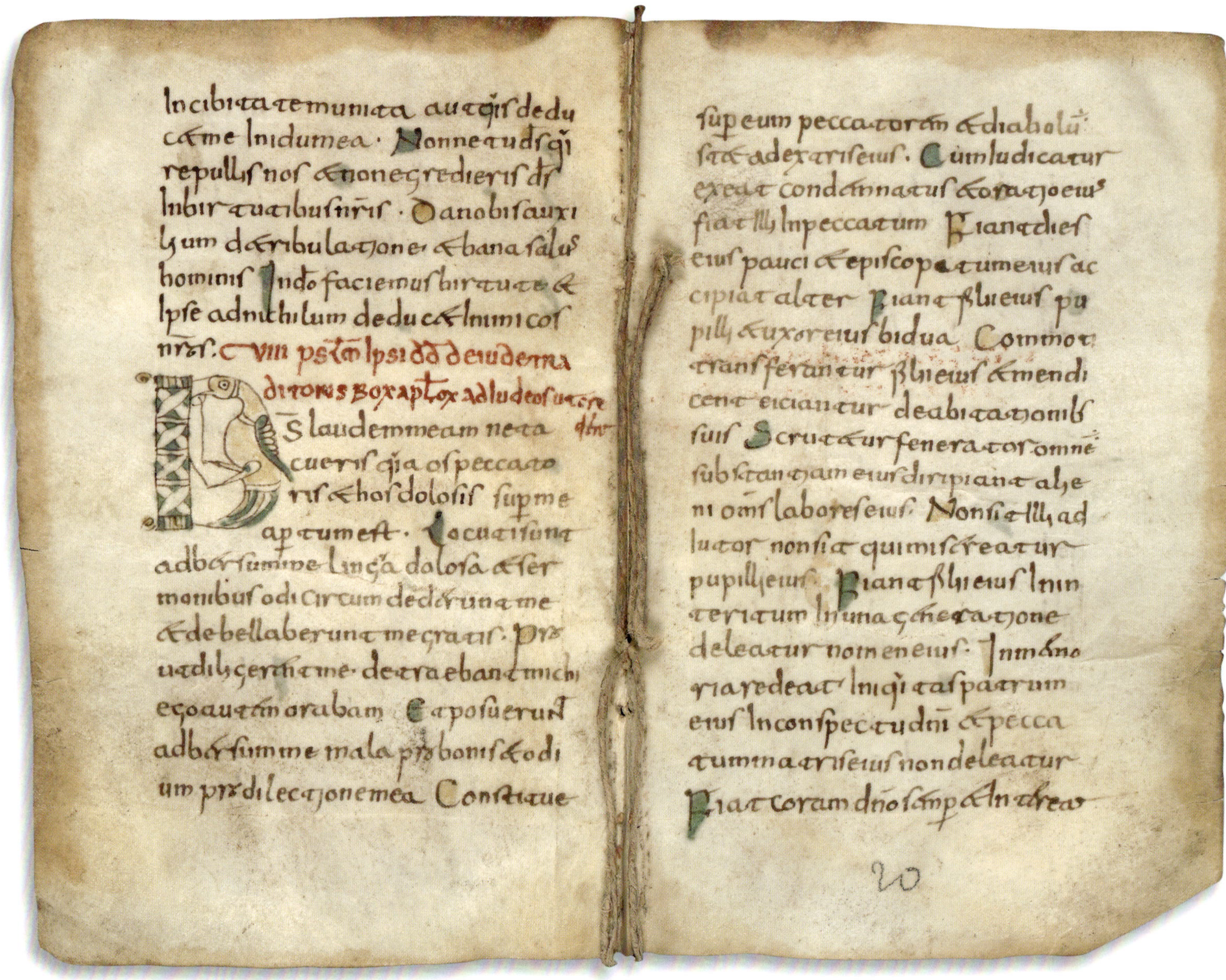

49

Glagolitic Euchologion.
Mt. Sinai, Holy Monastery of St. Catherine, Slavonic 37, ff. 85v–86r. Glagolitic; parchment. Macedonia or Croatia, eleventh century.

50

Georgian Gospelbook.
Mt. Sinai, Holy Monastery of St. Catherine, Georgian New Finds N. 12, ff. 107v–108r. Gospels. Georgian; parchment. Sinai, 1075.

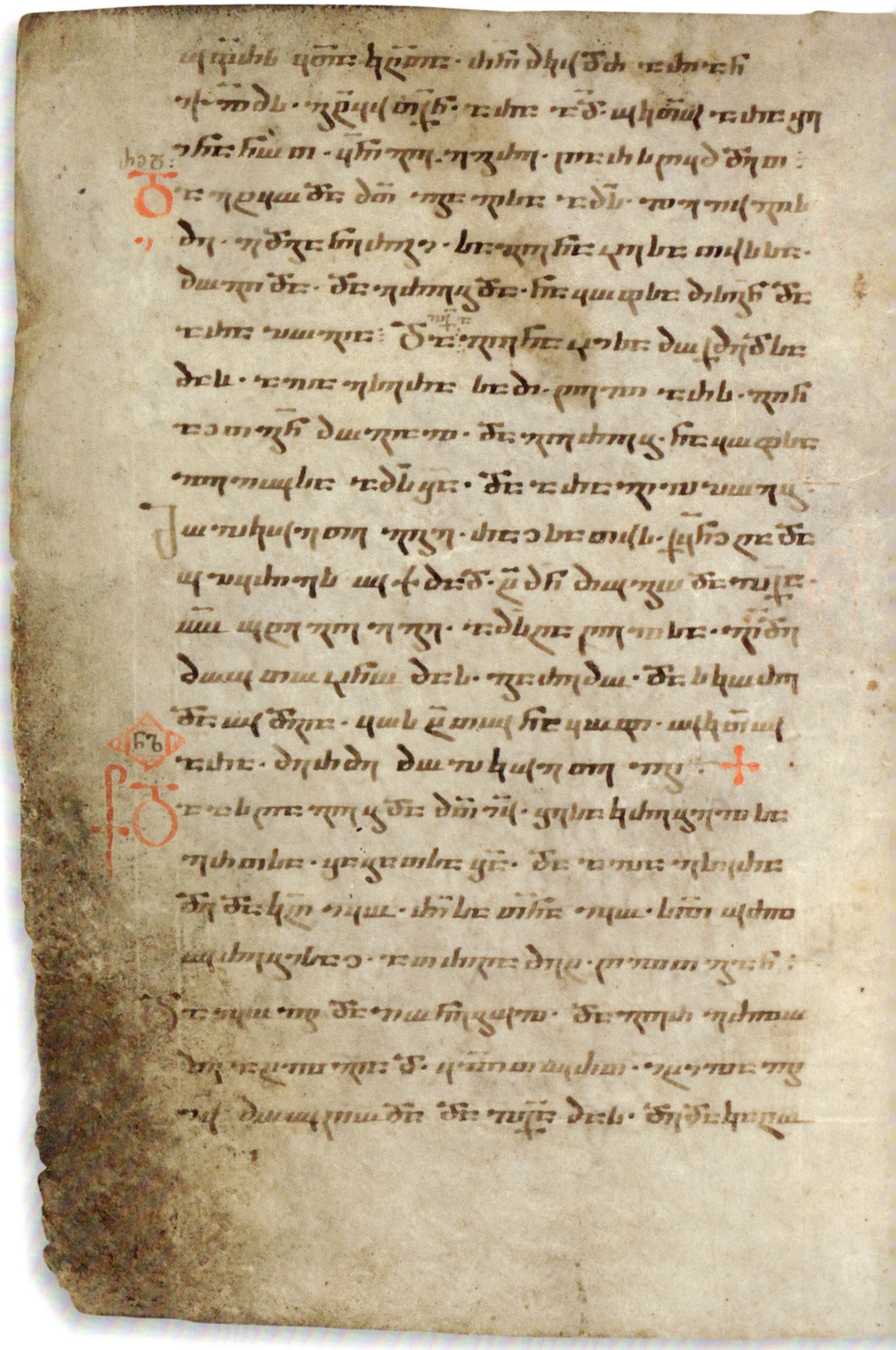

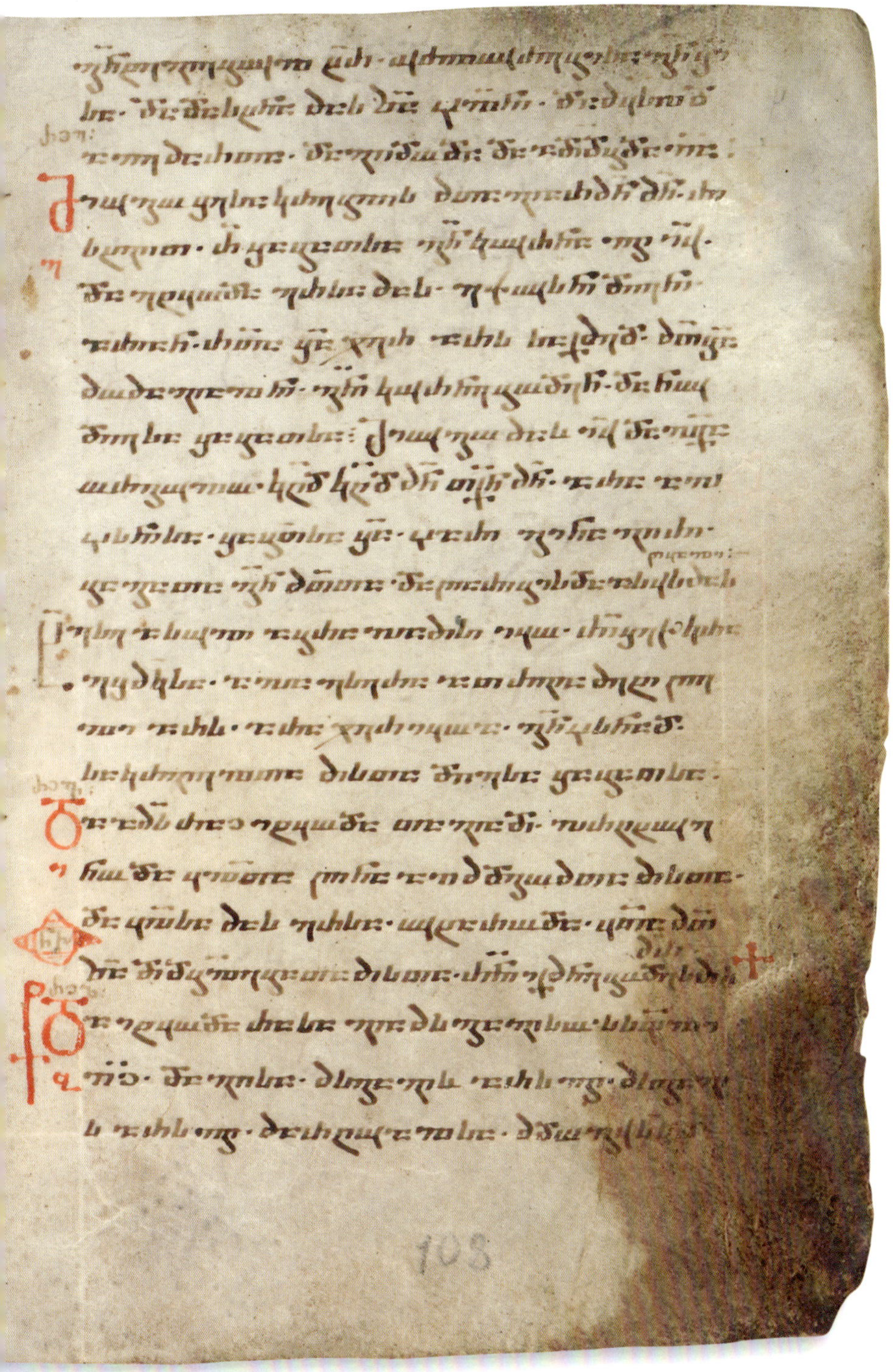

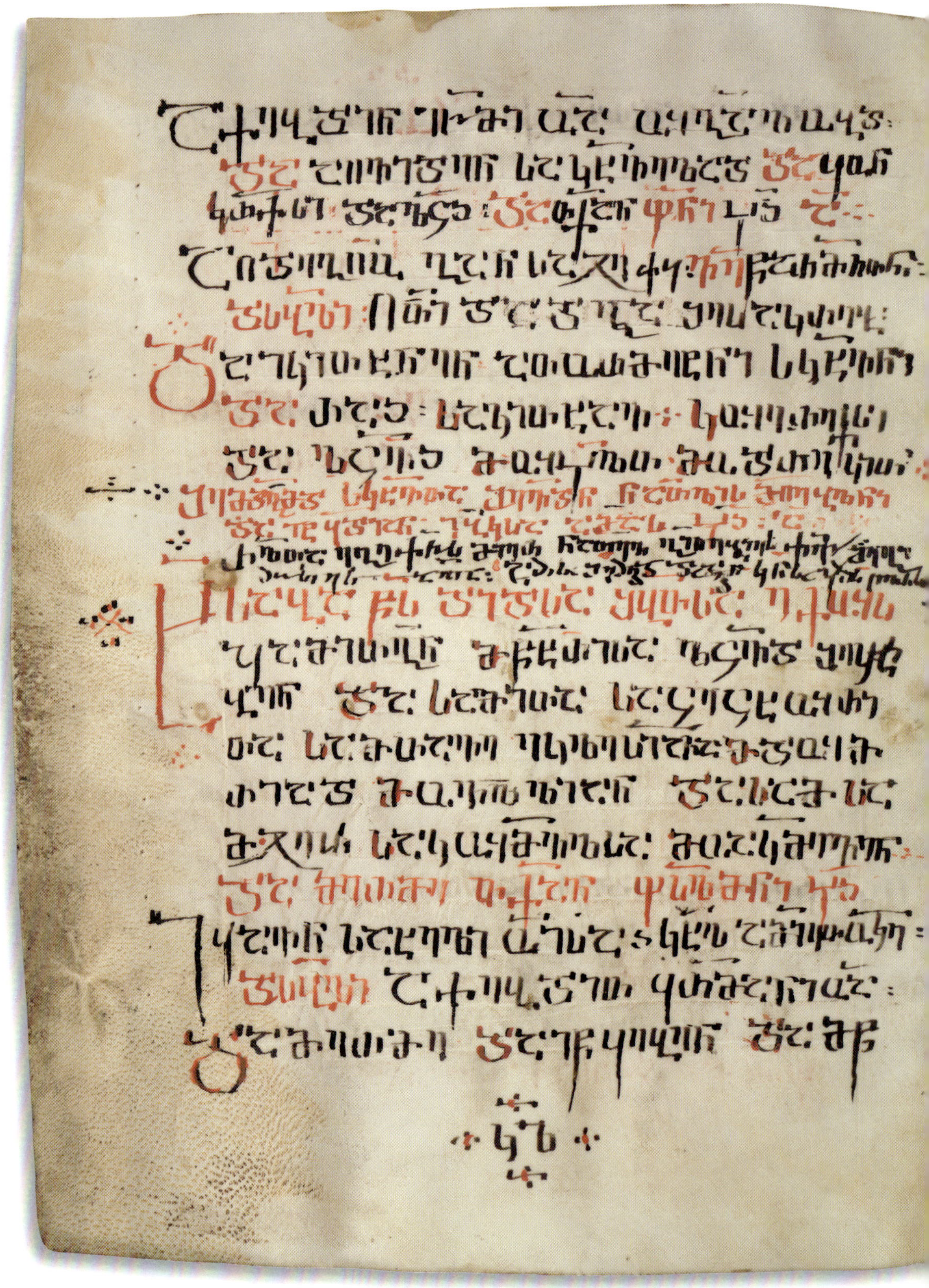

Georgian Lectionary.
Mt. Sinai, Holy Monastery of St. Catherine, Georgian 37, ff. 216v–217r. Georgian; parchment. Georgia or Sinai (?), tenth century.

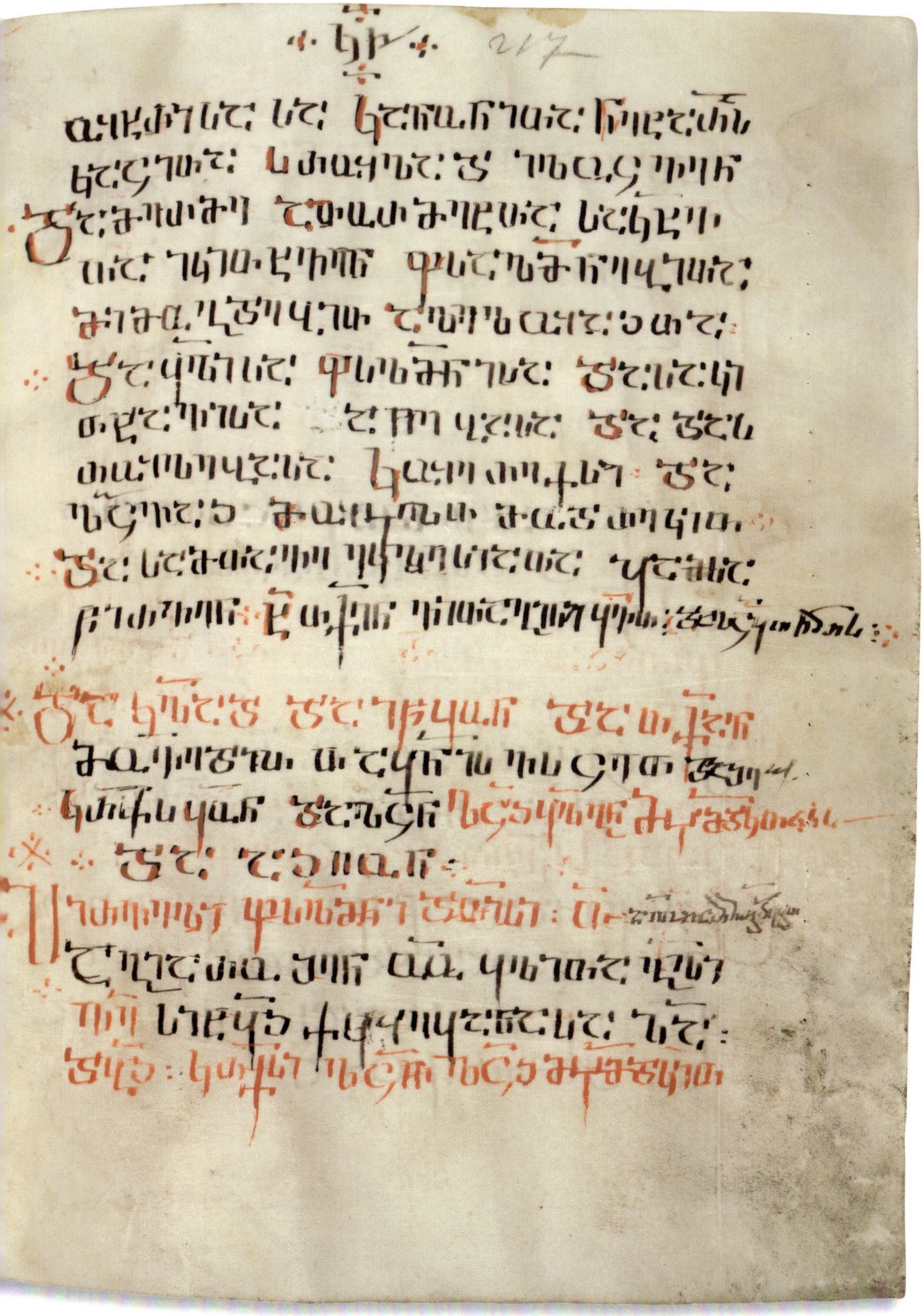

52

The Lectionary of Mount Horeb.
Mt. Sinai, Holy Monastery of St. Catherine, Greek 213, ff. 73v–74r. Greek; parchment. Near East Sinai (?), 967.

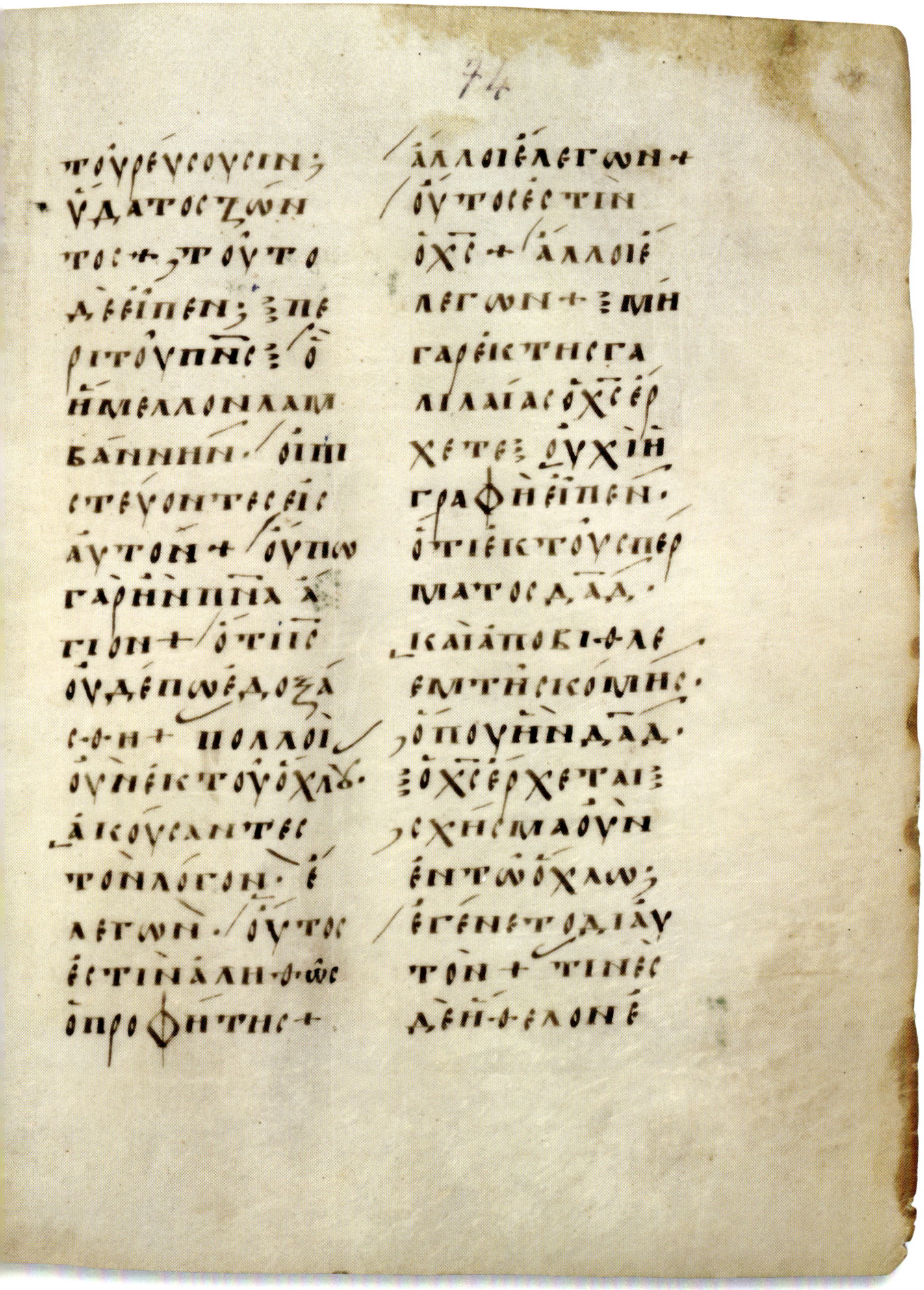
74

τουρευσουσιν·
υδατοσζων
τοσ· τουτο
δεειπεν· πε
ριτουπνσ· ο
ημελλονλαμ
βανειν· οιπι
στευοντεσεισ
αυτον· ουπω
γαρηνπνα α
γιον· οτιισ
ουδεπωεδοξα
σθη· πολλοι
ουνεκτουοχλου·
ακουσαντεσ
τονλογον· ε
λεγον· ουτοσ
εστιναληθωσ
οπροφητησ·

αλλοιελεγον·
ουτοσεστιν
οχσ· αλλοιε
λεγον· μη
γαρεκτησγα
λιλαιασοχσερ
χεται· ουχιη
γραφηειπεν·
οτιεκτουσπερ
ματοσδαδ·
καιαποβηθλεε
εκτησκωμησ·
οπουηνδαδ·
οχσερχεται·
σχισμαουν
εντωοχλω·
εγενετοδιαυ
τον· τινεσ
δεηθελονε

Spreading the Word:
Early Christian Britain and Ireland

BRITAIN FIRST RECEIVED CHRISTIANITY while part of the Roman Empire and in 314 was already sending bishops to Church councils across the Channel in Gaul. As the Empire contracted during the early fifth century England was increasingly settled by pagan immigrants from Germany and southern Scandinavia, who became known as the Anglo-Saxons. The Romano-British Church survived in southern Scotland, northwest England, Wales, and Cornwall but the conversion of the Anglo-Saxons only gained impetus with a mission sent from Rome by Pope Gregory the Great. This was led by Saint Augustine, who arrived in Kent in 597, accompanied by books from Italy and Gaul, of the sort represented by the Codex Oxoniensis (cat. no. 53). The English, as the Anglo-Saxons became known, were also evangelized by missionaries (notably Saint Columba and his followers) from Ireland, which had itself received Christianity during the fifth century. The monasteries they established, such as Iona and Lindisfarne, were influenced by the desert fathers of the East and introduced books exuberantly written and decorated in Celtic fashion (cat. no. 59). Along with English monks and nuns, who soon began making their own volumes, they blended elements from the Celtic, Germanic, and Mediterranean traditions with those from the Middle East, to form a distinctive cultural response known as "Insular" (a term applied to the culture of the islands of Britain and Ireland in the period ca. 550–850). English scribes produced striking copies of scripture such as the Cambridge–London Gospels (cat. no. 58), devised their own system of scripts and characteristic style of illumination, and followed the Irish example by introducing word-separation and systematic punctuation to clarify legibility.

Insular missionaries evangelized throughout Europe. During the 730s Saint Boniface, "Apostle to the Germans," wrote to his friend Abbess Eadburh of Minster-in-Thanet in Kent, asking her to supply copies of scripture for his mission. He also sent gold to be used in illumination to impress his potential converts, for making a visual impact could mean the difference between life and death. Notes probably written by Boniface and Eadburh survive in books owned by them, such as Boniface's copy of Primasius's *Commentary on the Apocalypse* (cat. no. 55).

The English and Irish fostered learning in Latin and in their own languages, which they used freely to share the "Good News" (in Old English, *godspell*). One of the greatest advocates of the use of the vernacular was the scholar Bede, a monk at the twin monasteries of Wearmouth–Jarrow in northeast England. Bede admired the generosity of the Jews in sharing their scriptures with the gentiles and encouraged the use of the English language to bring Christianity to others: on his deathbed in 735 he was translating Saint John's Gospel. Soon after his death the Wearmouth–Jarrow scriptoria published copies of his works, including his *Ecclesiastical History of the English People*, his scientific works on the nature of time, and his biblical commentaries (cat. no. 56) to satisfy domestic and foreign demand.

By the mid-tenth century gospelbooks were being translated into English by means of glosses written between the lines of the Latin texts in the Lindisfarne Gospels and the Macregol Gospels (cat. no. 59). And by the year 1000 parts of the Bible were being paraphrased in the vernacular alongside extensive cycles of illustration, as in the Junius Manuscript (cat. no. 61)—word and image working in harmony to expound the meaning of scripture.

Detail: The Old English Genesis, see cat. no 61.

53

Gospelbook (Codex Oxoniensis).
Oxford, Bodleian Library, MS. Auct. D. 2. 14, ff. 129v–130r.
Latin; parchment. Italy, sixth–seventh century.

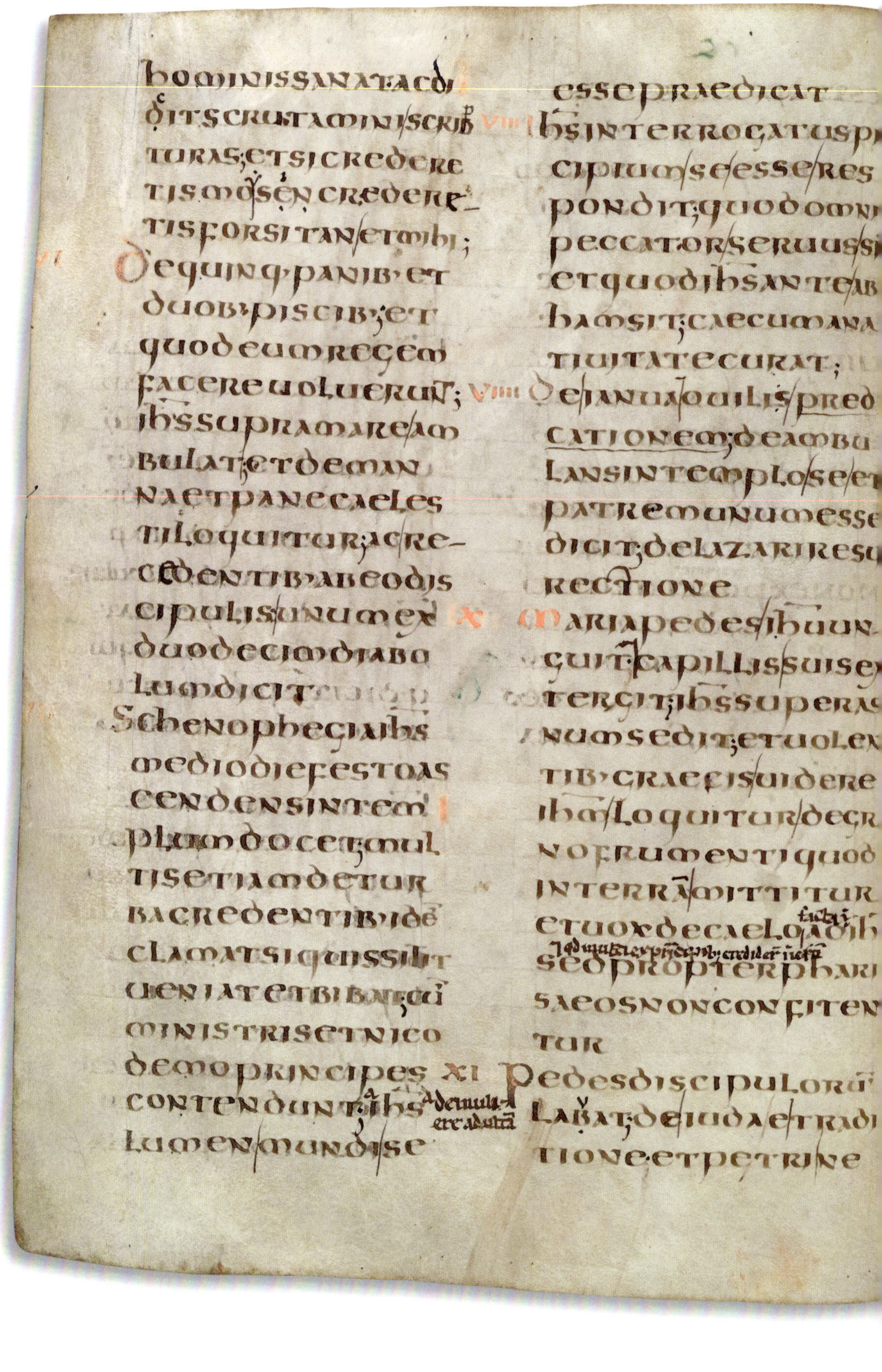

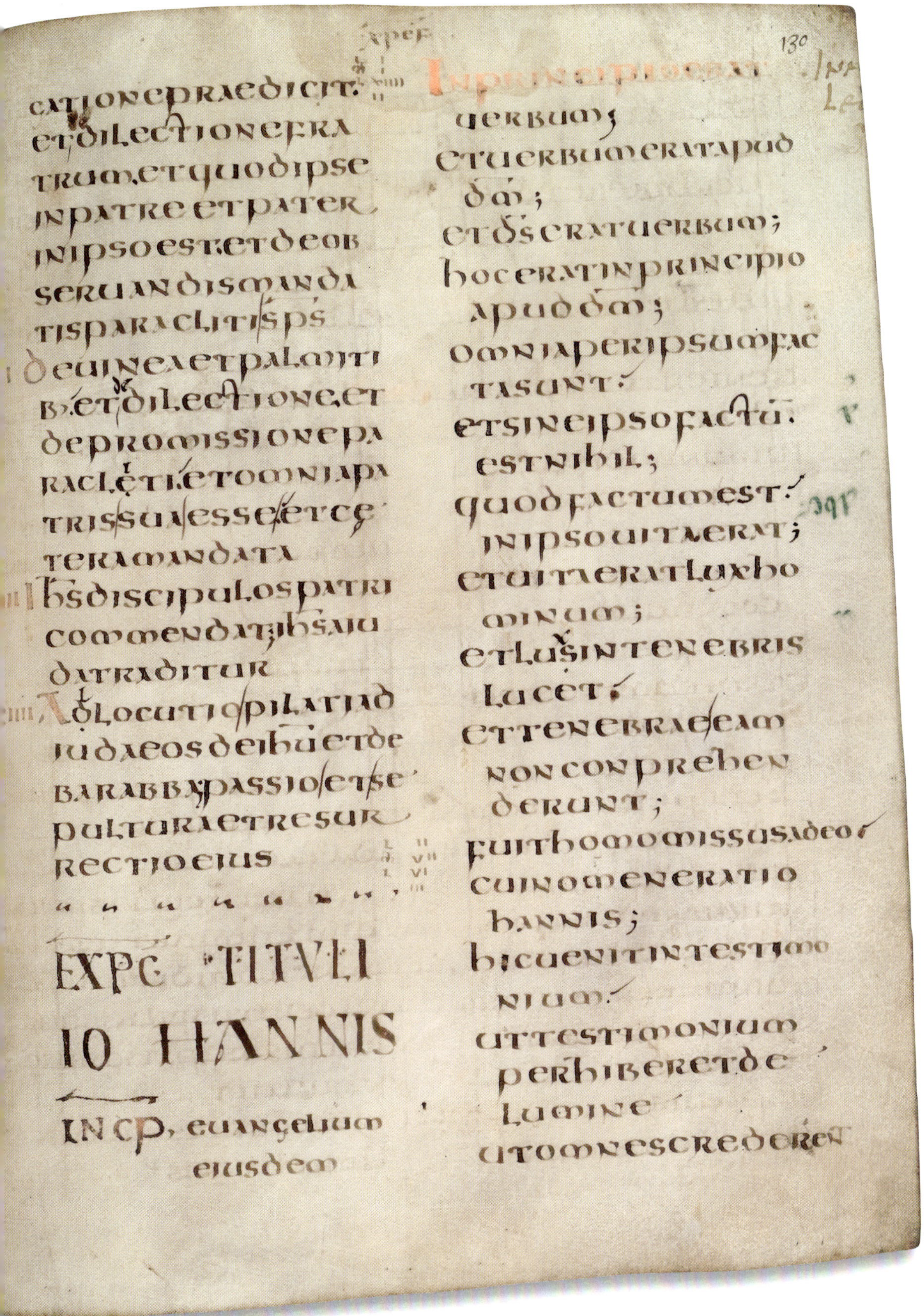
cationepraedicit.
etdilectionefra
trum.etquodipse
inpatreetpater
inipsoest.etdeob
seruandismanda
tisparaclitisps
deuineaetpalmiti
b.etdilectione.et
depromissionepa
racleti.etomniapa
trissuaesse.etce
teramandata
ihsdiscipulospatri
commendat.ihsaiu
datraditur
Adlocutiopilatiad
iudaeosdeihuetde
barabbapassioetse
pulturaetresur
rectioeius
EXPL TITULI
IOHANNIS
INCP. euangelium
eiusdem
Inprincipioerat
uerbum;
etuerbumeratapud
dm;
etdseratuerbum;
hoceratinprincipio
apuddm;
omniaperipsumfac
tasunt.
etsineipsofactum
estnihil;
quodfactumest.
inipsouitaerat;
etuitaeratluxho
minum;
etluxintenebris
lucet.
ettenebraeeam
nonconprehen
derunt;
fuithomomissusadeo
cuinomeneratio
hannis;
hicuenitintestimo
nium.
uttestimonium
perhiberetde
lumine
utomnescrederent

The Selden Acts of the Apostles.
Oxford, Bodleian Library, MS. Selden Supra 30, pp. 46–47. With lightly scratched inscription "EADB" (right), perhaps inscribed by Abbess Eadburh of Minster-in-Thanet in the early eighth century. Latin; parchment. Minster-in-Thanet, Kent (?), southern England, first half of the eighth century.

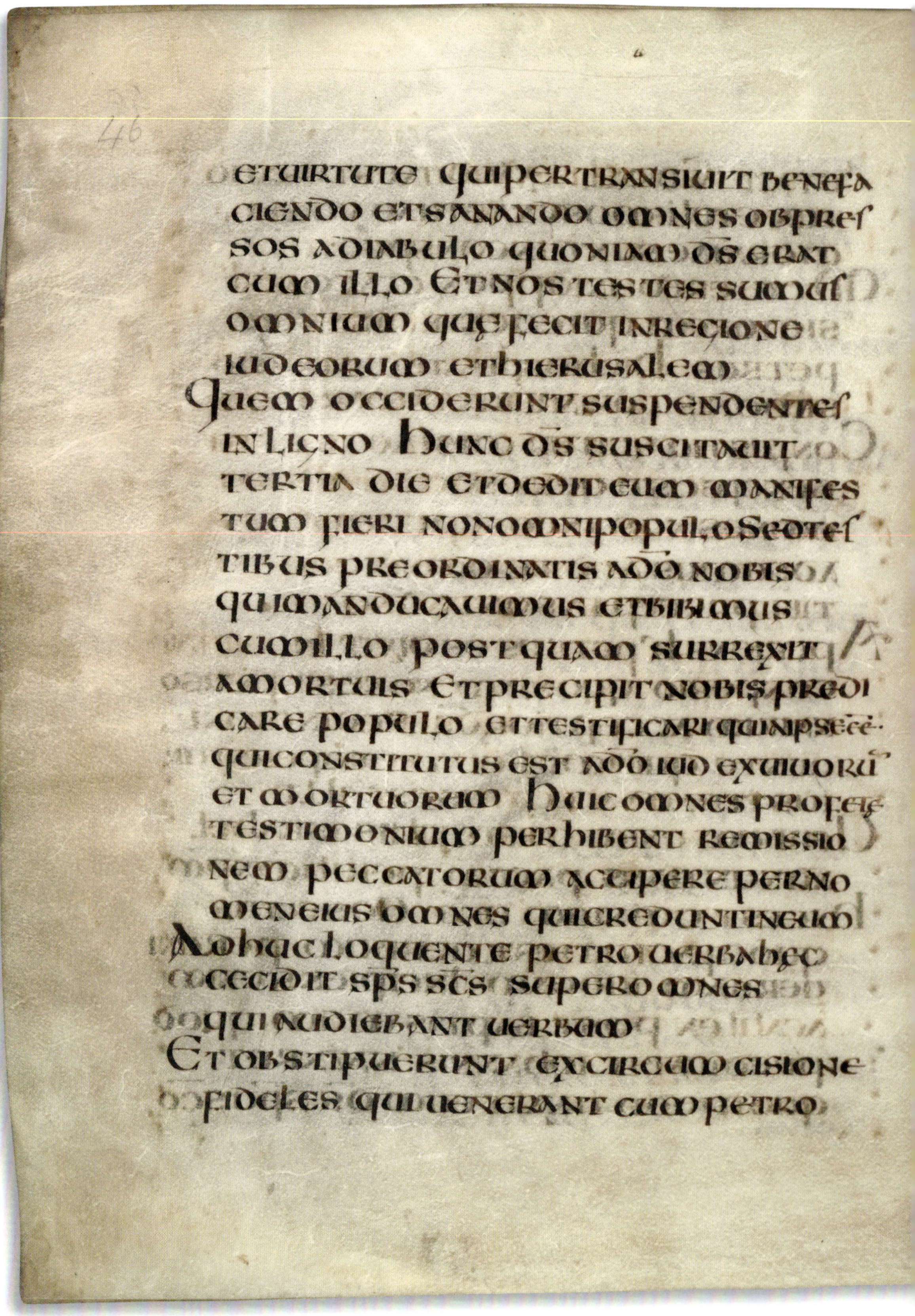

46

etuirtute quipertransiuit benefa
ciendo etsanando omnes obpres
sos adiabulo quoniam ds erat
cum illo Etnos testes sumus
omnium quaefecit inregione
iudeorum ethierusalem
Quem occiderunt suspendentes
in ligno Hunc ds suscitauit
tertia die etdedit eum manifes
tum fieri nonomnipopulo Sedtes
tibus preordinatis ado nobis
quimanducauimus etbibimus
cumillo postquam surrexit
amortuis Etprecipit nobis predi
care populo ettestificari quiaipse ē
quiconstitutus est ado iud exuiuorū
et mortuorum Huic omnes profete
testimonium perhibent remissio
nem peccatorum accipere perno
meneius omnes quicreduntineum
Adhuc loquente petro uerbahec
cecidit sps scs superomnes
qui audiebant uerbum
Et obstipuerunt excircumcisione
fideles quiuenerant cumpetro

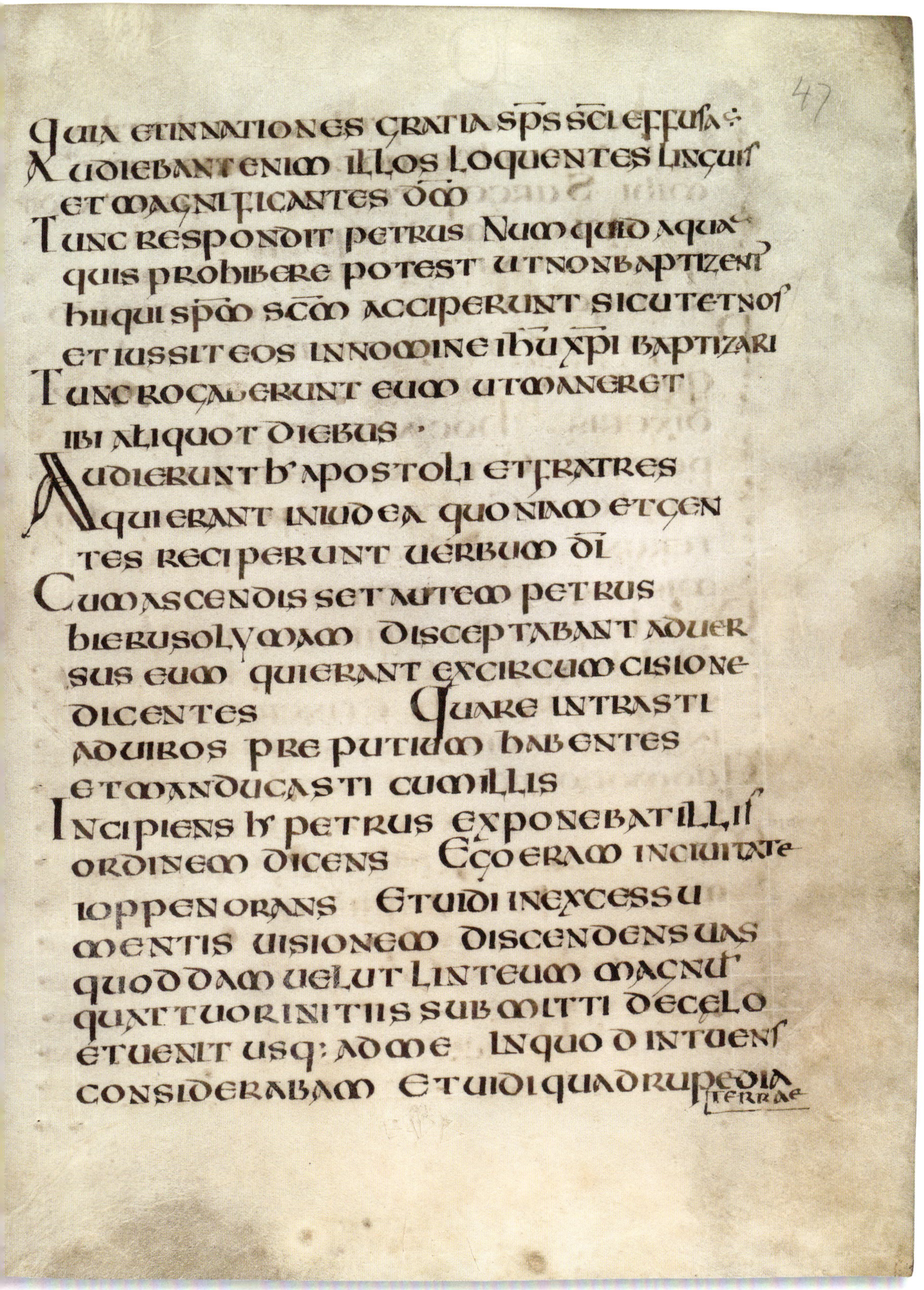
47
QUIA ETINNATIONES GRATIA SPS SCI EFFUSA ÷
AUDIEBANT ENIM ILLOS LOQUENTES LINGUIS
ET MAGNIFICANTES DM
TUNC RESPONDIT PETRUS NUMQUID AQUAM
QUIS PROHIBERE POTEST UTNONBAPTIZENT
HIQUI SPM SCM ACCIPERUNT SICUTETNOS
ET IUSSIT EOS INNOMINE IHU XPI BAPTIZARI
TUNC ROGAUERUNT EUM UTMANERET
IBI ALIQUOT DIEBUS
AUDIERUNT H' APOSTOLI ETFRATRES
QUI ERANT INIUDEA QUONIAM ETGEN
TES RECIPERUNT UERBUM DI
CUM ASCENDISSET AUTEM PETRUS
HIERUSOLYMAM DISCEPTABANT ADUER
SUS EUM QUIERANT EXCIRCUMCISIONE
DICENTES QUARE INTRASTI
ADUIROS PREPUTIUM HABENTES
ETMANDUCASTI CUMILLIS
INCIPIENS H' PETRUS EXPONEBAT ILLIS
ORDINEM DICENS EGO ERAM INCIUITATE
IOPPEN ORANS ETUIDI INEXCESSU
MENTIS UISIONEM DISCENDENS UAS
QUODDAM UELUT LINTEUM MAGNU
QUATTUOR INITIIS SUBMITTI DECELO
ETUENIT USQ: ADME INQUO D INTUENS
CONSIDERABAM ETUIDI QUADRUPEDIA
TERRAE

55

The Douce Primasius.
Oxford, Bodleian Library, MS. Douce 140, ff. 3v–4r. With marginal glosses added by St. Boniface (top right). Latin; parchment. Southern England (?), late seventh–early eighth century (before 718?).

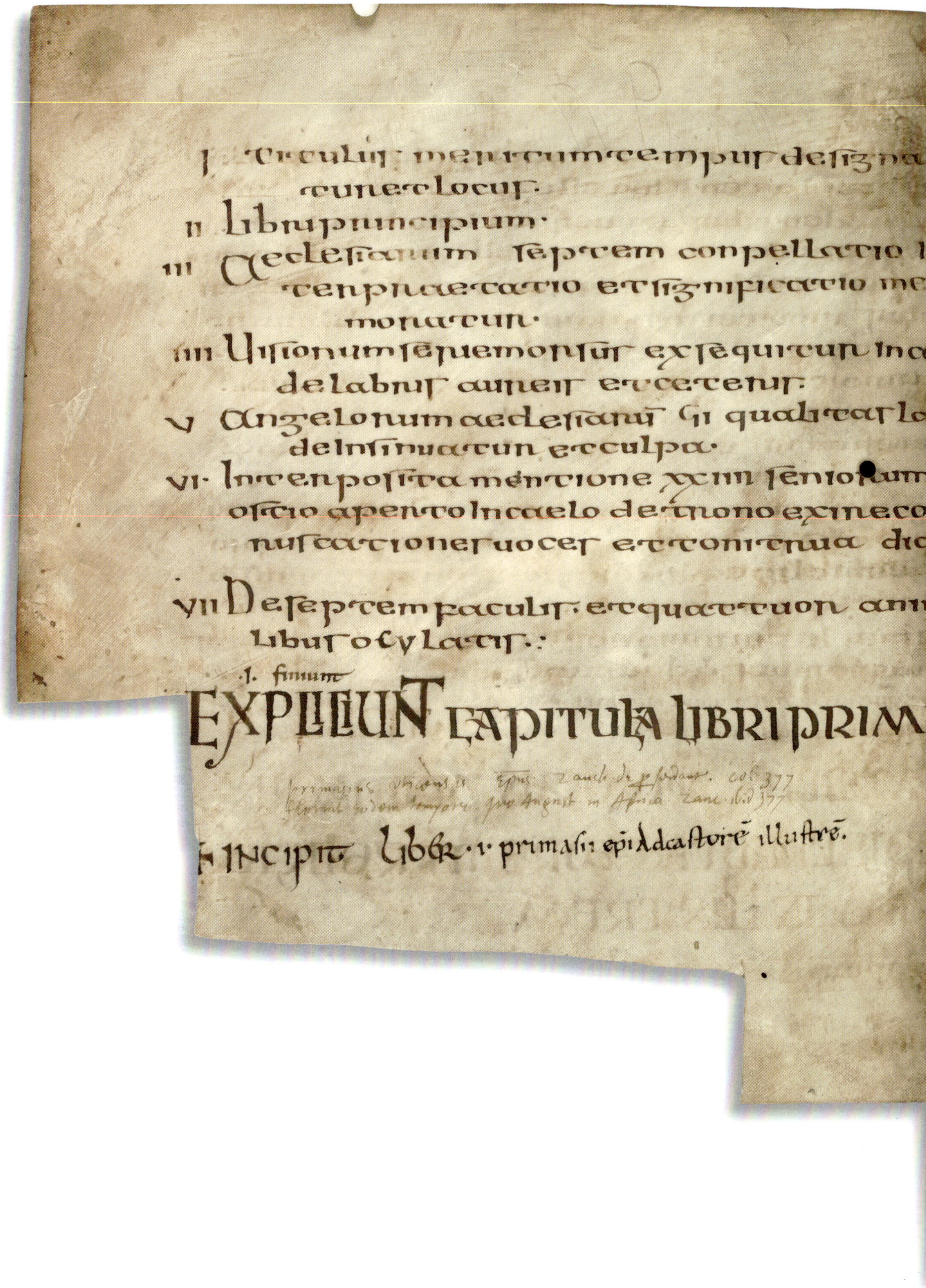

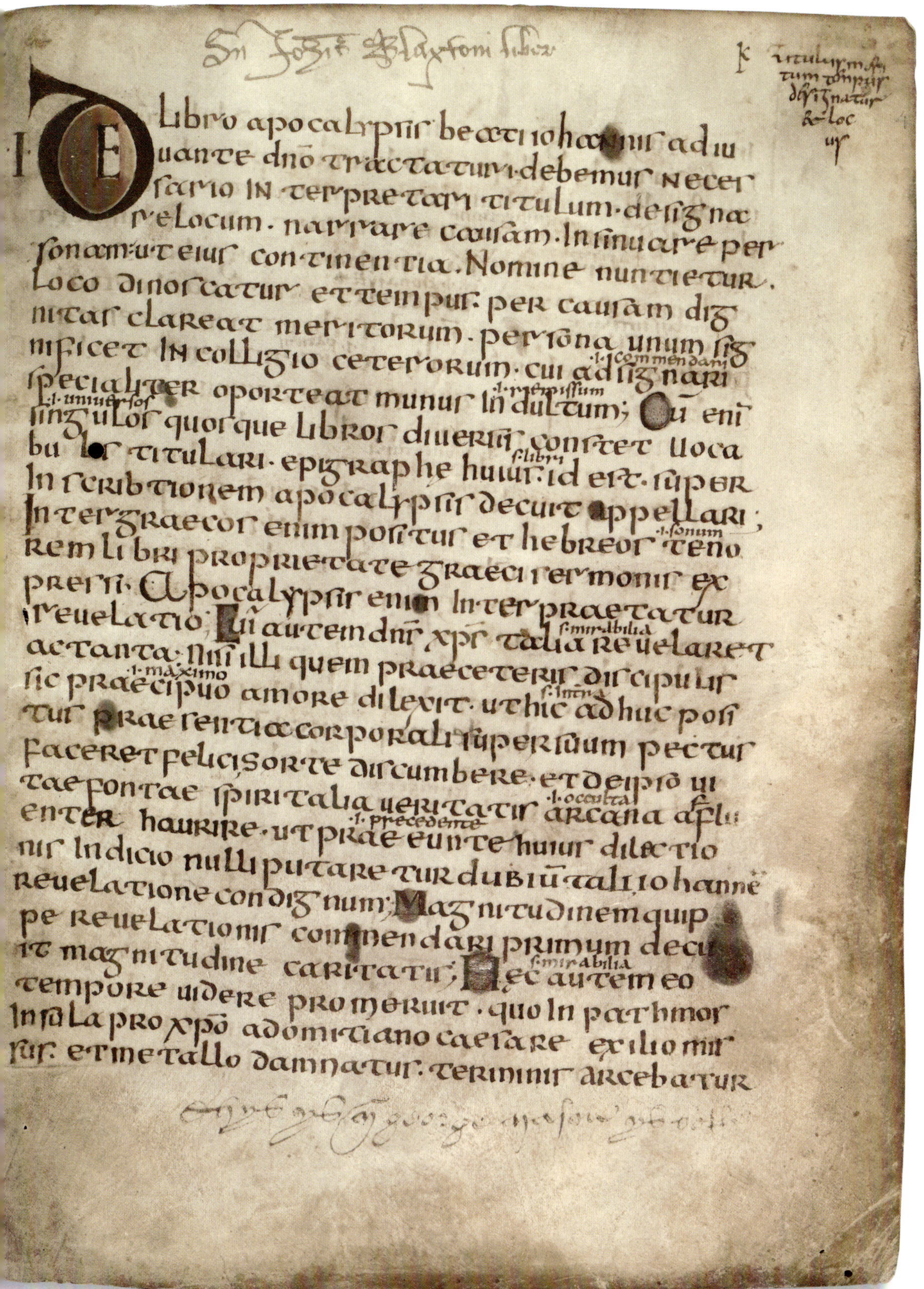
De libro apocalypsis beati iohannis adiu
uante dno tractaturi debemus neces
sario interpretatum titulum designa
re locum . narrare causam . insinuare per
sonam : ut eius continentia . Nomine nuntietur .
loco dinoscatur et tempus : per causam dig
nitas clareat meritorum . persona unum sig
nificet in collegio ceterorum . cui adsignari
specialiter oporteat munus indultum ; Qu eni
singulos quosque libros diuersis constet uoca
bu lis titulari . epigraphe huius : id est . super
inscribtionem apocalypsis decuit appellari ;
Inter graecos enim positus et hebreos teno
rem libri proprietate graeci sermonis ex
pressit . Apocalypsis enim interpraetatur
reuelatio ; Cui autem dns xps talia reuelaret
ac tanta : nisi illi quem praeceteris discipulis
sic praecipuo amore dilexit . ut hic adhuc posi
tus praesentiae corporali super suum pectus
faceret felici sorte discumbere . et de ipso ui
tae fonte spiritalia ueritatis arcana aflu
enter haurire . ut praeeunte huius dilectio
nis indicio nulli putaretur dubium tali iohanne
reuelatione condignum ; Magnitudinem quip
pe reuelationis commendari primum decu
it magnitudine caritatis ; Hec autem eo
tempore uidere promeruit . quo in pathmos
insula pro xpo adomitiano caesare exilio mis
sus . et metallo damnatus . terminis arcebatur

56

Bede's *Commentary on Proverbs.*

Oxford, Bodleian Library, MS. Bodl 819, ff. 28v–29r. Latin; parchment. Wearmouth–Jarrow, second half of the eighth century.

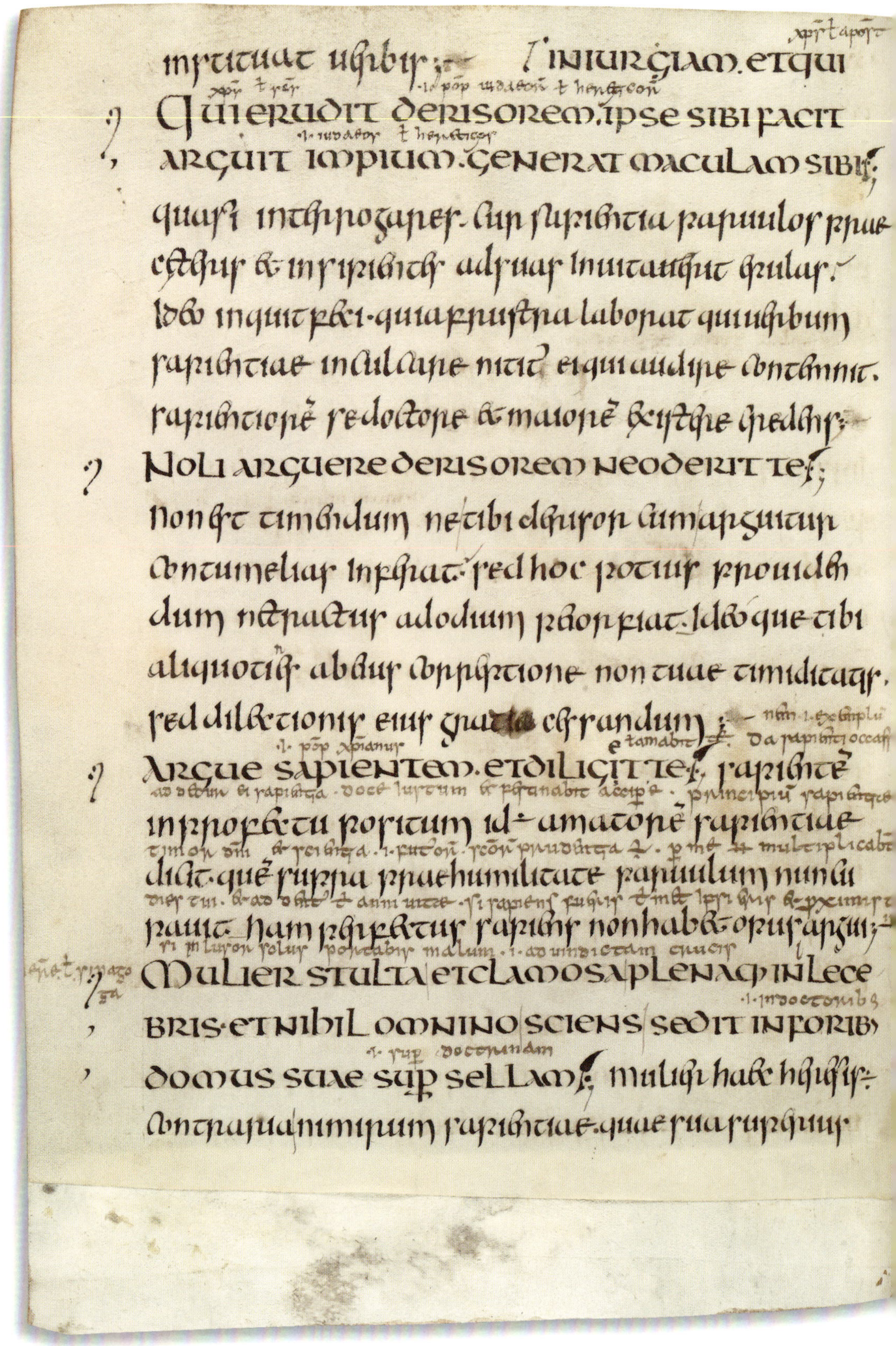

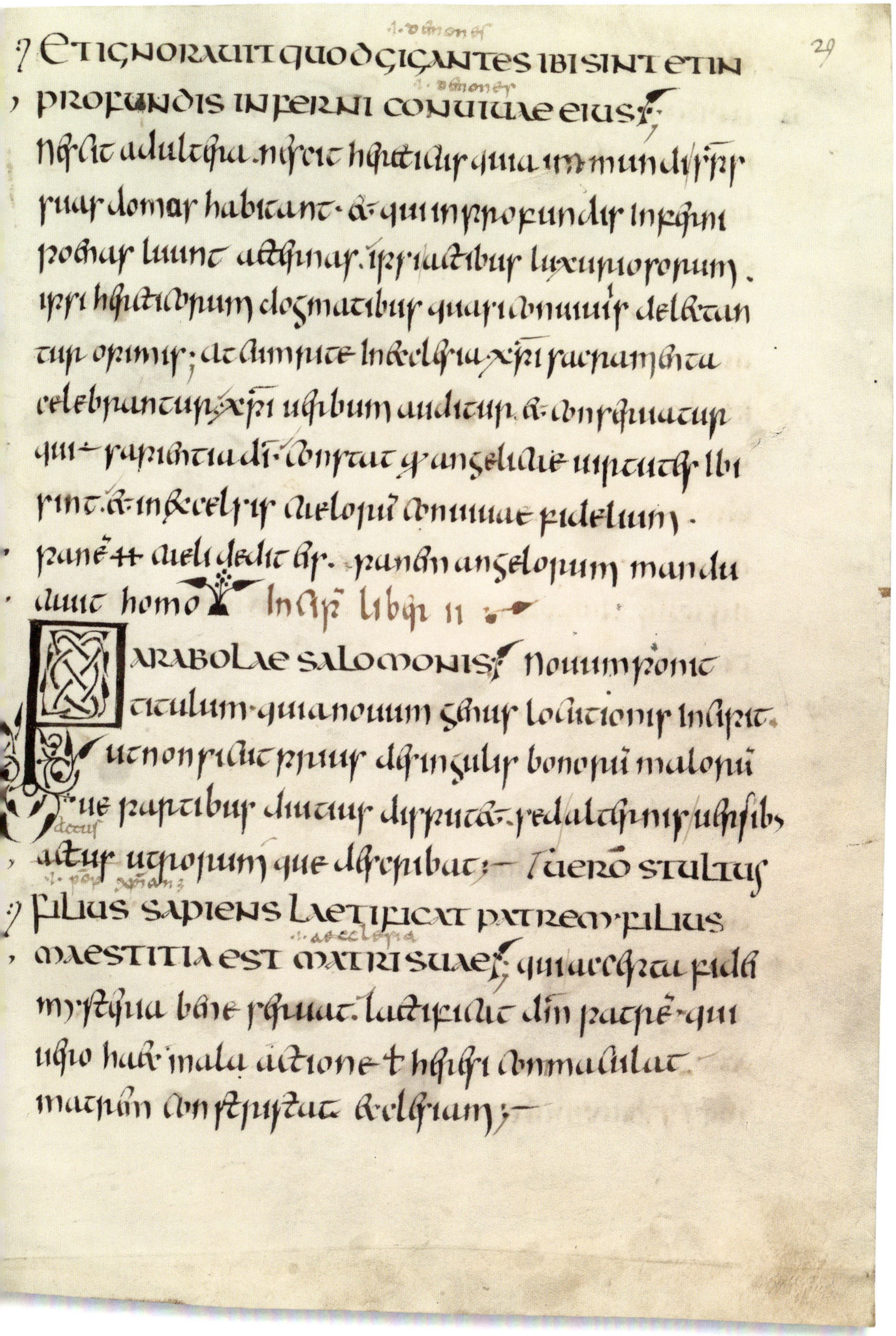
ET IGNORAUIT QUOD GIGANTES IBI SINT ET IN
PROFUNDIS INFERNI CONUIUAE EIUS
nescit adulter͂a. nescit hereticus quia inmundis sp͂r
ituas domos habitant. & qui inprofundis inferni
pocdas biuunt aeternas. ipsi lactibus luxuriosorum.
ipsi hereticorum dogmatibus quasi cōnuiuis delectan
tur opimis; At cumputet Inecclesia xp͂i sacramenta
celebrantur, xp͂i uerbum auditur. & confirmatur
qui sapientia d͂i. Constat q͂ angelicae uirtutes ibi
sint. & inecclesis caelorum conuiuae fidelium.
pane͂ tt͂ caeli dedit his. panem angelorum mandu
cauit homo✿ Incp͂t libr͂ II

PARABOLAE SALOMONIS Nouumpone
titulum. quianouum gn͂us locutionis Insipit.
utnonfiat prius dsingulis bonorum malorum
ue partibus diuturs disputa. sedalterius uersib;
altus ut rorum que describat;— Filius stultus
FILIUS SAPIENS LAETIFICAT PATREM, FILIUS
MAESTITIA EST MATRI SUAE; qui accepta fidei
mysteria bene seruat. laetificat d͂m patrem. qui
uero haec mala actione t heresi conmaculat.
matrem consistate͂ aecclesiam;—

57

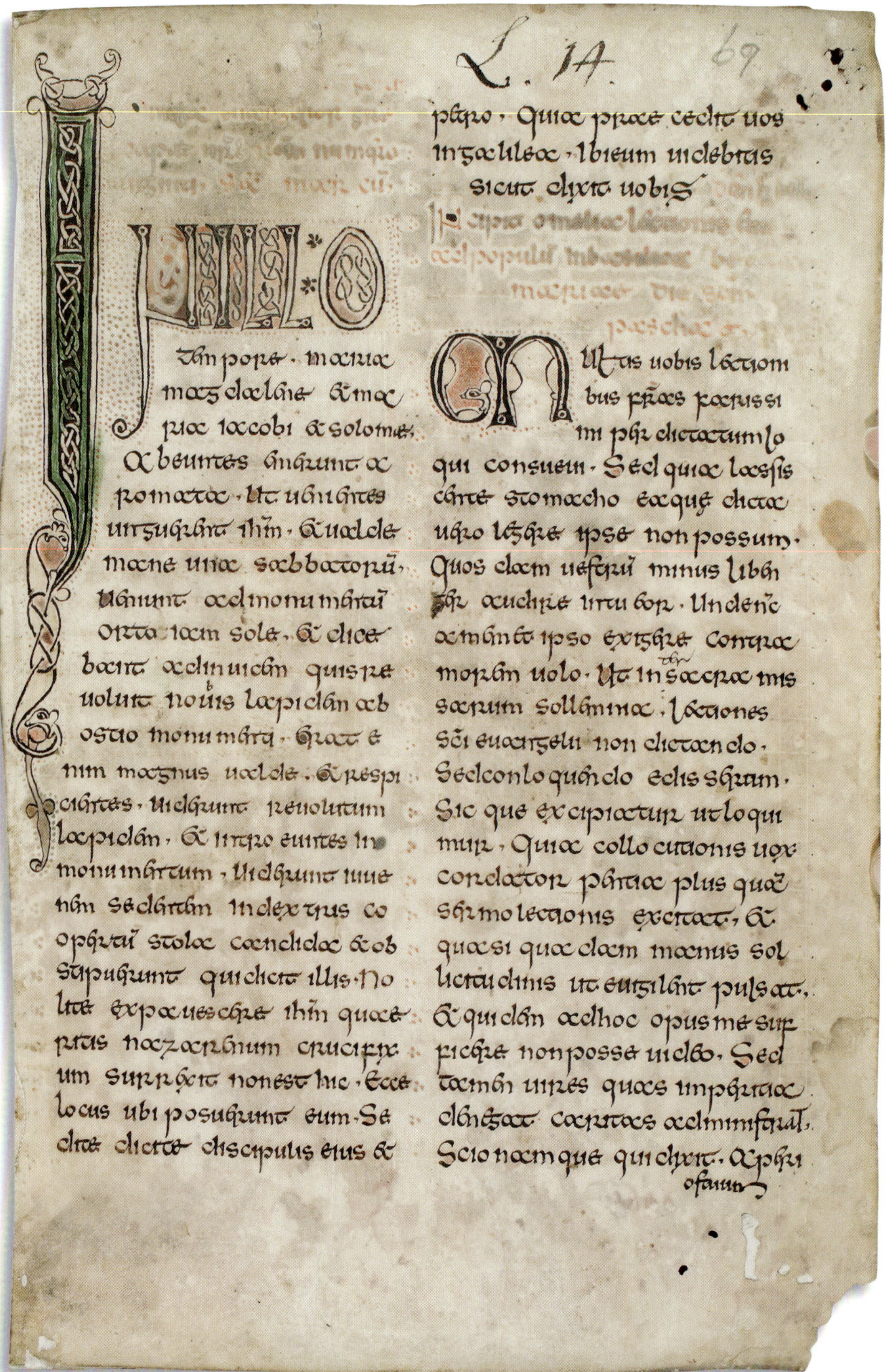

Pope Gregory the Great's Commentary on the Gospels.
Cambridge, Corpus Christi College, MS. 69, f. 1r. Latin; parchment. Kent, southeast England, late eighth–early ninth century.

Gospels.
Cambridge, Corpus Christi College, MS. 197b, f. 1r. Latin; parchment. Northumbria, northeast England, ca. 725–50.

59

The Macregol (Rushworth) Gospels.
Oxford, Bodleian Library, MS. Auct. D. 2. 19, ff. 51v–52r. Evangelist miniature and opening page (incipit) of St. Mark's Gospel. Latin with Old English interlinear gloss added in England in the second half of the tenth century; parchment. Birr, Ireland, late eighth or early ninth century.

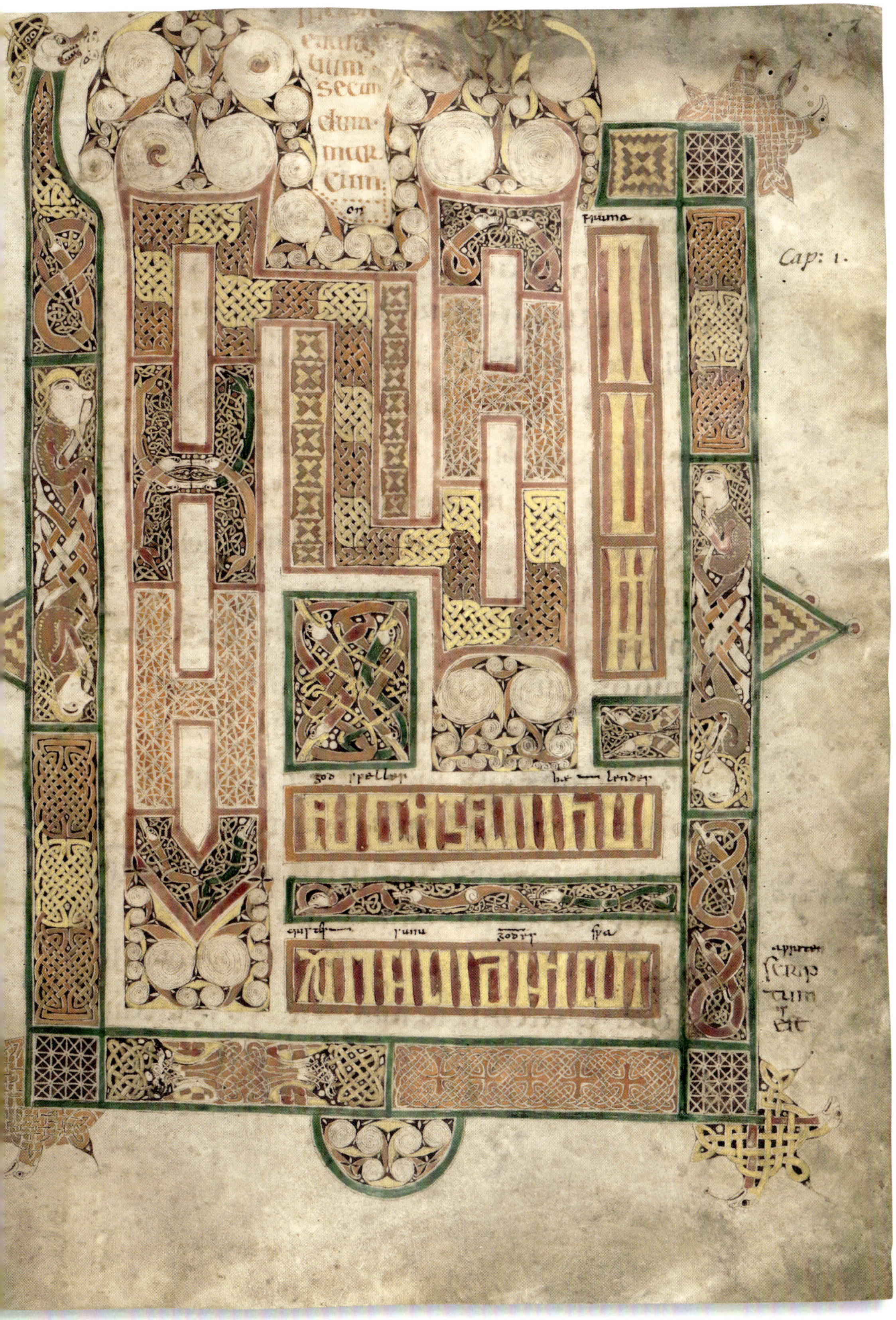
Cap: 1.

The Rawlinson Gospels.
Oxford, Bodleian Library,
MS. Rawl. G. 167, ff. 60v–61r.
Easter Sunday narrative at the end of St. Luke's Gospel. Latin; parchment. Ireland, second half of the eighth century.

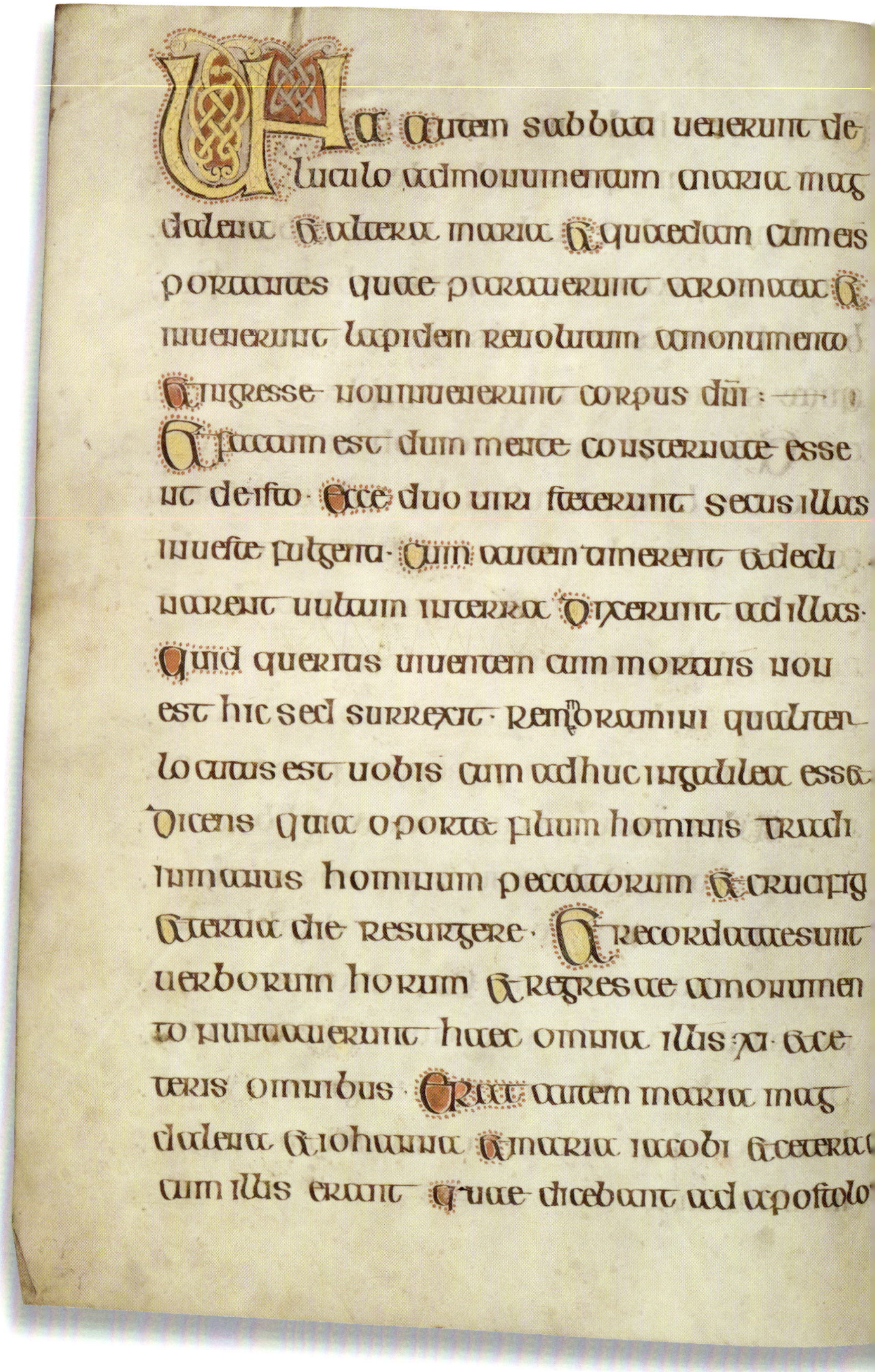

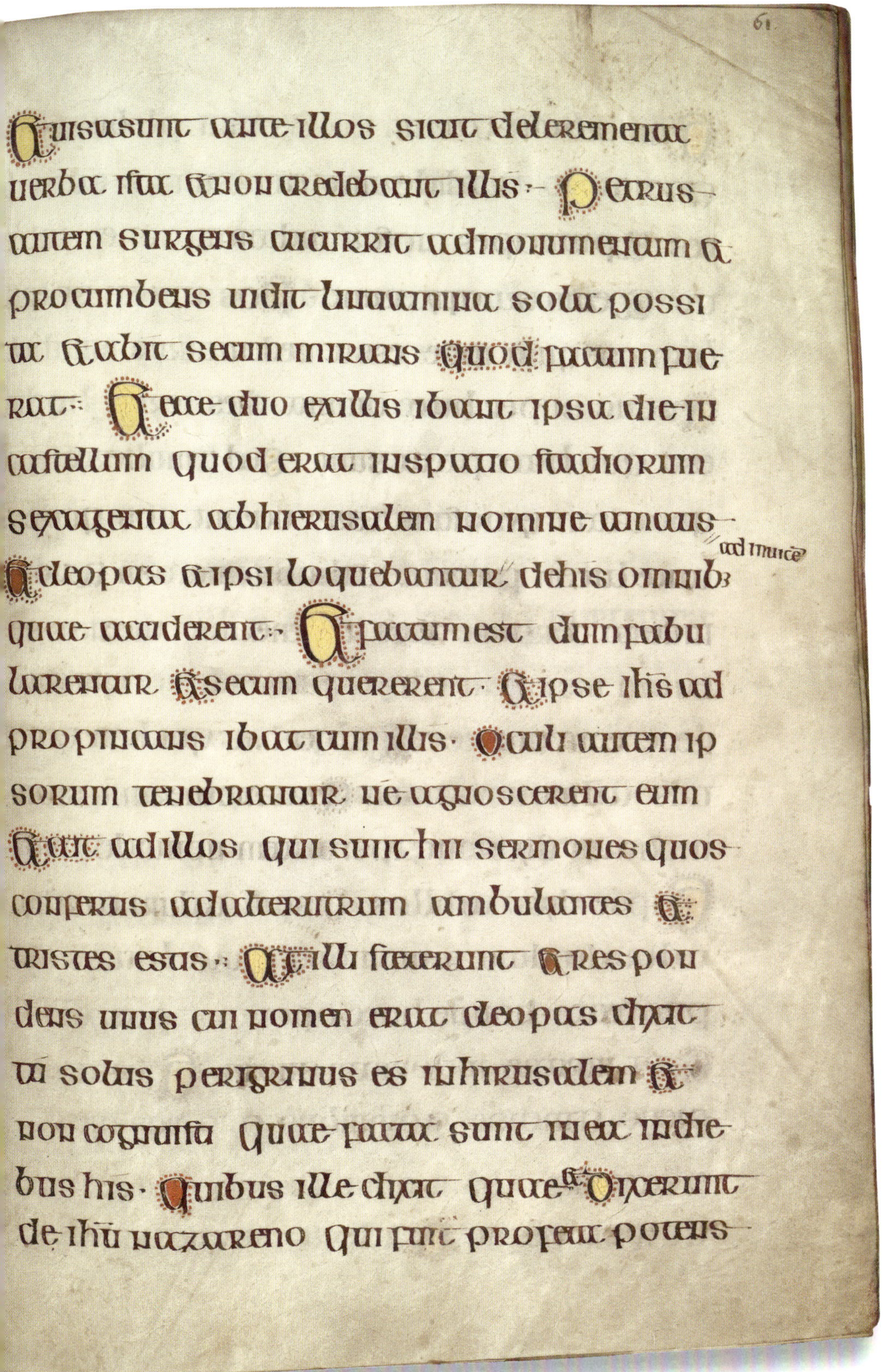
61
Et uisa sunt ante illos sicut deleramenta
uerba ista et non credebant illis. Petrus
autem surgens cucurrit ad monumentum et
procumbens uidit linteamina sola possi
ta et abiit secum mirans quod factum fue
rat. Et ecce duo ex illis ibant ipsa die in
castellum quod erat in spatio stadiorum
sexaginta ab hierusalem nomine emmaus
Cleopas et ipsi loquebantur de his omnib(us) ad inuicem
quae acciderant. Et factum est dum fabu
larentur et secum quaererent et ipse ihs ad
propinquans ibat cum illis. Oculi autem ip
sorum tenebrantur ne agnoscerent eum
Et ait ad illos qui sunt hii sermones quos
confertis ad alterutrum ambulantes et
tristes estis. Et illi steterunt et respon
dens unus cui nomen erat cleopas dixit
tu solus peregrinus es in hierusalem et
non cognouisti quae facta sunt in ea in die
bus his. Quibus ille dixit quae. Et dixerunt
de ihu nazareno qui fuit profeta potens

The Old English Genesis (*alias* The Junius Manuscript *or* The Caedmon Manuscript).
Oxford, Bodleian Library, MS. Junius 11, pp. 86–87.
Abraham builds an altar; Abraham makes an offering; the Lord appears to Abraham.
Old English; parchment.
England (Canterbury ?), ca. 1000.

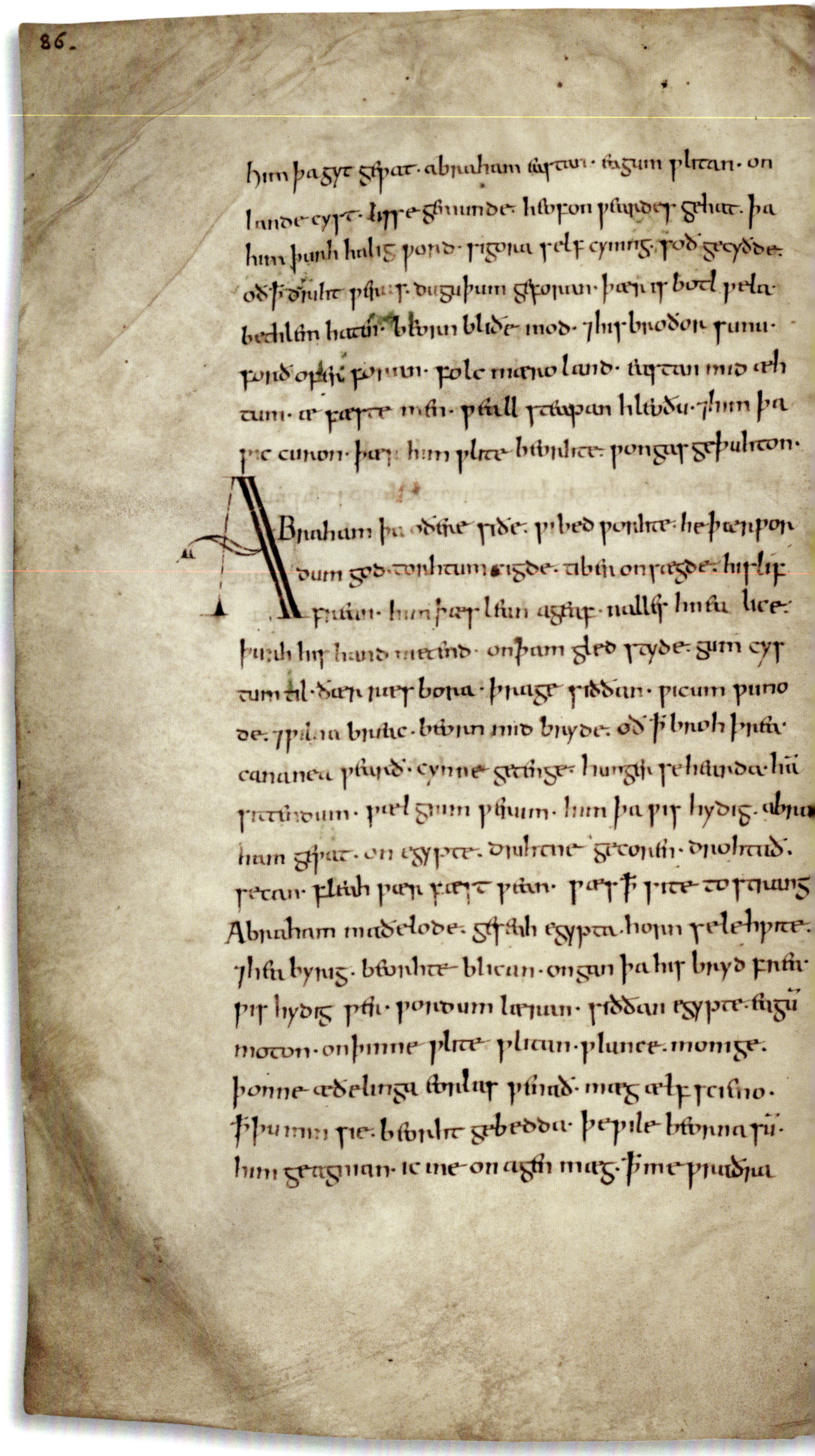

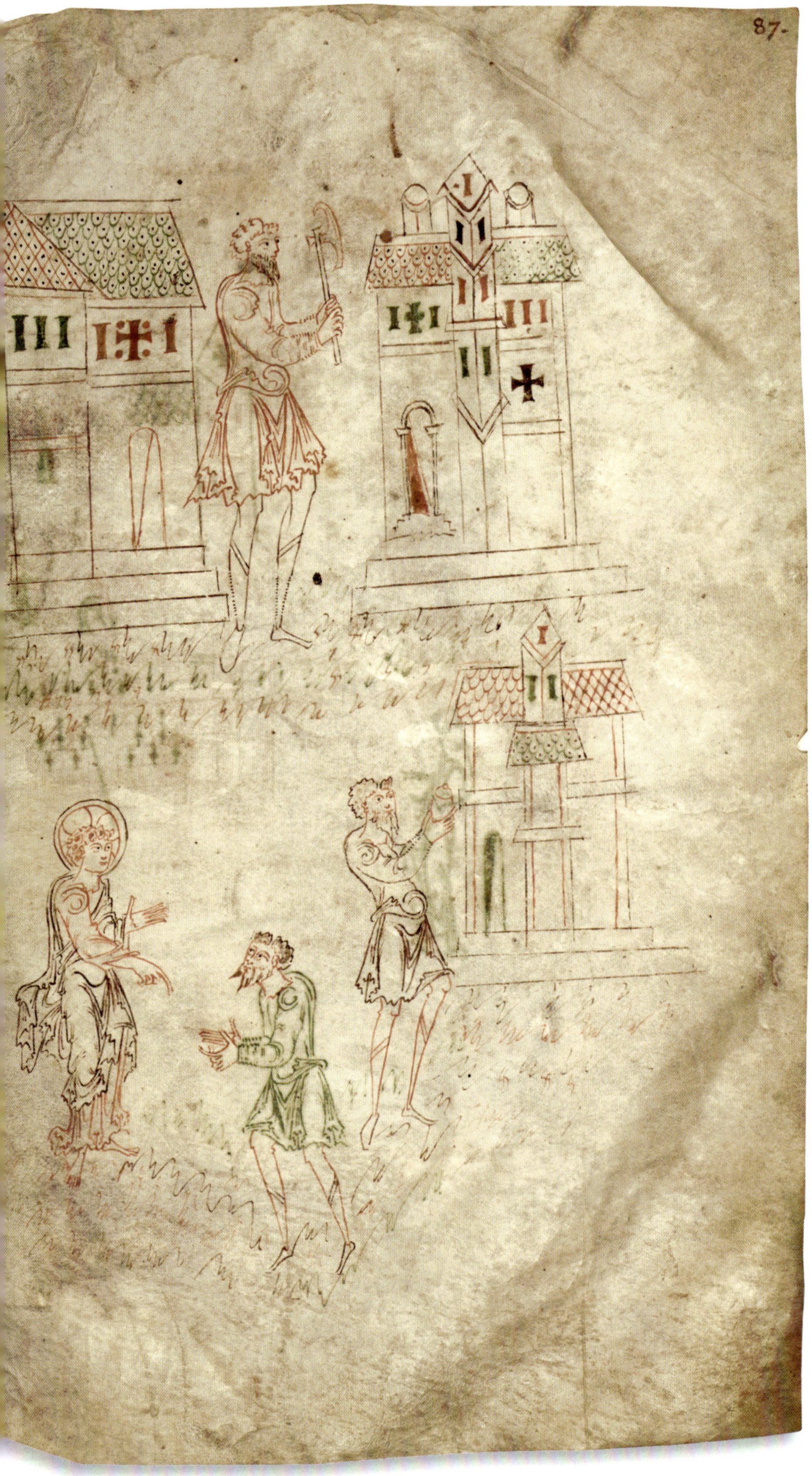

The book as icon

THE EARLIEST WRITTEN CHRISTIAN SCRIPTURES were simple, unadorned manuals for the use of faith communities: the cross and fish—cryptic Early Christian symbols used during times of persecution—were among the first images to appear in scriptural texts. After Christianity, and the book format, had achieved respectability during the fourth century following the Roman Empire's edicts of toleration, grander books were made for important churches. These were impressively made and written but did not usually contain much by way of decoration. During the fifth and sixth centuries, however, opulent materials such as purple-stained pages and gold and silver inks were increasingly employed to bestow prestige upon volumes such as the Codex Brixianus (cat. no. 70); and great didactic picture cycles illustrating biblical passages appeared on the walls of churches and in books such as the Rabbula Gospels (cat. no. 62) and the Codex Sinopensis (cat. no. 64).

Unease concerning idolatry occasioned debate in Jewish, Islamic, and Christian circles during the Middle Ages. It led to a refusal to include figural imagery in scriptural texts and eventually to the destruction of images in the movement known as iconoclasm, which beset Byzantium during much of the eighth and early ninth centuries. Western Church authorities, however, recognized the didactic value of illustration, especially among nations still to be converted: around 600 Pope Gregory the Great advised Serenus, the iconoclast bishop of Marseilles, that "in images the illiterate read." Accordingly, in the West images were used to help convey the meaning of scripture, as in the Valenciennes Apocalypse (cat. no. 72), in which the End of the World and Second Coming described in Saint John's vision are graphically portrayed in a long series of exciting scenes.

Meanwhile, enduring imperial and Early Christian imagery combined with a love of ornament among local cultures to produce distinctive forms of decoration to celebrate and beautify the Word of God. Canon tables, carpet pages, and incipit pages received lavish adornment and depictions of the evangelists and their symbols became popular. The Carolingians, though sometimes cautious about depicting the Divine, decorated their books lavishly with evangelist miniatures, biblical scenes, canon tables, initials, and display lettering and developed complex images of their rulers, inspired by those of imperial Rome. Their Ottonian successors, under renewed Byzantine influence now freed of the constraints of iconoclasm, created grand liturgical volumes in which images of monarchs, patrons, saints, evangelists, and Christ himself abound.

Books containing scripture could fulfill an equally powerful visual role when closed, through their ornamented bindings. Those associated with the shrines of saints served as relics themselves, enclosed in reliquaries and treasure bindings adorned with metalwork, such as the Mondsee Gospel Lectionary (cat. no. 74) or carved ivories, such as the Douce Ivory depicting Christ (cat. no. 73). The sacred book became an iconic object, seen carried ceremonially in procession, read from during the liturgy, and displayed on the high altar.

By the year 1000, imposing medieval books such as the Niketas Bible made in Constantinople (cat. no. 69) grandiosely embodied the formal codification of scripture and symbolized the ongoing transmission of the Word, with the authors of the biblical texts being shown in the act of receiving divine inspiration. In the course of the millennium had emerged the concept that the Christian Bible had been handed down as a powerful unified whole, graphically signaled by the very appearance of the books in which it was transcribed. The transition from the world of late Antiquity to that of the Middle Ages, and with it the process of formation of the Christian Bible, was complete.

Detail: Valenciennes Apocalypse, see cat. no. 72.

& ciuitas non eg& sol
nec luna nam claritas dī in
luminauit eam & lucer-na eius
est agnus

62

The Rabbula Gospels.
Florence, Biblioteca Medicea Laurenziana, MS. Plut. 1.56, ff. 12v–13r. Canon table and Crucifixion. Syriac; parchment. Beth Zagba, Syria, 586.

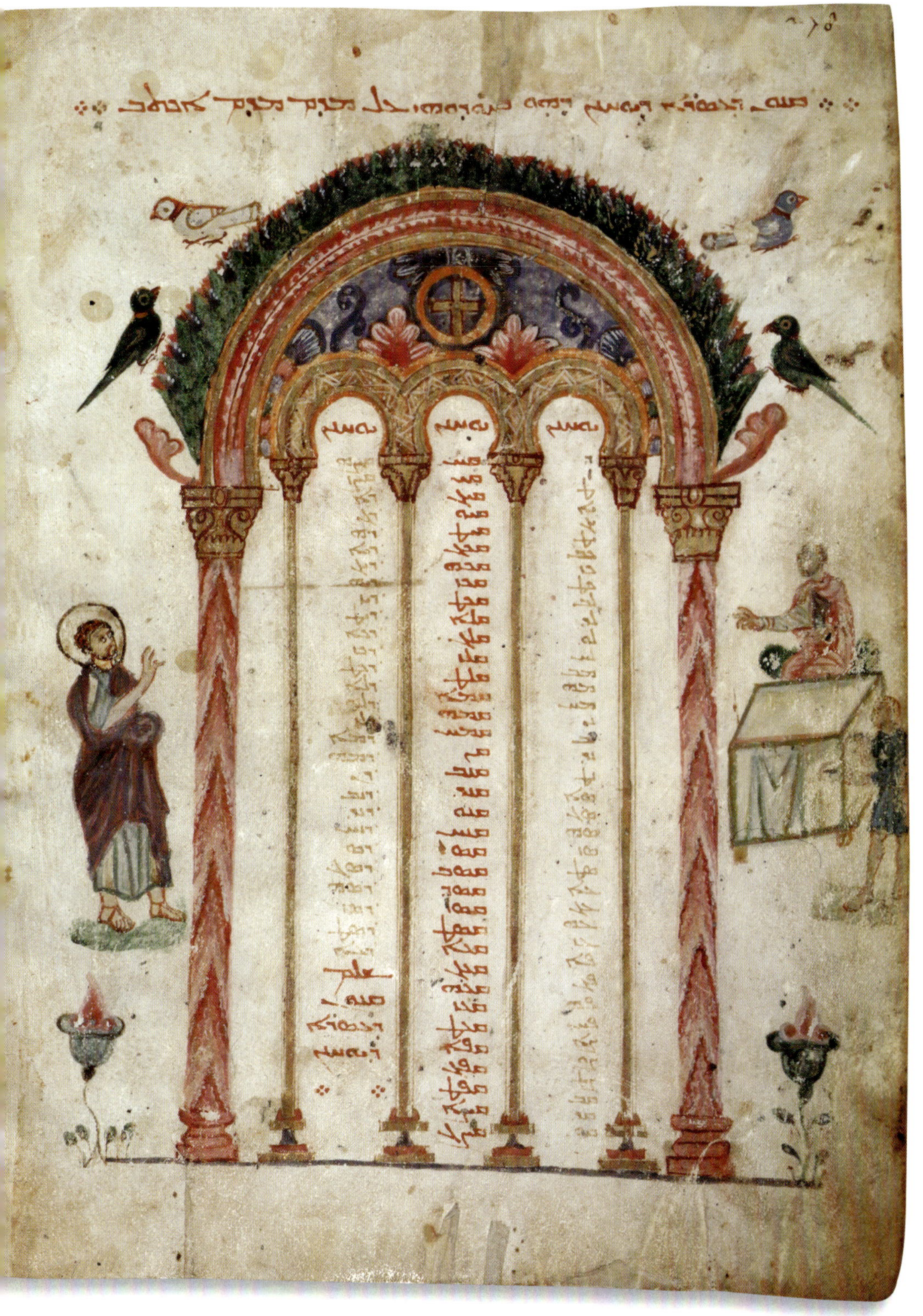

63

First Jrutchi Gospels.
Tbilisi, K. Kekelidze Institute of Manuscripts (Georgia), H1660, ff. 6v–7r. Georgian; parchment. Shatberdi Monastery, Georgia; 936–40.

64

Codex Sinopensis (*alias* The Sinope Gospels).
Paris, Bibliothèque nationale de France, MS. suppl. grec 1286, f. 10v. Greek; parchment. Constantinople or Syria, second half of the sixth century.

65

Codex Caesariensis (Codex Purpureus Petropolitanus).
New York, Morgan Library & Museum, MS. M.874, verso. Greek; parchment. Probably Syria, late sixth century.

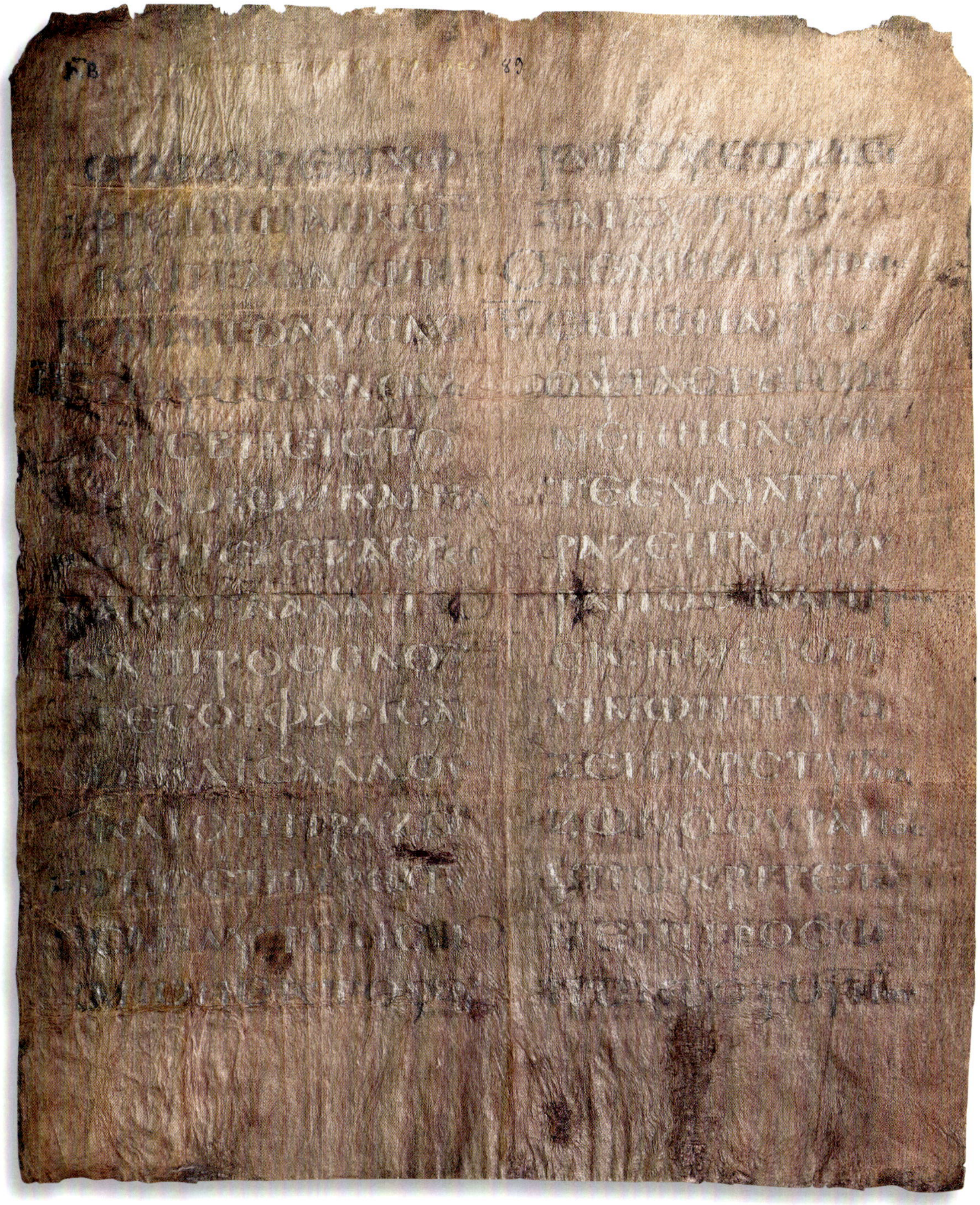

66

The Sion Treasure Book Covers (cross flanked by cypress trees).
Washington, D.C., Dumbarton Oaks, BZ.1963.36.9. (upper cover). Byzantine; silver and gilding. Constantinople (?), third quarter of the sixth century.

67

The Sion Treasure Book Covers (Christ between Sts. Peter and Paul)
Washington, D.C., Dumbarton Oaks, BZ.1963.36.8. (upper cover). Byzantine; silver and gilding. Constantinople (?), 550–560.

68

The Golden Canon Tables.
London, British Library,
Add. MS.5111, ff. 10v–11r.
Greek; gold-stained
parchment. Constantinople (?),
sixth or seventh century.

Florence, Biblioteca Medicea Laurenziana, MS. Plut. 5.9, ff. 128v–128Ar. Title page with portrait of Jeremiah. Greek; parchment. Constantinople, second half of the tenth century.

Θρήνων προφῆτα καὶ μετὰ κλαίων πόλιν·
πέπαυσο λοιπὸν τὴν φόνων πεπλησμένην·
ὁ μητρὸς ἔνδον γαστρὸς ἡγιασμένος·
καὶ μὴ πτοηθῇς εἰς ἔθνη τεθειμένος·
ὡς εἰς ἀπειθεῖς πρὶν κελευσθεὶς ἐκτρέχειν·
ἀλλ' ἐξαναστὰς ἀργὸν ὀφθαλμὸν κύκλῳ·
θρήνων ἔπαιρον δακρύων τὴν πλημμύραν·
ἐπείπερ οὐ τέθνηκας ἀλλ' ἔζησας ἄνω·
καὶ βλέψον ἔθνη τὰ πρὶν ἐκτὸς ἐννόμων·
ᾄδουσι Σιὼν τε τοὺς ὑπερτίμους κόνιν·
καὶ χαῖρε τῶν σῶν εἰς τελείωσιν λόγων·
οὓς τῇδε συντίθησιν εὐσεβὴς νόος:

44

The Stockholm Codex Aureus.

Stockholm, Royal Library, MS. A.135, ff. 115v–116r.
Gospelbook. Latin; parchment.
Canterbury or Minster-in-Thanet, Kent, southeast England, mid-eighth century.

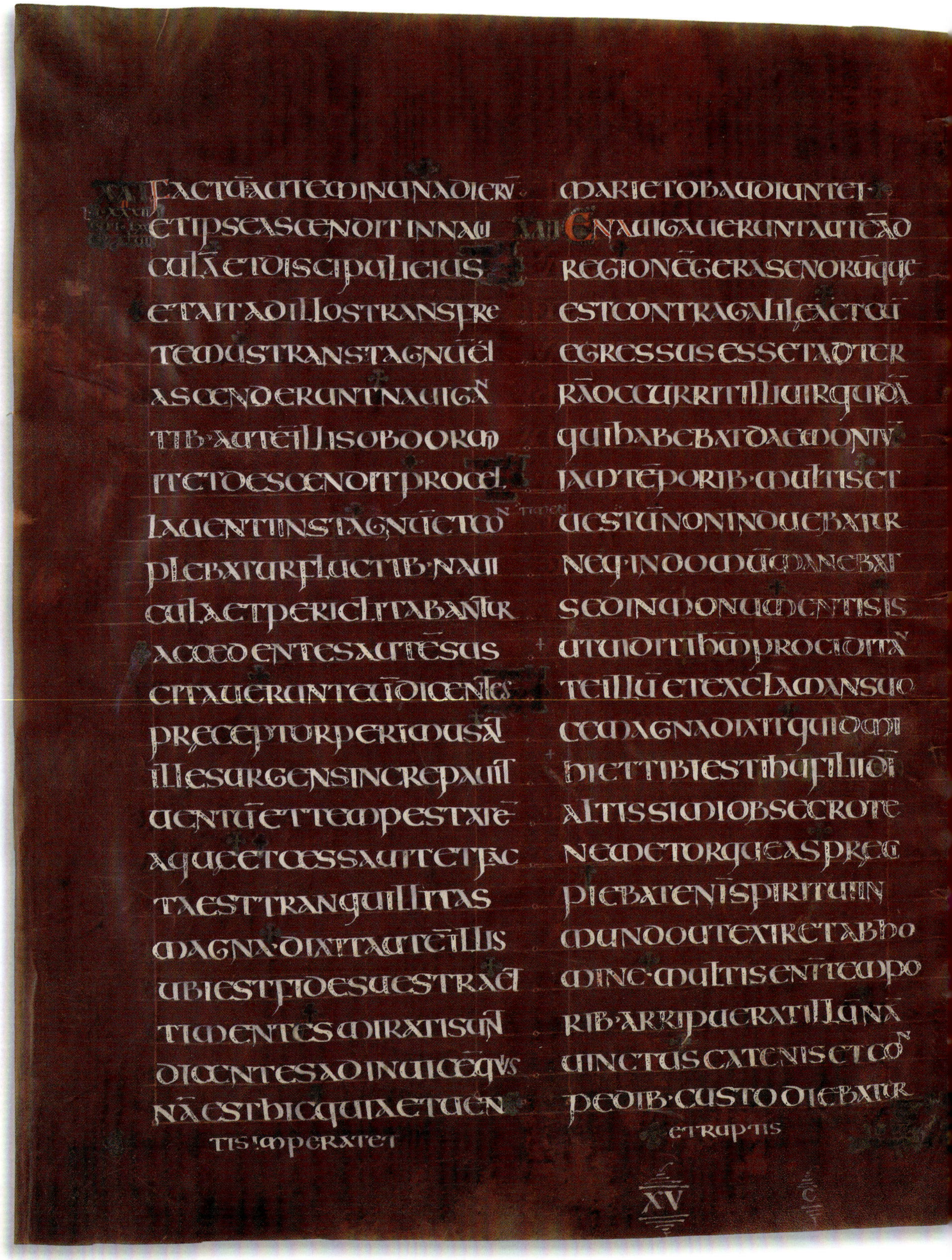

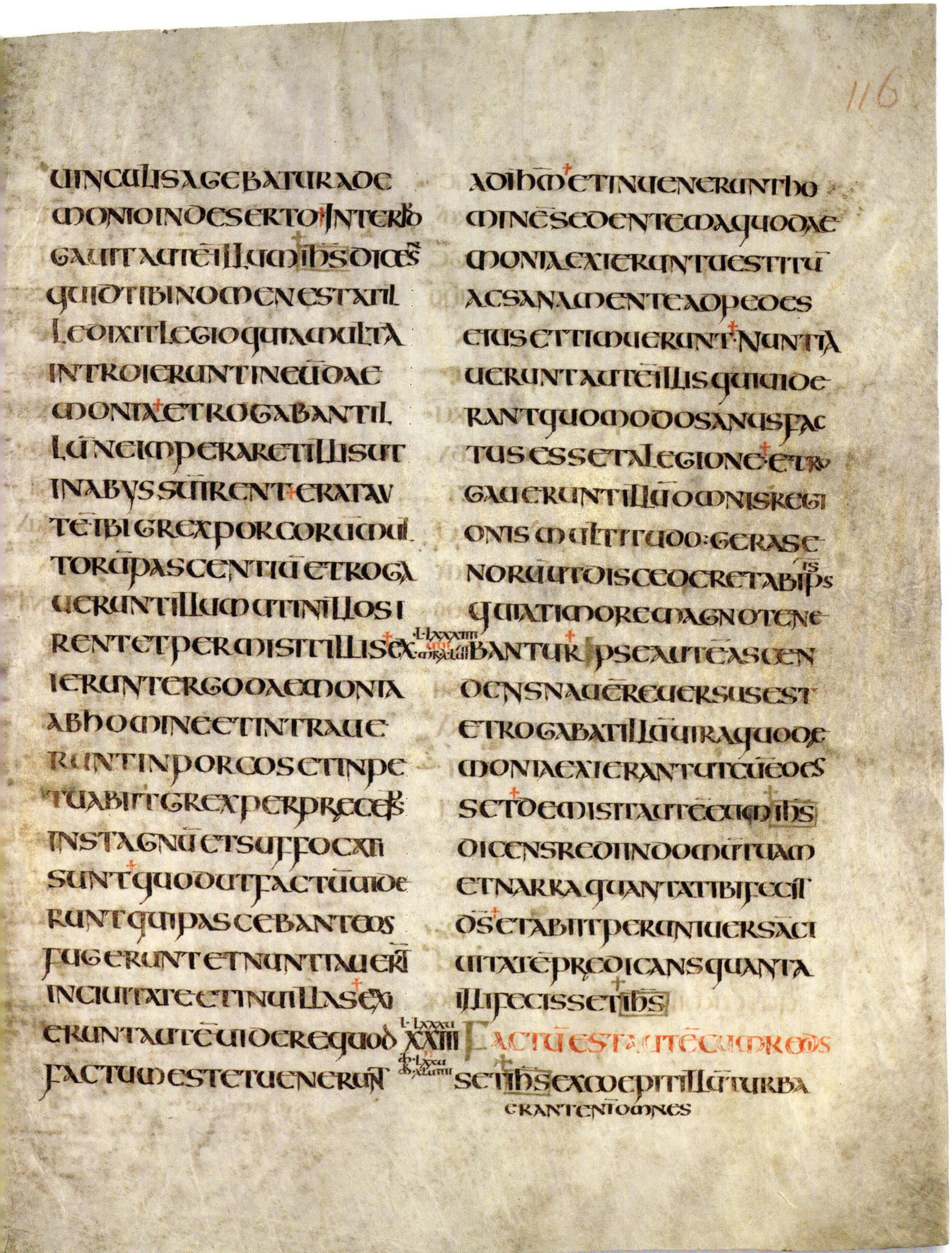
116

uinculis agebatur a dae
monio in deserto · Interro
gauit autem illum ihs dicens
quid tibi nomen est at il
le dixit legio quia multa
introierunt in eum dae
monia et rogabant il
lum ne imperaret illis ut
in abyssum irent · erat au
te ibi grex porcorum mul
torum pascentium et roga
uerunt illum ut in illos i
rent et permisit illis · ex
ierunt ergo daemonia
ab homine et intraue
runt in porcos et in pe
tu abiit grex per praeceps
in stagnum et suffocati
sunt · quod ut factum uide
runt qui pascebant eos
fugerunt et nuntiauerunt
in ciuitate et in uillas · ex
ierunt autem uidere quod
factum est et uenerunt
ad ihm et inuenerunt ho
minem sedentem a quo dae
monia exierunt uestitu
ac sana mente ad pedes
eius et timuerunt · nuntia
uerunt autem illis qui uide
rant quomodo sanus fac
tus esset a legione · et ro
gauerunt illum omnis regi
onis multitudo gerase
norum ut discederet ab ipsis
quia timore magno tene
bantur · ipse autem ascen
dens nauem reuersus est
et rogabat illum uir a quo dae
monia exierant ut cum eo es
set · dimisit autem eum ihs
dicens redi in domum tuam
et narra quanta tibi fecit
ds · et abiit per uniuersam ci
uitatem praedicans quanta
illi fecisset ihs
Factum est autem cum rediss
et ihs excepit illum turba
erant enim omnes

70

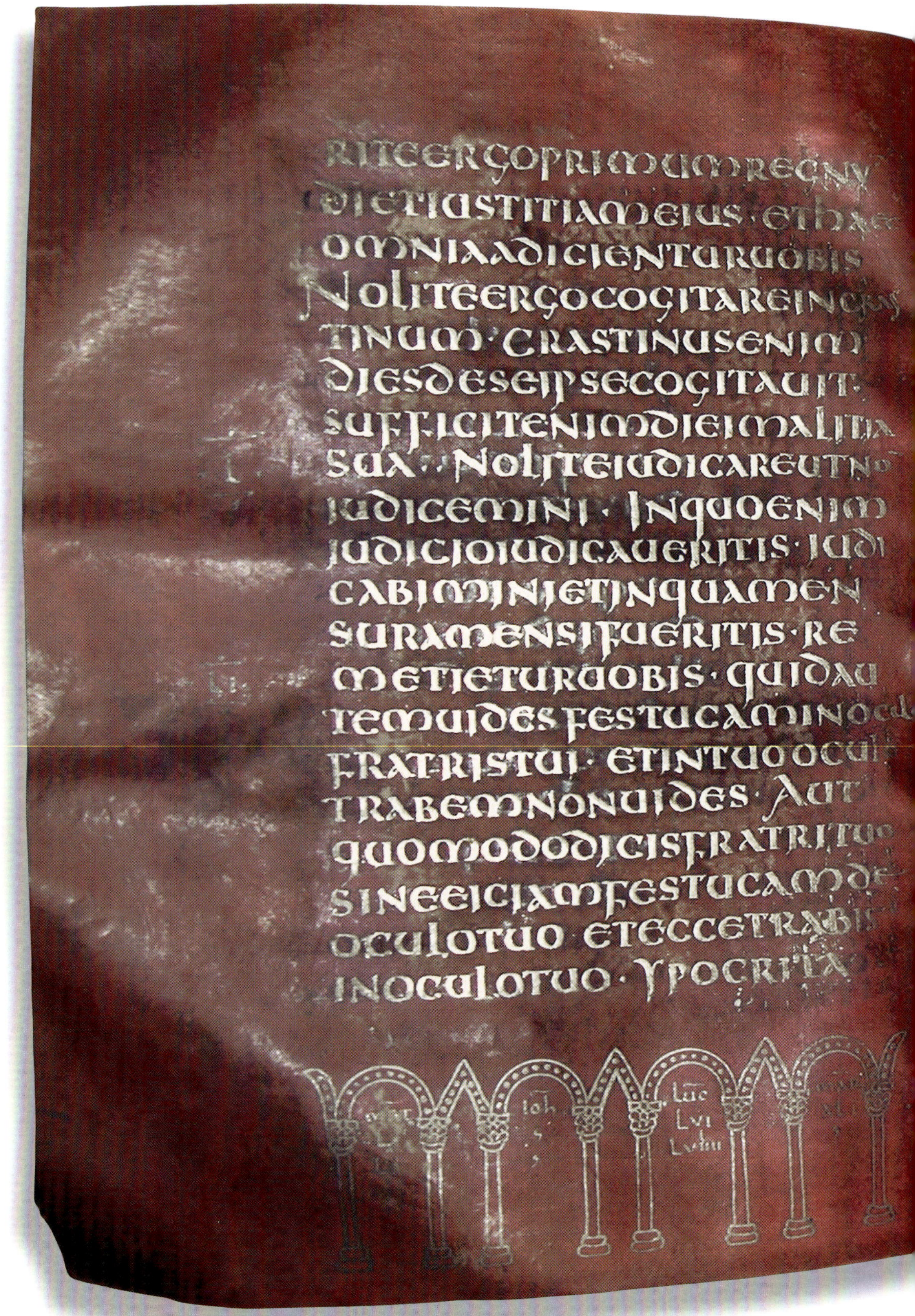

Codex Brixianus (Purple Gospels).
Brescia, Biblioteca Queriniana, s.n. Latin; parchment. Northern Italy, early sixth century.

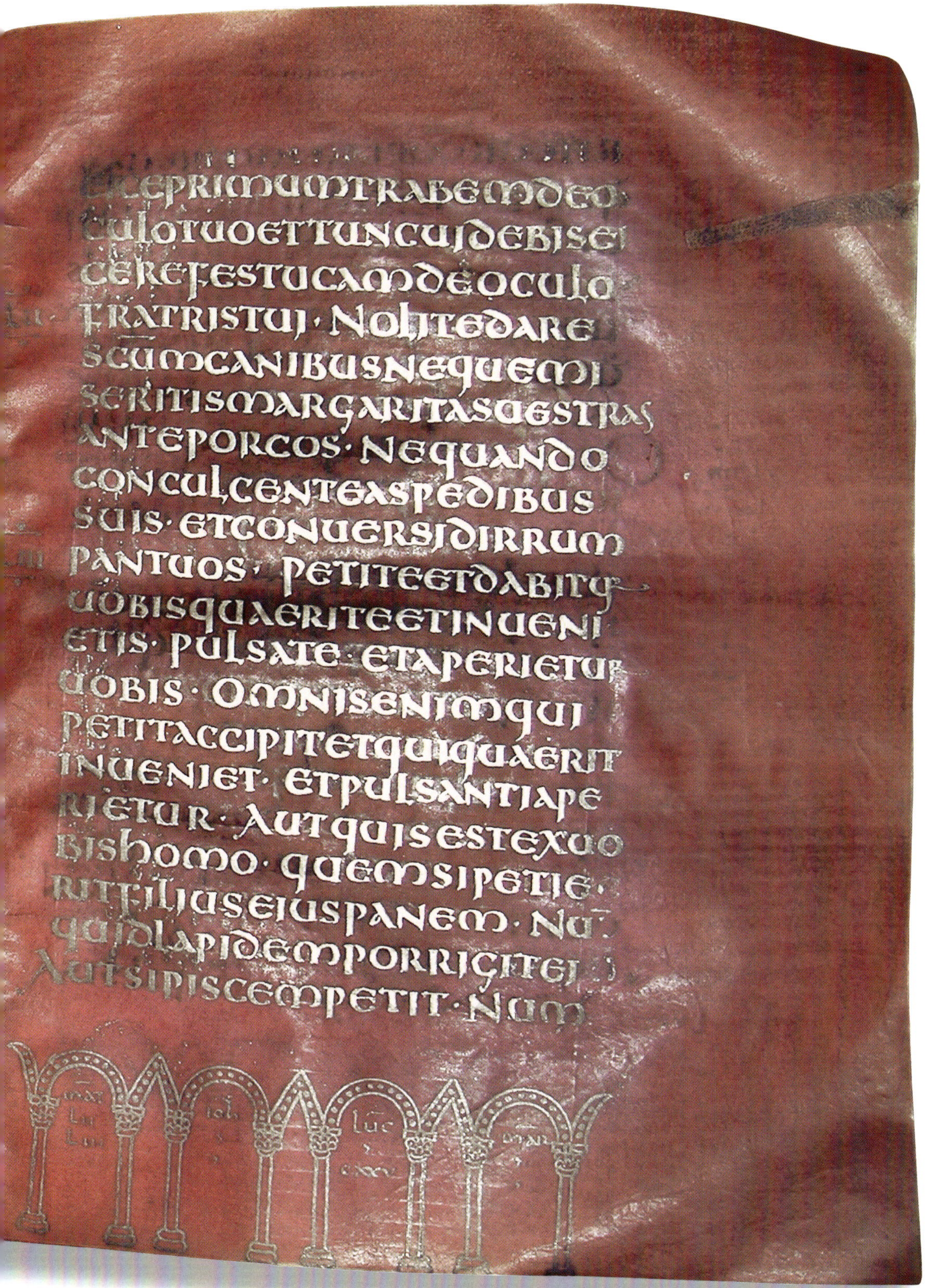
EICEPRIMUMTRABEMDEO
CULOTUOETTUNCUIDEBISEI
CEREFESTUCAMDEOCULO
FRATRISTUI· NOLITEDARE
SCUMCANIBUSNEQUEMI
SERITISMARGARITASUESTRAS
ANTEPORCOS· NEQUANDO
CONCULCENTEASPEDIBUS
SUIS· ETCONUERSIDIRRUM
PANTUOS· PETITEETDABITUR
UOBISQUAERITEETINUENI
ETIS· PULSATE· ETAPERIETUR
UOBIS· OMNISENIMQUI
PETITACCIPITETQUIQUAERIT
INUENIET· ETPULSANTIAPE
RIETUR· AUTQUISESTEXUO
BISHOMO· QUEMSIPETIE
RITFILIUSEIUSPANEM· NU
QUIDLAPIDEMPORRIGITEI
AUTSIPISCEMPETIT· NUM

71

The Psalter of Count Achadeus.
Cambridge, Corpus Christi College, MS. 272, ff. 153v–154r.
Litanies. Latin; parchment.
Reims, France, 883–84.

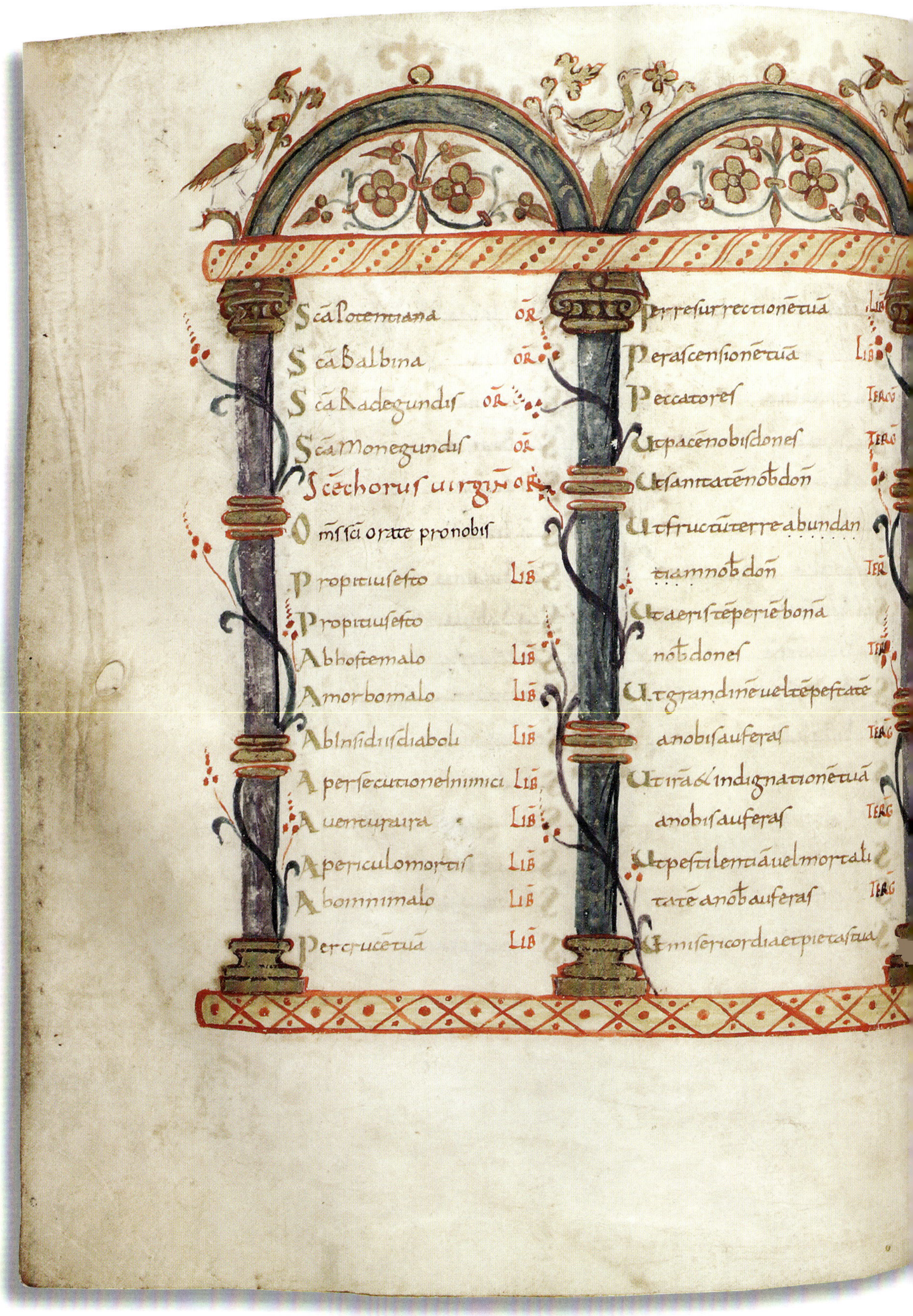

noscustodiat TERG
UtMarinuapostolicuinsca
religioneconseruare
digneris TERG
UtKarlomannuregẽ
perpetuaprosperitate
conseruaredigneris TERG
Ut regina
conseruaredigneris TERG
UtFolcone epm cuomni
gregesibicomissointuo
aptoseruitioconseruare
digneris TERG
Uteisuita&sanitatem
atquevictoriadon TERG
Utpopuloxpianopace
etunanimitatem
largiridigneris TERG
Utecclamtuamregere
ueldefensaredign TERG
Utnosexaudiredign TERG
Agnusdiquitollispeccata
mundiparcenobisdne
Agnusdiqtollispeccata
mundidonanobispace
Agnusdiqtollispeccata
mundimiserererenobis
XPEAUDINOSTER
KYRIELEISON
XPEELEISON
KYRIELEISON

Apocalypse.
Valenciennes, Bibliothèque municipale, MS. 99, ff. 37v–38r. Vision of Heavenly Jerusalem with the Lamb of God (*Agnus Dei*). Latin; parchment. Liège (?), ca. 800.

73

The Douce Ivory.
Oxford, Bodleian Library, MS. Douce 176 (upper cover). Christ Trampling the Beasts. Carolingian; ivory. Chelles, near Paris, ca. 800 (manuscript); Aachen, ca. 800 (ivory).

74

The Mondsee Gospels.
Baltimore, Walters Art Museum, MS. W.8, treasure binding (for use in the Benedictine Abbey of Mondsee, near Salzburg). Metalwork, ivories, and crystal over wooden boards. Regensburg, Germany, third quarter of the eleventh century, with later additions and modifications.

CAT. 1

1

Unconserved fragments from the Cairo Genizah

Cambridge University Library,
Taylor-Schechter Genizah Collection,
T-S unconserved fragments
Parchment, leather, paper; multiple leaves and fragments of leaves of varying sizes
Blank or with illegible text
Egypt; probably eleventh–sixteenth century

The Taylor-Schechter Genizah Collection is a priceless accumulation of centuries-old Hebrew manuscript material and Judaica, recovered from the *genizah* (storeroom) of the Ben Ezra Synagogue in Fustat (Old Cairo), Egypt, in 1896–97. The Collection was the gift in 1898 of the noted scholar Dr. Solomon Schechter and his friend and patron, Dr. Charles Taylor, Master of St. John's College, Cambridge. It has occupied a place of honor among the literary treasures of the University of Cambridge for more than a century and is housed at Cambridge University Library.

In 1896 Mrs. Agnes Lewis and Mrs. Margaret Gibson, two enthusiastic scholars of early Christian and Jewish manuscripts, showed some leaves of a hitherto unknown Hebrew manuscript of the book of Ben Sira (Ecclesiasticus) that they had purchased in Egypt to Schechter, then Reader in Talmudic and Rabbinic literature at Cambridge. Impressed by their unique discovery he traveled to Egypt to locate the source of the find and was shown the *genizah* of the thousand-year-old Ben Ezra Synagogue, into which worn-out Jewish books, documents, and other writings had continually been placed since the Middle Ages. Schechter described the scene thus in an article for the London *Times* of August 3, 1897:

It is a battlefield of books, and the literary productions of many centuries had their share in the battle, and their disjecta membra *are now strewn over its area. Some of the belligerents have perished outright, and are literally ground to dust in the terrible struggle for space, whilst others [...] are squeezed into big, unshapely lumps.*

Realizing the immense scholarly potential of these manuscripts, Schechter obtained the approval of the synagogue authorities to bring them back to Cambridge where they could be carefully conserved and studied. With financial backing from Taylor, he packed two-thirds of the contents of the *genizah*—he left what he thought was "recent" and of little scholarly interest—into tea-chests and shipped them to England.

Genizah fragments are present in many collections around the world, either acquired by visitors to the synagogue before Schechter's trip, by those who followed in his wake, or even bought on the open market. The largest collection after Cambridge is possessed by the Jewish Theological Seminary in New York, which has approximately 40,000 fragments; the Freer Gallery of Art holds one of the smallest, at 52 fragments.

Cambridge University Library's more than 137,000 separately classmarked items have now been conserved, a painstaking process. All that remain are a few hundred fragments of paper, parchment, and leather which have no visible text on them (or text so badly faded that it is completely illegible): these have been preserved in their original state, as a record of what faced Schechter when he opened the chests to begin the arduous task of examining, cataloguing, and describing what was to become the largest and most important collection of medieval Jewish manuscripts in the world.

BO

Bibliography:
Kahle, 1959; Reif, 2000.

Scroll and Codex: The earliest Hebrew scriptures

CAT. 2

2

Fragment of a Genesis scroll

Cambridge University Library,
Taylor-Schechter Genizah Collection,
T-S NS 4.3
Ink on parchment;
1 leaf (part of a scroll); 232 × 197mm
Torah (fragment); Hebrew
Palestine or Egypt; sixth–seventh century

This small fragment of a long biblical scroll contains text from the Book of Genesis chapters 4–6 (4:14–17; 5:10–18; 5:32–6:7). It is written in a calligraphic bookhand, embellished with early examples of *taggim* (crowns), ornamental strokes added to the letters of Torah scrolls. Parts of three columns are preserved in this fragment; the complete scroll, containing the Book of Genesis, would have had up to seventy columns and measured 9 meters in length. Another, larger, part of the same scroll is also preserved in the same collection (cat. no. 4). Evidently, at some point in the Middle Ages, the scroll became too worn out to be used or too badly damaged to repair and, in accordance with *halakhah* (Jewish law) that texts containing the name of God not be destroyed, it was consigned to a *genizah*, a storeroom for worn-out or otherwise unusable religious texts and objects.

This scroll was for liturgical use, rather than for private Bible study (for which, from the Islamic period onwards, the codex was preferred), and therefore follows the strict rules prescribed in the *halakhah* for the composition of Torah scrolls. If it originally consisted only of the Book of Genesis, then it resembles the many biblical scrolls found at Qumran that, with only one or two exceptions, contain just a single book each. It is not impossible, however, that these two fragments of Genesis are all that remain of a much larger *Sefer Torah*, perhaps 40 meters long. Very few Torah scrolls dating from before the tenth century have been identified, and this, if it did contain the entire Pentateuch, would be the earliest example by several centuries.
BO

Bibliography:
Sirat, 1992; Sirat, 1992a; Sirat, 1994; Sirat, 2002, pp. 27–28.

3

The Dead Sea Scrolls: Second Isaiah Scroll

Jerusalem, The Shrine of the Book,
95.57/26B, The Hebrew University of
Jerusalem (owner), MS. B (1QIsa[b] [1Q8])
Ink on leather; 1 leaf (part of a scroll);
220 × 430mm
Bible (fragment); Hebrew
Judaean Desert, Israel; before 73 C.E.

The Second Isaiah Scroll is part of an original repository of seven found by Bedouin of the Ta'amra tribe in a cave near Khirbet Qumran, on the northwestern shore of the Dead Sea, between late 1946 and mid-1947. This scroll was one of three subsequently purchased by a Bethlehem antiquities dealer, Faidi Salahi, who in turn sold them at the end of 1947 to Prof. Eliezer Lipa Sukenik of the Hebrew University of Jerusalem. The first publication of the scroll in English, by Sukenik in 1955, included a short introduction, a transcription of the text, and photographs.

Additional fragments of the scroll were found scattered in the same cave (now called Cave 1) in the excavations conducted in 1949 by the Dominican scholar, Fr. Roland de Vaux, of the École Biblique

CAT. 3

et Archéologique Française, under the auspices of the Jordanian Department of Antiquities. The fragments were published in 1955 by Barthélemy and Milik.

This scroll reached us in very poor condition. Regrettably, all that survived was the upper portion of the last third of the biblical book of Isaiah, and a few fragments of the early and middle sections. Written in a Herodian (that is, the period of Jewish history from 30 B.C.E. to 70 C.E.) Hebrew script and dated to the first century C.E., the section of the scroll illustrated here contains four columns (8–11) with an average of thirty-four lines each; an estimated fourteen lines at the bottom of the scroll have been lost. It contains Isaiah 52:7–8 to 61:2; it is the best-preserved of the four sheets found.

The text of this Isaiah scroll is close to the fixed Masoretic text of medieval codices, but not as close as appeared at first. Some differences are minor—column 9, line 18 reads *hanilvah al*, while the traditional text has *hanilvah el*, "has joined himself to" (56:3)—while others are more significant. The word *or*, "light," which appears in column 8, line 22 of this scroll, for example, is missing from the Masoretic text (53:3). Conversely, the Masoretic text includes the phrase *tze'u mitocha*, "go out of the midst of her" (52:11) while this scroll does not. On the other hand, there are passages in the scroll that are different from the Masoretic text, but identical to the Septuagint, the Greek translation of the Hebrew Bible in circulation at the time the scroll was written: *roshcha*, "your head" (column 10, line 12) rather than *rosho*, "his head" (58:5), for example. In addition, the scroll uses the mixed "plene" or full spelling *(ktiv malei)* and "defective" Hebrew spelling *(ktiv haser)*, as in the Masoretic text, rather than the plene form usually found in the other scrolls, biblical and sectarian alike, discovered in the Qumran caves between 1947 and 1956.

Apart from this scroll, parts of twenty separate copies of the book of Isaiah were found in the Qumran caves—one complete (1QIsa^{a}) and all the others fragmentary (4Q^{a-r}, 5QIsa)—and another manuscript in Wadi Muraba'at (MurIsa). Isaiah appears to have been the most popular biblical book of the Qumran community, after Psalms (thirty-six copies) and Deuteronomy (thirty copies). Six *pesharim* (sectarian commentaries) are devoted to it, and it is the most widely quoted in other scrolls. Most scholars recognize the Qumran community as a sect of Jewish separatists, perhaps a radical group of Essenes mentioned in the ancient writings of Flavius Josephus, Philo of Alexandria, and Pliny the Elder. The evident special status they accorded Isaiah—the eighth-century B.C.E. Judaean prophet who predicted the end-times—is consistent with their messianic and eschatological world-view.

AR

Bibliography:
Barthélemy and Milik, 1955; Sukenik, 1955; Ulrich, 2000; VanderKam and Flint, 2004.

4

Fragment of a Genesis scroll

Cambridge University Library,
Taylor-Schechter Genizah Collection,
T-S NS 3.21
Ink on parchment;
1 leaf (part of a scroll); 359 × 497mm
Torah (fragment); Hebrew
Palestine or Egypt; sixth–seventh century

This large fragment of scroll, written on the flesh-side of fine parchment in a calligraphic bookhand, contains portions of the biblical Book of Genesis (13:10; 14:9–22; 15:5–21; 16:5–17:2, 9–20) and is one of the earliest texts to emerge from the immense hoard of medieval Jewish manuscripts known as the Cairo Genizah. Another, smaller, part of this scroll is to be found in the same collection (cat. no. 2) and it contains portions of Genesis chapters 4–6. Together the two fragments represent only a small area of the complete scroll, which, if it contained the Book of

CAT. 4

Genesis alone, would have been 0.6 meters high and 8 or 9 meters in length.

Biblical scrolls were intended for liturgical use in the synagogue and were written by scribes steeped in the traditions of *hilkhot Sefer Torah* (rules of the Torah scroll). The rules, brought together in the medieval treatise *Masekhet Sofrim* (Tractate of the Scribes), govern everything from the preparation of parchment and ink to the correct writing of verse divisions and letter-ornaments (*taggim* or "crowns"). It should be no surprise, then, that the version of Genesis preserved in this fragment is practically identical to that of the standard Masoretic text of the Hebrew Bible (as exemplified in Codex Leningradensis in St. Petersburg, National Library of Russia). The only major textual difference occurs at Genesis 17:1, where the scroll reads שנה *(shana)*, "year," the singular, for the Masoretic text's plural, שנים *(shanim)*.

It is conceivable that this scroll contained not just a single biblical book, Genesis, but that the fragments were once part of a complete Torah scroll (probably about 40 meters long) containing the entire Pentateuch. If so, then this would represent the earliest known *Sefer Torah* by some centuries.

Accurate dating of the scroll is difficult. The hand is clearly earlier than that found in most Cairo Genizah manuscripts (the great majority of which date from the tenth to the thirteenth centuries), and is similar to that of Hebrew and Aramaic papyri from the Byzantine period (300–700 C.E.). The division of paragraphs *(parashah petuḥa and parasha setuma)* also differs slightly, but intriguingly, from the Masoretic text and resembles that found in biblical scrolls from Qumran. Ada Yardeni dates it to the eighth century, whereas Colette Sirat prefers the pre-Islamic period, the fifth to sixth century.

BO

CAT. 5

Bibliography:
Sirat, 1992; Sirat, 1992a; Sirat, 1994; Yardeni, 1990; Yardeni, 1997, pp. 79–80; Sirat, 2002, pp. 27–28 (pl. 11).

5

Palimpsest of Aquila's translation of the Bible

Cambridge University Library, Taylor-Schechter Genizah Collection, T-S 20.50
Ink on parchment; 2 ff;
folio 1) 270 × 216mm;
folio 2) 270 × 221mm
Biblical translation by Aquila, overwritten with poetry by Yannai; Greek beneath Hebrew
Palestine or Egypt; sixth century (lower script), ninth–tenth century (upper script)

This vellum manuscript from the Cairo Genizah contains copies of poems by the great Palestinian liturgical poet Yannai superimposed on a much earlier copy of Aquila's Greek translation of the Bible. The Greek text (2 Kings 23:11–27) is in an oriental biblical majuscule and has been dated paleographically to the sixth century. The upper script is harder to date and could be earlier than the estimated ninth–tenth century.

Aquila's ultra-literal translation of the Hebrew Bible (ca. 125 C.E.) was a product of the Greek-speaking Jewish world (his teacher was Rabbi Aqiva, the leading Jewish scholar of his age), but was incorporated by the Church Father Origen (along with the other revisions of the Septuagint, by Symmachus and Theodotion) into his multi-columned *Hexapla*. Since this manuscript is of Aquila alone there is no reason to assume that it came from a Christian context and it may well be evidence for the continued use of Aquila's translation by Greek-speaking Jews into the sixth century. Clearly, however, its Jewish religious credentials were not recognized by the (probably) Arabic-speaking Jewish scribe who washed it and overwrote it with Hebrew poetry some centuries later.

The lower script remains completely legible, and of particular interest in this manuscript is the use of Hebrew letters—

in actual fact, a stylized form of the paleo-Hebrew script—for the tetragrammaton (the holy name of God). The pronunciation of this form was evidently *kurios*, "lord" (like Hebrew *adonay*), for when the scribe ran out of room to write the tetragrammaton at the end of 2 Kings 23:24 (f. 2b, col. a, line 15), he simply wrote κυ, as an abbreviation of κύριος.

The upper script contains the works of Yannai, an early Palestinian poet renowned for having produced a poem for every single weekly portion *(seder*, pl. *sedarim)* of the Torah read in the synagogue. Prior to the discovery of the Cairo Genizah few of his poems were known to modern scholarship. Since then, hundreds have been discovered among the fragments, and his modern reputation as a master of the *piyyuṭ* (Hebrew liturgical poem) has been sealed. This fragment of his works, which contains *Qerovot* (liturgical poems incorporated into the recitation of the 'Amidah prayer) on four *sedarim* in Leviticus (13:29; 14:1; 21:1; 22:13), can be joined with other leaves in the Taylor-Schechter Genizah Collection to make a complete quire. Interestingly, each sheet of vellum used in the quire is a palimpsest, but not from the same original manuscript. Thus this fragment overwrites Aquila on Kings, another piece of the quire overwrites the Gospel of John in the Christian Palestinian Aramaic version, another Origen's *Hexapla* on Psalms. The scribe who wrote Yannai's poetry put his codex together from whatever odd sheets of vellum he had to hand.

BO

Bibliography:

Burkitt, 1897; Sokoloff and Yahalom, 1978; Tchernetska, 2002.

CAT. 6

6

The Aleppo Codex: Second Book of Chronicles

Jerusalem, The Shrine of the Book, 96.85/211, Ben-Zvi Institute (owner), f. 241r
Ink on parchment; ff. 1; 330 × 265mm
Bible (fragment); Hebrew
Tiberias, Israel; tenth century

The Aleppo Codex was apparently written in the tenth century in the most important Jewish city of its day—Tiberias, on the Sea of Galilee. It is known in Hebrew as *Ha-Keter*, "The Crown" (*el Taj* in Arabic), following the name given by Jewish communities of the region to ancient and venerated biblical manuscripts. According to its own dedicatory inscription, the codex was copied by Shlomo (Solomon) Ben-Buya'a (see also cat. no. 7), while the vocalization, the cantillation accents, and the Masorah were the work of the renowned scholar, Aaron ben Moshe ben Asher, last of a distinguished family of Masoretes. In the eleventh century, the codex was stolen from the Karaite synagogue in Jerusalem and smuggled to Egypt, but was redeemed there by the local Jewish community. In the fourteenth century, the codex was transferred from Egypt to the old synagogue of the Syrian city of Aleppo. Generations of scribes traveled to consult it as the ultimate authority on textual questions of the Hebrew Bible. In 1947 it was damaged in a riot and all trace of it was lost. It resurfaced in 1958, however, and was spirited out of Syria to Turkey, and thence to Israel.

The original codex evidently contained all the books of the Hebrew Bible, a total of some 487 pages; but the volume that finally reached Israel was no longer complete. It was missing the first and last sections of the text and several pages in the middle, a total of 193 pages, prompting enormous efforts to locate the missing pages, in response to a rumor that they had not entirely disappeared. The leaf shown here, covering 2 Chronicles 35:7 (middle) to 36:19 (except for the last word), was brought from the United States to Israel in 1981. The only other remnant that has surfaced since then is a small fragment of the book of Exodus.

This leaf was entirely preserved, except for a lower corner on its recto, which shows the same purple stain found on most of the pages of the codex. The text on this side, originally the flesh-side of the parchment, is badly faded and the letters are indistinct but the vocalization, cantillation accents, and Masorah are in better condition, suggesting that they were added using a different kind of ink. The text on the verso of the leaf, the hair-side of the parchment, is well preserved.

The external characteristics of this leaf are identical to those of the other pages of the Aleppo Codex: (1) it is divided into three columns (only the books of Job, Proverbs, and Psalms and the Song of

Moses [Deuteronomy 32] contain two columns per page); (2) each column contains twenty-eight lines and measures 235 by 55 millimeters; (3) it employs the Tiberias system of vocalization (*nikud*), in which the vowels are placed below the letters; (4) the cantillation accents, which provide phonetic information (whether a word should be accented on the last or the penultimate syllable), syntactic information (when the reader should pause), and musical information (how the words should be chanted) are inscribed above or beneath words; and (5) the text is accompanied by learned notes on various subjects, like "defective" or "plene" (full) Hebrew spelling (*ktiv haser* or *ktiv malei*), vocalization, and accentuation, of the type known as *Masorah Magna* (above and below the text) and *Masorah Parva* (between the columns and in the margins). However, in one respect this page does differ from the other pages of the codex: the form of a considerable number of the colons at the end of verses is different from that conventionally used in the codex, and they are thinner (a characteristic shared by one other page, that containing the text from Micah 5:1 through Nahum 1:4). It seems that these were not the work of the original scribe, but the reason for a second scribal hand is not known.

Among extant manuscripts of the Masoretic biblical text—such as the Codex Leningradensis (St. Petersburg, National Library of Russia) of the entire Hebrew Bible (1009), the British Library codex (MS Or. 4445) containing the Pentateuch (900–950), and the Codex Prophetarum Cairensis (Karaite Synagogue, Cairo) (895)—the Aleppo Codex is considered the finest. Its marvelous precision, without deviating from the Masoretic rules and precepts, was already recognized in the Middle Ages. The renowned religious legal expert and philosopher Maimonides (1138–1204) used it as a guide to the division of the Torah (i.e., Pentateuch) into "closed" and "open" *parshiyot* or sectional divisions, and to the way in which the Song at the Sea (Exodus 15) and the Song of Moses should be written, prompting him to refer to it as a dependable source (*Sefer Ahavah*, Laws of Torah Scrolls 8:4).

AR

Bibliography:
Beit-Arié, 1982; Yeivin, 1982; Shamosh, 1987; Offer, 2002.

CAT. 7

7

St. Petersburg Pentateuch

St. Petersburg, National Library of Russia, Firkovitch MS. Hebrew II B 17, f. 185v
Ink and pigments on parchment; ff. 242; 430–444 × 372–391mm
Pentateuch; Hebrew
Palestine or Egypt; 929

One of the earliest dated and most important complete Hebrew Pentateuchs, this manuscript is celebrated for its beautiful decoration. It is one of sixteen thousand Hebrew manuscripts acquired in the nineteenth century by Abraham Firkovitch (1787–1874), a collector and spiritual leader of the Crimean Karaite community, and sold to the Imperial Public Library in St. Petersburg between 1862 and 1876 (see also cat. no. 9). Firkovitch is believed to have acquired most of his collection from the Cairo Genizah, the collection of medieval writings produced by the city's Jewish community (cat. no. 1), and the Pentateuch most probably derived from that source.

Although substantially complete, the manuscript is missing portions of all five books, and has sustained damage to its margins. A colophon gives the name of the scribe, Solomon ha-Levi ben Rabbi Buya'a, who is also named as the scribe of the Aleppo Codex (cat. no. 6). In another colophon, Ephraim ben Rabbi Buya'a, Solomon's brother, writes that he "equipped this Torah with vowel points, cantillation signs, and Masorah, and [...] decorated and checked it." The Masorah refers to the corpus of notes and signs that appear in the margins and at the end of each biblical book in copies of the Masoretic text, the "authorized version" of the Hebrew Bible that has become the standard text in use today. Developed by the Masoretes of Tiberias—scholars who, beginning around 500 C.E., also established the Tiberian system of vowel and accent signs—these "masoretic notes" were intended to prevent changes and preserve the integrity of the biblical text.

In four books of this manuscript are gilt-framed end-pieces in which a number of verses are inscribed; the end-piece from the book of Numbers is shown here. Among the other illuminated folios, decorated in gold and color, are carpet pages and depictions of the Temple in Jerusalem (or the Tabernacle of the Covenant) with some of its implements, including a menorah and the Ark of the Covenant (see "Book as icon," fig. 20).

AG and OV

Bibliography:
Günzburg and Stassoff, 1905; Metzger 1958; Narkiss 1990; Beit-Arié, Sirat, and Glatzer 1997; Sirat 2002.

8

Bifolium from a biblical codex

Cambridge University Library,
Taylor-Schechter Genizah Collection,
T-S NS 246.26.2; Nehemiah 13:20–21
Ink on parchment; 2 ff;
folio 1) 94 × 127mm; folio 2) 94 × 97mm
Bible (fragment); Hebrew
Du Gunbadan, Iran; 903–904

This small, damaged vellum bifolium is the earliest dated medieval Hebrew manuscript. It contains the end of the biblical book of Nehemiah (13:20–31), vocalized with Babylonian vowel signs, a short, but carefully written colophon, and parts of Masoretic lists found customarily at the conclusion of biblical books. It is the remnant of a modest codex probably used for private study. Written originally in Iran, it ended its useful life in Egypt where it was deposited along with other worn-out texts in the storeroom *(genizah)* of the Ben Ezra Synagogue in Fustat, Old Cairo.

The colophon (f. 2a) states that the text was written by a certain Joseph ben נמורד (probably a Babylonian variant of the biblical name נמרוד, Nimrod) in the year 1215 in Gunbad-i-Mallgan (modern Du Gunbadan in Iran). Joseph does not state the system of dating he is employing in his colophon, but undoubtedly he is referring to the "Era of Documents" (usually indicated by writing *lishṭarot* after the year), the commonest method of dating found in Jewish documents from the classical Genizah period (tenth–thirteenth centuries C.E.). The Era of Documents (also known as the Era of the Greeks) was the Seleucid Era, which began in autumn 312 B.C.E. Therefore, the text was written in 903–4 C.E.

The small letters לאש מפחושט טיפק above the first line of the colophon simply duplicate the first line, יוסף בן נמורד כתב (written by Joseph ben נמורד) in the commonly used *atba"sh* code, where ת substitutes for א and ש for ב and so on. Similar wordplay often occurs in medieval biblical colophons.

The text is vocalized with supralinear Babylonian vowels signs and cantillated with Babylonian accents. The Babylonian system of vocalization was eventually eclipsed by the Tiberian system, which is still in use today. The pervasive influence of the more dominant system can be seen even here, for a second scribal hand has added to the text a small number of Tiberian vowels (placed beneath the letters), for instance Tiberian *ṣere* to *leqaddesh* (to sanctify) at Nehemiah 13:22 (f. 1a, line 5).
BO

Bibliography:
Rüger, 1966; Sirat, 2002, pp. 46–47 (pl. 20).

CAT. 8

9

Quire from the "Firkovitch Compilation"

St. Petersburg, National Library of Russia, Firkovitch MS. Hebrew II B 49, f.2v
Ink and pigments on parchment; ff. 2;
415 × 375mm
Pentateuch (?) (fragment); Hebrew
Egypt; late tenth century

This quire, produced in late tenth-century Egypt and bound with several unrelated texts, is a rare surviving example of Jewish luxury manuscript production. Excerpts from Psalms 33, 41, 99, and 119 are written in a monumental script formed by reserving the letters on the parchment ground and filling in the spaces between them with a painted gold diaper. A depiction of the Temple on f. 2v recalls the frontispiece in St. Petersburg, Public Library, Firk. MS II B 17, f. 5r (see "Book as icon," fig. 20), with its gabled structure, vines, and palmette medallions, and, in turn, the representations of the Temple on Late Antique synagogue pavements in Palestine. The diagram lacks the Temple implements, however, and pictures the Temple courtyard as closed off, suggesting that it is here a visionary building; indeed, Yaffa Levy has convincingly argued that it is the structure God showed to Ezekiel when he promised that:

...they shall know that I am the Lord their God because I sent them into exile among the nations and then gathered them into their own land. I will leave none of them behind; and I will never again hide my face from them.
Ezekiel 39:28–29

Quotations from Psalms and Proverbs outline the Temple and its parts; among these once again is Psalm 119:4 (fragmentary rectangle at right). These are rendered as micrography, that is, the figural designs are constructed from minutely written texts, a technique first encountered in the Moshe ben Asher Codex, a ninth-century Book of Prophets from Tiberias (Cairo, Karaite Synagogue). On the St. Petersburg leaf, the triangle at the top—formed from the text "The Lord is great in Zion; he is exalted over all the peoples" (Psalm 99:2)—suggests that, as it was in later Jewish manuscripts, micrography is used here to honor the prohibition of images in the Second Commandment and to figure God's essential unfigurability

Providing support for an intuition of Abraham Firkovitch, the eccentric nineteenth-century collector who sold his large collection of Hebrew manuscripts to the then Public Library in St. Petersburg, both Levy and Bezalel Narkiss have argued persuasively that the emphasis on literal adherence to scripture in the quoted texts, the repeated references in them to Zion and Jerusalem, and the visionary Temple itself all indicate that the quire was made for Karaite Jews, a messianic sect that promoted a plain reading of scripture as opposed to oral interpretation promoted by the rabbis and codified in the Talmud and other exegetical texts (see cat. no. 33). Even the absence of the Ark of the Covenant and other implements evokes Karaite fundamentalism, which considered bowing down before the Torah ark to be idolatry. The magnificent use of monumental letters on the carpet page and the elaborate micrography and Temple miniature, however, betray an artistic sensitivity typical of Jewish manuscripts produced in Islamic lands during the first millennium.
HLK

CAT. 9

Bibliography:
Günzburg and Stassoff, 1886; Revel-Neher, 1984; Narkiss, 1990, pp. 39, 60–61; Ernst, 1991, pp. 602–14; Levy, 1993/94.

Scroll and Codex: The earliest Christian scriptures

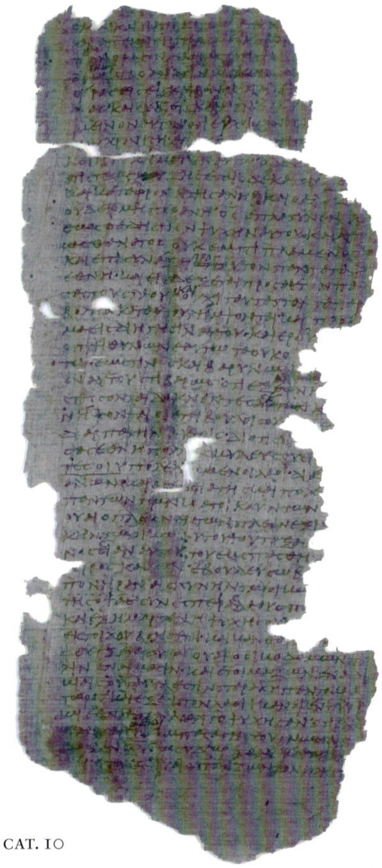

CAT. 10

10

The Washington Codex of the Minor Prophets

Washington D.C., Freer Gallery of Art, F1916.768 (MS. V), p. 37
Ink on papyrus; ff. 34 + fragments; 295 × 140mm
Minor Prophets; Greek with Coptic glosses
Egypt, Fayyum(?); third century, second half

This papyrus codex contains what is almost the oldest complete Christian copy of the Greek text of the twelve Minor Prophets (compare the more fragmentary first-century B.C.E. leather scroll from Nahal Hever). Only fragments of the first book (Hosea) are preserved, but part or whole of every page of the eleven other Minor Prophets survives. The codex was produced on papyrus of fine quality, and the scribe's work was corrected by another person against the parent manuscript with meticulous care.

Thirty-four leaves of the codex survive in some form. Based on how much of Hosea is lost at the beginning, the codex was almost certainly originally formed from twenty-four sheets of papyrus, folded and bound as a single quire (gathering) to make a ninety-six-page codex. After the end of Malachi, a fragmentary colophon of sorts in a different, later hand names the work ("Prophets and ...[?]") and notes "(it is) complete." This may serve to set the Minor Prophets off from the work that follows on the last preserved page of the codex. This text survives only in fragments, and more may have originally stood at the end of the manuscript. It was written, perhaps in the early fourth century, by a scribe different from the one who wrote the Minor Prophets (whose hand is, however, similar to that of some of the marginal notations). This text contains verbatim quotes from the books of Isaiah and Ezekiel (the latter in the version of Symmachus) surrounded (where the writer's sense can be followed) by development of the theme of the "new Jerusalem" of Revelation 21.

Indications both within the text and in one set of marginal notations of independence from the known Greek translations of the Hebrew scriptures suggest that the direct influence of the Hebrew is likely in some cases. A more certain linguistic influence is provided by the Coptic glosses that line many of the left, right, and bottom margins of fourteen pages (and probably originally many more, as one or more margins are lost entirely on a large number of pages).

The codex's ancient home is not known. Judging by the Sahidic (Upper Egyptian) dialect of the Coptic glosses, it may not have been the Fayyum, despite the fact it was acquired there. Wherever it was kept, a succession of people with close knowledge of the biblical books concerned had access to it and helped shape its text. Whether these were individual owners or members of a community in whose library the book was kept cannot be known. In its passage from a purely Greek production to a work adapted for use for preaching in Egyptian (one explanation for the Coptic glosses) the codex is a contemporary witness to the spread of Christianity in third- and fourth-century Egypt, from the Hellenized cultural centers in the Nile Delta and Valley into the native-speaking population.

The codex of the Minor Prophets was acquired in Egypt's Fayyum region by David Askren, a resident American missionary, and formed part of a large consignment of papyri that he sold through the Cairo antiquities dealer Maurice Nahman. These were purchased in 1916 by Charles Lang Freer in partnership with J. P. Morgan Jr., who (per agreement) took all the Coptic texts to the library founded by his father in New York. Freer received the lone Greek item, the Minor Prophets.
MC

Bibliography:
Sanders, 1921; Sanders, 1927; Sanders and Schmidt, 1927; Boak, 1959; Aland, 1976, no. 08; Haelst, 1976, no. 284; Rahlfs and Fraenkel, 2004, pp. 387–89; Choat, 2006.

CAT. 11

11

Early fragments of the Gospel of Saint Matthew

Oxford, Magdalen College Library, P. Magd. Gr. 17 (P 64)
Ink on papyrus; three fragments: a) 41 × 12mm; b) 16 × 16mm; c) 41 × 13mm
Gospel of Saint Matthew; Greek
Egypt (?); ca. 200 C.E. (possibly somewhat earlier)

These three fragments, containing the text of Matthew 26:7, 10, 14–15, 22–23 and 31–33, belonged to an early codex of the Gospel of Matthew. Other fragments from the same codex are designated P 67 (Barcelona, Fundacion San Lucas Evangelista, P. Barc. 1), containing Matthew 3:9, 15 and 5:20–22, 25–28, and P 4 (Paris, Bibliothèque nationale de France, Gr. 1120, suppl. 2°), containing Luke 1:58–59, 62–2:1, 6–7, 3:8–38, 4:2, 29–32, 34–35, 5:3–8, 30–38 and 6:1–16. From this it is clear that the codex from which all these fragments derive contained at least two gospels, and conceivably all four of the gospels that became canonical. It was a multiple-quire codex having pages originally about 200 by 130 millimeters, which were inscribed in two columns per page of thirty-five to thirty-nine lines. This was an unusual format in early Christian papyrus codices, which were commonly inscribed in one broad column to the page. The hand is an early form of the "biblical uncial" type, characterized by deliberate and carefully executed letters which are separated and somewhat rounded.

The *nomina sacra* "Lord" and "Jesus" are both seen here in Matthew 26:22–23: "Lord" (in the vocative) was apparently reduced to the first and last letters (fragment 3, recto, line 2), and "Jesus" is represented by the first two letters (fragment 1, recto, line 1). It was customary to draw a horizontal line over such abbreviations, but such lines are not to be seen here, perhaps because of damage to the papyrus. Also noteworthy is the use of letters to represent numbers (fragment 3, verso, line 2, where the letters *iota* and *beta* stand for the number twelve). This convention does not belong to Greek literary manuscripts or to Jewish manuscripts of the Septuagint, where numbers are fully written out, but is characteristic of early Christian manuscripts from Egypt.

These fragments arguably constitute the earliest manuscript witness to any of the synoptic gospels, although a close rival may be P 77 (P. Oxyrhynchus 2683, Oxford, Ashmolean Museum), which carries Matthew 23:30–39.

HYG

Bibliography:

Roberts, 1953; Roca-Puig, 1956; Head, 1990; Comfort, 1995; Skeat, 1997; Comfort and Barrett, 2000, pp. 42–71.

CAT. 12

12

The Unknown Gospel (*alias* The Egerton Gospel)

London, British Library,
Egerton Papyrus 2, 608
Ink on papyrus; three fragments:
1) 115 × 92mm; 2) 118 × 97mm;
3) 60 × 23mm
New Testament Apocrypha; Greek
Egypt; second century

Egerton Papyrus 2 consists of three small fragments of an early Christian gospel otherwise unknown, purchased from an Egyptian dealer in 1934 and published in 1935. The place of its discovery is not known, but it may have come from Oxyrhynchus. An additional fragment of this same manuscript, which fits together with Egerton fragment 1, was later found in Cologne (Papyrus-Sammlung, inv. 608, nr. 255) and published in 1987. The four fragments now known preserve parts of three leaves of the original codex. Fragment 1 carries parts of twenty lines of text on each side, fragment 2 preserves parts of seventeen lines on the recto and sixteen on the verso, and fragment 3 provides only small parts of six lines on each side, which cannot be made intelligible. The Cologne fragment (measuring 55 by 30 millimeters) offers parts of seven lines on each side, which continue the text of Egerton fragment 1.

The interest and value of this papyrus are far larger than the fragments themselves, and for several reasons. The manuscript is dated on paleographical grounds to the second century, and many have considered it to be not later than circa 150. It is among the earliest Christian papyri, and is the very earliest surviving manuscript of a noncanonical gospel. This papyrus displays the use of *nomina sacra*, some of which are conventional (for Lord, God, father, Jesus), but others of which are unique (for Moses, prophet, kings, Isaiah). This may point to a relatively early date before the *nomina sacra* became more standardized.

Fragment 1 verso (plus the Cologne fragment) gives part of a controversy between Jesus and Jewish leaders about the interpretation of scripture and the authority of Moses; fragment 1 recto (plus the Cologne fragment) offers the conclusion of a story of an attempt to stone and arrest Jesus, and a nearly complete story of Jesus's healing of a leper; fragment 2 recto gives part of an account of a controversy concerning tribute money; fragment 2 verso provides part of an account of a nature miracle of Jesus at the Jordan river. All but the last of these stories have parallels in the canonical gospels, some with the synoptic gospels (Matthew, Mark, and Luke), and some with John. Unusually, Jesus is addressed mainly as "teacher."

The similarities and differences between this "Unknown Gospel" and the canonical gospels present a puzzling picture. In its structure of loosely linked stories it resembles the synoptic gospels, and its vocabulary and style are on the whole closest to those of Luke, but its most striking similarities of content (including some verbatim agreements) are with John. Hence there is considerable controversy about whether the Egerton papyrus represents an early and independent gospel that draws on a larger stream of oral traditions, or whether it is dependent (through hearing and memory) on all the canonical gospels while enriching them with additional materials, or whether it may even be a source of one or another canonical gospel. These issues continue to be debated.

HYG

Bibliography:
Bell and Skeat, 1935; Mayeda, 1946; Bell, 1949; Crossan, 1985; Wright, 1985; Gronewald, 1987; Jon B. Daniels, "The Egerton Gospel: Its Place in Early Christianity," (dissertation, Claremont Graduate School, 1989); Pickering, 2003; Luhrmann, 2004.

13

An early codex of the Epistles of Paul

Ann Arbor, University of Michigan Library, 6238 (P 46), ff. 157v–158r
Ink on papyrus; ff. 30; 215 × 152mm
Epistles of Paul; Greek
Egypt (the Fayyum), ca. 200 C.E.

One of the earliest and most important manuscripts of the Pauline letters, and by far the most extensive, is a codex of which thirty leaves are held by the University of Michigan Library and fifty-six leaves are held by the Chester Beatty Library, Dublin (P. Chester Beatty II). This single-quire codex originally measured 280 by 165 millimeters and contained 104 leaves or 208 pages that were inscribed in a single column of twenty-five to thirty-two lines per page. Remarkably well preserved, the codex is missing seven leaves from the beginning, seven from the end, and four interior leaves. Some lines are lost at the bottom of each page. The script contrasts sharply with that of the Chester Beatty codex of the Gospels and Acts (cat. no. 14), and more closely approaches a good bookhand with its upright, square, and well-spaced letters. The complexion of the text is "Alexandrian," reflecting the influence of the careful editorial traditions of Alexandrian scholarship, and broadly agreeing with Codex Vaticanus, Codex Sinaiticus, and some earlier (proto-Alexandrian) papyrus manuscripts (P 66, P 75).

Notable features of this manuscript include page numbering, stichometric notes at the end of each epistle giving the number of lines in it, *nomina sacra* (some in early forms), paragraph marks, some diacritical marks, some punctuation, and occasional spacing between words.

The codex presented ten epistles of Paul in the order: Romans, Hebrews, 1–2 Corinthians, Ephesians, Galatians, Philippians, Colossians, 1–2 Thessalonians. Due to lost leaves the beginning of Romans (1:1–5:17) and all of 2 Thessalonians are missing, as are another part of Romans (6:14–8:15) and part of 1 Thessalonians (2:3–5:5). The inclusion of the (anonymous) Epistle to the Hebrews in so early a manuscript of Paul's letters is surprising, but Hebrews was early accepted in Egypt as a letter of Paul. Its placement after Romans is due to ordering the letters by length. The placement of Ephesians before Galatians is unusual but not unparalleled. It is generally believed that this

CAT. 13

codex did not contain the Pastoral Epistles (1–2 Timothy, Titus) since the remaining pages did not provide sufficient space for their inclusion.
HYG

Bibliography:
Kenyon, 1934–37; Sanders, 1935; Hoskier, 1937; Zuntz, 1953; Giversen, 1980.

CAT. 14

14

The Chester Beatty Codex of the Gospels and Acts

Dublin, Chester Beatty Library,
MS. Biblical Papyri I (P 45), f. 7r
Papyrus; ff. 30; 140 × 110mm
(original size 255 × 200mm)
Gospels and Acts; Greek
Fayyum or Aphroditopolis (modern Atfih), Egypt; ca. 250

The Chester Beatty Biblical Papyri, first brought to public attention in 1931, mark an epoch in the history of the Bible. As a group, the eleven codices form the largest single cache of early Christian manuscripts yet discovered, and individually each book has yielded evidence that places it in the forefront of textual research for the history of the New Testament and the Septuagint. The New Testament papyri are at least a hundred years older than the great vellum codices of the immediate post-Constantinian era such as Codex Vaticanus, Sinaiticus, and Alexandrinus. Moreover, the Beatty papyri contain much more substantial portions of the New Testament writings than any of the previously known papyrus fragments. They are thus able to provide a unique witness to the Greek text from the time before the mass destruction of the Christian scriptures under Diocletian at the start of the fourth century.

One of the most important of the Beatty papyri is the codex containing the four gospels and the Acts of the Apostles, known to scholars as P 45 and dated by some to the late second or early third century but certainly no later than 250 C.E. Until the discovery of this codex, only small fragments of individual gospels on papyrus were known, and it was commonly believed that all four gospels had not been collected together into one book until a much later date. The Beatty codex showed that both the four gospels and the Acts of the Apostles had been compiled in one volume much earlier than many had expected and although many more papyrus fragments have since been discovered, this codex remains the only surviving example of these texts together in a single volume. It is thought that the codex originally consisted of 220 or 224 pages of which only 60 survive. The most substantial losses occur at the beginning and end of the volume, and it is likely that it had only blank leaves as a protective cover rather than leather or cartonnage boards.

Textually P 45 is of great interest. The fragment shown is part of the text from the earliest extant witness of the Gospel of Mark, carrying the text of Mark 8:34–9:8 (and Mark 9:18–31 on the other side). The order of the gospels—Matthew, John, Luke, Mark—and Acts reflects the earlier "Western" sequence found in a number of very early manuscripts including the Freer Gospels (Codex Washingtonensis, cat. no. 29) and its scribal pattern and textual history have provided several generations of biblical scholars with material for many dissertations and publications. But, for all the evidence that the Chester Beatty papyri have provided, scholars are still divided on many issues, particularly in regard to the original context of the manuscripts, who created them and for what purpose. Divorced from their archaeological context many early papyri throw up as many questions as they provide answers.
CH

Bibliography:
Schmidt, 1931; Gerstinger, 1933; Schmidt, 1933; Kenyon, 1933–34; Hering, 1934; Merk, 1934; Zuntz, 1951; Huston, 1955; Skeat and McGing, 1991; Skeat, 1993; Horton, 2004.

15

The Sayings of Jesus (*Logia Jesou*)

Oxford, Bodleian Library,
MS. Gr. th. e. 7 (P),
Ink on papyrus; f. 1; 140–48 × 90–95mm
Gospel of Thomas (fragment); Greek
Oxyrhynchus, Egypt; third century.

Jesus says "… Raise the stone and there you shall find me, split the wood and there I am." (Logion 5)

Every Christian must feel a shiver of excitement at the new vistas suggested by these words. They are a translation of one

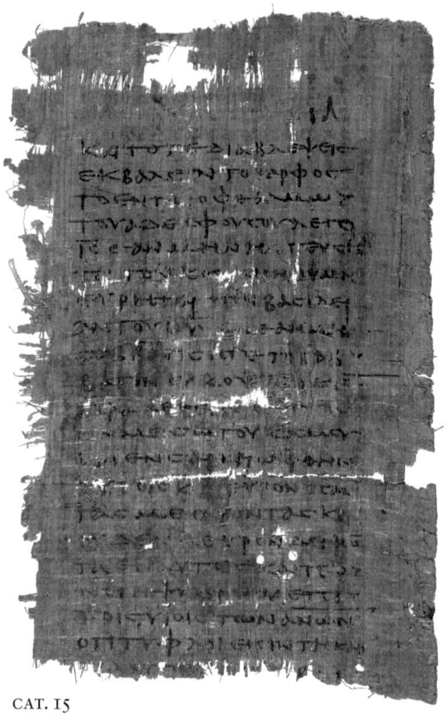

CAT. 15

of the eight Greek sayings *(logia)* of Jesus surviving on the two sides of this papyrus. Each begins "Jesus says ...," and though most of the material is duplicated in the canonical gospels, some is new or shows an unexpected turn of phrase:

Jesus says, "A prophet is not acceptable in his own country, nor does a physician work cures on those who know him." (Logion 6)

The papyrus derives from the Greco-Roman culture of Egypt, and was excavated in 1896–97 at Oxyrhynchus, a town about 190 kilometers south of Cairo. There, the ancient garbage mounds have yielded the largest surviving group of papyri containing documents and literary texts from the period of the Roman Empire. Nearly five thousand Oxyrhynchus papyri have been published so far, but this has the distinction of being the first: P.Oxy.I 1. Its discoverers, the Oxford scholars B. P. Grenfell and A. S. Hunt, dated it from its script "not much later than the year 200," and rushed it into print in 1897 under the title *Sayings of Our Lord*. The original was given to the Bodleian Library in 1900 by the Egypt Exploration Fund, which had financed the excavation.

The nature of the text was established more fully through the discovery in 1945 at Nag Hammadi in Upper Egypt of a papyrus codex of the later fourth century which includes, among various Gnostic texts in Coptic, a complete version in Coptic of the Gospel of Thomas (Cairo, Coptic Museum, Nag Hammadi Codex II). Textual parallels reveal that the Oxyrhynchus papyrus and other fragments in fact belong to the Greek version (close, but not identical) of the apocryphal text attributed in the Coptic to "Didymos Judas Thomas": it consists entirely of sayings attributed to Jesus, without narrative. Nevertheless, the Bodleian's papyrus remains of the highest value as the major witness to the original Greek version, first composed perhaps in the mid-second century—or earlier?

Like the Coptic find, this copy of the Greek Gospel of Thomas had been written in a papyrus codex. The format is immediately evident from the continuity of text and script on both sides: it is clearly one whole leaf, relatively little damaged, which had been numbered as the eleventh folio (equivalent to pages 21–22) of its book. By contrast, an ancient roll would have been written on one side only, with the other side either blank or perhaps reused for a different text and script. The fact that this early Christian text was here written in codex form is especially significant. Unlike the roll, the codex allows immediate access to any part of the text: the reader need no longer read a text continuously, but can leaf through it quickly, maybe to find a favorite Saying in a book like this. The adoption of the new format by the early Christians may have been the decisive factor in the development of the Western form of book.

BCBB

Bibliography:
Gospel of Thomas; *Summary Catalogue*, 1895–1953, no. 32901 (listing only); Grenfell and Hunt, 1897; Canberra Exhib., 2001, pp. 13, 36, 37 (pl.), 177.

16

An Early Christian bookroll

London, British Library, P2053r and v
Ink on papyrus; P18,
one fragment, 250mm high
Exodus and the Revelation of Saint John;
Greek. Oxyrhynchus, Egypt;
third–fourth century

This papyrus fragment (P.Oxy. 1079, P 18) is from a bookroll rather than a codex, and hence very unusual as the medium of an early Christian text, since Christians typically employed the codex format. Of the more than one hundred New Testament papyri now known, only four are from bookrolls (P 12, P 13, P 18, and P 22). All of

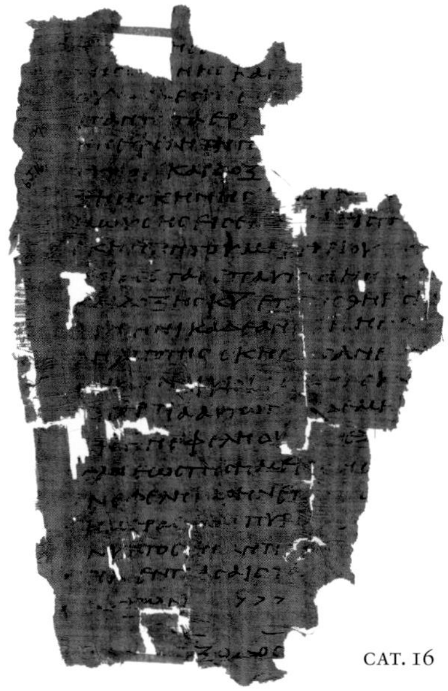

CAT. 16

these, however, are either opisthographs (written on the outside [or verso] of a previously inscribed bookroll) or palimpsests (written on papyrus from which the original writing has been erased). The reuse of papyrus in this way was a cost-saving measure.

The fragment shown here is an opisthograph. On the recto, usually the only side of a bookroll to carry writing, was inscribed the book of Exodus, of which this fragment contains Exodus 11:26–32. Subsequently, the Revelation of Saint John was inscribed on the verso, and hence runs in the opposite direction to the text of Exodus. This fragment preserves the text of Revelation 1:4–7. It is written in a clear hand of medium size with upright and heavily formed letters. Some punctuation is evident in the form of high and medial dots. The words "Jesus Christ" in Revelation 1:5 (line 6) are written as a *nomen sacrum* with superscriptive strokes. The scribe initially wrote out fully the word "God" in Revelation 1:10 (line 12) but then crossed out the central vowels and added the superscriptive stroke, thus converting this word, too, into a *nomen sacrum*.

It is generally assumed that the text of Exodus was written in a Christian context, for line 11 contains the *nomen sacrum* ku with a superscriptive stroke (for *kurios*, "Lord"). But because we are dealing with an opisthograph bookroll, it is at least conceivable that the text of Exodus was written for Jewish use, and that the manuscript was subsequently reused in a Christian setting by transcribing Revelation on the back (or outside) of the bookroll. In that case it would have to be thought that the *nomen sacrum* in line 11 was inserted into a space that had been left blank, perhaps for the later insertion of the divine name in a distinctive form, which was often done in Jewish Septuagintal manuscripts. That possibility could be supported by the observation that the *nomen sacrum* found here appears to be written in slightly larger letters than the surrounding text and is followed by a small space (though it seems to be written in the same hand). Whether or not this manuscript is evidence of it, Jewish manuscripts of the Septuagint are otherwise known to have been in the possession and use of Christians. HYG

Bibliography:

Hunt, 1911, pp. 13–14.

17

The Chester Beatty Numbers and Deuteronomy Codex

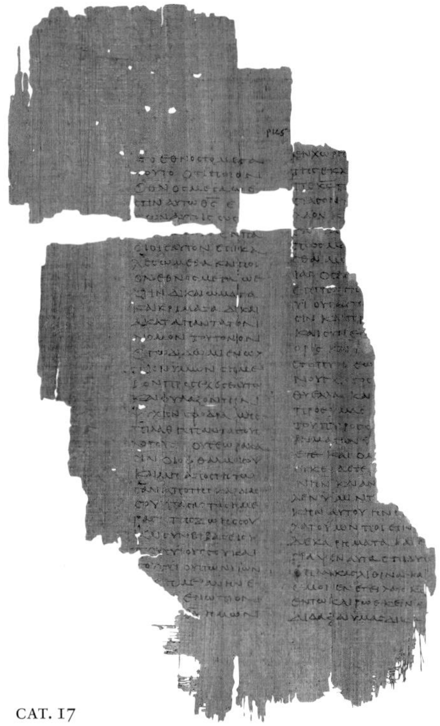

CAT. 17

Dublin, Chester Beatty Library, MS. Biblical Papyri VI (Rahlfs 963), ff. 63v, 64v
Papyrus; ff. 50; 280 × 180mm
(original size 330 × 190mm)
Numbers and Deuteronomy; Greek
Fayyum or Aphroditopolis (modern Atfih), Egypt; ca. 150 C.E.

Before the discovery of the Dead Sea Scrolls in the late 1940s, the earliest extant biblical manuscripts came from the Greek translation of the Hebrew Bible known as the Septuagint, and the pages exhibited here from the Chester Beatty Numbers and Deuteronomy Codex were regarded as the oldest extant manuscript of any bible. That accolade has now passed to other manuscripts but this codex, dating from the middle of the second century C.E. (or at the very latest the beginning of the third century), is still the most extensive second-century Christian codex. It is of great interest for providing evidence of the transition from roll to codex and is among the earliest examples in the world of the codex form of book production. It is possibly the earliest book to have page numbers, which are clearly visible written in Greek letters on the folios shown.

The portion of the text shown here is Deuteronomy 4:6–23. Analysis suggests that the scribe copied the biblical text from two different rolls, as the textual characteristics of Numbers are quite different from those of Deuteronomy. The exemplars were probably of varying dates and originated from different scribal centers. The text for Numbers largely corresponds to Codex Vaticanus but the Deuteronomy text does not; it largely agrees with the much later fifth-century Freer manuscript of Deuteronomy (cat. no. 27).

The codex originally consisted of 216 pages, of which about 100 survive. It is in a very fine hand, written by an accomplished scribe, on good-quality papyrus that has been carefully prepared so that the direction of the papyrus fibers aligns correctly on each facing page. Just as medieval scribes ensured that the hair side and flesh side of vellum manuscripts matched on each opening, so this earlier scribe has ensured that the direction of the papyrus fibers match. The elegance of the script and the generous margins mark it as a superior specimen of book production demonstrating that, even before Constantine's Edict of Toleration, a Christian community in Roman Egypt could occasionally command the services of skilled professional scribes. Several other characteristics of the manuscript point to its Christian origin, particularly the abbreviations used for the *nomina sacra* or holy names, where the abbreviation for Joshua is the same as that for Jesus.

CH

Bibliography:

Kenyon, 1935–58; Kenyon, 1939; Turner, 1977; Roberts and Skeat, 1983.

18

A tablet of texts

Vienna, Osterreichischen Nationalbibliothek, P. Vindob. KHT 1
Ink on wood; 230 × 560mm (text area 220 × 500mm)
Acts of the Apostles and the Epistles (selected texts); unknown origin; seventh century

This unique specimen is a wooden tablet that displays brief selections from several early Christian documents. One side carries James 5:16–20 and 2 Timothy 4:5–7, while the other carries Acts 1:1–5. The text is inscribed *transversa*, across the breadth of the tablet and thus with the grain of the wood, in an unskilled, labored, and irregular uncial hand on both sides. The lines are long and wavering and the margins variable. The writing has faded to obscurity at some points, especially at the lower edge. Two holes drilled near the center of the top edge indicate either that it was attached to additional tablets by a thong or perhaps was hung on a wall or suspended from a ceiling.

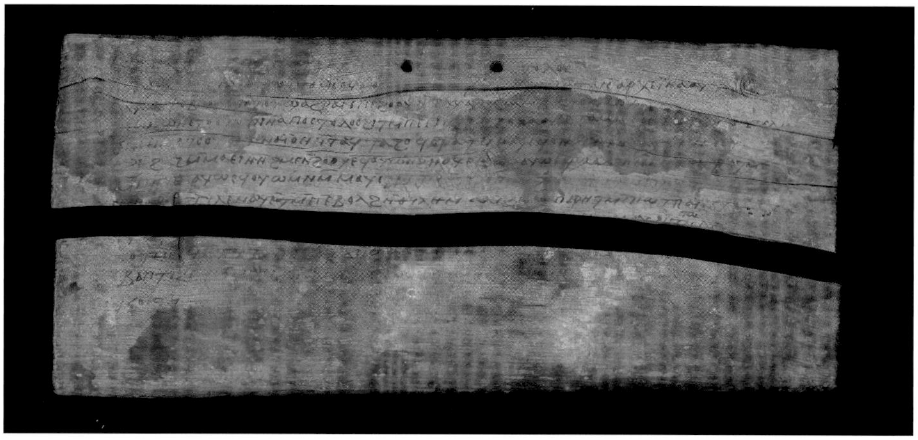

CAT. 18

It is difficult to discern why these texts may have been transcribed together since they have nothing in common by way of source or content. The selection, the medium, and the manner of inscription may indicate that we have to do with a writing exercise. The Austrian National Library has described this as a prayer tablet.

HYG

19

The Washington Codex of the Psalms

Washington, D.C., Freer Gallery of Art, F1906.273 (MS. II), p. 171
Ink on parchment; ff. 107; 355 × 280mm
Psalm 110; Greek
Egypt; fifth century

The Washington codex of the Psalms, like the Washington manuscript of Deuteronomy and Joshua (cat. no. 27), was purchased in Egypt by Charles Lang Freer in 1906. The Psalms manuscript was in a much more deteriorated condition, especially on the binding edge. This decay had affected more than half of each leaf and some whole leaves at the beginning of the manuscript, and had also caused the leaves to adhere to each other, which required a delicate procedure to separate them.

This codex has 107 leaves (or fragments of leaves), and is made up of quires of varying size (6, 8 or 10 leaves each). The leaves were carefully ruled, and inscribed in a single column per page with thirty lines to the column and twenty-five to thirty letters to the full line, though the lines are of unequal length by way of preserving the poetical versification of the Psalms. (There are, however, no stanza divisions.) The scribe wrote in a large, square uncial hand using broad strokes. Brown ink is used for the text, but the numeration and the customary titles of the Psalms are given in red ink. The Psalms are prominently numbered by large capital letters set into the left-hand margin, and these numbers are modestly ornamented both above and below. In about half of the Psalms where the beginning is preserved the initial letter of the Psalm is somewhat enlarged, but does not normally protrude into the margin. The manuscript is almost wholly lacking in punctuation, but the *nomina sacra* are regularly abbreviated, as was customary in early Christian manuscripts.

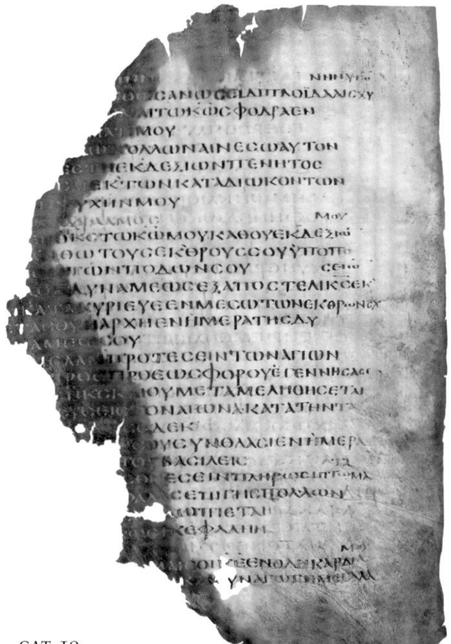

CAT. 19

At some point the last part of the manuscript, from Psalm 142:8 to Psalm 151, was lost. Subsequently, perhaps in the eighth century, a corresponding portion of another manuscript of the Psalms was pirated and used to replace what had been lost. The leaves of the added portion are somewhat smaller than those of the older manuscript, and, while they too are inscribed in one column per page, the columns have only twenty-four lines, the lines contain only eighteen to twenty-two letters, and the scribal hand is more sloping. The added leaves begin with Psalm 142:5, so that there is a textual overlap of some eight lines. The supplement extends to Psalm 151. On the back of the leaf containing Psalm 151 there is a portion of the first of the Psalms of Solomon, and the manuscript from which these leaves were taken probably originally contained all the Psalms of Solomon in addition to the biblical Psalms.

HYG

Bibliography:

Sanders, 1910–17, Part 2.

20

The Washington Manuscript of the Pauline Epistles

Washington, D.C., Freer Gallery of Art, F1906.275 (MS. IV), ff. 104v–105r
Ink on parchment; ff. 84; 160 × 105mm
Bible fragment (Epistles of Paul); Greek
Egypt; fifth or sixth century

This manuscript, sometimes called Codex Freerianus, was acquired in a much-decayed, fragmentary, and discolored condition, such that the pages were difficult to separate and much of the text had been lost. Because ten quire numbers survived, it can be calculated that the complete manuscript had between 208 and 212 leaves. This indicates that the codex was considerably larger than necessary for the Epistles of Paul, and suggests that originally it also contained the Acts of the Apostles and the catholic epistles. Of this large codex only 84 leaves (168 pages) are preserved in a fragmentary state. When produced, the leaves of the manuscript measured approximately 250 by 200 millimeters. In its present condition, only eight or nine lines remain on each page.

The codex was written on high-quality parchment in a single broad column (120 millimeters across) of thirty lines per page, with an average of twenty-five letters to the line. The parchment was carefully ruled before inscription, and the scribe, who was highly skilled, wrote very well-formed letters in an upright, square uncial hand. Thus the manuscript appears to have been produced to a relatively high standard. The *nomina sacra* are consistently used. There are no accent or breathing marks. Paragraph divisions are frequently shown by an enlarged letter that is set entirely into the margin. The scribe wrote with a brown ink, but the first line of each epistle (save one) was either written or, more probably, subsequently overwritten in red ink.

The extant leaves contain parts of all the Pauline Epistles except Romans, and include the Epistle to the Hebrews, which, as the leaves illustrated show, stands immediately after 2 Thessalonians rather than after the personal letters as was more customary. The titles of the epistles are all in the early form, that is, with the name of the Church addressed but without the name of Paul (e.g., "To the Galatians"). The titles, written in brown ink, are adorned with a Latin cross on the same line, between the title and the outer edge of the page, and by short ornamental strokes above and below. The text is of the Alexandrian type (see cat. no. 13), but agrees more closely with Codex Sinaiticus and Codex Alexandrinus than with Codex Vaticanus.

HYG

Bibliography:

Sanders, 1912–18, Part 2.

CAT. 20

Formation and codification: The evolution of the Bible

21

Coptic Psalter

Washington, D.C., Freer Gallery of Art, F1908.32, ff. 50r–51v
Inks on parchment; ff. 126, fragmentary Psalter; Coptic
Egypt; fifth–seventh century

The Freer Psalter is a Sahidic Coptic version of the Septuagint psalms. The Sahidic dialect was one of some dozen different Coptic dialects spoken in Egypt; and in the fourth and fifth centuries it became the standard literary form of Coptic. Although the books of the Christian Bible were among the most translated and copied works in Coptic, no complete collection of the books of the Coptic Old Testament has survived from Antiquity in any of the Coptic dialects. Relatively few Sahidic psalters have survived, and the Freer manuscript is a valuable witness to the Sahidic psalter tradition.

Charles L. Freer acquired this manuscript in Egypt in May 1908. It is associated with the site of the ancient Coptic monastery of Deir Nahya, which is located northwest of Giza in the Fayyum area of Egypt. Medieval Arabic sources named the monastery Deir el-Karram or the Monastery of the Vinedresser. According to the Arab historian al-Maqrizi (died 1441), the monastery was destroyed in 1354 or 1355. Other Coptic and Greek biblical manuscript holdings of the Freer, notably the Washington codex of the Gospels (Codex Washingtonensis), are also connected to this monastic site.

The psalter is miniature in size, measuring 7 by 8 centimeters. Only 126 folios remain of an estimated original 350 folios or 700 pages. The extant folios include most of Psalms 6–53. The small page dimensions, coupled with the large number of pages, would have made binding difficult. In fact, there is no indication of binding. The psalter may have been intended to be bound in several volumes; or, it may have been intended for use without binding. Such an arrangement would allow different sections of the text to be read or copied at the same time. William Worrell suggested that its small format was a way to make use of rough-haired and oddly shaped parchment trimmings from larger manuscripts.

The Freer Psalter is not a deluxe manuscript. The linear arrangement of text varies from page to page and ornament consists of simple paragraph marks. At times as many as three different scribal hands have been distinguished in the manuscript. Parchment shrinkage and the resulting distortion of individual letters may be partially responsible for this perception. The letters *alpha*, *mu*, and *upsilon* appear in two distinctive forms, round and square. The rounded forms are visible in the two leaves illustrated (Psalms 36:2–6 and 36:6–9). The codex is variously dated on paleographical evidence as early as the fifth century, or between 500 and 700.
MJB

CAT. 21

Bibliography:
Sanders, 1909; Worrell, 1916; Vaschalde, 1919; Worrell, 1923, p. i–xxvi, 1–106 (text), pl. I–IV; Petersen, 1954, esp. 298–99, no. 7a & b; Coquin and Martin, 1991; Horn, 2000; Schüssler, 2000, pp. 86–87, pl. 114.

22

Codex Bruce (Codex Brucianus)

Oxford, Bodleian Library, MS. Bruce 96, fol. 6r
Papyrus; ff. 71;
approx. 290 × approx. 170mm
The two books of Jeu(?), and Untitled Gnostic Treatise; Coptic
Region of Thebes, Upper Egypt;
fifth or sixth century C.E.

For most of the Christian era, the complex system of ancient religious thought known as Gnosticism (after the Greek word for "knowledge") could only be glimpsed through the attacks of its opponents. For early theologians such as Irenaeus and Tertullian it was a heresy, borrowing from Christianity but rooted in paganism and promoting a cult of

CAT. 22

secret rites and dangerous ideas: the duality of light and dark, flawed Creation by the Demiurge, personal salvation through "gnosis."

The Gnostic treatises preserved in this manuscript from ancient Egypt were among the first to reach modern Europe in pure form. The fragile remains of the papyrus codex are made up of two distinct parts, written perhaps in the fifth or sixth century. Although its texts may derive from earlier Greek originals, they are in Coptic, the native language and alphabet developed in Egypt with Greek assimilations in the first millennium C.E.

The goal of the Scottish traveler James Bruce of Kinnaird (1730–1794) had been to search in Ethiopia for the source of the Nile. The volume of pioneer travel-writing that he first published in 1790 makes no mention of his Coptic codex, but his biographer Alexander Murray later described its acquisition: "When Mr. Bruce was at ... Thebes, in Upper Egypt, he purchased a Coptic manuscript which had been found in the ruins near that place, in the former residence of some Egyptian monks." He had visited Thebes (modern Luxor) around 1769; he returned to London in 1774, and then home to Scotland. Later, he allowed the codex to be inspected and transcribed by the orientalist Charles G. Woide (1725–1790), a curator at the British Museum, who recognized its Coptic dialect as Sahidic. The manuscripts collected by James Bruce on his travels were bought by the Bodleian Library for £1000 in 1843: most are in Arabic or Ethiopic (including a copy of the Ethiopic Book of Enoch), but it is this single Coptic volume which now bears his name as "Codex Bruce" or "Codex Brucianus."

The contents of Codex Bruce suggest a late stage of Gnostic thought, developed and elaborated to a point that defies summary. The Coptic text is interspersed with symbolic diagrams. The most elaborate diagram consists of an overall design of the Coptic cross, incorporating monograms, symbols, and letters. It is carefully drawn, but entirely in ink, without colors. The papyrus is much damaged, and its dark brown color is often hard to distinguish from that of the fading ink; on some later pages, the writing has almost disappeared. Yet Codex Bruce was an astonishing find: maybe even more important, as a doorway to ancient thought, than the source of the Blue Nile.

BODLEIAN LIBRARY

Bibliography:
Bruce, 1813; Murray, 1842; Macray, 1890, pp. 344–45; Lamplugh, 1918; Baynes, 1933; Schmidt, 1959; Doresse, 1960, pp. 76–86; Schmidt, 1978.

23

Saint Ephrem's commentary on Tatian's *Diatessaron*

Dublin, Chester Beatty Library, MS. W 709
Ink on parchment; ff. 75; 250 × 165mm
Ephrem, *Evangelion Da-Meḥalleṭē*; Syriac
Deir el-Suriani, Egypt; ca. 480–500

The *Diatessaron*, meaning "through the four gospels," is the name the fourth-century Church historian Eusebius gave to a collation and combination of the gospels created by Tatian, a disciple of Justin Martyr, around 170 C.E. In this work, Tatian drew on the four canonical gospels to create a single, continuous narrative of Jesus's life that eliminated repetition of parallel passages and harmonized discrepancies and contradictions. Probably written in Tatian's native Syriac, the *Diatessaron* is one of the earliest witnesses to the text of the gospels, drawing on a form of the Greek text circulating in Rome in the mid-second century. It probably influenced many readings in the Old Syriac version of the New Testament, and enjoyed great popularity both within the Syriac- and Aramaic-speaking world and much farther afield. Not long after composing the *Diatessaron*, Tatian came to be considered a heretic, and by the mid-fifth century his work was finally suppressed.

Despite its enormous popularity and influence, no copy of the original text has survived, and reconstructions have necessarily drawn on translations, commentaries, and quotations. Among the most important of these was a commentary written by Ephrem of Edessa (ca. 306–373), a theologian who settled in this

CAT. 23

CAT. 24

important center of Christianity (now Urfa in eastern Turkey).

Until the late 1950s, Ephrem's commentary was available primarily through an Armenian version first published in the nineteenth century. It was then that Sir Alfred Chester Beatty, who had already assembled a remarkable collection of early biblical papyrus codices (cat. nos. 14, 17), acquired a manuscript containing a significant portion of the Syriac text of Ephrem's commentary. This was published in 1963 by Dom Louis Leloir, who had completed a critical edition of the Armenian version in 1953 and a Latin translation in 1954; a stray folio of the same manuscript now in Barcelona was published in 1966. Even more remarkably, the Chester Beatty Library acquired an additional five folios of the manuscript in 1984 and a further thirty-six in 1986. Approximately eighty percent of the original codex has now been reassembled, and a critical edition of the text and English translation have already been published.

AG

Bibliography:
Leloir, 1963; Leloir, 1990; McCarthy, 1993; Petersen, 1994; Petersen, 2004; Valdivieso, 1966.

24

Syriac Pentateuch

London, British Library, APA, Syriac MSS. Add. 14425, ff. 105r–106v
Ink and pigments on parchment;
273 × 218mm
Pentateuch; Syriac
Amida, Syria; 463

This is the oldest known dated biblical codex. It contains the Syriac Peshitta version of Genesis, Exodus, Numbers, and

Deuteronomy. The Peshitta or "simple" version of the Syriac text became the official translation used by the Syriac-speaking Churches in the fifth century. It is believed the New Testament portion was prepared by Rabbula, bishop of Edessa (411–435). He ordered copies of the separate gospels to be placed in every church instead of the *Diatessaron* of Tatian, which previously had been widely used.

The manuscript was written in 463 in a fine, bold *esṭrangelā* hand by the deacon John at Amida (now Diyarbakır in eastern Turkey). Amida was a strategic city on the Upper Tigris, seat of a bishop. Vowel points were added by a later hand.

From the Nitrian collection, British Library.

MPB after Nersessian, 1978, no. 19

Bibliography:
Nersessian, 1978, p. 28, no. 19 and pl. 2.

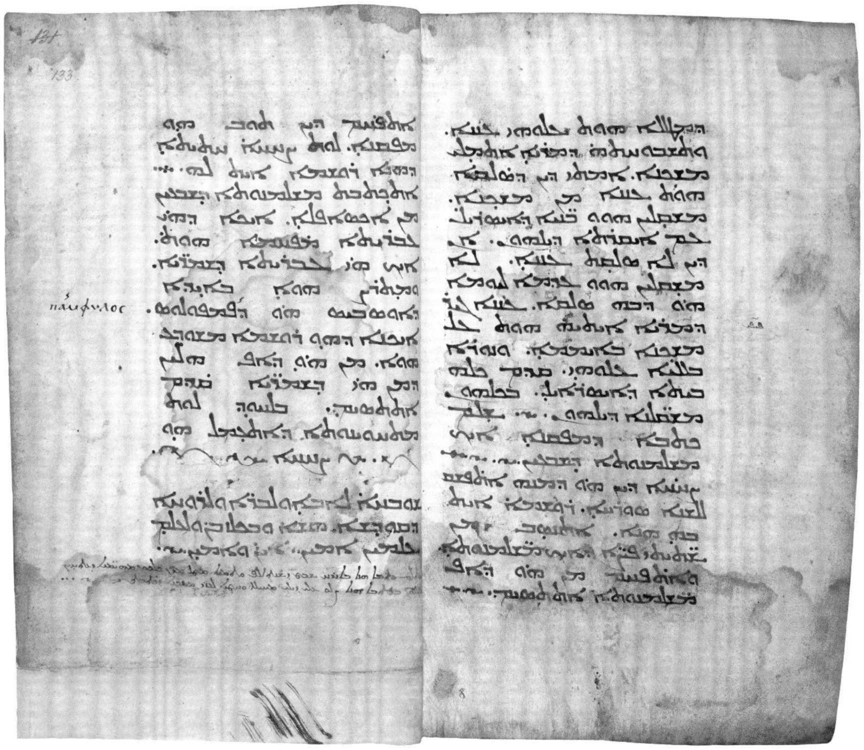

CAT. 25

25

Syrohexapla Exodus

London, British Library, APA, Syriac MSS. Add. 12134, ff. 132v–133r
Ink and pigments on parchment; ff. 134; 250 × 150mm
The Book of Exodus; Syriac
Syria; 697

The text is the Book of Exodus, translated from the Septuagint by Paul of Tella. It is divided into ten *capitula*, to which a summary of the contents is prefixed. The lessons (lections) are rubricated in the text and an index of them was prefixed to the volume, although the greater part of it is now lost as only one page (f. 2r) has survived. This page contains eighteen circles, arranged in three columns of six, surrounded by a double border of green and red. Each circle contains the indication of one lesson. The text is that of the *Hexapla* of Origen, with the critical marks and the various readings of Aquila, Symmachus, and Theodotion also indicated. The manuscript is copied in a fine, regular *esṭrangelā* hand dated in the year of the Greeks 1008 (697 C.E.).

The colophon (ff. 132v–133r) is most revealing, for it records an unusual amount of information concerning the scribe's sources and gives an insight into the importance attached to securing an authoritative text to copy. It reads:

The Book of Exodus, according to the translation of the LXX [Septuagint], ends here. In the Exemplar from which it was translated into the Syriac tongue, was this epigraph: "Taken from a copy of the hexapla, which was arranged according to the different versions, and collated with one which was furnished with the various readings of the versions. This copy of Exodus was also collated with an accurate exemplar, in which was this epigraph: "The translation of the LXX, was transcribed from a manuscript of the Hexapla, in which the Hebrew was collated according to the Hebrew text of the Samaritans. And this manuscript was corrected by the hand of Eusebius Pamphili, as the epigraph shows; from which manuscript also the things taken from the Samaritan text have been previously inserted, merely as an evidence that great pains were taken with the copy.

MPB after Nersessian, 1978, no.23

Bibliography:
Wright, 1870, pp. 29–31; Nersessian, 1978, pp. 28–29, no. 23.

Formation and codification: The earliest Christian bibles

26

Codex Sinaiticus

The Holy Monastery of Saint Catherine, Mount Sinai, Codex Sinaiticus; unnumbered bifolium
Ink on parchment; ff. 730 (originally); 363 × 332mm
Passages from the Book of Numbers; Greek
Uncertain provenance (Rome? Caesarea? Alexandria?); fourth century, second quarter

This most famous and important ancient manuscript of the Bible, named after the place of its discovery, Saint Catherine's Monastery at the foot of Mount Sinai (Jebel Musa, the Mount of Moses), originally contained the complete Greek Bible, both the Old Testament and the New Testament, as well as at least two early Christian writings later considered not to belong to the New Testament canon, namely the Epistle of Barnabas and the Shepherd of Hermas. Today, portions of the Old Testament have been lost, but the whole of the New Testament has been preserved, and consequently Codex Sinaiticus provides the only complete copy of the Greek New Testament that predates the ninth century. Hence it is also the only complete copy in an uncial script (although Codex Alexandrinus contains portions of every New Testament book).

Constantin von Tischendorf was the first European scholar to see the Codex Sinaiticus and understand its antiquity and importance. On his first visit to the monastery in 1844, he saw 128 leaves of the codex in the library, of which he managed to take forty-three. These were subsequently deposited in the library of the University of Leipzig where he was a *Privatdozent* (lecturer). Tischendorf returned to the monastery twice more, in 1853, and again in 1859 under the patronage of Alexander II, the Russian Czar, with the aim of discovering further parts of the same manuscript. On this last visit he was shown the rest of the codex, and, recognizing its immense value, undertook first to transcribe it. He then asked to take the original manuscript to Russia, where it would be published for the benefit of scholars, writing his famous promissory note, "This manuscript I promise to return, undamaged and in a good state of preservation, to the Holy Confraternity of Sinai at its earliest request." Instead, the codex was retained by the Russian Empire and, after the Revolution, was sold to the British Museum in 1933. In 1975 additional leaves and fragments of the Codex Sinaiticus were discovered at Saint Catherine's Monastery.

The remains of Codex Sinaiticus are therefore now held in four places: the larger part (347 leaves) is in the British Library; 43 leaves are in the Library of the University of Leipzig; parts of three leaves are held by the National Library of Russia in St. Petersburg; and a dozen or more leaves remain at Saint Catherine's Monastery. The two-best preserved leaves among those at Sinai are illustrated here.

Codex Sinaiticus is believed originally to have contained at least 730 leaves (1460 pages), measuring 381 by 345 millimeters. It was inscribed in four columns per page, and is the only biblical manuscript known in this format, with forty-eight lines to the column (but only two columns per page in Psalms, Proverbs, Ecclesiastes, Song of Songs, Wisdom of Solomon, Sirach, and Job). The manuscript was written by three scribes of very similar hand in a simple, regular, and upright uncial, the letters lacking ornamentation. There is no use of accents or breathing marks, but paragraphs are indicated by a slight extension of the initial letter of the line into the left margin, with the preceding line not filled out to the right margin. Sinaiticus is very heavily corrected. After the scribes finished their work it appears that the manuscript was reviewed and emended before it left the scriptorium. At a later time, perhaps in the sixth or seventh century, the manuscript was again subjected to thorough correction. A colophon at the end of Esdras and Esther indicates that at least some of these later changes were in accor-

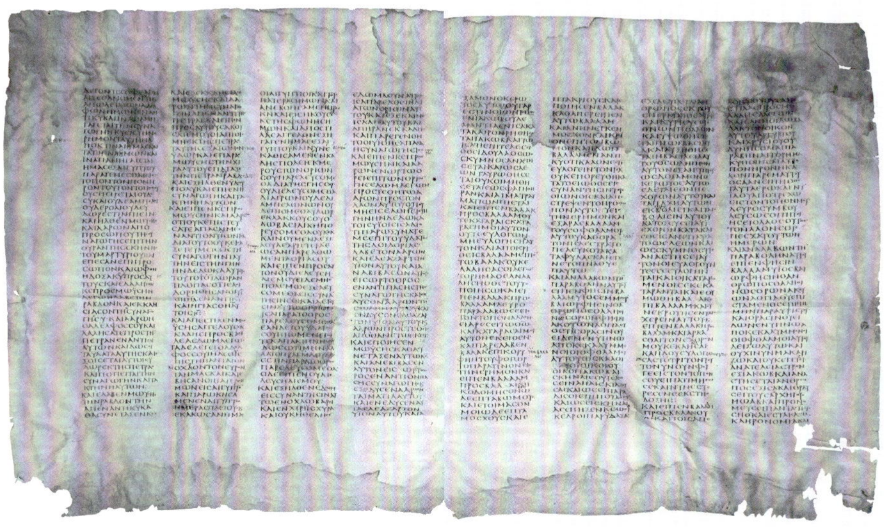

CAT. 26

dance with "a very ancient manuscript that had been corrected by the hand of the holy martyr Pamphilus." Pamphilus (240–309) had assembled the great Christian library at Caesarea, which housed many early Christian writings and was rich in biblical materials.

The character of the text of Codex Sinaiticus varies from one book to another, owing to the different manuscripts used as exemplars. In general it represents the Alexandrian text, but an appreciable number of readings, especially in the Gospel of John, are more closely related to the Western textual tradition, of which the principal early witnesses are Codex Bezae and a few earlier papyri (P 29, P 38, P 48).

Codex Sinaiticus incorporates numbers from the canon tables devised by Eusebius, bishop of Caesarea (ca. 260–ca. 339), and hence the manuscript cannot be dated earlier than the fourth century.

The bifolium illustrated here provides the passage in which Moses, leading the Hebrews through the Sinai desert after the exodus, strikes the rock to bring forth water (Numbers 20:2–13). The hole and pressure marks at the fore-edge of this folio suggest that at some point a tab, possibly of leather, was attached to it so that the codex might be readily opened at this passage, which would naturally have held particular interest for the monks of Saint Catherine's Monastery. It may be mentioned in this connection that the Spanish nun, Etheria (or Egeria), a fourth-century pilgrim to the Holy Land, visited Sinai among other sites, and remarked appreciatively in her travel diary (*Itinerarium Egeriae* or *Pereginatio Aetheriae*) that at the sacred places it was customary to read the biblical narratives relating to them.

HYG

Bibliography:
Lake and Lake, 1911–22; Milne and Skeat, 1938; Ševčenko, 1964; Charlesworth, 1981.

27

The Washington Codex of Deuteronomy and Joshua

Washington, D.C., Freer Gallery of Art, F1906.272 (MS I), ff. 117v and 119r
Ink on parchment; ff. 102; 306 × 258mm
Bible; Greek
Egypt; late fourth–fifth century

This parchment codex containing Deuteronomy and Joshua was acquired by Charles Lang Freer in 1906 from an Egyptian dealer and subsequently given to the Smithsonian Institution (see pages 6–9). It comprises 102 leaves. The quires of the codex are numbered in the upper right-hand corner of the first page of each quire. Because the numbers begin with 37 and continue through 60, it is clear that the first 36 quires are missing. They would doubtless have contained the books of Genesis through Numbers. Thus the manuscript would originally have had somewhere between 524 and 576 pages. Apart from the lost portion, the codex is relatively well preserved. Although the parchment has become crinkled and toughened with age and the leaves have been somewhat damaged along the bottom edge, this has caused only a small loss of text on the first two leaves and on the last leaf. There are, however, two sizable internal lacunae (Deuteronomy 5:16–6:18 and Joshua 3:3–4:10).

The codex was carefully ruled before it was written, and was inscribed in two columns per page with thirty-one lines to the column. The hand is a regular, upright uncial well executed by a practiced scribe. The *nomina sacra* are commonly used throughout. Punctuation is sparse and inconsistent, and there are no accent marks. Chapter divisions of irregular length, similar to those of Codex Vaticanus, are signaled by enlarging the initial letter and placing it slightly outside the left margin of the column. Notably, the first two or three lines of both Deuteronomy and Joshua, and presumably also of the other books that originally belonged to this codex, are written in red ink. Thus the manuscript offers an early example of rubrication (from the Latin, rubricare, "to color red"), writing in red ink by way of

CAT. 27

giving visual emphasis and calling attention to the divisions or headings of a text. Rubrication, whether of whole lines, of first words, or initial letters, became a common practice in European manuscripts from the seventh century on.

Beyond the hand of the original scribe, this manuscript betrays a number of additional hands. Only two of these hold much interest. A second hand, probably contemporary with the original scribe, was that of the corrector, who went over the manuscript and made some emendations. A century or two later, another hand added in a cursive script a set of notations providing directions for liturgical readings—where a reading was to begin and end, and when the reading was to be done. Such notations became known as "rubrics" since they were commonly written in red in order to distinguish them from the text proper, although in this manuscript they are not given in red.

By virtue of its careful layout, construction, inscription, and correction it is clear that this manuscript was intended as a high quality codex of the Hexateuch.
HYG

Bibliography:
Sanders, 1910–17, Part I.

28

Painted covers from the Freer Gospels

Washington, D.C., Freer Gallery of Art, F1906.297 (Matthew and John; left), F1906.298 (Mark and Luke; right) (MS. III; Codex Washingtonensis)
Covers from the Freer Gospels; Greek
Encaustic (wax) painting on wooden boards; 213 × 143 × 16mm (each board)
Coptic Egypt; seventh century

The Freer gospelbook, one of the earliest witnesses to the Greek Bible, was made in Egypt during the late fourth to early fifth century. It was purchased by Charles Lang Freer in Cairo in 1906. During the seventh century the book's wooden boards were adorned with images of the four evangelists whose gospels lie within. They are depicted bearded in Byzantine fashion, each head framed by a nimbus, and hold individual copies of their gospels bound in jeweled treasure bindings. Their hands are draped in the attitude of veneration adopted by the deacon when carrying the gospels in procession and reading from them during the liturgy.

The vibrancy of the colors has been retained due to the use of the encaustic painting technique that was particularly favored in Coptic Egypt. Encaustic paint consists of pigments mixed with beeswax that is worked when molten, applied to a surface, and reheated, giving an enamel-like finish. The term comes from the Greek term "to burn in," referring to the process of fusing the paint to its support. Encaustic painting was practised by the Greeks from the fifth century B.C.E. and Pliny the Younger, writing in the first century C.E., tells of Roman encaustic painting on wooden panels, marble, and ivory. Some of the finest examples of the art are the funerary portraits that adorned mummified burials in the Fayyum during the first and second centuries and the technique was perpetuated in Egypt during the early Middle Ages. It was a difficult process but one that permitted a building-up of paint in relief, with a jewel-like luminescence and a far better rate of preservation than tempera, as it is moisture-proof and does not fade, discolor, or require varnishing.

The binding boards are probably contemporary with the volume and were originally simply of wood, perhaps contained in an envelope binding, in accordance with early practice. Holes in the edges of

CAT. 28

the front cover show that, like the Glazier Codex (New York, Morgan Library & Museum, MS. G.67), the Freer Gospels were originally held closed by long leather bands, tied to prevent the parchment from cockling. These were removed to protect the paintings, which were added later to enhance the appearance and importance of the book. Traces of paint on the fore-edges suggest, as John Lowden notes, that the evangelist paintings were added in situ to the bound book.

The metalwork fittings at the head of the binding served to prevent the volume from being opened very far, thereby protecting its structure and contents but also effectively preventing the text from being read. Lowden has suggested that this later embellishment and chaining of the volume amounted to its enshrinement as a relic (perhaps protected by a fabric wrapping when not displayed), the images of the gospelers effectively serving as a substitute for their inaccessible gospels.

MPB

Bibliography:

Sanders, 1908; Sanders, 1913; Morey, 1914; Buchthal and Kurz, 1942; Mayer, 1962; Leroy, 1974, pp. 87–89, pl. 26; Metzger, 1992, pp. 56–57; Lowden, forthcoming.

29

The Four Gospels (Codex Washingtonensis or Freer Gospels)

Washington, D.C., Freer Gallery of Art, F1906.274 (MS. III), ff. 108v–109r
Ink on parchment; ff. 187; 208 × 143mm
Gospels; Greek
Egypt; fourth or fifth century

Variously known as Codex Washingtonensis or the Freer Gospels (after its purchaser, Charles Lang Freer), this multiple-quire codex is one of the more significant uncial manuscripts discovered in the last century. It originally contained the complete text of the four canonical gospels, which it presents in the Western order (Matthew, John, Luke, Mark), but is now missing pages containing part of Mark (15:13–38) and part of John (14:27–16:7). Moreover, the initial quire of John (1:1–5:11) is a later insertion: it shows a different script, a different method of punctuation, and a different sort of parchment. The pages are inscribed in a single column of thirty lines. The manuscript was written by one scribe in a small, sloping but clear and regular uncial that is pleasing to the eye.

The manuscript has many interesting features. It is carefully formatted, the readily legible script being complemented by paragraphing, punctuation, diacritical markings, and spacing between sense units, all of which suggest that it was prepared for public, liturgical reading.

The character of the text in this manuscript is, however, highly variegated and lacks any consistency. Throughout Matthew and in much of Luke (8:13–24:53) the text is of an ordinary Byzantine type; in the rest of Luke it is Alexandrian; the first five chapters of Mark have a Western character, while the rest of Mark is of a very mixed type; and in John the text is Alexandrian, save in the later insertion, where the text is of a mixed type. The highly heterogeneous textual character of this manuscript and the abrupt changes (even in the midst of individual gospels) from one text-type to another make this manuscript unique, and pose a standing puzzle to textual critics. Perhaps the best explanation is that the text of the gospels offered by this codex was compiled from a number of different, probably fragmentary, manuscripts of divergent textual types. It has been suggested that such a piecemeal reconstitution of gospel texts as we see in

CAT. 29

the Codex Washingtonensis was made necessary by the Great Persecution, during which the Emperor Diocletian ordered the destruction of Christian books.

A further and very notable feature of this manuscript is the addition near the end of the Gospel of Mark (after 16:14) of a statement attributed to Jesus that occurs in no other manuscript (though it was known to Jerome). This is the so-called Freer logion, which reads as follows:

And they excused themselves, saying, "This age of lawlessness and unbelief is under Satan, who does not allow the truth and power of God to prevail over the unclean things of the spirits. Therefore reveal your righteousness now"—thus they spoke to Christ. And Christ replied to them, "The term of years for Satan's power has been fulfilled, but other terrible things draw near. And for those who have sinned I was delivered over to death so that they may return to the truth and no longer sin, so that they may inherit the spiritual and incorruptible glory of righteousness that is in heaven."

HYG

Bibliography:
Gregory, 1908; Sanders, 1912–18, Part 1; Streeter, 1926; E. Helzle, *Der Schluss der Markusevangeliums und das Freer-Logion (Mk. 16,14 W)* (dissertation, Tubingen University, 1959); Hurtado, 1981.

30

Codex Claromontanus

Paris, Bibliothèque nationale de France, MS. Gr. 107
Ink on fine parchment;
ff. 533; 245 × 195mm
Bilingual manuscript of the Epistles of Paul; Greek and Latin
Provenance unknown (Sardinia?);
fifth to sixth century

Codex Claromontanus is a Greek–Latin bilingual manuscript that presents the letters of Paul, including the Epistle to the Hebrews, the Greek text being given on the left-hand pages, and the Latin on the right-hand pages. The leaves are inscribed in one column of twenty-one lines per page. The line lengths are irregular as the transcription is by sense units (*per cola et commata*). The hand is a simple uncial of somewhat archaic appearance. The manuscript originally lacked accents and breathing marks, though these were subsequently supplied by one of at least nine later correctors. Red ink (instead of brown) was employed for quotations from Jewish scripture (except in the Epistle to the Hebrews), and also for the first three lines of each letter. The codex is well-preserved, and lacks only the beginning of the letter to the Romans (1:1–7).

The origins of this codex are unknown. It was acquired, first examined, and named by the great French Calvinist scholar Theodore Beza, who reported that it had been discovered in a convent at Clermont-en-Beauvais north of Paris.

Codex Claromontanus is a significant witness to the history of the text of the Pauline Epistles. Together with its close relatives, Codex Boernerianus (Dresden, Sachischen Landesbibliothek, A 145b) and Codex Augiensis (Cambridge, Trinity College, B XVII.1), both ninth-century Greek–Latin bilinguals, it offers important testimony to a distinctly Western text of the epistles and often preserves early readings. Codex Sangermanensis (St. Petersburg, National Library of Russia, Greek 20) is a ninth- or tenth-century copy of Codex Claromontanus. The Greek text is far more correctly written than the Latin, which has numerous errors and seems relatively independent of the Greek. The Latin text is very closely similar to the Old Latin version cited by Lucifer of Cagliari (died 370) in Sardinia.

This codex is also important for the history of the New Testament canon, for inserted between Philemon and Hebrews is a Latin stichometric list of the books of the Bible, both Old Testament and New, the so-called *Catalogus Claromontanus*. This list is older than the codex itself, probably

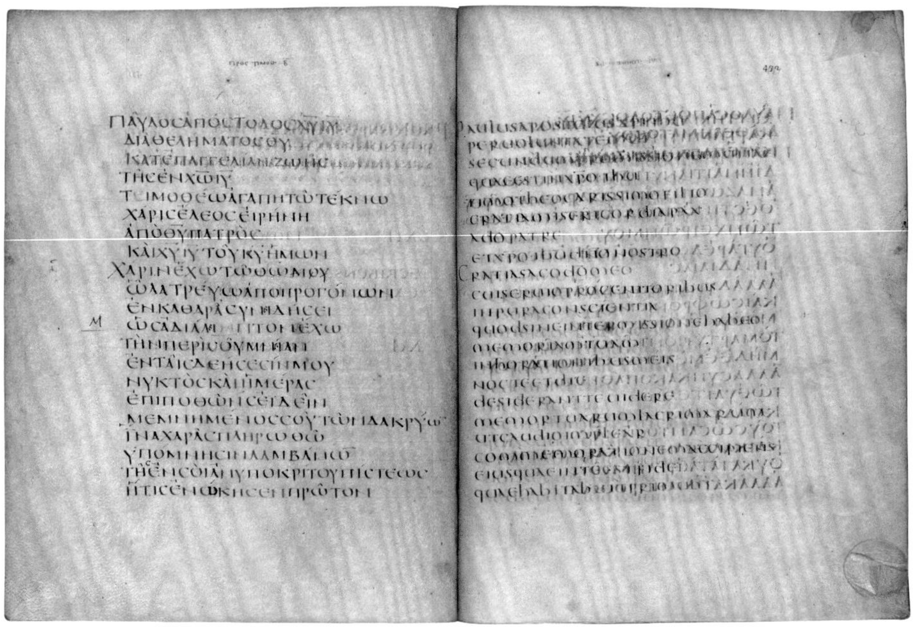

CAT. 30

dating to the fourth century, and had an Eastern origin. The list of New Testament books is divided into only two categories, "The Four Gospels" and "The Epistles of Paul" (and thus does not clearly distinguish the catholic epistles, Revelation, or Acts from the Epistles of Paul, although they are named). Moreover, the list omits (no doubt accidentally) Philippians and 1–2 Thessalonians in the enumeration of Paul's letters, and at the end it includes the Epistle of Barnabas, the Shepherd of Hermas, the Acts of Paul, and the Apocalypse of Peter, all of which have horizontal lines drawn beside them in the left margin, identifying them as books of disputed standing. When these points are considered, this list represents a New Testament of twenty-seven undisputed books.

HYG

Bibliography:
Souter, 1904–1905; Frede, 1964, pp. 15–39; Hahnemann, 1992.

31

Codex Harleianus (*alias* The Harley Gospels)

London, British Library, Western MSS. Harley MS. 1775, ff. 223v–224r
Ink on parchment; ff. 468; 177 × 120mm
Gospels with canon tables; Latin
Italy (northern?); late sixth century (possibly early seventh century)

This volume is an important early witness to the Vulgate text, although it also incorporates a number of Old Latin readings and has moved away somewhat from Jerome's original fourth-century text to become a "Mixed Vulgate." It was made in Italy (Wordsworth and White favored a northern Italian origin), probably during the late sixth century, although some scholars favor an early seventh-century date. It is small, but written on finely prepared parchment in a good uncial hand, with the text laid out *per cola et commata*, with the length of the line clarifying the sense, rather than punctuation symbols. The presentation is extremely elegant, even if decoration is confined to simple arcades around the canon tables, slightly enlarged initials, and the use of red ink for the first line of each gospel and colophon decoration for the incipit and explicit inscriptions. Running titles are written in rustic capitals.

Corrections in a contemporary hand in slanting uncial employ a Greek style of syllabification recalling the method of Victor of Capua (as in the Codex Fuldensis). Citations are marked by a *v*-shaped diple. There are eighteen canon tables of the First Latin Group proposed by Carl Nordenfalk. Each gospel begins on a new quire, in Eastern fashion.

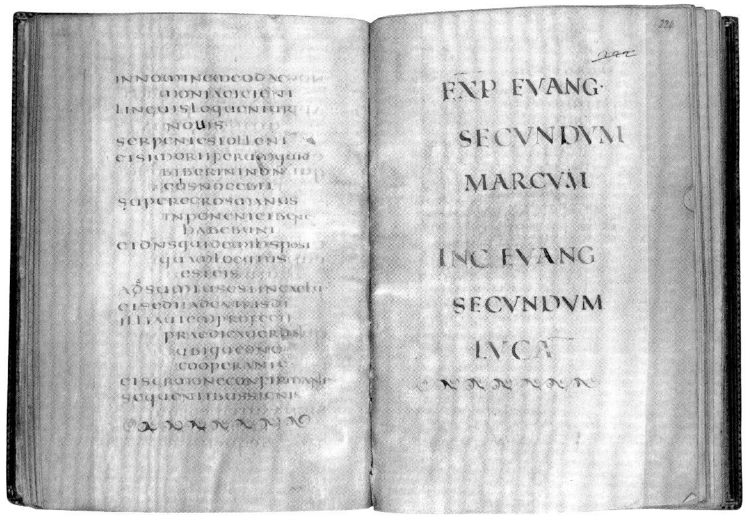

CAT. 31

The manuscript was in France by the ninth century, according to Elias Avery Lowe, when notes using Tironian shorthand symbols (invented by Cicero's secretary Tiro in the first century B.C.E. and used occasionally by Insular and Carolingian scribes) were added in a French hand to f. 11. It is representative of the sort of exemplars which may have been available to northern European biblical editors, such as Ceolfrith and his team and Alcuin (see cat. nos. 41, 43).

The book was owned by Cardinal Mazarin (died 1668) and then entered the Bibliothèque du Roi, formerly number 4582, from which it, together with other books, was stolen by the renegade priest Jean Aymon in 1707. It was subsequently purchased from him in Holland by Robert Harley, 1st Earl of Oxford (1661–1724); it was sold as part of the Harley Collection to the British Parliament in 1753 and incorporated into the Library of the newly founded British Museum.

MPB

Bibliography:
Ancient Manuscripts in the British Museum, 1888–94, Part 2, Latin, p. 14; Wordsworth and White, 1889–98, siglum "Z"; Scrivener, 1894, 2, p. 76; Kenyon, 1900; no. IX; Swarzenski, 1901, pp. 8, 17 n. 22; Chapman, 1908; Lowe, 1934–72, ii no. 197; Nordenfalk, 1938, pp. 209 ff; Micheli, 1939, pp. 31, 76, 93; Köhler, 1954; McGurk, 1961, pp. 35–36; Fischer, 1988–91, 1, pp. 13–14; Brown, 1990, pl. 5; McKitterick, 1990, (fig. 1); Farr, 1997, p. 120; McGurk, 1998, passim; Brown and Lovett, 1999, p. 44; Brown, 2003; Brown, 2005.

From Babel to Pentecost: "Sacred" languages and the vernaculars

32

Arabic Epistles and Acts

Mount Sinai, The Holy Monastery of Saint Catherine, Arabic MS. 151, ff. 171v–172r
Inks on parchment; ff. 269; 255 × 175mm
Epistles and Acts; Arabic
Damascus, Syria; A.H. 253 (867 C.E.)

This Arabic translation of and commentary on the Pauline Epistles, the Acts of the Apostles, and the catholic epistles by Bishr ibn al-Sirri is one of the oldest surviving dated Christian Arabic manuscripts. It is an autograph copy. A colophon at the end of the Pauline Epistles (ff. 186v–187r) states that Bishr ibn al-Sirri translated them from Syriac into Arabic, and that he commented on them for the benefit of his spiritual brother Solomon. The same colophon indicates that this work was completed in Damascus in the month of Ramadan, in the Hijrah year 253 (867 C.E). Bishr's Arabic translation was made from the standard Syriac version of the Bible called the Peshitta, which includes in its canon only James, 1 Peter, and 1 John from among the catholic epistles. The four minor catholic epistles (2 Peter, 2–3 John, and Jude) may have been translated into Arabic from a sixth-century Syriac version known today as the "Pococke Epistles," after William Pococke's 1630 edition.

The manuscript is shown here open to Hebrews 6:18–7:16. The translation is centered on the manuscript pages, with ample space below and in the margins for the commentary, which is arranged as notes. These notes are connected to the biblical text by special characters, much like modern footnotes. Other notes and interlinear glosses were also added to Bishr's translation and commentary. A colophon identifies Jirjis ibn Yuhanna ibn Sahl al-Yabrudi in this regard. It is dated A.H. 412 (1030 C.E) and, with two other notes dated A.H. 416 (1034 C.E), suggests the period during which Jirjis had access to Sinai Arabic MS. 151, which he used for collating other biblical manuscripts. Modern scholars have recognized Jirjis as the Christian physician and writer Abu'l Faraj al-Yabrudi (*floruit* first half of the eleventh century), who belonged to the Syrian Orthodox Church. Melkite lectionary notes, some of which were written in Greek, were also added throughout the manuscript. For example, a note on f. 172v identifies Hebrews 7:14 to be read at the Eucharist celebration on Christmas morning.

Sinai Arabic 151 shows the influence of yet another large church community of the Syriac tradition, that of the Church of the East. Bishr ibn al-Sirri's biblical commentary makes extensive use of the exegetical tradition of the Church of the East, including material that also appears in works by Theodore bar Koni (died 800) and Isho'dad of Merv (died circa 850). Bishr's own confessional affiliation remains to be established. He may have belonged to the Melkite Church or perhaps to the Church of the East. Subsequent use of his manuscript by Syrian Orthodox and Melkite readers demonstrates how the interpretative tradition of the Church of the East was shared more widely among the Arabic-speaking Christian communities resident in the Islamic world.

MJB

CAT. 32

Bibliography:

Dunlop Gibson, 1894, p. 22; Clark, 1952, p. 33; Atiya, 1955, p. 6; Staal, 1969; Kamil, 1970, p. 16; Nasrallah, 1976; Nasrallah, 1980; Staal, 1983; Staal, 1984; Samir, 1987; Brock, 2004.

CAT. 33

33

Karaite Book of Exodus

London, British Library,
APA, MS. Or. 2540, ff.18v–19r
Ink and pigments on paper;
ff. 21; 240 × 180mm
Exodus 1:1–8:5
Hebrew in Arabic characters
Palestine or probably Egypt;
ca. tenth century

The Karaites were a Jewish sect which, according to Karaite belief, was founded by Anan ben David in Babylonia in the eighth century C.E. They rejected rabbinic tradition and recognized the Hebrew Bible as the sole source of religious law. This led to a concentration on the study of the text of the Bible, on its "correct" pronunciation, translation, and interpretation. There is no certainty as to why the Karaites transcribed the Hebrew Bible into Arabic, but it may have represented an attempt to arrive at a correct reading tradition for the Bible, which they considered superior to the Masoretic text of rabbinical Jews.

Following the destruction of the Karaite centers of scholarship in Palestine by the Crusaders in 1099, the Karaite movement declined; its main center moved to Turkey and, later, to Lithuania and the Crimea. Nowadays communities of Karaite Jews can be found in Israel, particularly in Ramle, and in the United States.

This is a fragmentary manuscript comprising only Exodus 1:1–8:5. The Hebrew text was penned in a clear but rather unusual Arabic *naskhi* hand. The vowels, which are according to a system devised by the Tiberian Masoretes around the tenth century, have been added in red ink, the accents and the Arabic *tashdid* signs indicating long consonants in green.

The manuscript was copied on sturdy, brown, oriental paper and has two carpet pages of stylized flowers drawn in black ink and geometric borders in gold at the beginning of the volume (ff. 2v–3r). Spaces in the text indicating paragraphs, the end of verses, and other major divisions have been filled with stylized designs of foliage, leaves, intertwined chains, and rosettes in gold with red and green color in the Islamic style. The ornamentations used throughout the manuscript resemble decorations found in early Korans and have essentially a functional role, as illustrated in the opening shown here. These pages contain the text of Exodus 6:30–7:5 (f. 18v) and Exodus 7:5–10 (f. 19r). The gilded intertwined chain on the right-hand page marks the end of chapter 6; the gold filler with heart-shaped motifs on the opposite page indicates the start of a new paragraph (Exodus 7:8).

This significant and interesting manuscript is regarded as one of the earliest illuminated bibles in the Hebrew collection of the British Library. It was one of 145 mostly Karaite manuscripts that the British Museum acquired in July 1882 from the late Moses W. Shapira, a well-known antiquarian book-dealer from Jerusalem. Shapira had managed to obtain this collection partly at Hit in Iraq and partly at Cairo in Egypt. The addition of these invaluable handwritten works in the last quarter of the nineteenth century not only elevated the profile of the Hebrew manuscript collection of the British Museum, but also transformed it into one of the best Karaite resources in the world, rivaled only by the Abraham Firkovitch Karaite manuscript collection in St. Petersburg (see cat. nos. 7, 9).
IT

Bibliography:
Hoerning, 1889, pp. 1–20, and facsimile section at end; Margoliouth, 1965, vol. I, p. 77, no. 104; Sirat, 1993; Polliack, 2003, pp. 893–924.

CAT. 34

34

Pauline Epistles, from the Syriac Peshitta

London, British Library, APA, Syriac MSS. Add. 14478, End of Ephesians and beginning of Philippians, ff. 85v–86r
Ink and pigments on parchment; ff. 143; 235 × 170mm
The Epistles of Saint Paul, according to the Syriac Peshitta version; Syriac
Haluga in the district of Serug, Syria; 622

A note (f. 143r) states that the manuscript was written for one John bar Sergius, from the village of Haluga in the district of Serug, in the year of the Greeks 933 (622 C.E.), and that he paid the sum of 14 carats for the copying. The manuscript was brought to the Syrian Convent of Saint Mary Deipara by Abbot Moses of Nisibis.

The opening shown carries the end of Saint Paul's Letter to the Ephesians (6:21) and, in red, the title of the Epistles to the Philippians.

Syriac is an Aramaic dialect that became the principal literary vehicle for speakers of the Semitic languages within Near Eastern Christianity. This predominance stemmed from its origins in the important classical and Early Christian city of Edessa (now Urfa in eastern Turkey). The conversion of Edessa's populace is thought to date to the late second century, although tradition tells of one of its rulers, Abgar, who sent an embassy to Jesus which returned with a letter of instruction and a portrait which became the basis of a series of icons "not by human hand" *(acheropita)*. Missionary activity carried the Syriac tradition far into eastern Asia. Numerous manuscripts in the language dating from the fifth century onward have been preserved, including scriptures in the Old Syriac and Peshitta (revised, with reference to the Hebrew Bible and the Septuagint) versions.

Three types of script were developed: *esṭrangelā* (from Greek *stroggylē*, round); a less formal "Nestorian" hand probably originating in the eastern, Nestorian and Persian-dominated part of Syria (which favored the heretical teachings of Nestorius, distinguishing between the divine and human elements in Christ); and the more cursive *serṭā* or "script." As in older Aramaic, Syriac originally contained no vocalization system and phonetic and grammatical features were indicated by a system of dots, but the Greek vowels were subsequently introduced.

Syriac has remained as a written Church language to the present, although its use as a spoken language declined after the Muslim conquest. Syriac speakers served as a conduit for the preservation in Arabic of much of Hellenistic culture, which would later be transmitted to medieval Europe.

MPB

Bibliography:
Wright, 1870, pp. 90–92; Juckel, 2003.

35

Arabic Gospelbook

Mount Sinai, Holy Monastery of Saint Catherine, Arabic New Finds M.14, ff. 23v–24r
Inks on parchment; ff. 90; 216 × 160mm
Gospels; Arabic
Sinai, Holy Monastery of Saint Catherine; 859 (?)

The quire of which this bifolium is part is from the same manuscript as another item in the library at Mount Sinai (Sinai Arabic New Finds M.16), which is dated 859. This makes it the oldest dated Arabic manuscript at Sinai, and perhaps also the oldest dated copy of the gospels in Arabic now extant. Though incomplete, the manuscript is of the greatest importance, and the leaves that survive are in very good condition.

Of considerable interest and significance are the illuminations and depictions of the evangelists (portraits of Luke and John are preserved). Illuminations in Arabic manuscripts are very rare, and these are particularly important because of their early date. In the leaves shown here, Saint Luke stands in an arch supported by four columns of variegated marbles, each surmounted by a carved capital. The intertwined border of the archway is a decorative element used in the manuscript's other illuminations. The inscription above is the traditional one in Greek, *Ho Hagios Loukas*, with *Loukas* written below in Arabic. Luke raises his right hand in blessing, and in his left hand he holds the Gospel. The artist employs a limited color palette. The figure is drawn in ink, with color added in simple strokes.

The Arabic New Finds discovered at the monastery in 1975 consisted of 155 manuscripts and 345 documents. With these new finds, which are only now being studied by scholars, the number of Arabic manuscripts in the library at Mount Sinai has been increased to 756.

AG

Bibliography:
Meimaris, 1985, p. 27.

CAT. 35

36

Georgian Psalter

St. Petersburg, National Library of Russia, Gruz new series 10
Inks on papyrus; ff. 2; 200 × 170mm
Psalter (fragment); Georgian
Probably Palestine or Sinai, Egypt; eighth century

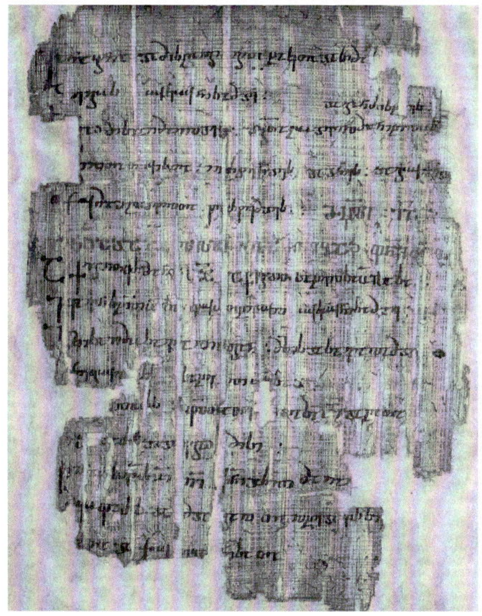

CAT. 36

This Georgian psalter fragment bears the text of Psalms 111–112 written in *nuskhury* script. It was acquired in 1883 by the Imperial Public Library (today the National Library of Russia) as part of the collection of Bishop Porphyry (Uspensky), who headed the Russian Orthodox Mission in Jerusalem from 1848 to 1854. In addition to his period of residence in Jerusalem, he also traveled through the Near East between 1843 and 1861, visiting Syria, Palestine, Sinai in Egypt, and Mount Athos in Greece. Porphyry acquired the psalter fragment in 1850 from Saint Catherine's Monastery in southern Sinai, where he also acquired two folios of the famous Codex Sinaiticus (see cat. no. 26).

In his *Second Journey to the Sinai Monastery in 1850* (1856), Porphyry noted that he had discovered the Georgian psalter "on the ceiling of one side-altar of the Cosmas and Damian [Church]." In his *Genesis of Mine* (1896), Porphyry wrote that the papyrus psalter had many lacunas and consisted of only eighty-four folios, and added: "I gave this remarkable manuscript ... to the sacristan, Father Vitaly, for safekeeping, taking two folios for myself."

The Porphyry collection consisted of 435 codices and fragments, of which 288 are Greek and 108 Old Russian and Slavonic. Its thirty-three Oriental manuscripts included four Georgian works,

three of which were transferred to Georgia in 1923. These three include one partly papyri, partly parchment servicebook dated to the ninth–tenth century and acquired by Porphyry in Palestine.
OV

Bibliography:
Porphyry, 1856, p.163; *Brief Survey...*, 1885, p. 176; Tsagareli 1988; Porphyry, 1896, vol. 4, pp. 57–58; Vasilyeva 1996.

CAT. 37

37

Armenian Gospelbook

Baltimore, Walters Art Museum, MS. W.537, f. 2
Ink and pigments on parchment; ff. 237; 305 × 250mm
Gospels; Armenian
Armenia; 966 C.E.

This is the oldest Armenian manuscript in an American collection and the fifth-oldest Armenian gospelbook in the world. Its colophon records that it was commissioned by a priest, "with all his family, for the adornment and glory of the holy church." The patron's name is unknown, but his scribe and fellow priest, who was called Sargis, added that he "wrote this holy Gospels in the year 415 of our Lord Jesus Christ." Formerly, the codex was known as "The Gospels of the Translators," because it was thought that its colophon date referred to the time of the first translation of the gospels into Armenian from Syriac, made in the early fifth century C.E. In fact, the date refers to the year 415 of the Armenian era (966 C.E.). Despite this confusion, the text remains a significant witness to both the first Armenian translation of the gospels and the earliest revision following the Council of Ephesus in 431. The angular uncial script in which Sargis wrote, called *erkat'agir*, or "iron-forged letters," was in use between the fifth and thirteenth centuries C.E.

Shown here is a minature of the Virgin and Child; on ff. 114v–115r are the portraits of the Evangelists Mark and Luke. They are clad in liturgical vestments, perhaps in response to the priestly occupations of the book's patron and its scribe. Indeed, Sargis the scribe might also have been the painter. The pairing of evangelist portraits between the gospel texts is rare: usually a single portrait appears before each gospel. This format, the preference for geometric design over figural modeling, and the largely earth-tone palette provide rare insight into early indigenous Armenian illumination.
RAL

Bibliography:
Der Nersessian, 1973, pp. 1–5; Alexanian, 1990–91; Mathews and Wieck, 1994, cat. no. 6; Nersessian, 2001, p. 224.

38

Armenian Gospelbook

London, British Library, APA, Armenian MSS. Add. 21932, ff. 118v–119r
Ink and pigments on parchment; ff. 244; 295 × 200mm
Gospels; Armenian
Armenia; ninth–tenth century

The age of this manuscript cannot be determined exactly, but the script (an archaic, leftwards-sloping *erkat'agir*) and textual features resemble the Lazarian Gospels (Yerevan, Matenadaran, MS. 6200), the oldest dated Armenian manuscript, which was made in 887 C.E. Both volumes lack decorated initials and numbers marking lections (although such numbers were added later in the Lazarian Gospels): during the eleventh or twelfth centuries this division of the text for liturgical use became a regular feature of Armenian gospelbooks.

The colophon, added later by the same hand in large uncials on f. 72v (at the end of Saint Matthew's Gospel) and here on f. 118v, states:

You who read this Holy Gospel remember in your prayers Tēr Eghise by whose order [this gospelbook was copied].

The text of this volume includes some interesting features. This opening shown carries the end of Saint Mark's Gospel and the beginning of Saint Luke's. The last twelve verses of Mark (Mark 16:9–20) are omitted and the scribe spread out verses 7–8 to occupy the whole first column of the page, the lines set twice as far apart as they are in the rest of the volume. This suggests that the scribe was aware of the last twelve verses but decided not to include them. In another Armenian gospelbook, the

CAT. 38

Ējmiacin Gospels (Matenadaran, MS. 2374/229), dated 989 C.E., this passage is ascribed to "Ariston the Presbyter," whom Conybeare identified with "Aristion the teacher of Papias" mentioned by Eusebius. Armenian awareness that these verses were by another author explains why they seldom included them prior to the thirteenth century. Another significant variation is that of the episode concerning the Woman Taken in Adultery, which is usually placed at the end of Saint John's Gospel, although many Greek and Latin manuscripts place it at John 7:53–8:11 (and sometimes after Luke 21:28). The present volume ends at John 27:1–3 and so we cannot tell if the passage was included here, but a marginal annotation notes the episode between John 7 and 8 (f. 220r).

The binding is contemporary, with brown leather covers, the upper cover tooled with a cross composed of interlace and the lower cover with a large rosette, and a rectangular flap to protect the book's fore-edge. The manuscript was purchased from Mr. J. Warington, on April 11, 1857.
MPB after Nersessian, 2001, no. 135

Bibliography:
Conybeare, 1893; Conybeare, 1913, pp. 1–3, no. 1; Nersessian 1978, no. 12; Nersessian, 2001, pp. 202–203, no.135.

39

Codex Zographensis

St. Petersburg, National Library of Russia, MS. Glag. 1, ff. 76v–77r
Ink and pigments on parchment, ff. 303; 183 × 260mm
Gospels; Glagolitic
Macedonia; late tenth–eleventh century

The oldest preserved Slavic texts, of which the Codex Zographensis is an important example, were written in Macedonia and date from the late tenth and eleventh centuries. These include several other early manuscripts in the Glagolitic language (Old Church Slavonic): Codex Assemianus, the Psalter of Sinai, the Euchologion of Sinai (cat. no. 49), the Bojana Palimpsest, and perhaps the Codex Marianus, which may have been copied from a Macedonian original on Serbo-Croatian territory. Ihor

CAT. 39

Ševčenko has suggested that they were influenced in their make-up and decoration by Italo-Byzantine manuscripts from southern Italy and that the Euchologion of Sinai and the Codex Zographensis are the earliest.

The origins of written Slavic are contentious. The invention of the Glagolitic alphabet and script, which gave rise in turn to Cyrillic, is commonly attributed to two brothers from Thessaloniki, Saints Cyril (or Constantine) and Methodius, "Apostles to the Slavs" during the ninth century. It has been argued, however, that there may have been some proto-writing system previously in use, as with the Gothic and Germanic experience of conversion and the reception of literacy. The possibility of earlier influence from the Gothic mission of Ulfilas, from Italy, and from the Carolingian Church has also been suggested.

The volume comprises 288 leaves of a gospelbook (known in Old Church Slavonic tradition as a tetraevangelion), followed by a synaxary or list of feasts of the saints, with short accounts of their significance, of sixteen leaves and a calendar of saints' days with an indication of the gospel for the day written in Cyrillic script of a later date. The illumination is brightly colored and features headpieces containing display lettering, in Byzantine fashion, and decorated initials with interlace and other infills and simplified acanthus-ornament extensions. It is related to that of the Euchologion of Sinai but is rather more rectilinear and refined, if somewhat less exuberant. On the pages illustrated, the headpiece contains the incipit of Saint Mark's Gospel, preceded by an image of Mark receiving inspiration for his work.

MPB

Bibliography:
Jagic, 1879; Ševčenko, 1982, pp. 131 fig. 26, 142, 145, 147.

CAT. 40

40

Ethiopic Gospelbook (Zir Ganela Gospels)

New York, Morgan Library and Museum, MS. M.828, Crucifixion, ff. 13v–14r
Ink and pigments on parchment; ff. 207; 362 × 251mm
Gospels; Ethiopic (Ge'ez)
Ethiopia, 1400–1401 (with eleventh-century canon tables)

This impressive gospelbook was written and illuminated in Ethiopia between August 29, 1400 and August 28, 1401, according to the colophon on f. 205v, which also states that it was made for Princess Zir G-anela, granddaughter of King 'Amda Seyon.

The decoration comprises twenty-six full-page miniatures, eight decorated canon tables, and four illuminated incipit pages. Ewa Balicka-Witakowska (1997, p. 130) mentions the observation by J. Pirenne (1982) that the canon table pages are earlier than the manuscript, and can be dated to the tenth/eleventh century. They may have been preserved because of their association with a valued earlier manuscript and included within the princess's new commission to emphasize the legitimacy of the rule of the dynasty from which she sprang by stressing links with the past. There are many splendid Ethiopic books dating from the fifteenth century onwards, but survivals from earlier periods are extremely rare.

This opening colorfully depicts the Crucifixion. The angels and the sun and moon watch on, the two thieves hang on their adjacent crosses, and the spear- and sponge-bearers (Stephaton and Longinus, according to apocryphal legend, here both shown holding spears) reach up to the body of Christ—which is absent, the empty cross serving to demonstrate his victory over death in the Resurrection.

The text is written in Ethiopic script in Ge'ez, the literary language of Ethiopia, in two columns of between twenty-five and twenty-nine lines. A note in Italian on f. 91 in purple ink, the same ink used for the earlier foliation, reads *Manca qualchecosa fra le due pagine* (something is missing between the two pages). The book was previously bound in wooden panels (a colophon on f. 207 indicates the manuscript had been rebound in the seventeenth century). It was rebound for the Pierpont Morgan Library in brick-red, native-dyed goatskin, tooled with a design of a cross standing upon a mound representing Golgotha, site of the Crucifixion.

The manuscript was owned by Léon Gruel of Paris in 1928 and then by Gregor Ahron; it was purchased by the Pierpont Morgan Library in December 1948 from Aron and Artim Hazarian through the Lewis Cass Ledyard fund.

MPB

Bibliography:
Skehan, 1954; Marilyn Eiseman Heldman, "Miniatures of the Gospels of Zir Ganela, an Ethiopian Manuscript dated A.D. 1400/01" (Ph.D. thesis, Washington University, St. Louis, 1972); Heldman, [1975], p. 52, figs. 4, 5; J. Pirenne, "Paleographic clues for classification of Geʿez writings from the 6th to 16th century," 1982, unpublished typescript, available at the Morgan Library and Museum, New York; Fitzgerald, 1992, p. 125a; Urbaniack-Walczak, 1992, pp. 143, 145; Heldman, 1994, pp. 85, 101, 192, fig. 46; Wilson, 1994, fig. 56; Balicka-Witakowska, 1997, pp. 5–7, 15, 16, 19, 21–25, 27–29, 31–33, 67, 69, 70, 72, 74–78, 80, 81, 87–90, 115, 130, 131, 185, pl. IX; Chojnacki, 2000. Further bibliography and typewritten notes can be viewed on the website of the Morgan Library and Museum, www.themorgan.org.

Spreading the Word: The single-volume bible

41

The Ceolfrith Bibles: Middleton Leaves

London, British Library, Western MSS., Add. MS. 45025, f. 2v–3r
Ink on parchment; ff. 11; 480 × 340mm
3 and 4 Kings; Latin
Northumbria (Wearmouth–Jarrow), northeast England; early eighth century (before 716)

Eyewitness accounts by Bede (died 735), in his *Historia Ecclesiastica* and *Lives of the Abbots*, and by an anonymous biographer tell us that in 716 Ceolfrith, abbot of the twin monasteries of Wearmouth–Jarrow, set off for Rome to retire, taking with him as a present for the pope a splendid single-volume bible. This was one of what Bede terms *tres pandects nouae translationis*—three bibles of the "new translation" made at Wearmouth–Jarrow. This gift, the Codex Amiatinus (Florence, Biblioteca Medicea Laurenziana, MS. Amiatinus 1), survives but was not recognized as an English work until the nineteenth century, so convincing is its mastery of Roman text, uncial script, and illusionistic painting. Its miniatures depict Ezra the Scribe (see fig. 7, page 57), Christ in Majesty, a plan of the Temple and diagrams outlining biblical transmission. The text is considered one of the best early examples of Jerome's Vulgate and represents one of the most scholarly editorial campaigns of the early Middle Ages, in which Bede (who also served as one of the team of scribes) played a leading role. Its layout is *per cola et commata*, in which length of line clarifies

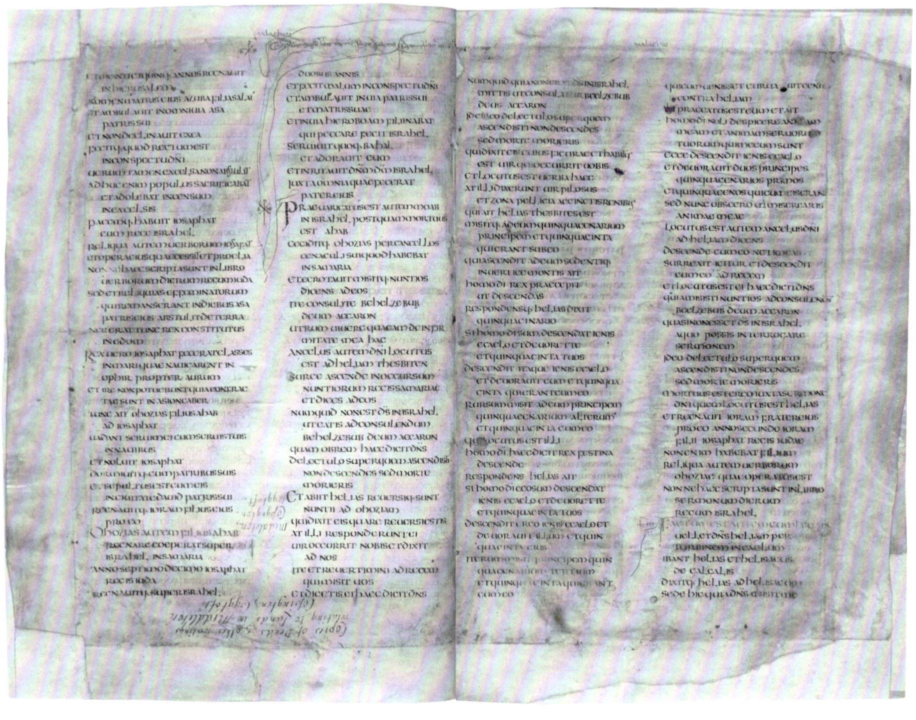

CAT. 41

sense. Textual models included at least one of Cassiodorus's biblical editions (Ceolfrith having brought a copy of one, the Codex Grandior, back from an earlier expedition to Rome) and a Neapolitan gospelbook, a copy of which was also the exemplar for the Lindisfarne Gospels. Wearmouth–Jarrow built up one of the finest libraries of its age and was a conduit for introducing Rome's influence into Britain. The Codex Amiatinus served as an ambassador for the English nation, demonstrating that the apostolic mission had reached the ends of the known world, where a key contribution was being made to Christian culture in turn.

Ceolfrith left two further pandects to be kept in the Wearmouth and Jarrow churches for study by their monks. Several fragments of one have been discovered. Part of the text of 3 Kings was found in a binding in a Newcastle bookshop by Canon Greenwell of Durham, who presented it to the British Museum in 1909 (now London, British Library, Add. MS. 37777). A single leaf from the apocryphal Book of Ecclesiasticus (now the "Bankes Leaf," British Library, Loan MS. 81) was identified in 1982 among estate papers at the National Trust property of Kingston Lacy, the Bankes family home in the county of Dorset. It served as a wrapper for deeds relating to land at Langton Wallis in Dorset and belonging to Sir Francis Willoughby of Wollaton Hall in Nottinghamshire. The portion illustrated consists of eleven leaves from 3 and 4 Kings, discovered as wrappers and flyleaves for documents compiled during the sixteenth century in the archives of Lord Middleton at Wollaton Hall (published by the Historical Manuscripts Commission, 1911).

Fragments from a late-eleventh-century Worcester cartulary (British Library, Add. MS. 46204), also found at Wollaton Hall, correspond (unusually for charter material, which generally observes a smaller, single-column format) to the dimensions and layout of the bible leaves. This Ceolfrith Bible was therefore probably the great bible recorded at Worcester Cathedral, to which Saint Wulfstan ordered copies of the cathedral's important documents to be added during the late eleventh century. Worcester tradition also asserted that an ancient bible, made in Rome, was donated by King Offa of Mercia in the late eighth century. Offa's daughter married into the Northumbrian royal house and it is not unlikely that one of Wearmouth–Jarrow's bibles should have traveled via this route—or that within a century it should already have been thought of as Italian.

MPB

Bibliography:

Lowe, 1934–72, ii, no. 177 and i.299 (Codex Amiatinus); Alexander, 1978, no. 7 (Codex Amiatinus); Bischoff and Brown, 1985, pp. 351–52; Henderson, 1987; Webster and Backhouse, 1991, nos. 87–88, this item no. 87a; Wood, 1995; Brown, 2003; Brown, 2003a; Brown, 2005; Brown, 2006.

42

The Theodulf Bible (Codex Hubertianus)

London, British Library, Western MSS., Add. MS. 24142, ff. 197v–198r
Ink and pigments on parchment; ff. 248; ff. 330 × 243mm
Bible pandect; Latin
Orléans or Fleury, France; ninth century, first third

The Spaniard Theodulf, abbot of the Carolingian monastery of Orléans (788–821), relied upon the "Mixed Spanish" textual tradition of his homeland, which conflated Old Latin and Vulgate readings, when preparing his revised edition of the Bible. Six copies of his text survive, and all differ in response to variation in the exemplars used for one part of the bible or another, as Theodulf

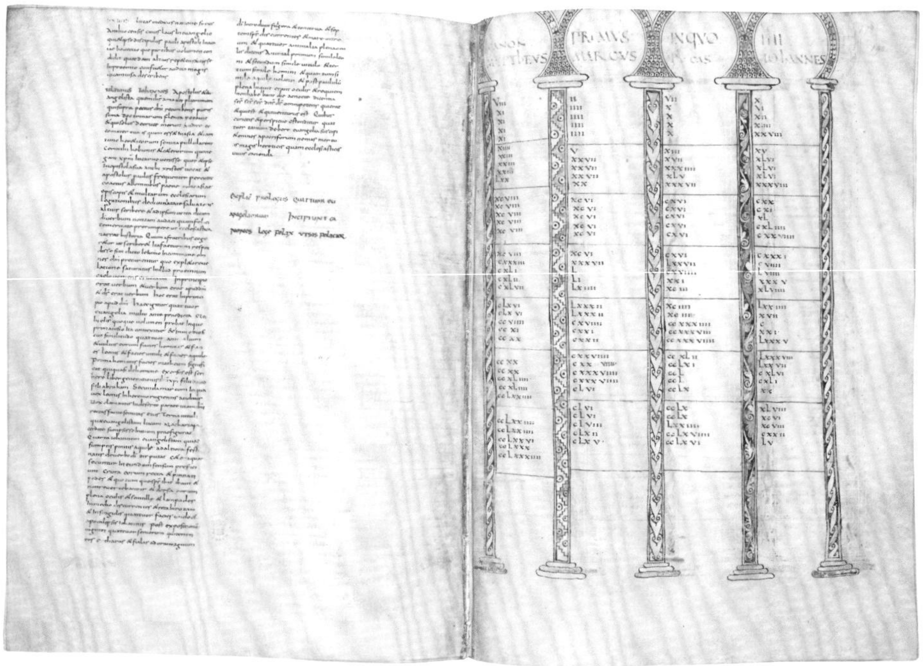

CAT. 42

encountered new models—this was a text for a scholar's use and reflects his ongoing research to reconstruct the fourth-century Vulgate. His arrangement of the biblical books was derived from Jerome and Cassiodorus and his complex cross-reference system of *capitula* (chapters) and marginal notes in the Pauline Epistles recalls that in Victor of Capua's *Diatessaron* and, earlier, writings from the circle of the heretic Pelagius (ca. 354–418).

This copy is written in three columns of sixty-two lines in a tiny, dense caroline minuscule script, with major text breaks marked only by slightly enlarged capital initials (some with modest foliate terminals) and incipits or explicits in rustic capitals, sometimes in red and surrounded by colophon decoration in ink and red. Rubrics are written in uncial script. An earlier copy of the Theodulf Bible is Paris, Bibliothèque nationale de France, MS. Lat. 9380 and the volumes have been corrected to agree more closely with each other. The British Library's volume was copied by several scribes and the sections of text written by the first hand tend to agree with the Vulgate text of the Codex Amiatinus, one of the Ceolfrith Bibles from early eighth-century northern England (cat. no. 41). There are some lengthy erasures by scraping (e.g., f. 179r).

The volume lacks images, which is not surprising, for Theodulf was also responsible for writing the *Libri carolini*, the Carolingian response to the Council of Nicaea of 787, which marked the end of iconoclasm in Byzantium. In the *Libri carolini* the primacy of the word was asserted over images, which were permitted but deemed to possess no inherent holiness or iconic value. The only element to be decorated is the set of canon tables (ff. 198r–201r), which are displayed beneath arcades, some arranged in two tiers. These take an unusual architectural form, with horseshoe-shaped heads that recall the Islamic influence apparent in the buildings of Theodulf's native Spain. The columns of the arcades are filled with fretwork, step, scroll, and foliate designs, painted with thin washes of blue, yellow, and red pigment.

The volume is known as the Codex Hubertianus because it was later owned by the monastery of Saint Hubert, Ardennes, Belgium. The seventeenth-century binding is blind-tooled with a cartouche of the Crucifixion and a Latin inscription recording ownership by the monastery on the upper cover and the arms, episcopal miter and crozier of Saint Hubert's on the lower cover. The book was purchased by the British Museum from Messrs. Boone on May 18, 1861.

MPB

Bibliography:

Ancient Manuscripts in the British Museum, 1881–94, Part 2. Latin: 5–8; Wordsworth and White, 1889–98, siglum "H"; Kenyon, 1900, xv; Quentin, 1922; Vulgate, 1926; Ayuso Marazuela, 1953, p. 362, no. 51; Fischer, 1985, pp. 57–66 and 101–202; Gibson, 1993, pp. 32–33.

43

Alcuin (Touronian) Bible

Los Angeles, J. Paul Getty Museum, 83.MA.50, ff. 8, 10
Ink and pigments on parchment; approx. 465 × 337mm; ff. 10
Bible pandect; Latin
Carolingian Empire, Tours; ca. 845–850

The English scholar Alcuin of York was Abbot of Tours (now in France) from 796 to 804. The tradition of biblical scholarship and publication that he established there was perpetuated by his successors from Fridugisius (807–834) to Vivian (843–851), as was his introduction of the

CAT. 43

concept of the pandect. Alcuin's revision of the Bible consisted mostly of minor corrections of orthography, punctuation, and grammar, although his substitution of the Gallicanum Psalter (that previously favored in Gaul), in preference to Jerome's Hebraicum or Romanum versions, ensured its subsequent popularity.

The text is in two columns of densely but elegantly written caroline minuscule. This multi-purpose script, which formed the basis of early modern typefaces, was developed at Corbie, Tours, and Aachen during the late eighth century as a replacement for the plethora of local styles of script favored in regional scriptoria. The promotion of such a standardized script, and of Alcuin's biblical edition, was designed to help foster unity throughout the disparate territories of the Carolingian Empire. The Tours scriptorium could produce as many as three pandects per year in its heyday, many of which were sent to other monasteries where they served as exemplars for further copies.

Each major text opens with a rubric written in square Roman capital script, in alternating lines of red and black, and the opening initial is followed by several lines of text in uncial script, before descending into the caroline minuscule of the main text. This hierarchy of scripts serves to emphasize the roots of the book, and of the scholarship that produced it, within the Roman world, as does the acanthus ornament of the major initials, which alludes to the art of Antiquity.

This bible belonged to the monastery of Saint Maximin in Trier (now in Germany). By the end of the fifteenth century it had been disbound and some of the leaves were being used as waste in the binding of an incunable printed in Nuremberg in 1474 by Anton Koberger. Fifty leaves from the manuscript have been discovered in Europe and the United States, including the ten leaves now at the J. Paul Getty Museum in Los Angeles, which were purchased as part of the collection of the German bibliophiles Peter and Irene Ludwig.

MPB

Bibliography:
J. Paul Getty Museum, 1991, no. 2 (leaf 10); Laufner, 1960; Fischer, 1971, p. 64; Mütherich, 1972; Kessler, 1977; von Euw and Plotzek, 1979, pp. 43–48; Nordenfalk, 1980; Fischer, 1985, pp. 203–403; Franz, 1985, pp. 15–43; de Hamel, 1994, pp. 49–50, pl. 39 (f. 7); Reiner, 2002, pp. 205, 214, 215, 217, 224, 226, 227, 233, 234, figs. 31, 32, 55–64, 75–78, 151–54, 172, 176, 179.

Spreading the Word: The book as desert, the scribe as evangelist

44

The Stockholm Codex Aureus

Stockholm, Royal Library, MS. A.135, ff. 9v–11r and ff. 115v–116r
Ink and pigments on parchment; ff. 193; 395 × 314mm
Gospelbook; Latin
Greater Mercia, Kent (Canterbury or Minster-in-Thanet?), southern England; mid-eighth century

This opulent gospelbook was made in Anglo-Saxon Kent during the mid-eighth century. Its text is of the mixed Old Latin / Vulgate variety and its script is a stately uncial based upon that of the Rome of Gregory the Great. Its two surviving evangelist portraits of Saint Matthew and Saint John, with their classicizing, modeled figure style, prominent tonsure, and architectural settings, recall author portraits from Early Christian Rome. They are identified by half-length evangelist symbols, perhaps based upon those in a late sixth-century Italian gospelbook thought to have accompanied Saint Augustine on his mission to the pagan kingdom of King Æthelberht of Kent in 597—the Saint Augustine Gospels (Cambridge, Corpus Christi College, MS. 286).

The usual white leaves alternate with purple-stained pages carrying text written in gold, white, silver, and red, with crosses and other designs overlaid. These recall picture poems *(carmina figurata)* in which superimposed images isolated the letters underlying them to form a poem within a

CAT. 44

poem; a genre popularized by Porphyry, court poet to Constantine. Archbishop Cuthbert of Canterbury is known to have borrowed a copy of Porphyry's works from the Archbishop of Mainz, who requested its return around the time this gospelbook was made. Such cultural allusions to the imperial dignity of the Roman and Byzantine Empires, fused with motifs from earlier Celtic and Germanic art, eloquently reflect the political aspirations of the expansionist rulers of the Anglo-Saxon kingdom of Mercia, which dominated central and parts of southern England: they engaged in international relations and would shortly claim kinship with Charlemagne.

The display lettering marking major text divisions, such as the *Chi-rho* (f. 11r), is covered with gold leaf and populated by tiny beasts. This ostentation ensured the book's survival, for an Old English inscription added in the margins of the *Chi-rho* page in the mid-ninth century records that it was ransomed from a Viking army, for bullion, by Ealdorman Alfred of Kent and his wife, Werburgh, and presented to the high altar of Christ Church Canterbury. The Vikings evidently considered it worth taking hostage for its gold, unlike so many other books that perished at their hands. (The will of Ealdorman Alfred [dating to ca. 871–89] bequeathed much of his wealth to Werburgh, providing that she went on pilgrimage to Rome and spent the remainder of her life there praying for the repose of his soul. We do not know if she complied, but this was an age when many people traveled on pilgrimage. In the 730s the Anglo-Saxon "Apostle to the Germans," Saint Boniface, wrote to the archbishop of Canterbury from the Germanic mission-fields asking that he restrain the hordes of unattached Englishwomen who journeyed throughout Europe, at great risk to life and honor.)

The style of the volume and the access probably enjoyed by its makers to the Saint Augustine Gospels, or something very similar, points to Kent as its birthplace. Its grandeur implies display at an important center—perhaps Canterbury Cathedral itself. It may have been copied there, but there is also an intriguing possibility that it was made by women. In Merovingian Gaul nuns supplied books for some important churches. Correspondence during the 730s between Saint Boniface and Eadburh, abbess of Minster-in-Thanet, includes requests that she have books made at her abbey for his mission. He even sent gold to be used in their illumination, in the hope of dazzling potential converts. The Codex Aureus was certainly a book that proclaimed the power and status of the new religion.

The volume came to Scandinavia not as Viking loot, but purchased for the Swedish Royal Library by Johan Gabriel Sparwenfeldt in Madrid in 1690. It had reached Spain during the sixteenth century, when it was owned by the scholar Jeronimo Zurita (1512–1580), and may have been taken there by a Catholic during the upheavals of the Reformation.

MPB

Bibliography:

Lowe, 1934–72, xi, no. 1642; McGurk, 1961, no. 111; Whitelock, 1970, no. 35; Alexander, 1978, no. 30; Henderson, 1987; Webster and Backhouse, 1991, no. 154; Brown, 2001a; Brown, 2001b; Gameson, 2003; Brown, 2006a.

45

Byzantine Gospels: Excerpt from St. Matthew's Gospel

Oxford, Bodleian Library, MS. Cromwell 16, ff. 30v–31r
Ink and pigments on parchment;
ff. iii + 357; 205 × 145mm
Gospels; Greek
Constantinople; tenth century, third quarter

Relatively few Byzantine gospelbooks contain narrative illustrations of scenes from the Life of Christ. More often they contain miniatures of each of the four evangelists, depicted, as Saint Matthew is here, at the beginning of the appropriate gospel text. The idea of such author portraits was a classical one, but in the new biblical context such "portraits" became the vehicle for an endlessly varied treatment of the author as inspired scribe. In this case Matthew, identified by an inscription, has started to write his Gospel—the opening words of the text already appear on the pages before him—but now pauses, stretching out his left hand towards the lectern, resting his right hand (which holds a reed pen) on his knee, and looking not at the book in front of him but out of the picture, perhaps towards the text on the facing page. Though much of the pigment has flaked from the figure's drapery and right arm, the high quality of the painting and its minute attention to detail are still to be seen in the face, hair, and beard.

The evangelist's location is not clear. The characteristic gold background seems to suggest a timeless spiritual realm, but that realm is not quite empty: as in some other portraits, the gold has been incised to suggest an architectural setting. Matthew is seated on a cushioned stool or bench, and rests his feet on a platform-like footstool. His writing desk, on which his implements (including a well of red and black ink) are visible, is of blue marble. Modern scholars scrutinize such pictures for the tantalizing evidence they provide of actual scribal hardware—though this involves fine judgments about the degree of realism to be expected.

The date of the silk curtain that covers the miniature when the book is closed is uncertain. Surviving curtains, or the telltale stitching-holes above miniatures that indicate their former presence, are quite frequently to be observed; though their primary function must always have been protective, one can also imagine the dramatic pleasure (and perhaps symbolic significance) for an owner of drawing the curtain aside to reveal the golden miniature beneath.

Only one evangelist portrait out of a presumed original set of four survives in this book, though there is also a set of decorated canon tables. Irmgard Hutter has attributed the production of the manuscript to the so-called Ephraim scriptorium; it was later adapted for liturgical use by the father of one Ioannes Doukas, whose birth in 1276 is recorded on f. 1v. Along with five others, it came to the Bodleian in 1727 from the Pantokrator monastery on Mount Athos, probably in connection with the community's request for financial support which had been made to Oxford University. The shelfmark is misleading in suggesting a connection with Oliver Cromwell.

MK

Bibliography:
Coxe, 1853, col. 443; Hutter, 1977–82, vol. I no. 5, vol. III, pp. 317–18; *Byzantium*, 1994, no. 149.

CAT. 45

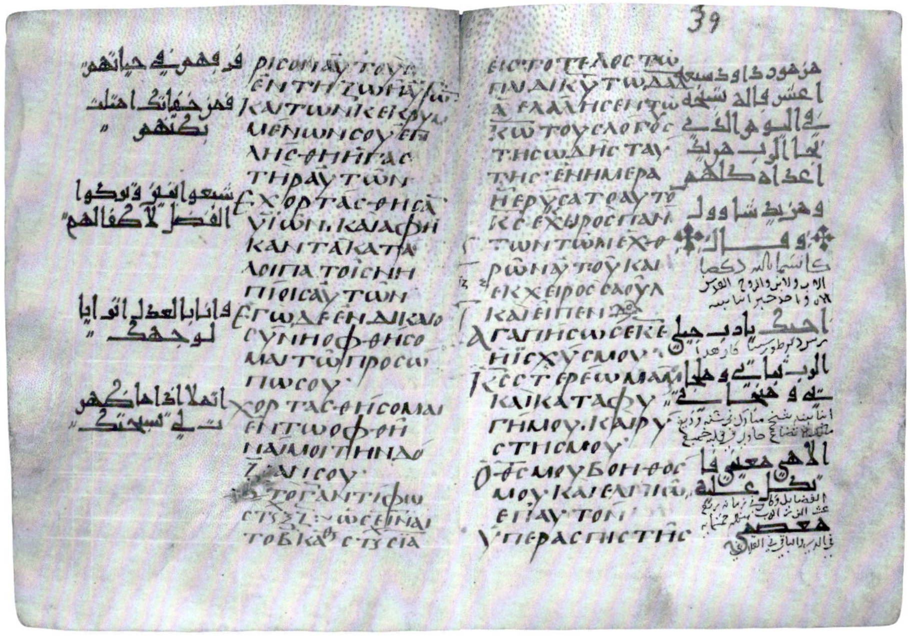

CAT. 46

46

Greek–Arabic Diglot of the Psalms and Odes

Mount Sinai, Holy Monastery of Saint Catherine, Greek 36, ff. 38v–39r
Inks on parchment; ff. 200, end lost; 205 × 156mm
Psalter and Odes; Greek and Arabic
Sinai (?); eighth–ninth century

This Greek and Arabic diglot is one of three bilingual psalters found at Saint Catherine's, Sinai (the others are Greek cods. 34, 35). They are important witnesses to the liturgical use of Arabic by Christians in the Holy Land and in Sinai in the eighth and ninth centuries. It was during that time that Christians living within the world of Islam, whose everyday spoken language was now Arabic, began to adopt Arabic as an ecclesiastical language. The Melkites (Byzantine or Rum Orthodox), for whom Greek had been the principal language of worship, were the first of the large church communities (Coptic, Syrian Orthodox, Church of the East, Melkite, Maronite) within the Islamic commonwealth to translate their scriptures and church literature into Arabic, and to produce original works in Arabic.

Codex 36 is shown here open at Psalm 16:14–15 to Psalm 17:1–3. Each page is divided into two columns: Arabic–Greek and on the facing page Greek–Arabic. The texts are marked off in rubrics for liturgical purposes. The Greek Septuagint text is written in a distinctive sloping uncial script with a marked rightward slant; the Arabic in a formal, pointed or voweled Kufic script with a tendency to slope downward to the left.

An undated Arabic note written in a later *naskhi* script was inserted between the Arabic verses of Psalm 17:1–3. It praises an unnamed head of the monastery and includes a count of the local monastic population during his headship—500 in the monastery of Saint Catherine's. Statistical information of this kind is interesting because most estimates of the number of monks at Mount Sinai from the tenth through nineteenth centuries have been gathered from accounts by Western travelers. The addition of the phrase "one God" to the customary Trinitarian doxology "the Father, and the Son, and the Holy Spirit" at the beginning of the note reflects Christian usage in an Islamic milieu.
MJB

Bibliography:
Gardthausen, 1886, p. 10; Graf, 1944–53, vol. 1, p. 115; Clark, 1952, p. 1; Kamil, 1970, p. 63; Nasrallah, 1979–, vol. 2, pt. 2, p.184.

47

Greek Psalter

The Holy Monastery of Saint Catherine, Mount Sinai, Greek 30, ff. 252v–253r
Ink on parchment; ff. 431; 180 × 106mm
Psalter; Greek
Sinai (?); ninth century

This early Greek codex contains the Psalms, the Canons of Saint Andrew of Crete (Migne, 1844–64, vol. 97, p. 1306 onwards) in a sixteenth-century hand, and prayers added by later hands. Three and a half verses have been deleted at the end of the psalter itself. It may have been written at Saint Catherine's Monastery, Sinai and be characteristic of the main style of book produced in its scriptorium during the early Middle Ages.

The script is written in an uncial hand with a distinctive slope to the right (a feature often encountered in works written at Sinai) and titles and rubrics are distinguished by being written in colored inks.

The psalm numbers are written in the margins and set within a lozenge formed of parallel lines. This device was also sometimes used to decorate the numbers that signaled the order of quires in early books; these were often written in the lower margin of the final page in a gathering.

The pages have not been cut down, as they so often are in medieval manuscripts trimmed during later rebindings, and the edges of the book retain an early example of fore-edge painting, in the form of marigolds set within red roundels.

MPB

Bibliography:
Kondakov, 1882, no. 89, p. 7; Gardthausen, 1886, no. 30, p. 9; Kamil, 1970, p. 63.

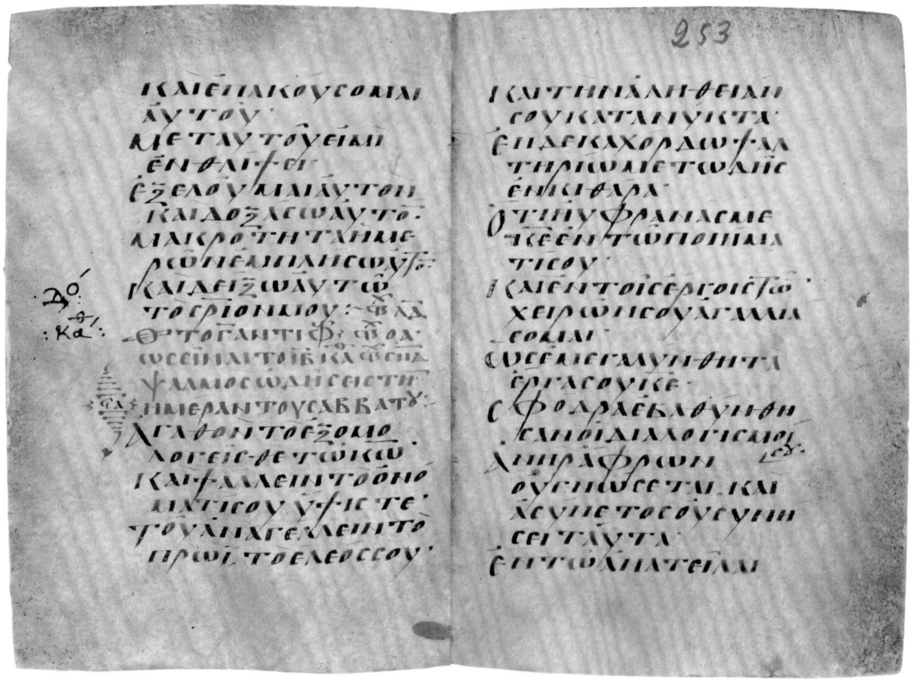

CAT. 47

48

Latin Psalter

Mount Sinai, The Holy Monastery of Saint Catherine, Latin New Finds 1, ff. 19v–20r
Ink and pigments on parchment; ff. 112; 156 × 102mm
Psalter; Latin
Sinai or Christian Orient; tenth century

This Latin manuscript, one of only a few from Sinai and the only one to have survived intact, was not recognized as such until the twentieth century because an earlier librarian had designated it as a Slavonic manuscript. It is remarkable in that it provides valuable evidence of the presence of Latin speakers in the region prior to the Crusades. On the first page is a note in Arabic referring to the surrender of Jerusalem to the Franks (1228 C.E.).

E. A. Lowe identified a scribal familiarity with Visigothic, Greek, Syriac, and Arabic palaeographical features in this and two other contemporary Latin fragments in

CAT. 48

the same collection, but I would suggest that the closest analogies for the script of this volume are perhaps to be found within the pre-Carolingian scriptoria of Gaul and of Irish foundations on the continent, such as Luxeuil, St. Gall and Bobbio—all founded by Saint Columbanus (ca. 543–615). The possibility of such Insular influence is suggested by features such as the *litterae notabiliores*, the tall *e* and the pointed *a*.

They are also reflected in the illumination, which consists of decorated initials composed of interlace ornament and of animals and birds, resembling those of pre-Carolingian Gaul, and provincial Greek illumination, such as that of southern Italy. In 599 Pope Gregory the Great dispatched a legate to Sinai bearing gifts and this would have been one possible route of influence, as would pilgrims visiting from Northern Europe.

MPB

Bibliography;

Lowe, 1955, pp. 177 ff.; Lowe, 1965, pp. 3 ff.; Kamil, 1970, p. 144; Weitzmann, 1973, pp. 12–13, pl. V, fig. 10; Altbauer, 1978.

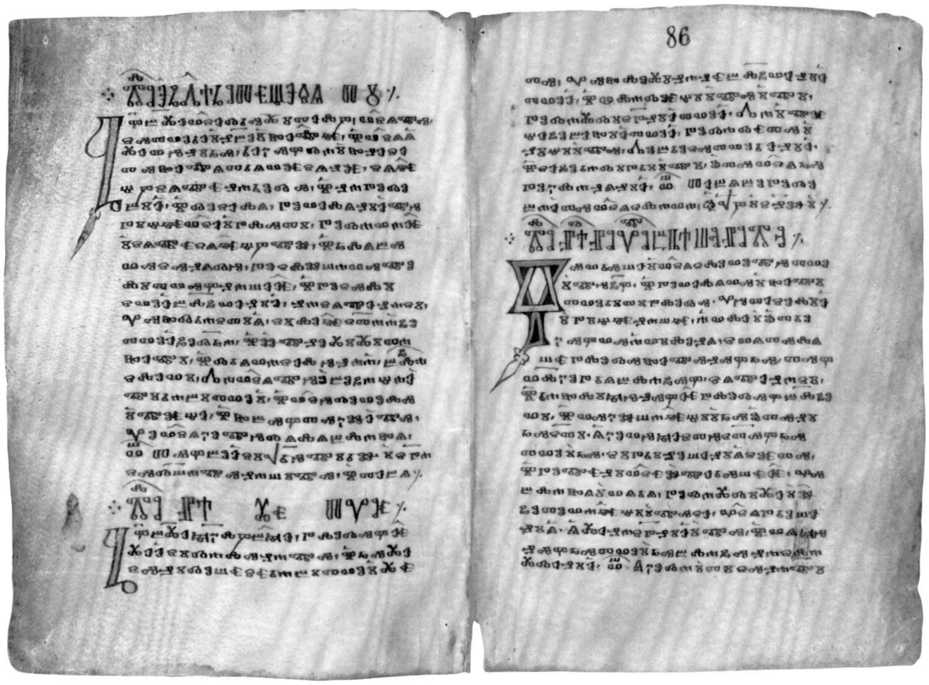

CAT. 49

49

Glagolitic Euchologion

Mount Sinai, The Holy Monastery of Saint Catherine, Slavonic 37, ff. 85v–86r
Ink and pigments on parchment; ff. 105; 146 × 106mm
Euchologion; Glagolitic
Macedonia or Croatia; eleventh century

The Sinai Euchologion (or *Euchologium*) is a text of prime importance for the study of Slavonic philology as it is one of the earliest manuscripts in the Glagolitic language. The original extent of the book has been estimated as 298 folia, of which 137 have now been found. It is known to have lost leaves from its beginning, middle, and end. Four of these are now in St. Petersburg, having been taken to Russia during the nineteenth century by scholars who had visited the Monastery of Saint Catherine's in Sinai; these were established as belonging to the Sinai Euchologion by Jan Frcek. Twenty-eight further missing leaves from the volume were amongst the manuscript fragments discovered at Saint Catherine's in 1975 and identified by Ioannis Tarnanidis; these are now known as Sinai, MS 1/N. One gathering of eight leaves survived intact and the other leaves were mixed up with fragments of different books. A later binding, with a piece of cloth still adhering to it, was also found.

A Euchologion contains prayers, parts of services and biblical passages used in the performance of the Holy Liturgy and is a type of book found in Byzantium from the eighth to the thirteenth centuries. The arrangement of their contents varies greatly and the Slavonic Euchologion was derived from several Byzantine versions. The scribe of this manuscript seems to have copied a Slavonic Euchologion and added other Slavonic texts with which he was familiar. However, the liturgy at its core has been thought to reflect the personal choice of Saints Cyril and Methodius concerning the books they took with them on their mission to the Slavs. It may therefore contain parts of the earliest Slavonic translations of the sacred texts, derived from the Byzantine tradition. Most of the Slavonic manuscripts at Saint Catherine's date from the thirteenth and fourteenth centuries, when the Slavic monastic tradition was flourishing, following a visit to Mount Sinai in 1235 by the Serbian Saint Sava. However, the presence of earlier volumes may indicate that Slavonic-speaking monks had already joined the community prior to this. This volume, along with the Codex Zographensis (cat. no. 39) has been identified by

Ihor Ševčenko as one of the first Glagolitic works, the earliest of which date from the late tenth to eleventh centuries and were made in Macedonia.

The text comprises prayers for hours, matins, vespers, special circumstances (such as earthquake and drought), prayers for the Blessing of the Waters, epistle and gospel readings for the whole week, epistle and gospel lections for particular occasions (such as illness and death) and for the major feasts. Some of the prayers are thought to exhibit the influence of the Western tradition, thereby assimilated into that of the Eastern Church.

The script is a rounded Glagolitic, carefully written by a single scribe in columns of between twenty-four and twenty-six lines. Headings are written on green or yellow grounds and initials are colorful with red, green, yellow, blue, and black pigments decorating angular letters filled with interlace and other ornament and terminating in acanthus leaves or zoomorphic and anthropomorphic motifs. Some major initials are half a page high. The decoration was considered by Ševčenko to exhibit influence from Italo-Byzantine illumination from southern Italy.

MPB

Bibliography;

Geitler, 1882; Frcek, 1933, pp. 611–12; Nahtigal, 1941–42; Dostál, 1966, p. 47; Altbauer, 1971; Weitzmann, 1973, p. 13; Sevcenko, 1982; Tarnanidis, 1988, pp. 65–87. The volume is not cited in Kamil, 1970, where Slavonic 37 appears as a fifteenth-century Psalterion.

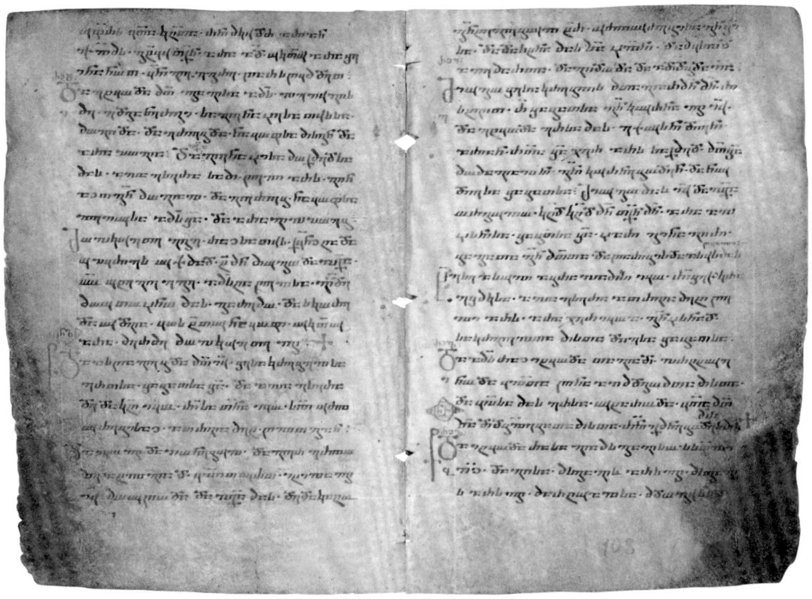

CAT. 50

50

Georgian Gospelbook

Mount Sinai, Holy Monastery of Saint Catherine, Georgian New Finds N.12, ff. 107v–108r
Inks on parchment; ff. 196; 192 × 137mm
Gospels; Georgian
Sinai, Holy Monastery of Saint Catherine; 1075

This manuscript of the four gospels was copied at Saint Catherine's monastery on Mount Sinai in 1075 by "Mikael the scribbler," whose colophons end each gospel and indicate that the text was following a "new translation," that is, the revised text by George the Hagiorite.

The main text is written in black ink in *nusxuri* script, with headings in red ink in *asomtavruli*. At the end of the manuscript (ff. 189r–196v) there is an index of lections for Lent and Easter, the title of which notes that the beginning of each reading is marked by a *kancili*, a monogram in red ink in the left margin, and the end by a cross, also in red, in the right margin. The numbers referring to Eusebian canons are written on star-like signs in the left margin. Pages illuminated with a large flowering cross preface the gospels of Matthew, Mark, and John, but only part of the cross on the first remains (f. 1r): the beginning and end of the manuscript are badly damaged, and in some cases only fragments of pages survive.

Mikael the scribe copied and signed another manuscript in the same collection in 1074 (Georgian O.19). The two manuscripts share many common features, and some of the people whom Mikael mentions here—"Beloved [saintly fath]ers and brothers, those whom this badly scribbled holy Evangelion reaches ... our magister David ..., and Mose, Mikael, Č̣ita and Simeon and Jerasime and Grigol and their parents and brothers"—are also named in the earlier volume.

ZA

Bibliography:

Garitte, 1956, pp. 255–6 (for Georgian O.19); Alexidze and others, 2005, pp. 382–84.

51

Georgian Lectionary

Mount Sinai, The Holy Monastery of Saint Catherine, Georgian 37, ff. 216v–217r
Ink on parchment; ff. 294; 260 × 205mm
New Testament; Georgian
Georgia (or Sinai?); tenth century

This early Georgian lectionary contains readings from the gospels, Acts and epistles read during church services. It falls into two sections, the first containing the lectionary and the second a collection of hymns. It is an important early witness to the New Testament in the Georgian language and is often designated in textual discussions by the siglum "L." The Georgian lectionary is thought to preserve the ancient liturgy of Jerusalem and this was one of four manuscripts that formed the basis of Michael Tarchnischvili's edition of the Great Lectionary of the Church of Jerusalem.

Strategically placed between the Black Sea, the Caucasus, Albania, and Armenia, Georgia (formed of two kingdoms, Lazica and Iberia) was contested between Rome and Persia in Antiquity. Its kings trod a delicate path between the two until 522, when King Tzathius received Christianity and his royal regalia from the Emperor Justinian, as a result of which the kingdom of Lazica became bound to Byzantium. Christianity had been practiced in the area earlier, however, and tradition links the conversion of King Mirian of Iberia to the missionary work of a slave woman, Saint Nino, in 337. The Georgian Church, which had a presence in Palestine from at least the fifth century, initially rejected the rulings of the Council of Chalcedon and favored Monophysitism, but in the early seventh century it returned to Orthodoxy and communion with Byzantium.

The text is written in a large majuscule hand in a single column of twenty lines. This hand has been identified as probably that of John Zosimus, who also wrote parts of two other manuscripts at Sinai in 979 (Georgian cod. 30 and 38). Tsagareli cited a colophon, now missing from the manuscript, which dated it to the year 982; this date would appear tenable as it corresponds with the period when the Georgian scribe Zosimus was working.
MPB

Bibliography:

Tsagareli, 1888, no. 30, p. 210; Garitte, 1955, pp. 18, 181–83; Garitte, 1956a; Garitte, 1957; Tarchnischvili, 1959–60; Kamil, 1970, p. 57; Garitte, 1972; Metreveli, 1978; van Esbroeck, 1981.

CAT. 51

52

The Lectionary of Mount Horeb

Mount Sinai, The Holy Monastery of Saint Catherine, Greek 213, ff. 73v–74r
Ink on parchment; ff. 340; 208 × 163mm
Gospel lectionary; Greek
Near East (possibly Saint Catherine's, Mount Sinai); 967

This lectionary is also known as the Gospels of Mount Horeb. A colophon (f. 1) states that it was written by Presbyter Eustathios in 967 C.E., although not explicitly on Mount Sinai. The attribution to Sinai rests upon an added Arabic inscription (f. 3r): "He sat at the Church of the Lord in the mountain of Horeb. No one has authority to dislodge Him from it or from inside it." Origins in Egypt or Palestine (Weitzmann, 1935) or southern Italy (Grabar, 1972) have been proposed, although a Near Eastern origin remains likely, perhaps even at Sinai itself (Weitzmann, 1973).

The volume is written in the distinctive local sloping uncial script with a marked rightwards slant that was favored in the

Sinai scriptorium. Added marginal annotations are in a cursive Arabic script.

The text contains decorated initials incorporating foliate and zoomorphic elements and the manipulum (pointing hand), along with finely decorated headpieces with foliate infill, some surmounted with peacocks (symbolic of resurrection), foliate and fretwork bars, and display lettering at major text breaks. In the lower margins are beasts, including particolored Sasanian-style griffins that recall the animal ornament and evangelist symbols in Insular manuscript illumination. The decoration is brightly painted in red, blue, yellow, and green pigments.
MPB

Bibliography:
Kondakov, 1882, p. 104, figs. 79–83, 89, 8; Gardthausen, 1886, no. 213, p. 42; Stassoff, 1887, p. 53, pls. 123, 3–7; Benesevitch, 1912, vol. 2, p. 41; Weitzmann, 1935, p. 73, pl. LXXX, pp. 495–96; Kamil, 1970, p. 70; Grabar, 1972, p. 73, figs. 321–26; Weitzmann, 1973, pp. 10–11, pl. III figs. 4–5l; Harlfinger, 1983, pl. 59; Elliott, 1989, p. 193; Aland, 1994, p. 269.

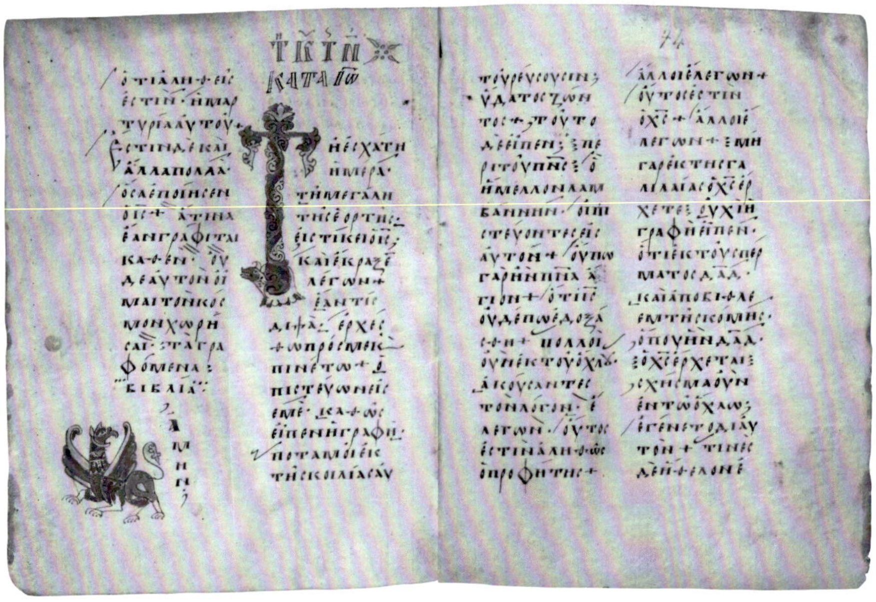

CAT. 52

Spreading the Word: Early Christian Britain and Ireland

53

Gospelbook (Codex Oxoniensis)

Oxford, Bodleian Library,
MS. Auct. D. 2. 14, ff. 129v–130r
Ink on parchment; ff. iii + 176;
230 × 195mm
Gospels; Latin
Italy (?); late sixth or seventh century

When Saint Augustine and his companions landed in Kent in 597 on their mission from Pope Gregory I to bring the Christian Gospel to the southern English, they must have carried with them books such as this. It is a Latin gospelbook written in uncial script of the late sixth or seventh century, probably of Italian origin but with additions that show that it had reached England by the eighth century at the latest. In date and character it closely resembles the Corpus Gospels (Cambridge, Corpus Christi College, MS. 286), to which it offers striking parallels in script-style, layout, and textual readings. Their version of the Latin text is primarily the Vulgate, but with some residue from the Old Latin translation. These two books are the earliest surviving copies of the gospels known to have been used in the British Isles.

Unfortunately the Oxford manuscript has lost its opening and closing leaves, and with them any clear evidence of its medieval origin and home. The surviving text comprises Matthew 4:14 to John 21:15. Saint Matthew's Gospel would no doubt have been preceded by prefaces, and also by canon tables to accompany the standard Eusebian section-numbers, which survive in the margins throughout the book: with the help of the tables, these indicate the parallels between the four gospels. The surviving core of the manuscript suggests that its decorative plan was relatively sparse. The start of Saint John's Gospel is here marked only by modest titles, with just its first line in red (f. 130r, col. II, top line). By contrast, the Corpus Gospels still preserve some pages of major illumination and were overall, therefore, a more lavish book. Both are laid out in double columns, without word-divisions but with frequent line-breaks to mark out clauses *per cola et commata*. Here, that system sometimes breaks down; and later readers trying to make sense of the text found it necessary to divide words and to add punctuation, perhaps to help them in reading aloud. In terms of production standards, neither manuscript is of the highest professional quality, with a smallish format, variable parchment, and a certain inelegance of script: perhaps the missionaries did not want to waste the finest Roman calligraphy on the heathen English.

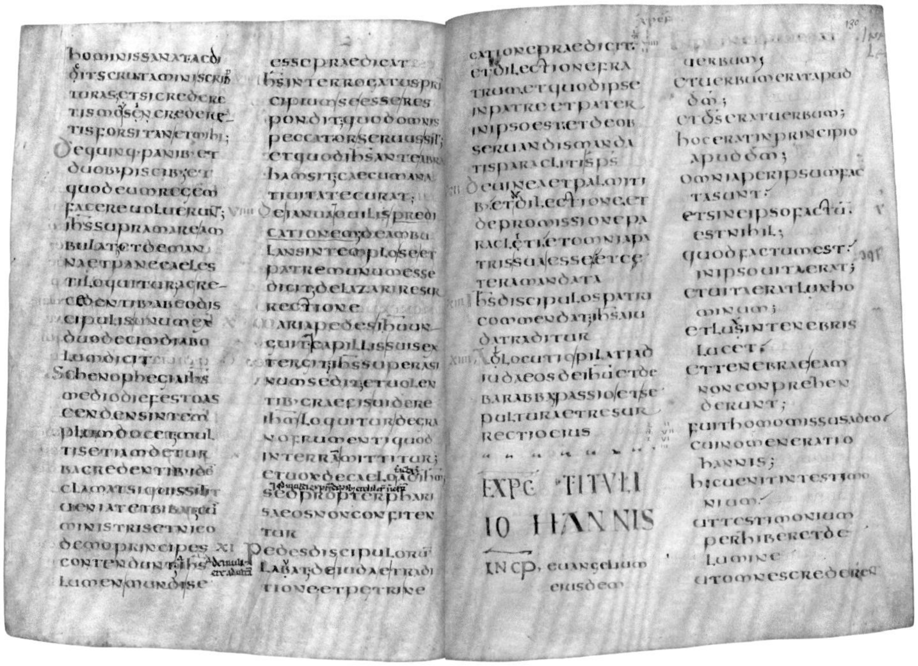

CAT. 53

In the margins of this manuscript, notes in Insular and Anglo-Saxon hands were added, mostly to mark the readings for specified feasts. The addition by an Insular hand of a few words celebrating Saint Chad (written upside down on f. 149v) might somehow link the manuscript by the eighth century with that saint's see of Lichfield in Mercia. It was still in liturgical use in the eleventh century, when neumatic musical notation was added for the chanting of Christ's genealogy at Luke 3:21–4:1 (ff. 79r–80r). A potential clue to the book's location around that period could lie in a book-list in Old English on a separate half-leaf at the end (f. 173r): this includes the name of an "Abbot Baldwin," probably of Bury St. Edmunds in Suffolk (1065–1097/8). Bury was not founded until the tenth century; but in any case, the evidence is inconclusive, since the end-leaf need not have joined the main volume until after the end of the Middle Ages. It could even have been added to the gospel-book by the great collector Sir Robert Cotton, before he gave the whole volume to the Bodleian Library in 1603, one year after the Library's opening.

The book's occasional modern nickname, "Gospels of Saint Augustine" (which it shares confusingly with the Corpus Gospels), is strictly forbidden at the Bodleian because it rests purely on speculation. Yet the idea has a curious, if unfounded persistence. The saint was buried at the abbey that he had founded outside the walls of Canterbury. Among relics dating back to the time of Pope Gregory I, Saint Augustine's Abbey preserved a number of ancient books: these were listed by the monk Thomas Elmham in 1414, when some were on display above the high altar in the abbey church. Elmham's chronicle describes three early copies of the gospels, of which one was almost certainly the book now at Cambridge. It remains not wholly beyond the bounds of possibility that one of the two others might have been the Oxford manuscript. Wherever its medieval home—Canterbury, Lichfield, Bury, or places unknown—a perfect summary of its character is given in the clumsy, eloquent words with which Elmham headed his Canterbury list: "the first-fruits of the books of the whole English church."

BCBB

Bibliography:

Summary Catalogue, 1895–1953, no. 2698; Lowe, 1934–72, ii, no. 230; Elmham; Wordsworth and White, 1889–98, siglum "O"; Nicholson, 1913, pp. xvii–xix, pls. I–III; Ker, 1957, no. 290; Lowe, 1960, p. 17, pl. 4; McGurk, 1961, no. 32; Pächt and Alexander, 1966–73, ii no. 1a; T. J. Brown, 1980, no. II. 5; McGurk, 1990, siglum "O"; Dumville, 1992, pp. 102–3, 121 and n. 191; Lapidge, 1996, pp. 428, 441; Sharpe et al., 1996, no. B12; Verey, 1998, pp. 112–14; Ganz, 2001; Gneuss, 2001, nos. 529, 529.1; *Bodley*, 2002, no. 35; Doane, 2002, pp. 62–6 (doc. 339); Emms, 2005, pp. 32–45.

54

The Selden Acts of the Apostles

Oxford, Bodleian Library,
MS. Selden Supra 30, pp. 46–47
Ink on parchment; pp. viii + 116;
approx. 225 × 175mm
Acts of the Apostles; Latin
Kent (?) (Minster-in-Thanet?),
southern England; eighth century, first half

In studying and transcribing the biblical books that Saint Augustine and his successors had brought to England, the new Christian communities copied scripts as well as texts. The Latin Vulgate text of the Acts of the Apostles is here written out entirely in lettering that directly imitates the rounded uncial style of Italian models. "English uncial" transmutes the quick, natural dexterity of the Italian script into something more artificial, often more monumental. Here, the script seems somehow labored, not yet natural to its scribes. Such slow, stately writing is so wasteful of parchment that even a single biblical book such as Acts could fill up an entire volume. Yet perhaps that is the point: the luxurious script-style, here touchingly uneven, represents the height of scribal ambition to proclaim reverence for the scriptures.

Underlying the imported script-style, the book still preserves elements of the native scribal traditions that it shares with the earliest books from Ireland and northern England. The parchment is thick, dark, and sometimes rough, with vertical rows of prickings in both inner and outer margins to guide the lines of hard-point ruling. There are numerous abbreviations of a type practised by the Irish and their pupils: for example, at p. 47, line 10, second word, *Audierunt autem apostoli et fratres* ... (Acts 11:1), where the single *h*-form with additional curved stroke is the Insular abbreviation for *autem*, meaning "however." In the letter-forms themselves, ancient features of the Italian style are subtly exaggerated, as in the pointed bow of *A*, the downstroke of *F*, and the trailing tail of *G*: such enhancements of script into calligraphy seem characteristic of an Insular spirit, glimpsed here through a delight in the abstract shapes of the letters.

The book was written by two scribes. The second, still writing uncial but less carefully, starts a new quire after leaving one side blank in mid-text (p. 70). This was soon filled up by two prayers, again in English uncial resembling that of the second scribe. The first prayer was written by or for a female petitioner, for it begs God not to despise *indignam famulam tuam*, "Thy unworthy handmaid" (p. 70, line 5). The woman's prayer places the book very likely in an eighth-century English nunnery, where it may all have been written.

Centuries later, the book belonged to the library of Saint Augustine's Abbey, Canterbury, as shown by inscriptions from the twelfth century onwards (p. 1) and by its entry added to the abbey's library-catalogue in the late fifteenth century: it seems first to have been shelved there amongst other copies of Acts, but then to have escaped initial cataloguing before transfer to another shelf in which very early manuscripts were jumbled alongside Old Testament texts. After the surrender of Saint Augustine's to Henry VIII in 1538, its library was left on site and its treasures raided, first for the king and then more gradually by anyone who could gain access. This book was given to the Bodleian by the executors of the historian John Selden (1584–1654).

There is one well-documented occasion when Saint Augustine's Abbey took over the property of an early nunnery. Around 1030, the relics of Saint Mildrith (died ca. 700) were translated to Saint Augustine's from Minster-in-Thanet, the nunnery on the Isle of Thanet where she had been abbess. It was probably at this time that Saint Augustine's took over the nuns' land-charters and perhaps a few books; if so, the Selden Acts was most likely among them. A supplementary clue, impossible to date or to verify, lies in the letters scratched in tiny capitals just below the text describing Saint Peter's vision at Joppa (Acts 11:5–6) on p. 47: *EADB* (with +*E*+ below at the edge). Around the period when this book was written, Minster had a saintly abbess (died 751), so learned that she corresponded with Saint Boniface and even copied manuscripts for his use. Her name was Saint Eadburh.

BCBB

Bibliography:
Summary Catalogue, 1895–1953, 3418; Lowe, 1934–72, ii, no. 257; Nicholson, 1913, pp. xx–xxi, pl. V; Lowe, 1960, p. 21, pl. XXV; Pächt and Alexander, 1966–73, iii no. 2; T. J. Brown, 1980, no. II. 6; Brown, 2001; Brown 2001a; Gneuss, 2001, no. 665.

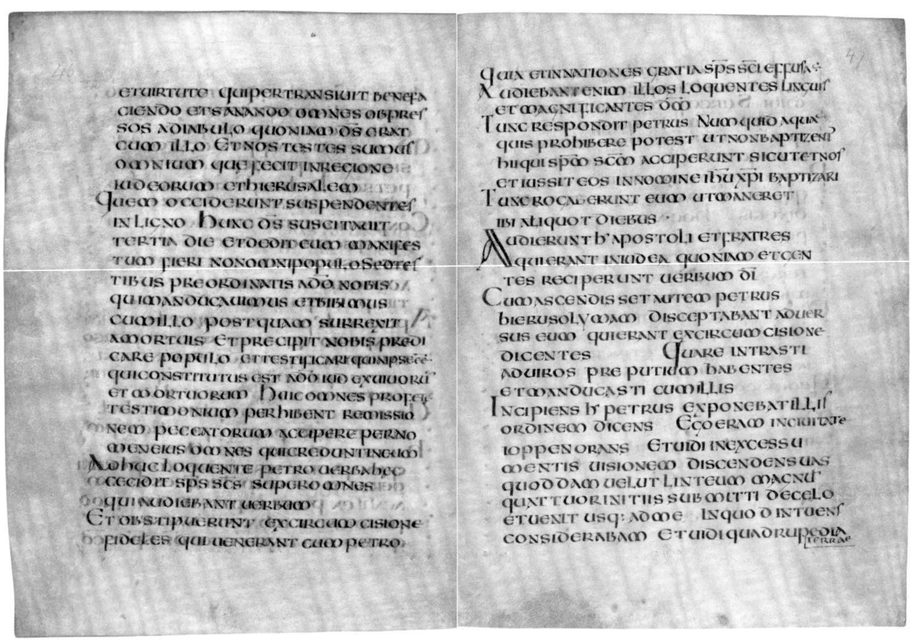

CAT. 54

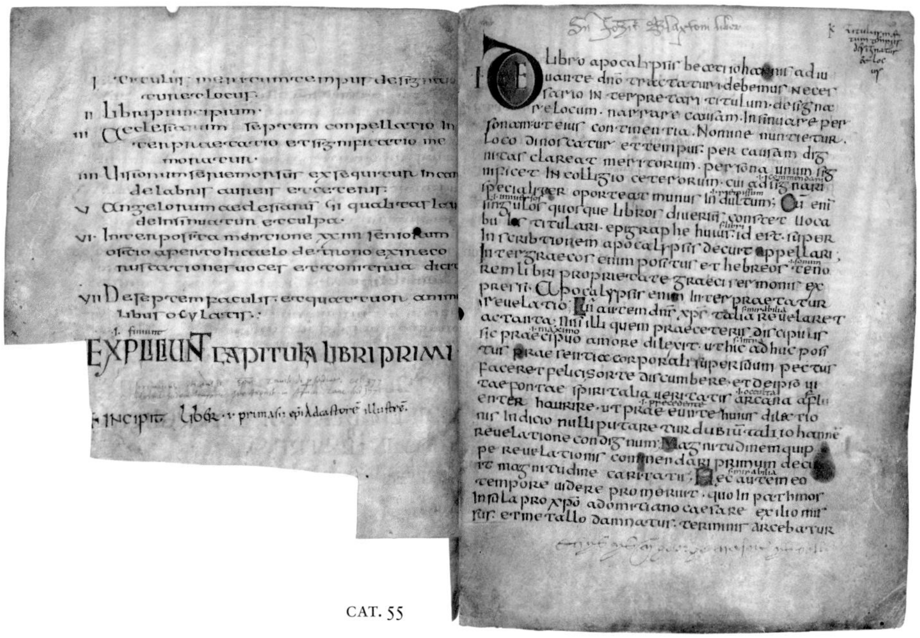

CAT. 55

55

The Douce Primasius

Oxford, Bodleian Library,
MS. Douce 140, ff. 3v–4r
Ink on parchment; ff. viii + 153;
335 × 180mm
Primasius, *Commentarius in Apocalypsin* (Commentary on the Apocalypse); Latin
Southern England (?); late seventh or early eighth century (before 718?)

The biblical scholarship of the early African Church may have been transmitted through this book to two of the greatest English saints and scholars: Saint Boniface (Wynfrith), the "Apostle to the Germans" (died 751); and Saint Dunstan, Archbishop of Canterbury (died 988). The manuscript itself was written out by a team of Insular scribes, most likely in southern England around the year 700.

Its text is the Latin commentary on the Book of Revelation by Primasius, bishop of Hadrumetum in modern Tunisia (died ca. 560). He had been summoned to Constantinople in the reign of Justinian; accordingly, his commentary draws both on Greek learning and on the theological traditions of his native North Africa. The version of the Latin biblical text that it embodies goes back to a type used by Saint Cyprian of Carthage (died 258); and Primasius's exposition both culls and expurgates the lost commentary of Tyconius, a member of the schismatic Donatist sect of the African Church in the late fourth century. The route by which Primasius's text was transmitted from the Byzantine Empire into this Insular book must remain a matter of speculation. It is the earliest and most important surviving manuscript of Primasius, and includes several passages (varying from a few words to as much as fifty-two of its lines) that survive nowhere else.

The script is an early imitation of ancient half-uncial, one grade down from the formality of uncial capitals: a style possibly brought to fruition in Primasius's own period and country, though here based on seventh-century French models. As an imitation rather than an adaptation, the script lacks the grace and charm of Insular calligraphy. Its clumsiness is to be contrasted with the elegance and strength of the marginal headings, added in quick cursive minuscule of southern English type and each starting *k* for "kapitulum" (e.g. f. 4r, top right). Annotations probably by the same hand occur also in the Capuan Codex Fuldensis (Fulda, Landesbibliothek, Bonifatianus 1), the sixth-century biblical manuscript which Saint Boniface had with him in Germany. The Primasius chapter-headings are therefore attributed to Boniface, at a period before 718 when he left southwest England on his second mission to the continent.

The inference that this copy of Primasius did not itself leave England to contribute to the conversion of Europe relies on the presence of further annotations by a tenth-century English hand, seen here (f. 4r) in the additions between the lines of one-word Latin explanations or alternatives. This hand is identifiable in turn with that found in the volume now known as Saint Dunstan's Classbook (Oxford, Bodleian Library, MS. Auct. F. 4. 32), which was evidently assembled and annotated by the saint himself. His scholarly interactions with these books seem more likely to belong to his time as abbot of Glastonbury in the 950s, before his elevation to the archbishopric of Canterbury. The later medieval home of the Primasius is unknown. In the mid-sixteenth century it belonged successively to the two men who wrote their names at the top and bottom of f. 4r, John Blaxton and George Mason, probably canons of Exeter Cathedral. It was the oldest manuscript in the great bequest of Francis Douce, which reached the Bodleian in 1834.

Dunstan's reading was perhaps less assiduous than Boniface's, for his additions peter out after the first three pages. It is nevertheless remarkable that the same pages by the African Primasius could have been studied and marked by these two magnificent and influential early English saints.

BCBB

Bibliography:

Primasius; *Summary Catalogue*, 1895–1953, no. 21714; Lowe, 1934–72, ii, no. 237; Clark, 1918, pp. 104–23; Bishop, 1968; Bishop, 1971, p. 2; Parkes, 1976; T. J. Brown, 1980, no. II. 2; *Douce Legacy*, 1984, no. 212; Watson, 1984, no. 461; Gneuss, 2001, no. 616.

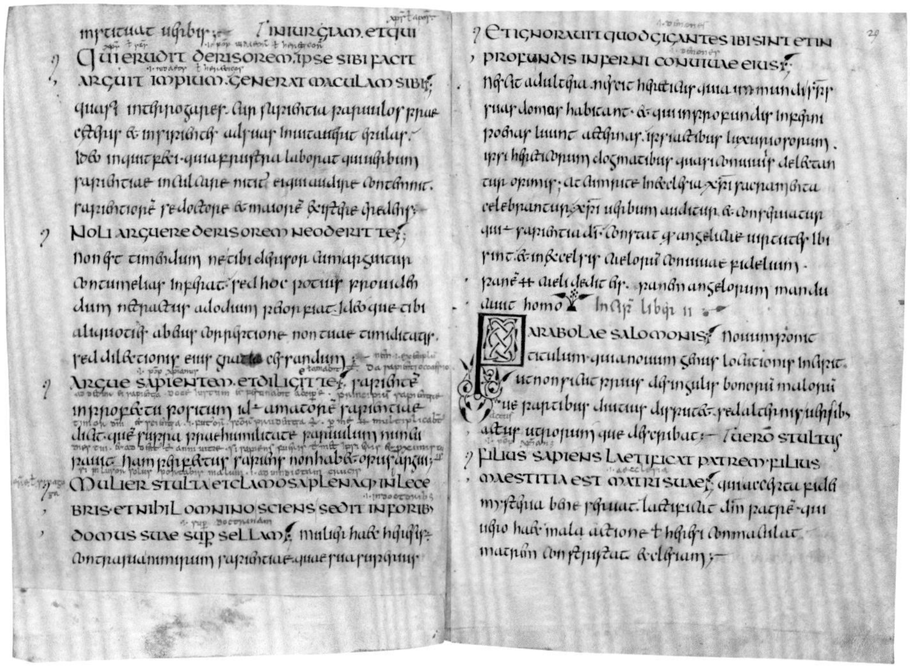

CAT. 56

56

Bede's *Commentary on Proverbs*

Oxford, Bodleian Library,
MS. Bodl. 819, ff. 28v–29r
Ink on parchment, ff. vii + 121; 252 × 185mm
Bede, *Super Parabolas Salomonis*; Latin
Northumbria (Wearmouth–Jarrow), northeast England; eighth century, second half

From his Northumbrian base at the twin monasteries of Wearmouth–Jarrow, Saint Bede (ca. 673–735) established himself as a scholar of pan-European stature and influence. Nowadays his best-known work is the *Ecclesiastical History of the English People*, completed in 731; but his range extended beyond history to science and the calendar, grammar and meter, saints' lives and cosmography. Above all, his biblical studies were extensive and systematic, producing commentaries on many books of the Bible. He paid critical attention to the texts themselves, by collecting and comparing the various Latin and even Greek versions, and drew on earlier patristic commentators to help explain their meaning.

The intensity of Bede's scholarship required not only the collecting of books from elsewhere, but also scribal copying of his own works. This manuscript of his commentary on the Old Testament Book of Proverbs is thought to have been written in the scriptorium of his own Wearmouth–Jarrow community, only a few decades after his death. The clear and intuitive layout of its text is accomplished through the use of two contrasting script-styles, written continuously by the same expert scribe. Here, at the start of a new section (f. 29r, line 13), the biblical text reiterates the title "PARABOLAE SALOMONIS" (Proverbs 10:1), to which Bede comments, "He puts a new title because he is beginning a new mode of saying …." The biblical text is written in English uncial, of a type developed at Wearmouth–Jarrow in the late seventh century for the chapter-headings of its great bibles. The Insular minuscule of Bede's commentary was a more recent development, an elegant, pointed style that had been perfected by the mid-eighth century, perhaps largely to disseminate Bede's own writings; at any rate, its earliest mature examples are devoted to his works. The decoration shows a similar duality of native and foreign influence: initials of Insular interlace, but with ivy-leaf shapes inherited ultimately from late Roman punctuation markings.

In its subsequent history, the manuscript seems to have traveled a familiar path for Northumbrian books. In the tenth century, it received interlinear Latin glosses (e.g., f. 29r, lines 1–2, identifying both "gigantes" and "conuiuae" at Proverbs 9:18 as "demones") by the same hand as the Old English gloss of the Lindisfarne Gospels (London, British Library, Cotton MS. Nero D. iv). This attentive Anglo-Saxon reader was Aldred, a member of the Lindisfarne community in its temporary refuge at Chester-le-Street. Later, once the community had found its permanent home at Durham Cathedral Priory, the manuscript was still of use: its punctuation and abbreviations were modernized to allow it to be used there in the early twelfth century as the exemplar for a copy that still survives (British Library, Harley MS. 4688), and a replacement leaf (f. 74) was inserted around the same time. Unlike many works of Bede, the text was thus transmitted directly from Insular to Norman England, without the need to re-import it from the continent. Eight centuries after it was written, and with some leaves lost, the manuscript was given to the Bodleian Library as a foundation gift by Sir Walter Cope in 1602.

BCBB

Bibliography:
Summary Catalogue, 1895-1953 no. 2699; Lowe, 1934–72, ii, no. 235; Lowe, 1960, pp. 9, 24, pl. XXXVIII*e*; Pächt and Alexander, 1966–73, iii no. 8; T. J. Brown, 1980, no. II. 7, fig. 2; Watson, 1987, pp. 263, 276 n. 13, 296 no. B26; Gneuss, 2001, no. 604.

57

Pope Gregory the Great's *Commentary on the Gospels*

Cambridge, Corpus Christi College, MS. 69, f. 1r
Ink and pigments on parchment; ff. 83; 305 × 215mm
Gregory the Great, *Homilae in Euangelia*; Latin
Greater Mercia (probably in a Kentish monastery), southern England; late eighth to early ninth century

This is a good example of an Anglo-Saxon monastic library book. The script is an Insular half-uncial, written informally by an accomplished scribe who lets the script descend into cursive minuscule at the ends of pages. The major and minor initials and display lettering are ornamented with interlace and animal-headed terminals and are painted in red, green, and yellow, the characteristic palette used in earlier Coptic, Frankish, and Insular illumination. The practice of using patterns of triple red dots to frame each of the two columns on the page is unusual. The style of decoration, with its distinctive playful animal heads that bite on to parts of letters to link them together, places the volume within what is known as the "Tiberius Group" of manuscripts (its name derived from a characteristic representative of this style, a copy of Bede's *Historia Ecclesiastica*, British Library, Cotton MS. Tiberius C.ii), made in southern England during the eighth and early ninth centuries.

The role of Pope Gregory the Great (died 604) in sending Saint Augustine and his mission to help convert the pagan Anglo-Saxon settlers of England made him a particularly popular figure there, especially in Kent where Augustine landed in 597. Gregory was an influential Church Father and a notable author. His exegetical commentary on the nature and symbolic meaning of the four gospels influenced the work of later scholars such as Bede.

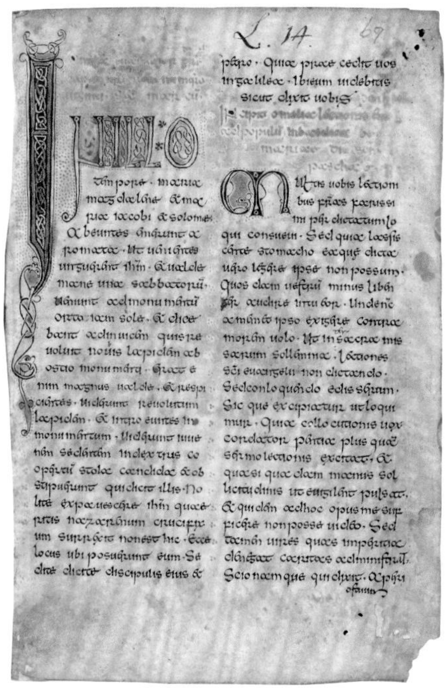

CAT. 57

Gregory interpreted Saint Matthew's symbol, the man or angel, as representing Christ's Incarnation; Saint Mark's symbol, the lion, as signifying kingship and the Resurrection; Saint Luke's symbol, the calf or bull, as representing the sacrificial offering of the Crucifixion; and Saint John's symbol, the eagle, as flying to the throne of God for inspiration and representing the Second Coming and Last Judgment. This was the interpretation also favored by Bede and it subsequently became the medieval norm, rather than the order and imagery of the symbols advanced by Irenaeus.

MPB

Bibliography:
Lowe, 1934–72, ii.121; Chazelle, 1990; Markus, 1997; Brown, 1998a; O'Reilly, 1998; Étaix, 1999; Brown, 2001.

58

The Cambridge–London Gospels

Cambridge, Corpus Christi College, MS. 197b, Symbol of St. John, f. 1r
Ink and pigments on parchment; ff. 36; 285 × 215mm
Gospels; Latin
Northumbria (Lindisfarne?), northeast England; ca. 725–50

This once striking gospelbook now survives only in two fragmentary portions: London, British Library, Cotton MS. Otho C.v, badly damaged by fire in 1731; and the present item. Its half-uncial script, decoration, and text, which used "Mixed Celtic" and Vulgate versions as models for

CAT. 58

different gospels, suggest that it was probably made in the monastery of Lindisfarne or a daughter house, circa 725–50, shortly after the famous Lindisfarne Gospels. Founded by Irish followers of Saint Columba, the Lindisfarne scriptorium skillfully blended Celtic, Pictish, Germanic, Roman, and eastern Mediterranean influences to reflect its unifying role in the British Isles and an ecumenical tradition stretching from the deserts of the Near East to the Atlantic coast of Ireland. It is a masterpiece of "Insular" art. The term "Insular" appertains, in this context, to the islands of Britain and Ireland, circa 550–850, a time when their various cultures were blending to form a new, distinctive Christian identity in the wake of the Roman Empire.

Two evangelist miniatures remain: the sadly charred lion of Saint Mark (Otho C.v, f. 27r), which closely resembles its splendid rampant counterpart in the Echternach Gospels (Paris, Bibliothèque nationale de France, MS. lat. 9389, f. 75v); and a powerful depiction of the eagle of Saint John, symbolizing the visionary nature of his Gospel—flying directly to the throne of God for inspiration and representing the Second Coming. Its striking design recalls vigorous Pictish carvings from Scotland and Anglo-Saxon enamelwork. Crosses point towards it, connecting the concepts of Crucifixion and Second Coming.

On f. 2r is a magnificent incipit page across which the opening words of John's Gospel explode, becoming an iconic image in their own right: an Insular artist's version of sacred calligraphy. Such symbolic solutions to depicting the Divine obliquely, through sign and symbol, may have been a response to the international debate concerning idolatry.

Tradition claims that this gospelbook was owned by Saint Augustine, who led the Roman mission to convert the Anglo-Saxons in 597 (as recorded in an inscription added above the Saint John miniature). This cannot be the case, but evidence suggests that the book may have been at Saint Augustine's Abbey, Canterbury, during the Anglo-Saxon period. During the sixteenth century it entered the collection of Matthew Parker, Archbishop of Canterbury (died 1575), who did much to preserve the Christian book culture of England in the wake of the Reformation and helped lay the foundations of Anglican biblical scholarship. His collection forms the core of the Parker Library at Corpus Christi College. The other portion of the book entered the collection of the great bibliophile and parliamentarian, Sir Robert Cotton (died 1631), partially destroyed in the Ashburnham House fire in 1731. This became one of the foundation collections of the British Museum in 1753. Fortunately, a hand-painted facsimile of one of the volume's decorated pages was made in the early eighteenth century, before the fire, conveying its splendor (British Library, Stowe MS. 1061, f. 36r).

MPB

Bibliography:
Lowe, 1934–72, ii, no. 125; McGurk, 1961, no. 2; Alexander, 1978, no. 12; Henderson, 1987; Verey, 1989; Webster and Backhouse, 1991, no. 83; Verey, 1999; Brown, 2003; Brown, 2003a; Brown, 2005; Brown, 2006.

59

The Macregol Gospels (*alias* The Rushworth Gospels)

Oxford, Bodleian Library,
MS. Auct. D. 2. 19, ff. 51v–52r
Ink and pigments on parchment,
ff. ii + 171; 348 × 264mm
Gospels; Latin, with Old English gloss (added in England in the second half of the tenth century)
Co. Offaly (?) (Birr ?), Ireland; late eighth or early ninth century (before 822?)

"Macregol painted this gospelbook. Whoever shall have read or understood that story prays for Macreguil the scribe." This is a translation of the Latin colophon, written by the main scribe within a decorative border on the last page of the book (f. 169v). The inscription seems to treat painting and writing as two separate activities, each to be signed for; yet the name given for both illuminator and scribe is apparently the same, except for the minor spelling variant (perhaps between Latin and Old Irish). It is unusual in illuminated manuscripts of any period to find script and decoration credited together to one person.

A probable match for the name occurs in the Annals of Ulster for the year 821: "Macriagoil nepos Magleni (Macriaghoil ua Magléni), scribe and bishop, abbot of

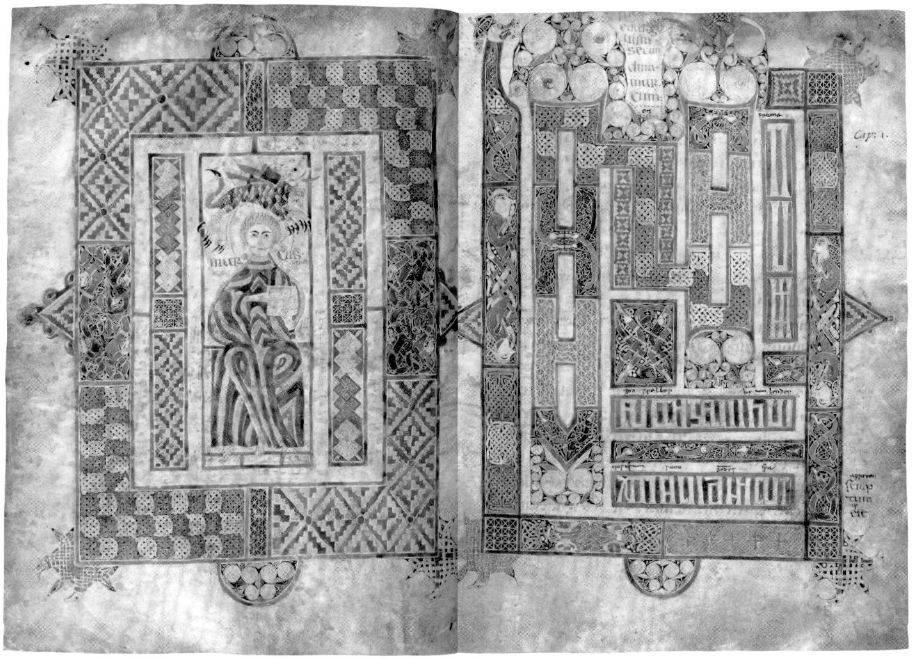

CAT. 59

Birr, perished." A shorter version of this entry appears in the Annals of Inisfallen for the year 822. Although the identification must depend on the relative rarity of the name, it is supported by the annalistic characterization of the abbot as scribe, and is now generally accepted. The manuscript's alternative name, the Rushworth Gospels, derives from the historian John Rushworth, who gave it to the Bodleian Library, perhaps in 1681.

Macregol's death-date confirms this as one of the latest of the luxury gospelbooks of Ireland. The script is half-uncial like that of the Rawlinson Gospels (cat. no. 60), if rather less well controlled. Though its craftsmanship lacks the magical finesse of the Book of Kells, the treatment of colors and patterns has a raised, enameled quality of its own, especially vivid when seen in the original. As always, the decorative scheme concentrates on the evangelist portrait and facing incipit page at the start of each gospel. The first surviving page contains the incipit for Saint Matthew's Gospel (f. 1r), his portrait being lost. Shown here, at the next main opening, "Marcus" sits holding his book; overhead flies his symbol, a winged lion with prominent claws. Set within heavy panels of interlace- or fret-patterns and intertwining creatures, the evangelist's robes are stylized to the point where his body and knees are almost absorbed into the abstract design. The same principle applies to the opening words of his Gospel, *Initium euangelii Jesu Christi, Filii Dei. Sicut [scriptum est]* (The beginning of the gospel of Jesus Christ, the Son of God; As [it is written]), with only the last two words in plain text at lower right. Both the evangelist's image and his words are transfigured into color, for the greater glory of God.

Macregol's gospelbook has been in English hands for over a millennium. It must have been brought over the Irish Sea by the second half of the tenth century, when its Latin text was glossed with a word-for-word translation in Old English by two named scribes, Farmon and Owun. The linguistics of their two stints are distinguishable: while the Old English words naturally follow the order of the Latin words over which they were written, Farmon's gloss on Matthew is in a form of Mercian dialect, and goes further than Owun's towards making continuous sense. Here at the start of Mark, Farmon inserts his English words in plain script over the Irish calligraphic fantasies of the Latin. Both men are named in a colophon at the end (ff. 168v–169r), which describes Farmon as a priest at "Harewood"; there are places of this name in both Yorkshire and Herefordshire. Around the same time, an Old English gloss was similarly added to the Lindisfarne Gospels (London, British Library, Cotton MS. Nero D. iv) by Aldred at Chester-le-Street, north of Durham. The sets of glosses in these two manuscripts are evidently related, with Owun's work especially close to the Northumbrian; together, they are the earliest surviving translations of the gospels into the English language.

BCBB

Bibliography:

Summary Catalogue, 1895–1953, no. 3946; Lowe, 1934–72, ii, no. 231; Skeat, 1871–87; Hennessy, 1887–1901, vol. 1, pp. 314–15; Wordsworth and White, 1889–98, siglum "R"; Mac Airt, 1951, pp. 124–25; Ker, 1957, no. 292; McGurk, 1961, no. 33; Pächt and Alexander, 1966–73, iii no. 1269; Alexander, 1978, no. 54; Byrne, 1979, no. 2; O'Neill, 1984, no. VI; Watson, 1984, no. 43; Ohlgren, 1986, no. 54; McGurk, 1990, siglum "R"; Gneuss, 2001, no. 531; Brown, 2003.

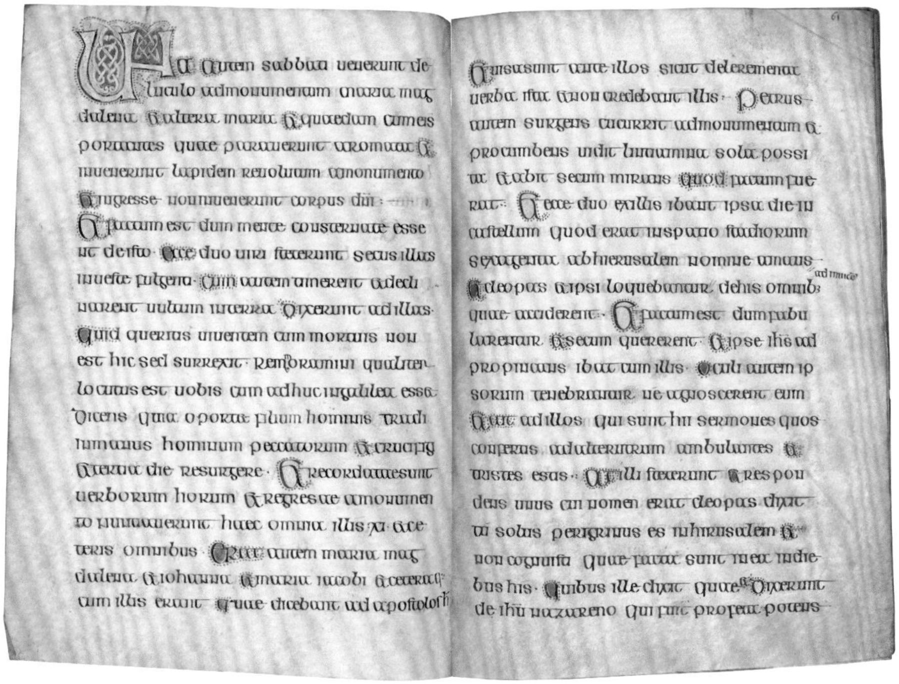

CAT. 60

60

The Rawlinson Gospels

Oxford, Bodleian Library,
MS. Rawl. G. 167, ff. 60v–61r
Ink and pigments on parchment,
ff. v + 109; 325 × 230mm
Gospels (fragment); Latin
Ireland (?); eighth century, second half (?)

The noble script and fine initials show that this must once have been one of the major Insular gospelbooks. Over a hundred leaves remain, containing most of Saint Luke's and Saint John's gospels. The first page of Luke survives with full-page illumination (f. 1r), including a huge *Q* for the opening Latin word *Quoniam* ("Inasmuch") and a full interlace border: but it is so stained, faded, and rubbed that it retains only a shadow of its former splendor.

In the body of the manuscript the leaves are well preserved, though the power of their design is reduced by the severe trimming of the margins by a later binder. At f. 60v, the first two words, *Una autem*, offer an example of well-controlled "diminuendo," as the size is reduced letter by letter from the largest illuminated capitals to normal script. The first two letters are joined together, with a fine example of Insular interlace. The red dots that surround the initials are an easy and common form of early decoration. The style of script, which used to be categorized as "Insular majuscule," is perhaps better described as Insular half-uncial, written boldly for display at nearly the highest degree of formality. The manuscript is generally assumed to be of Irish origin, though stylistic links have been detected with books of equivalent status from elsewhere in the British Isles such as the Lichfield or Saint Chad Gospels (Lichfield, Cathedral Library, MS. 1) or even the Lindisfarne Gospels (London, British Library, Cotton MS. Nero D. iv). Its medieval home remains unknown. It reached the Bodleian Library through the bequest of Richard Rawlinson (1690–1755), who also owned other major Irish manuscripts originally collected by Sir James Ware (1594–1666); however, there is no evidence that Ware owned this gospelbook.

The illuminated letters at the top of f. 60v begin the Easter narrative at the last chapter of Luke (24:1–): *Una autem sabbati uenerunt deluculo ad monumentum Maria Magdalena et altera Maria* … (But on the first day of the week, at early dawn, they went to the tomb …). In this version of the Latin text, the protagonists are named at once as Mary Magdalene and "the other Mary" rather than as the usual "they": so the reading starts here with more immediate clarity. From these pages, a deacon might thus have proclaimed the Easter message in an Irish church, over twelve hundred years ago.

BCBB

Bibliography:
Summary Catalogue, 1895–1953, no. 14890; Lowe, 1934–72, ii, no. 356; McGurk, 1961, no. 35; Pächt and Alexander, 1966–73, iii no. 1268; Alexander, 1978, no. 43; Byrne, 1979, no. 1; Ohlgren, 1986, no. 43; McGurk, 1990, siglum "Ho"; Gneuss, 2001, no. 664.5.

61

The Old English Genesis (*alias* The Junius Manuscript, *or* The Caedmon Manuscript)

Oxford, Bodleian Library, MS. Junius 11, pp. 86–87
Ink on parchment; ff. 116;
323 × 195mm
Biblical poetry; English
England (Canterbury?); ca. 1000

Of the four major sources of Old English poetry, the Junius manuscript is the only one to contain an extensive cycle of pictures. The alliterative poems it preserves—testimony to the precocious development of vernacular religious literature in Anglo-Saxon England—are paraphrases of biblical narratives: "Genesis A"; "Genesis B," an interpolation derived from an Old Saxon poem on the Fall of the Rebel Angels and of Man; "Exodus"; "Daniel"; and "Christ and Satan." The attractive but unlikely connection with the seventh-century illiterate herdsman Caedmon of Whitby, whose miraculous poetic gifts are recorded by Bede, was first made by Francis Junius, the pioneering philologist who acquired the manuscript in the seventeenth century. The manuscript may be identifiable in the early-fourteenth-century library catalogue of Christ Church, Canterbury—though this does not constitute proof that the manuscript was produced there. A medallion portrait on p. 2 of the manuscript is inscribed "Aelfwine" and appears to depict a layman, but too little is known about the relations between lay patrons and monastic book producers at this period to be certain of its significance.

Much of Genesis is illustrated with an extensive but incomplete series of drawings. In the later parts of Genesis, and throughout Exodus and Daniel, spaces were left by the scribe for drawings that were never inserted. No such spaces were left in the text of Christ and Satan. Two distinct styles can be identified in the drawings. The first artist uses brown and red inks with occasional washes, and draws figures in a firm outline. The second artist, whose work is shown here, draws with red, blue, and green inks in a lighter, sketchier, and more fluent style. It has been observed that text and pictures do not proceed smoothly together from page to page; sometimes they are jarringly out of step. Some scholars have inferred that the artists were struggling to adapt earlier cycles of biblical illustrations to the particular demands of this vernacular version. The composition of the drawings must in reality have involved a complex mixture of borrowing, adaptation, and invention.

Page 87 illustrates Abraham building an altar (top) and making an offering (center), and the Lord appears to Abraham (bottom). The drawing on p. 84 (see page 205) illustrates three crucial moments in the relationship between God and Abraham (Genesis 12:1–7), employing a vivid vocabulary of gesture to indicate the communication between them. In the top register the beardless figure of God commands Abraham to leave his home in Haran, watched from Abraham's house on the right by Sarah and Lot. In the middle register Abraham leads Sarah, Lot, and their followers into the land of Canaan. Finally, God returns to announce that he will give the land to Abraham's seed. The Anglo-Saxons drew parallels between their own migration from the European continent to England and the journeys of the Israelites, identifying themselves as a chosen people under God's protection. Their royal genealogies traced their ancestry back to the Old Testament patriarchs, and their law codes contained extensive quotations from the Pentateuch.

MK

Bibliography:
Summary Catalogue, 1895–1953, no. 5123; Gollancz, 1927 (facsimile); Krapp, 1931; Ker, 1957, no. 334; Evans, 1963; Pächt and Alexander, 1966–73, iii no. 34; Henderson, 1975; Blum, 1976; Hall, 1976; Raw, 1976; Temple, 1976, no. 58; Doane, 1978; Lucas, 1979; Bergman, 1980, pp. 13, 25–27, 31–35, 45–47; Lucas, 1980–81; Broderick, 1983; Raw, 1984; Doane, 1991; Ohlgren, 1992, no. 16; Amtower, 1993; Lucas, 1994; Zimmermann, 1995; Remley, 1996; Lucas, 2000; Liuzza, 2002; Muir, 2004 (digital facsimile); Karkov, 2001.

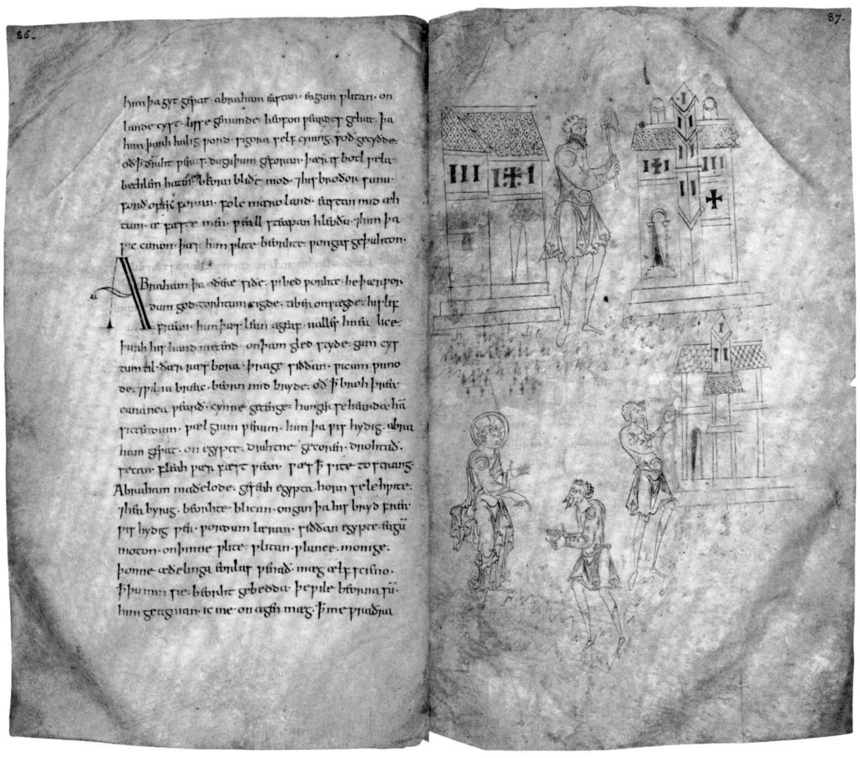

CAT. 61

62

The Rabbula Gospels

Florence, Biblioteca Medicea Laurenziana, MS. Plut. I. 56, ff. 12v–13r
Ink and pigments on parchment; 336 × 266mm
Gospels; Syriac
Syria (Beth Zagba); 586

A colophon near the end (f. 291r) records the completion of this exceptionally luxurious manuscript by an otherwise unknown scribe (perhaps also the painter) named Rabbula in the year 586 at the monastery of Saint John in Beth Zagba, an obscure place apparently inland from the Mediterranean coast between Antioch and Damascus. Its Syriac Peshitta version of the gospels is written in beautiful *esṭrangelā* script (literally "to write the Gospels"), like other Semitic languages written from right to left. Hence the book itself proceeds in a fashion opposite to that of Greek and Latin manuscripts.

The opening illustrated presents two of the types of decoration found in the Rabbula Gospels. On the right is the last of ten canon tables, listing passages unique to John's text. On the left is one of several full-page miniatures, this one devoted to the Crucifixion and events immediately following: the Marys at the Tomb and the resurrected Christ Appearing to the Two Marys. The canon table is adorned by paradisiacal symbols—birds and a cross set in foliage; and in the margins an illustration of Christ Before Pilate, the culmination of a continuous series of narrative pictures that begins with the Annunciation to Zacharias on the first canon table and conveys the sense of unity underlying the charts themselves. Most of the other canon tables also picture Old Testament prophets, leading to the portraits of the evangelists on ff. 9v and 10r, thus figuring the harmony of all scripture. Other full-page miniatures include the Choosing of Matthias (f. 1r), the Ascension of Christ (f. 13v), and Pentecost (f. 14v), three episodes actually drawn from the Book of Acts, not the Gospels, portraits of Eusebius and Ammonius who devised the canon tables and the numbering of the gospel passages (f. 2r), the giving of the manuscript to Christ (f. 14r), and an icon of Mary and Christ framed by a double arch and two peacocks (f. 1v). Such anomalies as the transposition of the Dedication and Selection of Matthias suggest that the Rabbula Gospels may have been copied from an exemplar. The model may have been Palestinian; in its general characteristics, the iconography conforms to that on a pilgrim's box in the Vatican (Museo Sacro) and lead *ampullae* (pilgrim flasks) commemorating sites in the Holy Land.

A group of Florentine scholars led by Massimo Bernabò of the University of Cremona has recently been studying the Rabbula Gospels' extensive repainting, which seems not simply to have been a restoration but a concerted attempt to normalize many unusual Syriac features. On the Crucifixion page, for example, Christ was originally portrayed with a spade-shaped face and curly red hair, the so-called "semitic" type found in the dedication page and in the depiction of Christ Before Pilate. The sarcophagus on which the angel sits is also a replacement; originally, he was seated on a rock, which would have worked better with the *tholos* tomb, its doors shown open to indicate that the Lord had risen.

HLK

CAT. 62

Bibliography:

Cecchelli, 1959; Leroy, 1964, pp. 139–206; Wright, 1973; Mango, 1983; Sörries, 1993, pp. 94–100; Lowden, 1999, pp. 26–30; Nersessian, 2001, no. 108.

CAT. 63

63

First Jrutchi Gospels

Tbilisi, K. Kekelidze Institute of Manuscripts (Georgia), H1660, St. Matthew and the Virgin and Child, ff. 6v–7r
Ink on parchment; ff. 297; 210 × 160mm
Gospels; Georgian
Shatberdi Monastery, Georgia; 936–40

One of the oldest surviving biblical manuscripts written in Georgian, this is the earlier of two copies of the gospels housed until the early twentieth century in the Jrutchi Monastery (Sachkhere, Western Georgia). It represents one of the ancient versions of the gospel text known as the "proto-Vulgate." The second Jrutchi Gospels manuscript (K. Kekelidze Institute of Manuscripts, H 1667) dates to the twelfth century, and its text reflects the "Vulgate" version of the Georgian gospels.

The First Jrutchi Gospels includes colophons by Gabriel, "the hasty scribe"; Grigol, son of Mirdat, the patron; and Tevdore, the illuminator. These colophons establish that work on the manuscript took place over a period of four years at the Shatberdi Monastery (now in Turkey), with the miniatures added in the fourth year (940). It was written using two forms of Georgian script: *asomtavruli* (majuscule), the earliest known Georgian script; and *nusxuri* (minuscule), which came into wide use beginning in the ninth century. From the ninth to the end of the eighteenth century, most manuscripts were written in *nusxuri* while headings and beginnings of paragraphs used *asomtavruli*. Thus, as here, the two scripts coexist in different parts of the same manuscript. The gospels and the illuminator's colophon are written in *asomtavruli*, while the colophons by the scribe and patron, and an index of the gospel lections at the end of the manuscript, are in *nusxuri* script.

The text of the gospels is introduced by eight canon tables (ff. 2r–5v), with a portrait of Matthew opposite the Virgin and Child on the next opening (ff. 6v–7r). There are three scenes of healing: the Healing of the Blind, with a portrait of Mark (ff. 92v–93r); the Healing of a Man Possessed by the Devil, with a portrait of Luke (ff. 143v–144r); and the Healing of a Man Suffering from Palsy, with a portrait of John (ff. 228v–229r). Each scene has two inscriptions: one naming Jesus Christ, in three languages (Georgian, Armenian, and Greek); and the other describing the miracle depicted (Georgian). In the scene of the blind man's healing Christ is named in only two languages, Georgian and Armenian, the Greek having been omitted due to lack of space.

Christianity was established as the state religion in Georgia in the 320s. How soon afterward a translation of the scriptures was made in the native language is not certain, but at least the gospels and other Christian writings were translated before the mid-fifth century (see "The Christian Orient," page 39). The oldest Georgian manuscripts, which date from the fifth to sixth century, are palimpsests, and contain mostly biblical texts; they include fragments of a gospel, an apocryphal version of the Acts of the Apostles, a lectionary, hagiographical writings, and the books of Jeremiah and Ezra. Early Georgian manuscripts were typically written on parchment made from the skin of a sheep, goat, calf, or deer, although examples on papyrus are also known (cat. no. 36). Most Georgian manuscripts had a wooden binding covered with tooled leather, although lavishly decorated covers made of precious metal and stones have also survived.

The oldest known illuminated Georgian manuscripts date to the ninth century, and the First Jrutchi Gospels are therefore an early example. From this point on, several stages in the development of Georgian manuscript decoration can be identified, each characterized by distinctive styles. Most are of ecclesiastical content, such as psalms and gospels; but secular illuminated works also survive, including astronomical treatises, indigenous literature, and

Georgian versions of Firdawsi's Persian epic *Shahnameh* (Book of Kings) and the fables known as *Kalila wa Dimna*.
ZA

Bibliography:
Brosset, 1849–51, vol. 12, pp.83–85; Kondakov, 1890; Shanidze, 1945; Amiranashvili, 1966; Schmerling, 1967–79, vol. 1.

CAT. 64

64

Codex Sinopensis (*alias* The Sinope Gospels)

Paris, Bibliothèque nationale de France, MS. Suppl. grec. 1286, Beheading of John the Baptist, f. 10v
Gold ink on purple parchment; ff. 44; 300 × 250mm
Gospel of Saint Matthew; Greek
Constantinople or Syria; sixth century, second half

Given the extraordinarily large layout of text in this fragment, it is entirely possible that the manuscript originally included only the Gospel of Saint Matthew. In that case, it would be a unique surviving example of a four-volume edition of the gospels. In style and conception it is closely related to the Rossano Gospels (Rossano, Museo dell'Arcivescovada); precisely where these luxurious illustrated codices were produced is a matter of speculation, though a consensus favors the eastern part of the Empire.

Each of the five surviving miniatures in the Sinope Matthew (so-called because found at Sinop on the Black Sea) follows the text that describes the subject and is framed by two prophets who present texts from their scriptures as prophecies of the pictured events.

In the case of the Feast of Herod and Beheading of John the Baptist, Moses is portrayed at the left holding the text of Exodus 16:15: "It is the bread that the Lord has given you to eat"; at the right, David displays Psalm 116:15: "Precious in the sight of the Lord is the death of his faithful ones." Labeled with the chapter heading "On the daughter of Herodias," the miniature proper represents Herod's feast; at a sigma-shaped table, the king and his guests look on as a servant delivers the Baptist's head to Salome while John's disciples discover the decapitated body left behind in the prison (Matthew 14:6–11).

The dramatic conception and vivid handling of light and dark relies on classical conventions, but the concentration on the overly large heads and exaggerated gestures is a Late Antique device to convey the essence of the story. The arrangement realizes the notion that the "old covenant" was transmitted in words that, having been realized in actual events and recorded in the gospels, could not only be described but also rendered in pictures.
HLK

Bibliography:
Muñoz, 1906; Grabar, 1948; Sörries, 1993, pp. 78–80; Lowden, 1999, pp. 21–24; D'Aiuto, Morello, and Piazzoni, 2000, pp. 125–29.

CAT. 65

65

Codex Caesariensis (Codex Purpureus Petropolitanus)

New York, Morgan Library and Museum, MS. M.874; gift of the Fellows, 1955, recto?
Inks on purple parchment; f. 1v;
309 × 260mm
Gospels; Greek
Syria; late sixth century

This leaf was once part of a luxurious gospelbook variously known as the Codex Purpureus Petropolitanus, Codex N, or Codex Caesariensis. The gospel text, part of the Gospel of Saint Matthew (15:38–16:7), is written in large, silver, uncial letters; each page contains two columns of sixteen lines. The abbreviated *nomina sacra* (IC) on the verso, which stand for Christ's name (IHCOVC), and the small running title on the recto, are written in gold. The origin of the *nomen sacrum* has been connected with the Jewish reluctance to write out the name of God. (The page numbers on the leaf [89, 90] were added in 1820 and do not reflect the original order.)

We can be grateful that all did not share Saint Jerome's view of such luxury volumes as "written burdens rather than books". Indeed, the writing of sacred scripture in gold and silver was also a way to glorify it, and three other sixth-century gospelbooks written in Greek uncials on purple parchment have survived: the Rossano Gospels or Codex Rossanensis (Rossano, Museo dell'Arcivescovada), the script and text of which are most closely related to the present leaf; the Codex Beratinus (Berat, Albania); and the Codex Sinopensis (cat. no. 64), which is written entirely in gold. All four gospelbooks belong to the same, Byzantine textual family. According to Robert Fuchs, who analyzed the leaf in 1977, the purple color is not the Tyrian purple obtained from murex shells, as was once thought, but comes from lichen.

The leaf includes Christ's remarkable quotation regarding ancient weather prophecy: "When it is evening, you say, 'It will be fair weather, for the sky is red.' And in the morning, 'It will be stormy today, for the sky is red and threatening.'" The verses (Matthew 16:2–3) are not found in the famous fourth-century Greek uncial codices, Vaticanus (Vat. gr. 1209) and Sinaiticus (London, British Library, Add. MS. 43725), but they are common to the three purple manuscripts cited above and to both the Vulgate and King James editions of the Bible.

The Codex Purpureus Petropolitanus is now widely dispersed. The name derives from the largest surviving part (182 folios), which is in St. Petersburg (National Library of Russia, MS. Gr. 537); it was acquired in Sarumsahly (Cappadocia) for Czar Nicholas II's imperial library in 1896. Codex N was the collective designation used by Casper René Gregory for all the surviving leaves. The others are in Patmos, Monastery of Saint John the Evangelist (MS. 67, 33 folios); Athens, Byzantine Museum (Fragment 21, 1 folio); Lerma, Spinola Library (1 folio); London, British Library (MS. Cotton Titus C.XV, 4 folios, which had been in the possession of Sir Robert Cotton before his death in 1631); Thessaloniki, Archeological Museum (MS. Am 25.14, 1 folio, which surfaced in the district of Caesarea in the late nineteenth century); Vienna, Österreichische Nationalbibliothek (MS. Vindob. Theol. Gr. 31, 2 folios bound with the Vienna Genesis); and Vatican Library (MS. Vat. Gr. 2305, 6 folios, acquired between 1548 and 1596). The Morgan leaf was purchased through Prof. Stanley Rypins, then of Brooklyn College, who had discovered it in the possession of a rural schoolteacher while traveling in an eastern Mediterranean country. The Morgan and Athens leaves once belonged to the St. Petersburg portion, and were evidently removed after the foliation made in 1820 (see above), presumably in Ephesus, where it first came to light. In 2002 all of the surviving folios were reproduced and correctly ordered in a color facsimile.

WMV

Bibliography:

Gregory, 1909, pp. 56–9; Rypins, 1956; Adams, 1957, pp. 11–14, illus; Faye and Bond, 1962, p. 367; Richard, 1964, p. 43; Weitzmann, 1979, p. 493 no. 444, illus; Mango, 1986, p. 258 no. 87, fig. 87.1; Aland and Aland, 1989, p. 113 [N 022]; Plotzek and others, 1992, p. 60; Εὐάγγελος, Ὀ Πέρλης, and others, 2002, p. 26 no. 6, p. 34 (bibliography), p. 73. The Morgan leaf is reproduced on pp. 93 and 94 in the facsimile.

CAT. 66

66

The Sion Treasure Book Covers (cross flanked by cypress trees)

Washington, D.C., Dumbarton Oaks, inv. nos. BZ.1963.36.9, upper cover
Silver with gilding;
372 × 300 mm and 375 × 276 mm
Constantinople (?); sixth century, third quarter

This cover, one of a pair (the back cover is less well preserved), is part of an enormous treasure of silver furnishing for a Church of the Holy Sion, almost certainly at Korydalla in what is now southern Turkey. Buried during the seventh-century Muslim raids, the treasure was unearthed in 1963 and divided between Dumbarton Oaks and the Archaeological Museum in Antalya. It includes some seventy other pieces, among which are book covers featuring Christ (cat. no. 67), and such ecclesiastical furnishing as patens, chalices, lamp-holders, and architectural revetments.

Like the binding featuring Christ between Peter and Paul (cat. no. 67), these virtually identical covers feature aedicules consisting of horseshoe arches atop columns and filled with great conches. Instead of the three figures on the other binding, these depict the cross at the center of each aedicule and two trees.

Drawing on a long tradition that the cross was "a tree of life" through which paradise was regained, the covers reveal what awaits the faithful beyond this world. The flanking trees have been identified as cypresses, but the vine-like stock from which new growth emerges may be a generic metaphor for the renewed life offered by Christ. The distinct in-turning of the leaves, a feature of later representations of the motif on a marble parapet in Torcello and the ivory Harbaville Triptych in Paris (Musée du Louvre, inv. no. OA3247), may allude to an ancient tradition describing wind passing through cypress trees that perpetually sings the trishagion: Holy, Holy, Holy.

HLK

Bibliography:

Kitzinger, 1973; Boyd and Mango, 1992; Iacobini, 1994, pp. 255–58.

67

The Sion Treasure Book Covers (Christ between Saints Peter and Paul)

Washington, D.C., Dumbarton Oaks, inv. no. BZ.1963.36.8, upper cover
Silver with gilding; 250 × 238mm
Constantinople (?); 550–60

Inscribed "For the memory and repose of Prinkipios, deacon, and Staphane and Leontia," the binding seems to have been made in the Byzantine capital as an ex-voto to a shrine on the route to the Holy Land.

Like the Freer Gospels' binding (Codex Washingtonensis; cat. no. 28), the two covers were nearly identical; but in this case the figures are the same, front and back. Christ is portrayed holding a book and blessing, standing between the two apostles who seem to be listening to him while raising their hands in gestures of preaching. The cover thus identifies the gospels with Christ himself and the lessons contained in them with the teachings of the Lord's disciples. While the five bosses on the pictured book symbolize Christ and the four gospels that recount his life and teachings, the aedicule (niche or doorway) that dominates the actual cover introduces the theme that scripture is the gateway to eternal life. The great conch or half-dome flanked by stars above the three men symbolizes heaven; the peacocks—also found on the Rabbula Gospels canon tables—stand for the paradise, lost when Adam and Eve sinned, to which Christ will return the faithful. Christ teaching, flanked by Paul at the left and Peter at the right, was a theme often represented in church apses and so allusion may have been intended to the Church, which safeguards and disseminates scripture.

HLK

CAT. 67

Bibliography:

Boyd and Mango, 1992.

68

The Golden Canon Tables

London, British Library, Add. MS. 5111, ff. 10v, 11r
Ink and pigments on gilded parchment; ff. 2; 220 × 170mm (fragmentary), original size at least 300 × 260mm
Canon tables from a gospelbook; Greek
Eastern Mediterranean, Constantinople (?); sixth or seventh century

These fragments of a manuscript are bound into a twelfth-century Latin gospelbook. Precisely where and when they were made is not certain, but their extraordinary lavishness suggests a major center and the style of the paintings indicates sixth- or early seventh-century date. The parchment is actually impregnated with powdered gold.

One of the leaves begins with Eusebius's letter to Carpianus and continues with the first canon; the other comprises the eighth and tenth canons. The concordances are framed by architectural columns and arches adorned with delicate, though entirely flat, ornament. Portraits of the apostles or evangelists are inserted in roundels where the arches meet or in the spandrels. Their faces are well modeled, if flatly painted. Plant ornament, comprising acanthus-type forms and marigolds, fills the frames and sprouts from them, and fish and birds fill out the pages, as in the Rabbula Gospels (cat. no. 62) and other early medieval canon tables. The use of the same ink for the script and for details of the

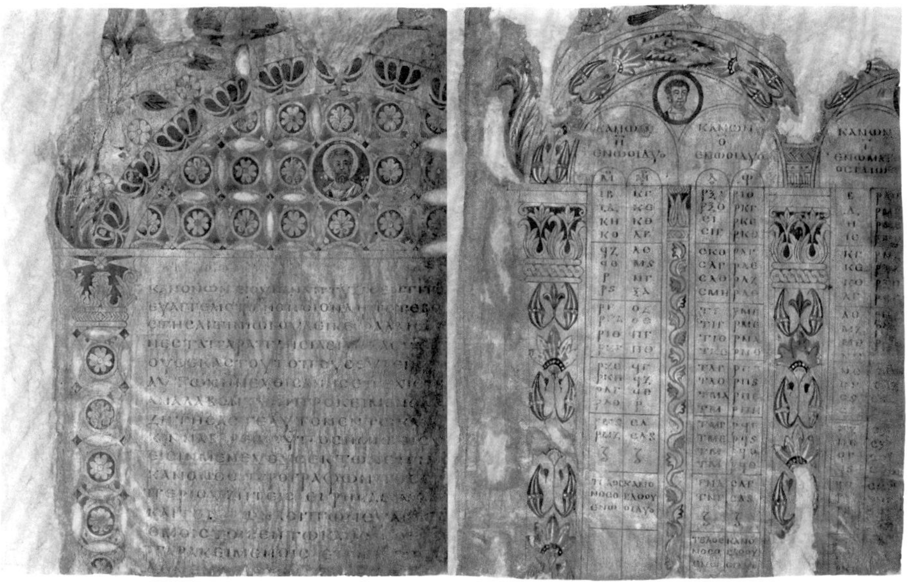

CAT. 68

decoration has led to the suggestion that they are the work of an artist-scribe.
MPB

Bibliography:
Nordenfalk, 1938, pp. 127–46; Cavallo, 1975, p. 125; Buckton, 1994, no. 69, p. 77; Lowden, 1999, pp. 24–26.

69

Major Prophets (*alias* The Niketas Bible)

Florence, Biblioteca Medicea Laurenziana, MS. Plut.5.9, ff. 128v–128Ar
Ink and pigments on parchment;
ff. 339; 355 × 275mm
Major prophets, prefaces and catena; Greek
Constantinople; tenth century, second half

One volume of a set of books, of which other parts are preserved in Turin (Biblioteca Nazionale, cod. B.I.2; Minor Prophets) and Copenhagen (Kongelige Bibliotek, cod. GKS 6; Wisdom Books), this magnificent manuscript contains the books of the four Major Prophets with catena (commentaries on bibilical passages) and lives of the prophets. Of the four full-page portraits, only that of Jeremiah remains; a fragmentary manuscript in Oxford (Bodleian Library, MS. Auct. T. inf. 2.12) containing the Life of Isaiah almost certainly once belonged to the volume in Florence.

Produced during the period of artistic regeneration in the wake of Iconoclasm (726–87, 815–43), the Niketas Bible recreates the aura of a great sixth-century biblical codex through the use of such archaizing features as "Alexandrian uncial" in prefatory texts and classical ornament and iconography. A colophon in the Turin Minor Prophets (f. 93v) reinforces the effect by naming the Emperor Justinian and the Consul Belisarius and giving the date of 535; but these grand manuscripts are surely confections of Niketas, a member of the tenth-century imperial court, who is named on f. 3v of the Florence manuscript and who drew on ancient materials in a creative fashion. Niketas seems also to have authored the poems, including the verses about Jeremiah written in majestic gold uncials on f. 128Ar.

The statuesque Jeremiah painted in a subtle and controlled modeling technique conjures up classical portraits and his swarthy face fully captures a sense of mental intensity that is characteristic of the finest classical art; but the closest comparison is with the tenth-century mosaic of

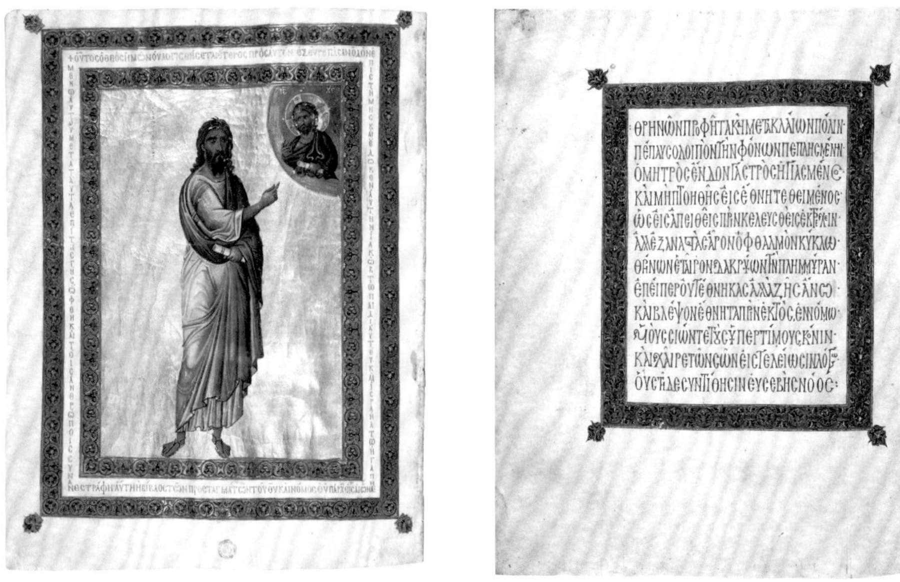

CAT. 69

Jeremiah in Hagia Sophia in Constantinople, where the prophet is shown holding the very text from the apocryphal book of Baruch that in the Florence manuscript frames the icon. A reading in the Christmas liturgy, the passage was considered a prophecy of the Incarnation:

This is our God; no other can be compared to him. He found the whole way to knowledge, and gave her to his servant Jacob and to Israel, whom he loved. Afterwards she appeared on earth and lived with humankind (3:35–37).

The prophecy is realized in the miniature by the figure of Christ that appears half-length in the celestial arc, the scroll he holds and his gesture suggesting that he is simultaneously both Jeremiah's inspiration and the fulfillment of his words.
At the end of the first millennium, golden letters and brilliant icons are deployed to assert the glory and mysterious unity of the Holy Word.

HLK

Bibliography:
Hutter, 1977–82, vol. 3, pp. 28–29; Belting and Cavallo, 1979; Lowden, 1983; Lowden, 1988, pp. 14–22 and 112–14.

CAT. 70

70

Codex Brixianus (Purple Gospels)

Brescia, Biblioteca Queriniana (not numbered)
Inks on purple parchment; ff. 419; 280 × 215mm
Gospels; Latin
Northern Italy; early sixth century

The Codex Brixianus contains the Old Latin version of the gospels, which continued to circulate after Jerome's Vulgate had gained wide acceptance during the fifth century; but it includes some peculiar readings, which it shares with the closely related Codex Argenteus (Uppsala, Universitetsbibliotek, DG 1), a Gothic translation of the gospels from the Greek that has been associated with patronage of the Arian Ostrogothic Emperor Theodoric. It is quite possible that both manuscripts were derived from a bilingual Gothic–Latin edition of the gospels; indeed, a preface bound into the Codex Brixianus stresses the importance of meaning over textual accuracy, referring specifically to variations found in Greek, Latin, or Gothic versions.

The beautiful and homogeneous appearance of this manuscript belies its complicated textual contents. In itself, that is telling: to a certain extent at least, a lavish physical presentation worked against textual correctness. Jerome himself recognized this when he disapproved of such manuscripts and advocated accuracy instead of luxury.

Purple-dyed vellum was highly prized during Antiquity and was associated with the court; the third-century emperor Gaius Julius, for instance, had a copy of Homer written in gold on purple; and Constantine the Great transferred the tradition to scripture. The sole ornament here, as in the Codex Argenteus, consists of canon tables, many in the lower margins and in some instances comprising alternating round and (smaller) pointed arches of a type also found in a sixth-century Greek gospelbook in Ravenna (Vienna, Nationalbibliothek, cod. 847). The true decoration is scripture itself, the word of the Lord written in the most precious materials.

HLK

Bibliography:
Burkitt, 1899; von Friesen and Grape, 1927; Nordenfalk, 1938, pp. 263–69; Kenyon, 1939, p. 168; Cavallo, Gribomont and Loerke, 1987.

71

The Psalter of Count Achadeus

Cambridge, Corpus Christi College, MS. 272, ff. 153v–154r
Ink and pigments on parchment; ff. 183; 265 × 210mm
Gallicanum Psalter; Latin
Reims, France; 883–84

In addition to the Psalms, this manuscript includes three of Jerome's prefaces and, at the end, canticles, creeds, the Lord's Prayer, litanies, collects after each Psalm, and several short prayers. These suggest that the manuscript may have been made as a private prayerbook, presumably for the patron mentioned in a golden inscription at the end of the Psalms proper and just before the litanies (f. 150r): "Achadeus, count by the grace of God, had this psalter written." The precise date is indicated by prayers to Pope Marinus (882–84), King Carloman (879–84) and his queen, and Fulco, archbishop of Reims (883–90); and the origin in Reims is secured by the emphasis in the litanies on Mary, Remigius, Columbanus, and Abundus, as well as other local saints included in the lists. Glosses written in an English script make it virtually certain that the manuscript had already been taken abroad by the tenth century.

Reims had been the principal center of manuscript illumination in France during the middle decades of the ninth century; but by the 880s, its production had declined. With its fine minuscule and handsome initials decorated with vines (many now removed), the Achadeus Psalter is an exceptional witness to the final phase of Reims production. The columnar frames of the litanies capped by arches and pediments and adorned with tendrils, birds, and fantastic animals recall the canon tables in such earlier Reims manuscripts as the Gospels in New York (Morgan Library and Museum, MS. M 728) and, ultimately, the old tradition of embellishing such charts represented by the Golden Canon Tables (cat. no. 68). In the Achadeus Psalter, the ancient tradition takes on a new meaning, here associated not with the correlation of diverse texts, but with lists of saints believed to be alive in heaven and able, through Christ, to offer the hope of eternal life to those who pray to them.

HLK

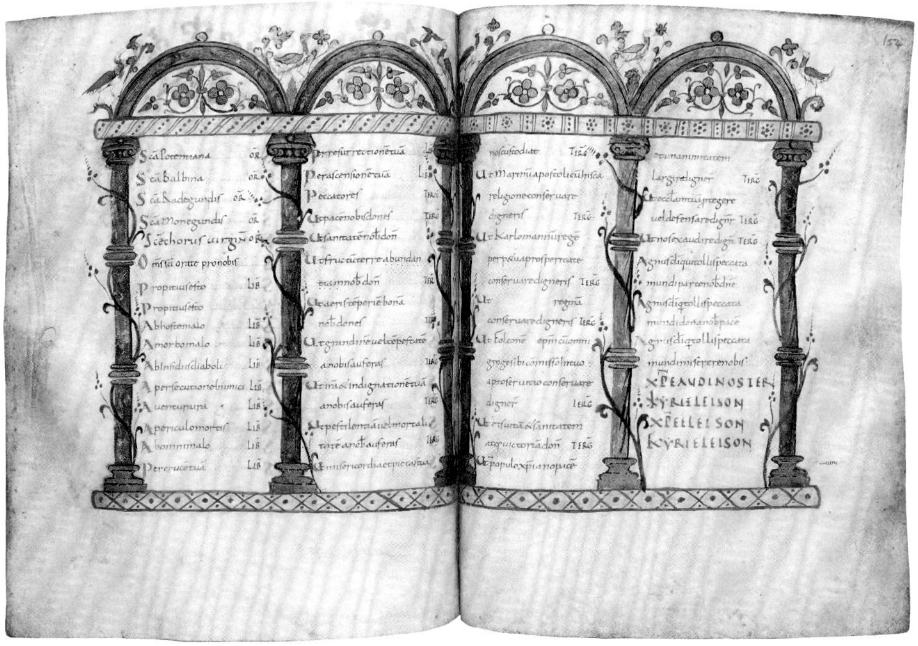

CAT. 71

Bibliography:
Van der Horst, Noel and Wüstefeld, 1996, pp. 21, 116–18; Koehler and Mütherich, 1999, pp. 200–206 et passim; McKitterick, 2005.

72

The Valenciennes Apocalypse

Valenciennes, Bibliothèque municipale, MS. 99, ff. 37v–38r
Ink and pigments on parchment; ff. 40; 270 × 200mm
Book of Revelation; Latin
Liège (?); ca. 800

Recorded in the mid-twelfth-century catalogue of the library of the Abbey of Saint Amand near Valenciennes, this manuscript was probably written and illuminated in northwestern France a quarter of a millennium earlier. It was also copied there during the early tenth century, as witnessed by a manuscript in Paris (Bibliothèque nationale de France, MS. nouv. acq. lat. 1132). An early eleventh-century fragment in Munich (Bayerische Staatsbibliothek, MS. Clm 29270.I2), perhaps North Italian, is also closely related.

The pictorial lineage is quite complicated. The Valenciennes Apocalypse seems to have been based on an exemplar produced

CAT. 72

in Wearmouth–Jarrow early in the eighth century which, in turn, was presumably based on the "pictures of the Apocalyptic visions" brought to England from Rome by Benedict Biscop in 676. Pictures of Saint John's graphic visions are illustrated in this manuscript as equals to the scripture itself and in a reciprocal relationship to it in each opening. Folios 37v–38r, for example, oppose the description of the Heavenly Jerusalem in Revelation (21:9–20) to a visualization of the text, in which the angel appears to the Evangelist while John, in turn, points to the city encircled by twelve walls and opened by twelve portals, in which the Lamb appears. The picture's *titulus* is little more than a paraphrase of the words on the facing page (21:10–11); and the caption inside the city introduces a text repeated on the verso: "And the city has no need of sun or moon to shine on it, for the glory of God is its light, and its lamp is the Lamb" (21:23). The depiction itself departs from the written description, however, most notably in representing the New Jerusalem as a city built of twelve concentric circles of different colors opened by gates grouped on the four cardinal points and hence forming a cross. The circular rendering may have been derived from drawings of the Holy Sepulcher, providing an apposite culmination for the tabernacle that serves as the frontispiece for the entire manuscript (f. 2r); this, by contrast, is an empty rectilinear diagram rendered in red ink, also marked with the cardinal points and surrounded by the names of the twelve tribes. The illustrations at beginning and end thus construct the manuscript of John's revelation as the completion of sacred history, initiated by the Jewish covenant transmitted in words and culminating in the Second Coming when God would again appear to the chosen people.

HLK

Bibliography:

Omont, 1922, pp.64 ff.; Goldschmidt, 1947; Bischoff, 1966–81, vol. 3, p. 8; Nordenfalk, 1983; Laufner and Klein, 1975; Alexander, 1978, pp. 82–83; Kühnel, 1987, pp. 128–38; Klein, 1992; Christe, 1996.

73

The Douce Ivory

Oxford, Bodleian Library,
MS. Douce 176, upper cover
Ivory plaque set within the binding of a parchment codex; ff. ii + 129; 290 × 195mm (manuscript), 210 × 125mm (ivory)
Gospel lectionary; Latin
Chelles, near Paris, France;
ca. 800 (manuscript)
Aachen; ca. 800 (ivory)

The illuminated manuscripts produced in the Court School of the Emperor Charlemagne at Aachen are relatively reticent in illustrating the events of the New Testament in painted form; but on this ivory panel, made to adorn a liturgical book, scenes from the Life of Christ are displayed. The panel represents at its center the triumphant Christ trampling on the lion and the serpent, in fulfillment of the prophecy of Psalm 90 (91):13: "You will tread on the lion and the adder, the young lion and the serpent you will trample underfoot." Christ, clothed in richly modeled draperies and represented as a handsome, young, beardless savior, carries his cross-staff over his shoulder as an emblem of victory and holds an open book inscribed "IHS XPS" and "SVP[er] ASP[idem]." The small scenes surrounding the central figure begin at the top left with the figure of the prophet Isaiah holding a scroll inscribed "ECCE VIRGO CONC[ipiet]," and continue clockwise with scenes from the Life of Christ: the Annunciation; the Nativity; the Adoration of the Magi; the Massacre of the

CAT. 73

Innocents; the Baptism; the Wedding at Cana; the Stilling of the Storm on the Sea of Galilee; the Raising of Jairus's Daughter; the Healing of the Gerasene Demoniac; the Healing of the Paralytic; and the Healing of the Woman with an Issue of Blood.

The overall organization of the panel, the type of Christ figure, and the lively narrative of the smaller scenes are typical of the ivories produced in the Court School in being modeled on Late Antique ivory diptychs; as such, they exemplify the intense engagement with Late Antique art that characterizes the "Carolingian renaissance." Indeed, six of the small scenes seem to be directly inspired by two surviving fragments from the early fifth century, now preserved in Paris and Berlin. The Carolingian plaque, however, is carved from a single piece of ivory, rather than being composed of separate parts in the manner of a Late Antique diptych.

The ivory is set into the upper cover of a gospel lectionary. The distinctive form of its Caroline minuscule script connects this book to a group of manuscripts, some of them signed by female scribes, which has been located by Bernhard Bischoff to the nunnery at Chelles, near Paris. At this period the abbess of Chelles was Charlemagne's sister, Gisla, who exchanged letters with her brother's advisor Alcuin about biblical and patristic texts. It cannot be proved that ivory and manuscript were originally joined together—the ivory is now set into an eighteenth-century French binding—but Gisla's connections with the court circle at Aachen, the closeness in date between the manuscript and the ivory, and the general appropriateness of the ivory's subject matter for a book containing gospel readings for the Mass through the year, are suggestive of an early conjunction. A note in the manuscript states that before the French Revolution it had belonged to the nunnery of Saint Faro at Meaux, also near Paris.

MK

Bibliography:

Summary Catalogue, 1895–1953, no. 21750; Lowe, 1934–72, ii, no. 238; Goldschmidt, 1914, no. 5; Zimmermann, 1916, pp. 11, 13, 17, 83–85, 220–21, 226, pls. 138, 142–43; Bischoff, 1957; Pächt and Alexander, 1966–73, no. 412; Volbach, 1976, no. 221; *Douce Legacy*, 1984, no. 39; Fischer, 1985, p. 149; McKitterick, 1989a; Lasko, 1994, pp. 23–24; Paderborn, 1999, cat. X.7.

CAT. 74

74

The Mondsee Gospels

Baltimore, Walters Art Museum, MS. W 8, upper cover
Silver, ivory, rock crystal, gilt copper, and silk cover for a parchment codex; ff. 230; 283 × 220mm
Gospel lectionary; Latin
Regensburg, Germany; eleventh century, third quarter, with later additions and modifications to the covers

Attributed to the scribe Othlon, who was active in Regensburg between 1032 and 1055, the text inside this elaborate binding is unadorned except for a few initials. It is a gospel lectionary, made for use in the Benedictine abbey of Mondsee (near Salzburg).

Developing a tradition going back to the Early Christian period and represented by the Sion Treasure gospel covers (cat. nos. 66,67), the front cover features a cross highlighted in gold; and, following the pattern that had been represented at Regensburg by the magnificent ninth-century cover of the Codex Aureus of Saint Emmeram (Munich, Bayerische Staatsbibliothek, cod. lat. 14000, Cim. 55), it holds between the cross's arms depictions of the evangelists writing their gospels to suggest the unity in Christ of the four inspired accounts. The depiction of Mark at the lower left is a nineteenth-century replacement; originally, John was probably the only evangelist shown in contemplation rather than actively writing, to distinguish his more spiritual Gospel from the three synoptic texts. The corner bosses are also modern, most likely substitutes for semi-precious stones or enamels that, like the gems at the ends of the cross, were lost through wear or theft.

By referring to an organic form, the filigree symbolizes the life-giving quality of scripture and Christ's cross, a theme realized on the Sion Treasure covers half a millennium earlier, making visible the belief that through Christ's sacrifice, humankind was redeemed and returned to everlasting life. It is a theme to which the enormous cabochon rock crystal at the cover's center also alludes: painted on gold beneath the crystal is the Crucified Christ, with a splinter of wood across his chest. An imitation of Early Christian gold glass, the Crucifix is encircled by a paraphrase of Hosea 13:14: *Mors XPI mors mortis erat tuus infere morsus* (The death of Christ was the death of death, rendering its sting impotent). Triumph over death is also the theme of the back cover, which is adorned with an engraved gilt-copper plaque of uncertain date picturing the Archangel Michael, dressed in military garb and standing atop a dragon while plunging a cross-lance into its mouth. The abbey at Mondsee was dedicated to Saint Michael; but the iconography is not simply parochial. Christ Trampling the Beasts was commonly pictured on book covers, as on the Oxford Douce Ivory (cat. no. 73). The two covers are attached to one another by an incised silk twill woven in an Islamic or Byzantine center.

Heterogeneous and, perhaps, extensively rearranged during modern times, the Mondsee binding is typical of medieval treasure bindings that render bibles as objects capable, in themselves, of providing an elevating experience. Looking at the Codex Aureus of Saint Emmeram (at the very moment the Mondsee Gospels were being fashioned in Regensburg), the author of the *Liber translationis Dionysii Areopagite* saw in the disposition of its materials and subjects an icon that "leads to the heavenly city constructed of living stones."

HLK

Bibliography:

Goldschmidt, 1914–26, vol. 4, p. 58; Steenbock, 1965, pp. 181–83; Muthesius, 1978; Randall, 1985, p. 172; Fillitz and Pippal, 1987, pp. 96–100.

Manuscripts and lenders in the exhibition

Biblioteca Medicea Laurenziana, Florence
MS. Plut. 1.56 (Rabbula Gospels)
MS. Plut. 5.9 (Niketas Bible)

Bibliothèque municipale, Valenciennes
MS. 99 (Valenciennes Apocalypse)

Bibliothèque nationale de France, Paris
MS. Gr. 107 (Codex Claromontanus)
MS. Suppl. grec 1286 (Codex Sinopensis; Sinope Gospels)

Bodleian Library, University of Oxford
MS. Auct. D. 2. 14 (Gospels; Codex Oxoniensis)
MS. Auct. D. 2. 19 (Macregol Gospels, alias the Rushworth Gospels)
MS. Bodl 819 (Bede's *Commentary on Proverbs*)
MS. Bruce 96 (Codex Bruce; Codex Brucianus)
MS. Cromwell 16 (Byzantine Gospels)
MS. Douce 140 (Douce Primasius)
MS. Douce 176 (Douce Ivory)
MS. Gr. th. e. 7 (P) (Sayings of Jesus, *Logia Jesou*)
MS. Junius 11 (Old English Genesis; Junius Manuscript; Caedmon Manuscript)
MS. Rawl. G. 167 (Rawlinson Gospels)
MS. Selden Supra 30 (Selden Acts of the Apostles)

British Library, London
Add. MS 5111 (Golden Canon Tables)
Armenian MSS. Add. 21932 (Armenian Gospelbook)
Egerton Papyrus 2, 608 (Unknown Gospel, alias The Egerton Gospel)
MS. Or. 2540 (Karaite Book of Exodus)
P2053r (Exodus 11:26–32) and 2053v (Revelation 1:4–7) (P 18) (Early Christian bookroll)
Syriac MSS. Add. 12134 (Syrohexapla Exodus)
Syriac MSS. Add. 14425 (Syriac Pentateuch)
Syriac MSS. Add. 14478 (Pauline Epistles, from the Syriac Peshitta)
Western MSS. Add. MS 24142 (Theodulf Bible; Codex Hubertianus)
Western MSS. Add. MS 45025 (Ceolfrith Bibles: Middleton Leaves)
Western MSS. Harley MS. 1775 (Codex Harleianus; Harley Gospels)

Cambridge University Library
T-S unconserved fragments (from the Cairo Genizah)
T-S 20.50 (Palimpsest of Aquila's translation of the Bible)
T-S NS 3.21 (fragment of a Genesis scroll)
T-S NS 4.3 (fragment of a Genesis scroll)
T-S NS 246.26.2 (bifolium from a biblical codex)

Chester Beatty Library, Dublin
MS. Biblical Papyri VI (Rahlfs 963) (Chester Beatty Codex of Numbers and Deuteronomy)
MS. Biblical Papyrus I (P 45) (Chester Beatty Codex of the Gospels and Acts)
MS.W709 (Saint Ephrem's commentary on Tatian's *Diatessaron*)

Corpus Christi College, Cambridge
MS. 69 (Pope Gregory the Great's *Commentary on the Gospels*)
MS. 197b (Cambridge–London Gospels)
MS. 272 (Psalter of Count Achadeus)

Dumbarton Oaks, Washington, D.C.
BZ.1963.36.8 (Sion Treasure Book Covers [Christ between Sts. Peter and Paul])
BZ.1963.36.9 (Sion Treasure Book Covers [cross flanked by cypress trees])
BZ.1963.36.10 (Sion Treasure Book Covers [cross flanked by cypress trees])

Freer Gallery of Art, Smithsonian Institution, Washington, D.C.
Coptic fragments
F1906.272 (Washington Codex of Deuteronomy and Joshua)
F1906.273 (Washington Codex of the Psalms)
F1906.274 (Washington Codex of the Four Gospels; Codex Washingtonensis; Freer Gospels)
F1906.275 (Washington Manuscript of the Pauline Epistles)
F1906.297 (Freer Gospels, right cover)
F1906.298 (Freer Gospels, left cover)
F1908.32 (Coptic Psalter)
F1916.768 (Washington Codex of the Minor Prophets)

J. Paul Getty Museum, Los Angeles
83.MA.50 (Alcuin [Touronian] Bible)

Holy Monastery of Saint Catherine, Mount Sinai, Egypt
Arabic 151 (Arabic Epistles and Acts)
Arabic New Finds M.14 (Arabic Gospelbook)
Codex Sinaiticus (passage from the Book of Numbers)
Georgian 37 (Georgian Lectionary)
Georgian New Finds N.12 (Georgian Gospelbook)
Greek 30 (Greek Psalter)
Greek 36 (Greek–Arabic Diglot of the Psalms and Odes)
Greek 213 (Lectionary of Mount Horeb)
Latin New Finds 1 (formerly Slavonic 5; Latin Psalter)
Slavonic 37 (Glagolitic Euchologion)

K. Kekelidze Institute of Manuscripts, Tbilisi, Georgia
H1660 (First Jrutchi Gospels)

National Library of Russia, St. Petersburg
Gruz new series 10 (Georgian Psalter)
Firkovitch MS. Hebrew II B 17 (St. Petersburg Pentateuch)
Firkovitch MS. Hebrew II B 49 (Quire from the "Firkovitch Compilation")
MS. Glag. 1 (Codex Zographensis)

Magdalen College, Oxford
P. Magd. Gr. 17 (P 64) (Gospel of Saint Matthew)

Morgan Library & Museum, New York
MS. M.828 (Ethiopic Gospelbook; Zir Ganela Gospels)
MS. M.874 (Codex Caesariensis; Codex Purpureus Petropolitanus)

Österreichischen Nationalbibliothek, Vienna
P. Vindob. KHT 1 (tablet of texts)

Royal Library, Stockholm
MS. A.135 (Stockholm Codex Aureus)

The Shrine of the Book, The Israel Museum, and Ben-Zvi Institute, Jerusalem
96.85/211 (Aleppo Codex: Second Book of Chronicles)

The Shrine of the Book, The Israel Museum, and the Hebrew University, Jerusalem
95.57/26B (Second Isaiah Scroll)

University of Michigan, Ann Arbor
6238 (P46) (Epistles of Saint Paul)

Walters Art Museum, Baltimore
MS. W.8 (Mondsee Gospels)
MS. W.537 (Armenian Gospelbook)

Chronology

ca. 600 B.C.E. | Ezra the Scribe reconstructs the Hebrew scriptures destroyed by the Babylonians

ca. 250 B.C.E. | Formation of the Septuagint commences; according to legend, with the Hebrew Bible translated into Greek in Alexandria at the command of Ptolemy II Philadelphus (285–246 B.C.E.)

ca. 3 B.C.E. | Birth of Christ

ca. 30 C.E. | Crucifixion of Christ

ca. 50–60 | First Christian texts (some of the Pauline Epistles) written

ca. 65–70 | Gospel of St. Mark composed

ca. 80–90 | Gospels of St. Matthew and St. Luke, and Acts of the Apostles composed

ca. 85–95 | Gospel of St. John composed

late 1st century | Other letters composed (of James, of Peter, of John, to the Hebrews)

ca. 95 | Apocalypse / Revelation of John composed

ca. 100 | Council of Jamnia determines the canonical text of the Hebrew Bible, subsequently known as the "Masoretic" text

ca. 125 | Earliest surviving manuscript of a gospel written (St. John, known from fragments)

2nd century | Old Testament books start to be individually translated from Hebrew into Syriac

first half 2nd century | Christian writings—letters, gospels, and apocalypses—multiply; Pauline Epistles circulate as a collection

ca. 180 | Irenaeus, bishop of Lyon, asserts the primacy of the four gospels (St. Matthew, St. Mark, St. Luke and St. John); Tatian, a Syrian, produces the *Diatessaron*, a single narrative drawn from the gospels and additional material

early 3rd century | Origen of Alexandria compiles a comparative edition of the Old Testament in Hebrew and Greek, the *Hexapla*

late 3rd century | St. Anthony retreats into the eastern desert of Egypt, beginning a trend towards ascetic desert monasticism

303 | Emperor Diocletian orders the destruction of Christian books during the "Great Persecution"

312 | Constantine sees a vision of the Cross and triumphs at the Battle of the Milvian Bridge

313 | Edict of Milan: Emperors Constantine and Licinius grant freedom of worship throughout the Western Empire

early 4th century | Armenia becomes the first nation to adopt Christianity as its state religion; Gregory the Illuminator ordained bishop of Armenia (ca. 314); Christianity introduced to Ethiopia from Egypt

324 | Constantine defeats Emperor Licinius and reunites the Empire's two halves, extending religious toleration throughout

325 | Council of Nicaea, the first ecumenical council, condemns Arianism

330 | Constantinople (now Istanbul) founded by Constantine as a bridgehead between East and West

332 | Constantine commissions Bishop Eusebius to supply the churches he has founded in Constantinople with complete bibles

ca. 337 | Georgia accepts Christianity as its state religion

mid-4th century | Codex Sinaiticus, the earliest surviving complete Christian bible, is made, perhaps in Caesarea

363 | Council of Laodicea lists 26 canonical books for reading in church (omitting Revelation)

ca. 372 | St. Martin of Tours introduces monasticism to Europe

381 | First Council of Constantinople declares that this city exerts an equal authority in the East to that of Rome in the West

ca. 382 | St. Jerome enters the service of Pope Damasus and is commissioned to produce a standardized Latin edition of the Bible—the Vulgate

383 | Death of Ulfilas, "Apostle to the Goths," who translated the Bible into the Gothic language

392 | Emperor Theodosius bans pagan worship, and Christianity effectively becomes the state religion of the Roman Empire

393 | Council of Hippo and Council of Carthage (397) both name the 27 books of the New Testament we know today

ca. 400 | Roman Empire begins to contract

5th century | Syriac translations of Old Testament and New Testament books combined to form the Peshitta,the standard text for Syriac-speaking Churches

early 5th century | Greek alphabet adapted by the missionary St. Mesrob to produce those of Armenia and Georgia

431 | Council of Ephesus condemns the views of Nestorius on the nature of Christ; Bishop Palladius is sent from Rome to believers in southern Ireland

451 | Council of Chalcedon condemns Monophysitism (the belief that Christ has only one, divine nature) and establishes five patriarchates—Constantinople, Rome, Alexandria, Antioch, and Jerusalem

ca. 460–90 | St. Patrick's mission from the northern British Church to Ireland

ca. 529 | St. Benedict founds the monastery of Montecassino in Italy

548–65 | Emperor Justinian founds the monastery now known as St. Catherine's on Mt. Sinai

563 | St. Columba leaves Ireland on voluntary exile to evangelize the Picts, and founds the monastery of Iona in western Scotland

580 | Death of Cassiodorus, biblical scholar and founder of the monastery called the Vivarium in southern Italy

588 | Patriarch John IV of Constantinople declares himself Ecumenical Patriarch, a title still retained by the leader of the Greek Orthodox Church

597 | Death of St. Columba; Pope Gregory the Great sends a Roman mission led by St. Augustine to England to convert the Anglo-Saxons

599 | Pope Gregory the Great sends a legate bearing gifts to Sinai

604 | Death of Pope Gregory the Great

ca. 610 | The Prophet Muhammad begins preaching in Mecca

615–17 | Paul of Tella makes the Syrohexapla, a translation into Syriac of Origen's *Hexapla*

635 | Monastery of Lindisfarne is founded in northeast England by St. Aidan, a follower of St. Columba

ca. 641 | Islamic conquest of eastern and southern Mediterranean complete

687 | Death of St. Cuthbert of Lindisfarne

716 | Abbot Ceolfrith of Wearmouth–Jarrow sets off for Rome in retirement, taking one of three great complete bibles made by his community as a gift for the pope

720s–787 | Period of Iconoclasm in Byzantium

735 | On his deathbed the scholar Bede, a monk at Wearmouth–Jarrow in Northumbria, translates St. John's Gospel into English

754/5 | Death of St. Boniface, "Apostle to the Germans," at Dokkum (now in The Netherlands)

787 | Council of Nicaea reinstates the use of images in Byzantium

793 | Viking raids on Europe commence with the sacking of Lindisfarne

late 8th century | Theodulf of Orléans asserts the primacy of the word over images in his *Libri carolini*

800 | Emperor Charlemagne crowned in Rome, solemnizing the creation of a Carolingian Empire; Abbot Alcuin of Tours completes a single-volume edition of the Vulgate Bible, copied throughout the Carolingian Empire

814–43 | Resurgence of iconoclasm in Byzantium

869 | Byzantine Emperor Constantine sends St. Cyril as a missionary to the Slavs; Cyril invents the Glagolitic alphabet from which Cyrillic is descended

ca. 950–60 | Aldred glosses the Lindisfarne Gospels into Old English—the oldest surviving translation of the Gospels into English

ca. 962–1056 | Ottonian Empire succeeds the Carolingian in Europe

Glossary

aedicule | From the Latin for "miniature house." A niche or opening framed by two columns, an entablature, and usually a pediment.

Alexandrian text | One of several broad text-types associated with New Testament manuscripts that share a relatively high proportion of distinctive or characteristic readings. So-called because it appears to reflect the careful editorial methods of Alexandrian scholarship, it is mainly represented by Codex Vaticanus, Codex Sinaiticus, some earlier papyrus manuscripts (P 66, P 75), and a few later manuscripts (Codex Regius, 33, 1739). It is generally a careful and controlled textual tradition. *See also* Byzantine text, Western text

antiphonal | A servicebook containing the sung portions of the Divine Office. During the Middle Ages they were often large (so that they could be used by a choir) and included decorated and historiated initials, depicting saints and key events of the liturgical year.

apocalypse | The biblical book known in the Protestant tradition as the Book of Revelation. During the Middle Ages, Apocalypse manuscripts were produced in Latin and Anglo-Norman versions often accompanied by commentaries, and sometimes with picture cycles. They became particularly popular from the tenth century onwards, although some earlier manuscript examples and picture cycles are known.

apocryphal | From the Greek for "hidden things." Used for texts of disputed canonical status.

apotropaic | Serving to ward off evil.

bibliotheca | Greek, literally a "box for storing books."

bookroll | A manuscript, generally consisting of several sheets of papyrus pasted together, on which the writing is in many columns written side by side, with lines running parallel to the length of the papyrus.

book-shrine | In Coptic Egypt and in Ireland (where it was called a *cumdach*), a box designed to protect and exalt a sacred manuscript. It was made of wood covered with decorative metalwork and sometimes precious stones.

breviary | A servicebook containing the texts necessary for the celebration of the Divine Office. During the high Middle Ages it might be adorned with decorated and historiated initials and more luxurious copies contain miniatures depicting biblical scenes or the performance of the Office.

Byzantine text | One of several broad text-types associated with New Testament manuscripts that share a relatively high proportion of distinctive or characteristic readings. Also known as the Majority or Koine (i.e., "common") text, it is a late and secondary form of the text that aims to smooth out difficulties through conflation, harmonization, and verbal alterations. Found in no early papyri, its earliest witness is Codex Alexandrinus (in the Gospels only), but it is represented in many late uncial manuscripts and the vast majority of Greek minuscule manuscripts. *See also* Alexandrian text, Western text

canon | A list of sacred or other writings acknowledged as genuine and/or authorized for standard use.

canon table | A system indicating the concordance of passages among the gospels, devised in the fourth century by Eusebius of Caesarea. Gospel passages are numbered, generally in the margins, in accordance with "Ammonian sections." (The division of passages is usually ascribed to Ammonius of Alexandria, ca. 220, although he may merely have inspired Eusebius to create his own divisions.) These numbers are also arranged in columnar form to create the tables, which are often set within ornamental surrounds of an architectural character. Canon tables were generally placed at the beginning of a volume and were popular in gospelbooks, whole bibles, and New Testaments, especially during the early Middle Ages.

canticle | A song derived from the Bible.

cantillation | Textual marks found in the Masoretic text of the Hebrew Bible that indicate how words should be chanted and accented, and where the reader should pause. *See also* vocalization

***capitula* (sing. *capitulum*)** | Latin. Lists of chapters, often found preceding the gospels.

caroline | Of or relating to Charlemagne or the Carolingian dynasty and its culture.

Carolingian | A dynasty of Frankish kings (751–962), whose empire expanded under Charlemagne (emperor from 800) and came to embrace much of northern Europe (excluding Britain and much of Spain and Italy). Charlemagne and his successors promoted the Carolingian cultural renaissance and ecclesiastical reform, which resulted in the scholarly revision of sacred texts, the production of large illuminated bibles, and the development of a new script, caroline minuscule. In 843, the empire was divided into three parts by the Treaty of Verdun and the Ottonian dynasty assumed imperial power in 962.

carpet page | An ornamental page, without text, the patterns on which resemble those of an Oriental carpet. It sometimes incorporates a cross in its design. Such pages generally separate the four gospels in a manuscript, or might serve to introduce the book. They are perhaps of Coptic origin.

cartonnage | A material made of layers of gummed linen or waste papyrus soaked in plaster.

cartulary | A collection of charters or deeds, especially relating to the property of a monastery or other large estate.

Chi-rho | A Christian symbol consisting of the first two letters of Christ's name in Greek, *chi* and *rho*.

chrysography | From the Greek, literally "writing in gold." The technique used powdered gold (or silver), mixed with glair or gum to create an ink; when dry, the ink was usually burnished. Gold leaf was also sometimes used. Such writing on parchment is known from the Early Christian period and from the sixth century was often used on pages stained purple.

codex (pl. codices) | From the Latin *caudex*, for tree bark. A book consisting of sheets of papyrus or parchment stacked and sewn along one side. Originating in the first century, the codex was popular among Christians for its portability and ease of use and eventually supplanted the bookroll as the favored vehicle for literary texts after the Christianization of the Roman Empire.

codicology | The study of the physical structure of books, including the number of leaves used in a gathering, the way in which they are pricked and ruled, and how the book is sewn and bound. This examination can shed considerable light on a book's method of production, place of origin, and provenance, and can help to reconstruct its original appearance.

colophon | A term originally meaning the label on the outside of a bookroll, identifying its contents. In the Middle Ages, however, it denotes an inscription recording information relating to the circumstances of a book's production, which might include the place of manufacture and the people involved and, less frequently, the date. Colophons are generally located at the end of a book.

colophon decoration | A late Roman practice of drawing attention to titles, colophons, and the like by framing them with patterns formed by dots and commas.

Coptic | A language written in the Greek alphabet but descended from ancient Egyptian; the ancient Christian Church of Egypt; appertaining to the Christian inhabitants of early medieval Egypt.

cross-carpet page | *See* carpet page

cursive | A rapidly written script, with many letters joined together and sometimes including loops.

display script | Decorative, sometimes colored, script often used to emphasize the opening of a major section of text.

Divine Office | The canonical prayers and psalms recited daily by priests, monks, and nuns at certain prescribed hours (matins, lauds, prime, tierce, sext, none, vespers, compline).

Early Christian | The period from apostolic times to around 600, when Pope Gregory the Great established a strong, independent Western Church. It overlapped with Late Antiquity and began the transition into the Middle Ages.

epistolary | A servicebook containing readings from the epistles (the letters in the New Testament) for the Mass, arranged according to the liturgical year.

esṭrangelā | From the Greek for "rounded"; in Syriac, literally "to write the Gospels." A formal script used to write the Syriac language, running from right to left.

euchologion | A servicebook containing prayers, parts of services, and biblical passages for use in the performance of the liturgy.

evangelary/evangelistary | *See* lectionary

evangelist portrait | A depiction of one of the "authors" of the canonical gospels—Matthew, Mark, Luke, and John—perhaps identified by his accompanying symbol (a man or angel, lion, ox, and eagle respectively). The symbols could also be depicted alone.

exegete | A person who explains or interprets a written work.

explicit | From the Latin *explicitus*, for "unrolled." A title marking the closing of a major section of text, sometimes written in display script.

floruit | Latin for "flourished." The period of time during which a person (whose birth and death dates are not known) was productive.

Frank | A member of one of a number of Germanic tribal federations, who began to invade Roman territory in the third century C.E. and established an empire in northern Europe from the fifth century onward.
See also Carolingian, Merovingian

gathering | The booklets or "quires" of which a book is formed. Initially, single sheets of papyrus were cut square, stacked, folded at the middle, and then stitched together along the fold. A single gathering could comprise as many as fifty sheets. Many early codices consisted of single gatherings with a large number of sheets, but later multiple gatherings with fewer sheets were stacked and sewn together, especially after parchment or vellum replaced papyrus.

Glagolitic | A language with a 40-character Greek-based alphabet, the invention of which is ascribed to Saint Cyril (ca. 827–869) and his companion Saint Methodius. It formed the basis of Cyrillic script.

gloss | A word or words commenting on, clarifying, or translating those of the main text. Glosses were often written in the margins or between the lines.

gospel | From Old English *godspell*, "good news." The message of a religious teacher; in particular the story of Christ's life, teachings and Resurrection as narrated in one of the canonical gospels (attributed to Matthew, Mark, Luke, and John), the first four books of the New Testament.

gospelbook | A book containing the full text of the canonical gospels, often accompanied by introductory matter such as the prefaces of Saint Jerome, Eusebius's canon tables, and chapter lists *(capitula)*. From the sixth or seventh century on, carpet pages, incipit pages, *Chi-rho* pages, evangelist portraits or symbols, and other illustrations appeared in gospelbooks. From the late eighth century, gospelbooks were partially replaced in liturgical use by lectionaries.

half-uncial | A script derived from uncial. In Ireland and Britain it developed independently to form the basis of Insular formal book-script.

Hebrew Names | A list, often found prefacing Irish/Celtic gospelbooks, explaining the Hebrew names contained in the biblical text. Saint Jerome regularized these in accordance with the Hebrew originals.

historiated initial | A large letter framing a pictorial subject.

incipit | The opening of a major section of text, sometimes marked by a whole decorative page, embellished with a large initial or monogram and display script.

incunable | A book printed before 1501.

Insular | Referring to the culture of Britain and Ireland from around 550 to 850, which fused Celtic, Germanic, Antique, Early Christian, and Mediterranean elements to form something new. Developments in book production first occurred in sixth- to seventh-century Ireland, then in England and Scotland, where Irish influence mixed with Germanic and Pictish styles to produce Hiberno-Saxon art. Southern England produced its own distinctive styles of decoration and script, while other areas such as Wales preserved their late Roman legacy. A characteristic feature of Insular books is the integration of decoration, script, and text. Insular art and learning in turn helped stimulate the Carolingian renaissance.

Karaite | A Jewish sect originating in eighth-century Baghdad. Their belief that the Hebrew Bible was the sole source of religious law led to a concentration on the close study of the text of the Bible.

lectionary | A servicebook containing readings for the Mass, arranged according to the liturgical year; also known as an evangelary or pericope book. The lectionary became increasingly popular from the Carolingian period on.

liturgy | The rites, observances, or procedures prescribed for public worship and for the public prayer-life of the Church. At the core of Christian liturgy are the Mass and the Divine Office.

Masoretic text | Canonical text of the Hebrew Bible, as determined at the Council of Jamnia (ca. 100 C.E.). The Masorah, a body of notes on the traditions of the text, was compiled 600–900 C.E. by Jewish scribes called the Masoretes.

Mass | The celebration of the Eucharist (the consecration and consumption of bread and wine in commemoration of the Last Supper).

Merovingian | A dynasty of Frankish kings (480–751), predecessors of the Carolingians.

minuscule | A script in "lower case" (rather than capital) letters, with longer strokes called ascenders and descenders that extend above and below the body of the letter (as in *d* and *q*). Caroline minuscule, developed in Carolingian scriptoria in the late eighth century, was used even for more formal manuscripts that earlier would have been written in capitals, uncials, or half-uncials.

missal | A servicebook containing the texts necessary for the performance of the Mass (including chants, prayers, and readings), together with ceremonial directions. Introduced in the early Middle Ages, it eventually supplanted the sacramentary, gradual, evangelary, and epistolary, which had previously been used together.

Monarchian prologue | A prologue to each of the gospels, attributed to the Spanish theologian and heretic Priscillian (died 386). It summarizes the authority from which each evangelist received his gospel's teachings.

Mozarab | A Christian inhabitant of Spain under Muslim rule.

neume, neumatic | An early form of musical notation used for plainsong in the Middle Ages. The marks, written above the text rather than on stave lines, indicate the general shape of the music but not precise notes or rhythms.

ogam | An alphabet (perhaps of Irish origin but inspired by Roman script) used by the Celts for short inscriptions. Letters consist of straight or diagonal marks written along or across a single line.

orthography | Spelling, study of the variants of which can help locate the origins of a manuscript, or identify a scribe.

Ottonian | A ruling dynasty in Germany (919–1024), whose empire succeeded that of the Carolingians (from 962).

palimpsest | From the Greek *palimpsestos*, "scraped again." A reused document from which the original writing might be erased by washing (in the case of papyrus) or scraping, with pumice or a knife (in the case of parchment), before being written over. Sometimes the underlying text can be read in ultraviolet light or using electronic image-enhancing techniques.

pandect | From the Greek, "all receiver." A single volume containing the complete biblical text.

papyrus (pl. papyri) | A writing support material made from a species of rush that grows in marshes along the River Nile.

parchment | From Pergamon (Bergama in modern Turkey), an early production centre. A writing support material made from prepared sheep and goat skin. The skin was defleshed, stretched, and scraped, and might be treated with pumice and whitened with chalk before being cut to size. Parchment supplanted papyrus as the most popular writing support material in the fourth century, and was itself largely replaced by paper in the sixteenth century with the rise of printing, thought it remained in use for certain high-grade books. Parchment is the term used generically in the present work to indicate prepared membrane. *See also* vellum

paschal | Relating to Passover or Easter.

patristic | Relating to texts written by the Church Fathers or other Early Christian writers whose authority was particularly respected in later periods. Well-known patristic authors include Saint Augustine, Saint Jerome, and Saint John Chrysostom.

Pentecost | From the Greek for "fifty." In Judaism, the fiftieth day after Passover; in Christianity, the descent of the Holy Spirit to the apostles and their speaking in tongues.

psalter | A volume containing the Psalms. Medieval psalters were used in the liturgy and for private devotion. Depictions of King David, author of many of the Psalms, frequently introduce the psalter, which might also feature a calendar, canticles, creeds, a litany of the saints, and prayers. Byzantine psalter illustration exerted an important influence on the West.

quire | *See* gathering

rubric | From the Latin *rubrica*, "red." A title, chapter heading, or instruction, often written in red ink, that is not part of the text but which helps to identify its components or instructs on their use.

rune | A letter from one of a number of alphabets used by the Germanic tribes of northern Europe before Christianization. Some runes were combined with the Latin alphabet in written Old English.

Sasanian | Of the Sasanid dynasty (224–651 C.E.) in Iran, Iraq, and neighboring areas.

scriptorium | A writing room, usually (but not exclusively) in a monastery or church, where books are made.

scriptura continua | Latin. Writing in which the letters are written one after the other without spaces between the words. This was usual during Antiquity, until Insular scribes introduced word-separation and more systematic punctuation, which was in turn developed further in Carolingian scriptoria.

scroll | *See* bookroll

stylus | A pointed tool, generally of metal or bone, used for writing on wax tablets, and also for pricking and ruling manuscripts.

treasure-binding | An elaborately decorated, often bejeweled, front cover for a codex, indicating the value of the text within.

troper | A servicebook containing tropes, that is, musical and textual additions to the chants of the Mass or Divine Office, sung by a soloist. Tropers are known from the early Middle Ages onward.

typology | An interpretive system in Christian thought, designed to prove that the New Testament is a fulfillment of the Old. The sacrifice of Isaac, for example, foretells the Crucifixion; and the stories of Daniel in the lions' den and Jonah and the whale prefigure Christ's Passion and Resurrection. Encountered during the early Middle Ages, and favoured by Saint Jerome, such juxtapositions become increasingly frequent in art from the eleventh century on.

uncial | A formal script with letters based on Roman capitals but with more rounded forms. It was introduced in the third century C.E.

vellum | A writing support material made from calfskin. Uterine vellum, the skin of stillborn or very young calves, is particularly fine and white in appearance, but was rarely used. The term is often used generally to indicate prepared membrane. *See also* parchment

vernacular | From the Latin for "vulgar." A regional language, as distinct from an international literary language, such as Latin and Greek. Throughout the Middle Ages biblical texts were only gradually translated into the vernacular, although development of Western vernacular literacy began at least as early as the sixth to eighth century in Ireland and Anglo-Saxon England.

vocalization | Textual marks indicating vowels in languages (such as Hebrew, Arabic) whose alphabets do not contain them. *See also* cantillation

Western text | One of several broad text-types associated with New Testament manuscripts that share a relatively high proportion of distinctive or characteristic readings. So-called because it can be traced back to mainly Western early Christian thinkers of the second and third centuries (Marcion, Irenaeus, Tertullian, Cyprian), it is mainly represented by Codex Bezae (D), some earlier papyrus manuscripts (P 29, P 48, P 38), and some Old Latin manuscripts. It is an uncontrolled textual tradition characterized by various additions and omissions. *See also* Alexandrian text, Byzantine text

Who's Who

Alcuin of York (ca. 732–804), Anglo-Saxon churchman and scholar. As abbot of Tours (from 796) he made a single-volume revision of the Vulgate Bible that was to become the norm in much of Europe.

Augustine, Saint (died 604), missionary sent by Gregory the Great to convert the English. He arrived in Kent in 597 and became first archbishop of Canterbury from 601.

Bede, The Venerable (ca. 672–735), Anglo-Saxon priest and scholar. He lived at the monasteries of Wearmouth–Jarrow almost all his life, but became the foremost scholar of his age. His writings include the *Ecclesiastical History of the English People* and *On the Nature of Time*.

Boniface, Saint (Wynfrith; ca. 675–755), "Apostle to the Germans." Born at Crediton in southwest England, he was first a monk and scholar but in 718 left England to preach the gospel to the Germanic tribes. He reformed the Frankish Church and became archbishop of Mainz. He eventually directed his mission to Holland, and was killed at Dokkum. A number of his letters survive.

Caesaria, Saint (died ca. 530), first abbess of the convent founded in 512 by her brother, Saint Caesarius of Arles. He addressed his Nuns' Rule to her and related how she taught and supervised the copying of scripture at the convent. Other contemporaries also testified to her gifts.

Cassiodorus (Senator), Flavius Magnus Aurelius (ca. 485–580), Roman politician and writer. On retiring from public life he founded a monastery known as the Vivarium ("the fishponds") on his estate at Squillace in southern Italy, and instigated there an influential program of Bible study, copying, and correction.

Ceolfrith (ca. 642–716), first abbot of the twin monasteries of Wearmouth–Jarrow. He traveled to Rome in 679 to collect books for this foundation, greatly enlarged its libraries, and oversaw the production of three complete copies of the Bible. He died on his way to Rome to present one of these copies (now known as the Codex Amiatinus) to the pope.

Charlemagne (742–814), Frankish king (from 768) and emperor (from 800), who sponsored a cultural renaissance that included editorial programs revising biblical texts and the making of luxurious codices.

Church Fathers. A number of early Christian writers and teachers, whose works are considered of special authority. They include Saint Augustine of Hippo, Saint Jerome, and Saint John Chrysostom.

Columba, Saint (ca. 521–597), monastic founder and missionary. Born in Ireland, he became a monk and priest and founded monasteries at Derry and Durrow. In 563 he left his country to preach to the Picts of Scotland. He settled on the island of Iona, which became a very influential monastery.

Constantine the Great (died 337), the first Roman emperor to promote Christianity. In 312 he defeated his rival Maxentius after having a vision that he would triumph under the sign of the Cross. In 313 his Edict of Milan allowed freedom of worship throughout the Western Empire. From 324 he ruled the whole Empire and moved its capital to Constantinople. He was baptized at his death.

Desert Fathers. The first Christians to live as hermits or monks in the deserts of Egypt, Palestine, and Syria, from the third century C.E., influencing the development of the Christian monastic way of life. They include Saints Anthony of Egypt, Basil, Pachomius, and Paul the Hermit.

Diocletian (245–316), Roman emperor (284–305) who instigated the "Great Persecution" as part of his efforts to stabilize the Roman Empire. From 303 he expelled Christian soldiers from the army, confiscated Church property, and finally demanded that Christians worship the imperial cult or face death. The persecutions ended in 313 with Constantine's Edict of Milan.

Eadburh, Saint (died 751), churchwoman and scribe. Of the Kentish royal family, she became abbess of Minster-in-Thanet, Kent. She is known largely from her correspondence with Saint Boniface, whose mission she, or her double monastery (male and female), supplied with copies of scripture, including luxuriously gilded volumes.

Eusebius of Ceasarea (ca. 260–ca. 339), bishop and historian. He wrote the early history of the Church from apostolic times, devised a concordance system with canon tables allowing comparison of episodes across the gospels, and was involved in the early ecumenical councils.

Godescalc (active 781–83), Frankish scribe. He was commissioned by Charlemagne and his wife Hildegard to write the lectionary that now bears his name; it is the earliest known manuscript produced at the Court School at Aachen.

Gregory the Great, Saint (ca. 540–604), pope (from 590) and statesman. He secured the Church's position in Italy, influenced worship and Church music, and wrote widely on the Christian life. As part of his vision for the conversion of western Europe he dispatched Augustine to preach to the English.

Irenaeus (ca. 130–ca. 202), bishop of Lyon and theologian. His writings aimed at refuting heresy and establishing the canon of scripture, especially the primacy of the four gospels.

Jerome, Saint (ca. 347–419/20), a Father of the Church and biblical scholar. From 382 to 385 he was the secretary of Pope Damasus I in Rome, at whose request he began his revision and translation of the Old Latin Bible. In 386 he retired to Bethlehem to continue the work, which eventually led to the completion of his "Vulgate" Bible.

Maurdramnus (active 772–81), abbot of Corbie. During work on his six-volume revision of the Bible his scriptorium experimented with a new form of script, which could be rapidly copied and easily read—the earliest dateable example of caroline minuscule.

Tatian (active ca. 170), Syrian convert to Christianity and author, regarded by some as heretical. Only two of his works survive, the most important being the *Diatessaron*, a gospel harmony in which all the events of Christ's life are recounted in a single narrative.

Theodulf (ca. 760–821), bishop of Orléans and theologian. A distinguished member of the court of Charlemagne, he prepared a revision of the Vulgate and wrote the *Libri carolini*, making pronouncements against idolatry.

Ulfilas (ca. 311–383), "Apostle to the Goths." He is credited with inventing the Gothic script and wrote the first translation of the Bible in a Germanic language.

Notes to the essays

The following abbreviations are used in the notes:

CCCM	Corpus Christianorum Continuatio Mediaevalis
CCSL	Corpus Christianorum Series Latina
CISAM	Centro italiano di studi sull'alto medioevo
CSCO	Corpus Scriptorum Christianorum Orientalium
MGH	Monumenta Germaniae Historica
PG	J.-P. Migne, *Patrologiae Cursus Completus, Series Graecae*, 161 vols. (Paris, 1857–66)
PL	J.-P. Migne, *Patrologiae Cursus Completus, Series Latina*, 221 vols. (Paris, 1844–55, 1862–65)

Charles Lang Freer's biblical manuscripts
(pages 6–9)

1. Charles Lang Freer to Frank J. Hecker, 19 December 1906, Charles Lang Freer Papers, Freer Gallery of Art Archives, Smithsonian Institution, Washington, D.C.
2. H. A. Sanders, "Age and Ancient Home of Biblical Manuscripts in the Freer Collection," *American Journal of Archaeology* 13 (1909): 130–41.
3. 23 January 1908. Diary, Francis W. Kelsey Papers, Bentley Historical Library, University of Michigan, Ann Arbor.
4. Charles Lang Freer to Francis W. Kelsey, 23 May 1908, Francis W. Kelsey Records, Kelsey Museum Archives, Bentley Historical Library, University of Michigan, Ann Arbor.
5. Freer to Kelsey, 14 April 1908, Francis W. Kelsey Records.
6. Freer to Hecker, 16 May 1908, Charles Lang Freer Papers.
7. R. Gottheil and W. H. Worrell, *Fragments from the Cairo Genizah in the Freer Collection*, University of Michigan Studies, Humanistic Series 13 (New York and London: Macmillan, 1927).
8. Freer to Kelsey, 18 June 1912, Charles Lang Freer Papers.
9. Freer to Worrell, 17 July 1912, Charles Lang Freer Papers.
10. Freer to Kelsey, 1 August 1909, Francis W. Kelsey Records.
11. W. H. Worrell, *The Coptic Psalter in the Freer Collection* (New York and London: Macmillan, 1916), fragment 9.

Bible and book (pages 15–35)

1. On the development of this collection see, among many resources, S. Z. Leiman, *The Canonization of Hebrew Scripture: The Talmudic and Midrashic Evidence* (Hamden, Conn.: Archon Books, 1976); R. T. Beckwith, *The Old Testament Canon of the New Testament Church* (Grand Rapids, Mich.: Eerdmans, 1985); J. C. Trebolle Barrera, *The Jewish Bible and the Christian Bible* (Leiden: Brill, 1998); and the essays by J. C. Vanderkam, S. Mason, J. C. Trebolle Barrera, J. Lewis and J. Lightstone in *The Canon Debate*, ed. L. M. McDonald and J. A. Sanders (Peabody, Mass.: Hendrickson, 2002).
2. On the Septuagint generally, see S. Jellicoe, *The Septuagint and Modern Study* (Oxford: Clarendon Press, 1968); A. C. Sundberg, *The Old Testament of the Early Church* (Cambridge, Mass.: Harvard University Press, 1964); M. Hengel, *The Septuagint as Christian Scripture: Its Prehistory and the Problem of Its Canon* (Edinburgh: T & T Clark, 2002); and, more briefly, A. C. Sundberg, "The Septuagint: The Bible of Hellenistic Judaism," in McDonald and Sanders, *The Canon Debate*, 68–90.
3. The Latin term *septuaginta* was first applied to the translation (as distinct from the translators) by Augustine (*City of God* 18.42), but the Greek equivalent *(hebdomenkonta)* had earlier been used of the translation by Eusebius (*Ecclesiastical History* 6.16.1), and so this designation seems to have arisen in the fourth century C.E. For an English translation of the *Letter of Aristeas* see R. H. Charles, *Apocrypha and Pseudepigrapha of the Old Testament* (repr. Oxford: Oxford University Press, 1968), 2:94–122.
4. The Septuagint itself is known also in several distinct revisions, associated with the names of Aquila, Symmachus, and Theodotion, which appeared between 200 B.C.E. and 200 C.E.
5. There are, however, differences even between these. The Latin Vulgate (see p. 56) has one more deuterocanonical book than the Greek Septuagint, namely 2 Esdras, which belonged to the Old Latin version. The Eastern Orthodox Churches, for their part, recognize the additional books of 3 Maccabees and Psalm 151.
6. There is a large literature on the construction and inscription of ancient bookrolls. The most recent and well-founded is W. A. Johnson, *Bookrolls and Scribes in Oxyrhynchus* (Toronto: University of Toronto Press, 2004), on which much of the following discussion depends. Older but variously useful studies include W. Schubart, *Das Buch bei den Griechen und Romern*, 3rd ed., ed. P. von Eberhard (Heidelberg: Lambert Schneider, 1962); F. G. Kenyon, *Books and Readers in Ancient Greece and Rome*, 2nd ed. (Oxford: Clarendon Press, 1951); E. G. Turner, *Greek Manuscripts of the Ancient World*, 2nd ed., rev. P. Parsons (London: University of London Institute of Classical Studies, 1987); and H. Blanck, *Das Buch in der Antike* (Munich: Beck, 1992).
7. See the highly instructive discussion of this issue by W. A. Johnson, "Toward a Sociology of Reading in Classical Antiquity," *American Journal of Philology* 121 (2000): 593–627. Further, on the commonality of reading aloud, R. Starr, "*Lectores* and Book Reading," *Classical Journal* 86 (1990–91): 337–43.
8. For the manufacture of papyrus the *locus classicus* is Pliny the Elder, *Natural History* 13.74–82. The standard study of papyrus is N. Lewis, *Papyrus in Classical Antiquity* (Oxford: Clarendon Press, 1974), repr. with corrections and additions in *Papyrus in Classical Antiquity: A Supplement* (Brussels: Fondation Egyptologique reine Elisabeth, 1989).
9. On Greek scribal hands see Turner, rev. Parsons, *Greek Manuscripts*, 1–23.
10. All the books that were subsequently included in the Hebrew Bible are represented among the Qumran scrolls, with the exception of Esther and Nehemiah (though Ezra is found). The books of the Hebrew Bible found in the largest numbers of copies are Psalms (36), Deuteronomy (32), Isaiah (22), Exodus (17) and Genesis (15). Some non-canonical books were also present, both apocryphal (Tobit, Ben Sira, Epistle of Jeremiah) and pseudepigraphical (Enoch, Jubilees, Testaments of the Twelve Patriarchs). Notably, eight Septuagint manuscripts were also among the books at Qumran.
11. Scholars who have edited and published the materials from the Judaean Desert have not been highly attentive to or informative about the physical characteristics of the manuscripts and no study focuses closely on these. See, however, E. Tov, "Hebrew Biblical Manuscripts from the Judean Desert: Their Contribution to Textual Criticism," *Journal of Jewish Studies* 39 (1988): 5–37; and especially H. Stegemann, "Methods for the Reconstruction of Scrolls from Scattered Fragments," in *Archaeology and History in the Dead Sea Scrolls*, ed. L. Schiffman (Sheffield, UK: Sheffield Academic Press, 1990), 189–220.

12. The lengths of the Qumran scrolls run from 2m up to more than 8m, the longest of the manuscripts being 1QIsaiah(a) at 7.34m and 11QTemplel at 8.75m. The official Torah Scroll of ancient Judaism, retained in the sanctuary of the Jerusalem Temple, read on solemn occasions, and serving as the authoritative master copy, would presumably have been of the largest size, but statements about it and the illustration of it on the Arch of Titus in Rome indicate that it was no taller than about 45cm. See L. Blau, *Studien zum althebraischen Buchwesen* (Strasbourg: E. K. J. Trubner, 1902), 71–78.
13. The reason is that Hebrew, Arabic, and Syriac were written in consonants only, making words hard to recognize without separation.
14. The use of such parchment notebooks is mentioned, for example, by Horace (*Satirae* 2.3.2) and Quintilian (*Institutio* 10.3.31–2). It should be noted, however, that among the Romans waxed tablets were also employed for legal and archival purposes, being inscribed with wills, birth certificates, marriage records, compacts, etc. See now E. A. Meyer, *Legitimacy and Law in the Roman World: Tabulae in Roman Belief and Practice* (Cambridge: Cambridge University Press, 2004).
15. Of the remains of non-Christian Greek books that can be dated before the third century, more than 98 percent are bookrolls. The codex does not begin to show up significantly until the third century, when fewer than 20 percent are codices, and only in the fourth century are codices found in a number (48 percent) almost equal to rolls. For statistical tables see C. H. Roberts and T. C. Skeat, *The Birth of the Codex* (Oxford: Oxford University Press, 1983).
16. Of the nearly 100 early Christian scriptural papyri, only four are from rolls rather than codices, and all of those (P 12, 13, 18, and 22) are either opisthographs (written on the outside [or verso] of a previously inscribed bookroll) or are written on reused papyrus. Christianity's decided predilection for the codex began to be recognized by Kenyon, *Books and Readers*, 94–99, but was first carefully documented by C. H. Roberts, "The Codex," *Proceedings of the British Academy* 40 (1954): 169–204.
17. All in the Chester Beatty Library, Dublin.
18. P 47 is in Dublin, The Chester Beatty Library; P 52 is in Manchester, The John Rylands Library; and P 5 is in London, The British Library.
19. P 66 is in the Bibliothèque Bodmer, Geneva; P 4 is in the Bibliothèque nationale de France; P 64 is in the Library of Magdalen College, Oxford; and P 67 is in the Fundacíon San Lucas Evangelista, Barcelona.
20. P 75 is in the Bibliothèque Bodmer, Geneva.
21. Only occasionally in early Christian papyrus codices do we find two columns per page: P 4+64+67, P 8, P 50, P 78.
22. Such conclusions are also supported by the fact that the vast majority of the textual variants in those books that ultimately came to be included in the New Testament seem to have arisen in the first two centuries, that is, before 200 C.E., when the texts of these documents were still somewhat fluid. On the identity, training, and work of early Christian scribes, see now K. Haines-Eitzen, *Guardians of Letters: Literacy, Power and the Transmitters of Early Christian Literature* (Oxford and New York: Oxford University Press, 2000).
23. E. G. Turner, *The Typology of the Early Codex* (Philadelphia: University of Pennsylvania Press, 1977), 84–87.
24. On this practice, see B. M. Metzger, *Manuscripts of the Greek Bible: An Introduction to Palaeography* (New York: Oxford University Press, 1981), 36–37; and, more fully, C. H. Roberts, *Manuscript, Society and Belief in Early Christian Egypt*, The Schweich Lectures of the British Academy, 1977 (London: Oxford University Press for the British Academy, 1979), 26–48. In time, this scribal practice was extended to eleven additional terms (Spirit, Man, Cross, Father, Son, etc.), but with much less regularity. The use of such abbreviations or contractions was common in documentary texts, but rare in well-written literary texts.
25. Thorough discussion of the Nag Hammadi covers is given in J. M. Robinson, "The Construction of the Nag Hammadi Codices," in *Essays on the Nag Hammadi Texts in Honor of Pahor Labib*, ed. M. Krause (Leiden: Brill, 1975), 170–90; and *The Facsimile Edition of the Nag Hammadi Codices* (Leiden: Brill, 1984), 71–86.
26. Of the seventeen non-Christian codices that seem to date from the second century, eleven contain literary texts and six contain grammatical, lexical, and medical texts. Some of those with literary texts may have been working copies for educational use, that is, teachers' manuals.
27. The first place in which anything else is meant is 2 Peter 3:16 where Paul's letters are implicitly regarded as scripture. 2 Peter is usually considered the latest document of the New Testament, belonging to the late first or early second century.
28. Indicative of this, among other things, is that the various genres of early Christian literature have no correspondence to the genres of Jewish scripture.
29. For the evidence, see D. Rensberger, "As the Apostle Teaches: The Development and Use of Paul's Letters in Second Century Christianity" (Ph.D. dissertation, Yale University, 1981); and A. Lindemann, *Paulus im altesten Christentum: Das Bild des Apostels und die Rezeption der Paulinischen Theologie in der frühchristlichen Literatur bis Marcion* (Tübingen: Mohr, 1978). Marcion's collection seems to be derivative from a still earlier collection: J. J. Clabeaux, *A Lost Edition of the Letters of Paul: A Reassessment of the Text of the Pauline Corpus Attested by Marcion* (Washington, D.C.: Catholic Biblical Association of America, 1989).
30. It is in consideration of relative length that P 46 places Hebrews between Romans and 1 Corinthians.
31. On the number and variety of these see H. Koester, *Ancient Christian Gospels: Their History and Development* (Philadelphia: Trinity Press International, 1990); and H.-J. Klauck, *Apocryphal Gospels: An Introduction* (London and New York: T & T Clark, 2003). The non-canonical gospels are easily accessible in English translation in R. Cameron, ed., *The Other Gospels: Non-Canonical Gospel Texts* (Philadelphia: Westminster Press, 1982).
32. From the second century right up through the fifth century Christian thinkers were exercised by the many divergences among the gospels and sought to rationalize them, as we can see, for example, from comments of Papias, Irenaeus, Augustine, and others. See O. Cullmann, "The Plurality of the Gospels as a Theological Problem in Antiquity," in *The Early Church* (Philadelphia: Westminster Press, 1956), 39–54. The relevant texts are gathered and discussed by H. Merkel, *Die Pluralitat der Evangelien als theologisches und exegetisches Problem in der alten Kirche* (Berne: Lang, 1978).
33. P 1 is at the University of Pennsylvania Museum, Philadelphia; P 70 and P 77 are at the Ashmolean Museum, Oxford.
34. P 52 is at the John Rylands University Library, Manchester; P 66 is at the Bibliothèque Bodmer, Geneva.
35. P 75 is at the Bibliothèque Bodmer, Geneva.
36. See note 19 above.
37. T. C. Skeat has claimed, perhaps too boldly, that all the early papyrus gospel fragments, which appear to come from single-gospel codices, actually derive from codices containing all four gospels ("The Origins of the Christian Codex," *Zeitschrift für Papyrologie und Epigraphik* 102 (1994): 263–68).

38. Although this was not, of course, the attribution of the symbols to the named evangelists actually favored by Irenaeus (the "Western order," in which John and Mark were reversed), but rather, that promoted by Augustine and Gregory the Great.
39. The name, "through four," was a musical term (an interval of a fourth), but here should be understood as "through four [gospels]." On the *Diatessaron*, see W. L. Petersen, *Tatian's Diatessaron: Its Creation, Dissemination, Significance and History in Scholarship*, Supplements to Vigiliae Christianae 25 (Leiden: Brill, 1994). Tatian was certainly not the first to create a harmony of (some) gospels (Petersen, 26–34). There are indications that his teacher, Justin Martyr, had earlier used a gospel harmony in Rome, though he also knew some gospels (at least those of Matthew and Luke) as discrete documents.
40. This explanation is favored by H. A. Sanders, *The New Testament Manuscripts in the Freer Collection*, Part 1: *The Washington Manuscript of the Four Gospels* (New York: Macmillan, 1912), who thinks the ancestor manuscript of the Washington codex was written from fragments of various manuscripts gathered up after the persecution of Diocletian (on which see below).
41. "And they excused themselves, saying 'This age of lawlessness and unbelief is under Satan, who does not allow the truth and power of God to prevail over the unclean things of the spirits. Therefore reveal your righteousness now'—thus they said to Christ. And Christ replied to them, 'The term of years for Satan's power has been fulfilled, but other terrible things draw near. And for those who have sinned I was delivered over to death so that they may return to the truth and no longer sin, so that they may inherit the spiritual and incorruptible glory of righteousness that is in heaven.'"
42. Thus, for example, Clement of Alexandria, writing in the late second century, regarded 1 Clement and the Epistle of Barnabas as apostolic in origin and fully authoritative as scripture, and, with Irenaeus and Tertullian, Clement considered the Shepherd of Hermas authoritative. It is not merely accidental that the Shepherd of Hermas is strongly represented among early papyrus manuscripts.
43. This fluidity is given valuable statistical documentation by F. Stuhlhofer, *Der Gebrauch der Bibel von Jesus bis Euseb: Eine statistische Untersuchung zur Kanongeschichte* (Wuppertal: Brockhaus, 1988).
44. *Ecclesiastical History* 2.23.25.
45. For discussion of these terms and their application, see L. M. McDonald, *The Formation of the Christian Biblical Canon*, rev. ed. (Peabody, Mass.: Hendrickson, 1995), 6–21; and J. Barton, *Holy Writings, Sacred Texts: The Canon in Early Christianity* (Louisville, Ky.: Westminster / John Knox Press, 1997), 1–14.
46. This alone sharply posed for Christians the problem of which books they could turn over without scruple, and which, on account of their scriptural value, should be withheld from the authorities. Decisions that were made about this had long-lasting repercussions in the Church, and there was great reluctance to restore to community the *traditores* who had surrendered scriptural books under persecution.
47. For Codex Sinaiticus, see cat. no. 26. Codex Vaticanus is Vatican, Biblioteca Apostolica, MS. Vat. Or. 1209.
48. G. A. Robbins, "*Peri ton Endiathekon Graphon*: Eusebius and the Formation of the Christian Bible" (Ph.D. dissertation, Duke University, 1986), 186–216.
49. Note also that the third large early codex, the fifth-century Codex Alexandrinus (London, British Library, Royal MSS 1.D.v-viii) contains in its New Testament portion two other early Christian documents, 1 and 2 Clement.
50. Even then the Syrian sector of the Church lagged behind, continuing to use the *Diatessaron*, and recognizing besides this only Acts and the community letters of Paul (but not the personal ones). The catholic epistles had no standing in the Syrian region before the late fourth and early fifth centuries, and of them only James, 1 Peter and 1 John secured any acceptance. Thus even by the early fifth century the Syrian Church admitted only twenty-two books.

The Christian Orient (pages 37–43)

1. M. Le Quien, *Oriens christianus, in quatuor patriarchatus digestus quo exhibentur ecclesiae, patriarchae, caeterique praesules totius Orientis. Studio & opera ... Opus posthumum...*, 3 vols. (Paris: ex Typographia regia, 1740).
2. The terms "Monophysite," "Jacobite," and "Nestorian" are polemical and misleading in this context. Instead, the names Syrian Orthodox Church and the Church of the East, or the Assyrian Church of the East are used. West and East Syrian are broader-based designators. In order to avoid associations with the modern state of Syria and to draw attention to the language, West and East Syriac are used as general descriptors for the Churches.
3. They include differences in the pronunciation and writing of Syriac. Syriac has three major scripts: *esṭrangelā*, the monumental script seen in all Syriac manuscripts on display; *serṭā* or West Syriac script; and East Syriac or Nestorian script. Syriac was first written consonantally with very few diacritic marks. Over time, West and East Syriac systems of vowel marks and diacritical marks were added to manuscripts to avoid ambiguous or mistaken readings. A Syriac text of the ninth/tenth century can look very different from a fourth/fifth-century one because of this.
4. Since the Old Testament books seem to have been translated individually rather than together, it is possible that the Syriac translation of some books may be dependent on earlier Aramaic *Targums*, i.e., Jewish translations of the Bible into Aramaic. But see M. P. Weitzman, *The Syriac Version of the Old Testament: An Introduction* (Cambridge: Cambridge University Press, 1999), 86–163.
5. See collected articles in S. Brock, *From Ephrem to Romanos: Interactions between Syriac and Greek in Late Antiquity*, Variorum Collected Studies Series, CS664 (Aldershot, UK: Ashgate, 1999).
6. See introduction and bibliography in C. McCarthy, *Saint Ephrem's Commentary on Tatian's Diatessaron: An English Translation of Chester Beatty Syriac MS 709 with Introduction and Notes*, Journal of Semitic Studies Supplement 2 (Oxford: Oxford University Press on behalf of the University of Manchester, 1993).
7. See M. J. Blanchard and R. D. Young, *A Treatise on God Written in Armenian by Eznik of Kolb (floruit c.430–c.450): An English Translation, with Introduction and Notes*, Eastern Christian Texts in Translation 2 (Louvain: Peeters, 1998), 1–11.
8. Saint Bartholomew is also claimed as an apostolic founder of the Armenian Church. See M. van Esbroeck, "The Rise of Saint Bartholomew's Cult in Armenia from the Seventh to the Thirteenth Centuries," in *Medieval Armenian Culture: Proceedings of the Third Dr. H. Markarian Conference on Armenian Culture*, ed. T. J. Samuelian and M. E. Stone, University of Pennsylvania Armenian texts and studies 6 (Chico, Calif.: Scholars Press, 1984), 161–78; R. Thomson, "Mission, Conversion, and Christianization: The Armenian Example," *Harvard Ukrainian Studies* 12–13 (1988–89): 28–45, esp. p. 29.
9. *The Teaching of Addai*, trans. G. Howard, Texts and Translations 16; Early Christian Literature Series 4 (Ann Arbor, Mich.: Scholars Press, 1981).

10. M. van Esbroeck, "Le roi Sanatrouk et l'apôtre Thaddée," *Revue des études arméniennes* n.s. 9 (1972): 241–83.
11. R. W. Thomson, "Syrian Christianity and the Conversion of Armenia," in *Die Christianiserung der Kaukasus / The Christianisation of the Caucasus (Armenia, Georgia, Albania)*, ed. W. Seibt (Vienna: Österreichischen Akademie der Wissenschaften, 2002), 159–69.
12. N. G. Garsoïan, trans. and commentary, *The Epic Histories attributed to P'awstos Buzand (Buzandaran Patmut'iwnk')* (Cambridge, Mass.: Distributed for the Dept. of Near Eastern Languages and Civilizations, Harvard University by Harvard University Press, 1989), 84.
13. The earliest Armenian letters were written in an uncial or *erkat'agir* form; the rounded *bolorgir* minuscule appeared in the eleventh century; later in the seventeenth century the *notragir* script was developed.
14. Koriwn, *Vark' Mashtots'i: a Photoreproduction of the 1941 Yerevan Edition with a Modern Translation and Concordance, and with a new Introduction by Krikor H. Maksoudian* (Delmar, N.Y.: Caravan Books, 1985), 43 [English translation].
15. D. Marshall Lang, *Lives and Legends of the Georgian Saints Selected and Translated from the Original Texts* (London and New York: George Allen & Unwin / Macmillan, 1956), 13–39, esp. 20–25. See too N. Thierry, "Sur le culte de Sainte Nino," in *Die Christianisierung des Kaukasus*, 151–58.
16. See G. Tseret'eli, "The Most Ancient Georgian Inscriptions in Palestine," *Bedi Kartlisa: Revue de Kartvélologie* 7 (1961): 111–30. On Peter the Iberian see C. B. Horn, *Asceticism and Christological Controversy in Fifth-Century Palestine: The Career of Peter the Iberian*, Oxford Early Christian Studies (Oxford: Oxford University Press, 2006).
17. See T. Mgaloblishvili, ed., *Ancient Christianity in the Caucasus*, Caucasus World (Surrey, UK: Curzon Press, 1998); G. Garitte, *Scripta Disiecta, 1941–1977*, Publications de l'Institut Orientaliste de Louvain 21–22 (Louvain-la-Neuve: Université Catholique de Louvain, Institut Orientaliste, 1980); D. M. Lang, *The Georgians*, Ancient Peoples and Places 51 (Bristol: Thames & Hudson, 1966).
18. On the proliferation and production (until the tenth or even the twelfth century) of Greek–Coptic bilingual gospel lectionaries and other biblical books used in the liturgy of the Coptic Church, see R. S. Bagnall, *Egypt in Late Antiquity* (Princeton, N. J.: Princeton University Press, 1993), 253–55.
19. It has been suggested that the *Life of St. Anthony of Egypt* written by Athanasius indicates the existence of a Coptic translation of the gospels by ca. 270 when Anthony, a Copt who did not know Greek (according to Athanasius), was inspired by readings from the Gospel of Matthew. But see the remarks of D. Brakke, *Athanasius and Asceticism* (Baltimore and London: The Johns Hopkins University Press, c1995), 253–60.
20. For an overview of Coptic dialects, see R. Kasser, "Dialects," and "Dialects, Grouping and Major Groups of," in *The Coptic Encyclopedia*, ed. A. S. Atiya, 8 vols. (New York: Macmillan, c1991), 87–97, 97–101.
21. These lists are still helpful: A. Vaschalde, "Ce qui a été publié des versions coptes de la Bible," *Revue biblique* n.s. 16, 28 (1919): 220–43, 513–31; 29 (1920): 91–106, 241–58; 30 (1921): 237–46; 31 (1922): 81–88, 234–58; continued in *Le Muséon* 43 (1930): 409–31; 46 (1933): 299–306; 46 (1933): 306–13; also W. C. Till, "Coptic Biblical Texts after Vaschalde's Lists," *Bulletin of the John Rylands Library* 42 (1959–1960): 220–40; P. Nagel, "Editionen koptischer Bibeltexte seit Till 1960," *Archiv für Papyrusforschung* 35 (1989), 43–100.
22. L. Depuydt, *Catalogue of Coptic Manuscripts in the Pierpont Morgan Library*, 2 vols., Corpus of Illuminated Manuscripts, vol. 4; Oriental Series 1 (Louvain: Peeters, 1993). Depuydt dates the collection ca. 822/23–913/14 using the earliest and latest dated manuscripts as termini.
23. B. Layton, *The Gnostic Scriptures: A New Translation with Annotations and Introductions* (Garden City, N.Y.: Doubleday, 1987), xv–xxvii.
24. It has been suggested that the sayings of Jesus in the Gospel of Thomas influenced the *Diatessaron*; also that the Coptic Gospel of Thomas is a translation of a Syriac text dependent on the *Diatessaron*. See N. Perrin, *Thomas and Tatian: The Relationship between the Gospel of Thomas and the Diatessaron*, Academia Biblica 5 (Atlanta: Society of Biblical Literature, 2002). See also C. Lange, *The Portrayal of Christ in the Syriac Commentary on the Diatessaron*, CSCO vol. 616. Subsidia tom. 118 (Louvain: Peeters, 2005).
25. See Layton, *Gnostic Scriptures*, 376–77; A. Siverstev, "The Gospel of Thomas and Early Stages in the Development of the Christian Wisdom Literature," *Journal of Early Christian Studies* 8 (2000): 319–40.
26. The chronology is anchored by the letter of the emperor Constantius II to the rulers of Axum, written ca. 356 in an unsuccessful attempt to replace Frumentius with an Arian bishop. The text is preserved in Athanasius's *Apology to the Emperor Constantius* 31 (ca. 356/7).
27. On the Ethiopic Bible, see E. Ullendorff, *Ethiopia and the Bible*, The Schweich Lectures of the British Academy 1967 (London: Oxford University Press for the British Academy, 1968); M. A. Knibb, *Translating the Bible: the Ethiopic Version of the Old Testament*, The Schweich Lectures of the British Academy 1995 (London: Oxford University Press for the British Academy, c1999); S. Uhlig, "Bible: Time and Context," in S. Uhlig, ed., *Encyclopaedia Aethiopica* (Wiesbaden: Harrassowitz, 2003), 1: 563–64.
28. See I. Shahid, "The Kebra Nagast in the Light of Recent Research," *Le Muséon* 89 (1976): 133–78; D. W. Johnson, "The Kebra Nagast: Another Look," in *Peace and War in Byzantium: Essays in Honor of George T. Dennis*, ed. T. S. Miller and J. Nesbitt, (Washington, D.C.: Catholic University of America Press, 1995): 197–208.
29. See E. Balicka-Witakowska, *La Crucifixion sans crucifié dans l'art éthiopien: recherches sur la survie de l'iconographie chrétienne de l'Antiquité tardive*, Bibliotheca nubica et aethiopica 4 (Warsaw: Zaś Pan, 1997), esp. 15–17; C. Lepage, "Reconstitution d'un cycle protobyzantin à partir des miniatures de deux manuscrits éthiopiens du XIVe siècle," *Cahiers archéologiques* 35 (1987): 159–96. See also B. Kühnel, "The Holy Land as a Factor in Christian Art," in *Christians and Christianity in the Holy Land: From the Origins to the Latin Kingdoms*, ed. O. Limor and G. G. Stroumsa, Cultural Encounters in Late Antiquity and the Middle Ages (Turnhout: Brepols, c2006): 463–504.
30. See S. H. Griffith, "From Aramaic to Arabic: The Languages of the Monasteries of Palestine in the Byzantine and Early Islamic Periods," *Dumbarton Oaks Papers* 51 (1997): 11–31; S. H. Griffith, "The Church of Jerusalem and the 'Melkites': The Making of an 'Arab Orthodox' Christian Identity in the World of Islam (750–1050 CE)" in *Christians and Christianity in the Holy Land*, 175–204.
31. See S. Brock, "A Neglected Witness to the East Syriac New Testament Commentary Tradition: Sinai, Arabic MS 151," in *Studies on the Christian Arabic Heritage in Honour of Father Prof. Dr. Samir Khalil Samir S.J. at the Occasion of his Sixty-Fifth Birthday*, ed. R. Ebied and H. Teule, Eastern Christian Studies 5 (Louvain: Peeters, 2004), 205–215, esp. 215.
32. Overviews include: J.-M. Fiey, "Coptes et syriaques: contacts et échanges," *Studia Orientalia Christiana. Collectanea* 15 (1972–73, i.e. 1976): 297–365; M. J. Blanchard, "Moses of Nisibis (fl. 906–943) and the Library of Deir Suriani," in *Studies in the Christian East in Memory of Mirrit Boutros Ghali*, ed. L. S. B. MacCoull, Publications of the Society for Coptic Archaeology (North America), 1 (Washington, D.C., 1995),

13–24; K. Innemée and L. Van Rompay, "La présence des Syriens dans le Wadi al-Natrun (Egypte)," *Parole de l'Orient* 23 (1998): 167–202; S. Brock, "Without Mushē of Nisibis, Where would we be? Some Reflections on the Transmission of Syriac Literature," *Journal of Eastern Christian Studies* 56 (2004): 15–24. The history of the monastery is presented in H. G. E. White, *The Monasteries of the Wadi 'n Natrun*, 3 vols. (New York: Metropolitan Museum of Art, 1926–33), esp. vols. 2 and 3.

33. See now the listing by Brock in "Without Mushē of Nisibis, Where Would We Be?", 18–21.
34. White, *The Monasteries of the Wadi 'n Natrun*, 2:17–42.
35. At Deir el-Suriani lives of the founders of the four great monasteries of the Wadi Natrun, Macarius, John the Little, Bishoi, and the Romaioi Maximus and Dometius, appear together in a small group of Syriac manuscripts mostly from the twelfth and thirteenth centuries. Along with them are lives of Egyptian desert fathers and monks, including the *Life of Shenute*, whose fame was limited to Coptic Egypt. These biographies testify to ongoing translation from Arabic into Syriac of Coptic originals. We know that such work was already in progress at the Deir el-Suriani in the tenth century from a manuscript note that the *Life of John the Little* was translated from Arabic into Syriac here in 936. See M. Blanchard, "Saint Ephrem's Coptic Friend, Apa Bishoi," *The Harp: A Review of Syriac and Oriental Ecumenical Studies* 16 (2003): 43–55.
36. On the attraction of the Egyptian monasteries, see S. H. Griffith, "The Handwriting on the Wall: Graffiti in the Church of St. Antony," in *Monastic Visions: Wall Paintings in the Monastery of St. Antony at the Red Sea*, ed. E. S. Bolman, (New Haven and London: Yale University Press, 2002), 185–93.

Spreading the Word (pages 45–75)

1. G. W. H. Lampe, ed., *The Cambridge History of the Bible*, vol. 2, *The West from the Fathers to the Reformation* (Cambridge: Cambridge University Press, 1969); C. de Hamel, *The Book: A History of the Bible* (London and New York: Phaidon, 2001).
2. There is no "authentic" witness to the Septuagint's text: versions circulated by Hesychius and Lucian and in Origen's *Hexapla*. Recognition of this led Jerome, in his revision of the Old Latin, to acknowledge the value of a new version direct from the Hebrew texts. This was very controversial, due to limited knowledge of Hebrew among other ecclesiastics, who could not evaluate the work themselves. Other Greek versions also circulated, including those by Aquila, Symmachus and Theodotion. See Lampe, *Cambridge History of the Bible*, 95; de Hamel, *The Book*, 17–18.
3. The subject of biblical transmission is a vast, complex, and debated one. For good general introductions suited to this particular context see, for example, Lampe, *Cambridge History of the Bible*; R. G. Gameson, ed., *The Early Medieval Bible* (Cambridge: Cambridge University Press, 1994); R. Marsden, *The Text of the Old Testament in Anglo-Saxon England*, Cambridge Studies in Anglo-Saxon England 15 (Cambridge: Cambridge University Press, 1995); de Hamel, *The Book*; H. Y. Gamble, *Books and Readers in the Early Church: A History of Early Christian Texts* (New Haven and London: Yale University Press, 1995).
4. Codex Sinaiticus consists of several portions now in the Holy Monastery of St. Catherine, Mount Sinai; London; St. Petersburg; and Leipzig. Codex Vaticanus is Vatican, Biblioteca Apostolica, MS. Vat. Or. 1209. Codex Alexandrinus is London, British Library, Royal MSS 1.D.v-viii. See C. H. Roberts and T. C. Skeat, *The Birth of the Codex* (Oxford: Oxford University Press, 1983).
5. On the Vienna Genesis (Vienna, Österreichische Nationalbibliothek, Cod. Theol. Gr. 31) and Rabbula Gospels (Florence, Biblioteca Medicea Laurenziana, MS. Plut. I.56) see K. Weitzmann, *Late Antique and Early Christian Book Illumination* (London: Chatto & Windus, 1977); O. Pächt, *Book Illumination in the Middle Ages: An Introduction* (London: Harvey Miller, 1986); C. Nordenfalk, *Early Medieval Book Illumination* (New York: Rizzoli, 1988); C. de Hamel, *A History of Illuminated Manuscripts* (Oxford: Phaidon, 1986); J. J. G. Alexander, *Medieval Illuminators and Their Methods of Work* (New Haven: Yale, 1992).
6. Weitzmann, *Late Antique and Early Christian Book Illumination*; D. H. Wright, *The Vatican Virgil* (Berkeley: University of California Press, 1993).
7. Codex Brixianus is in Brescia, Biblioteca Civica Queriniana; the Golden Canon Tables are London, British Library, Add. MSS 5111–2.
8. A. Badawry, *Coptic Art and Archaeology* (Cambridge, Mass.: MIT Press, 1978); G. Gabra, *Cairo: The Coptic Museum and Old Churches* (Cairo: Longman, 1993); V. Nersessian, ed., *Treasures from the Ark: 1700 Years of Armenian Christian Art* (London: British Library, 2001).
9. L. Avrin, *Scribes, Script and Books* (London and Chicago: British Library / Chicago University Press, 1991); F. Déroche and F. Richard, *Scribes et manuscrits du Moyen-Orient* (Paris: Bibliothèque nationale de France, 1997).
10. W. Ong, *Orality and Literacy: The Technologizing of the Word* (London: Methuen, 1981); R. I. Page, *Runes and Runic Inscriptions* (Woodbridge: Boydell & Brewer, 1995); M. P. Brown, *The British Library Guide to Writing and Scripts* (London and Toronto: British Library / Toronto University Press, 1998).
11. Also introduced into Hebrew texts for public reading. On the history of punctuation and word-separation, see M. B. Parkes, *Pause and Effect: An Introduction to the History of Punctuation in the West* (Aldershot, UK: Scolar Press, 1992).
12. M. P. Brown, *A Guide to Western Historical Scripts from Antiquity to 1600* (London and Toronto: British Library and Toronto University Press, 1990), 32–33; R. Walker, *Views of Transition: Liturgy and Illumination in Medieval Spain* (London and Toronto: British Library and Toronto University Press, 1998).
13. Brown, *Guide to Western Historical Scripts*, 32–33, 116–119.
14. London, British Library, Add. MS. 5463.
15. R. Markus, *Gregory the Great and His World* (Cambridge: Cambridge University Press, 1997); D. Ganz, "Roman Manuscripts in Francia and Anglo-Saxon England," in *Roma fra Oriente e Occidente*, Settimane di studio del centro italiano di studi sull'alto medioevo 49 (Spoleto: CISAM, 2002); M. P. Brown, *How Christianity Came to Britain and Ireland* (Oxford: Lion Hudson, 2006).
16. Brown, *How Christianity Came to Britain and Ireland*.
17. Parkes, *Pause and Effect*; M. B. Parkes, "*Rædan, areccan, smeagan*: how the Anglo-Saxons read," *Anglo-Saxon England* 26 (2000): 1–22.
18. Brown, *Guide to Western Historical Scripts*; J. Bately, M. P. Brown and J. Roberts, eds., *A Palaeographer's View: Selected Papers of Julian Brown* (London: Harvey Miller, 1993); M. P. Brown, "Fifty Years of Insular Palaeography, 1953–2003: An Outline of some Landmarks and Issues", in *Archiv für Diplomatik 50, Schriftgeschichte Siegel- und Wappenkunde*, ed. W. Koch and T. Kölzer (Vienna: Böhlau, 2004), 277–325.
19. S. Kelly, "Anglo-Saxon Lay Society and the Written Word," in *The Uses of Literacy in Early Mediaeval Europe*, ed. R. McKitterick (Cambridge: Cambridge University Press, 1990), 36–62.

20. For an overview of the conversion period in England, see H. Mayr-Harting, *The Coming of Christianity to Anglo-Saxon England* (Oxford: Oxford University Press, 1977) and Brown, *How Christianity Came to Britain and Ireland*.
21. H. Buchthal and O. Kurz, *A Handlist of Illuminated Oriental Christian Manuscripts*, Warburg Oriental Studies 12 (London: Warburg Institute, 1969); Déroche and Richard, *Scribes et manuscrits du Moyen-Orient*.
22. The Aramaic language used by Christ was recalled by the survival of a genre known as the *Targum*, an interpretative reading of the Hebrew Bible into Aramaic.
23. Gabra, *Cairo*.
24. Brown, *Writing and Scripts*, 39.
25. G. H. Forsyth and K. Weitzmann, *The Monastery of Saint Catherine at Mount Sinai: The Church and Fortress of Justinian* (Ann Arbor: University of Michigan Press, 1973).
26. K. W. Clark, *Checklist of Manuscripts in St Catherine's Monastery, Mount Sinai. Microfilmed for the Library of Congress, 1950* (Washington: Library of Congress, 1952).
27. So far, only one Armenian manuscript of the *Categoras* of Aristotle, and one Coptic *Horologion* have been identified, along with six Ethiopic volumes. See M. Kamil, 'Les Manuscrits Éthiopiens du Sinai', *Annales d'Éthiopie* 2 (1957): 83–90; M. Kamil, *Catalogue of all Manuscripts in the Monastery of St. Catharine on Mount Sinai* (Wiesbaden: Otto Harrassowitz, 1970), 53–5.
28. A. Smith Lewis, *Catalogue of the Syriac MSS. In the Convent of St Catharine on Mount Sinai*, Studium Sinaitica 1 (London: C. J. Clay & Sons, 1894).
29. H. Lake and K. Lake, *Codex Sinaiticus Petropolitanus* [facsimile], 2 vols. (Oxford: Clarendon Press, 1911–22); J. R. Harris, *Biblical Fragments from Mount Sinai* (Cambridge: Cambridge University Press, 1890); W. H. P. Hatch, *The Greek Manuscripts of the New Testament at Mount Sinai*, American Schools of Oriental Research. Publications of the Jerusalem School, vol. 1 (Paris, 1932); H. J. M. Milne and T. C. Skeat, eds., *The Codex Sinaiticus and the Codex Alexandrinus* (London: British Museum, 1938; repr. 1963); J. K. Elliott, ed., *The Collected Biblical Writings of T. C. Skeat* (Leiden: Brill, 2004); S. Mckendrick and O. A. O'Sullivan, eds., *The Bible as Book: The Transmission of the Greek Text* (London: British Library, 2003).
30. V. E. Gardthausen, *Catalogus codicum graecorum Sinaiticorum* (Oxford: Clarendon Press, 1886); V. N. Benesevitch, *Catalogus codicum manuscriptorum graecorum, qui in monasterio Sanctae Catherinae in monte Sinai asservantur*, 3 vols. (Hildesheim: Georg Olms, 1911–1917); M. Dunlop Gibson, *Catalogue of the Arabic MSS. In the Convent of St. Catharine on Mount Sinai* (London: C. J. Clay & Sons, 1894); A. S. Atiya, *The Arabic Manuscripts of Mount Sinai. A Hand List of Arabic Documents and Scrolls Microfilmed at the Library of the Monastery of St. Catherine Mount Sinai in 1954* (Baltimore: Johns Hopkins Press, 1955); A. S. Atiya, *Catalogue raisonné of the Mount Sinai Arabic Manuscripts* (Alexandria: Galal Hazzi and Co. Al Maaref Establishment, 1970).
31. K. Weitzmann, *Illustrated Manuscripts at St Catherine's Monastery on Mount Sinai* (Collegeville, Minn.: St John's University Press, 1973).
32. N. IA. Marr, *Opisanie gruzinskich rukopisei Sinaiskogo monastyrja* (Moscow: Izdatelstvo Akademii nauk SSSR, 1940); G. Garitte, *Catalogue des Manuscrits Géorgiens Littéraires du Mont Sinai*, CSCO vol. 165, Subsidia tom. 9 (Louvain: L. Durbecq, 1956).
33. E. A. Lowe, "An Unknown Latin Psalter on Mount Sinai," *Scriptorium* 9 (1955); E. A. Lowe, "Two Other Unknown Latin Liturgical Fragments on Mount Sinai," *Scriptorium* 19 (1965).
34. R. A. B. Mynors, *Cassiodori Senatoris Institutiones* (Oxford: Clarendon Press, 1937), 5–6.
35. See M. P. Brown, "The Tower of Babel: the architecture of the early western written vernaculars," in *Omnia Disce: Medieval Studies in Memory of Leonard Boyle, O.P.*, ed. A. J. Duggan, J. Greatrex and B. Bolton (Aldershot, UK: Ashgate, 2005), 109–128.
36. Jerome also advocated "tropology", in which the spiritual develops naturally out of the literal, and "typology," the practice of identifying Old Testament symbolic precursors or "types" for the New Testament, such as King David as a "type" for Christ; see Lampe, *Cambridge History of the Bible*, 90–91; de Hamel, *The Book*, ch. 1.
37. PL 29, 526c; Lampe, *Cambridge History of the Bible*, 83–4.
38. See Lampe, *Cambridge History of the Bible*, 83–84, 99–100, 108; deHamel, *The Book*, ch. 1.
39. For an overview of textual "families," see J. Wordsworth and H. J. White, *Nouum Testamentum ... secundum editionem Sancti Hieronymi: pars prior – Quattuor Euangelia* (Oxford: Clarendon Press, 1889–98) and B. Fischer, *Die lateinischen Evangelien bis zum 10.Jahrhundert*, 4 vols., Vetus Latina. Aus der Geschichte der lateinischen Bibel 13, 15, 17, 18 (Freiburg: Herder, 1988–91).
40. Codex Amiatinus is Florence, Biblioteca Medicea Laurenziana, MS. Amiatino 1. The Lindisfarne Gospels are London, British Library, Cotton MS. Nero D.iv.
41. de Hamel, *The Book*, ch. 1.
42. Lampe, *Cambridge History of the Bible*, 109.
43. Biblical quotations from *The Holy Bible: New Standard Revised Version*, (New York, 1995).
44. Bede, *Expositio Actuum Apostolorum*, CCSL 121 (1983), 3–99; Bede, *Commentary on the Acts of the Apostles*, trans. L. T. Martin, Cistercian Studies Series 117 (Kalamazoo: University of Western Michigan, 1989).
45. Bede, *Retractio*, CCSL 121 (1983), 110.
46. To give a modern example, in 1821 and following his conversion to Christianity, the Native American, Sequoya, assisted by his wife and child, devised the Cherokee script. This was done mainly by assigning syllabic values to the letters of the Roman alphabet and supplementing them with new symbols to form an eighty-five sign writing system.
47. Uppsala, Universitetsbibliotek, DG I; O. von Friesen and A. Grape, *Codex Argenteus Uppsaliensis jussu senatus universitatis phototypice editus* [facsimile], (Uppsala and Malmö: Almqvist and Wiksell, 1927). See Brown, *Writing and Scripts*, 43; L. Webster and M. P. Brown, eds., *The Transformation of the Roman World AD 400–900* (London: British Museum Press, 1997), 242–43.
48. These arcades are comparable, for example, to those in an early Byzantine purple gospelbook, the Codex Brixianus (see note 7, above, and cat. no. 70).
49. Bede, *Historia Ecclesiastica*; *Bedae Opera Historica*, ed. C. Plummer (Oxford: Heinemann, 1956); *Bede's Ecclesiastical History*, ed. B. Colgrave and R. A. B. Mynors (Oxford: Clarendon Press, 1969); *Ecclesiastical History of the English People*, ed. D. H. Farmer, transl. L. Sherley-Price, revd. R. E. Latham (London: Penguin, 1990). Gregory's guidelines for Christianization of pagan festivals and shrines were conveyed via his letter to Abbot Mellitus in 601, related by Bede, *Historia Ecclesiastica* I.30; see Bede, ed. Farmer, *Ecclesiastical History*, 92–93.
50. Bede, *Epistola ad Ecgberctum*; *Baedae Opera Historica*, ed. C. Plummer, (Oxford: Clarendon Press, 1896), 1:405–423; Bede, ed. Farmer, *Ecclesiastical History*, 337–351.

51. S. Connolly, *Bede. On Tobit and on the Canticle of Habbakkuk* (Dublin, Ireland and Portland, Oreg.: Four Courts Press, 1997), 24–25. On Caedmon, see Bede, *Historia Ecclesiastica* IV.24.
52. M. P. Brown, *"In the beginning was the Word": Books and Faith in the Age of Bede*, Jarrow Lecture Series (Jarrow, Tyne & Wear).
53. M. P. Brown, *The Lindisfarne Gospels: Society, Spirituality and the Scribe* (Lucerne, London and Toronto: Faksimile Verlag / British Library / Toronto University Press, 2003).
54. L. Webster and J. M. Backhouse, eds., *The Making of England: Anglo-Saxon Art and Culture AD 600–900* (London: British Museum, 1991), 71–74; M. Lapidge, ed., *Archbishop Theodore: Commemorative Studies on his Life and Influence* (Cambridge: Cambridge University Press, 1995).
55. The Old English Hexateuch is London, British Library, MS. Cotton Claudius B.iv: see C. R. Dodwell and P. Clemoes, *The Old English Illustrated Hexateuch*, Early English Manuscripts in Facsimile 18 (Copenhagen: Rosenkilde & Bagger, 1974); R. Barnhouse and B. Withers, eds, *The Old English Hexateuch: Aspects and Approaches* (Kalamazoo and Ann Arbor: University of Western Michigan, 2000). The Old English Genesis is Oxford, Bodleian Library, MS. Junius 11: see C. Karkov, *Intertextuality and Intervisuality: Narrative Strategies in the Junius 11 MS* (Cambridge: Cambridge University Press, 2006); B. J. Muir, *A digital facsimile of Oxford, Bodleian Library, MS Junius 11* [CD-ROM], Bodleian Digital Texts 1 (Oxford: Bodleian Library, 2004).
56. Brown, *Guide to Western Historical Scripts*, 32–33, 46–47, 116–119.
57. J. Nelson, *The Frankish World, 750–900* (London: Hambledon Press, 1996), 10.
58. On lections see M. Andrieu, *Les Ordines Romani du Haut Moyen Age*, vol. 2, *Les Textes*, Specilegium sacrum lovaniense 23 (Louvain: Peeters, 1948); A. Chavasse, *Les Lectionnaires Romains de la Messe*, Spicilegii Friburgensis, 'Subsidia' 22 (Fribourg-en-Suisse: Spicilegii Friburgensis, 1993); U. Lenker, *Die Westsächsische Evangelienversion und die Perikopenordnungen im angelsächsischen England*, Münchener Universitätsschriften, Texte und Untersuchungen zur Englischen Philologie 20 (Munich: Munich University Press, 1997); C. Farr, *The Book of Kells: Its Function and Audience* (London and Toronto: British Library / University of Toronto Press, 1997); Brown, *Lindisfarne Gospels*; E. Ó Carragáin, *Ritual and the Rood: Liturgical Images and the Old English Poems of the Dream of the Rood Tradition* (London and Toronto: British Library / University of Toronto, 2005).
59. Paris, Bibliothèque nationale de France, MS. lat. 1, fol. 3v: see R. McKitterick, "Essai sur les representations de l'écrit dans les manuscrits carolingiens," *Révue française d'histoire du livre*, nos 86–87 (1995): 37–64, at 50–51 and pl. 8.
60. P. McGurk, *Latin Gospel Books from AD 400 to AD 800*, Les Publications de Scriptorium 5 (Paris–Brussels, Anvers–Amsterdam: Scriptorium, 1961), 6–7.
61. See C. Nordenfalk, *Studies in the History of Book Illumination* (London: Pindar Press, 1992), 17.
62. The numbered sections are known as Ammonian sections after Ammonius of Alexandria, who is thought to have compiled them around 220 C.E., although his work may simply have inspired Eusebius to create his own divisions. Lampe, *Cambridge History of the Bible*, 115; P. McGurk, "The Canon Tables in the Book of Lindisfarne," *Journal of Theological Studies* 6 (1955): 192–8; McGurk, *Latin Gospel Books*, 12; P. McGurk, "The disposition of numbers in Latin Eusebian canon tables," in R. Gryson, ed., *Philologia Sacra* 1 (Freiburg: Herder, 1993): 242–58.
63. McGurk, *Latin Gospelbooks*, 7–8.
64. These also occur in the Durham Gospels (Durham Cathedral Library, MS. A.ii.17) and the Echternach Gospels (Paris, Bibliothèque nationale de France, MS. Lat. 9389). See C. D. Verey and others, *The Durham Gospels*, Early English Manuscripts in Facsimile 20 (Copenhagen: Rosenkilde & Bagger, 1980).
65. Lampe, *Cambridge History of the Bible*, 100.
66. Nordenfalk, *Studies in the History of Book Illumination*, 16.
67. Nordenfalk, *Studies in the History of Book Illumination*, 30 and 18; Brown, *Lindisfarne Gospels*, ch. 5.
68. Bede, *Historia Abbatum*, ed. C. Plummer (Oxford: Clarendon Press, 1896), 2:16; Bede, *Bedae Opera Historica*, ed. C. Plummer (Oxford: Heinemann, 1956), 1:379; PL 94, 725a and 91, 454c; Cassiodorus, *in Psalmos* 15:14, see PL 70, 109a,b. Lampe (*Cambridge History of the Bible*, 115) gives a useful bibliography for Cassiodorus and books from his library (some reached the Lateran and Ceolfrith obtained his copy of the Codex Grandior in Rome). See B. Fischer, "Codex Amiatinus und Cassiodor," *Biblische Zeitschrift*, N.F. 6 (Paderborn: F. Schöning, 1962), 57ff.
69. Lampe, *Cambridge History of the Bible*, 116–7. See especially the full discussion by Marsden, *Text of the Old Testament*, ch. 5; Brown, *Lindisfarne Gospels*; P. Meyvaert, "The Date of Bede's *In Ezram* and His Image of Ezra in the Codex Amiatinus," *Speculum* 80 (2005): 1087–1133.
70. For a recent appraisal of the relationship of the Codex Amiatinus to works by Cassiodorus, see P. Meyvaert, "Bede, Cassiodorus and the Codex Amiatinus," *Speculum* 71 (1996): 827–83 and "The Date of Bede's *In Ezram*." See also K. Corsano, "The First Quire of the Codex Amiatinus," *Scriptorium* 41 (1987), pt 1:3–34; G. Henderson, "Cassiodorus and Eadfrith Once Again," in *The Age of Migrating Ideas*, ed. M. Spearman and J. Higgitt (Edinburgh: National Museums of Scotland, 1993), 82–91; R. Marsden, "Job in his place: the Ezra miniature in the *Codex Amiatinus*," *Scriptorium* 49 (1995): 3–15; Marsden, *Text of the Old Testament*; C. Chazelle, "Christ and the Vision of God: The Biblical Diagrams of the Codex Amiatinus," in *The Mind's Eye: Art and Theological Argument in the Middle Ages*, ed. J. F. Hamburger and A.-M. Bouché (Princeton: Princeton University Press, 2006), 84–111. See also Corsano, "The First Quire of the Codex Amiatinus."
71. The Codex Amiatinus has, in the absence of fuller evidence, been taken as representative of the other two Ceolfrith Bibles. Bede simply says that Ceolfrith added the three locally produced pandects to the one he brought back from Rome.
72. See C. Roth, "Jewish Antecedents of Christian Art," *Journal of the Warburg and Courtauld Institutes* 16 (1953): 37. For a thorough discussion of the issue, see Meyvaert, "Bede, Cassiodorus and the Codex Amiatinus" and "The Date of Bede's *In Ezram*."
73. Brown, *Lindisfarne Gospels*, where the extension of the multivalent reading of this image to include the contemporary scribe—i.e. Bede and his brethren—was proposed; for further exploration of the Bedan identification, see Meyvaert, "The Date of Bede's *In Ezram*."
74. Alcuin's *Carmina* 69 quotes the couplet above Amiatinus's Ezra miniature as part of his description of a bible punctuated *per cola et commata* (see "Bible and book," p. 34) like the Ceolfrith pandects, which he may have seen. See Corsano, "The First Quire of the Codex Amiatinus," 3–4 and 20–22.
75. See P. McGurk, "The Oldest Manuscripts of the Latin Bible" in Gameson, *Early Medieval Bible*, 1–23; on the introduction of caroline minuscule see, for example, D. Ganz, *Corbie in the Carolingian Renaissance* (Sigmaringen: Thorbecke, 1990); R. McKitterick, *The Carolingians and the Written Word* (Cambridge: Cambridge University Press, 1989).

76. Lampe, *Cambridge History of the Bible*, 133–42; de Hamel, *The Book.*
77. "Vita sancti Caesarii," I, ch. 58, in B. Krusch, ed., *Passiones Vitaeque Sanctorum aevi Merovingici et antiquiorum aliquot*, MGH, Scriptorum rerum Merovingicarum 19 (Hannover: Hahn, 1896).
78. McKitterick, *Carolingians and the Written Word*, 30–31. G. Morin, ed., *S. Caesarii arelatensis episcopi. Regula sanctarum virginum aliaque opuscula ad sanctimoniales directa*, Florilegium Patristicum Fasc. 34 (Bonn: P. Hanstein, 1933), ch. 32, 12.
79. For the correspondence, see D. Whitelock, ed., *English Historical Documents* I, rev. ed. (London: Oxford University Press, 1979), 811–812, nos. 172–173. On the Vespasian Psalter and the Stockholm Codex Aureus, see J. J. G. Alexander, *Insular Manuscripts: 6th to the 9th Century* (London: Harvey Miller, 1978) and on the latter R. G. Gameson, *The Stockholm Codex Aureus*, Early English Manuscripts in Facsimile 28 (Copenhagen: Rosenkilde & Bagger, 2003); on the evidence for female literacy in an Insular milieu, see M. P. Brown, "Female book-ownership and production in Anglo-Saxon England: the Evidence of the Ninth-Century Prayerbooks," in *Lexis and Texts in Early English: Papers in Honour of Jane Roberts*, ed. C. Kay and L. Sylvester (Amsterdam: Brepols, 2001), 45–68.
80. See McKitterick, *Carolingians and the Written Word*, 22–26. For contextualization, see M. P. Brown, "Mercian Manuscripts? The 'Tiberius' Group and its Historical Context," in *Mercia: An Anglo-Saxon Kingdom in Europe*, ed. M. P. Brown and C. A. Farr (London: Leicester University, 2001; 2nd ed. 2005), 278–91; Brown, "Anglo-Saxon Manuscript Production"; and Brown, "Female book-ownership."
81. On St. Harlindis and St. Relindis, see L. D'Achéry and J. Mabillon, *Acta Sanctorum Ordinis Sancti Benedicti* (Paris: J. Billaine, 1668–1701), March III, 386.
82. Brown, "Female book-ownership."
83. S. Keynes and M. Lapidge, *Alfred the Great* (Harmondsworth, UK: Penguin, 1983).
84. Bede, *Expositio in Lucam*, ed. D. Hurst, CCSL 120 (Turnhout: Brepols, 1960), prol. 93–115; M. Stansbury, "Early Medieval Biblical Commentaries, Their Writers and Readers," in *Frümittelalterliche Studien, Herausgegeben von H. Keller und C. Meier*, ed. K. Hauck (Berlin and New York: Frümittelalterliche Studien, 1999), 50–82 at p. 72.
85. Scripture lends the scribal analogy to the Lord himself (see Jeremiah 31:33; Hebrews 10:16; Psalms 44/45:1–2).
86. Cassiodorus, *De Institutione Divinarum Litterarum*, ch. 30; see *Magni Aurelii Cassiodori Variarum Libri XII*, ed. A. Fridh, CCSL 96 (Turnhout: Brepols, 1973); PL 70, cols 1144–1145; D. Ayerst and A. S. T. Fisher, *Records of Christianity* (Oxford: Basil Blackwell, 1977), 14. See also J. O'Reilly, "The Library of Scripture: Views from the Vivarium and Wearmouth-Jarrow," in *New Offerings, Ancient Treasures: Essays in Medieval Art for George Henderson*, ed. P. Binski and W. G. Noel (Stroud: Alan Sutton, 2001); and Brown, *Lindisfarne Gospels*, ch. 5.
87. See O'Reilly, "Library of Scripture."
88. Brown, *Lindisfarne Gospels.*
89. I have spoken to a number of contemporary scribes on this matter, including some of the team currently working with Donald Jackson on a complete hand-produced bible for the Benedictine monastery of St. John's, Collegeville, Minnesota.
90. J. Mellors and A. Parsons, *Ethiopian Bookmaking* (London: New Cross Books, 2002) and J. Mellors and A. Parsons, *Scribes of South Gondar* (London: New Cross Books, 2002).
91. Brown, "*In the Beginning was the Word*"; Brown, *Lindisfarne Gospels.*
92. Brown, "*In the Beginning was the Word*"; Brown, *Lindisfarne Gospels*; and R. G. Gameson, *The Scribe Speaks? Colophons in Early English Manuscripts*, H. M. Chadwick Memorial Lectures 12 (Cambridge: University of Cambridge, Department of Anglo-Saxon, Norse and Celtic, 2001).
93. See M. Walsh and D. Ó Cróinín, eds., *Cummian's Letter De Controversia Paschale* (Toronto: Pontifical Institute, 1988), 15–18, 57–59. See O'Reilly, "Library of Scripture."
94. For the writings of Columbanus, see T. O'Fiaich, *Columbanus in His Own Words* (Dublin: Veritas Publications, 1974; repr. 1990).
95. People traveled during this period. Traditions in Britain and Ireland and in the Christian Orient hint at visits in both directions, and British and Irish liturgy and litanies include numerous references to practices and figures from the Near East. For discussion of the transmission of eastern influences to these western isles, see C. Plummer, *Irish Litanies*, Henry Bradshaw Society 67 (London: Henry Bradshaw Society, 1925), 54–75; N. Chadwick, *The Age of the Saints in the Early Celtic Church* (Oxford: Oxford University Press, 1961); A. S. Atiya, *History of Eastern Christianity* (South Bend, Ind.: Methuen, 1967), 55 onwards; Fr. G. Telepneff, *The Egyptian Desert in the Irish Bogs. The Byzantine Character of Early Celtic Monasticism* (Etna, CA: Center for Traditionalist Orthodox Studies, 1998), esp. 14–15. Telepneff and Atiya are inclined to overestimate the reliability and extent of the sources. A more measured discussion occurs in J. Wilkinson, *Jerusalem Pilgrims Before the Crusades* (Warminster, UK: Aris & Phillips, 1977). See also Brown, *Lindisfarne Gospels*, esp. 28–32; and Brown, *How Christianity Came to Britain and Ireland.*

    Bede relates that Benedict Biscop, founder of Wearmouth–Jarrow, went to Rome on a number of occasions, sometimes accompanied by Abbot Ceolfrith. In the late seventh century a Frankish bishop named Arculf was returning from pilgrimage to Judaea and northern Africa, when his ship was blown off course. Finding himself on the island of Iona, off western Scotland, he dictated his recollections to his host, Abbot Adomnán. The account was subsequently reworked by Bede to form *De locis sanctis*—one of the best early guidebooks to the holy places. Adomnán, *De locis sanctis*, ed. D. Meehan, *Scriptores Latini Hiberniae* 3 (Dublin: Dublin Institute of Advanced Studies, 1958).
96. Brown, *Lindisfarne Gospels.*
97. The Theodore Psalter is London, British Library, Add. MS. 19352. See E. Kitzinger, *The Place of Book Illumination in Byzantine Art* (Princeton: Princeton University Press, 1975); D. Buckton, ed., *Byzantium: Treasures of Byzantine Art and Culture* (London: British Museum, 1994); J. Lowden, *Early Christian and Byzantine Art* (London: Phaidon, 1997); L. Safran, ed., *Heaven on Earth: Art and the Church in Byzantium* (University Park: Pennsylvania State University Press, 1998).
98. W. J. Diebold, *Word and Image: A History of Early Medieval Art* (Boulder, Colo.: Westview Press, 2000), 100–101, 117–118.
99. F. Mütherich and J. Gaehde, *Carolingian Painting* (London: Chatto & Windus, 1976); R. Deshman, "The Exalted Servant: The Ruler Theology of the Prayerbook of Charles the Bald," *Viator* 11 (1980): 385–417; P. Dutton and H. Kessler, *The Poetry and Paintings of the First Bible of Charles the Bald* (Ann Arbor: University of Michigan Press, 1997).
100. For the First Bible of Charles the Bald, see note 59 above. The Lothar Gospels are Paris, Bibliothèque nationale de France, MS. Lat. 266.
101. London, British Library, Cotton MS. Tiberius A.ii: see J. M. Backhouse, D. H. Turner and L. Webster, eds., *The Golden Age of Anglo-Saxon Art* (London: British Museum, 1984), no. 3.
102. Now Lichfield Cathedral, MS. 1: see Alexander, *Insular Manuscripts*; Webster and Backhouse, *Making of England*; Brown, *Lindisfarne Gospels.*

103. A. Boeckler, *Deutsche Buchmalerie vorgotischer Zeit* (Königstein: Langewiesche, 1953); H. Mayr-Harting, *Ottonian Book Illumination: An Historical Study*, 2 vols. (London: Harvey Miller, 1991).
104. The Gospels of Otto III are Aachen, Domschatzkammer (s. n.); the Sacramentary of Henry II is Munich, Bayerische Staatsbibliothek, Clm 4456; the Hitda Gospels are Darmstadt, Hessische Landes- und Hochschulbibliothek, Hs. 1640.
105. Important treasure bindings include the Lindau Gospels (New York, Morgan Library & Museum, MSM 1) and the Codex Aureus of Charles the Bald (Munich, Bayerische Staatsbibliothek, Clm 14000).
106. R. Ó Floinn, *Irish Shrines and Reliquaries of the Middle Ages* (Dublin: National Museum of Ireland, 1994).
107. Formerly known as the Stonyhurst Gospel (London, British Library, Loan MS. 74). See T. J. Brown and others, ed., *The Stonyhurst Gospel of St John* (Oxford: Roxburghe Club, 1969); B. van Regemorter, *Binding Structures in the Middle Ages* (Brussels: Bibliotheca Wittockiana, 1992), transl. J. Greenfield (London: Maggs, 1992).
108. Cairo, Coptic Museum, MS. Lib. 6614; see Gabra, *Cairo*.
109. Perhaps also of relevance in this connection, in Ethiopia a short text known as the *Lefafa Sedq* (Bandlet of Righteousness) is still often carried on the person throughout life, read at your funeral and buried with you.
110. E. P Kelly, "The Lough Kinale Book Shrine: the Implications for the Manuscripts," in *The Book of Kells. Proceedings of a Conference at Trinity College Dublin, 6–9 September 1992*, ed. F. O'Mahony (Aldershot, UK: Scolar Press for Trinity College Library, 1994), 280–89.

Book as icon (pages 77–103)

1. Paris, Bibliothèque nationale de France, MS. nouv. acq. lat. 1203, ff. 126v–127r: translation Paul E. Dutton. See W. Koehler, *Die Hofschule Karls des Grossen* (Berlin: Deutscher Verlag für Kunstwissenschaft, 1958), 22–28; B. Brenk, "Schriftlichkeit und Bildlichkeit in der Hofschule Karls des Grossen," in *Testo e immagine nell'alto medioevo*, Settimane di studio del centro italiano di studi sull'alto medioevo 41 (Spoleto: CISAM, 1994), 2:631–82; B. Reudenbach, *Das Godescalc-Evangelistar: Ein Buch für die Reformpolitik Karls des Grossen* (Frankfurt am Main: Fischer Taschenbuch, 1998).
2. Tivoli, Cattedrale di S. Lorenzo: H. L. Kessler, "The *Acheropita* Triptych in Tivoli," *Festschrift Arturo C. Quintavalle* (forthcoming). See M. Büchsel, *Die Entstehung des Christusporträts* (Mainz: Philipp von Zabern, 2003), 146.
3. For example, John of Damascus *On the Divine Images*, Book II.14; trans. D. Anderson (Crestwood, N.Y.: St. Vladimir's Seminary Press, 1980), 16–17; *Opus caroli regis contra synodum (Libri Carolini)*, ed. A. Freeman, MGH, Concilia 2, suppl. 1 (Hannover: Hansche Buchhandlung, 1998), 126, 249.
4. *Hadrianum* 25 (56.11–14); see D. Appleby, "Instruction and Inspiration through Images in the Carolingian Period," in *Word, Image, Number: Communication in the Middle Ages*, ed. J. J. Contreni and S. Casciani (Florence: Sismel, 2002), 85–111.
5. Dublin, Trinity College, MS. 58: C. Farr, *The Book of Kells: Its Function and Audience* (London and Toronto: British Library / University of Toronto Press, 1997).
6. The identity of the figure is disputed; Farr, *Book of Kells*, 147–52.
7. See G. Cavallo, "Testo e immagine: Una frontiera ambigua," in *Testo e immagine nel alto medioevo*, Settimane di studi del centro italiano di studi sull'alto medioevo 41, 1:31–62.
8. Brescia, Biblioteca civica Queriniana.
9. Badia, Cava dei Terreni: F. D'Aiuto, G. Morello, A. M. Piazzoni, eds., *I vangeli dei popoli* (Vatican: Edizioni Rinnovamento nello Spirito Santo, 2000), 181–83.
10. Paris, Bibliothèque nationale de France, MS. lat. 9384; Yerevan, Archaeological Museum, Gospels 299; Milan, Duomo treasury: F. Steenbock, *Der kirchliche Prachteinband im frühen Mittelalter von Anfängen bis zum Beginn der Gotik* (Berlin: Deutscher Verlag für Kunstwissenschaft, 1965), 69–71, 77–78.
11. The Lorsch Gospels cover is in the Vatican, Musei Vaticani, Museo Sacro: Steenbock, *Der kirchliche Prachteinband*, 82–83. The relief of Justinian is in Paris, Musée du Louvre, inv. no. OA 9063: W. F. Volbach, *Elfenbeinarbeiten der spätantike und des frühen Mittelalters*, Kataloge vor- und frühgeschichtlicher Altertümer 7, 3rd ed. (Mainz: Philipp von Zabern, 1976), 47–48.
12. St. Gall, Stiftsbibliothek, MS. 53: Johannes Duft and Rudolf Schnyder, *Die Elfenbein-Einbände der Stiftsbibliothek St. Gallen* (Beuron: Beuroner Kunstverlag, 1984), 55–93.
13. Porphyry, *Publilii Optatiani Porphyrii Carmina*, ed. Johannes Polara (Turin: G. B. Paravia, 1973); U. Ernst, *Carmen Figuratum. Geschichte des Figurengedichts von den antiken Ursprüngen bis zum Ausgang des Mittelalters* (Cologne and Vienna: Weimer / Böhlau, 1991).
14. Stockholm, Kungliga Biblioteket, A.135: R. Gameson, ed., *Codex Aureus. An Eighth-Century Gospel Book (Stockholm, Kungliga Biblioteket, A.135)* (Copenhagen: Rosenkilde & Bagger, 2001).
15. S. Der Nersessian, "Une apologie des images du septième siècle," *Byzantion* 17 (1944–45): 58–87 (at p. 63); A. B. Schmidt, "Gab es einen armenischen Ikonoklasmus? Rekonstruktion eines Dokuments der Kaukasisch-Albanischen Theologiegeschichte," in *Das Frankfurter Konzil von 794. Kristallisationspunkt karolingischer Kultur* (Mainz: Gesellschaft für Mittelrheinische Kirchengeschichte, 1997), 947–64.
16. Carmen 1, ll.1–12, Porphyry, ed. Polara, 7; Ernst, *Carmen Figuratum*, 97.
17. Letter 22.32; *Select Letters of St Jerome*, trans. F. A. Wright (Cambridge, Mass. and London: Harvard University Press, 1980), 130–33, 364–65.
18. Letter 107.12; *Select Letters of St Jerome*, 364–65. Jerome criticized Rome itself in a similar way, and also decorated churches; see D. S. Wiesen, *St. Jerome as a Satirist: A Study in Christian Latin Thought and Letters* (Ithaca: Cornell University Press, 1964), 34–36.
19. *Opus caroli regis*, 509–10.
20. Florence, Biblioteca Medicea Laurenziana, MS. Amiatino 1; *La Bibbia Amiatina / The Codex Amiatinus, Complete Reproduction on CD-Rom of the Manuscript Firenze, Bibloteca Medicea Laurenziana, Amiatino 1* (Florence: Sismel, 2000).
21. Paris, Bibliothèque nationale de France, MS. lat. 9380; L. Nees, "Problems of Form and Function in Early Medieval Illustrated Bibles from Northwest Europe," in *Imaging the Early Medieval Bible*, ed. J. Williams (University Park: Pennsylvania State University Press, 1999), 125–31.
22. E. Dahlhaus-Berg, *Nova antiquitas et antiqua novitas. Typologische Exegese und isidorianisches Geschichtsbild bei Theodulf von Orléans* (Cologne and Vienna: Böhlau, 1975).
23. See C. de Hamel, *The Book: A History of the Bible* (London and New York: Phaidon, 2001), 54.
24. Vatican, Biblioteca Apostolica Vaticana, MS. lat. 3256E.
25. London, British Library, Royal MS. 1.D.vi.
26. Paris, Bibliothèque nationale de France, MS. lat. 9427: E. H. Zimmermann, *Vorkarolingische Miniaturen* (Berlin: Deutscher Verein für Kunstwissenschaft, 1916), 171–72.

27. P. Saenger, *Space between Words: The Origins of Silent Reading* (Stanford, Calif.: Stanford University Press, 1997).
28. H. Y. Gamble, *Books and Readers in the Early Church: A History of Early Christian Texts* (New Haven and London: Yale University Press, 1995), 74–78.
29. Munich, Bayerische Staatsbibliothek, MS. lat. 6224.
30. Paris, Bibliothèque nationale de France, MS. lat. 9389.
31. Bede *De templo*, Book II, 19.10.
32. See M. P. Brown, *The Lindisfarne Gospels: Society, Spirituality and the Scribe* (Lucerne, London and Toronto: Faksimile Verlag / British Library / Toronto University Press, 2003), 370–86 *et passim*.
33. J. F. Hamburger, *St John the Divine: The Deified Evangelist in Medieval Art and Theology* (Berkeley and Los Angeles: University of California Press, 2002), 9; M. Krasnodebska-D'Aughton, "Decoration of the *In principio* Initials in Early Insular Manuscripts: Christ as a Visible Image of the Invisible God," *Word and Image* 18 (2002): 105–21.
34. Wolfenbüttel, Herzog August Bibliothek, Cod. Guelf. 3.1.300 Aug. 2°, f. 284v: J. Leroy, *Les manuscrits syriaques à peintures conservés dans les bibliothèques d'Europe et d'Orient: contribution à l'étude de l'iconographie des églises de langue syriaque*, Bibliothèque archéologique et historique 77 (Paris: P. Geuthner, 1964), 1:117; J. Lowden, "The Beginnings of Biblical Illustration," in *Imaging the Early Medieval Bible*, ed. J. Williams (University Park: Pennsylvania State University Press), 9–59.
35. Washington, Dumbarton Oaks, inv. nos. 63.36.9, 63.36.10: E. Kitzinger, "A Pair of Silver Book Covers in the Sion Treasure," in *Gatherings in Honor of Dorothy E. Miner*, ed. U. E. McCracken, L. M. C. Randall, and R. H. Randall, Jr. (Baltimore: Walters Art Gallery, 1973), 3–17.
36. É. P. Kelly, "The Lough Kinale Book Shrine: The Implications for the Manuscripts," in *The Book of Kells. Proceedings of a Conference at Trinity College Dublin 6–9 September 1992*), ed. F. O'Mahony (Aldershot, UK: Scolar Press for Trinity College Library), 280–89.
37. New York, Morgan Library & Museum, MS. 585: J. Leroy, *Les manuscrits coptes et coptes-arabes illustrés*, Bibliothèque archéologique et historique 96 (Paris: P. Geuthner, 1974), 54–55.
38. Mount Sinai, Holy Monastery of St. Catherine: K. Weitzmann, *The Monastery of Saint Catherine at Mount Sinai: The Icons* (Princeton: Princeton University Press, 1976), 13–15.
39. Dublin, National Museum of Ireland, inv. no. R.4006. See Brown, *Lindisfarne Gospels*, 317–25 *et passim*.
40. New York, Morgan Library & Museum, MS. G. 67: Leroy, *Manuscrits coptes*, 60.
41. Vatican, Biblioteca Apostolica Vaticana, MS. Reg. gr. 1, f. 3v: P. Canart and S. Dufrenne, eds., *Die Bibel des Patricius Leo: Codex Reginensis Graecus I B* (Zurich: Belser, 1988).
42. London, British Library, Cotton MS. Nero, D.iv: Brown, *Lindisfarne Gospels*, 312–31 *et passim*.
43. Paris, Bibliothèque nationale de France, MS. lat. 12048, f. 143v: L. Nees, "On the Image of Christ Crucified in Early Medieval Art," in *Il Volto Santo in Europa*, ed. M. C. Ferrari and A. Meyer (Lucca: Istituto storico Lucchese, 2005), 345–85.
44. Durham, Cathedral Library, Cod. A.II.17, f. 38[3]v: J. J. G. Alexander, *Insular Manuscripts: 6th to the 9th Century* (London: Harvey Miller, 1978), 40–42; Nees, "Image of Christ Crucified," 350–51.
45. Würzburg, Universitätsbibliothek, Cod. M. p.th. f. 69, f. 7v: Nees, "Image of Christ Crucified," 351.
46. Paris, Bibliothèque nationale de France, MS. lat. 257, f. 12v; M.-C. Sepière, *L'image d'un Dieu souffrant: Aux origines du crucifix* (Paris: Éditions du Cerf, 1994), 151 *et passim*.
47. Munich, Bayerische Staatsbibliothek, MS. Clm. 13601: A. S. Cohen, *The Uta Codex: Art, Philosophy and Reform in Eleventh-Century Germany* (University Park: Pennsylvania State University Press, 2000); J. F. Hamburger, "Body vs. Book: The Trope of Visibility in Images of Christian-Jewish Polemic," in *Ästhetik des Unsichtbaren: Bildtheorie und Bildgebrauch in der Vormoderne*, ed. David Ganz and Thomas Lentes (Berlin; Dietrich Reimer, 2004), 112–25.
48. New York, Morgan Library & Museum, MS. 1: Steenbock; *Kirchliche Prachteinband*, 92–96.
49. *Bibbia Amiatina / The Codex Amiatinus*; C. Chazelle, "Christ and the Vision of God: The Biblical Diagrams of the Codex Amiatinus," in *The Mind's Eye: Art and Theological Argument in the Middle Ages*, ed. J. F. Hamburger and A.-M. Bouché (Princeton: Princeton University Press, 2006), 84–111.
50. D. de Bruyne, *Préfaces de la Bible Latine* (Namur: Auguste Godenne, 1920), 8–9.
51. See H. L. Kessler, "Images of Christ and Communication with God," in *Communicare e significare nell'alto medioevo*, Settimane de studio della fondazione centro italiano di studi sull'alto medioevo 52 (Spoleto: CISAM, 2005): 1099–1136.
52. Messina, Biblioteca Regionale Universitaria, Fondo vecchio 18, f. 1v: A. Iacobini and L. Perria, *Il Vangelo di Dionisio* (Rome: Àrgos, 1998).
53. H. L. Kessler, "Through the Temple Veil: The Holy Image in Judaism and Christianity," *Kairos: Zeitschrift für Religionswissenschaft und Theologie* 32/33 (1990/91): 53–77; Hamburger, "Body vs. Book."
54. I owe this information to Dr. Marilyn Heldman. See P. A. Underwood, "The Fountain of Life in Manuscripts of the Gospels," *Dumbarton Oaks Papers* 5 (1950): 43–138.
55. Valenciennes, Bibliothèque municipale, MS. 99, f. 2r.
56. Cohen, *Uta Codex*, 77–96.
57. London, British Library, Additional MS. 5111; Lowden, "Beginnings of Bible Illustration," 24–26.
58. Florence, Biblioteca Medicea Laurenziana, MS. Plut. I.56.
59. Paris, Bibliothèque nationale de France, MS. Syr. 341: R. Sörries, *Die Syrische Bibel von Paris* (Wiesbaden: Dr. Ludwig Reichert, 1991); Lowden, "Beginnings of Bible Illustration," 34–37.
60. London, British Library, MS. Add. 10546, f. 25v: H. L. Kessler, *The Illustrated Bibles from Tours* (Princeton: Princeton University Press, 1977), 59–68.
61. A. St. Clair, "A New Moses: Typological Iconography in the Moutier-Grandval Bible Illustrations of Exodus," *Gesta* 26 (1987): 19–28.
62. Copenhagen, Kongelige Bibliotek, Cod. Haun., GKS 6, f. 83v: H. Belting and G. Cavallo, *Die Bibel des Niketas: Ein Werk der höfischen Buchkunst in Byzanz und sein antikes Vorbild* (Wiesbaden: Dr. Ludwig Reichert, 1979); J. Lowden, *Illuminated Prophet Books: A Study of Byzantine Manuscripts of the Major and Minor Prophets* (University Park and London: Pennsylvania State University Press, 1988), 14–22 and 112–14.
63. Florence, Biblioteca Medicea Laurenziana, Cod. Plut. 5.9, f. 128v.
64. See I. Marchesin, *L'image organum: La représentation de la musique dans les psautiers médiévaux 800–1200* (Turnhout: Brepols, 2000).
65. Moscow, State Historical Museum, Cod. 129, f. 1v.
66. Munich, Bayerische Staatsbibliothek, Cod. lat. 14345, f. 7v.
67. Rossano, Museo dell'Arcivescovada, f. 5r; G. Cavallo, J. Gribomont and W. Loerke, eds., *Codex Purpureus Rossanensis* (Rome and Graz: Salerno Editrice / Akademische Druck u. Verlaganstalt, 1987); Lowden, "Beginnings of Bible Illustration," 18–21.

68. The precise date of this interpolated portrait is debated; see Lowden, "Beginnings of Biblical Illustration," 20–21.
69. Washington, D.C., Freer Gallery of Art, Smithsonian Institution, F1906.297–98: see H. Wenzel, "Die Schrift und das Heilige," in *Die Verschriftlichung der Welt* (Milan: Skira, 2000), 15–57.
70. G. Galavaris, *The Illustrations of the Prefaces in Byzantine Gospels* (Vienna: Österreichischen Akademie der Wissenschaften, 1979); R. Nelson, *The Iconography of Preface and Miniature in the Byzantine Gospel Book* (New York: New York University Press, 1980).
71. A.-O. Poilpré, *Maiestas Domini: Une image de l'Église en Occident Ve–IXe siècle* (Paris: Éditions du Cerf, 2005).
72. Brown, *Lindisfarne Gospels*, 349.
73. Alcuin, *Commentarium in Joannis evangelium* (PL, 100, cols. 741–44).
74. Dublin, Trinity College Library, MS. 52, ff. 32v and 90r: F. Mütherich, "Der Adler mit dem Fisch," in *Zum Problem der Deutung frühmittelalterlicher Bildinhalte*, ed. H. Roth (Sigmaringen: J. Thorbecke, 1986), 317–40.
75. H. L. Kessler, "'Facies bibliothecae revelata': Carolingian Art as Spiritual Seeing," in *Testo e immagine*, 2:533–94.
76. *Adversus Elipandum*, Book I, section 99; ed. B. Löfstedt, CCCM 59 (Turnhout: Brepols, 1984), 76.
77. K. Weitzmann and M. Bernabò, *The Byzantine Octateuchs* (Princeton: Princeton University Press, 1999).
78. Paris, Musée du Louvre, inv. nos. MR 370, 371; K. Holter, *Der goldene Psalter "Dagulf-Psalter"* (Graz: Akademische Druck u. Verlaganstalt, 1980).
79. The First Bible of Charles the Bald is Paris, Bibliothèque nationale de France, MS. lat. 1. The San Paolo Bible is in Rome, Monastero di San Paolo. See Kessler, *Bibles from Tours*, 84–95.
80. See M. P. Brown, *"In the Beginning was the Word": Books and Faith in the Age of Bede*, Jarrow Lecture Series (Jarrow, Tyne & Wear, 2000); P. Meyvaert, "The Date of Bede's *In Ezram* and His Image of Ezra in the Codex Amiatinus," *Speculum* 80 (2005): 1087–1133. Meyvaert connects the portrait to Bede himself.
81. See L. Nees, "The Colophon Drawing in the Book of Mulling: A Supposed Irish Monastery Plan and the Tradition of Terminal Illustration in Early Medieval Manuscripts," *Cambridge Medieval Celtic Studies* 5 (1983): 67–91.
82. Bremen, Universitätsbibliothek, MSB 21, f. 124v. See C. Nordenfalk, *Codex Caesareus Upsaliensis: An Echternach Gospel-Book of the Eleventh Century* (Stockholm: Alqvist & Wiksell, 1971).
83. Paris, Bibliothèque nationale de France, MS. lat. nouv. acq. 2334: D. Verkerk, *Early Medieval Bible Illumination and the Ashburnham Pentateuch* (Cambridge: Cambridge University Press, 2004).
84. B. Narkiss, "Towards a Further Study of the Ashburnham Pentateuch (Pentateuque de Tours)", *Cahiers archéologiques* 19 (1969): 45–59.
85. London, British Library, MS. Cotton Otho B vi: K. Weitzmann and H. L. Kessler, *The Cotton Genesis*, Illustrations in the Manuscripts of the Septuagint 1 (Princeton: Princeton University Press, 1986); Lowden, "Beginnings of Bible Illustration," 13–16.
86. Weitzmann, *Monastery of Saint Catherine: Icons*, 31–32, 69–71, 73–76.
87. John of Damascus, *On the Divine Images*, Book I.5 (PG 94, cols. 1236); trans. Anderson, 16.
88. G. D. Mansi, *Sacrorum conciliorum nova et amplissima collectio* (repr. Graz: Akademische Druck u. Verlagsanstalt, 1960–61), vol. 13, cols. 373–80.
89. Mt. Athos, Holy Monastery of Pantokrator, MS. 61, f. 165r: K. Corrigan, *Visual Polemics in the Ninth-Century Byzantine Psalters* (Cambridge: Cambridge University Press, 1992), 33–34.
90. Stuttgart, Württembergische Landesbibliothek, Bibl. f. 23, f. 116v: *Der Stuttgarter Bilderpsalter: Bibl. fol. 23 Württembergische Landesbibliothek Stuttgart* (Stuttgart: E. Schreiber Graphische Kunstantstalten, 1968).
91. Utrecht, Rijksuniversiteit, MS. 32: C. Chazelle, *The Crucified God in the Carolingian Era: Theology and Art of Christ's Passion* (Cambridge: Cambridge University Press, 2001).
92. Paris, Bibliothèque nationale de France, MS. lat. 8850; W. Koehler, *Die Hofschule Karls des Grossen*, 2:70–82.
93. Berlin, Staatliche Museen-Preussischer Kulturbesitz, inv. no. 8505: W. J. Diebold, "'Except I shall see … I will not believe' (John 20:25): Typology, Theology, and Historiography in an Ottonian Ivory Diptych," in *Images, Objects and The Word: Art in the Service of the Liturgy*, ed. C. Hourihane (Princeton: Princeton University Press, 2003), 257–73; Hamburger, "Body vs. Book", 117–18.
94. Cavallo, Gribomont and Loerke, *Codex Purpureus Rossanensis*.
95. Yerevan, Matenadaran, MS. 2734; T. F. Mathews, "The Early Armenian Iconographic Program of the Ējmiacin Gospel (Erevan, Matenadaran MS. 2374, *olim* 229)," in *East of Byzantium: Syria and Armenia in the Formative Period*, ed. N. G. Garsoïan, T. F. Mathews, and R. W. Thomson (Washington, D.C.: Dumbarton Oaks, 1980), 201–203; Lowden, "Beginnings of Bible Illustration," 37–40.
96. Mathews, "The Early Armenian Iconographic Program," 199–215.
97. H. Schreckenberg and K. Schubert, *Jewish Historiography and Iconography in Early and Medieval Christianity* (Assen and Maastricht and Minneapolis: Van Gorcum / Fortress Press, 1992), 241–43.
98. Oxford, Bodleian Library, Junius MS. 11: C. E. Karkov, *Text and Picture in Anglo-Saxon England: Narrative Strategies in the Junius 11 Manuscript*, Cambridge Studies in Anglo-Saxon England 31 (Cambridge: Cambridge University Press, 2001).
99. J. Lowden, "The Royal/Imperial Book and the Image or Self-Image of the Medieval Ruler," in *Kings and Kingship in Medieval Europe*, ed. A. J. Duggan (London: King's College Centre for Late Antique and Medieval Studies, 1993), 213–40.
100. Canart and Dufrenne, *Bibel des Patricius Leo*, 20–22; T. F. Mathews, "The Epigrams of Leo Sacellarios and an Exegetical Approach to the Miniatures of Vat. Reg. gr. 1," *Orientalia Christiana Periodica* 43 (1977), 126–27.
101. K. van der Horst, W. Noel and W. C. M. Wüstefeld, eds., *The Utrecht Psalter in Medieval Art: Picturing the Psalms of David* (Westrenen: HES Publishers, 1996).
102. Leiden, Bibliotheek der Rijksuniversiteit, MS. Perizoni 17: S. Wittekind, "Die Makkabäer als Vorblid des geistlichen Kampfes: Eine kunsthistorische Deutung des Leidener Makkabäer-Codex Perizoni 17," *Frühmittelalterliche Studien*, 37 (2003): 47–71.
103. Canart and Dufrenne, *Bibel des Patricius Leo*; trans. T. Matthews, "Epigrams," 107. See A. Arnulf, *Versus ad picturas: Studien zur Titulusdichtung als Quellengattung der Kunstgeschichte von der Antike bis zum Hochmittelalter* (Berlin: Deutscher Kunstverlag, 1997), 322–24.
104. Canart and Dufrenne, *Bibel des Patricius Leo*, 26–28; trans. T. Mathews, "Epigrams," 107.
105. See C. Little, "A New Ivory of the Court School of Charlemagne," in *Studien zur mittelalterlichen Kunst 800–1250* (Munich: Prestel, 1985), 11–28.
106. Paris, Bibliothèque nationale de France, Cod. lat. 266, f. 2v; Nancy, Cathédrale.
107. Kessler, *Illustrated Bibles from Tours*, 45–47.
108. P. E. Dutton and H. L. Kessler, *The Poetry and Paintings of the First Bible of Charles the Bald* (Ann Arbor: University of Michigan Press, 1997).

109. P. E. Dutton and É. Jeauneau, "The Verses of the 'Codex Aureus' of Saint-Emmeram," *Studi Medievali*, third series, 24 (1983): 75–120; *Iohannis Scotti Eriugenae Carminae*, ed. M. W. Herrin (Dublin: School of Celtic Studies of the Dublin Institute for Advanced Studies, 1993), 128–33.
110. Paris, Bibliothèque nationale de France, MS. lat. 817, f. 13r: H. Mayr-Harting, *Ottonian Book Illumination: An Historical Study* (London: Harvey Miller, 1991), vol. 2, 117–23.
111. See, for example, Peter Damian, Sermon 63.5; *Sancti Petri Damiani Sermones*, ed. J. Lucchesi, CCCM 57 (Turnhout: Brepols, 1983), 365.
112. PL, 78, col. 940.
113. PL, 115, col. 677.
114. Tournai, Cathédrale Notre-Dame, treasury; Steenbock, *Kirchliche Prachteinband*, 36–38.
115. St. Petersburg, National Library of Russia, MS. Firk. Hebr. II B 17; B. Narkiss, *Hebrew Illuminated Manuscripts* (New York: Leon Amiel, 1969), 42–43; Y. Levy, "Ezekiel's Plan in an Early Karaite Bible, *Jewish Art* 19–20 (1993/94): 68–85.
116. See Z. Weiss, *The Sepphoris Synagogue: Deciphering an Ancient Message through Its Archaeological and Socio-Historical Contexts* (Jerusalem: Hebrew University of Jerusalem, 2005), 87.
117. Der Nersessian, "Une apologie," 65.
118. O. K. Werckmeister, *Der Deckel des Codex Aureus von St. Emmeram* (Baden-Baden and Strasbourg: P.H. Heitz, 1963), 81.
119. Translation by Paul E. Dutton.

Bibliography

The following list includes both works cited in the endnotes and others of particular relevance.

Adams, J., F., 1957. *Seventh Annual Report to the Fellows of the Pierpont Morgan Library*. New York.

Addai [Thaddeus], 1981. *The Teaching of Addai*, trans. G. Howard, Texts and Translations 16; Early Christian Literature Series 4. Ann Arbor, Mich.: Scholars Press.

Adomnán, 1958. *De locis sanctis*, ed. D. Meehan, *Scriptores Latini Hiberniae* 3. Dublin: Dublin Institute of Advanced Studies.

Aland, B., 1989. "Die Rezeption des neutestamentlichen Textes in den ersten Jahrhunderten," in *The New Testament in Early Christianity*, ed. J.-M. Severin, 55–70. Leuven: Leuven University Press.

Aland, K., 1976. *Repertorium der griechischen christlichen Papyri*, vol. 1, *Biblische Papyri: Altes Testament, Neues Testament, Varia, Apokryphen*. Berlin and New York: Walter de Gruyter.

—, 1994. *Kurzgefasste liste der griechischen Handschriften des Neuen Testaments*. Berlin and New York: Walter de Gruyter.

Aland, K. and B. Aland, 1987. *The Text of the New Testament*. Grand Rapids: Eerdmanns. [2nd ed., 1989]

Alexander, J. J. G., 1978. *Insular Manuscripts: 6th to the 9th Century*. London: Harvey Miller.

—, 1992. *Medieval Illuminators and Their Methods of Work*. New Haven: Yale University Press.

Alexanian, J. M., 1990–91. "The Text of the Oldest Armenian Gospel Manuscript in America: A Reappraisal of Walters Art Gallery MS 537," *Journal of the Society for Armenian Studies* 5:55–64.

Alexidze, Z., and others, 2005. *Catalogue of Georgian Manuscripts Discovered in 1975 at Saint Catherine's Monastery on Mount Sinai*. Athens: Greek Ministry of Culture and the Mount Sinai Foundation.

Altbauer, M., 1971. *Psalterium Sinaiticum: An 11th Century Glagolitic Manuscript from St. Catherine's Monastery Mt. Sinai*. Skopje: Goce Delcer.

—, 1978. *Psalterium latinum hierosolymitanum. Eine frühmittelalterliche lateinische Handschrift Sin. Ms. No.5* [partial facsimile]. Vienna: Böhlau. [Orig. pub. Jerusalem: Masada Press, 1977]

Amiranashvili, Sh., 1966. *Gruzinskai'a'miniati'u'ra* (Pami'a'tniki drevnego iskusstva). Moscow: Iskusstvo.

Amtower, L., 1993. "Some codicological considerations in the interpretation of the Junius poems," *English Language Notes* 30:4–10.

Ancient Manuscripts in the British Museum, 1881–84. [E. M. Thompson and G. F. Warner], *Catalogue of Ancient Manuscripts in the British Museum*, Part 1: *Greek*; Part 2: *Latin*. London: British Museum.

Andrieu, M., 1948. *Les Ordines Romani du Haut Moyen Age*, vol. 2, *Les Textes*. Spicilegium sacrum lovaniense 23. Louvain: Peeters.

Appleby, D., 2002. "Instruction and Inspiration through Images in the Carolingian Period," in *Word, Image, Number: Communication in the Middle Ages*, ed. J. J. Contreni and S. Casciani, 85–111. Florence: Sismel.

Arnulf, A., 1997. *Versus ad picturas: Studien zur Titulusdichtung als Quellengattung der Kunstgeschichte von der Antike bis zum Hochmittelalter*. Berlin: Deutscher Kunstverlag.

Atiya, A. S., 1955. *The Arabic Manuscripts of Mount Sinai. A Hand List of Arabic Documents and Scrolls Microfilmed at the Library of the Monastery of St. Catherine Mount Sinai in 1954*. Baltimore: Johns Hopkins Press.

—, 1967. *History of Eastern Christianity*. South Bend, Ind.: Methuen.

—, 1970. *Catalogue raisonné of the Mount Sinai Arabic Manuscripts*. Alexandria: Galal Hazzi and Co. Al Maaref Establishment.

Avrin, L., 1991. *Scribes, Script and Books*. London and Chicago: British Library / Chicago University Press.

Ayerst, D. and A. S. T. Fisher, 1977. *Records of Christianity*. Oxford: Basil Blackwell.

Ayuso Marazuela, T., 1953. *La Vetus Latina Hispana*, vol. 1, *Prolegómenos*. Madrid: C.S.I.C.

Backhouse, J. M., D. H. Turner and L. Webster, eds., 1984. *The Golden Age of Anglo-Saxon Art, 966–1066*. London: British Museum.

Badawry, A., 1978. *Coptic Art and Archaeology*. Cambridge, Mass.: MIT Press.

Bagnall, R. S., 1993. *Egypt in Late Antiquity*. Princeton, N. J.: Princeton University Press.

Bailey, R., 1979. *The Durham Cassiodorus*, Jarrow Lecture Series. Jarrow, Tyne & Wear.

Balicka-Witakowska, E., 1997. *La Crucifixion sans crucifié dans l'art éthiopien: recherches sur la survie de l'iconographie chrétienne de l'Antiquité tardive*, Bibliotheca nubica et aethiopica 4. Warsaw: Zaś Pan.

Barnhouse, R. and B. Withers, eds., 2000. *The Old English Hexateuch: Aspects and Approaches*. Kalamazoo and Ann Arbor: University of Western Michigan.

Barthélemy, D. and J. T. Milik, 1955. *Discoveries in the Judean Desert*, vol. 1, *Qumran Cave I*. Oxford: Oxford University Press.

Barton, J., 1997. *Holy Writings, Sacred Text: The Canon in Early Christianity*. Louisville, Ky: Westminster / John Knox Press. [Published in the UK as *The Spirit and the Letter: Studies in the Biblical Canon*. London: Society for Promoting Christian Knowledge.]

Bately, J., M. P. Brown and J. Roberts, eds., 1993. *A Palaeographer's View: Selected Papers of Julian Brown*. London: Harvey Miller.

Baynes, C. A., 1933. *A Coptic Gnostic Treatise contained in the Codex Brucianus*. Cambridge: Cambridge University Press.

Beatus of Liébana, 1984. *Adversus Elipandum*, ed. B. Löfstedt, Corpus Christianorum Continuatio Mediaevalis 59. Turnhout: Brepols.

Beckwith, R. T., 1985. *The Old Testament Canon of the New Testament Church*. Grand Rapids, Mich.: Eerdmans.

Bede, 1946. *Historia Abbatum*, ed. C. Plummer, 2 vols. 2d ed. Oxford: Clarendon Press.

—, 1956. *Bedae Opera Historica*, ed. C. Plummer. Oxford: Heinemann.

—, 1960. *Expositio in Lucam*, ed. D. Hurst, Corpus Christianorum Series Latina 120. Turnhout: Brepols.

—, 1969. *Bede's Ecclesiastical History*, ed. B. Colgrave and R. A. B. Mynors. Oxford: Clarendon Press.

—, 1989. *Commentary on the Acts of the Apostles*, trans. L. T. Martin, Cistercian Studies Series 117. Kalamazoo: University of Western Michigan.

—, 1990. *Ecclesiastical History of the English People*, ed. D. H. Farmer, trans. L. Sherley-Price, revd. R. E. Latham. London: Penguin.

Beit-Arié, M., 1982. "A Lost Leaf from the Aleppo Codex Recovered," *Tarbiz* 51:171–74. [Hebrew]

—, C. Sirat, and M. Glatzer, 1997. *Codices hebraicis litteris exarati quo tempore scripti fuerint exhibentes* 1. Monumenta Palaeographica Medii Aevi, Series Hebraica. Turnhout: Brepols.

Bell, H. I., 1949. "The Gospel Fragments P. Egerton 2," *Harvard Theological Review* 42:53–63.

—, and T. C. Skeat, 1935. *Fragments of an Unknown Gospel and Other Early Christian Papyri*. London: British Museum.

Belting, H. and G. Cavallo, 1979. *Die Bibel des Niketas: Ein Werk der höfischen Buchkunst in Byzanz und sein antikes Vorbild*. Wiesbaden: Dr. Ludwig Reichert.

Benesevitch, V. N., 1911–17. *Catalogus codicum manuscriptorum graecorum, qui in monasterio Sanctae Catherinae in monte Sina asservantur*, 3 vols. Hildesheim: Georg Olms.

—, 1912. *Monumenta Sinaitica*. St. Petersburg.

—, 1937. "Les Manuscrits Grecs du Mont Sinaï et le Monde Savant de l'Europe depuis le XVIIe siècle jusq'à 1927," *Texte und Forschungen zur Byzantinisch-Neugriechischen Philologie* 21.1–114.

Bergman, R. P., 1980. *The Salerno ivories: ars sacra from medieval Amalfi*. Cambridge, Mass., and London: Harvard University Press.

Bibbia Amiatina, 2000. *La Bibbia Amiatina / The Codex Amiatinus, Complete Reproduction on CD-Rom of the Manuscript Firenze, Bibloteca Medicea Laurenziana, Amiatino 1*. Florence: Sismel.

Bischoff, B., 1957. "Die Kölner Nonnenhandschriften und das Skriptorium von Chelles," in *Karolingische und ottonische Kunst. Werden, Wesen, Wirkung. VI. internationaler Kongress für Frühmittelalterforschung, 1954*, 395–411. Wiesbaden: F. Steiner. [Reissued in expanded form in Bischoff, 1966–81, 1:16–34.]

—, 1966–81. *Mittelalterliche Studien. Ausgewählte Aufsätze zur Schriftkunde und Literaturgeschichte*, 3 vols. Stuttgart: Hiersemann.

—, 1979. *Paläographie des römischen Altertums und des abendlandischen Mittelalters.* Berlin: Schmidt. [English ed. and trans. by D. Ganz and D. Ó Cróinín, *Latin Paleaography*. Cambridge: Cambridge University Press, 1989]

—, and V. Brown, 1985. "Addenda to Codices Latini Antiquiores," *Mediaeval Studies* 47:317–66.

Bishop, T. A. M., 1968. "An Early Example of Insular-Caroline," *Transactions of the Cambridge Bibliographical Society* 4:396–400.

—, 1971. *English Caroline Minuscule*. Oxford Palaeographical Handbooks. Oxford: Clarendon Press.

Blanchard, A., ed., 1989. *Les debuts du codex*. Brepols: Turnhout.

Blanchard, M. J., 1995. "Moses of Nisibis (fl. 906–943) and the Library of Deir Suriani," in *Studies in the Christian East in Memory of Mirrit Boutros Ghali*, ed. L. S. B. MacCoull, Publications of the Society for Coptic Archaeology (North America) 1:13–24. Washington, D.C.

—, 2003. "Saint Ephrem's Coptic Friend, Apa Bishoi," *The Harp: A Review of Syriac and Oriental Ecumenical Studies* 16:43–55.

—, and R. D. Young, 1998. *A Treatise on God Written in Armenian by Eznik of Kołb (floruit c.430–c.450): An English Translation, with Introduction and Notes*, Eastern Christian Texts in Translation 2. Louvain: Peeters.

Blanck, H., 1992. *Das Buch in der Antike*. Munich: Beck.

Blau, L., 1902. *Studien zum althebraischen Buchwesen*. Strasbourg: E. K. J. Trubner.

Blum, P., 1976. "The cryptic creation cycle in MS Junius XI," *Gesta* 15:211–26.

Boak, A. E. R., 1959. "The Building of the University of Michigan Papyrus Collection," *Michigan Alumnus Quarterly Review* 66, no.10 (Autumn): 35–42.

Bodley, 2002. *Sir Thomas Bodley and his Library: An Exhibition to Mark the Quatercentenary of the Bodleian*. Oxford: Bodleian Library, University of Oxford.

Boccklcr, A., 1953. *Deutsche Buchmalerie vorgotischer Zeit*. Königstein: Langewiesche.

Boyd, S. A., and M. M. Mango, eds., 1992. *Ecclesiastical Silver Plate in Sixth-Century Byzantium*, Papers of the Symposium Held May 16–18 at the Walters Art Gallery, Baltimore and Dumbarton Oaks. Washington, D.C.: Dumbarton Oaks Research Library and Collection.

Boyle, L., 1984. *Medieval Latin Palaeography: A Bibliographical Introduction*. Toronto: Pontifical Institute of Mediaeval Studies.

Brakke, D., c1995. *Athanasius and Asceticism*. Baltimore and London: The Johns Hopkins University Press.

Brenk, B. 1994. "Schriftlichkeit und Bildlichkeit in der Hofschule Karls des Grossen," in *Testo e immagine nell'alto medioevo*, Settimane di studio del centro italiano di studi sull'alto medioevo 41, 2:631–82. Spoleto: CISAM.

Brief Survey . . . , 1885. *Kratkiy obzor sobraniya rykopisey, prinadlejashego pre-osvyashennomu episkopu Porfiriyu, a nine hranyashegosia v Imperatorskoy Publichnoy biblioteke* [The Brief Survey of the Manuscript Collection [that] belonged to Right Reverend Bishop Porphyry and Is Now Kept in the Imperial Public Library]. St. Petersburg.

Brock, S., 1999. *From Ephrem to Romanos: Interactions between Syriac and Greek in Late Antiquity*, Variorum Collected Studies Series, CS664. Aldershot, UK: Ashgate.

—, 2004. "A Neglected Witness to the East Syriac New Testament Commentary Tradition: Sinai, Arabic MS 151," in *Studies on the Christian Arabic Heritage in Honour of Father Prof. Dr. Samir Khalil Samir S.J. at the Occasion of his Sixty-Fifth Birthday*, ed. R. Ebied and H. Teule, Eastern Christian Studies 5, 205–215. Louvain: Peeters.

—, 2004a. "Without Mushē of Nisibis, Where would we be? Some Reflections on the Transmission of Syriac Literature," *Journal of Eastern Christian Studies* 56:15–24.

Broderick, H., 1983. "Observations on the method of illustration in MS. Junius 11 and the relationship of the drawings to the text," *Scriptorium* 37:161–77.

Brosset, M. F, 1849–51. *Rapports sur un voyage archéologique dans la Géorgie et dans L'Arménie executé en1847–1848*. St. Petersburg.

Brown, M. P., 1990. *A Guide to Western Historical Scripts from Antiquity to 1600*. London and Toronto: British Library / Toronto University Press. [Rev. eds., 1994; 1999.]

—, 1998. *The British Library Guide to Writing and Scripts*. London and Toronto: British Library / Toronto University Press.

—, 1998a. "Embodying Exegesis: Depictions of the Evangelists in Insular Manuscripts," in *Le Isole Britanniche e Roma in Età Romanobarbarica*, ed. A. M. Luiselli Fadda and E. Ó Carragáin, 109–128. Rome: Herder.

—, 2000. *"In the Beginning was the Word": Books and Faith in the Age of Bede*, Jarrow Lecture Series. Jarrow, Tyne & Wear.

—, 2001. "Anglo-Saxon Manuscript Production: Issues of Making and Using," in *Anglo-Saxon Literary Culture*, ed. P. Pulsiano and E. Traherne. Oxford: Oxford University Press.

—, 2001a. "Female book-ownership and production in Anglo-Saxon England: the Evidence of the Ninth-Century Prayerbooks," in *Lexis and Texts in Early English: Papers in Honour of Jane Roberts*, ed. C. Kay and L. Sylvester, 45–68. Amsterdam: Brepols.

—, 2001b. "Mercian Manuscripts? The 'Tiberius' Group and its Historical Context," in *Mercia: An Anglo-Saxon Kingdom in Europe*, ed. M. P. Brown and C. A. Farr, 278–91. London: Leicester University. [2nd ed. 2005.]

—, 2003. *The Lindisfarne Gospels: Society, Spirituality and the Scribe*. Lucerne, London, and Toronto: Faksimile Verlag / British Library / Toronto University Press. [Facsimile and commentary volume, also published as a monograph]

—, 2003a. "House-Style in the Scriptorium: Scribal Reality and Scholarly Myth," in *Anglo-Saxon Styles*, ed. G. Brown and C. Karkov, 131–50. New York: State University of New York.

—, 2004. "Fifty Years of Insular Palaeography, 1953–2003: An Outline of some Landmarks and Issues," in *Archiv für Diplomatik 50, Schriftgeschichte Siegel- und Wappenkunde*, ed. W. Koch and T. Kölzer, 277–325. Vienna: Böhlau.

—, 2005. "Predicando con la penna: il contributo Insulare alla transmissione dei testi sacri dal VI al IX secolo," in *Forme e Modelli della Tradizione Manoscritta della Bibbia*, ed. P. Cherubini, 61–108. Vatican City: Vatican.

—, 2005a. "The Tower of Babel: the architecture of the early western written vernaculars," in *Omnia Disce: Medieval Studies in Memory of Leonard Boyle, O.P.*, ed. A. J. Duggan, J. Greatrex, and B. Bolton, 109–128. Aldershot, UK: Ashgate.

—, 2006. *How Christianity Came to Britain and Ireland*. Oxford: Lion Hudson.

—, 2006a. *Manuscripts from the Anglo-Saxon Age*. London and Toronto: British Library / University of Toronto.

—, and P. Lovett, 1999. *The Historical Source Book for Scribes*. London: British Library.

Brown, T. J., 1980. "Late Antique and Early Anglo-Saxon books," in *Manuscripts at Oxford: An Exhibition in Memory of Richard William Hunt*, ed. A. C. de la Mare and B. C. Barker-Benfield, 9–14 art. II, figs. 2, 5–6. Oxford: Bodleian Library.

—, and others, ed., 1969. *The Stonyhurst Gospel of St John*. Oxford: Roxburghe Club.

Bruce, F. F., 1988. *The Canon of Scripture*. Downers Grove, Ill.: Intervarsity.

Bruce, J., 1813. *Travels to discover the source of the Nile*, 3rd ed., corrected [by A. Murray]. Edinburgh: Archibald Constable.

Büchsel, M., 2003. *Die Entstehung des Christusporträts*. Mainz: Philipp von Zabern.

Buchthal, H. and O. Kurz, 1942. *A Handlist of Illuminated Oriental Christian Manuscripts*, Warburg Oriental Studies 12. London: Warburg Institute. [2nd. ed., 1969.]

Buckton, D., ed., 1994. *Byzantium. Treasures of Byzantine Art and Culture*. London: British Museum.

Bullough, D. A., 2004. *Alcuin*. Leiden, Boston and Brill: Brepols.

Burkitt, F. C., 1897. *Fragments of the Books of Kings according to the translation of Aquila, from a MS. formerly in the Geniza at Cairo*. Cambridge: Cambridge University Press.

—, 1899. "The Vulgate Gospels and the *Codex Brixianus*," *Journal of Theological Studies*, o.s. 1:129–34.

Byrne, F. J., 1979. *1000 years of Irish Script* [exhibition catalogue]. Oxford: Bodleian Library.

Byzantium, 1994. *Byzantium. Treasures of Byzantine art and culture from British collections* [exhibition catalogue], ed. D. Buckton. London: British Museum.

Cameron, R., ed., 1982. *The Other Gospels: Non-Canonical Gospel Texts*. Philadelphia: Westminster Press.

Campenhausen, H. von, 1972. *The Formation of the Christian Bible*. ET: Philadelphia: Fortress.

Canart, P. and S. Dufrenne, 1988. *Die Bibel des Patricius Leo: Codex Reginensis Graecus I B*. [facsimile]. Zurich: Belser.

Canberra, 2001. *Treasures from the World's Great Libraries* [exhibition catalogue]. Canberra: National Library of Australia.

Cassiodorus, 1973. *Magni Aurelii Cassiodori Variarum Libri XII*, ed. A. Fridh, Corpus Christianorum Series Latina 96. Turnhout: Brepols.

Cavallo, G., 1967. *Richerche sulla maiuscola biblica*. Studi e testi di papirologia, no. 2. Florence: Edmond Le Monnier.

—, 1975. "Libro e pubblico alla fine del mondo antico," in *Libri, editori e pubblico nel mondo antico*, 83–132. Rome and Bari: Laterza.

—, 1994. "Testo e immagine: Una frontiera ambigua," in *Testo e immagine nell'alto medioevo*, Settimane di studio del centro italiano di studi sull'alto medioevo 41, vol. 1:31–62. Spoleto: CISAM.

—, J. Gribomont and W. Loerke, eds., 1987. *Codex Purpureus Rossanensis*. Rome and Graz: Salerno Editrice / Akademische Druck u. Verlaganstalt.

Cecchelli, C., ed., 1959. *The Rabbula Gospels*. Olten and Lausanne: Urs Graf.

Chadwick, N., 1961. *The Age of the Saints in the Early Celtic Church*. Oxford: Oxford University Press.

Chapman, J., 1908. *Notes on the Early History of the Vulgate Gospels*. Oxford: Clarendon Press.

Charles, R. H., 1968. *Apocrypha and Pseudepigrapha of the Old Testament*. 2 vols. Repr. Oxford: Oxford University Press. [Orig. pub. Oxford: Clarendon Press, 1913]

Charlesworth, J. H., 1981. *The New Discoveries in St. Catherine's Monastery. A Preliminary Report on the Manuscripts*. Winona Lake, Ill.: American Schools of Oriental Research.

Chavasse, A., 1993. *Les Lectionnaires Romains de la Messe*, Spicilegii Friburgensis, 'Subsidia' 22. Fribourg-en-Suisse: Spicilegi Friburgensis.

Chazelle, C., 1990. "Pictures, Books and the Illiterate: Pope Gregory I's Letters to Serenus of Marseilles," *Word and Image* 6, no. 2:138–53.

—, 2001. *The Crucified God in the Carolingian Era: Theology and Art of Christ's Passion*. Cambridge: Cambridge University Press.

—, 2006. "Christ and the Vision of God: The Biblical Diagrams of the Codex Amiatinus," in *The Mind's Eye: Art and Theological Argument in the Middle Ages*, ed. J. F. Hamburger and A.-M. Bouché, 84–111. Princeton: Princeton University Press.

Choat, M. 2006. "The Unknown Work on Prophecy in the Freer Minor Prophets Codex," *The Freer Biblical Manuscripts: Fresh Studies of the Greek Biblical Manuscripts Housed in the Freer Gallery*, ed. L. Hurtado. Atlanta: Society for Biblical Literature Publications.

Chojnacki, S., 2000. *Ethiopian Icons: Catalogue of the Collection of the Institute of Ethiopian Studies, Addis Ababa University*. Milan: Skira.

Christe, Y., 1996. *L'Apocalypse de Jean*. Paris: Picard.

Clabeaux, J. J., 1989. *A Lost Edition of the Letters of Paul: A Reassessment of the Text of the Pauline Corpus Attested by Marcion*. Washington, D.C.: Catholic Biblical Association of America.

Clark, A. C., 1918. *The Descent of Manuscripts*. Oxford: Clarendon Press. [Repr. 1969.]

Clark, K. W., 1952. *Checklist of Manuscripts in St Catherine's Monastery, Mount Sinai. Microfilmed for the Library of Congress, 1950*. Washington, D. C.: Library of Congress.

Cohen, A. S., 2000. *The Uta Codex: Art, Philosophy and Reform in Eleventh-Century Germany*. University Park: Pennsylvania State University Press.

Comfort, P. W., 1995. "Exploring the Common Identification of Three New Testament Manuscripts: P 4, P 64 and P 67," *Tyndale Bulletin* 46:43–54.

—, and D. P. Barrett, eds., 2000. *The Complete Text of the Earliest New Testament Manuscripts*. Grand Rapids, Mich.: Baker.

Connolly, S., 1997. *Bede. On Tobit and on the Canticle of Habbakkuk*. Dublin, Ireland and Portland, Oreg: Four Courts Press.

Conybeare, F. C., 1893. "Aristion, the author of the last twelve verses of Mark," *The Expositor* (7 October): 241–54.

—, 1913. *A Catalogue of the Armenian Manuscripts in the British Museum*. London: British Museum.

Coquin, R.-G., and M. Martin, 1991. "Dayr Nahya," in *The Coptic Encyclopedia*, ed. A. S. Atiya, vol. 3, 843–44. New York: Macmillan.

Corrigan, K., 1992. *Visual Polemics in the Ninth-Century Byzantine Psalters*. Cambridge: Cambridge University Press.

Corsano, K., 1987. "The First Quire of the Codex Amiatinus," *Scriptorium* 41, pt 1:3–34.

Coxe, H. O., 1853. *Catalogi codicum manuscriptorum Bibliothecae Bodleianae pars prima recensionem codicum Graecorum continens*. Oxford: Oxford University Press. [Repr. with corrections, 1969.]

Crossan, J. D., 1985. *Four Other Gospels*. New York: Winston.

Crum, W. E., 1905. *Catalogue of the Coptic Manuscripts in the British Museum*. London: Trustees of the British Museum.

Cullmann, O., 1956. "The Plurality of the Gospels as a Theological Problem in Antiquity," in *The Early Church*, 39–54. Philadelphia: Westminister Press.

D'Achéry, L. and J. Mabillon, 1668–1701. *Acta Sanctorum Ordinis Sancti Benedicti*. Paris: J. Billaine.

Dahlhaus-Berg, E., 1975. *Nova antiquitas et antiqua novitas. Typologische Exegese und isidorianisches Geschichtsbild bei Theodulf von Orléans*. Cologne and Vienna: Böhlau.

D'Aiuto, F., G. Morello and A. M. Piazzoni, eds., 2000. *I vangeli dei popoli* [exhibition catalogue]. Vatican: Edizioni Rinnovamento nello Spirito Santo.

de Bruyne, D., 1920. *Préfaces de la Bible Latine*. Namur: Auguste Godenne.

de Hamel, C., 1986. *A History of Illuminated Manuscripts*. Oxford: Phaidon. [2nd ed., London: Phaidon, 1994.]

—, 2001. *The Book: A History of the Bible*. London and New York: Phaidon.

Depuydt, L., 1993. *Catalogue of Coptic Manuscripts in the Pierpont Morgan Library*, 2 vols., Corpus of Illuminated Manuscripts, vol. 4; Oriental Series 1. Louvain: Peeters.

Der Nersessian, S., 1944–45. "Une apologie des images du septième siècle," *Byzantion* 17:58–87.

—, 1973. *Armenian Manuscripts in the Walters Art Gallery*. Baltimore: Trustees of the Walters Art Gallery.

Déroche, F. and F. Richard, 1997. *Scribes et manuscrits du Moyen-Orient*. Paris: Bibliothèque nationale de France.

Deshman, R., 1980. "The Exalted Servant: The Ruler Theology of the Prayerbook of Charles the Bald," *Viator* 11:385–417.

Diebold, W. J., 2000. *Word and Image: A History of Early Medieval Art*. Boulder, Colo.: Westview Press.

—, 2003. "'Except I shall see . . . I will not believe' (John 20:25): Typology, Theology, and Historiography in an Ottonian Ivory Diptych," in *Images, Objects and The Word: Art in the Service of the Liturgy*, ed. C. Houirhane, 257–73. Princeton: Princeton University Press.

Dines, J., 2004. *The Septuagint*. London: T & T Clark.

Doane, A. N., 1978. *Genesis A. A new edition*. Madison: University of Wisconsin Press.

—, 1991. *The Saxon Genesis: An edition of the West Saxon Genesis B and the Old Saxon Vatican Genesis*. Madison: University of Wisconsin Press.

—, ed., 2002. *Anglo-Saxon Manuscripts in Microfiche Facsimile* 7, Medieval and Renaissance Texts and Studies 187. Tempe: Arizona Center for Medieval and Renaissance Studies.

Dodwell, C. R. and P. Clemoes, 1974. *The Old English Illustrated Hexateuch*, Early English Manuscripts in Facsimile 18. Copenhagen: Rosenkilde & Bagger.

Doresse, J., 1960. *The Secret Books of the Egyptian Gnostics*, rev. English trans. London: Hollis & Carter.

Dostál, A., 1966. "L'Eucologe slave du Sinai," *Byzantion* 36, 1:1–52.

Douce Legacy, 1984. *The Douce Legacy: An Exhibition to Commemorate the 150th Anniversary of the Bequest of Francis Douce (1757–1834)*. Oxford: Bodleian Library.

Duft, J. and R. Schnyder, 1984. *Die Elfenbein-Einbände der Stiftsbibliothek St. Gallen*. Beuron: Beuroner Kunstverlag.

Dumville, D. N., 1992. *Liturgy and the Ecclesiastical History of Late Anglo-Saxon England: Four Studies*, Studies in Anglo-Saxon History 5. Woodbridge: Boydell Press.

Dunlop Gibson, M., 1894. *Catalogue of the Arabic MSS. In the Convent of St. Catharine on Mount Sinai*. London: C. J. Clay & Sons.

Dutton, P. E., 2004. *Charlemagne's Mustache and other Cultural Clusters of a Dark Age*. New York and Basingstoke, UK: Palgrave Macmillan.

—, and É. Jeauneau, 1983. "The Verses of the 'Codex Aureus' of Saint-Emmeram," *Studi Medievali*, third series, 24:75–120.

—, and H. Kessler, 1997. *The Poetry and Paintings of the First Bible of Charles the Bald*. Ann Arbor: University of Michigan Press.

Dvornik, F., 1962. *The Slavs in European History and Civilization*. New Brunswick, N.J.: Rutgers University Press.

—, 1970. *Byzantine Missions Among the Slavs*, Rutgers Byzantine Series. New Brunswick, N.J.: Rutgers University Press.

Easterling, P. E. and B. M. W. Knox, eds., 1985. "Books and Readers in the Greek World," in *The Cambridge History of Classical Literature* 1:1–41. Cambridge: Cambridge University Press.

Ehrman, B. D., 1993. *The Orthodox Corruption of Scripture: The Effect of Early Christological Controversies on the Text of the New Testament*. Oxford: Oxford University Press.

Elliott, J. K., 1989. *A Bibliography of Greek New Testament Manuscripts*. Cambridge: Cambridge University Press.

—, ed., 2004. *The Collected Biblical Writings of T. C. Skeat*. Leiden: Brill.

Elmham, Thomas [of], 1858. *Historia Monasterii S. Augustini Cantuariensis*, Rolls Series 8, ed. C. Hardwick. London.

Emms, R., 2005. "St Augustine's Abbey, Canterbury, and the 'First Books of the Whole English Church'", in *The Church and the Book*, ed. R. N. Swanson, Studies in Church History 38. Woodbridge: Boydell & Brewer, for the Ecclesiastical History Society.

Epp, E. J., 1989. "The New Testament Papyrus Manuscripts in Historical Perspective," in *To Touch the Text: Biblical and Related Studies in Honor of Joseph P. Fitzmyer*, ed. M. P. Horgan and P. Kobelski, 261–88. New York: Crossroads.

Ernst, U., 1991. *Carmen Figuratum. Geschichte des Figurengedichts von den antiken Ursprüngen bis zum Ausgang des Mittelalters*. Cologne and Vienna: Weimer / Böhlau.

Étaix, R. ed., 1999. *Gregorius Magnus, Homiliae in Evangelia*, Corpus Christianorum Series Latina 141. Turnhout: Brepols.

Evans, J. M., 1963. "Genesis B and its background," *Review of English Studies* 14:1–16, 113–23.

Εὐάγγελος, Ὁ Πέρλης, et al., *Ο ΠΟΡΦΥΡΟΥΣ ΚΩ ΙΣ ΤΩΝ ΕΥΑΓΓΕΛΩΝ ΠΑΤΜΟΥ ΚΑΙ ΠΕΤΠΡΟΥΠΟΛΕΩΣ* [The Purple Codex of the Gospels of Patmos and Petroupolis], ΑΘΗΝΑ [Athens], ΜΙΛΗΤΟΣ ΕΚ ΟΣΕΙΣ [Militos Editions], 2002, 26 no. 6, 34 (bibliography),73.

Farr, C., 1997. *The Book of Kells: Its Function and Audience*. London and Toronto: British Library / University of Toronto Press.

Faye, C. U. and W. H. Bond, 1962. *Supplement to the Census of Medieval and Renaissance Manuscripts in the United States and Canada*. New York: The Bibliographical Society of America.

Fernandez Marcos, N., 2000. *The Septuagint in Context: Introduction to the Greek Version of the Bible*. Leiden: Brill.

Fiey, J.-M., 1972–73, i.e. 1976. "Coptes et syriaques: contacts et échanges," *Studia Orientalia Christiana. Collectanea* 15:297–365.

Fillitz, H. and M. Pippal, 1987. *Schatzkunst: Die Goldschmiede- und Elfenbeinarbeiten aus österreichische Schatzkammern des Hochmittelalters*. Salzburg and Vienna: Residenz.

Fischer, B., 1962. "Codex Amiatinus und Cassiodor," *Biblische Zeitschrift*, N.F. 6. Paderborn: F. Schöning.

—, 1971. *"Die Alkuin-Bibeln" Die Bibel von Moutier-Grandval: British Museum Add. Ms. 10546*. Bern: Verein Schweizerischer Lithographiebesitzer.

—, 1985. *Lateinische Bibelhandschriften im frühen Mittelalter*, Vetus Latina. Aus der Geschichte der lateinischen Bibel 11. Freiburg: Herder.

—, 1988–91. *Die lateinischen Evangelien bis zum 10.Jahrhundert*, 4 vols., Vetus Latina. Aus der Geschichte der lateinischen Bibel 13, 15, 17, 18. Freiburg: Herder.

Fitzgerald, W., 1992. *Ocelli Nominum: Names and Shelf Marks of Famous / Familiar Manuscripts*. Toronto: University of Toronto / Pontifical Insititute of Mediaeval Studies.

Forsyth, G. H. and K. Weitzmann, 1973. *The Monastery of Saint Catherine at Mount Sinai: The Church and Fortress of Justinian*. Ann Arbor: University of Michigan Press.

Franz, G., ed., 1985. *Trevirensia: Beiträge zur Trierer Bibliotheksgeschichte*. Wiesbaden: Reichert.

Frcek, J., 1933. "Euchologium Sinaiticum. Texte slave avec sources grecques et traduction françaises," *Patrologia Orientalis* 24. Paris: Firmin-Didot.

Frede, H.-J., 1964. *Altlateinische Paulus-Handschriften*, Vetus Latina, Aus der Geschichte der lateinischen Bibel 4. Freiburg: Herder.

Gabra, G., 1993. *Cairo: The Coptic Museum and Old Churches*. Cairo: Longman.

Galavaris, G., 1979. *The Illustrations of the Prefaces in Byzantine Gospels*. Vienna: Österreichischen Akademie der Wissenschaften.

Gamble, H. Y., 1985. *The New Testament Canon: Its Making and Meaning*. Philadelphia: Fortress.

—, 1995. *Books and Readers in the Early Church: A History of Early Christian Texts*. New Haven and London: Yale University Press.

Gameson, R. G., ed., 1994. *The Early Medieval Bible*. Cambridge: Cambridge University Press.

—, ed., 2001. *Codex Aureus. An Eighth-Century Gospel Book (Stockholm, Kungliga Biblioteket, A.135)*. Copenhagen: Rosenkilde & Bagger.

—, 2001a. *The Scribe Speaks? Colophons in Early English Manuscripts*, H. M. Chadwick Memorial Lectures 12. Cambridge: University of Cambridge, Department of Anglo-Saxon, Norse and Celtic.

—, 2003. *The Stockholm Codex Aureus*, Early English Manuscripts in Facsimile 28. Copenhagen: Rosenkilde & Bagger.

Ganz, D., 1990. *Corbie in the Carolingian Renaissance*. Sigmaringen: Thorbecke.

—, 1994. "Mass Production of Early Medieval Manuscripts: The Carolingian Bibles from Tours," in *The Early Medieval Bible*, ed. R. G. Gameson, 53–62. Cambridge: Cambridge University Press.

—, 2001. "The Annotations in Oxford, Bodleian Library, Auct. D. II. 14," in *Belief and Culture in the Middle Ages: Studies Presented to Henry Mayr-Harting*, ed. R. Gameson and H. Leyser, 35–44, pls. 1–2. Oxford: Oxford University Press.

—, 2002. "Roman Manuscripts in Francia and Anglo-Saxon England," in *Roma fra Oriente e Occidente*, Settimane di studio del centro italiano di studi sull'alto medioevo 49. Spoleto: CISAM.

Gardthausen, V. E., 1886. *Catalogus codicum graecorum Sinaiticorum*. Oxford: Clarendon Press.

Garitte, G., 1955. *L'Ancienne Version Géorgienne des Actes des Apôtres*. Louvain: Publications Universitaires.

—, 1956. *Catalogue des Manuscrits Géorgiens Littéraires du Mont Sinai*, Corpus Scriptorum Christianorum Orientalium, vol. 165, Subsidia tom. 9. Louvain: L. Durbecq.

—, 1956a. "Les manuscrits géorgiens du Sinai," *La Nouvelle Clio* 7–9:105–111.

—, 1957. "Les manuscrits géorgiens du Sinai', *Bedi Karthlisa* 23:7–11.

—, 1961. "Les récents catalogues des manuscripts géorgiens de Tiflis," *Le Muséon* 74:387–422.

—, 1972. "Un index géorgien des lectures évangelique selon l'ancien rite de Jérusalem," *La Muséon* 85:337–98.

—, 1980. *Scripta Disiecta, 1941–1977*, Publications de l'Institut Orientaliste de Louvain 21–22. Louvain-la-Neuve: Université Catholique de Louvain, Institut Orientaliste.

Garsoïan, N. G., trans. and commentary, 1989. *The Epic Histories attributed to P'awstos Buzand (Buzandaran Patmut'iwnk')*. Cambridge, Mass.: Distributed for the Dept. of Near Eastern Languages and Civilizations, Harvard University by Harvard University Press.

Geitler, L., 1882. *Euchologium Glagolski spomenik manastira Sinai Brda*. Zagreb: Zagres.-Jugoslavenska Akademija.

Gerster, G., 1970. *Churches in Rock: Early Christian Art in Ethiopia*. London: Phaidon.

Gerstinger, H., 1933. "Ein Fragment des Chester Beatty-Evangelienkodex in der Papyrussammlung der Nationalbibliothek in Wien," *Aegypus* 13:67–72.

J. Paul Getty Museum, 1991. *A Thousand Years of the Bible: Medieval and Renaissance Manuscripts* [exhibition catalogue]. Malibu, Calif.: J. Paul Getty Museum.

Gibson, M. T., 1993. *The Bible in the Latin West*. Notre Dame, Ind.: University of Notre Dame.

Giversen, S., 1980. "The Pauline Epistles on Papyrus," in *Die paulinische Literatur und Theologie*, ed. S. Pedersen, 201–212. Gottingen: Van den Hoeck & Ruprecht.

Gneuss, H., 1996. *Books and Libraries in Early England*. Aldershot, UK: Ashgate.

—, 2001. *A Handlist of Anglo-Saxon Manuscripts: A List of Manuscripts and Manuscript Fragments Written or Owned in England up to 1100*, Medieval and Renaissance Texts and Studies 241. Tempe: Arizona Center for Medieval and Renaissance Studies. [An earlier version was printed in *Anglo-Saxon England* 9 (Cambridge: Cambridge University Press, 1981), with a supplement in *Anglo-Saxon England* 32 (Cambridge: Cambridge University Press, 2004).]

Goldschmidt, A., 1914. *Die Elfenbeinskulpturen aus der Zeit der Karolingischen und Sächsischen Kaiser*, vol. 1. Berlin: Cassirer. [Reissued Berlin: Deutscher Verlag für Kunstwissenschaft, 1969]

—, 1914–26. *Die Elfenbeinskulpturen aus der romanischen Zeit XI.–XIII. Jahrhunderts*, 4 vols. Berlin: Deutscher Verlag für Kunstwissenschaft.

—, 1947. *An Early Manuscript of the Aesop Fables of Avianus and Related Manuscripts*. Princeton: Princeton University Press.

Gollancz, I., 1927. *The Caedmon Manuscript of Anglo-Saxon Biblical Poetry* [facsimile]. Oxford: Oxford University Press.

Gospel of Thomas, 1959. Coptic text ed. A. J. P. Guillaumont and others, *Evangelium nach Thomas*. Leiden: Brill.

Gospel of Thomas, 1997. R. Valantasis, *The Gospel of Thomas (New Testament Readings)*. London and New York: Routledge.

Gospel of Thomas, 2003. E. H. Pagels, *Beyond Belief: the Secret Gospel of Thomas*. New York: Random House.

Gottheil, R., and W. H. Worrell, 1927. *Fragments from the Cairo Genizah in the Freer Collection*, University of Michigan Studies, Humanistic Series 13. New York and London: Macmillan.

Grabar, A., 1948. *Les peintures de l'évangile de Sinope*. Paris: Bibliothèque nationale.

—, 1972. *Les manuscrits grecs enluminés de provenance italienne*. (IXe–XIe siècle) Bibliothèque des Cahiers Archéologiques 8. Paris.

Graf, G., 1944–53. *Geschichte der christlichen arabischen Literatur*, 5 vols., Studi e Testi 118, 133, 146, 147, 172. Vatican City: Biblioteca Apostolica Vaticana.

Gregory, C. R., 1908. *Das Freer-Logion, Versuche und Entwurfe I*. Leipzig: Hinrichs.

—, 1909. *Textcritik des Neuen Testaments*. Leipzig: J. C. Hinrichs'sche Buchhandlung.

Grenfell, B. P. and A. S. Hunt, 1897. *Logia Iesou. Sayings of Our Lord from an Early Greek Papyrus*. London: Egypt Exploration Fund.

Griffith, S. H., 1997. "From Aramaic to Arabic: The Languages of the Monasteries of Palestine in the Byzantine and Early Islamic Periods," *Dumbarton Oaks Papers* 51:11–31.

—, 2002. "The Handwriting on the Wall: Graffiti in the Church of St. Antony," in *Monastic Visions: Wall Paintings in the Monastery of St. Antony at the Red Sea*, ed. E. S. Bolman, 185–93. New Haven and London: Yale University Press.

—, c2006. "The Church of Jerusalem and the 'Melkites': The Making of an 'Arab Orthodox' Christian Identity in the World of Islam (750–1050 CE)," in *Christians and Christianity in the Holy Land: From the Origins to the Latin Kingdoms*, ed. O. Limor and G.G. Stroumsa, Cultural Encounters in Late Antiquity and the Middle Ages, 175–204. Turnhout: Brepols.

Gronewald, M., 1987. "Unbekanntes Evangelium oder Evangeliumharmoonie (Fragment aus dem 'Evangelium Egerton')," in *Kolner Papyri*, ed. M.Gronewald and others, Abhandlungen der Rheinische-Westfalischen Akademie der Wissenschaften, Sonderreihe, Papyrologica Coloniensia 7.6, 136–45. Opladen: Westdeutscher.

Günzburg, D. and V. Stassoff, 1886 and 1905. *Ornementation des anciens manuscrits Hébreux de la Bibliothèque Impériale Publique de Saint-Pétersbourg*. St. Petersburg, 1886 and Berlin: S. Calvary and Co., 1905. [Plates reissued in Narkiss, 1990]

Haelst, J. van, 1976. *Catalogue des papyrus littéraires juifs et chrétiens*. Paris: Sorbonne.

Hahneman, G., 1992. *The Muratorian Fragment and the Development of the Canon*. Oxford: Clarendon Press.

Haines-Eitzen, K., 2000. *Guardians of Letters: Literacy, Power and the Transmitters of Early Christian Literature*. Oxford and New York: Oxford University Press.

Hall, J. R., 1976. "The Old English epic of redemption: the theological unity of MS Junius 11," *Traditio* 32:185–208.

Hamburger, J. F., 2002. *St John the Divine: The Deified Evangelist in Medieval Art and Theology*. Berkeley and Los Angeles: University of California Press.

—, 2004. "Body vs. Book: The Trope of Visibility in Images of Christian-Jewish Polemic," in *Ästhetik des Unsichtbaren: Bildtheorie und Bildgebrauch in der Vormoderne*, ed. D. Ganz and T. Lentes, 112–25. Berlin: Dietrich Reimer.

Harlfinger, D., D. R. Reinsch and J. A. M. Sonderkamp, 1983. *Specimina Sinaitica: die datierten griechischen Handschriften des Katharinen-Klosters auf dem Berge Sinai: 9. bis 12. Jahrhundert*. Berlin: D. Reimer.

Harris, J. R., 1890. *Biblical Fragments from Mount Sinai*. Cambridge: Cambridge University Press.

Hatch, W. H. P., 1932. *The Greek Manuscripts of the New Testament at Mount Sinai*, American Schools of Oriental Research. Publications of the Jerusalem School, vol. 1. Paris, 1932.

—, 1939. *The Principal Uncial Manuscripts of the New Testament*. Chicago: University of Chicago Press.

Head, P. M., 1990. "Observations on Early Papyri of the Synoptic Gospels, especially on the 'Scribal Habits'," *Biblica* 71:240–47.

Heldman, M. E., [1975]. "Christ's Entry into Jerusalem in Ethiopia," *Proceedings of the First United States Conference on Ethiopian Studies, 1973*, ed. H. G. Marcus, 43–60. East Lansing: African Studies Center, Michigan State University.

—, 1994. *The Marian Icons of the Painter Fre Seyon: A Study of Fifteenth-Century Ethiopian Art, Patronage, and Spirituality*. Wiesbaden: Harrassowitz.

Henderson, G., 1975. "The programme of illustrations in Bodleian MS Junius XI," in *Studies in Memory of David Talbot Rice*, ed. G. Robertson and G. Henderson, 113–45. Edinburgh: Edinburgh University Press. [Repr. in G. Henderson, *Studies in English Bible Illustration* 1:138–83. London: Pindar Press, 1985]

—, 1987. *From Durrow to Kells, the Insular Gospel-books 650–800*. London: Thames & Hudson.

—, 1993. "Cassiodorus and Eadfrith Once Again," in *The Age of Migrating Ideas*, ed. M. Spearman and J. Higgitt, 82–91. Edinburgh: National Museums of Scotland.

Hendriks, I. H. M., 1980. "Pliny, *Historia Naturalis XIII 74–82*, and the Manufacture of Papyrus," *Zeitschrift für Papyrologie und Epigraphik* 37:121–36.

Hengel, M., 2002. *The Septuagint as Christian Scripture: Its Prehistory and the Problem of Its Canon*. Edinburgh: T & T Clark.

Hennessy, W. M., 1887–1901. *Annals of Ulster*, 4 vols. Dublin: Her Majesty's Stationery Office.

Hering, J., 1934. "Observations critiques sur le texte des Évangiles et des Actes de P45," in *Revue d'Histoire et de Philosophie religieuses* 14:144–54.

Herren, M., ed., 1988. *The Sacred Nectar of the Greeks: The Study of Greek in the West in the Early Middle Ages*. London: University of London.

Hoerning, R., 1889. *British Museum Karaite MSS. Description and collation of six Karaite Manuscripts of portions of the Hebrew Bible in Arabic Characters with a complete reproduction by the autotype process of one, Exodus I.1–VIII. 5, in 42 facsimiles*. London and Edinburgh: Williams & Norgate.

Holter, K., 1980. *Der goldene Psalter "Dagulf-Psalter."* Graz: Akademische Druck und Verlaganstalt.

Horn, C. B., 2006. *Asceticism and Christological Controversy in Fifth-Century Palestine: The Career of Peter the Iberian*, Oxford Early Christian Studies. Oxford: Oxford University Press.

Horn, J., 2000. "Die koptische (sahidische) Überlieferung des alttestamentlichen Psalmenbuches—Versuch einer Gruppierung der Textzeugen für die Herstsellung des Textes," in A. Aejmelaeus and U. Quast, eds., *Der Septuaginta-Psalter und seine Tochterübersetzungen: Symposium in Göttingen 1997*. Mitteilungen des Septuaginta-Unternehmens 24: 97–106. Göttingen: Vandenhoeck & Ruprecht.

Horton, C., ed., 2004. *The Earliest Gospels: The Origins and Transmission of the Earliest Christian Gospels—The Contribution of the Chester Beatty Gospel Codex P45*, Journal for the Study of the New Testament Supplement Series 258. London and New York: T & T Clark.

Hoskier, H. C., 1937. "A Study of the Chester Beatty Codex of the Pauline Epistles," *Journal of Theological Studies* 38:148–63.

Hubert, J., J. Porcher and W. F. Volbach, 1970. *Carolingian Art*. London: Thames & Hudson.

Hunt, A. S., 1911. *The Oxyrhynchus Papyri, Part VIII*. London: Egypt Exploration Fund.

Hurtado, L.W., 1981. *Text-critical Methodology and the Pre-Caesarean Text: Codex W in the Gospel of Mark*, Studies and Documents 43. Grand Rapids, Mich.: Eerdmans.

Huston, H. W., 1955. "Mark 6 and 11 in P45 and in the Caesarean Text," in *Journal of Biblical Literature* 74:262–71.

Hutter, I., 1977–1982. *Corpus der Byzantinischen Miniaturenhandschriften. Oxford Bodleian Library*, 3 vols. in 4. Stuttgart: Hiersemann.

Iacobini, A., 1994. "L'albero della vita nell'immaginario medievale: Bisanzio e l'Occidente," in *L'architettura medievale in Sicilia: la cattedrale di Palermo*, 241–90. Rome: Istituto della Enciclopedia Italiana.

—, and L. Perria, 1998. *Il Vangelo di Dionisio*. Rome: Àrgos.

Innemée, K. and L. Van Rompay, 1998. "La présence des Syriens dans le Wadi al-Natrun (Egypte)," *Parole de l'Orient* 23:167–202.

Jagic, V., 1879. *Quattuor evangeliorum codex glagoliticus olim Zographensis nunc Petropolitanus*. Berlin: Weidmann. [Repr. Graz: Akademischer Druck- und Verlagsanstalt, 1954]

Jellicoe, S., 1968. *The Septuagint and Modern Study*. Oxford: Clarendon Press.

Jerome, Saint, 1980. *Select Letters of St Jerome*, ed. and trans. F. A. Wright. Cambridge, Mass. and London: Harvard University Press.

John of Damascus, Saint, 1980. *On the Divine Images*, trans. D. Anderson. Crestwood, N.Y.: St. Vladimir's Seminary Press.

John Scottus Eriugena, 1993. *Iohannis Scotti Eriugenae Carminae*, ed. M. W. Herrin. Dublin: School of Celtic Studies of the Dublin Institute for Advanced Studies.

Johnson, D. W., 1995. "The Kebra Nagast: Another Look," in *Peace and War in Byzantium: Essays in Honor of George T. Dennis*, ed. T. S. Miller and J. Nesbitt, 197–208. Washington, D.C.: Catholic University of America Press.

Johnson, W. A., 2000. "Toward a Sociology of Reading in Classical Antiquity," *American Journal of Philology* 121:593–627.

—, 2004. *Bookrolls and Scribes in Oxyrhynchus*. Toronto: University of Toronto Press.

Juckel, A., 2003. "Ms. Schoyen 2530 / Sinai syr. 3 and the New Testament Peshitta," *Hugoye Journal of Syriac Studies* 6, no.2 (July): 1–25.

Junack, K., 1981. "Abschreibpraktiken und Schreibergewohnheiten in ihrer Auswirkung auf die Textuberlieferung," in *New Testament Textual Criticism: Its Significance for Exegesis. Essays in Honor of Bruce M. Metzger*, ed. E. J. Epp and G. D. Fee, 277–95. Oxford: Clarendon Press.

Kahle, P., 1959. *The Cairo Geniza*, 2nd ed. Oxford: Basil Blackwell.

Kamil, M., 1957. "Les Manuscrits Éthiopiens du Sinai', *Annales d'Éthiopie* 2:83–90.

—, 1970. *Catalogue of all Manuscripts in the Monastery of St. Catharine on Mount Sinai*. Wiesbaden: Otto Harrassowitz.

Karkov, C. E., 2001. *Text and Picture in Anglo-Saxon England: Narrative Strategies in the Junius 11 Manuscript*, Cambridge Studies in Anglo-Saxon England 31. Cambridge: Cambridge University Press.

Kasser, R., c1991. "Dialects," and "Dialects, Grouping and Major Groups of," in *The Coptic Encyclopedia*, ed. A.S. Atiya, 8 vols., 87–97, 97–101. New York: Macmillan.

Kelly, É. P., 1994. "The Lough Kinale Book Shrine: The Implications for the Manuscripts," in *The Book of Kells. Proceedings of a Conference at Trinity College Dublin 6–9 September 1992*, ed. F. O'Mahony, 280–89. Aldershot, UK: Scolar Press for Trinity College Library.

Kelly, S., 1990. "Anglo-Saxon Lay Society and the Written Word," in *The Uses of Literacy in Early Mediaeval Europe*, ed. R. McKitterick, 36–62. Cambridge: Cambridge University Press.

Kenney, E. J., ed., 1982. "Books and Readers in the Roman World," in *The Cambridge History of Classical Literature* 2: 3–32. Cambridge: Cambridge University Press.

Kenyon, F. G., ed., 1900. *Facsimiles of Biblical Manuscripts in the British Museum*. London: British Museum.

—, ed., 1933–34 *The Chester Beatty Biblical Papyri: Descriptions and Texts of Twelve Manuscripts on Papyrus of the Greek Bible*, Fasc. I: General Introduction (1933); Fasc. II: The Gospels and Acts, Text (1933); Fasc. II: The Gospels and Acts, Plates (1934) (London, Emery Walker).

—, ed., 1934–37. *The Chester Beatty Biblical Papyri: Descriptions and Texts of Twelve Manuscripts on Papyrus of the Greek Bible*, Fasc. III/1: Pauline Epistles and Revelation, Text (1934); Fasc. III/3: Pauline Epistles, Text (1936); Fasc. III/4: Pauline Epistles, Plates (1937) (London: Emery Walker).

—, ed., 1935–58. *The Chester Beatty Biblical Papyri: Descriptions and Texts of Twelve Manuscripts on Papyrus of the Greek Bible*, Fasc.V: Numbers and Deuteronomy, Text (London: Emery Walker, 1935); Fasc. V: Numbers and Deuteronomy, Plates (Dublin, Hodges Figgis, 1958).

—, 1939. *Our Bible and the Ancient Manuscripts*, 4th ed. London: Eyre & Spottiswoode.

—, 1951. *Books and Readers in Ancient Greece and Rome*, 2nd ed. Oxford: Clarendon Press.

Ker, N. R., 1957. *Catalogue of Manuscripts Containing Anglo-Saxon*. Oxford: Clarendon Press. [Reissued with Supplement, 1990]

Kessler, H. L., 1977. *The Illustrated Bibles from Tours*. Princeton: Princeton University Press.

—, 1990/91. "Through the Temple Veil: The Holy Image in Judaism and Christianity," *Kairos: Zeitschrift für Religionswissenschaft und Theologie*, 32/33:53–77.

—, 1994. "'Facies bibliothecae revelata': Carolingian Art as Spiritual Seeing," in *Testo e immagine nell'alto medioevo*, Settimane di studio del centro italiano di studi sull'alto medioevo 41, vol. 2:533–94. Spoleto: CISAM.

—, 2005. "Images of Christ and Communication with God," in *Communicare e significare nell'alto medioevo*, Settimane de studio della fondazione centro italiano di studi sull'alto medioevo 52:1099–36. Spoleto: CISAM.

—, forthcoming. "The *Acheropita* Triptych in Tivoli," *Festschrift Arturo C. Quintavalle*.

Keynes, S. and M. Lapidge, 1983. *Alfred the Great*. Harmondsworth, UK: Penguin.

Kitzinger, E., 1973. "A Pair of Silver Book Covers in the Sion Treasure," in *Gatherings in Honor of Dorothy E. Miner*, ed. U. E. McCracken, L. M. C. Randall, and R. H. Randall, Jr., 3–17. Baltimore: Walters Art Gallery.

—, 1975. *The Place of Book Illumination in Byzantine Art*. Princeton: Princeton University Press.

Klauck, H.-J., 2003. *Apocryphal Gospels: An Introduction*. London and New York: T & T Clark.

Klein, P. K., 1992. "Introduction: The Apocalypse in Medieval Art," in *The Apocalypse in the Middle Ages*, ed. R. K. Emmerson and B. McGinn, 159–99. Ithaca, N. Y.: Cornell University Press.

Knibb, M. A., c1999. *Translating the Bible: The Ethiopic Version of the Old Testament*, The Schweich Lectures of the British Academy, 1995. London: Oxford University Press for the British Academy.

Koehler, W., 1954. "The Fragments of an Eighth-century Gospel Book in the Morgan Library (M. 564)," in *Studies in Art and Literature for Belle da Costa Greene*, ed. D. Miner, 238–65. Princeton, N. J.: Princeton University Press.

—, 1958. *Die Hofschule Karls des Grossen (Die karolingischen Miniaturen)* vol. 2. Berlin: Deutscher Verlag für Kunstwissenschaft.

— and F. Mütherich, 1999. *Die Schule von Tours (Die karolingischen Miniaturen)* vol. 6. Berlin: Deutscher Verlag für Kunstwissenschaft.

Koester, H. 1990. *Ancient Christian Gospels: Their History and Development*. Philadelphia: Trinity Press International.

Kondakov, N., 1890. *Opis' pami'a'tnikov drevnosti v ni'e'kotorykh kramakh I monastyri'a'kh Gruzīī*. St. Petersburg: Tip. Minsterstva puteĭ soobshchenīī'a'.

Kondakov, V. P., 1882. *Putestvie na Sinai v 1881 godu*. Odessa.

Koriwn, 1985. *Vark' Mashtots'i: a Photoreproduction of the 1941 Yerevan Edition with a Modern Translation and Concordance, and with a new Introduction by Krikor H. Maksoudian*. Delmar, N.Y.: Caravan Books.

Krapp, G. P., 1931. *The Junius manuscript*, Anglo-Saxon Poetic Records 1. London and New York: Routledge / Columbia University Press.

Krasnodebska-D'Aughton, M., 2002. "Decoration of the *In principio* initials in Early Insular Manuscripts: Christ as a Visible Image of the Invisible God," *Word and Image* 18:105–21.

Krusch, B., ed. 1896. *Passiones vitaeque sanctorum aevi Merovingici et antiquiorum aliquot*, Monumenta Germaniae Historica, Scriptorum rerum Merovingicarum 19. Hannover: Hahn.

Kühnel, B. 1987. *From the Earthly to the Heavenly Jerusalem: Representations of the Holy City in Christian Art of the First Millennium*. Rome: Herder.

—, c2006. "The Holy Land as a Factor in Christian Art," in *Christians and Christianity in the Holy Land: From the Origins to the Latin Kingdoms*, ed. O. Limor and G. G. Stroumsa, Cultural Encounters in Late Antiquity and the Middle Ages, 463–504. Turnhout: Brepols.

Lake, H. and K. Lake, 1911–22. *Codex Sinaiticus Petropolitanus* [facsimile], 2 vols. Oxford: Clarendon Press.

Lampe, G. W. H., ed., 1969. *The Cambridge History of the Bible*, vol. 2, *The West from the Fathers to the Reformation*. Cambridge: Cambridge University Press.

Lamplugh, F., 1918. *The Gnôsis of the Light: A Translation of the Untitled Apocalypse Contained in the Codex Brucianus*. London: J. M. Watkins. [Repr. 1994]

Lang, D. M., 1966. *The Georgians*, Ancient Peoples and Places 51. Bristol: Thames & Hudson.

Lange, C., 2005. *The Portrayal of Christ in the Syriac Commentary on the Diatessaron*, Corpus scriptorum Christianorum Orientalium vol. 616. Subsidia tom. 118. Louvain: Peeters.

Lapidge, M., ed., 1995. *Archbishop Theodore: Commemorative Studies on his Life and Influence*. Cambridge: Cambridge University Press.

—, 1996. *Anglo-Latin Literature 600–899*. London and Rio Grande, Ohio: Hambledon Press.

Lasko, P., 1994. *Ars Sacra 800–1200*, 2nd edition. New Haven and London: Yale University Press.

Laufner, R., 1960. "Vom Bereich der Trierer Klosterbibliothek St. Maximin im Hochmittelalter," *Armaria Trevirensia: Beiträge zur Trierer Bibliotheksgeschichte. Zum 50. Deutschen Bibliothekartag in Trier*, ed. H. Schiel, 9–35. Trier: Stadtbibliothek Trier.

—, and P. K. Klein, 1975. *Trierer Apokalypse*. Graz: Akademische Druck u. Verlagsanstalt.

Layton, B., 1987. *The Gnostic Scriptures: A New Translation with Annotations and Introductions*. Garden City, N.Y.: Doubleday.

—, 1989. *Nag Hammadi Codex II, 2–7, Together with XIII, 2. Brit Lib. Or. 4926 (1) and P. Oxy. 1, 654, 655*. 2 vols. Nag Hammadi Studies 20–21. Leiden: Brill.

Leiman, S. Z., 1976. *The Canonization of Hebrew Scripture: The Talmudic and Midrashic Evidence*. Hamden, Conn.: Archon Books.

Leloir, L., 1963. *Saint Ephrem, Commentaire de l'Evangile concordant, texte syriaque (Manuscrit Chester Beatty 709)*, Chester Beatty Monographs 8. Dublin: Hodges Figgis.

—, 1990. *Saint Ephrem, Commentaire de l'Evangile concordant, texte syriaque (Manuscrit Chester Beatty 709), Folios additionels*, Chester Beatty Monographs 8(b). Louvain: Peeters.

Lenker, U., 1997. *Die Westsächsische Evangelienversion und die Perikopenordnungen im angelsächsischen England*, Münchener Universitätsschriften, Texte und Untersuchungen zur Englischen Philologie 20. Munich: Munich University Press.

Lepage, C., 1987. "Reconstitution d'un cycle protobyzantin à partir des miniatures de deux manuscrits éthiopiens du XIVe siècle," *Cahiers archéologiques* 35:159–96.

Le Quien, M., 1740. *Oriens christianus, in quatuor patriarchatus digestus quo exhibentur ecclesiae, patriarchae, caeterique praesules totius Orientis. Studio & opera … Opus posthumum…*, 3 vols. Paris: ex Typographia regia.

Leroy, J., 1964. *Les manuscrits syriaques à peintures conservés dans les bibliothèques d'Europe et d'Orient: contribution à l'étude de l'iconographie des églises de langue syriaque*, 2 vols., Bibliothèque archéologique et historique 77. Paris: P. Geuthner.

—, 1974. *Les manuscrits coptes et coptes-arabes illustrés*, Bibliothèque archéologique et historique 96. Paris: P. Geuthner.

Levison, W., 1946. *England and the Continent in the Eighth Century*. Oxford: Clarendon Press.

Levy, Y., 1993/94. "Ezekiel's Plan in an Early Karaite Bible, *Jewish Art* 19–20:68–85.

Lewis, N., 1974. *Papyrus in Classical Antiquity*. Oxford: Clarendon Press. [Repr. with corrections and additions in *Papyrus in Classical Antiquity: A Supplement* (Brussels: Fondation Egyptologique reine Elisabeth, 1989)]

Lindemann, A., 1978. *Paulus im altesten Christentum: Das Bild des Apostels und die Rezeption der Paulinischen Theologie in der frühchristlichen Literatur bis Marcion*. Tübingen: Mohr.

Little, C., 1985. "A New Ivory of the Court School of Charlemagne," in *Studien zur mittelalterlichen Kunst 800–1250*, 11–28. Munich: Prestel.

Liuzza, R. M., 2002. *The poems of MS Junius 11: basic readings*. New York and London: Routledge.

Lowden, J., 1983. "An Alternative Interpretation of the Manuscripts of Niketas," *Byzantion*, 53:559–74.

—, 1988. *Illuminated Prophet Books: A Study of Byzantine Manuscripts of the Major and Minor Prophets*. University Park and London: Pennsylvania State University Press.

—, 1992. "Concerning the Cotton Genesis and other illustrated manuscripts of Genesis," *Gesta* 3:40–53.

—, 1993. "The Royal/Imperial Book and the Image or Self-Image of the Medieval Ruler," in *Kings and Kingship in Medieval Europe*, ed. A. J. Duggan, 213–40. London: King's College Centre for Late Antique and Medieval Studies.

—, 1997. *Early Christian and Byzantine Art*. London: Phaidon.

—, 1999. "The Beginnings of Biblical Illustration," in *Imaging the Early Medieval Bible*, ed. J. Williams, 9–59. University Park: Pennsylvania State University Press.

—, forthcoming. "The Exterior of the Early Christian Book as Visual Argument," in *The World Made Visible*, W. Klingshirn and L. Safran, eds. Washington, D. C.:Catholic University of America Press.

Lowe, E. A., ed., 1934–72. *Codices Latini Antiquiores*, 11 vols. and suppl. Oxford: Clarendon Press.

—, 1955. "An Unknown Latin Psalter on Mount Sinai," *Scriptorium* 9.

—, 1960. *English Uncial*. Oxford: Clarendon Press.

—, 1965. "Two Other Unknown Latin Liturgical Fragments on Mount Sinai," *Scriptorium* 19.

Lucas, P. J., 1979. "On the blank Daniel-cycle in MS. Junius 11," *Journal of the Warburg and Courtauld Institutes* 42:207–13.

—, 1980–81. "Junius 11 and Malmesbury," *Scriptorium* 34:197–220; 35:3–22.

—, 1994. *Exodus*. Rev. ed. Exeter: Exeter University Press.

—, ed., 2000. *Franciscus Junius, Caedmonis monachi paraphrasis poetica Genesios ac praecipuarum sacrae paginae historiarum, abhinc annos M.LXX. Anglo-Saxonicè conscripta, et nunc primum edita*, Early Studies in Germanic Philology 3. Amsterdam and Atlanta: Rodopi.

Luhrmann, D., 2004. *Die apokryph gewordenen Evangelien: Studien zu neuen Texten und zu neuen Fragen*, Supplements to Novum Testamentum 112. Leiden: Brill.

Mac Airt, S., 1951. *The Annals of Inisfallen (MS. Rawlinson B. 503)*. Dublin: The Dublin Institute for Advanced Studies.

Macray, W. D., 1890. *Annals of the Bodleian Library Oxford*, 2nd ed. Oxford: Clarendon Press.

Mango, M. M., 1983. "Where Was Beth Zagba?," *Okeanos* (Festschrift für Ihor Ševčenko), *Harvard Ukrainian Studies* 7:405–30.

—, and others, 1986. *Silver from Early Byzantium: The Kaper Koraon and Related Treasures* [exhibition catalogue]. Baltimore: Walters Art Gallery.

Mansi, G. D., 1960–61. *Sacrorum conciliorum nova et amplissima collectio.* Repr. Graz: Akademische Druck u. Verlagsanstalt.

Marchesin, I., 2000. *L'image organum: La représentation de la musique dans les psautiers médiévaux 800–1200*. Turnhout: Brepols.

Margoliouth, G., 1965. *Catalogue of the Hebrew and Samaritan manuscripts in the British Museum*, 4 vols. London: British Museum.

Markus, R., 1997. *Gregory the Great and His World*. Cambridge: Cambridge University Press.

Marr, N. IA., 1940. *Opisanie gruzinskich rukopisei Sinaiskogo monastyrja.* Moscow: Izdatelstvo Akademii nauk SSSR.

Marsden, R., 1995. "Job in his place: the Ezra miniature in the *Codex Amiatinus*," *Scriptorium* 49:3–15.

—, 1995a. *The Text of the Old Testament in Anglo-Saxon England*, Cambridge Studies in Anglo-Saxon England 15. Cambridge: Cambridge University Press.

Marshall Lang, D., 1956. *Lives and Legends of the Georgian Saints Selected and Translated from the Original Texts*. London and New York: George Allen & Unwin / Macmillan.

Mathews, T. F., 1977. "The Epigrams of Leo Sacellarios and an Exegetical Approach to the Miniatures of Vat. Reg. gr. 1," *Orientalia Christiana Periodica* 43:94–133.

—, 1980. "The Early Armenian Iconographic Program of the Ejmiacin Gospel (Erevan, Matenadaran MS 2374, *olim* 229)," in *East of Byzantium: Syria and Armenia in the Formative Period*, ed. N. G. Garsoïan, T. F. Mathews, and R. W. Thomson, 199–212. Washington, D.C.: Dumbarton Oaks.

—, and R. S. Wieck, 1994. *Treasures in Heaven. Armenian Illuminated Manuscripts*. New York: The Pierpont Morgan Library and Princeton University Press.

Mayeda, G., 1946. *Das Leben-Jesu-Fragment Papyrus Egerton 2 und seine Stellung in der urchristlichen Literaturgeschichte*. Bern: Haupt.

Mayer, R., 1962. *The Artist's Handbook of Materials and Techniques*. London: Faber.

Mayr-Harting, H., 1977. *The Coming of Christianity to Anglo-Saxon England*. Oxford: Oxford University Press.

—, 1991. *Ottonian Book Illumination: An Historical Study*, 2 vols. London: Harvey Miller.

Mazal, O., 1999. *Geschichte der Buchkultur*, vol. 1, *Griechische-romische Antike*. Graz.

McCarthy, C., 1993. *Saint Ephrem's Commentary on Tatian's Diatesseron: An English Translation of Chester Beatty Syriac MS 709 with Introduction and Notes*, Journal of Semitic Studies Supplement 2. Oxford: Oxford University Press on behalf of the University of Manchester.

McCormick, M., 1985. "The Birth of the Codex and the Apostolic Lifestyle," *Scriptorium* 39:150–58.

McDonald, L. M., 1995. *The Formation of the Christian Biblical Canon*. Rev. ed., Peabody, Mass.: Hendrickson.

—, and J. A. Sanders, eds., 2002. *The Canon Debate*. Peabody, Mass: Hendrickson.

McGurk, P., 1955. "The Canon Tables in the Book of Lindisfarne," *Journal of Theological Studies* 6:192–8.

—, 1961. *Latin Gospel Books from AD 400 to AD 800*, Les Publications de Scriptorium 5. Paris–Brussels, Anvers–Amsterdam: Scriptorium.

—, 1990. "The Gospel text," in *The Book of Kells, MS 58 Trinity College Library Dublin, Commentary*, ed. P. Fox, 59–152. Lucerne: Fine Art Facsimile Publishers of Switzerland / Faksimile Verlag Luzern.

—, 1993. "The disposition of numbers in Latin Eusebian canon tables," in R. Gryson, ed., *Philologia Sacra* 1:242–58. Freiburg: Herder.

—, 1994. "The Oldest Manuscripts of the Latin Bible," in R. G. Gameson, ed., *The Early Medieval Bible*, 1–23. Cambridge: Cambridge University Press.

—, 1998. *Gospel Books and Early Latin Manuscripts*, Variorum Collected Studies Series. Aldershot, UK: Ashgate.

McKendrick, S. and O. A. O'Sullivan, eds. 2003. *The Bible as Book: The Transmission of the Greek Text*. London: British Library.

McKitterick, R., 1989. *The Carolingians and the Written Word*. Cambridge: Cambridge University Press.

—, 1989a. "Nuns' scriptoria in England and Francia in the eighth century," *Francia* 19:1–35. [Reprinted in R. McKitterick, *Books, scribes and learning in the Frankish kingdoms, 6th–9th centuries*, no. VII (Aldershot, UK and Brookfield, Vt.: Variorum / Ashgate, 1994)]

—, 1990. "Carolingian Uncial: A Context for the Lothar Psalter," *British Library Journal* 16:1–15.

—, ed. 1990a. *The Uses of Literacy in Early Medieval Europe*. Cambridge: Cambridge University Press.

—, ed., 1994. *Carolingian Culture: Emulation and Innovation*. Cambridge: Cambridge University Press.

—, 1995. "Essai sur les representations de l'écrit dans les manuscrits carolingiens," *Révue française d'histoire du livre*, nos 86–87:37–64.

—, 2005. "Psalter of Count Achadeus," in *The Cambridge Illuminations: Ten Centuries of Book Production in the Medieval West*, ed. P. Binski and S. Panayotova, 68–69. London: Harvey Miller.

Meimaris, I. E., 1985. *Catalogos ton Neon Arabikon Xeirographon tes Ieras Mones Hagias Aikaterines tou Orous Sina*. Athens: Greek Ministry of Culture.

Mellors, J. and A. Parsons, 2002. *Ethiopian Bookmaking*. London: New Cross Books.

—, 2002a. *Scribes of South Gondar*. London: New Cross Books.

Merk, A., 1934. "Codex Evangeliorum et Actuum ex collectione Papyrorum Chester Beatty," in *Miscellanea Biblica* 2:375–406.

Merkel, H., 1978. *Die Pluralitat der Evangelien als theologisches und exegetisches Problem in der alten Kirche*. Berne: Lang.

Metreveli, H., 1978. "Les manuscripts liturgiques Géorgiens des IXe–Xe siècles et leur importance pour l'étude de l'hymnographie Byzantin," *Bedi Kartlisa* 36:43–48.

Metzger, B. M., 1981. *Manuscripts of the Greek Bible: An Introduction to Palaeography*. New York: Oxford University Press.

—, 1987. *The Canon of the New Testament: Its Origin, Development and Significance*. Oxford: Clarendon Press.

—, 1992. *The Text of the New Testament: Its Transmission, Corruption and Restoration*, 3rd ed. New York and Oxford: Oxford University Press.

Metzger, M., 1958. "Quelques caractères iconographiques et ornementaux de deux manuscripts hébraïques du Xe siècle," *Cahiers de civilisation médiévale* 1 (1958): 205–13.

Meyer, E. A., 2004. *Legitimacy and Law in the Roman World: Tabulae in Roman Belief and Practice*. Cambridge: Cambridge University Press.

Meyvaert, P., 1996. "Bede, Cassiodorus and the Codex Amiatinus," *Speculum* 71:827–83.

—, 2005. "The Date of Bede's *In Ezram* and His Image of Ezra in the Codex Amiatinus," *Speculum* 80:1087–1133.

Mgaloblishvili, T., ed., 1998. *Ancient Christianity in the Caucasus*, Caucasus World. Surrey, UK: Curzon Press.

Micheli, G. L., 1939. *L'enluminure du haut moyen age et les influences irlandaises*. Brussels: Editions de la connaissance.

Milne, H. J. M. and T. C. Skeat, 1938. *Scribes and Correctors of Codex Sinaiticus*. London: Trustees of the British Museum.

—, eds., 1963. *The Codex Sinaiticus and the Codex Alexandrinus*. Repr. London: British Museum. [Orig. pub. 1938]

Morey, C. R., 1914. "The Painted Covers of the Washington Manuscript of the Gospels," in *East Christian Paintings in the Freer Collection*, 63–81. Ann Arbor: University of Michigan.

Morin, G., ed., 1933. *S. Caesarii arelatensis episcopi. Regula sanctarum virginum aliaque opuscula ad sanctimoniales directa*, Florilegium Patristicum Fasc. 34. Bonn: P. Hanstein.

Muir, B. J., 2004. *A digital facsimile of Oxford, Bodleian Library, MS Junius 11* [CD-Rom], Bodleian Digital Texts 1. Oxford: Bodleian Library.

Muñoz, A., 1906. "Codex Purpureus Sinopensis," *Nuovo Bullettino di Archeologia Cristiana*, 12:215–37.

Murray, A., 1842. [Descriptions of James Bruce's manuscripts in] an auction catalogue of G. Robins of Covent Garden, *A catalogue of a valuable collection of Oriental literature, collected by James Bruce, of Kinnaird* (London, 30 May).

Mütherich, F., 1972. "Die touronishe Bibel von St. Maximin in Trier," *Kunsthistorische Forschungen Otto Pächt zu seinem 70. Geburtstag*, ed. A. Rosenauer and G. Weber, 44–54, pl. 3. Munich: Residenz.

—, 1986. "Der Adler mit dem Fisch," in *Zum Problem der Deutung frühmittelalterlicher Bildinhalte*, ed. H. Roth, 317–40. Sigmaringen: J. Thorbecke.

—, and J. Gaehde, 1976. *Carolingian Painting*. London: Chatto & Windus.

—, and A. Weiner, 1989. *Illuminierte Handschriften der Agilolfinger-und früheren Karolingerzeit*. Munich: Prestel.

Muthesius, A., 1978. "The Silk over the Spine of the Mondsee Gospel Lectionary," *Journal of the Walters Art Gallery* 37:51–73.

Mynors, R. A. B., ed., 1937. *Cassiodori Senatoris Institutiones*. Oxford: Clarendon Press.

Nagel, P., 1989. "Editionen koptischer Bibeltexte seit Till 1960," *Archiv für Papyrusforschung* 35:43–100.

Nahtigal, R., 1941–42. *Euchologium Sinaiticum*, 2 vols. Ljubljana: University of Ljubljana.

Narkiss, B., 1969. *Hebrew Illuminated Manuscripts*. New York: Leon Amiel.

—, 1969a. "Towards a Further Study of the Ashburnham Pentateuch (Pentateuque de Tours)", *Cahiers archéologiques* 19:45–59.

—, 1990. *Illuminations from Hebrew Bibles of Leningrad: Decorations in Hebrew Mediaeval Manuscripts from the Imperial Public Library in St. Petersburg, now the Saltykov Shchedrin Collection at the State Public Library in Leningrad*. Jerusalem: The Bialik Institute.

Nasrallah, J., 1976. "Abūl-Farağ al-Yabrūdī ; médecin chrétien de Damas (X^e^-XIe s.)," *Arabica* 23:13–22.

—, 1979–. *Histoire du mouvement littéraire dans l'église Melchite du Ve au XXe siècle: contribution à l'étude de la littératire arabe chrétienne*, 3 vols. in 6 to date. Louvain: Peeters.

—, 1980. "Deux versions Melchites partielles de la Bible du IXe et du Xe siècles," *Oriens Christianus* 64:202–215.

Nees, L., 1983. "The Colophon Drawing in the Book of Mulling: A Supposed Irish Monastery Plan and the Tradition of Terminal Illustration in Early Medieval Manuscripts," *Cambridge Medieval Celtic Studies* 5:67–91.

—, 1999. "Problems of Form and Function in Early Medieval Illustrated Bibles from Northwest Europe," in *Imaging the Early Medieval Bible*, ed. J. Williams, 125–31. University Park: Pennsylvania State University Press.

—, 2005. "On the Image of Christ Crucified in Early Medieval Art," in *Il Volto Santo in Europa*, ed. M. C. Ferrari and A. Meyer, 345–85. Lucca: Istituto storico Lucchese.

Nelson, J., 1996. *The Frankish World, 750–900*. London: Hambledon Press.

Nelson, R., 1980. *The Iconography of Preface and Miniature in the Byzantine Gospel Book*. New York: New York University Press.

Nersessian, V., ed., 1978. *The Christian Orient*. London: British Library.

—, 1987. *Armenian Illuminated Gospel Books*. London: British Library.

—, ed., 2001. *Treasures from the Ark: 1700 Years of Armenian Christian Art*. London: British Library.

Netzer, N., 1994. *Cultural Interplay in the Eighth Century: The Trier Gospels and the Making of a Scriptorium at Echternach*. Cambridge: Cambridge University Press.

Nicholson, E. W. B., 1913. *Introduction to the Study of Some of the Oldest Latin Musical Manuscripts in the Bodleian Library, Oxford*, Early Bodleian Music [3]. London and New York: Novello / H. W. Gray. [Repr. Farnborough: Gregg, 1967]

Nordenfalk, C., 1938. *Die spätantiken Kanontafeln* Göteborg: Oscar Isacsons Boktryckeri.

—, 1971. *Codex Caesareus Upsaliensis: An Echternach Gospel-Book of the Eleventh Century*. Stockholm: Alqvist & Wiksell.

—, 1977. *Celtic and Anglo-Saxon Painting*. London: Chatto & Windus.

—, 1980. Review of von Euw and Plotzek, 1979, *Kunstchronik* 33:57.

—, 1983. "Ein unveröffentlichtes Apokalypsenfragment," *Pantheon* 36:114–18.

—, 1988. *Early Medieval Book Illumination*. New York: Rizzoli.

—, 1992. *Studies in the History of Book Illumination*. London: Pindar Press.

Ó Carragáin, E., 1987. "A Liturgical Interpretation of the Bewcastle Cross," in *Medieval Literature and Antiquities: Studies in Honour of Basil Cottle*, ed. M. Stokes and T. C. Burton, 15–42. Cambridge: Cambridge University Press.

—, 1994. *The City of Rome and the World of Bede*. Jarrow Lecture Series. Jarrow, Tyne & Wear.

—, 2005. *Ritual and the Rood: Liturgical Images and the Old English Poems of the Dream of the Rood Tradition*. London and Toronto: British Library / University of Toronto.

Offer, Y., 2002. "The History and Authority of the Aleppo Codex," in *Jerusalem Crown. Companion Volume*, ed. M. Glatzer, 25–50. Jerusalem: N. Ben-Zvi Printing Enterprises.

O'Fiaich, T., 1974. *Columbanus in His Own Words*. Dublin: Veritas Publications. [Repr. 1990]

Ó Floinn, R., 1994. *Irish Shrines and Reliquaries of the Middle Ages*. Dublin: National Museum of Ireland.

Ohlgren, T. H., 1986. *Insular and Anglo-Saxon Illuminated Manuscripts: An Iconographic Catalogue c. A.D. 625 to 1100*, Garland Reference Library of the Humanities 631. New York and London: Garland.

—, 1992. *Anglo-Saxon textual illustration. Photographs of sixteen manuscripts with descriptions and index*. Kalamazoo: Medieval Institute Publications, Western Michigan University.

Omont, H., 1922. "Manuscrits illustrés de l'Apocalypse aux IXe et Xe siècles," *Bulletin de la Société française de reproductions de manuscrits à peintures* 6:62–95.

O'Neill, T., 1984. *The Irish Hand*. Portlaoise: Dolmen Press.

Ong, W., 1981. *Orality and Literacy: The Technologizing of the Word*. London: Methuen.

Opus caroli regis, 1998. *Opus caroli regis contra synodum (Libri Carolini)*, ed. A. Freeman, Monumenta Germaniae Historia, Concilia 2, suppl. 1. Hannover: Hansche Buchhandlung.

O'Reilly, J., 1998. "Patristic and Insular Traditions of the Evangelists: Exegesis and Iconography," in *Le Isole Britanniche e Roma in Età Romanobarbarica*, ed. A. M. Luiselli Fadda and E. Ó Carragáin, 49–94. Rome: Herder.

—, 2001. "The Library of Scripture: Views from the Vivarium and Wearmouth-Jarrow," in *New Offerings, Ancient Treasures. Essays in Medieval Art for George Henderson*, ed. P. Binski and W. G. Noel. Stroud: Alan Sutton.

Pächt, O., 1986. *Book Illumination in the Middle Ages: An Introduction*. London: Harvey Miller.

—, and J. J. G. Alexander, 1966–73. *Illuminated Manuscripts in the Bodleian Library Oxford*, 3 vols. Oxford: Clarendon Press.

Pack, R. A., 1965. *The Greek and Roman Literary Texts from Greco-Roman Egypt*. 2nd ed. Ann Arbor: University of Michigan Press.

Paderborn, 1999. *799. Kunst und Kultur der Karolingerzeit: Karl der Grosse und Papst Leo III. in Paderborn* [exhibition catalogue], ed. C. Stiegemann and M. Wemhoff, 2 vols. Mainz: Philipp von Zabern.

Page, R. I., 1995. *Runes and Runic Inscriptions*. Woodbridge: Boydell & Brewer.

Parker, D. C., 1997. *The Living Text of the Gospels*. Cambridge: Cambridge University Press.

Parkes, M. B., 1976. "The Handwriting of St Boniface: A Reassessment of the Problems," *Beiträge zur Geschichte der deutschen Sprache und Literatur, Tübingen* 98:161–79.

—, 1992. *Pause and Effect: An Introduction to the History of Punctuation in the West*. Aldershot, UK: Scolar Press.

—, 2000. "*Rædan*, *areccan*, *smeagan*: how the Anglo-Saxons read," *Anglo-Saxon England* 26:1–22.

Perrin, N., 2002. *Thomas and Tatian: The Relationship between the Gospel of Thomas and the Diatessaron*, Academia Biblica 5. Atlanta: Society of Biblical Literature.

Perruchon, J., 1965. *Vie de Lalibela, roi d'Éthiopie. Texte éthiopien publié d'après un manuscrit du Musée Britannique et traduction française … et la description des églises monolithes de Lalibala*, Publications de l'Ecole des Lettres d'Alger. Paris: E. Leroux.

Peter Damian, 1983. *Sancti Petri Damiani Sermones*, ed. J. Lucchesi, Corpus Christianorum Continuatio Mediaevalis, 57. Turnhout: Brepols.

Petersen, T., 1954. "The Paragraph Mark in Coptic Illuminated Ornament," in D. Miner, ed., *Studies in Art and Literature for Bella Da Costa Greene*, 295–330. Princeton: Princeton University Press.

Petersen, W. L., 1994. *Tatian's Diatessaron: Its Creation, Dissemination, Significance, and History in Scholarship*, Supplements to Vigiliae Christianae 25. Leiden: Brill.

—, 2004. "The Diatessaron and the Fourfold Gospel," in *The Earliest Gospels*, ed. C. Horton, *Journal for the Society of the New Testament*, Supplement Series 258:50–68. London and New York: T & T Clark.

Pickering, S. R., 2003. "The Egerton Gospel and New Testament Textual Transmission," in *The New Testament Text in Early Christianity (Proceedings of the Lille Colloquium, July 2000)*, ed. C. B. Amphoux and J. K. Elliott, 215–34. Lausanne: Zebre.

Plotzek, J. M., and others, 1992. *Biblioteca Apostolica Vaticana: Liturgie und Andacht im Mittelalter* [exhibition catalogue], Erzbischöfliches Diözesan-museum Köln. Stuttgart: Belser.

Plummer, C., 1925. *Irish Litanies*, Henry Bradshaw Society 67. London: Henry Bradshaw Society.

Poilpré, A.-O., 2005. *Maiestas Domini: Une image de l'Église en Occident Ve–IXe siècle*. Paris: Éditions du Cerf.

Polliack, M., ed., 2003. *Karaite Judaism: a guide to its history and literary sources*. Leiden and Boston: Brill.

Porphyry, 1973. *Publilii Optatiani Porphyrii Carmina*, ed. J. Polara. Turin: G. B. Paravia.

Porphyry, Bishop, 1856. *Vtoroye puteshestviye arhimandrita Porfiriya Uspenskogo v Sinayskiy monastir v 1850 godu*. [Second Journey to the Sinai Monastery in 1850]. St. Petersburg.

—, 1896. *Kniga bitiya moego* [Genesis of Mine]. St. Petersburg.

Prescott, A. J., 2002. *The Benedictional of St Ethelwold* [facsimile]. London: British Library / Folio Society.

Primasius, 1847. J.-P. Migne, *Patrologiae Cursus Completus, Series Latina* 68, cols. 793–936. Paris: Garnier.

Primasius, 1887. Haussleiter, J., *Leben und Werke des Bischofs Primasius von Hadrumetum*. Progr., Erlangen.

Primasius, 1891. Haussleiter, J., *Die lateinische Apokalypse der alten afrikanischen Kirche*, Forschungen zur Geschichte des neutestamentlichen Kanons und der altkirchlichen Literatur, ed. T. Zahn and others, 4, 1–224. Erlangen and Leipzig: A. Deichert.

Primasius, 1985. *Primasius Episcopus Hadrumetinus, Commentarius in Apocalypsin*, ed. A. W. Adams, Corpus Christianorum Series Latina 92. Turnhout: Brepols.

Quentin, H., 1922. "Mémoire sur l'établissement du texte de la Vulgate," in *Collections Biblica Latina*, 6:249–59.

Rahlfs, A. and D. Fraenkel, 2004. *Verzeichnis der griechischen Handschriften des Alten Testament*, vol. 1. Göttingen: Vandenhoeck & Ruprecht.

Randall, R. R. Jr., 1985. *Masterpieces of Ivory from the Walters Art Gallery*. New York: Hudson Hills Press.

Raw, B., 1976. "The probable derivation of most of the illustrations in Junius 11 from an illustrated Old Saxon Genesis," *Anglo-Saxon England* 5:133–48.

—, 1984. "The construction of Oxford, Bodleian Library, Junius 11," *Anglo-Saxon England* 13:187–207.

Reed, R., 1972. *Ancient Skins, Parchments and Leathers*. London: Seminar.

Reif, S. C., 2000. *A Jewish Archive from Old Cairo: The History of Cambridge University's Genizah Collection*. Richmond, UK: Curzon.

Reiner, N., 2002. *Die Touronische Bibel der Abteil St. Maximin von Trier*. Trier.

Remley, P. G., 1996. *Old English Biblical Verse: Studies in* Genesis, Exodus, *and* Daniel, Cambridge Studies in Anglo-Saxon England 16. Cambridge: Cambridge University Press.

Reudenbach, B., 1998. *Das Godescalc-Evangelistar: Ein Buch für die Reformpolitik Karls des Grossen*. Frankfurt am Main: Fischer Taschenbuch.

Revel-Neher, E., 1984. *L'arche d'alliance dans l'art juif et chrétien du second au dixième siècles*. Paris: Association des Amis des Études Archéologiques Byzantino-Slaves et du Christianisme Oriental.

Reynolds, L. D., and N. G. Wilson, 1974. *Scribes and Scholars: A Guide to the Transmission of Greek and Latin Literature*. 2nd ed. Oxford: Oxford University Press.

Richard, M., 1964. *Répertoire des bibliothèques et des catalogues de manuscrits grecs, Supplément I*, 1958–63. Paris: Centre Nationale de la Recherche Scientifique.

Roberts, C. H., 1953. "An Early Papyrus of the First Gospel," *Harvard Theological Review* 46:233–37.

—, 1954. "The Codex," *Proceedings of the British Academy* 40:169–204.

—, 1955. *Greek Literary Hands 350 BC–AD 400*. Oxford: Clarendon Press.

—, 1979. *Manuscript, Society and Belief in Early Christian Egypt*, The Schweich Lectures of the British Academy, 1977. London: Oxford University Press for the British Academy.

—, and T. C. Skeat, 1983. *The Birth of the Codex*. Oxford: Oxford University Press.

Robinson, J. M., 1975. "The Construction of the Nag Hammadi Codices," in *Essays on the Nag Hammadi Texts in Honor of Pahor Labib*, ed. M. Krause, 170–90. Leiden: Brill.

—, 1984. *The Facsimile Edition of the Nag Hammadi Codices*. Leiden: Brill.

—, and R. Smith, eds., 1988. *The Nag Hammadi Library in English*. 3rd rev. ed. San Francisco: Harper & Row.

Roca-Puig, R., 1956. *Un Papiro Griego del Evangelio de San Mateo*. Barcelona.

Roth, C., 1953. "Jewish Antecedents of Christian Art," *Journal of the Warburg and Courtauld Institutes* 16:24–44.

Royse, J. R., 1979. "Scribal Habits in the Transmission of New Testament Texts," in *The Critical Study of Sacred Texts*, ed. W. D. O'Flaherty, 139–61. Berkeley: Graduate Theological Union.

Rüger, H. P., 1966. "Ein Fragment der bisher ältesten datierten hebräischen Bibelhandschrift mit babylonischer Punktation," in *Vetus Testamentum* 16:65–73.

Rypins, S., 1956. "Two inedited leaves of Codex N," *The Journal of Biblical Literature* 75, Part I: 27–39, 2 illus.

Saenger, P., 1997. *Space between Words: The Origins of Silent Reading.* Stanford, Calif.: Stanford University Press.

Safran, L., ed., 1998. *Heaven on Earth: Art and the Church in Byzantium.* University Park: Pennsylvania State University Press.

Samir, K., 1987. "Michel évêque melkite de Damas au 9e siècle. A propos de Bišr Ibn al-Sirrī," *Orientalia Christiana Periodica* 53:439–41.

Sanders, H. A., 1908. "New Manuscripts of the Bible from Egypt," *American Journal of Archaeology* 12:49–55 and pl. III.

—, 1909. "Age and Ancient Home of Biblical Manuscripts in the Freer Collection," *American Journal of Archaeology* 13:130–41.

—, 1910–17. *The Old Testament Manuscripts in the Freer Collection*, Part I: *The Washington Manuscript of Deuteronomy and Joshua* (New York: Macmillan, 1910); Part 2: *The Washington Manuscript of the Psalms*, University of Michigan Studies, Humanistic Series 8 (New York: Macmillan).

—, 1912–18. *The New Testament Manuscripts in the Freer Collection*, Part 1: *The Washington Manuscript of the Four Gospels* (New York: Macmillan, 1912); Part 2: *The Washington Manuscript of the Epistles of Paul*, University of Michigan Studies, Humanistic Series 9 (New York and London: Macmillan, 1918).

—, 1913. Introduction to *Facsimile of the Washington Manuscript of the Four Gospels in the Freer Collection*. Ann Arbor: University of Michigan.

—, 1921. "A Papyrus Manuscript of the Minor Prophets," *Harvard Theological Review* 14:181–87.

—, 1927. *Facsimile of the Washington Manuscript of the Minor Prophets in the Freer Collection and the Berlin Fragment of Genesis*. Ann Arbor: University of Michigan.

—, 1935. *A Third-Century Papyrus Codex of the Epistles of Paul*, University of Michigan Studies, Humanistic Series 38. Ann Arbor: University of Michigan.

—, and C. Schmidt, 1927. *The Minor Prophets in the Freer Collection and the Berlin Fragment of Genesis*. New York: Macmillan.

Sawyer, J. F. A., 1999. *Sacred Languages and Sacred Texts*. London: Routledge.

Schmerling, R., 1967–79. *Khudozhestvennoe oformlenie gruzinksko rukopisno knigi IX–XI vv.* [Georgian: K'art'uli xelnaceri cignis mxatvruli gap'ormeba IX–XI saukuneebi], 2 vols. Tbilisi: Met's'niereba.

Schmidt, A. B., 1997. "Gab es einen armenischen Ikonoklasmus? Rekonstruktion eines Dokuments der Kaukasisch-Albanischen Theologiegeschichte," in *Das Frankfurter Konzil von 794. Kristallisationspunkt karolingischer Kultur*, 947–64. Mainz: Gesellschaft für Mittelrheinische Kirchengeschichte.

Schmidt, C., 1931. "Die neuesten Bibelfunde aus Ägypten," in *Zeitschrif für die neutestamentliche Wissenschaft* 30:285–93.

—, 1933. "Die Evangelienhandschrift der Chester Beatty-Sammlung," in *Zeitschrif für die neutestamentliche Wissenschaft* 32:225–32.

—, 1959. *Koptisch-Gnostische Schriften*, ed. W. Till, Die Griechischen Christlichen Schriftsteller der ersten Jahrhunderte 45 (13). 3rd ed. Berlin: Akademie.

—, 1978. *The Books of Jeu and the Untitled Text in the Bruce Codex*, English trans. V. Macdermot. Leiden: Brill.

Schneemelcher, W., 1991. *New Testament Apocrypha*, 2 vols. Rev. ed. Louisville: Westminster / John Knox.

Schreckenberg, H. and K. Schubert, 1992. *Jewish Historiography and Iconography in Early and Medieval Christianity.* Assen and Maastricht and Minneapolis: Van Gorcum / Fortress Press.

Schubart, W., 1962. *Das Buch bei den Griechen und Romern*, 3rd ed., ed. P. von Eberhard. Heidelberg: Lambert Schneider. [Orig. pub. Berlin: Königliche Museen. Handbücher, 1907]

Schüssler, K., ed., 2000. *Biblica Coptica: Die koptischen Bibeltexte. Bd. 1. Das sahidische Alte und Neue Testament: Vollständiges Verzeichnis mit Standorten, 1–120, Lieferung 4, 93–120.* Forschungsinstitut für Koptologie und Ägyptenkunde der Universität Salzburg. Wiesbaden: Harrassowitz.

Scrivener, F. H. A., 1894. *A Plain Introduction to the Criticism of the New Testament*, 4th ed., ed. Edward Miller, 2 vols. London: George Bell and Sons.

Sepière, M.-C., 1994. *L'image d'un Dieu souffrant: Aux origines du crucifix.* Paris: Éditions du Cerf.

Ševčenko, I., 1964. "New Documents on Constantine Tischendorf and the Codex Sinaiticus," *Scriptorium* 18:55–80.

—, 1982. "Report on the Glagolitic Fragments (of the Euchologium Sinaiticum?) Discovered on Sinai in 1975 and Some Thoughts on the Models for the Make-up of the Earliest Glagolitic Manuscripts," *Harvard Ukrainian Studies* 6, no.2 (June): 119–51.

Shahid, I., 1976. "The Kebra Nagast in the Light of Recent Research," *Le Muséon* 89:133–78.

Shamosh, A., 1987. *Ha-Keter: The Story of the Aleppo Codex*. Jerusalem: Ben-Zvi Institute. [Hebrew]

Shanidze, A., 1945. *Two Ancient Versions of the Georgian Gospels*, Monuments of the Old Georgian Language 2:017–132. Tbilisi: Academy of Sciences. [Georgian]

Sharpe, R., and others, 1996. *English Benedictine Libraries: the Shorter Catalogues*, Corpus of British Medieval Library Catalogues 4. London: The British Library in association with the British Academy.

Sirat, C., 1992. "Genesis discovery," in *Genizah Fragments* 23 (April): 2.

—, 1992a. "Earliest known Sefer Torah," in *Genizah Fragments* 24 (October): 3.

—, 1993. "Par l'oreille et par l'oeil: la Bible hébraïque et les livres qui la portent," in *The Frank Talmage memorial volume*, ed. B. Walfish, 1, 233–49. Haifa and Hanover, N. H.: Haifa University Press / University Press of New England in association with Brandeis University Press.

—, 1994. "Rouleaux de la Tora antérieurs à l'an mille," with the collaboration of M. Dukan and A. Yardeni, in *Comptes Rendus de séances de L'Academie des Inscriptions et Belles Lettres* 1994:861–87.

—, 2002. *Hebrew Manuscripts of the Middle Ages*, ed. and trans. N. de Lange. Cambridge: Cambridge University Press.

Siverstev, A., 2000. "The Gospel of Thomas and Early Stages in the Development of the Christian Wisdom Literature," *Journal of Early Christian Studies* 8:319–40.

Skeat, T. C., 1982. "The Length of the Standard Papyrus Roll and the Cost Advantage of the Codex," *Zeitschrift fur Papyrologie und Epigraphik* 45, 169–75.

—, 1993. "A Codicological Analysis of the Chester Beatty Papyrus Codex of Gospels and Acts (P45)," in *Hermathena (A Trinity College Dublin Review)* 155:27–43.

—, 1994. "The Origins of the Christian Codex," *Zeitschrift für Papyrologie und Epigraphik* 102:263–68.

—, 1997. "The Oldest Manuscript of the Four Gospels?" *New Testament Studies* 43:1–34.

—, and B. C. McGing, 1991. "Notes on Chester Beatty Biblical Papyrus I (Gospels and Acts)," in *Hermathena (A Trinity College Dublin Review)* 150:21–25 and plates.

Skeat, W. W., 1871–87. *The Four Gospels in Anglo-Saxon, Northumbrian, and Old Mercian Versions*, 4 vols. Cambridge: Cambridge University Press. [Repr. Darmstadt, 1970]

Skehan, P. W., 1954. "An Illuminated Gospel Book in Ethiopic," in *Studies in art and literature for Belle da Costa Greene*, ed. D. Miner, 350–57. Princeton, N.J.: Princeton University Press.

Smith Lewis, A., 1894. *Catalogue of the Syriac MSS. In the Convent of St Catharine on Mount Sinai*, Studium Sinaitica 1. London: C. J. Clay & Sons.

Snyder, H. G., 2000. *Teachers and Texts in the Ancient World: Philosophers, Jews and Christians*. London: Routledge.

Sokoloff, M. and J. Yahalom, 1978. "Christian palimpsests from the Cairo Geniza," in *Revue d'histoire des textes* 8:109–32.

Sörries, R., 1991. *Die Syrische Bibel von Paris*. Wiesbaden: Dr. Ludwig Reichert.

—, 1993. *Christlich-Antike Buchmalerei im Überblick*. Wiesbaden: Dr. Ludwig Reichert.

Souter, A., 1904–1905. "The Original Home of Codex Claromontanus Paul," *Journal of Theological Studies* 6:240–43.

Staal, H., 1969. *Codex Sinai Arabic 151, Pauline Epistles (Rom., I & II Cor., Phil.)*, 2 vols., Studies and Documents 40. Salt Lake City: University of Utah Press.

—, ed. and trans., 1983. *Mt. Sinai Arabic Codex 151*. I. *Pauline Epistles*, Corpus Scriptorum Christianorum Orientalium 452–3. Scriptores Arabici t. 40–41. Louvain: Peeters.

—, ed. and trans., 1984. *Mt. Sinai Arabic Codex 151:* II. *Acts of the Apostles, Catholic Epistles*, Corpus Scriptorum Christianorum Orientalium 462–3. Scriptores Arabici t. 42–43. Louvain: Peeters.

Stansbury, M., 1999. "Early Medieval Biblical Commentaries, Their Writers and Readers," in *Frümittelalterliche Studien, Herausgegeben von H. Keller und C. Meier*, ed. K. Hauck, 50–82. Berlin and New York: Frühmittelalterliche Studien.

Starr, R., 1990–91. "*Lectores* and Book Reading," *Classical Journal* 86:337–43.

Stassoff, W., 1887. *L'Ornement Slave et oriental*. St. Petersburg.

St. Clair, A., 1987. "A New Moses: Typological Iconography in the Moutier-Grandval Bible Illustrations of Exodus," *Gesta* 26:19–28.

Steenbock, F., 1965. *Der kirchliche Prachteinband im frühen Mittelalter von Anfängen bis zum Beginn der Gotik*. Berlin: Deutscher Verlag für Kunstwissenschaft.

Stegemann, H., 1990. "Methods for the Reconstruction of Scrolls from Scattered Fragments," in *Archaeology and History in the Dead Sea Scrolls*, ed. L. Schiffman, 189–220. Sheffield, UK: Sheffield Academic Press.

Strakhovsky, L. I., 1949. *A Handbook of Slavic Studies*. Cambridge: Harvard University Press.

Streeter, B. H., 1926. "The Washington Manuscript of the Gospels," *Harvard Theological Review* 19:165–72.

Stuhlhofer, F., 1988. *Der Gebrauch der Bibel von Jesus bis Euseb: Eine statistische Untersuchung zur Kanongeschichte*. Wuppertal: Brockhaus.

Stuttgarter Bilderpsalter, 1968. *Der Stuttgarter Bilderpsalter: Bibl. fol. 23 Württembergische Landesbibliothek Stuttgart*. Stuttgart: E. Schreiber Graphische Kunstantstalten.

Sukenik, E. L., 1955. *The Dead Sea Scrolls of the Hebrew University*. Jerusalem: The Magness Press, The Hebrew University of Jerusalem.

Summary Catalogue, 1895–1953. F. Madan and others, *A Summary Catalogue of Western Manuscripts in the Bodleian Library at Oxford which have not Hitherto been Catalogued in the Quarto Series*, 7 vols. in 8 [vol. 2 in 2 parts]. Oxford: Clarendon Press. [Repr. Munich: Kraus-Thomson, 1980]

Sundberg, A. C., 1964. *The Old Testament of the Early Church*. Cambridge, Mass.: Harvard University Press.

Swarzenski, G., 1901. *Die Regensburger Buchmalerei des X. und XI. Jahrhunderts*. Leipzig: Hiersemann.

Tarchnischvili, M. ed., 1959–60. *Le Grand Lectionaire de L'Eglise de Jerusalem (Ve–VIIIe S.)*, Corpus Scriptorum Christianorum Orientalium 189, 205. Louvain: Peeters.

Tarnanidis, I. C., 1988. *The Slavonic Manuscripts Discovered in 1975 at St Catherine's Monastery on Mount Sinai*. Thessaloniki: Hellenic Association for Slavic Studies.

Tchernetska, N., 2002. "Greek-oriental palimpsests in Cambridge: problems and prospects," in *Literacy, education and manuscript transmission in Byzantium and beyond*, ed. C. Holmes and J. Waring, 243–56. Leiden and Boston: Brill.

Telepneff, Fr. G., 1998. *The Egyptian Desert in the Irish Bogs: The Byzantine Character of Early Celtic Monasticism*. Etna, Calif.: Center for Traditionalist Orthodox Studies.

Temple, E., 1976. *Anglo-Saxon manuscripts 900–1066*, A Survey of Manuscripts Illuminated in the British Isles 2. London: Harvey Miller.

Thierry, N., 2002. "Sur le culte de Sainte Nino," in *Die Christianisierung des Kaukasus / The Christianization of Caucasus (Armenia, Georgia, Albania)*, ed. W. Seibt, 151–58. Vienna: Österreichischen Akademie der Wissenschaften.

Thomson, R., 1988–89. "Mission, Conversion, and Christianization: The Armenian Example," *Harvard Ukrainian Studies* 12–13:28–45.

—, 2002. "Syrian Christianity and the Conversion of Armenia," in *Die Christianisierung des Kaukasus / The Christianization of Caucasus (Armenia, Georgia, Albania)*, ed. W. Seibt, 159–69. Vienna: Österreichischen Akademie der Wissenschaften.

Till, W. C., 1959–60. "Coptic Biblical Texts after Vaschalde's Lists," *Bulletin of the John Rylands Library* 42:220–40.

Tov, E., 1986. "Jewish Greek Scriptures," in *Early Judaism and Its Modern Interpreters*, ed. R. A. Kraft and G. W. E. Nickelsburg, 223–37. Atlanta: Scholars Press.

—, 1988. "Hebrew Biblical Manuscripts from the Judean Desert: Their Contribution to Textual Criticism," *Journal of Jewish Studies* 39:5–37.

Trebolle Barrera, J. C., 1998. *The Jewish Bible and the Christian Bible*. Leiden: Brill.

Tsagareli, A. A., 1888. *Gruzine na Sinayé I vi svyatoï Zemlyé*. St. Petersburg: 2 Vip.

—, 1888a. "Pamyatniki gruzinskoy starini v Sviatoy Zemle i na Sinaye" [Monuments of Georgian Antiquity in the Holy Land and Sinai], in *Pravoslavniy Palestinskiy sbornik* 10:193–95. St. Petersburg.

Tseret'eli, G., 1961. "The Most Ancient Georgian Inscriptions in Palestine," *Bedi Kartlisa: Revue de Kartvélologie* 7:111–30.

Turner, E. G., 1977. *The Typology of the Early Codex*. Philadelphia: University of Pennsylvania Press.

—, 1980. *Greek Papyri: An Introduction*. 2nd ed. Princeton: Princeton University Press.

—, 1987. *Greek Manuscripts of the Ancient World*, 2nd ed., rev. P. Parsons. London: University of London Institute of Classical Studies. [Orig. pub. Oxford: Clarendon Press, 1971]

Uhlig, S., 2003. "Bible: Time and Context," in *Encyclopaedia Aethiopica*, ed. S. Uhlig, 1:563–64. Wiesbaden: Harrassowitz.

Ullendorff, E., 1968. *Ethiopia and the Bible*, The Schweich Lectures of the British Academy, 1967. London: Oxford University Press for the British Academy.

Ulrich, E., 2000. s.v. "Isaiah, Book of," in *Encyclopedia of the Dead Sea Scrolls*, ed. L. H. Schiffman and J. C. VanderKam, 1:384–88. Oxford: Oxford University Press.

Underwood, P. A., 1950. "The Fountain of Life in Manuscripts of the Gospels," *Dumbarton Oaks Papers* 5:43–138.

Urbaniack-Walczak, K., 1992. *Die "conceptio per aurem": Untersuchungen zum Marienbild in Ägypten unter besonderer Berücksichtigung der Malereien in El-Bagawat*, Arbeiten zum spätantiken und koptischen Ägypten 2. Altenberge: Oros.

Valdivieso, P. O., 1966. "Un neuvo fragmento siriaco del Comentario de san Efrén al Diatésaron (PPalau-Rib. 2)," *Studia Papyrologica* 5:7–17.

van der Horst, K., W. Noel, and W. C. M. Wüstefeld, eds., 1996. *The Utrecht Psalter in Medieval Art: Picturing the Psalms of David*. Westrenen: HES Publishers.

VanderKam, J. and P. Flint, 2004. *The Meaning of the Dead Sea Scrolls*. New York: Harper San Francisco.

van Esbroeck, M., 1972. "Le roi Sanatrouk et l'apôtre Thaddée," *Revue des études arméniennes* n.s. 9:241–83.

—, 1981. "Les manuscrits de Jean Zosime Sin. 34 et Tsagareli 81," *Bedi Kartlisa* 39:63–75.

—, 1984. "The Rise of Saint Bartholomew's Cult in Armenia from the Seventh to the Thirteenth Centuries," in *Medieval Armenian Culture: Proceedings of the Third Dr. H. Markarian Conference on Armenian Culture*, ed. T. J. Samuelian and M. E. Stone, University of Pennsylvania Armenian texts and studies 6:61–78. Chico, Calif.: Scholars Press.

van Regemorter, B., 1992. *Binding Structures in the Middle Ages*. Brussels: Bibliotheca Wittockiana. [Trans. J. Greenfield, London: Maggs, 1992]

Vaschalde, A., 1919. "Ce qui a été publié des versions coptes de la Bible," *Revue biblique* n.s. 16, 28 (1919): 220–43, 513–31; 29 (1920): 91–106, 241–58; 30 (1921): 237–46; 31 (1922): 81–88, 234–58; continued in *Le Muséon* 43 (1930): 409–31; 46 (1933): 299–306; 46 (1933): 306–13.

Vasilyeva, O., 1996. "Oriental Manuscripts in the National Library of Russia," *Manuscripta Orientalia* 2, 2 (June): 19–35.

Verey, C. D., 1989. "The Gospel Texts at Lindisfarne at the Time of St Cuthbert," in *St Cuthbert, His Cult and His Community*, ed. G. Bonner and others, 143–150. Woodbridge: Boydell & Brewer.

—, 1998. "A Northumbrian Text Family," in *The Bible as Book: the Manuscript Tradition*, ed. J. L. Sharpe III and K. Van Kampen, 105–22. London and New Castle, Del.: The British Library / Oak Knoll Press.

—, 1999. "Lindisfarne or Rath Maelsigi? The Evidence of the Texts," in *Northumbria's Golden Age*, ed. J. Hawkes and S. Mills, 327–35. Stroud: Alan Sutton.

—, and others, 1980. *The Durham Gospels*, Early English Manuscripts in Facsimile 20. Copenhagen: Rosenkilde & Bagger.

Verkerk, D., 2004. *Early Medieval Bible Illumination and the Ashburnham Pentateuch.* Cambridge: Cambridge University Press.

Volbach, W. F. 1976. *Elfenbeinarbeiten der spätantike und des frühen Mittelalters*, Kataloge vor- und frühgeschichtlicher Altertümer 7. 3rd ed. Mainz: Philipp von Zabern.

von Euw, A. and J. M. Plotzek, eds., 1979. *Die Handschriften der Sammlung Ludwig I*. Cologne: Schnütgen Museum.

von Friesen, O. and A. Grape, 1927. Introduction to *Codex Argenteus Upsaliensis jussu senatus universitatis phototypice editus* [facsimile], 11–118. Uppsala and Malmö: Almqvist and Wiksell.

Vulgate, 1926. *Biblia Sacra iuxta Latinam Vulgatam versionem ad codicum fidem*. Rome: Vatican.

Walker, R., 1998. *Views of Transition: Liturgy and Illumination in Medieval Spain*. London and Toronto: British Library / Toronto University Press.

Walsh, J. and T. Bradley, 1991. *A History of the Irish Church 400–700 AD*. Blackrock: Columba Press.

Walsh, M. and D. Ó Cróinín, eds., 1988. *Cummian's Letter De Controversia Paschale*. Toronto: Pontifical Institute of Mediaeval Studies.

Watson, A. G., 1984. *Catalogue of Dated and Datable Manuscripts* c.*435–1600 in Oxford Libraries*, 2 vols. Oxford: Clarendon Press.

—, 1987. "The Manuscript Collection of Sir Walter Cope (d. 1614)," *The Bodleian Library Record*, 12 pt. 4:262–97.

Webster, L. and J. M. Backhouse., eds., 1991. *The Making of England: Anglo-Saxon Art and Culture AD 600–900*. London: British Museum.

—, and M. P. Brown, eds., 1997. *The Transformation of the Roman World AD 400–900*. London: British Museum Press.

Weiss, Z., 2005. *The Sepphoris Synagogue: Deciphering an Ancient Message through Its Archaeological and Socio-Historical Contexts*. Jerusalem: Hebrew University of Jerusalem.

Weitzman, M. P., 1999. *The Syriac Version of the Old Testament: An Introduction*. Cambridge: Cambridge University Press.

Weitzmann, K., 1935. *Die Byzantinische Buchmalerei des 9 und 10 Jahrhunderts*. Berlin.

—, 1973. *Illustrated Manuscripts at St Catherine's Monastery on Mount Sinai*. Collegeville, Minn.: St John's University Press.

—, 1976. *The Monastery of Saint Catherine at Mount Sinai: The Icons*. Princeton: Princeton University Press.

—, 1977. *Late Antique and Early Christian Book Illumination*. London: Chatto & Windus.

—, 1979. *Age of Spirituality: Late Antique and Early Christian Art, Third to Seventh Century* [exhibition catalogue]. New York: Metropolitan Museum of Art.

—, and M. Bernabò, 1999. *The Byzantine Octateuchs*. Princeton: Princeton University Press.

—, and H. L. Kessler, 1986. *The Cotton Genesis*, Illustrations in the Manuscripts of the Septuagint 1. Princeton: Princeton University Press.

Wenzel, H., 2000. "Die Schrift und das Heilige," in *Die Verschriftlichung der Welt*, 15–57. Milan: Skira.

Werckmeister, O. K., 1963. *Der Deckel des Codex Aureus von St. Emmeram*. Baden-Baden and Strasbourg: P.H. Heitz.

White, H. G. E., 1926–33. *The Monasteries of the Wadi 'n Natrun*, 3 vols. New York: Metropolitan Museum of Art.

Whitelock, D., ed., 1970. *Sweet's Anglo-Saxon Reader*. 2nd. ed. Oxford: Clarendon Press.

—, ed., 1979. *English Historical Documents* 1. Rev. ed. London: Oxford University Press.

Wiesen, D. S., 1964. *St. Jerome as a Satirist: A Study in Christian Latin Thought and Letters*. Ithaca: Cornell University Press.

Wilkinson, J., 1977. *Jerusalem Pilgrims Before the Crusades*. Warminster, UK: Aris & Phillips.

Wilson, E. B., 1994. *Bibles and Bestiaries: A Guide to Illuminated Manuscripts*. New York: Farrar, Straus & Giroux.

Wittekind, S., 2003. "Die Makkabäer als Vorblid des geistlichen Kampfes: Eine kunsthistorische Deutung des Leidener Makkabaer-Codex Perizoni 17," *Frühmittelalterliche Studien*, 37:47–71.

Wood, I., 1995. *The Most Holy Abbot, Ceolfrid*, Jarrow Lecture Series. Jarrow, Tyne & Wear.

Wordsworth, J. and H. J. White, 1889–98. *Nouum Testamentum ... secundum editionem Sancti Hieronymi: pars prior – Quattuor Euangelia*. Oxford: Clarendon Press.

Worrell, W. H., 1916. *The Coptic Psalter in the Freer Collection*. New York and London: Macmillan.

—, 1923. *The Coptic Manuscripts in the Freer Collection*. University of Michigan Humanistic Series, vol. 10. New York: Macmillan.

Wright, D., 1973. "The Date and Arrangement of the Illustrations of the Rabbula Gospels," *Dumbarton Oaks Papers* 27:199–208.

Wright, D. F., 1985. "Apocryphal Gospels: The 'Unknown Gospel' (Pap. Egerton 2) and the Gospel of Peter," in *Gospel Perspectives*, ed. D. Wenham, 207–32. Sheffield: Journal for the Study of the Old Testament.

Wright, D. H., 1993. *The Vatican Virgil*. Berkeley: University of California Press.

Wright, W., 1870. *Catalogue of Syriac Manuscripts in the British Museum* [now The British Library]. London: British Museum.

Yardeni, A., 1990
פתוחות וסתומות בקטע חדש של ספר בראשית מן הגניזה שעטנ"ז ג"ץ ופרשות, *Proceedings of the Tenth World Congress of Jewish Studies*, division D, vol. 1 (Jerusalem): 173–80.

—, 1997. *The Book of Hebrew Script: History, Palaeography, Script Styles, Calligraphy & Design*. Jerusalem: Carta. [Republished London: British Library Publishing Division, 2002]

Yeivin, I., 1982. "The Vocalization and Accentuation of the Recently Recovered Leaf of Ms. Aleppo," *Tarbiz* 51:174–76. [Hebrew]

Zimmermann, E. H., 1916. *Vorkarolingische Miniaturen*. Berlin: Deutscher Verein für Kunstwissenschaft.

Zimmermann, G., 1995. *The four Old English poetic manuscripts: Texts, Contexts, and Historical Background*, Anglistische Forschungen 230. Heidelberg: C. Winter.

Zuntz, G., 1951. "Reconstruction of one leaf of the Chester Beatty Papyrus of the Gospels and Acts (Mt. 25,41–26,39)," in *Chronique d'Égypte* 26:191–211.

—, 1953. *The Text of the Epistles: A Disquisition upon the Corpus Paulinum*. London: Oxford University Press.

Contributors

Dr. Zaza Alexidze (ZA)
Professor and Head of the Scientific Department of the K. Kekelidze Institute of Manuscripts in Tbilisi, Georgia

Dr. Bruce C. Barker-Benfield (BCBB)
Senior Assistant Librarian, Department of Special Collections and Western Manuscripts, Bodleian Library, University of Oxford

Monica J. Blanchard, Ph.D. (MJB)
Curator, Semitics/Institute of Christian Oriental Research Collections, The Catholic University of America, Washington, D.C.

Michelle P. Brown (MPB)
Professor of Medieval Manuscript Studies, University of London; Visiting Professor, Leeds University; Regional Programmes (and formerly Curator of Illuminated Manuscripts), British Library; Lay Canon and Chapter Member of Saint Paul's Cathedral, London; and curator of the *In the Beginning: Bibles Before the Year 1000* exhibition.

Dr. Reg Carr
Director of University Library Services & Bodley's Librarian, Bodleian Library, University of Oxford

Dr. Malcolm Choat (MC)
Associate Lecturer, Department of Ancient History, Macquarie University, Sydney, Australia

Harry Y. Gamble (HYG)
Professor and Chair, Department of Religious Studies, University of Virginia, Charlottesville

Ann C. Gunter, Ph.D. (AG)
Head of Scholarly Publications and Programs and Curator of Ancient Near Eastern Art, Freer Gallery of Art & Arthur M. Sackler Gallery, Smithsonian Institution, Washington, D.C.

Charles Horton (CH)
Curator of the Western Collections of the Chester Beatty Library, Dublin

Dr. Martin Kauffmann (MK)
Assistant Librarian, Department of Special Collections and Western Manuscripts, Bodleian Library, University of Oxford

Dr. Herbert L. Kessler (HLK)
Professor of the History of Art, Zanvyl Krieger School of Arts and Sciences, Johns Hopkins University, Baltimore

Richard A. Leson (RAL)
Zanvyl Krieger Curatorial Fellow, Department of Manuscripts and Rare Books, The Walters Art Museum, Baltimore

Dr. Vrej Nersessian (VN)
Head of Christian Middle East Section, British Library, London

Dr. Ben Outhwaite (BO)
Head of the Taylor-Schechter Genizah Research Unit, Cambridge University Library

Dr. Julian Raby
Director, Freer Gallery of Art & Arthur M. Sackler Gallery, Smithsonian Institution, Washington, D.C.

Adolfo Roitman, Ph.D. (AR)
Curator of the Dead Sea Scrolls and Head of the Shrine of the Book, The Israel Museum, Jerusalem

Ilana Tahan, M.Phil. (IT)
Curator of Hebrew Collections, British Library, London

Olga Vasilyeva (OV)
Curator of Oriental Collections, Manuscript Department, National Library of Russia, St. Petersburg

William M. Voelkle (WMV)
Department Head and Curator of Medieval and Renaissance Manuscripts, Pierpont Morgan Library, New York

Photo Credits

Permission to reproduce the following photographs is gratefully acknowledged.

Frontispiece and pp. 120, 254
The President and Fellows of Magdalen College, Oxford, United Kingdom

pp. 6, 8, 119, 132, 133, 135, 136, 145, 148–149, 150, 151, 152–153, 253, 261, 262, 267, 268, 269
Freer Gallery of Art, Smithsonian Institution, Washington, D.C.

pp. 14, 18, 21,
© The Israel Museum, Jerusalem

p. 17
The Scheide Library at Princeton University Library, Princeton, N.J.

p. 25
Institute for Antiquity and Christianity, Claremont, California; courtesy of Jean Doresse

pp. 37, 39, 42, 48
Courtesy of Anne Gunter

p. 41
Courtesy of The Coptic Museum, The Supreme Council of Antiquities, Cairo, Egypt

pp. 44, 63, 78, 84, 85, 154–155, 228, 270, 302 (left)
Bibliothéque nationale de France

pp. 47, 260
Courtesy of the Osterreichische Nationalbibliothek, Vienna, Austria

p. 48
Courtesy of Elizabeth S. Bolman

p. 49 (MS. 644, ff. 117v–118r); pp. 174–175, 278 (MS. M828, ff. 13v–14r, photo by Joseph Zehavi); pp. 229, 302 [right] (MS. M874v)
The Pierpont Morgan Library, New York

pp. 50, 61, 71, 72, 74, 121, 126, 127, 140–141, 142–143, 156–157, 162–163, 164–165, 170–171, 178–179, 180–181, 232–233, 255, 258, 264 (bottom), 265, 271, 273, 274, 277 (left), 279, 280, 305 (top)
Courtesy of the British Library, London, United Kingdom

pp. 50, 214, 215, 240–241, 295, 296, 307
© Master and Fellows of Corpus Christi College, Cambridge, United Kingdom

pp. 57 (MS. Amiatino 1, f. Vr); 88 (MS Amiatino 1, f. 6/VIIr); 224–225, 300 (MS. Plut. 1.56, ff. 12v–13r); 234–235, 305 [bottom] (MS. Plut. 5.9, ff. 128v–128r)
© Biblioteca Medicea Laurenziana, Florence, Italy. Reproduced with permission of the Italian Ministry of Culture. Any publication without permission from the ministry is strictly prohibited.

p. 69
Durham Cathedral, Durham, United Kingdom

p. 70 (top)
© Jean Guichard/CORBIS

p. 70 (bottom)
Courtesy of Michelle P. Brown

p. 72
Reproduced by kind permission of the Dean and Chapter of Lichfield Cathedral, Lichfield, United Kingdom

p. 75 (top)
Courtesy of The Coptic Museum (Supreme Council of Antiquities), Cairo, Egypt

p. 75 (bottom)
Reproduced with the kind permission of the National Museum of Ireland, Dublin

pp. 76, 81, 98
Erich Lessing/Art Resource, New York

pp. 78, 91, 92, 93, 96, 98, 99
Courtesy of Herbert L. Kessler

p. 80
The Board of Trinity College, Dublin; courtesy of Herbert L. Kessler

p. 82
Courtesy of St. Gall Stiftsbibliothek, Switzerland

pp. 85, 87
Bayerishce Staatsbibliothek, Munich, Germany

pp. 94, 95
© Biblioteca Apostolica Vaticana

p. 97
Bildarchiv Preussischer Kulturbesitz/Art Resource, New York

pp. 101, 115, 117, 168, 172–173, 251, 253, 275 (right), 277 (right)
Courtesy of the National Library of Russia, Saint Petersburg

pp. 105, 107, 110–111, 112–113, 116, 246, 247, 248, 249, 252
Courtesy of Cambridge University, Cambridge, United Kingdom

pp. 108–109, 247
© The Israel Museum, Jerusalem; photo by David Harris

p. 114, 250
Published courtesy of the Ben Zvi Institute of Yad Izhak Ben-Zvi and the Hebrew University of Jerusalem; digital photography by Ardon Bar-Hama, with the support of George Blumenthal

pp. 122, 123, 256
Image digitally reproduced with the permission of the Papyrology Collection, Graduate Library, University of Michigan, Ann Arbor

pp. 124, 128, 129, 138–139, 257, 259, 264 (top),
© The Trustees of the Chester Beatty Library, Dublin, Ireland

pp. 125, 137, 185, 188–189, 205, 206–207, 208–209, 210–211, 212–213, 216–217, 218–219, 220–221, 243, 258, 263, 284, 291–294, 297–299, 308 (right)
Bodleian Library. University of Oxford,
United Kingdom

pp. 130–131
Courtesy of the Department of Papyri, Osterreichische Nationalbibliothek, Vienna, Austria

pp. 146–147, 159, 160–161, 166–167, 191, 192–193, 194–195, 196, 197, 198–199, 200–201, 202–203, 266, 272, 275 (left), 285–290
Courtesy of the Holy Monastery of Saint Catherine at Mount Sinai, Egypt

pp. 169, 244, 276, 309
The Walters Art Museum, Baltimore

pp. 177, 182, 183, 281
The J. Paul Getty Museum, Los Angeles

pp. 186–187, 236–237, 283
The National Library of Sweden, Stockholm

pp. 223, 242, 308 (left)
© Bibliothèque municipale de Valenciennes, France; photos by F. Leclercq

pp. 226–227, 301
K. Kekelidze Institute of Manuscripts, Tbilisi, Georgia

pp. 230, 231, 303, 304
Dumbarton Oaks, Byzantine Collection, Washington, D.C.

pp. 238–239, 306
Courtesy of Biblioteca Querina, Brescia, Italy

Index

C

D

E